reflective teaching

in further, adult and vocational education

4th edition

reflective teaching

in further, adult and vocational education

4th edition

Margaret Gregson and Yvonne Hillier
with Gert Biesta, Sam Duncan, Lawrence Nixon, Trish Spedding and Paul Wakeling

B L O O M S B U R Y
LONDON • NEW DELHI • NEW YORK • SYDNEY

Bloomsbury Academic

An imprint of Bloomsbury Publishing Plc

50 Bedford Square	1385 Broadway
London	New York
WC1B 3DP	NY 10018
UK	USA

www.bloomsbury.com

BLOOMSBURY and the Diana logo are trademarks of Bloomsbury Publishing Plc

First published 2015

British Library Cataloguing-in-Publication Data
A catalogue record for this book is available from the British Library.

ISBN: HB: 978-1-7809-3815-8
PB: 978-1-7809-3792-2
ePDF: 978-1-7809-3681-9
ePub: 978-1-7809-3665-9

Library of Congress Cataloging-in-Publication Data
Gregson, Margaret.
Reflective teaching in further, adult and vocational education / Margaret Gregson and Yvonne Hillier with Gert Biesta [and four others].– Fourth edition.
pages cm
ISBN 978-1-78093-792-2 (paperback)– ISBN 978-1-78093-815-8 (hardback)
1. Adult education–Planning. 2. Adult education teachers–Training of. 3. Effective teaching. 4. Adult learning. I. Hillier, Yvonne. II. Biesta, Gert. III. Hillier, Yvonne. Reflective teaching in further and adult education. IV. Title.
LC5219.H54 2015
374–dc23
2014035137

Series: Reflective Teaching

Typeset by Fakenham Prepress Solutions, Fakenham, Norfolk NR21 8NN
Printed and bound in Great Britain

For our children and our grandchildren

Contents

Part four Reflecting on consequences

Part five Deepening understanding

Foreword

The Education and Training Foundation promotes high quality teaching and learning in England's further education and training sector. The new Professional Standards for Teachers and Trainers in our sector (see **et-foundation.co.uk/our-priorities/professional-standards/professional-standards-2014/**) are at the heart of everything that we do, and are reflected in the design of every programme through which we support the sector and its workforce. The Standards emphasise the importance of professional reflection, of practitioners developing and refining their own expertize and judgement in applying theory to practice, and of identifying where practice needs to improve in order to ensure best outcomes for learners.

Those working in our sector cannot be expected to achieve these demanding standards on their own. Practitioners need time, space and support, including the support of their management and leadership, as well as their peers, in order to be able to operate at this level.

In our support for the sector we therefore design-in peer learning and practitioner-led activities, which legitimize practitioners' having time for reflection, trying things out, and sharing problems and learning with their colleagues. And we want to promote a culture that recognizes that learning also results from when things don't work out as expected.

This is why the Foundation is supporting the Joint Practice Development programme, which has been delivered by the University of Sunderland since 2009 and is integrated into this book on reflective teaching.

JPD is based on mutual respect, a willingness to learn from each other, equality in argument, and a desire to improve everyone's practice for the sake of getting better at teaching so as to improve the quality of students' learning.

Since its inception we have seen this programme demonstrate the benefits of the JPD approach, and its impact on professional practices and on learner outcomes; these examples are drawn on throughout this volume.

I am delighted that the significantly revised edition of this volume, but now with its new companion book of readings and related website, are available to support practitioners in our sector. Their publication is very timely for us at the Foundation. They demonstrate a practical and practitioner-led approach to professional development that is completely in tune with the new Professional Standards and also our vision for how we support education and training practitioners, whatever their role and position.

I thoroughly recommend these volumes and their website, and I'm delighted that the Foundation's investment in the JPD programme, and the work undertaken by its many participants over the years, have generated such rich material that can now be drawn on and support the broader workforce within further education throughout the UK and even beyond.

David Russell
Chief Executive Officer
The Education and Training Foundation
September 2014

Introduction

We have written this book for people who work in the Further Adult and Vocational Education (FAVE) sector – a context which is particularly diverse and dynamic.

We recognize the challenges and opportunities which practitioners across FAVE are faced with on a regular basis. The book offers support for student teachers new to the sector, student teachers who have experience in the sector undergoing programmes of professional development, teacher educators and managers and education leaders. It draws primarily on our experiences of working in the English FAVE system. However we have tried to set out the issues in a sufficiently broad way to enable connections to be made by readers working in other countries and contexts.

There are two main messages in this book. The first is about the moral purpose of education and our commitment to an *educational* practice that seeks social justice and personal empowerment for all our students and colleagues. The second is that teaching in FAVE is a *professional* practice that has an ethos and responsibilities. We argue that it is by critically reflecting on our practice, taking action and testing out our ideas and theories through working with our colleagues and our students that we can foster these two aims.

As this book is part of a series on Reflective Teaching across the education system, it also draws upon the work of the Teaching and Learning Research Programme (TLRP) which was managed by the Economic and Social Science Research Council (ESRC) in the United Kingdom. The TLRP established a series of principles, dimensions and concepts that address the enduring issues that confront us in our professional practice, in whatever part of the education system we work. The ten principles are:

Principle 1: Effective teaching and learning equips learners for life in its broadest sense. Learning should aim to help people develop the intellectual, personal and social resources that will enable them to participate as active citizens and flourish as individuals in a diverse and changing society. This implies adopting a broad view of learning outcomes and ensuring that equity and social justice are taken seriously.

Principle 2: Effective teaching and learning engages with valued forms of knowledge. Teaching and learning should engage with the big ideas, facts, processes, language and narratives of subjects so that learners understand what constitutes quality and standards in particular disciplines.

Principle 3: Effective teaching and learning recognizes the importance of prior experience and learning. Teaching and learning should take account of what the learner knows already in order to plan their next steps. This includes building on personal and cultural experiences of different groups of learners.

Principle 4: Effective teaching and learning requires teachers to scaffold learning. Teachers should provide activities which support learners as they move forward, not just intellectually but also socially and emotionally, so that once these supports are removed, learning is secure.

Principle 5: Effective teaching and learning needs assessment to be congruent with learning. Assessment should help to advance learning as well as determine whether learning has taken place. It should be designed and carried out so that it measures learning outcomes in a dependable way and also provides feedback for future learning.

Principle 6: Effective teaching and learning promotes the active engagement of the learner. A chief goal of teaching and learning should be the promotion of learners' independence and autonomy. This involves acquiring a repertoire of learning strategies and practices, developing positive attitudes towards learning, and confidence in oneself as a good learner.

Principle 7: Effective teaching and learning fosters both individual and social processes and outcomes. Learning is a social activity. Learners should be encouraged and helped to work with others, to share ideas and build knowledge together. Consulting learners about their learning and giving them a voice is both an expectation and a right.

Principle 8: Effective teaching and learning recognizes the significance of informal learning. Informal learning, such as learning outside of college and other formal educational settings, should be recognized as at least as significant as formal learning and should therefore be valued and used appropriately in formal processes.

Principle 9: Effective teaching and learning depends on teacher learning. The need for lecturers, teachers, trainers and co-workers to learn continuously in order to develop their knowledge and skill, and to adapt and develop their roles, especially through practice-based inquiry, should be recognized and supported.

Principle 10: Effective teaching and learning demands consistent policy frameworks with support for teaching and learning as the primary focus. Policies at national, institutional and local levels need to recognize the fundamental importance of teaching and learning. They should be designed to create effective learning environments in which all learners can thrive.

Such models or frameworks can help us understand our professional practice, but the context in which we teach is shifting and changing and subject to many demands from numerous groups with an interest in what we do. Think, for example, how many different policies currently affect what we do in FAVE. For example, we have to comply with health and safety and safeguarding regulations, equality and diversity legislation, a qualification system, professional body requirements in many specialist subjects, inspection and quality frameworks, not to mention the demands of trying to meet the hopes and needs of our students and their families. There are, therefore, a number of enduring issues we must take account of in our professional practice. These include:

- Our role in working towards society's educational goals.
- Identifying the elements of learning in formal education: knowledge, concepts, skills values and attitudes.
- Examining the community context in which we work with parents, community, employers and society.
- Examining the institutional context; working towards a shared vision to extend educational experiences and inspire learners.
- Understanding processes for our learners' social needs; building on relationships, cultural understandings and learner identities.
- Understanding processes for our learners' affective needs; taking account of our learners' views, feelings and characteristics.
- Using processes for learners' cognitive needs; matching learners' cognitive needs and providing appropriate challenges.
- Identifying outcomes for continuing improvement and learning; providing educational experiences which will lead to development in knowledge, concepts, skills and attitudes.
- Identifying outcomes for certification and the life-course; equipping learners for life. (TLRP, 2010: 11)

We also need to be able to step back from the day-to-day aspects of our teaching and examine the wider aspects of our professional practice by looking at three broad domains of activity: the curriculum, pedagogy and assessment. Underpinning these are numerous concepts that deepen our understanding, knowledge and experience of working in FAVE. All of the ideas presented in this book are subject to further testing and debate and we therefore think of our engagement in educational and professional practice as a journey, with challenges, surprises, and moments of satisfaction and joy along the way.

We offer an approach to examining our practice through working jointly with our colleagues and, where possible, with our learners. This approach is known as Joint Practice Development (JPD) and throughout the book we provide examples from projects that have been undertaken by a variety of teachers and managers in FAVE. JPD moves away from solitary reflection to a collaborative and collegiate approach to change and improvement. It has four guiding principles, which invite practitioners to:

1 Make space for trust, openness and honesty.
2 Work to establish a shared understanding of the education problem and how it makes educational sense for it to be addressed.
3 Share the experience of trying out interventions/innovative practices.
4 Critically review overall progress together.

The book is divided into five sections. Part One focuses on what it means to become a reflective teacher in FAVE. Part Two examines the conditions, circumstances and contexts in which we teach and offers a range of ideas and practical suggestions that readers can test out in their daily practice. Part Three considers three broad domains of teaching: curriculum, pedagogy and assessment. Part Four explores different approaches to assessment and evaluation and the consequences of each. Part Five integrates major concepts that underpin the development of teacher expertise and professionalism.

PART ONE: BECOMING A REFLECTIVE PROFESSIONAL **recognizes the significance of the contribution we can make as professional teachers in FAVE.** In Chapter 1 we introduce ourselves to you and acknowledge the many reasons that have influenced our decision to teach in FAVE. We draw on our own journeys into the FAVE sector to explain why it is important to us that our practice is imbued with educational values and principles. We discuss the characteristics of the sector and acknowledge the complexity and challenges that arise from this diverse and interesting part of the education system. We introduce key principles that we will refer to throughout the book, which we suggest can be used to examine and further develop professional educational practice. We also introduce a particular approach to educational change and improvement and teachers' professional development which involves undertaking research and development jointly with colleagues and students – a process known as Joint Practice Development (JPD). Chapter 2 offers ways of understanding 'learning' because, despite much complexity, a commitment to *learning* and the pursuit of good educational practice is what it is all about! Given the many competing theories of learning, we examine a number of theories, including, behaviourism, cognitivism, social constructivism and multi-disciplinary understandings of how people learn. We then explore taxonomies of learning and finally show how even the way we talk about learning shapes current educational practice. Chapter 3 introduces ideas about reflecting on our practice and why this is so important. We introduce the work of Dewey, who advocated experimenting in a reflective manner when we want to change or develop aspects of our teaching. We offer insights into processes of reflection and illustrate the JPD process of working with our colleagues and our students to improve teaching and learning. We outline seven principles and values of reflective practice and suggest that these important characteristics can guide the development of our practice in FAVE. On the website, **reflectiveteaching.co.uk**, there are supplementary chapters offering practical advice on how to conduct classroom enquiries into practice. Chapter 4 provides an overview of ten principles to guide teaching and learning which come from the Teaching and Learning Research Programme, TLRP. We signal underlying concepts that are more fully explored in the subsequent chapters in the book.

PART TWO: CREATING CONDITIONS FOR LEARNING **concerns the creation of environments to support high-quality teaching and learning.** In this part of the book we focus upon the conditions, circumstances and contexts in which we teach. Chapter 5 examines the social context of teaching, learning and assessment in FAVE. We argue that teachers need to be aware of social structures and contexts because they shape much of our practice. The chapter also explores principles and concepts which take account of the relationship between individuals and society. Chapter 6 then examines the particular relationships between teachers and students in FAVE and argues that such relationships are crucial for successful learning. Chapter 7 builds further and illustrates how positive cycles of behaviour can be created to engage students in the curriculum. Finally, we consider a range of learning spaces in FAVE in Chapter 8 and the affordances they offer for formal and informal learning. As well as the basic dimensions of classroom organization, this chapter also addresses the use of technology and team-working with other educational professionals including learning support assistants, librarians, technicians, and curriculum managers and education leaders.

PART THREE: TEACHING FOR LEARNING supports the development of practice across the three classic dimensions of teaching – curriculum, pedagogy and assessment. Chapter 9 reviews aspects of curriculum design and development and the role of subject knowledge. Chapter 10 puts these ideas into action and supports the development and evaluation of programmes of study, schemes of work and lesson plans. Chapter 11 offers ways of understanding the art, craft and science of pedagogy and the development of a pedagogic repertoire. Chapter 12 extends this with an introduction to the vital role of talking, listening, and the development of literacies across the curriculum. We argue that communication plays a central role in the development of thinking and learning for teachers and their students. Finally, this part concludes by demonstrating how assessment can underpin teaching and learning processes in very constructive ways (Chapter 13).

PART FOUR: REFLECTING ON CONSEQUENCES examines what is achieved, and by whom, in FAVE and the consequences of what we do. Chapter 14 reviews educational assessment and evaluation, paying particular attention to measuring achievement and managing accountability. Chapter 15 considers various dimensions of difference and the ways in which routine processes differentiate between people. It emphasizes accepting difference as part of the human condition and how to build more inclusive communities in FAVE.

PART FIVE: DEEPENING UNDERSTANDING integrates major themes through discussion of teacher expertise and professionalism. Chapter 16 integrates key themes from previous chapters into a holistic conceptual framework of enduring issues in teaching and learning. It examines these through three case studies relating to the dimensions of teaching, curriculum, pedagogy and assessment. The chapter also presents dimensions of expert thinking. In Chapter 17, we show how professionalism is a contested concept, but we offer a variety of ways in which readers can foster their own professional practice.

At the beginning of each chapter we draw your attention to TLRP principles which we believe are particularly relevant to the chapter under consideration. The enduring issues and concepts that relate to these principles are embedded throughout the book and enable another level of analysis.

At the end of each chapter, we offer 'key readings' that you may wish to consult and use to follow up references from points we have made within the chapters.

Supplementary resources are available on the website, **reflectiveteaching.co.uk**, and a companion book of readings, *Readings for Reflective Teaching in Further and Vocational Education.*

As the FAVE sector is so diverse, we have chosen to use the term 'student' or 'learner' to denote any learner, including trainees on apprenticeships and similar initial vocational programmes, adults learning informally in an adult education setting, employees in the workplace, as well as students on traditional formal qualification programmes in colleges and other educational institutions. Likewise, we have decided to use the term 'teacher' for those of you who may be called trainers, lecturers, tutors, facilitators, technicians, librarians, managers or learning support staff in your organization. We hope that whatever your title, role or experience, this book will be helpful in developing your knowledge and understanding about your professional practice and will lead you to further enquiry and insights as you continue to work in FAVE.

You may find that you will read this book systematically from beginning to end. However, you may also want to dip in and out of different sections or chapters, particularly if you have an interest in developing an aspect of your practice, or want to use this book to support the professional development of your colleagues or student teachers. Whatever your strategy, we suggest that the first section provides the overall theoretical underpinning for the book, whereas the next three sections provide a more practical stance. The final section offers a drawing together of many of the deeper underlying concepts, as well as ideas for further development. It is always difficult to introduce and then develop ideas when the field is so diverse and complex, but we hope that our approach, coupled with the accompanying website and companion book of readings, will enable you to apply many of the suggestions in your own setting, whatever your role and wherever you practise.

part one

Becoming a reflective professional

Part One recognizes the significance of the contribution we can make as professional teachers in FAVE.

In Chapter 1 we introduce ourselves and acknowledge the many reasons that have influenced our decision to teach in FAVE and discuss the characteristics, complexity and challenges of the sector. We offer an approach to undertaking research and development jointly with our colleagues, known as Joint Practice Development. Chapter 2 offers ways of understanding 'learning' because, despite much complexity, *learning* is what it is all about! We examine a number of theories, including, behaviourism, cognitivism, social constructivism and multi-disciplinary understandings of how people learn. We discuss taxonomies of learning and show how the way we talk about learning shapes current educational practice. Chapter 3 introduces ideas about reflecting on our practice and why this is so important. We offer processes of reflection and the Joint Practice Development process of working with our colleagues to improve teaching and learning. We outline seven principles and values of reflective practice and suggest that these important characteristics can guide the development of our practice in FAVE. Chapter 4 provides an overview of ten principles to guide teaching and learning which come from the Teaching and Learning Research Programme, TLRP. We signal underlying concepts that are more fully explored in the subsequent chapters in the book.

Identity
Who are we, and what do we stand for?

1

Introduction

This chapter focuses upon how we are drawn to the profession of teaching and how we become good teachers. Goodson (2003) identifies how the forms of knowledge that we produce, use and develop as teachers are closely related to the feelings and perceptions we hold about ourselves and others, including what we believe to be the purposes of education and what we think education is 'for' (Biesta, 2015, Reading 1.1).

A key issue here concerns our 'identities' as unique individuals and how our identities are influenced by our personal biographies as well as by the cultural, social and political factors operating within and beyond the educational settings in which we work at different stages in our careers (Brookfield, 1995). In recognition of the importance of biography and the different ways in which each of us has come into teaching (and also by way of a personal introduction), we begin this chapter with our stories of our journeys into the profession and the values which continue to inform and sustain our professional practice.

1 Understanding ourselves as teachers

1.1 Becoming a teacher

The Further, Adult and Vocational Education (FAVE) system is broad and far-reaching. It provides educational opportunities in various places and spaces for a very wide range of people. Teachers across the sector also come from equally broad walks of life, as do their students. Many people come to study in this sector having had less than positive experiences in their formal schooling. Most people who have chosen to work in this sector do not usually start out by making a decision to train to teach there at the beginning of their early careers. Yet the rich diversity of its settings and people is one of the most enduring strengths of the sector. Even the terminology used to describe the sector has changed over the years. The FAVE sector has been known variously in different counties as the Further Education (FE) sector, Post-compulsory Education and Training (PCET), Lifelong Learning (LLL), Permanent Education (*éducation permanente*), Vocational Education and Training (VET), Technical Adult and Further Education (TAFE), Adult and Community Learning (ACL), Learning and Skills (LS), and more recently in England as the Education and Training sector.

Throughout this book we advocate a principled approach to the initial and continuing professional development of teachers. This means that we do not support the view that the role of the teachers and teaching can be reduced to the technical delivery of other people's purposes. For us, teaching is a moral act concerned with the pursuit of individual and collective good framed by a concern for equity and social justice. That is why we look to educational values and principles to guide what we do.

The Economic and Social Research Council-funded Teaching and Learning Research Programme (TLRP) took place over a period of ten years, involving over 100 educational research projects. This large-scale longitudinal research study developed and refined ten evidence-informed principles distilled from the outcomes of its many research projects and extensive consultations with UK practitioners in each major education sector. The programme also compared its findings with other research from around the world to produce ten guiding principles (see James and Pollard, 2012). The ten TLRP principles can be used to support the development of teachers' professional judgement and contribute to educational policymaking (see Chapter 4). The principles focus upon important and enduring issues in education and present what the TLRP programme found to be important regarding guiding principles for effective teaching and learning. The TLRP principles do not however seek to tell teachers what to do. Each principle is expressed at a level of generality which calls for contextual interpretation by a teacher 'in the light of their knowledge of the educational needs of their students and the circumstances in which they work' (Pollard, 2014: 92).

TLRP principles

Two TLRP principles are of particular relevance to this chapter on identity and values in education:

Principle 1: Effective teaching and learning equips learners for life in its broadest sense. Learning should aim to help people develop the intellectual, personal and social resources that will enable them to participate as active citizens and flourish as individuals in a diverse and changing society. This implies adopting a broad view of learning outcomes and ensuring that equity and social justice are taken seriously.

Principle 9: Effective teaching and learning depends on teacher learning. The need for lecturers, teachers, trainers and co-workers to learn continuously in order to develop their knowledge and skill, and to adapt and develop their roles, especially through practice-based inquiry, should be recognized and supported.

So who are the teachers who work in the FAVE sector and how do they arrive at different points in their careers? We represent some of the diversity of teachers in the sector. We have travelled along different paths to become teachers. We have in turn gone on to teach and then professionally develop others to teach. Our personal journeys represent a number of purposes and values. We believe that by sharing these with you, the reader, you will begin to appreciate our different perspectives as authors and the diversity of the sector you are joining or already working within. We hope that this will give you some insights into our reasons for writing this book.

1.2 Journeys into teaching: Our stories

Yvonne's story

Yvonne did not mean to end up where she is today. She didn't even mean to study psychology, but following a year's exchange at a Californian High School she realized that she could go straight to university back in England. By then she had become interested in psychology, although her initial love of science has never wavered. What do you do with a degree in psychology? At the time, teaching seemed to be the right thing to do and following her postgraduate teaching certificate in primary education, she fell into working in a special school for children with learning difficulties, having spent a little time teaching maths on supply and working with young women who were unemployed.

Starting her family early then provided her with a desire to keep busy and so began her experience of initially volunteering and then teaching adult literacy and numeracy in the evenings. She was fortunate enough to begin this work after the initial launch of the adult literacy campaign in England and so became part of this story, which she has captured with Mary Hamilton in the Changing Faces research project (Hamilton and Hillier, 2006). Notwithstanding a stint at a comprehensive school pretending to be a music teacher and subsequently a science teacher, Yvonne continued working part-time in the adult literacy and numeracy field for a number of years before taking on an organizing role. It was at this point that she became involved in training volunteers and tutors, and eventually moving into managing training of adult education teachers and trainers. This broadened her experience of watching people teach across a very wide range of contexts and when she finally moved into working in higher education, she was able to draw upon this knowledge when she began researching and writing about the policy and practice of post-compulsory education.

The enduring lessons that Yvonne still draws upon from her experience of being a part-time tutor includes understanding the precariousness of being casually employed, never quite knowing if there would be work in the following year. She began early on to seek ways to improve what she was doing in her literacy and numeracy classes and this desire to continually improve guides her still. She has a strong sense of wanting to help people who have not been successful in their schooling or who now need, for a variety of reasons, support to engage in education.

Lawrence's story

Lawrence left school not being able to spell or write very well. In those post-punk, free festival-traveller days he read *Zen and the Art of Motorcycle Maintenance*. Pirsig went on about motorbikes, a university lecturer, quality, values and Aristotle. It was the first time Lawrence had thought of teachers as real people! He subsequently became a student of philosophy. His writing got better as he read more; even his spelling marginally improved. At university he helped out at the adult education centre in the literacy class. It was an inclusive and fun place – lots of education going on, led by two wonderful teachers.

The Basic Skills initiative provided the funding for Lawrence to study to become a literacy tutor. Things had changed; there was a nationally imposed curriculum, mapping, diagnostics and Individual Learning Plans (ILPs). Literacy teaching looked more professional, better resourced, but had less heart. He worked in a college and in adult and community education settings. Lawrence finally finished his philosophy doctorate – it had been rumbling on for eight years! But it's hard studying as a full-time worker with a family. He moved to the University of Sunderland and still teaches on the Postgraduate

Certificate in Education and masters programmes. He has never owned a motorbike, but the issues of quality, values and education Pirsig talked about still seems to require a great deal of maintenance.

Sam's story

Sam studied literature and film and was never exactly sure what she wanted to do with her life, apart from read and watch films. In her early twenties she was living in Edinburgh, working in what was probably quite an interesting job in arts administration, but was feeling stuck and frustrated. It wasn't quite the right job for her. One day she was off on a long walk around the city, trying to stomp off her annoyance, when she came across a small dusty-looking office which gave out information on voluntary jobs. She remembers looking through an old, heavy lever-arch file. She found something on adult literacy teaching, made some calls, and soon was taking part in training to be a volunteer adult literacy and numeracy tutor.

She started working with a group once a week and had never been happier. She had finally found what she'd been searching for, what she wanted to do with her life. It was that dramatic; she remembers it well. But there was still the problem of money (it was a voluntary job), so she continued other kinds of work, did a Certificate in English Language Teaching (CELTA) and taught English language overseas. Just over a year later, she arrived in London in that first full force of 'Skills for Life', when miraculously money had been poured into adult literacy teaching. Within a month she found full-time paid (paid!) work as an adult literacy teacher and she started an English Postgraduate Certificate in Education (PGCE) for adult literacy specialists soon after. She taught adult literacy, poetry, cinema and drama for the next eight years, and now mainly works in teacher education. It was, and is, hard of course, as it should be, but it also made her feel like the luckiest person alive.

Trish's story

As the eldest girl in a family of seven girls and two boys, Trish adopted a teacher's role from an early age, a situation stemming from necessity rather than design! She was a quick learner with lots of support from her family and followed a pretty traditional path from school to university. University life was emancipatory. She loved the emphasis on self-direction although she often strayed off the path, the challenges of critical thinking both academic and political, the freedom and fun of student life; loads of personal space away from an overcrowded home was pretty welcome too! More than anything, it opened up a life of opportunity that a girl from working-class roots only a short time earlier would never have had access to. However the late seventies were not the easiest of times to begin a career, so she thought she had better hedge her bets and secured a place on a PGCE to start in 1978.

However her teaching career was not destined to begin quite yet. She worked in the USA following graduation and didn't make it back in time to take up her place. Soon after her return, she was lucky enough to begin work as a chartered librarian. Returning to work after babies was not so easy in the eighties and she found herself, three children later, with a series of part-time jobs and little confidence up until 1992.

A full-time masters programme which encouraged applications from women provided her with the opportunity to re-enter higher education and focus on a return to work. Researching her dissertation led Trish into working with pupils with special educational needs (SEN) and a job in a large secondary school. An advertisement in the *Times Higher Education Supplement* for PhD studentships in Education at the University of Sunderland presented the most amazing opportunity to study and receive a bursary. She'd found her place – educational research, which led into posts as a teacher educator in two FE colleges and then back to the University of Sunderland in 2002.

Of course these life chances were at a time before the introduction of university course fees and when a sense of possibility prevailed through hard work for anyone brave enough to seize the opportunity. So in the end Trish was not so very different from her younger self, a teacher, the design of which sprang from necessity to prolong a lifelong love of education and a desire to help shape the education of others.

Margaret's (Maggie's) story

Maggie went to school in Lanarkshire in Scotland. At primary school she loved the way her reception and early years teachers used stories, art, music, poems and dance to bring learning to life and spark imagination. Later on, however, she learned that the education system also served other purposes in the form of the dreaded 'eleven plus' exam which loomed over children and which everyone was terrified of 'failing'. Thanks to her primary school teacher and with the encouragement and support of her father John, she passed the exam and was the first person in her family to gain access to a grammar school. She left school at 16. Her Scottish 'O' Levels and 'Highers' helped to get a job with the Department of Employment and for the next twenty years she played a part in implementing a range of employment and training policies in various posts across Scotland and England. She successfully completed her first degree through full-time study (while on unpaid sabbatical leave from the Department) in 1981.

As she became involved in education and training policy in her work with the Department, she became more aware of the difference between policy and educational discourses and felt that she needed to know more about educational theory and practice to do her job well, so she studied for an MA in Education through part-time study which she completed in 1986. She moved to the FE sector in 1990 and worked full-time as a senior, then a Principal lecturer and then as Director of Access Studies at a large FE college in the north-east of England. She taught on teacher education programmes there for ten years before moving to the University of Sunderland in 2000. She was awarded her Doctoral degree through part-time study by Newcastle University in 2003 while working full-time at the University of Sunderland. She was particularly fortunate in the initial financial support she received as an undergraduate from the Scottish Education Authority. This funding paid university fees and provided a maintenance grant which gave her the means to begin a degree in education at the age of 26. She is also grateful to the employers throughout her career who have supported her in engaging with educational issues at higher degree level. Sadly she knows that very few people these days receive the levels of financial, moral and employer support that she did. She also knows that the quality of professional knowledge and the standards of educational practice achieved by teachers of vocational and academic subjects across the sector make such a difference to the lives of so many others who have not had the same advantages in life that she had. That is why being a teacher educator in the field of post-compulsory education and training means so much to her. The birth of her son in 1993 brought a whole new dimension to her life as a teacher and a mother. Maggie's son realized his childhood ambition to become a primary school teacher on 17 July 2014. Watching him graduate and become a member of the teaching profession – the profession of which she still feels very proud and privileged to be a part – is one of the happiest moments of her life.

Gert's story

From an early age Gert wanted to be a teacher, but it took two aborted university studies, a car accident, a job in the radiography department of a hospital and someone who expressed belief in his abilities to get him there. For about ten years he taught physics to student radiographers. During this time he obtained a teaching certificate and eventually a degree in Education and a degree in Philosophy, all through part-time study and evening classes alongside his job. He was part of the last generation of undergraduate students in The Netherlands who still were able to obtain a government grant for their studies, although he had to fight hard for his case given his earlier trajectory of failure. He was lucky to receive a scholarship for doing a PhD which, again, he did alongside a number of part-time jobs. After this he taught at a number of Dutch universities. In 1999 he moved with his family to England to take up a post at the University of Exeter, where he became involved in teacher education in post-16 education. This brought him into contact with the rich and diverse field of further education in Britain. He developed a deeper interest in this through his involvement in a major research project – the *Transforming Learning Cultures in Further Education* project, with colleagues from colleges and universities around Exeter, Bristol, Leeds and Warwick (James and Biesta, 2007). A second major project, *Learning Lives: Learning, identity, and agency in the lifecourse* (Biesta et al., 2011) gave him an understanding of the complexities of learning in people's lives, showing both the transformative potential of education and the way in which people's encounter with the educational system can actually be 'uneducational', frustrating and even deeply damaging. Over the years he has become even more passionate about education and even more convinced about the importance of the role of teachers in the process. He remains highly critical of attempts by policymakers at all levels to make education into a machine for the production of learning outcomes, which he sees as a 'sausage factory' conception of education. He is also sceptical about what research can actually contribute to the improvement of educational practice, and tends to think that the first priority should be to support teachers in thinking with clarity and a sense of purpose about their practice.

Paul's story

Having completed his degree in English and Philosophy at Keele University in the early 1990s, Paul was dedicated to education and learning. This was partly due to the approach at Keele with the broad foundation year, joint honours degree and requirement to study something outside of your home faculty. He chose astronomy of all things! Hooked on learning, Paul completed a Masters in Language, Culture and Communication at Southampton and then a PGCE back at Keele. Paul remembers his first job in a sixth form college as a delicious time, teaching English and Media to young people with their life ahead of them. Mostly he remembers the conversations with other teaching staff. There were constant, engaging conversations involving deep thinking about how to teach better, how to help the students to learn. There seemed to be time and inclination for professional discourse.

Wanting to learn and feeling restless, Paul moved to east London to teach Media and then lead and manage in south London. He is now Principal at Havering Sixth Form College, which partly reflects the culture of east London and partly of Essex.

During his time in London colleges, Paul has always wanted to create time to learn for himself and for others. This is probably because of his experiences at Keele and because of his early experiences as a teacher. He has made time to study at the Kennedy School of Government at Harvard, to complete and contribute to leadership programmes, to study for a Certificate in Advanced Educational Studies at Southampton University, to contribute to teacher education programmes and to complete a research fellowship. At college he tries to create time for meaningful professional dialogue and through supporting JPD. Increasingly he finds this hard. Sometimes this leads to despair. Paul finds the challenge of improving teaching and learning in post-compulsory education, at this time, very demanding. However, he is determined not to give up, but to continue to focus on enabling professionals to develop their practice.

1.3 Values informing practice

What do our stories tell? Firstly, the metaphor of a journey is very strong, but it is fair to say that most of these were not intentional, rather meandering with false starts and some cul-de-sacs. What they also represent, though, is that we have made choices which relate to our underlying principles and taken decisions not to follow certain paths. A career in the FAVE system is unlikely to yield very high salaries, but it also brings its own rewards. None of us would have wanted the kind of career that only brought a sense of achievement through gaining more and more financial reward (although most of us would have liked a higher salary!).

Serendipity is a strong element within our stories. Chance encounters account for many of the pathways which led to us working in the field. Inspirational teachers, parents or colleagues, a financial and moral support system for us while studying full-time, also played an important role in helping us and many of our colleagues to change course or begin in a new direction. For those of us who had families, we have encountered a number of challenges, not least in having low confidence at the beginning of our careers but also being flexible enough to take small steps through part-time work into more substantial involvement in the sector.

Our stories show just how different the sector is and how open and permeable it is to people becoming teachers. You do not have to decide upon leaving school to study a certain suite of subjects and train to teach in the FAVE sector, although that is certainly one option. It is more common to have had a career in a different occupation and then enter the sector to help develop others in a chosen field. It is more likely that ways into the sector occur through small amounts of hourly paid teaching. The field draws upon a large cadre of casually employed staff (Hillier and Jameson, 2004, 2006) and figures in 2010 showed that of a total of 268,310 staff, 82,211 were on casual or fixed-term contracts (Lifelong Learning UK, 2010).

One of the main features emerging from our stories is that we do appear to share common values. There is a deep sense of social justice running through our accounts. We all believe that teaching has an important purpose in working towards a just and free society, even though we acknowledge that these are contested ideas. The values that we hold about the purpose and importance of education were critical to our decisions to become teachers in the first place and to sustaining our motivation and resilience throughout our careers. Being clear about our values can guide us in ensuring that we are fair in our practice and that we can justify the actions we take as we work with our students and with colleagues. Values can also help us to evaluate and respond appropriately to external pressures, policy imperatives and other professional requirements. Finally, being clear about our professional values can also help us to check if the values we stand for are reflected in what we actually do in practice in the classrooms, workshops and other educational settings in which we teach. In other words they are a means of judging whether what we really do in the world matches what we say we value. Gaps between what we aspire to and what we achieve are common in many walks of life. However, as teachers, we need to recognize that shortcomings in our practice can have profound and damaging consequences for our students. That is why it is particularly important for us to think carefully about how we can improve what we do, together with a strong commitment to realize continuing improvement in our practice. As improvements in teaching and learning are often based upon the collection and analysis of evidence, we need to be prepared and able to test out our value positions and beliefs, not only in the light of evidence from theory and research but also from evidence from our own experiences of practice.

We believe that teaching is, in essence, not only an art and a craft but also a principled, moral practice, which can serve different purposes. We believe that it is experimental (of which more later). It is also an activity that always requires careful judgement. To make good judgements we need wisdom, and we will explain throughout the book what we mean by this and what we are hoping to achieve in writing about the practice of teaching.

Alongside an awareness of the values we held when we entered the profession (see Reflective activity 1.1), we are also required to work by values shared within and across the profession. These are often presented in the form of national standards and codes of conduct and practice, which set out clear expectations regarding the values that should underpin the work of teachers. One of the reasons for developing codes or standards of professional practice is that they frame our practice and development in purposive ways.

Most of you reading this book will have a national or state set of standards that you are expected to adhere to. In many cases, these will include the standards of the values and principles that are considered to underpin national standards of teaching. We believe that your own values are a fundamental component of your professional practice and that it is important for you to be able articulate what these are, as well as thinking about how a more formally expressed set of standards, values and principles apply to your own context. We will say more about this in Chapter 4.

An important step in becoming a reflective teacher is to understand how your own values beliefs and practices are influenced by your previous experiences, circumstances and understanding. As teachers we need to be able to question and challenge our own assumptions and taken-for-granted practices. This 'reflexivity' is an important aspect of reflective practice. While reflective practice can help us to address a wide range of social, organizational and pedagogic factors in our teaching, reflexivity focuses upon our self-awareness and our ability to reflect upon ourselves (Moore, 2004). Reflective educational practice requires an interesting and sometimes courageous combination of moral commitment to do the right thing at the right time, open-mindedness, tenacity and a dedication to the pursuit of social justice and equity of educational opportunity for all (Pollard et al., 2014).

Reflective activity 1.1

Aim: To develop an awareness of your own biography into teaching

Think about your own journey into teaching. Write a brief summary of your story as we have done at the beginning of this chapter. Ask a colleague to do the same. Together, look at the influences on your decisions and decide if there are any factors that relate to your own students and indeed family members. If you are already teaching, what advice would you give to someone thinking about becoming a teacher? If you are just beginning your teaching career, what questions do you have about this profession that you could ask a more experienced colleague?

1.4 Teacher identities

In this section we focus upon how we form and maintain our professional identities as teachers. In exploring teacher identity, it may be helpful to ask yourself what kind of person you think you are and what kind of teacher you would like to become. We are using the concept of identity here as a shorthand for the ways in which we think about who we are as teachers, what we do and how we go about doing it. Our sense of personal identity develops throughout our lives and is often influenced by identification with 'significant others' such as parents, friends and, as we move into the world of work, colleagues. However it is worth noting how we often think about our personal and professional selves as being separate, when in teaching contexts they are, in practice, closely related.

In the FAVE sector teachers often associate themselves with their specialist subject or cluster of subjects, for example as a teacher of English, Mathematics, Sociology, Psychology, Accounts, Business Studies, Art, Drama, Engineering, Hairdressing, etc.

Our stories of our journeys into teaching outlined above show how most people enter the profession of teaching with a strong sense of personal commitment to try to live up

Research Briefing

Teacher careers and effectiveness

A large-scale and comprehensive TLRP project on teachers' work, lives and effectiveness, VITAE, researched teachers' professional identities through career phases. Teachers' sense of professional identity is affected by tensions between: their personal values and life experiences; the situated leadership and cultures of their schools; and the impact of external policies on their professional work. Outcomes, in terms of well-being, commitment and resilience, and hence effectiveness, depend on teachers' capacity to manage interactions between personal, work and professional factors.

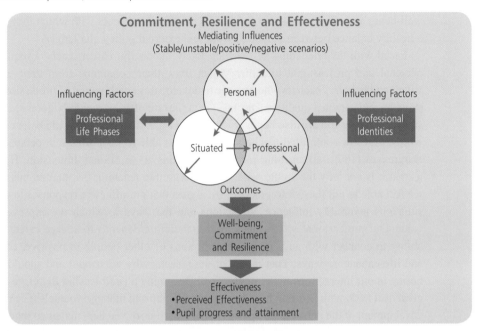

Commitment, Resilience and Effectiveness
Mediating Influences
(Stable/unstable/positive/negative scenarios)

Influencing Factors — Professional Life Phases

Personal

Situated — Professional

Influencing Factors — Professional Identities

Outcomes

Well-being, Commitment and Resilience

Effectiveness
• Perceived Effectiveness
• Pupil progress and attainment

Key findings:	Implications:
Pupil attainment: Pupils of teachers who are committed and resilient are likely to attain more than pupils whose teachers are not.	Policy makers, national associations and head teachers concerned with raising standards in schools need to consider the connections between teachers' commitment, resilience and effectiveness.
Professional identity: Teachers' sense of positive professional identity is associated with well-being and job satisfaction and is a key factor in their effectiveness.	Strategies for sustaining commitment in initial and continuing professional development programmes should distinguish between the needs of teachers in different phases of their professional lives.
Challenge: The commitment and resilience of teachers in schools serving more disadvantaged communities are more persistently challenged than others.	Schools, especially those which serve disadvantaged communities, need to ensure that their continuing professional development (CPD) provision is relevant to the commitment, resilience and health needs of teachers.
Experience: Teachers do not necessarily become more effective over time. Teachers in later years are likely to be less effective.	National organizations and schools need strategies for professional learning and development to support teachers in the later stages of their careers.
Sustainability: Sustaining and enhancing teachers' commitment and resilience is a key quality and retention issue.	Efforts to support and enhance teacher quality should focus upon building, sustaining and retaining their commitment and resilience.

Further information:
Day, C., Stobart, G., Sammons, P., Kington, A., Gu, Q., Smees, R,. Mujtaba, T. and Woods, D. (2006) *Factors that make teachers more effective across their careers.* TLRP Research Briefing No 20 (at **tlrp.org/pub**).
Day, C., Stobart, G., Sammons, P. and Kington, A. (2007) *Teachers Matter.* Maidenhead: Open University Press.
This TLRP Associate Project was funded by DfES and directed from the University of Nottingham.

T·L·R·P
TEACHING
& LEARNING
RESEARCH
PROGRAMME

E·S·R·C
ECONOMIC
& SOCIAL
RESEARCH
COUNCIL

to the values and guiding principles of good educational practice. The same values and principles are affirmed and expected as characteristics of the professional teacher. However the journey from early idealism to long-term professionalism is not straightforward and at each stage in our careers we need to balance tensions between vocational commitment and practical challenges. In the course of your initial teacher education, you may be encountering or have already encountered some of these challenges in your teaching career.

Day and Gu (2010), in a large-scale study of teachers' work and lives (see **TLRP Research Briefing p. 13),** show that the key factor in achieving satisfaction, commitment, well-being and effectiveness for teachers is the relative success with which they can strike a healthy balance between personal, work and external policy challenges.

Faced with the challenges of teaching today, successful career teachers require strong personal and professional identities which draw their coherence from their underlying values and beliefs. Teachers who manage to develop this combination of professional understanding and personal qualities, Day and Gu argue, are often particularly good in supporting student learning and are also better able to achieve a sustainable work–life balance. In other words, they are committed teachers who are also able to keep things in perspective. For Hargreaves (1998) all teaching inevitably contains an emotional dimension. He reminds us that it is not only the values with which we go into teaching that matter, but the extent we feel able to put these into practice. He argues that our affective responses to classroom situations invariably influence our actions and the ways in which we express what we value. Our professional success as a teacher therefore depends to a large extent upon our ability to connect with and 'move' the emotions of other people in positive, educational and life-enhancing ways. That is one of the reasons why we cannot and should never be boring in our interactions with our students! Becoming a good teacher therefore also has a great deal to do with learning how to support, develop and manage yourself. The nature and development of the personal and professional identities of teachers matter so much because how we are in ourselves can deeply influence how our students are in themselves. Each of us reflects the uniqueness of our past experiences and circumstances and this is part of the uniqueness we bring to our teaching. In addition, our teacher colleagues can influence and support the development of our identity and self-confidence by giving feedback to us on our work and by providing encouragement and support in our continuing professional development. If we do not relate well to our colleagues, then that might inhibit both our personal and professional development. On the other hand, collaboration with colleagues in open and trusting relationships can enable us to help each other to improve our practice and sustain our energies. Building on the work of Lave and Wenger (1991), Coffield (2014) points to the importance of the value of participating in a community of practice where the central value lies in *becoming* part of the community (original emphasis).

> Newcomers to a trade or profession gain a sense of belonging and identity … In this way participation in the activities of the group plays a powerful role in … [this case the teacher's] … motivation and identity: they begin to talk think and act like experts. (Coffield, 2014: 106)

Coffield argues that by working collaboratively with other teachers and with our students, we can begin to build such communities of practice where we can improve teaching and learning together. Later in this book (see Chapters 16 and 17) we offer some ideas about how you might begin to create the conditions which might nurture the development of a community of practice in the context of your own work through JPD (Fielding et al., 2005).

Pollard et al. (2014: 12) draw attention to how 'for teachers the personal and the professional interrelate to a considerable extent'. They also point to how 'the nature and resilience of our identity over time can make a significant contribution to our professional success'.

1.5 Teachers' work

Teachers' work is often set out in terms of their roles and responsibilities in the form of contracts of employment. Indeed teachers have a right to receive particulars of their employment setting out their role. Contractual conditions are very important in setting out how many days/hours a teacher is expected to be engaged in direct teaching, how much time is allocated for preparation, planning, assessment, administration, annual leave and performance review, etc. However a key question concerns how we interpret such contracts and the role of the teacher more generally. Teaching is a complex activity requiring personal and professional qualities, which are not easy to capture in formal contracts of employment. The use of metaphor can help to bring some of these qualities to light, as well as drawing attention to the complexities of teaching. For example, the most common metaphors are 'the *art* of teaching' (see for example Eisner, 1985; Woods, 1986; Brighouse, 1987; Barker, 1987), 'the *science* of teaching' (see for example Sockett, 1976; Simon, 1985; Hattie, 2012) and 'the *craft* of teaching' (see for example Brown and McIntyre, 1993).

The metaphor of 'art' foregrounds the multidimensional, emotional, creative, imaginative, visual, melodic and poetic (to name but a few!) of the more subtle aspects of teaching, including the use of intuition in forming judgements. The 'science' of teaching emphasizes instruction, factual knowledge organized by academic discipline, the application of tested knowledge, systematization, structured learning, clear objectives, formal testing, 'a yearning for prediction through control' (Eisner, 1985: 91) alongside a drive to discover the 'laws of learning' (Woods, 1996: 20), while the emphasis on the teacher's 'craft' gives particular significance to the importance of practical experience. These are just a few of the metaphors used to try to capture the essence of teaching. Other metaphors include teacher as gardener, drawing attention to the nurturing of the personal development of learners, and 'teacher as (musical) conductor', bringing to mind the image of teachers orchestrating multiple, simultaneous classroom activities. The metaphors we use to describe teachers and teaching are important because they bring to the fore different aspects of the teacher's expertise. These include professional knowledge and decision-making, creating, instructing, directing, coordinating, navigating, encouraging, coaching, nurturing, supporting, facilitating, inspiring, leading, protecting, defending etc.

Reflective activity 1.2

Aim: To develop insight into our identity and work as a teacher.

The most established metaphors to describe teachers' work foreground the art, science and craft of teaching. Listed below are some additional metaphors that people have used to describe the work of teachers.

- Architect
- Conductor
- Gardener
- Engineer
- Director

Choose a couple of the metaphors listed above and explore their strengths and limitations. For example, the conductor of an orchestra coordinates diverse contributions to create a symphony, but follows a musical score often composed by someone else. A gardener nurtures and tends, but also weeds … Look over your lists. What does it reveal about how you understand the nature of teachers' work?

Extension: The issues raised could be discussed and analysed with colleagues. It might be helpful to try to identify aspects which are core to the role of teachers and those which are more supplementary.

So far in this chapter we have explored personal and professional values and demonstrated how teachers' own sense of identity is drawn upon and develops during initial training and beyond. In a sense, the whole of this book is dedicated to helping us to analyse our own behaviour and its consequences. As we bring evidence to bear on our practice, we can progressively reflect upon our values and aspirations and, in doing so, contribute to the development of our expertise as teachers.

We now move on to consider the nature of our sector and our students.

2 Knowing our sector and our students

2.1 A broad and far-reaching sector

Given that our journeys have begun to demonstrate some of the complexity and turbulence of the FAVE sector, we can now turn to a brief description of the sector itself. Hyland and Merrill (2003) provide a helpful summary of the history of education and training in post-compulsory education.

Some FAVE provision occurs in formal settings, like schools, colleges, universities and training organizations. Other learning takes place entirely independently, through reading magazines, belonging to an interest group, watching television or surfing the internet. Huge funds are available from the government to support learning in more formal settings, much of this directed at younger adults, to encourage them to gain qualifications which will enable them to be economically active. In the UK, most of this provision is found in further education colleges. You may think that all of further education is aimed at young people and helps them gain qualifications. In 2012, 3.25 million students aged 19 or over were studying in FE in England. There were nearly 2.25 million students registered for a higher education qualification in further education. There were 858,900 apprenticeships in 2012. In addition, 89,500 offenders were engaged in some form of education or training. It is more difficult to quantify the participation of adults in adult and community learning, but in 2012, 683,000 adult students were involved in ACL provision (Skills Funding Agency, 2013).

A much smaller proportion of funds is available for those who simply want to learn about a new hobby or interest. Much of this kind of provision takes place in local education authority institutions and school premises. Trying to map what opportunities are available, and where and how these are funded, is a difficult task. Not all learning is funded through the government's Department for Education, (DfE) or the Department for Business, Innovation and Skills (BIS). People who work in the health sector, for example, may be able to have their studies funded through hospital trusts and health authorities. Trades' unions are now involved in funding learning, particularly through the Learning Fund. Unison, the union for local government workers, is heavily involved in providing 'opportunities for learning', through its work with shop stewards and in recent years with its Return to Learning campaign, in association with the Workers' Educational Association (WEA). Other forms of learning can be quite informal (McGivney, 2001), including non-course-based activities, planned short courses delivered in informal ways and settings, and learning taking place outside dedicated learning environments which is often not recognized as learning. There are approximately 50,000 groups of people who meet to read and discuss books in book clubs, for example, let alone those who use Wikipedia, YouTube and other forms of social media to share knowledge and support each other's learning.

Voluntary organizations are involved in the provision of learning opportunities. Housing associations enable those involved in tenants' associations to develop the skills of working in committees and urging action by local government. Prisoners can learn while serving their sentences. People in care can take part in learning programmes, as can people in community groups. A very successful non-formal provision is offered through the University of the Third Age (U3A), which is organized for members who are primarily retired or working part-time in an entirely voluntary basis. People have opportunities to learn in an ever-increasing number of ways. The education programmes of television, radio and of course the opportunities from the internet bring learning opportunities into the home and workplace.

Figure 1.1 shows many of the settings for education and training, demonstrating that provision of learning covers a range of different purposes.

Places where people can learn

- Adult and community learning institutions
- Armed forces and uniformed services
- Children's centres
- Community provision by organizations such as football clubs
- Churches, temples and mosques
- Further education colleges
- Distance and open learning, e.g. Learndirect, National Extension College (NEC)
- Libraries
- The Open University
- Prisons and offender learning
- Public venues including pubs and drop-in centres in shopping centres
- Specialist and designated colleges
- Training organizations
- University extramural classes
- Voluntary organizations
- Web-based learning
- Work-based learning programmes

2.2 Who are our learners?

In England, the FAVE sector officially begins when young people finish their schooling. In many countries, young people are 18 years old at this point, but the age at which they begin school occurs later, too. In England, the leaving age has been 16 since 1971. The government has raised this leaving age to 18 from 2015. However, young people have been learning in further education colleges, school sixth forms or sixth form colleges after they turn 16 and indeed, there has been a small but significant group of younger school-aged students who have been studying in FE colleges, either because of vocational programmes being available there or because they have not thrived in a school environment (see Chapter 5). In 2012, the average participation for young people aged 17 in England was 88.7 per cent but there was a wide variation between local authorities. Thirty-three per cent of young people studied in further education colleges, 37 per cent in schools and 12 per cent in sixth form colleges (DfE, 2013). FAVE clearly ranges wider than provision for those who have just left school or sixth form college. Adults of any age engage in learning, although there are peaks of activity, for example, among people in their thirties and forties. They also engage in different ways. Some attend a formal course at set times for a specified duration. Others 'drop in' when they can. They can dip in and out of provision, their journeys can be 'untidy' (DIUS, 2008: 21), and they can decide for themselves when they want to progress to new activities rather than being expected to follow a set curriculum. People 'follow a common human impulse to satisfy their curiosity and thirst for knowledge' (DIUS, 2008: 31).

Not everyone participates in learning opportunities and one of the challenges for people working in FAVE is how to encourage people to become involved. One of the most intransigent problems facing the sector is the lack of participation among young people. Those not in education, employment or training (NEET) is approximately 5 per cent of young people aged between 14–16, rising to 18.2 per cent for 19–24-year-olds (DfE, 2013). The overall figure of 15 per cent for 16–24-year-olds is similar to the Organisation for Economic Cooperation and Development (OECD) average for the 15–29-year-old population. Numerous projects and initiatives have attempted to tackle this intransigent problem (see DfE, 2011) and colleges, community providers and employers have worked together to encourage young people to participate.

Just how difficult it is to foster the learning culture can be seen from an Adult Participation in Learning Survey in the UK (NIACE, 2013). Only one in five adults surveyed had undertaken any learning in the past year and only 38 per cent within the last three years. A large number of adults surveyed had not engaged in any learning activity through lack of time, lack of funds or childcare commitments, and some simply did not want to do so. Those who did participate may have interpreted learning as that associated with formal learning. The OECD figures show that there is a wide disparity between participation rates in member countries, with the Nordic countries exceeding 60 per cent participation. The Programme for the International Assessment of Adult Competencies (PIAAC) report (OECD, 2013a) argues that such variation is explained by major differences in learning cultures, learning opportunities at work and adult education structures.

2.3 Why do people learn?

When you first meet a group of learners, you may spend a little time asking them what they want to achieve from their learning programme. Even if you are running a one-day workshop, it is always helpful to find out something about your learners' motivations and aspirations.

Professionals have developed their own views about why adults learn. These views constitute models of how people learn. One such model, known as liberal education, assumes that people want to learn for learning's sake. In other words, they enjoy learning and they continually wish to do so (Brookfield, 1988; Jarvis, 1990; Schuller and Watson, 2009). They are not driven by some functional need, such as seeking a qualification in order to find work or advance their career; they simply enjoy finding out about things. This model of adult education is one which can be seen in many local authority forms of provision and in university extramural departments. It can also be seen in courses put on by art galleries, museums and a host of societies. It is, however, the area of lifelong learning which is most subject to cuts in funding from governmental sources, because it is seen as being less important than learning for employment. Schuller and Watson (2009) argue strongly for a change in the way that lifelong learning is funded, precisely because a small rebalancing of funding away from younger learners will have a profound effect on provision for adults.

A second model known as the radical model of adult education subscribes to the view that education has a transformative potential. Here, people learn in order to make changes to their social and political situation. Theories of radical education derive particularly from the work of Paulo Freire (1972), who worked with peasants in Brazil and enabled them to gain literacy skills through a process of 'conscientization' – in other words, becoming aware of their disadvantaged position. The radical model of adult education is particularly strong in community education, where workers facilitate the empowerment of local people to fight for improvements in their situation. The work of Lovett in Northern Ireland and Liverpool is an example of this type of community education (Lovett, 1988; Westwood and Thomas, 1991; Mayo and Thompson, 1995), where local people learnt together about local issues which enabled them to develop strong community links as well as take steps to improve the lives of their families and neighbours. Radical approaches to adult education continue to actively seek to transform people's lives and more recently have developed strong links with more global issues, including sustainability and the eradication of the wide disparity between rich and poor (Jackson, 2011; Derrick et al., 2011).

There are *work-related* purposes for learning. Traditionally, further education has been the site of vocational learning, through full-time programmes for young people, day-release programmes for people in work, and evening courses for those who cannot have time off during the day to study. Increasingly, further education has expanded its provision to cover even younger people from 14–19 years, adults wanting evening classes similar to those in adult education institutes, and continuing professional development for a large number of professions. Generally, but not exclusively, further education has always offered accredited programmes. The more liberal adult education providers have also found ways to offer credit for their programmes, often with Open College credits or through awarding bodies which are more prescriptive in what they accredit. Some courses disappear from the curriculum and others take their place. The rise and rise of technology courses, and the increasing demand for these, replaces other previously popular courses.

Reflective activity 1.3

Collect and review a number of prospectuses from local colleges and other FAVE providers to see if you can identify whether there is an explicit model of adult education reflected in the range of learning opportunities advertised. Compare them with the prospectus from your own organization. What are the main similarities and differences?

Extension: You might like to reflect on your own values and beliefs about why your students participate in the educational activities that you are involved in.

What counts as learning and who provides the opportunities to do so keeps changing. Edwards (1997) challenges the idea that people learn in neat categories of provision and that provision comes solely from formal educational institutions. Many people do not choose or wish to learn in any formal educational provision but may wish to learn together in informal groups – something that is not always possible or even encouraged within the current FAVE system. Yet all models of adult education draw upon the underlying cultural and ideological forces that direct and, to some extent, control our lives. Thus, the purposes of what we do as educators and the reasons why people wish to engage in learning must also be considered in light of the ideological context (see, for example, Collins, 1991).

2.4 The wider context

The range of provision, how it is funded and how learning opportunities are devised, accredited and evaluated partly depend on the education and training policies that have been created and implemented. These policies are written on a grand scale, such as those devised by government, and on a smaller, local level by individual institutions, course teams and individual tutors and trainers. Policies, too, can be seen to be part of a much wider strategy based upon political ideology (see Hillier and Jameson, 2003; Fawbert, 2008; Hillier, 2006; Avis, 2010).

Each country will have its own story about how FAVE has been shaped. Fieldhouse (1996) provides an interesting chronological account of the history of British education. In England an important influence on FAVE came from a report commissioned in 1973 known as the Russell Report. Although many of its recommendations were not introduced, it urged government to take account of the need for such provision.

> Although permanent education is as much concerned with infants as with adults, it has marked implications for adult education, staking a claim for it as an integral part of total provision, not as something for the less fortunate or more studious, but as something to be expected and experienced by the whole nation, 'permanent education' is a long-term concept and *we have not time to wait for it.* (DES, 1973: para. 50) (our italics)

The Russell Report's description of the range of provision in FAVE is testament to the depth and complexity of the sector, a complexity which continues to this day.

Coffield's (2007) inaugural lecture at the Institute of Education provides more recent critical analysis of lifelong learning policy in England.

A major influence on policymaking for lifelong learning in England has been the increasing interest in education and training of adults by the European Union (EU). In 1995, a White Paper was produced on Education and Training by the EU, and in 1996 the education ministers from the countries of the OECD adopted a 'lifelong learning for all' policy framework (OECD, 2001: 9). Key components of this policy include the acknowledgement of different forms of learning such as informal learning, accreditation of learning, developing foundations for learning and resourcing learning. Linked strongly to these areas is a commitment to access and equity (see also Chapters 5 and 14).

It is important to recognize that many challenges facing the UK are also experienced worldwide. Given its membership of the European Union, the UK is particularly influenced by policies and strategies with a European focus. In 2000, the Lisbon Strategy for the European Commission stated its goal that Europe would be the most competitive and dynamic knowledge-based economy in the world, capable of sustainable economic growth with more and better jobs, and social cohesion (EU, 2000). The OECD provides a wealth of data and analysis on how its member countries are faring on a variety of indicators in relation to such goals. Its annual *Education at a Glance* is a rich source of information (OECD, 2013b). The Inquiry into the Future for Lifelong Learning (IFLL) also provides analysis of how well the UK is doing by taking data from Eurostat, the statistical arm of the European Union, as well as national data from the UK Commission for Employment and Skills (UKCES) and the Office for National Statistics (ONS). These analyses help inform national government about how much more they need to do to ensure that their countries are performing well. The EU Adult Education Survey (Eurostat, 2008; OECD, 2013b) shows that the UK generally fares well in the level of participation compared with other European Countries. However, in other surveys, particularly the Programme for International Student Assessment (PISA), the UK has slipped its position in the past few years, partly because other countries are investing heavily in education and training.

Despite the focus on education provision for economic success, there is a need for educational opportunities that satisfy other needs and interests (Biesta, 2015, Reading 1.1; Coffield, 2014, Reading 1.2). As Russell stated over forty years ago:

> At times, especially where economies were being sought, there has been a tendency, even in official pronouncements, to depreciate many [subjects] as recreational and therefore of little educational value; to assume that people go for social intercourse rather than to learn and to dismiss certain kinds of activity (like classes in bridge, golf and entertaining in the home) as pandering to petit-bourgeois aspirations. (DES, 1973: para. 13)

We may not call our activities 'entertaining in the home' but people do continue to want to learn about cooking, as the many television programmes and celebrity chefs testify!

2.5 Different people, different students, ages and stages

Many educational policies focus on encouraging people to participate fully in society through work, civic life and through lifelong learning. If you are new to teaching, or primarily working with students, your role in this is clearly at the 'sharp end' where you work with people who wish to learn. If you are an education manager, your role will be primarily focused on creating opportunities for students to learn even if you are responsible for managing teams of colleagues or resources. However, you may have begun to wonder whether the policies which heavily influence where you work, how you are paid and what you are asked to provide do achieve their goals of encouraging all adults to participate in learning opportunities. Just how difficult it is to foster the learning culture can be seen from the Adult Participation in Learning Survey in the UK (NIACE, 2013) where participation is highest among those from the top socioeconomic groups and also high among younger learners. We must be very careful with such a survey. Those who did participate may have interpreted learning as that associated with formal learning. Even though figures show that people from the higher social classes take up learning opportunities in formal settings, we suggest that adults from other backgrounds have not 'learned nothing' in recent years, but they may not think that what they have learnt 'counts'. However, it is clear that simply providing learning opportunities is not going to encourage certain people to participate.

The challenge for those of us who work in developing learning provision for young people and adults is to find ways to foster an interest in learning for a much wider group of people, while at the same time respecting an individual's decision not to participate. Yet the main focus of government policy is on engaging people to achieve economic success and social cohesion (see Chapters 4 and 5). This causes tension between those who are responsible for funding such a huge sector of education, i.e. government, and the professionals who work in it.

There have been numerous educational research initiatives in the past two decades which have sought to address how best to increase economic competitiveness, social well-being, globalization and the demands of a changing population. These include the Evidence for Policy and Practice Information and Co-ordinating Centre (EPPI) and the Centre for Skills, Knowledge and Organisational Performance (SKOPE). Longitudinal studies of a cohort of people born in one week in March 1958 (the National Child Development Survey) are beginning to show the economic and social returns of education (Brynner and Parsons, 2006; Vorhaus, Feinstein and Sabates, 2008). Individual decision-making is influenced by intrinsic motivation, a key factor in whether or not people participate in more formal education provision as adults. This longitudinal study, supplemented now by two later cohort studies, has given us a wealth of information about the effects of early and subsequent education on the life chances and experiences of the cohort members. It shows that education is mediated by individuals' skills, competences, social interactions, as well as their qualifications, as our own biographies at the start of this chapter show. The Centre for Research in the Wider Benefits of Learning has demonstrated a variety of benefits from education including improved health and well-being, community and social cohesion (Vorhaus, Feinstein and Sabates, 2008). Such research provides important evidence that has shaped subsequent work, for example the TLRP principles (Pollard et al., 2013, see also Chapter 4) and provides arguments to inform and influence government policymaking.

Our professional knowledge, based upon experience and research (Bathmaker and Avis, 2005; Hillier and Jameson, 2003; Coffield, 2008; Appleby and Hillier, 2012) is often compromised by the funding constraints and urgent performance demands that governments with limited resources have. Our professional knowledge and practice is centred on working within a notion of participation, and we have an understanding of why people want to engage in learning and also why they do not. The existence of research centres, as well as networks to support research in our field, provides an important source of information and knowledge that we can draw upon when we consider how best to meet the challenges of helping people learn. The British Educational Research Association (BERA) succinctly argues that educational research should question assumptions, discard old myths, consider whether activities and polices are worthwhile, set agendas and reconceptualize problems (BERA, 2013: 5).

2.6 Different wants and needs

We have already introduced a number of terms to capture the breadth and scope of the FAVE sector. One prevalent term, 'lifelong learning', as the name implies, is about learning that takes place throughout a person's life. It is meant to be continuous, and therefore does not stop at the end of compulsory schooling. Lifelong learning is also called lifetime learning, continuing education, and within Europe terms like '*éducation permanente*' attempt to capture the meaning of learning throughout life. For the purposes of this book we will concentrate on learning that takes place primarily in institutions set up to help young people and adults learn. However, as you will see below, the boundary between childhood, young adulthood and adulthood is becoming more blurred as far as the learning opportunities provided for them in institutions are concerned.

The second challenge is defining what counts as learning. The *Oxford English Dictionary* (OED) defines learning as 'to get knowledge of (subject) or skill in (art etc.) by study, experience or being taught'. The definition of learning is very fluid and allows us to focus on what is being learned, by whom and how. What about people who go on holiday and take a trip to a local museum, escorted by their tour guide? They find out all sorts of things they did not know about before. They have learned a great deal. Does this count as learning? Is the tour guide therefore a teacher? If you ask your colleagues to name the ways in which adults can learn, you will probably find that you have a long and varied list. In most cases, the learners do not *have* to learn. They are no longer in a compulsory education sector. In fact, they are taking up learning opportunities that are on offer in the post-compulsory sector and in many cases they learn outside the formal education and training sectors. Our definition of informal learning has a defining characteristic that it is always occurring. It may be unplanned, it may be a result of serendipity. It is *prevalent* but often unrecognized. People would not be able to use mobile phones, find their way in strange cities or use new foods without learning informally how to do so (Hillier, 2010).

When we teach a group of students, it makes sense to take account of the learning environment that we are within. If we are in a formal setting, possibly where our students are engaged on a programme leading to a qualification, then we are going to need to abide by some strict rules about what subjects we cover, what they must be able to do and understand and demonstrate in order to successfully gain the qualification and even to be able to aim for a particular level of qualification. If we are working in a community learning capacity, we may have a wide range of adults who have joined our class for very different reasons, not least because they want to do something socially. Our role in such a learning environment is still one of enabling people to achieve their goals, but we will not necessarily have a strict syllabus set out by a particular awarding body (of which more later) to abide by. We will, almost certainly, need to meet certain criteria about setting out a scheme of what will be covered in our classes and how we will help students learn and achieve.

In formal education provision with clearly defined outcomes, we will also have to meet a number of other requirements. If we teach in a further education college or one of its community satellite centres, we will need to keep track of our students, register their attendance, monitor their progress throughout the programme and give them information about what each session involves, what they can expect to achieve and what kinds of assessment will be undertaken. We will most likely be observed by a manager in the college and if there is an inspection by an external body (for example, in England it would be the Office for Standards in Education – Ofsted [see Chapter 14]) we must ensure that all our records are in order, as well as that we are abiding by the standards set out for us.

However, when we think about non-formal learning contexts, then our role becomes more elastic. We may not have a set syllabus or even an agreed plan of what we will cover with our learners at the outset. We may even be more of a member of the group itself rather than its tutor. Yet this does not mean that we can ignore basic principles of good education and how best to help people learn. Indeed, our experience may be particularly helpful for members of informal learning groups that have no particular guidelines to follow. The U3A is an example of such informality. This organization is wholly voluntary and was set up to encourage older people who are usually retired or working part-time to engage in an immense variety of activities such as walking, learning a new language, painting, discussing literature, making music or simply discussing current affairs. In this organization, one member will lead a group simply because of a shared interest and the format is decided among those who want to attend.

There are people that many formal and indeed informal learning provisions seek to work with, but who are reluctant to participate for various complex reasons. When they do agree to become involved, they may have a number of challenging factors that require careful and specialist support. Finding ways to encourage such 'reluctant' learners is often undertaken through a non-formal or informal route in the first instance. For example, community provision may welcome young mothers to a toddler and baby play session while aiming to draw them into parenting classes or other provision that may help them develop a range of activities to use with their children in the home. Professionals in health care provision try to encourage their clients to learn healthy ways to eat, to look after their bodies and even stop harmful habits. The support they offer, even on an individual basis rather than in groups, is also very much part of the informal learning process, with clear goals such as giving up smoking or losing weight.

When we work with people who have not necessarily chosen to be involved in our provision, then we face challenges of motivation. Many young people decide to stay on after school and gain a qualification because they feel that they have no choice. There may be very few job opportunities for them. Their reason for taking a particular programme is then not motivated by an interest in the subject *per se* but as a quite rational decision to enhance their chances in a future labour market. Our role, in such a situation, is to encourage them to learn successfully and to endeavour to make the subject as interesting and accessible as possible.

Prison education provides a different example where people are not entirely 'free' in their choice to learn. Inmates in most prisons are offered a range of opportunities to gain skills, including vocational subjects and functional literacy, numeracy and language. There are sessions aimed at helping them manage personal challenges such as anger management and assertiveness, as well as life skills for when they are released. Clearly, prisoners face a number of difficulties and many suffer from mental health problems or addiction. Finding ways to work effectively in such a confined and constrained environment requires particular skill, yet teachers in this context gain great satisfaction from their work.

As you can see, our role, in any of these contexts, is to enable people to learn, taking account of their personal circumstances, the requirements of the learning programmes, institutions and organizations and of sector-wide and national performance criteria. Finding the most effective means to meet these demands is a constant challenge for professionals in the field.

Reflective activity 1. 4

Think about your own students and why they have chosen to participate in the programme of learning you are offering. Are there similarities with the liberal, radical or work-based models outlined above? You may also want to reflect upon your own reasons for engaging in any form of learning and your views about the purposes of education more widely.

3 Learning and teaching through life: Introducing reflection

Given the need to take account of the diversity and range of the field and the varying desires and purposes that teachers and students bring, how do we begin to understand an appropriate way to proceed? Throughout this book you will encounter ideas for you to introduce into your own practice. You may not teach across the range of contexts that we describe, but we hope that you will draw lessons that you can apply in your own situation. Yet simply introducing new ideas will not help develop your professional practice. We believe that a fundamental component of professional practice is the deep and considered examination of such practice in a careful way. To achieve this, we suggest that we all need to reflect on our teaching. We do not mean by this that we simply think back over our last teaching session and mull over what happened and decide what to do in the following session. We will explain, in Chapter 3, what we mean by reflection, why it is important and ways to undertake it. Here, we wish to set out a rationale for our book. Let us think about the following two scenarios

Case study 1.1 Challenging behaviour

Lisa just can't win. Every week she goes into her class with a group of young students who are not in school but come to college to learn numeracy and literacy. She tries to gain their interest by making the maths that they need to cover relevant to their own interests. She has used football league tables, pool and snooker competitions, music charts, and even considered covering more illicit subjects such as drugs from a numeracy perspective (but backed away from that idea!). Yet every week the students swear, mess around and pay her very little attention. Lisa has to ensure that her learners gain a qualification within the specified timescale set down by the college. She is given regular updates on a number of indicators such as the students' attendance. Although this information is useful, she feels constantly monitored and compared with national figures, college figures and departmental figures. There is a manager responsible for her area of work in the college but he is so busy that he is not able to meet with her often. Lisa works part-time as she has a young family and so finds that she is now dreading her teaching and thinking of giving up.

   What advice would you give Lisa?

Case study 1.2 Challenging circumstances

Joshua runs an art workshop for people recovering from a stroke. His students are often unable to speak and may have use of only one hand. The sessions are open to all patients in the local hospital trust and he is never sure how many will attend at any session. Sometimes patients are so frustrated by the effect that their stroke has had that they throw down their paint brushes or even shout obscenities. He can see the power of art therapy for stroke patients but he is not sure that he has yet fully developed a range of approaches that are accessible for the requirements of the people he sees on a weekly basis. The workshop is funded by the local community centre which has just been informed that it has to reduce its provision by 10 per cent. He is worried that his workshop will be one of the first casualties.

What advice would you give Joshua?

What challenges do you see Lisa and Joshua facing? How can they address the questions they are asking themselves? Lisa and Joshua could set out all the issues that they believe they are being confronted by and think of ways to tackle these. This is an important avenue to follow but it is not the only one. The first solution that they think of is not always the best and, indeed, there may not be solutions as such, but ways to try out ideas and find if, on some days, certain activities work more effectively than others. We believe that to reflect carefully on our practice, we need to do this not only by our own thoughts and insights but also through the eyes, ears and thoughts of others.

An obvious way forward is for Lisa and Joshua to go and talk to someone who has experience in their fields. It is helpful to observe someone else teach in a similar context. It is surprising how much we can gain from simply taking time to look at a familiar situation – in this case, an educational experience but through the eyes of an observer, not the practitioner. There are opportunities to look at what the students are doing while the teacher is giving a presentation, demonstrating a practical skill or even working with individual students or small groups. It is hard when teaching a session to be aware of what every student is doing and an observer provides useful information about the interactions that take place.

Both of the case studies show that pedagogical problems are seldom simple and 'solutions' are rarely arrived at through 'recipes'. This is why being and feeling part of a professional community of practice is so important. By watching someone else, we can think about what we would do in that situation. We can draw ideas from our colleague's practice and decide whether we want to try them out in our own teaching. We can also decide not to do something and this, too, is an important lesson.

Yet these fairly obvious ways to help us develop our practice in response to the challenges set out in the examples of Lisa and Joshua still do not go far enough. There is a wealth of experience and professional knowledge that has been built up within the education community that we can draw upon, and our book is just one source within many. In Chapter 3 we explain more fully what we mean by reflection and why it is important.

There are other challenges for Joshua and Lisa that are not directly related to their own teaching practice but to the wider world of funding, accreditation and information management. An hourly paid sessional teacher is not usually in a position to influence decisions about the funding of their classes or whether their students can enrol for the programme without taking a qualification. These decisions are made both institutionally and nationally. Knowing what factors affect the teaching in the classroom, though, is an important part of being professional. Knowing what action can be taken and what needs to be referred to colleagues for a wider decision-making process is part of the role of a professional. We will discuss this more fully in Chapter 4. What we do need to do, though, is to think about what we mean by teaching and why we think it important to develop particular approaches to this professional practice.

3.1 Our view about teaching – provisional, contested and hugely experimental!

The chapters in this book are informed by our particular view of what teaching is, which also means that we have ideas about how teaching should not be understood or approached. We cannot learn for other people. Each individual can only learn for him/herself. We can learn from other people and therefore we see the practice of teaching first and foremost as social interaction between human beings and as a living process of meaning-making, interpretation and understanding, rather than a mechanical process of causes and effects or inputs and outcomes. Although we believe that teachers will generally do a better job if they have more knowledge of the complexities of educational processes and practices, such knowledge is never a matter of cookbook recipes that simply tell us what we should do. We believe we should want to influence what and how people learn and for what purpose. We are suggesting we could create possible worlds in which we help people encounter ideas, other people and other contexts. We discuss our ideas more fully in the next two chapters.

Unlike the laws of physics, there are no universal laws of teaching because teaching is an interaction between human beings who can think for themselves and can make up their own minds. We suggest that teaching is, to a certain degree, always an experiment, because we can never entirely predict how we or our students will respond. Yet we also believe that teaching is an art, a craft *and* a science which requires an ability to act in the light of evidence – that is, to adjust our knowledge in view of evidence and in situations that in some respect are always new and unique. This also means that the consequences of our teaching can never be fully predicted. In this regard teaching is always open towards a changing future.

Knowledge about educational purposes, processes and practices can help us to make better decisions about how to act. These decisions cannot be simply prescribed and they always involve judgement. This is why we believe that it is so important that we think about what we do and why we believe we should reflect on our practice but in a critical manner (see Chapter 3). By being critical, we mean that we should not simply accept what other people tell us but make up our own minds, draw our own conclusions, and come to our own judgements, based on our professional knowledge, evidence and expertise. Much of the professional knowledge and expertise we have as teachers is knowledge about *how* to do things, what we call *practical knowledge*. Such knowledge is partly gained through experience – both our own experience and the way in which we learn from the experience of other teachers and partly from the insights of others, for example in the form of research and theory.

Just as with knowledge, we see research and theory as resources that teachers can use to think *with*, rather than prescriptions we should simply follow. The professional knowledge and expertise of teachers is not only about how to do things, but also has to do with the question of the purposes of teaching – that is, the question of what it is we aim to achieve with our teaching (Biesta, 2011, 2012). This is not a matter of 'how' knowledge but of 'why' knowledge. We believe that teachers should also be able to make judgements about the ways and means of teaching and the wider purposes of their educational activities. Only if we know what it is that we want to achieve with our students and what we want our students to achieve, can we make good judgements about the best way of trying to get there. When, for example, we want our students to become good bricklayers or good nursery nurses, we do not simply want them to have the knowledge and skills, but we also want them to understand what they are doing and why they are doing it, so that they can act independently and professionally.

We believe that teaching is not only about giving students what they want. It is not simply about meeting their 'needs'. Teaching should also challenge students, should expand their horizons, and should help them to question *their* ideas about what they think they want or need. While teachers generally act in the best interests of their students, we need to recognize that power plays an important role in teaching. This, first of all, means that we should be aware of our own power in relation to our students, and we should always aim to use this power in ways that are justifiable and ethical. It also means that we work within situations where other people have power over us. It is important for teachers to understand the wider dynamics of the situations they work in, so that they can act in a manner that is responsible and responsive. Chapter 4 discusses the underlying principles that help us manage the complex relationship of acting in the best interests of our students within local, national and international constraints.

Throughout this book we will be offering a view about teaching, learning and education where practice is at the fore. This practice is a *social practice* which has goals, principles and a search for ways to help people learn. We do not offer this as a cook book approach with quick fixes for tricky situations. Practice can't be reduced solely to a set of skills. We believe that our professional practice should include thinking carefully about what constitutes good teaching, good learning and good education. We know that these are difficult ideas and will be contested, but we also believe that we should not shirk these challenging questions. We will draw upon a number of frameworks and ideas that have been developed through research and practice to help us think and talk about educational practice. These include the ten TLRP principles – the set of ten teaching and learning principles mentioned earlier. These and other views we believe will provide a helpful starting point for your journey of discovery and experience as a teacher in the FAVE sector.

3.2 What does all this mean for a teacher in FAVE?

How are you affected by the issues above? There are numerous factors which fundamentally affect your teaching. How does the funding of your programmes affect what you do? How does your work fit into the qualifications framework? Obviously, as a teacher or trainer, the places and spaces in which you work are inextricably linked to the kinds of provision that are funded, by the learners that are targeted to attend, by the outcomes, particularly in qualification terms, that you are asked to help them work towards (Coffield, 2014, Reading 1.2).

Not only is the range of learning programmes that you may be asked to work with varied, so are the people that you will work with. You may have old and young learners in the same group, and almost certainly they will have a range of abilities, motivations and personalities. You may have people who have never studied in a formal institution joining a course with those who have attended classes for the past 20 years. You may have people who have many qualifications sitting next to people with none. You may be asked to work with people who have learning difficulties. You may be asked to work with people who are no longer working but who wish to keep their minds and bodies active. There are people who want to know about the demands of a new lifestyle, such as new parents, parents with adolescent children, people with relatives who have developed a range of physical or mental disabilities.

What you do have is people who, for whatever reason, are hoping to learn about the subject you are going to teach.

Reflective activity 1.5

If you need to write a professional journal as part of your initial teacher training or CPD, you might start this by including your own journey into teaching, the reasons why you want to belong to this profession and the challenges that you foresee/are facing. Whether you are new to FAVE or an experienced practitioner, drawing upon and noting your journey can help you to outline some of the challenges that you are facing in your professional practice and discuss these with a colleague or your mentor. You may like to refer to this list as you read through this book and identify where you are gaining ideas to introduce into your teaching.

Conclusion

This chapter has examined our own identities as practitioners, as well as the contexts in which we teach, the people that we teach and the varied reasons they have for wanting to learn. Our next chapter focuses on what we know about learning: the theories that we can draw upon and the models of learning that can direct our teaching in these varied contexts. We have shown how complex the sector is, with its wide variety of settings and myriad reasons why people choose to teach and learn there. We have shown how policies at national and international level influence the practice of teaching and we have introduced an approach to help us scrutinize our professional role in FAVE.

Key readings

Becoming a teacher

For detailed and insightful accounts of the importance of biography in the development of teachers and teaching see:

Brookfield, S. D. (1995) *Becoming a Critically Reflective Teacher*. San Francisco: Jossey-Bass.

Goodson, I. (2003) *Professional Knowledge Professional Lives*. Maidenhead: Open University Press.

James and Pollard (2012) offer ten useful guiding principles for effective teaching based on evidence from a large-scale longitudinal research Teaching and Learning Research Programme (TLRP).

James, M. and Pollard, A. (2012) *Principles for Effective Pedagogy. International Response to Evidence for the UK Teaching and Learning Research Programme*. London: Routledge.

Journeys into teaching and values informing practice

For a interesting discussion of the history of adult literacy and numeracy and how changes in national policies influenced educational values and practice and changed the working conditions and the status of this specialist branch of the teaching workforce see:

Hamilton, M. and Hillier, Y. (2006) *The Changing Faces of Adult Literacy, Language and Numeracy*. Stoke-on-Trent: Trentham Books.

Teacher identities

For insightful discussion of teacher identity and the emotional dimension of teaching see:

Day, C and Gu, Q. (2010) *The New Lives of Teachers*. London: Routledge.

Hargreaves, A. (1998) 'The emotional practice of teaching', *Teaching and Teacher Education*, 14 (8), 835–54.

On the importance of belonging to a community of research and practice as an integral part of teachers' initial and continuing professional development see:

Coffield, F. (ed.) (2014) *Beyond Bulimic Learning*. London: London University, Institute of Education (IOE).

Teachers' work

For a detailed consideration of the extent to which teaching might be considered to be an art, a craft or a science see:

Eisner, E. W. (1985) *The Art of Educational Evaluation: A Personal View*. Lewes: Falmer Press.

Woods, P. (1986) *Researching the Art of Teaching*. London: Routledge.

A broad and far-reaching sector

Hyland and Merril (2003) provide a helpful summary of the history of education and training in post-compulsory education.

> Hyland, T. and Merrill, B. (2003) *The Changing Faces of Further Education.* Abingdon: Routledge.

Books that discuss the development, governance and growth of the FAVE sector in general:

> Avis, J. (2010) 'Education, governance and the "new" professionalism: radical possibilities?', *Power and Education*, 2 (2), 197–208.
>
> Bathmaker A. and Avis, J. (2005) 'Becoming a lecturer in further education in England: The construction of professional identity and the role of communities of practice', *Journal of Education for Teaching*, 31 (1), 47–62.

For a critical analysis of the development of policy in the FAVE sector see:

> Coffield, F. (2007) *Running Ever Faster Down the Wrong Road.* Inaugural Professorial Lecture. London: London University, Institute of Education (IOE).

Who are our learners?

For an overview of the FAVE system in England and recommendations on how best to sustain adults and their learning see:

> Schuller, T. and Watson, D. (2009*) Learning Through Life: Inquiry into the Future for Lifelong Learning.* Leicester: NIACE.

Why do people learn?

For a useful analysis and examples of radical emancipatory adult education see:

> Freire, P. (1972) *Pedgagogy of the Oppressed.* London: Penguin Books.

For explanations of why people learn, Curzon offers clear accessible overviews, including discussions of behaviourism, constructivism and social constructivism in the context of FAVE settings.

> Curzon, L. B. (2003). *Teaching in Further Education. An Outline of Principles and Practice.* 6th edn. London, Continuum.

The wider context

For a discussion of how policies, can be seen to be part of a much wider strategy based upon political ideology see:

> Fawbert, F. (2008) *Teaching in Post Compulsory Education.* London: Continuum.

Despite the focus on education provision for economic success, there is a need for other educational opportunities that satisfy other needs and interests – see:

Biesta, G. (2015) 'Expertise: Becoming Educationally Wise'. In M. Gregson, L. Nixon and A. Pollard (eds) *Readings for Reflective Teaching in Further, Adult and Vocational Education.* London: Bloomsbury (see Reading 1.1).

Different people – different wants and needs

For longitudinal studies which are beginning to show the economic and social returns of education see:

Feinstein L., Vorhaus, J. and Sabates, R. (2008) *Living Through Life: Future Challenges.* Foresight Capital Well Being Project. London: The Government Office for Science.

For an engaging discussion of important issues in policy and pedagogy in the sector see:

Coffield, F. (2014) 'Beyond Bulimic Learning'. In M. Gregson, L. Nixon and A. Pollard (eds) *Readings for Reflective Teaching in Further, Adult and Vocational Education.* London. Bloomsbury (see Reading 1.2).

Learning and teaching through life

A thought-provoking discussion and analysis of how learning cultures develop in FAVE contexts:

James, D. and Biesta, G. (2007) *Improving Learning Cultures in Further Education.* London: Routledge.

For an insightful exploration of dominant discourses surrounding the nature of good teachers and good teaching see:

Moore, A. (2004) *The Good Teacher*. Abingdon: Routledge.

The associated website, **reflectiveteaching.co.uk**, offers a wealth of supplementary resources including reflective activities, research briefings, advice on further reading and downloadable diagrams, figures and checklists from the book. It also features a compendium of educational terms, links to useful websites, policy and curriculum documents, and showcases examples of excellent research and practice.

Learning
How can we understand learner development?

2

Introduction

Learning can be considered as the process by which people acquire, understand, apply and extend knowledge, concepts, skills and attitudes. Adults and learners in the FAVE sector have already, through their past experience of education, acquired feelings toward themselves, towards each other and towards learning itself. Learning is thus a combination of cognitive, social and affective elements. In the FAVE sector it is crucial that we recognize and respond to what learners of any age bring to their education. Theories of learning and education will help us to see more clearly the needs of our learners. These theories will also suggest how these needs can be met. It is only then we can plan carefully and creatively to ensure that our teaching environment will engage, inspire and support learners to achieve and that negative attitudes toward learning can be overcome. This chapter will introduce some of the technical aspects of applying learning theory in practice. The TLRP principles 3, 6 and 7 indicate how we can promote achievement and encourage positive attitudes toward lifelong learning.

TLRP principles

Three principles are of particular relevance to this chapter on learning and education:

Principle 3: Effective teaching and learning recognizes the importance of prior experience and learning. Teaching and learning should take account of what the learner knows already in order to plan their next steps. This includes building on personal and cultural experiences of different groups of learners.

Principle 6: Effective teaching and learning promotes the active engagement of the learner. A chief goal of teaching and learning should be the promotion of learners' independence and autonomy. This involves acquiring a repertoire of learning strategies and practices, developing positive attitudes towards learning, and confidence in oneself as a good learner.

Principle 7: Effective teaching and learning fosters both individual and social processes and outcomes. Learning is a social activity. Learners should be encouraged and helped to work with others, to share ideas and to build knowledge together. Consulting learners about their learning and giving them a voice is both an expectation and a right.

There are numerous factors which may influence how people learn: their ability, motivation, personality, attitude, age, previous experience of learning, life experiences, physical well-being and the time available for learning. Some of these factors are determined at birth, and others influenced by the environment in which people live. If we are not sure how people learn, then our teaching remains more of an uninformed experiment. Although we may have an idea of what seems to work when we facilitate the learning of a group of individuals, we may only be getting it right by chance.

Theories of learning often come from careful and systematic research and their widespread popularity indicates their usefulness. Each theory can help us see different things about the ways in which people learn. It is important to remember that our theories are not fully tested and complete: they are the best descriptions and explanations that we have so far. This means that when you read about theories of learning, they are not statements of fact as such. There is a danger that theories often become 'reified' – in other words, the ideas promoted are treated as if they exist in practice.

A second difficulty is that we do not know about all of the theoretical developments in the field of learning while we continue to practise. We therefore operate in a messy everyday situation, applying our own informal theories and continually finding new challenges in situations that we have not met before. This need not be a depressing scenario: rather it is a challenge, a journey to find new ways of doing things and new ideas to add to our current repertoire.

Learning can happen in the classroom, in the workplace, the home, anywhere. Learning happens all the time. We are sometimes aware that we have learnt something and sometimes it is so subtle that we are not aware of it. However, there is always a change in the way that we think, feel or act when we have learnt something. It is not easy to capture all the ways in which we learn. What do we mean by learning? Many attempts have been made to describe, explain and predict the processes that are at work when we learn. Yet we need to be able to think and talk about the processes of learning in meaningful ways so that we can help our students learn. This means that when we plan our sessions, when we think about our different students and their needs and when we think about how we know that they have learnt anything, we are drawing upon the up-to-date, relevant and research-informed ideas about how people learn.

The range of competing theories of learning can be mystifying. This chapter focuses on a number of theories of learning, that have been particularly influential in education: behaviourism, cognitivism, social constructivism and what we call multidisciplinary theories. Attempts have been made to place structure on this complexity through the construction of taxonomies of learning (a system for categorizing things). We discuss three main domains (i.e. overarching categories): cognitive, affective and psychomotor, that can be used in taxonomies. We then discuss two taxonomies currently used in education: Bloom's taxonomy and the Structure of Observed Learning Outcomes (SOLO) taxonomy. The chapter then shows that the way we talk about learning shapes current educational practice. We illustrate this through Biesta's work on 'learnification'. Looking at learning theory in relation to the TLRP principles helps to keep in mind that learning is a social activity, which needs to take account of the prior experience and learning of our students and ensures that they are actively engaged in the process.

Learning in a FAVE education setting is a fascinating, but highly complex, aspect of human activity. If you search Google or look down the shelves in any library, you will see the huge range of theories about how people learn. For example, *Frameworks for Thinking* (Moseley et al., 2005) reviews and evaluates 42 different accounts of the thinking processes necessary for learning! There is no single grand theory of how people learn. For anyone, but especially a student teacher, this situation can appear frustrating. If we had one grand theory of learning then we could become fluent in it, build our confidence in applying it in the classroom and then any problem we faced could be addressed in an assured way. The grand theory of learning would guarantee the results of our practice.

The philosopher Jacques Derrida drew an analogy between the idea of a grand theory and a magic compass that would point us in the right direction at every turn. He called this device the compass for universal orientation (Derrida, 1987: 42).

1 Theories of learning

There are many ways in which to categorize the theories of learning. They can be divided into those which deal with learning from a physiological stance, those that deal with learning from a psychological point of view, those that deal with learning from a socio-political and those that deal with learning from other multidisciplinary points of view. Within each of these main categories there are numerous subdivisions. Figure 2.1 outlines a selection of these theories.

Figure 2.1 Principal theories of learning

Theories of learning			
Physiological	**Psychological**	**Sociological**	**Multidisciplinary**
Neurological	Behaviourist	Radical	Deep and surface
Chemical	Cognitive	Transformative	Experiential
	Humanist	Liberal	Andragogy
	Developmental	Human/social capital	Situated learning
	Psychoanalytical	Group dynamics	

It is not our intention to describe in detail each of the theories shown in Figure 2.1; full discussions of these can be obtained from a variety of sources, which are listed at the end of this chapter. However, we do want to draw attention to one important distinction. Many of the theories discuss how learning *should* take place – they are predicated on a basic scientific assumption that if one does *x* then *y* will occur. Yet, as Brockbank and McGill (1998) cogently argue, 'there is no science or theory of learning which embraces all the activities involved in human learning' (p. 32).

Theory offers a description of the phenomenon, an explanation for it being this way, and can be used to predict what will happen when it is applied. For example, a theory about global warming firstly describes the features of what is occurring, such as increased extreme weather patterns; it explains these by showing how this is a direct result of increase in the earth's temperature, and it predicts that these weather patterns will increase as the temperature rises. Theories about human learning tend to be less precise and indeed there is an ongoing debate in philosophical circles about knowledge and the use of universal laws to explain these. The next section will now discuss overarching theories that have been particularly influential in education. We also introduce a range of approaches that draw upon a multidisciplinary foundation.

1.1 Behaviourism

In its simplest form, this theory is about behaviour and its consequences and its beginning stems from the work of Watson (1913), who wanted to overcome difficulties in explaining what goes on in people's minds through concentrating on what can be seen, i.e. a person's behaviour. This theory reached its zenith through the work of B. F. Skinner (1938, 1959, Reading 2.1) and has subsequently been criticized by educators who feel that his work takes no account of human cognition and free will. Skinner's work drew upon his experiments with animals, usually pigeons or rats. If a pigeon was placed in a box (known as a Skinner box) and pecked at a key, food would follow. The pigeon would increase its pecking of that key and the food would therefore always follow. The pigeon's behaviour was, then, shaped by the consequences of its action: more pecking resulted in more food. If the food was subsequently withdrawn, the pigeon would not receive this 'reinforcement' and eventually the behaviour would decline and cease. Behaviourism is a complex theory of how behaviour is shaped by reinforcement. We recommend readers consult Tennant (1997) for full analysis.

According to the behaviourist theory, behaviour is shaped by the consequences of its action. If, for example, every time a student tries to answer a question but the teacher doesn't wait long enough for the student to answer, the student will end up not bothering to engage. The consequence of trying to respond has not been positively rewarded. If some students are always late for the start of a class and the teacher waits until they are all present before beginning the session, the other students will not try to be on time. These are all direct consequences of the original behaviour. The behaviourist theory is predicated on two main premises: the law of effect and the law of exercise. The law of effect argues that:

> The greater the satisfaction or discomfort, the greater the strengthening or weakening of the bond.

Second, the law of exercise argues that:

> The probability of a response occurring in a given situation increases with the number of times that response has occurred in that situation in the past.

Thorndike claimed that these 'laws' emerged clearly from 'every series of experiments on animal learning and in the entire history of the management of human affairs' (Thorndike, 1911: 244). Behaviourist theory focuses on observable, measurable features of human activity rather than upon what is going on inside people's heads. The theory claims that effective teaching requires the best stimulus that will reinforce patterns of action – in other words, it will condition students' behaviour. The result of this process is that students learn to respond in the desired way. The 'law of exercise' asserts that the link between stimulus and response is strengthened by repetition. For example, apprentice car mechanics students can learn the parts of a car engine through behaviourist teaching techniques. Here, they might be rewarded positively when they identify appropriate engine parts, take part in quizzes in teams and build up their repertoire of diagnosing problems and identifying solutions which become more complex over time.

Many of the teaching and learning practices we use are behaviourist in nature. The importance of reinforcing students' work is well established. Something as simple as giving praise to a student's answer can be seen from a behaviourist perspective as giving positive reinforcement. The use of teacher-controlled explanation and of question-and-answer routines are important parts of any teacher's pedagogic repertoire. They can be found, for instance, when new topics are being introduced and when taking stock of achievements.

Behaviourism has also been influential in work with students who experience emotional and behavioural difficulties, achieving significant success through reinforcement of appropriate actions (Wheldall, 1991).

Case study 2.1 Behaviourist learning in action

Madge is learning how to make tea. She has learning difficulties and is at college one day a week. Her tutor, Frances, starts by showing her how to boil water in a kettle, put out cups, milk and sugar on a tray, warm the pot when the water has boiled, empty the pot and then place tea in it before pouring the boiled water in. Finally, she shows Madge how to wait a few minutes for the tea to 'brew' before pouring it into the cups. When it is Madge's turn, each step that Madge takes draws comments from the tutor. 'That's right, fill the water up to the level of cups you need.' 'Good, now what comes next?' 'That's right – don't forget to warm the pot.' 'Well done, you remembered that bit.' 'Good, now you have put the tea in.' 'Brilliant, a nice cup of tea for you and me.'

Throughout this case study, Frances is reinforcing Madge's behaviour verbally. The process of making the tea has been broken down into discrete steps that Madge can perform. Every step can be reinforced so that it is more likely that Madge will remember and execute them next time. This process of encouragement, which has been formalized in behaviourist terms, works on the principle that if people behave in ways prescribed for them by their teachers, then they can have certain rewards. For example, if you want your teenage children to help with housework, you may well set up an agreed regime where they can earn extra pocket money or allowance, or stay out later if they have helped with stacking a dishwasher or doing the laundry. This process is very effective, but the behaviour does not last once the regime has stopped. As you may have begun to realize, there are issues of power operating in such situations. The respect of the individual is not necessarily considered when devising ways to shape certain behaviours and deter others, as can be seen in many regimes of torture and imprisonment.

When we use the behaviourist theory of learning to reflect on what happened in the classroom, we tend to focus on what the teacher is doing. This is because it is the teacher who sets up the stimulus for the students and the activities. It is also the teacher who monitors the responses of students and the outputs from the activities.

Behaviourism has often been applied to what are commonly termed 'traditional' teaching methods, and particularly those associated with whole-class, subject-based teaching. Careful programmes of reinforcement can meet particular needs. Some computer programs are particularly successful in reinforcing and shaping learning. They are often very popular with students. However, behaviourism is often oversimplified as a 'training' model. Some policymakers and journalists often expect behaviourist techniques to be applied to almost all teaching contexts. Perhaps it is popular because of its association with tight discipline and strong subject teaching. Indeed, recent developments in applications for iPads and handheld devices attest to the prevalence of behaviourist approaches to learning.

The influence of the behaviourist way of looking at education has been significant. In the early part of the twentieth century, it provided the foundation for the science of teaching based on whole-class, didactic approaches through which knowledge and skills were to be taught. The 'law of effect' was reflected in elaborate systems and rituals for the reinforcement of correct student responses. The law of exercise was reflected in an emphasis on practice and drill. In the 1960s, Skinner continued to promote behaviourism in a variety of contexts including education (1968, Reading 2.1). Skinner, through his work with animals, developed a sophisticated theory of the role in learning of stimulus, response, reinforcement and consequence. Behaviourist learning theory casts the learner in a relatively passive role, leaving the selection, pacing and evaluation of learning activity to the teacher. The theoretical application led to a particularly didactic and tightly controlled approach to teaching (or, perhaps more accurately, instruction) based on the idea that teachers were going to shape and reinforce what they wanted their students to learn. Looking at learning in this way, concentrating on inputs and outputs tends to ignore what is going on inside the black box of students' minds as well as assuming they do not need control over their own learning.

Reflective activity 2.1

Think how a behaviourist approach would apply in your own teaching context:

- What will be the priorities for you?
- What will be expected of your students?
- What kind of practices will you prioritize?
- What kind of assessment/evaluation practices will be appropriate?
- What does behaviourist learning theory ignore/overlook in your context?

1.2 Cognitivism

Cognitive approaches are concerned with how people gain knowledge about the world. These approaches therefore deal with the aspects that behaviourism ignored, i.e. the mind. Here the learner is the focus of the theory, not the task. Cognitive approaches incorporate ideas of intelligence and the psychometric tradition of using IQ tests. There is an assumption that once people become adult, their intelligence is less fluid and more stable or crystallized. In childhood, thinking develops through a series of stages (Piaget, 1978) until adulthood, where people are able to use and develop abstract ideas.

Cognitive approaches are generally structuralist – in other words, there is an assumption that there are stages of development and then stability. There are many analogies used by cognitive theorists. One of the more prevalent is that of the computer, where people are seen to process information which has been 'input' into their brains. People do not simply receive the information but do something with it, thereby actively engaging with the initial stimulus. People do not necessarily learn what they are taught; rather they make sense of what they are taught and recreate or reframe this information to construct their own knowledge. The theory therefore acknowledges individual autonomy. It is on the basis of this sense-making that theories of teaching have been derived. Key writers in the field of cognitive theory include Ausubel et al. (1978), Chomsky (2002, 2004), Kyriacou (1998), Hattie and Yates (2014). All articulate the importance of students and how they organize knowledge.

Ausubel emphasizes the importance of people developing their understanding of a topic. Ausubel's most influential idea is that of meaningful learning. He explains this notion in terms of cognitive structures of knowledge and how these are organized and reorganized when learning takes place. In order for meaningful learning to take place, the student's cognitive structures of knowledge need to be reorganized in order to accommodate the new information. The learning is meaningful when the new learning becomes integrated into how the student thinks. One way to picture these structures of knowledge is as a spider's web where each section is connected to the others and the web can be extended by building on existing connections. It is no use starting a new web each time a new topic is introduced when it is better to build on an existing one and create a more robust structure. Newly learnt facts and knowledge need to play meaningful roles that relate to and then become part of what is already understood.

Many vocational subjects start from scratch when being taught. This means that the cognitive structures that are required early on in a programme of learning can be built upon when the level of learning and complexity of the subject area is covered. For example, many young people may decide to train to be chefs. They may already be able to cook their own dinner but they need to develop a range of concepts about food technology as well as hospitality if they are to succeed in their chosen profession. A catering teacher, therefore, can make use of the existing concepts and ideas to make links to the more complex demands that this specialist subject requires. It would not help the students if they were asked to cook a soufflé if they hadn't yet understood the nature of working with egg whites and air within the mixture when being cooked. This theory of learning draws attention to the need to relate new knowledge to what students already know – that is, to their already existing cognitive structures, and make those links to the relevant parts of the cognitive structure.

The cognitivist theory casts the student in an active role. Students have to work hard to make sense of new knowledge, to make links between what they already know and what they need to learn or incorporate into their cognitive structures. Students therefore need to be given tasks that help them to explore the knowledge from many different angles. This will help them make links to what they already know.

Cognitivism and deep and surface learning

The ideas of deep and surface learning can also be applied to task of helping us reflect on an individual learner's cognitive development. Originally developed by Marton and Saljö, and Entwistle (1997), this theory suggests people have different approaches to their learning. Those who take a surface approach simply want to 'pass the test' and do not develop strategies for permanent learning. Those who adopt a deep approach devise their own models from the information they have to learn. The approaches have been identified from higher education learners who initially were asked to read a passage and answer questions. Those who used a deep approach to their analysis of the passage created concepts and related these to emerging themes, whereas those who used a surface approach simply memorized disparate items. Further work by Marton, Hounsell and Entwistle (1997) and Biggs (1999) has expanded the theory. Biggs developed a taxonomy of learning which identifies five levels of learning:

1 *Pre-structural:* no knowledge.
2 *Unistructural:* limited knowledge about one aspect.
3 *Multistructural:* knowledge about a number of aspects.
4 *Relational:* knowledge about aspects related to each other.
5 *Extended abstract:* knowledge about aspects synthesized to form hypotheses.

If we want our learners to make connections between different ideas or concepts, then we want them to be learning at the relational level of learning. If we simply want them to list a set of ideas or characteristics, then we want them to perform at the multistructural level. If we want people to think critically and analytically about a topic, weighing up different ideas and creating a coherent argument for a point of view, then we are asking them to perform at an extended abstract level. Biggs argues that it is no good setting people tasks that will encourage them to adopt a surface approach to learning; they will simply remember at the time and then forget. Identifying tasks that encourage a deep approach to learning will be more effective in enabling them to apply their knowledge in future, undefined, ways.

Many of you will be working with individuals rather than whole groups, or will spend some of your time working with individuals when they are learning in a group. In certain learning situations, you will be working with individuals, within a group such as those working in functional skills or study skills groups, or on a one-to-one basis, e.g. in tutorials, guidance sessions or learning support sessions. If you are working with individuals who are dropping in to a resource centre, or who each have an individual learning programme, you will need to track carefully what learners are doing each time they visit you, and you will not know when they will return. Here is selection from a typical adult basic skills group attending a two-hour session in a learning resource centre.

Case study 2.2 The cognitivist model of learning in practice

Phyllis works as a tutor of literacy. She has four new students who have already had an in-depth interview with the Skills for Life co-ordinator. They have all agreed their learning objectives for a ten-week term. Gary is working towards his Level One literacy certificate, Rajdeep is attending courses to help him with his full-time Foundation Degree and Nikolaos is improving his English language skills having recently emigrated from Greece. Camille is very unconfident about her spelling and she needs to take messages at work. The students can attend the learning resource centre on any session they choose. This means that they might see up to five different tutors in any one week.

The students each have a record of activities they have undertaken with comments from the tutors recommending further work. How can Phyllis plan for a session? She can look at the students' records as they arrive for the session. She can set up the computers so that they can be used immediately. The resource centre will have a range of web-based and paper-based material that they can be directed to. She will know which resources are appropriate for the different levels of basic skill.

Phyllis will need to plan time to work with each student. She can do this in various ways. She may quickly 'start everyone off' with activities based on her analysis of their individual records. She can then decide when to introduce the group activity and when to introduce the individual work that arises from this. Finally, she will need to set aside time for them to record their work covered in the session and to negotiate what they should work on next time they come along.

Throughout her plan, Phyllis will need to consider the time allowed for individual work, what each person will be doing, when, and to allow opportunities for negotiating content. Often, students will arrive with something they have to deal with at home, a letter from school, a bill, a request for information. Phyllis will have to set aside time when she moves around the group for such spontaneous requests for help.

Phyllis can also plan for people to work together. She can decide that there may be a group activity with which all the learners can engage. This is where the idea of working with topics, themes or issues is useful. Often, there will be an item from the day's news that could be discussed. Students could read this information from the daily paper and then write their own views. They could then discuss these in the group, thereby enabling those working towards the literacy qualification to cover the units on speaking and listening. Although students may have different goals, the way for them to achieve these may be by doing similar activities. For example, four students – Camille, Rajdeep, Nikolaos and Gary – all have difficulty spelling. They will need to learn strategies for spelling and the context in which they learn these can be shared. By writing a response to a controversial news item, they will be using their spelling strategies. Gary will count his work towards his Level One certificate, Rajdeep will be refining his ability to structure a written assignment and Nikolaos will be able to concentrate on his use of grammar. Camille will be able to practise spellings she is most likely to need for her role as a receptionist in a busy office.

When we look at learning from a cognitivist perspective it is easy to overlook the importance of students working together to make meaning. The emphasis on the individual, isolated learner makes it hard to acknowledge the importance of empathy and supporting other students in the group. The students in the classroom appear as isolated students working to develop their individual thinking and knowledge. What is missed here is the social nature of learning. Finally, this way of talking about learning encourages us to see the learner's mind as an inner place. The picture is powerful, because it helps us to imagine what happens when students work hard to get something in their head but the image is dangerous because it separates the individual from the world.

Reflective activity 2.2

Think of a situation when you could use cognitive learning theory in the context of your practice

- What will be your priorities?
- What will you be expecting your students to be doing?
- What kind of classroom practices would you prioritize?
- What kind of assessment/evaluation practices would you use?
- What does cognitivist learning theory ignore or overlook?
- What does cognitivism ignore/overlook?

Cognitivism and humanistic approaches

Humanistic psychology places the individual in the centre. It is a theory concerned with the 'self'. Maslow (1968) was the main protagonist of humanistic psychology, and he argued that there is a hierarchy of need by which people are motivated. The lowest level consists of basic needs: food, water, shelter, warmth. This is followed by safety needs, then love and belongingness needs, self-esteem needs, and finally the need for self-actualization. Only when lower-level needs are satisfied can an individual become motivated to satisfy the higher level. The highest level can be seen to be a state of equilibrium, where people are making full use of their capabilities, are 'rooted' in self-knowledge, and are in control of the direction of their lives. Applied to adult learning, Maslow's theory would predict that people who are hungry or thirsty are not likely to learn effectively because their energy will be directed to satisfying their basic needs. Adults will learn when they are motivated to reach the higher levels of the hierarchy, because they will then be active participants in the learning situation. One can criticize this theory, because we know that we can learn even if we are cold or hungry, and that our survival skills depend on our being able to learn when we are in extremely challenging situations. In fact, as anyone familiar with Buddhism will know, the way to enlightenment is achieved by specifically eschewing physical comforts which Maslow argues must be satisfied before moving towards self-actualization. The model, then, is culturally bound.

Carl Rogers was a clinical psychologist, like Maslow, whose theory proselytizes respect for an individual and the development of genuine feelings. For a tutor of adults, this means that we should be ourselves, and not try to develop a facade. We should have a warm regard for our learners, but accept our learners as individuals in their own right. We need to treat them with empathy – that is, to 'understand the learner's reactions from the inside' (Rogers, 1983: 129). Rogers' work has been particularly influential in group dynamics and the study of how people behave in group learning situations, covered more fully in Chapter 7.

1.3 Multidisciplinary

Some theorists have developed what we call 'multidisciplinary' theories of adult learning. These theories therefore draw upon sociological and psychological theories. They take account of both the individual as an actor in the world and the world in which the individual lives.

Andragogy

The psychological theories covered so far could apply to any person, at any age. There are far more theories about learning by children and we do not intend to examine these. Many of these theories do not account well for the way *adults* learn. Adults are busy people, with experience gained from living through their transition from childhood to adulthood. When they join a programme of learning, they come with a foundation of knowledge, skills and attitude, including habits of learning acquired in the past. One theorist, Malcolm Knowles (1978, 1984), argued that the theory of how adults learn is different from that of children. The study of how children learn is called pedagogy, and Knowles coined the term 'andragogy' for the study of how adults learn.

Knowles applies a range of theories in his pragmatic approach to the facilitation of learning in adults. His main argument is that people are 'self-directed' and the role of the adult educator is to help adults to move from being the type of dependent learner from their childhood days to self-directed learners as adults. This means that people should be able to control and negotiate their own learning environment and goals. Knowles' ideas draw heavily upon the Rogerian notions of respect and empathy.

Experiential learning

The most influential theory in recent years for adult learning has been the experiential theory, particularly Kolb's learning cycle, drawn from the fuller discussion found in John Dewey's work. Here it is shown as a cycle of learning from a concrete experience. Kolb's cycle accounts for the way in which people can abstract generalizations from a concrete experience and devise ideas for future experimentation based on their reflections. Although experiential learning is often defined as learning by doing, it actually refers to the learning as a result of thinking about the doing.

Kolb's cycle has been adapted to take account of many of the criticisms of this earlier model. Cowan (1999) describes loops of learning, almost like coiled springs, where people do not simply have an experience, reflect on it, generalize about it and then start experimenting with their new ideas. He argues that people bring their experiences to any new learning situation and that not only is there reflection on the recent experience itself, but the assimilation of this into previous experience. People can then consolidate their reflections when they put their new learning into action, which thereby creates opportunities for them to gain new experiences that can be assimilated into their now-previous experiences. He also shows how this form of learning is compatible with behaviourist approaches where learning is programmed, and with cognitive approaches where the more traditional approach of 'tell them what to do, get them to do it and then

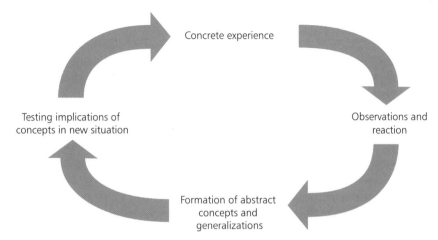

Figure 2.2 Kolb's Learning Cycle, from Kolb, D. (1984) *Experiential Learning: Experience as the Source of Learning and Development*, New Jersey: Prentice Hall.

remind them what they have done' helps learners develop cognitive abilities (Cowan, 1999: 41).

Situated learning

When we learn about something it is not usually in a sterile environment. In fact, Lave and Wenger (1991) argued that we need to look at the context in which people learn to maximize the effectiveness of our teaching and facilitation of learning. They proposed that our learning is situated within the social context. In other words, when people learn, they do so through acquiring the social knowledge within which they are situated. For example, apprentices acquire technical knowledge and skills but they do so by being steeped in a particular environment with taken-for-granted ways of working which they need to learn, even though these ways are not normally specified or articulated. Lave and Wenger, then, like Biggs, would argue that we need to think of learning in terms of its application in the real world, something which is far more complex than working at the unistructural level. New attempts to embed basic skills within a vocational curriculum, for example, would fit with the model of situated learning

Lave and Wenger noted that we live in a number of communities which have their ways of doing things and proposed that as professionals we work in such a community of practice, in this case, of post-compulsory education. In fact, this is too broad a term and we actually belong to various communities – for example, we may belong to one that relates to our subject specialism, and another that relates to the kind of institution. Being a numeracy tutor would involve belonging to the functional skills community, to the numeracy and maths specialist community and, quite likely, the FE, adult and community or work-based vocational community. These communities overlap and interrelate. Newcomers to a community of practice need to acquire the tacit knowledge about what they need to do and understand. You will be part of a community of practice as you undertake your professional development, as Chapter 17 discusses.

Social constructivist theory

This learning theory takes two main forms. On the one hand, it draws attention to the language and forms of understanding that are embedded in particular contexts and social practices and sees these as important 'cultural resources' that are available to a student. Theories which emphasize this approach to learning are often referred to as *sociocultural*. On the other hand, it draws attention to the key role of experienced participants in inducting less competent learners, and in 'mediating', 'scaffolding' and extending their understanding. Studies with this emphasis are known as *social constructivist*, because they retain the constructivist concern with learner activity, but also recognize the significance of social processes.

The seminal writer on this approach was Vygotsky (1962, 1978, Reading 2.2), whose work in particular led to the concept of scaffolding, whereby knowledge is gradually built up through the introduction of certain basic concepts that are then developed. It is easy to see this approach in mathematics and science, where students need to be able to manipulate the basic arithmetic functions of addition and subtraction before they can begin to work with multiplication and division. Indeed, given that multiplication and division are more advanced ways to add and subtract, it would be extremely difficult to help someone multiply if they could not yet add.

We might say then, that theories of social constructivism affirm the importance of recognizing and building on students' family and community knowledge, while also emphasizing the role of teaching and instruction in extending such knowledge. Psychologists such as Bruner (1986), Wood (1988) and Wertsch (1985) have been able to demonstrate the considerable relevance of Vygotsky's work to modern education by highlighting important links between thought and language. His work offers key insights into the role of the culture and the social context of the student in influencing understanding (Wells, 1999, Reading 2.3). This influence starts in informal ways from birth. Thus infants and young children interact with their parents and family and, through experiencing the language and forms of behaviour of their culture, also assimilate particular cognitive skills, strategies, knowledge and understanding (Dunn, 1988; Richards and Light, 1986). The focus here is upon the meanings people make between themselves as they live together. Children, teenagers and adults make meanings in the family, with friends, with work colleagues and as part of a community. The key point is that the things we talk about and how we tend to think about them depend on our culture and social history as well as on any particular instruction which may be offered at any point in time. For example, Colley, James and Diment (2007) explore how teachers in the FAVE sector find themselves having to fit into an educational culture that shapes their workplace. Ideas, language and concepts derived from interaction with others structure, challenge, enhance or constrain thinking.

The practical conclusion to be drawn from this is that teachers must engage with students' existing cultural and conceptual understandings (and misunderstandings) before attempting further instruction. A review from the US indicates that: 'if initial understanding is not engaged, students may fail to grasp new information and concepts, or may learn for the purposes of the test, but fail to transfer the learning to new situations' (Bransford et al., 1999: 25). As we discuss in this chapter, this argument for 'deep' and 'connected' learning is also linked to learner identity. Do students feel comfortable with new knowledge? Can they incorporate it and feel supported by the significant others in their lives (such as parents, partners or their peers), or do they experience apathy or even disapproval?

The second major aspect of social constructivism concerns the mediation of understanding by more knowledgeable others. This is best illustrated through Vygotsky's concept of the 'zone of proximal development' (the ZPD) (1978, Reading 2.2). This is:

> … the distance between the actual developmental level (of the student) as determined through problem solving and the level of potential development as determined through problem solving under adult guidance or in collaboration with more capable peers. (Vygotsky, 1978: 86)

The ZPD concerns each person's potential to 'make sense'. Given a learner's present state of understanding, what developments can occur if he or she is given appropriate assistance by more capable others? If support is appropriate and meaningful, then, it is argued, the understanding of students can be extended far beyond that which they could reach alone.

Such assistance in learning can come in many ways. It may take the form of an explanation by or discussion with a knowledgeable teacher; it may reflect debate among a group of students as they strive to solve a problem or complete a task; it might come from discussion with an employer or from watching a particular television programme. In each case, the intervention functions to extend and to 'scaffold' the students' understanding across their ZPD for that particular issue. An appropriate analogy, suggested by Bruner, is that of building a house. Scaffolding is needed to support the process as the house is gradually constructed from its foundations, but when it has been assembled and all the parts have been secured, the scaffolding can be removed. The building – the student's understanding – will stand independently.

The influence of social constructivism has grown steadily since the early 1980s. Perhaps this is because the approach seems to recognize both the needs of learners to construct their own, meaningful understandings and the strength of teaching itself. Indeed, a key to the approach lies in specifying constructive relationships between these factors. As Tharp and Gallimore (1988) suggest, learning can be seen as 'assisted performance'.

Figure 2.3 below, elaborated from Rowland (1987), represents the roles of students and adults in social constructivist teaching and learning processes. Negotiation, focused perhaps on a topic, is followed by activity and discussion by students. However, the teacher then makes a constructive intervention to provide support and instruction – a role which Rowland named as that of the 'reflective agent'. This draws attention to the fact that any intervention must be appropriate. It must connect with the understandings and purposes of the students so that their thinking is extended. If this is to happen, teachers need to draw on both their subject knowledge and their understanding of people in general and of their students in particular. They must make an accurate judgement themselves about the most appropriate form of input. In this, various techniques of formative assessment (see Chapter 13) are likely to be helpful. If such judgements are astute then the input could take students thinking forward, across the ZPD and beyond the level of understanding which they would have reached alone. Clearly there could be successive cycles of this process.

Figure 2.3
A social
constructivist
model of roles
in the teaching–
learning process
(adapted from
Rowland, 1987).

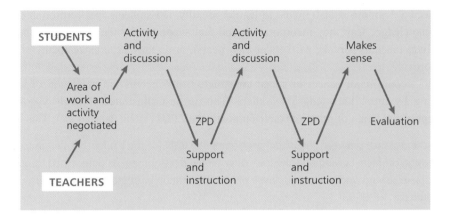

Reflective activity 2.3

Think how you might use social constructive learning theory in your context.

- What will be your priorities?
- What will you expect of your students in a social constructivist setting?
- What kind of educational practices will social constructivists prioritize?
- What kind of assessment/evaluation practices will you use?
- What does social constructivism ignore/overlook?

2 Domains and taxonomies of learning

So far in this chapter we have considered three groups of learning theory: behaviourist, cognitivist and multidisciplinary, including social constructivist theories of learning. These accounts of the process of learning are useful because they help us to see how people learn. They are not as good at helping to reflect on how people feel in the learning environment or how they feel as they learn. Many of you will have personal experience of finding something so difficult that it becomes threatening and it prevents you from making progress. When we learn to ride a bicycle we are doing something very different from learning to speak a new language or calculating the necessary paint to decorate a community hall. We suggest that the kind of learning we do in these examples is not the same. One way to capture this difference is to identify categories in which learning occurs. These categories are often presented as domains of learning and we now discuss how thinking about these can help us plan and organize teaching, learning and assessment.

Figure 2.4 provides a very simple summary of some key points in the previous discussions of learning theory and the insights they offer into educational practice.

Cognitive psychologists Bloom, Krathwohl and Dave (1956) named three domains of learning: cognitive, affective and psychomotor. The cognitive focuses upon the

Figure 2.4 Comparative overview of three theories of learning

	Behaviourism	Cognitivism	Social constructivism
How learner is viewed	• Passively learns correct response • Focus on the individual • Extrinsically motivated	• Actively builds understanding • Focus on the individual • Intrinsically motivated	• Collaboratively builds understanding through dialogue • Focus on working together • Socially motivated
Characteristics of teaching	• Teacher transmits knowledge and skills • Learning depends on teaching and systematic reinforcement of correct behaviour	• Teachers give learners individual opportunities to build their understanding of the topic • Sets problems to solve • Real life examples	• Teacher plans activities that allow learners to gradually build understanding through experience interaction and adult support
Characteristics of learning	• Students follow teacher's instructions • Students respond in the desired way	• Building knowledge of the topic by solving problems • Learning can be independent of teacher	• Group discussion, problem-solving and feedback
Examples of T&L methods and resources	• Recall of names • Simple motor skills • Multiple choice test • Lower levels of Bloom	• Note-taking, reading, evaluating information and justifying decisions made • Essay writing (compare and contrast ...) • Higher level of Bloom	• Group discussion • Group activities • Paired mind mapping • Higher level of Bloom
Strengths of the model	• Easy to plan and administer • Focus on clear targets • Progress easy to monitor • Can be fast and efficient way to learn	• Makes links between everyday life and classroom • Motivates learners through links to everyday life • Builds understanding on the experience of learners • Individual students' deep learning can be assessed	• Learning comes through interdependence of teacher and students • Encourages collaboration and language development • Clarifies thinking and extends understanding • Supports differentiation
Weaknesses of the model	• Risk of superficial learning • Difficult to adapt Teaching and Learning to meet the varied needs of students • Motivation seen in terms of reward systems	• Planning and managing learning challenging • Significant resource and organizational implications • Management of classroom can dominates teacher's time • Requires the active participation of learners	• Harder to assess the deeper learning of individual learners • Planning and managing learning challenging • Students may need preparing to fully participate in these activities (learning to learn)
Major theorists	• Watson • Skinner • Thorndike	• Dewey • Bruner • Ausubel	• Vygotsky ZPD • P4C (Lipman) • Lave and Wenger

development of 'mind'; the affective concerns attitudes and emotions; the psychomotor focuses on the development of physical skills.

The cognitive domain focuses on developing understanding of concepts and ideas and the practice of thinking skills: explain, identify, how, why, when, what – for example, naming the major bones in the body, evaluating the impact of the banking crisis on the economy of a local region. The affective domain focuses on developing attitudes, emotions and feelings: how we feel about ourselves and how we get along with other people – for example, the need to feel safe and welcome, to feel included, to feel one's opinions are valued and for equality of opportunity for all. Krathwohl's (1956) taxonomy categorizes or maps out the levels within the *affective* domain. The psychomotor domain focuses on developing physical dexterity – for example, changing a wheel, giving an injection or taking a goal kick. These are skills that need practice. Dave's taxonomy categorizes or maps out the levels within the *psychomotor* domain.

Seeing learning in terms of these three different domains will help you to think more carefully about how adult learners and others feel about themselves, each other and toward the learning itself. Using these ideas will help you to provide opportunities for differentiation and progression. For example, you may be teaching a programme on publishing using a particular software brand. Your group may have different previous experience and levels of achievement in linked areas such as word processing and using spreadsheets. You will need to identify how best to support their learning and think not only about the cognitive aspect of how to use the publishing software, but also about their levels of confidence and anxiety, as well as their ability to type efficiently. In particular, keeping in mind these three different domains will help you to include and justify activities that aim to achieve more than just cognitive outcomes.

2.1 Bloom's taxonomy: Focusing in more detail on the cognitive domain

Bloom's taxonomy can help when considering the level of challenge associated with a task and how this might make your learners feel. For example, common sense suggests that adult learners who have left school with little confidence with writing could feel very threatened by a 'low level' cognitive task such as picking out nouns and verbs from sentences in a word search activity.

Bloom's cognitive taxonomy helps us to see that the tasks teachers give to learners imply different levels of 'cognitive demand'. That is, asking people to describe or recall what they have just learnt does not require as much of learners as does higher 'cognitive demand' tasks that ask learners to evaluate or make judgements about, for example, a historical event, a scientific experiment or educational policy. Each of these levels of tasks has implications for how learners feel about what they are asked to do. The more demanding the task the more potential there is for learners to feel threatened.

Figure 2.5 Bloom's taxonomy: thinking about levels cognitive challenge

Level of Bloom's taxonomy	Level of cognitive challenge associated with the task	Affective implications of the activity
Knowledge and Comprehension	Can students find, define list, give examples of, sort and reorganize examples of, for example, key terms such as nouns?	Low level of challenge. Likely to raise less feelings of discomfort but soon becomes tedious.
Application and Analysis	Can students use, apply or demonstrate their use of these terms to express fairly straightforward ideas? They can analyse more complex text and use a bigger range of technical vocabulary to describe the text.	Medium level of challenge. More demanding so more potential to raise feelings of discomfort.
Synthesis and Evaluation	Either creating an original piece of work, making good use of, for example, nouns. Or evaluating a complex piece of writing, justifying the evaluations made with evidence from the text.	High level of challenge and demand. Risk of high levels of discomfort unless carefully supported by prior work.

Reflective activity 2.4

Use the idea of three domains of learning to help you review a lesson or a series of sessions. Does one domain dominate? Should this domain dominate? What could be gained from including activities that develop other domains?

2.2 SOLO taxonomy

As we noted earlier in this chapter, Biggs and Collis (Biggs and Collis, 1982; Biggs, 1995, 1999) developed the SOLO taxonomy (Structure of the Observed Learning Outcomes). This taxonomy pictures how the learner's performance grows in complexity and abstraction as they complete more complex tasks. The SOLO taxonomy is based on the idea that there is a general sequence, or set of steps, related to learning many concepts and skills. This basic assumption helps teachers to plan a series of related targets for students to achieve and to assess outcomes against these pre-defined levels. The taxonomy gives us a way to describe the increasing development of a student's understanding of a topic. It indicates the level of demand the task will place on the student. It allows teachers to recognize the complexity and quality of thinking expected of students (Mosley, 2005: 88). The SOLO taxonomy has proved useful in helping teachers plan and moderate assessment. It is used by teachers planning for teaching, learning and assessment with adult learners and for those working in higher education. A key strength of this taxonomy is that it enables a close alignment of learning outcomes with assessment methods (see Chapter 13).

Figure 2.6 SOLO taxonomy

SOLO taxonomy and assessing levels of achievement				
SOLO descriptor	**General description**	**Particular features**	**Consistency of argument**	**Assessment outcome**
Pre-structural	This is where the learner 'misses the point' or does not show any evidence for having learnt anything about the topic.	Acquire bits of unconnected information. Remain focused on own opinion about what is important. Failing to see the problem.	Very inconsistent. Almost random selection of material.	Fail/minimal pass
Unistructural	This is where the learner can identify items and undertake simple procedures.	Limited ability to generalize. Tends to stick to specific cases. Simple obvious connections made.	Little consistency. Tends to jump to conclusion to quickly.	Minimal pass
Multistructural	This is where the learner can describe, make lists, do simple algorithms.	Beginning to generalize. Connections made but not generalized. But only with limited examples.	Attempt to present a consistent discussion. But isolated facts and data not clearly related to conclusion.	Pass
Relational	This is where the learner can make comparisons, explain causes, and relate ideas.	Can generalize with a given context. Parts appreciated in relation to whole.	Consistent discussion range of examples relevant but limited to one area.	Good pass
Extending abstract	This is where the learner can theorize, generalize and reflect.	Can generalize to situations not experienced. Connections made beyond given subject area.	Conclusions left open to allow logically possible alternatives.	Outstanding pass

Adapted from Mosley et al., 2005

Each level of response identified in the above table does not replace the previous one but adds to it. Essentially this is an attempt to help the learner and teacher identify what has been achieved from the original learning objectives and how well this has been covered. The flexibility in this model ensures that some people will provide more evidence of learning at higher levels than the original learning outcomes specified. We have seen this occur in numerous adult education classes where the participants displayed deep levels of analysis which went beyond the requirements for the course.

3 Learning and education

In the final part of this chapter we look more critically at the current preoccupation with learning in the FAVE sector. In England in particular, the focus is concentrated on learning and its 'facilitation'. Students have become 'learners', student teachers 'trainees', and we assess the 'impact' of classroom activities on learners. This way of looking at education does foreground important aspects of what teachers and students do. It is of central importance that students achieve their qualifications. This section aims to help deepen reflection on learning by exploring some of the difficulties we are likely to encounter if we only focus on learning. Talk of learning can easily slip into seeing students as consumers. We draw attention to some familiar and important features of what goes on in the classroom that are not easily accommodated by talk of learning. We need other ways of approaching education if we are to make a fuller sense of what goes on in the classroom.

The rise of the new language of learning: Learnification

Biesta has named a phenomenon that is widespread within education and the FAVE sector in particular, characterized by the 'translation of everything there is to say about education in terms of learning and learners' (2009: 38). He calls this phenomenon *learnification*. What this 'ugly' term captures is the way our thinking, talk and practice as teachers has been reduced to a narrow and constraining set of learning priorities (2005: 56–7).

Our everyday conversations show we already 'know' a great deal about learning. This everyday talk often involves, according to Sfard, one or two metaphors (1995: 5). First, there is the metaphor of learning as acquisition, and second there is the metaphor of learning as participation. Learning 'conceived as the acquisition of something', whether this be knowledge *per se* or conceptual development, pictures the 'human mind as a container to be filled with certain materials and of the learner becoming an owner of these materials' (p. 5). These entities may include knowledge, concepts, skills, facts, understanding, meaning and attitudes. They are to be acquired through remembering, internalization, construction, appropriation, development and with the help of teachers who guide, support, deliver, explain, mediate, test and so forth. Once acquired, the capabilities can be applied, transferred, shared with others.

The second metaphor Sfard identifies is learning as participation. The emphasis is on the learner as 'a person interested in participation in certain kinds of activities' (p. 6), including learning through activity, through direct engagement in an applied situation, and learning through practice as a participant. For example, the student on a work-based apprenticeship or the student teacher working with a mentor to develop teaching 'skills' is learning through the activity of the workplace. Instead of prioritizing formal knowledge, one becomes a participating member of a practice community (see Lave and Wenger, 1990). The learning as participation metaphor has particular resonance in respect of informal and tacit learning, including through use of new technologies, where people often share tips with each other or learn through trial and error (Buckingham, 2005). These are important ways in which learning theories can help us to reflect more thoughtfully and productively.

Striking a balance

Thinking about what you plan to do in terms of different theories of learning and education can help you to evaluate the teaching resources, methods and strategies you use or which are widely promoted in your organization. When you look at what you do in terms of the learning theories, you might, for example, come to realize that your classroom practice prioritizes the individual student's development of new understanding (constructivism). This realization might also help you to see that you are not making the most of the kinds of understanding that come from talk between students (social constructivism) or from learning by repeatedly practising recalling or 'memorizing' information (an aspect of behaviourism). Reflecting on what goes on in terms of the theories considered in the chapter will help you, as a professional teacher, to decide where the balance should be struck in particular circumstances and situations.

Planning

We need to consider whether the tasks or questions we are setting groups of students or individuals are at the right level so that they are challenged but can also achieve. Theories of learning can also help us to reflect on whether our session or series of sessions is following a logical sequence, i.e. whether the activities are organized in such a way that learners can build confidence in a topic by engaging with the basic knowledge before moving on to critically evaluate a topic. Taxonomies of learning as systems for categorizing different kinds of thinking or learning are useful in planning for inclusion and progression.

Overall, this pause to consider the range of learning theories available could be summed up by drawing an analogy between educational learning and a city such as London. The first thing this comparison helps us to see is the size and complexity of the task of getting to know either. Such a comparison invites us to see learning theories as if they were like the walking tours that reveal parts of the metropolis to visitors. For example, the Royal Walking Tour would show sites such as Buckingham Palace, Westminster Abbey and Kensington Palace and include tales about royal intrigues and memorable events. By contrast, the Marxist Walking Tour might take you to Highgate cemetery, the Karl Marx Memorial Library in Clerkenwell, the old Reading Room of the British Library, as well as telling you about various struggles of working people against entrenched power and privilege. This analogy helps us to see the differences in emphasis and limits of learning theories. One learning theory will help us to pick out what is significant, to see the relationship between different features and to plan a journey toward the picked-out destination. Following one theory will also push other things out of view. It will leave other parts of the city unexplored. This analogy suggests that the importance of learning theories is not to be found in their potential to give us *the answer*. Rather their strength lies in their ability to help us pick out and see relationships between aspects of our educational practice and ask focused questions about what is happening and how we can develop what we do.

These ways of talking about learning are typically developed by the learning theories that have been considered in this chapter. They add depth to these everyday ways of talking about learning and, by so doing, help us to better appreciate how we, as teachers, can plan for and deliver effective acquisition and participation. Learning theories appear to give us control over these processes. For example, behaviourist learning theory explains how to plan and deliver learning so that students acquire new skills. Social constructivist theory explains how we can organize participation so that students acquire new knowledge. The higher levels of Bloom's taxonomy help us to think about how acquisition and participation can be organized to support students to evaluate current practice, decide and be able to justify what to do. These learning theories enhance ideas of acquisition and participation so that we can picture students going through a process, a series of stages, either by themselves or by working with others, that result in new knowledge and/or skills being learned. In part the theories of learning gain some of their popularity from their potential to clarify the things we already say about learning.

We should remember that teaching involves not just applying theories unproblematically to our practice. We need to remember also that the social practice of teaching must take account of the inequalities in our system and in our society. If we unquestioningly adopt a particular learning theory, we are in danger of using a superficial quick fix approach to our practice. Theories can inform practice but cannot and should not determine practice. Theories can tell us in general what we could do but they cannot tell us if, when and how we should act. As teachers we are ultimately responsible for making judgements and we now turn to examining how we could develop our ability to make good judgements in complex and unfolding situations in practice.

Reflective activity 2.5

When you reflect on your discussions of teaching and learning, what metaphors or assumptions about education can you identify? Now take a step further back: what are the benefits and challenges associated with these ways of talking about and doing education? What do they help us to see? What do they make it harder to acknowledge? You might want to draw this visually and then discuss with your colleagues or mentor.

Conclusion

Learning is an immensely complex topic and this chapter has simply touched the surface of some of the many issues involved. As teachers we always need to make judgements about the assumptions underpinning different theories of learning, the strengths and shortcomings of each, when, where and to what extent each should be used, and how some need to be treated with particular caution because, although they might appear intuitively appealing, they may not have any significant support from robust independent empirical research (Nixon et al., 2007, Reading 2.5). In one sense, perhaps the provisional nature of our understanding is no bad thing, because, if we knew it all, then one of the greatest sources of fascination and fulfilment in teaching would be diminished. The vocation of teaching will certainly always include this element of intellectual challenge as teachers seek to understand what students understand, and then to provide personalized support.

In this chapter we have reviewed a number influential theories of learning and related these to aspects of practice in the FAVE sector. We considered in some detail behaviourism, cognitivism and theories which foreground the social construction of knowledge. We then extended our discussion to include different domains of learning and taxonomies of thinking, focusing in particular on Bloom's Taxonomy and Biggs' SOLO Taxonomy. Finally through the work of Biesta, we briefly explored the relationship between learning and education.

One of our most important professional responsibilities as teachers is to enhance the lives of our students and improve the education system. This depends upon our commitment to enhancing the learning capacities of our students whatever their circumstances. In this chapter we have shown how important it is to use theory to reflect carefully on the learning experiences of our students as we support them to achieve their goals. Central to this chapter is the view that teachers should help students to become autonomous thinkers, independent learners and active citizens.

Key readings

Theories of learning

On psychological approaches to learning, both Tennant and Curzon offer clear introductory overviews, including discussions of behaviourism, constructivism and social constructivism. Both texts discuss the implications of psychological accounts of learning for teaching in FAVE settings.

> Curzon, L. B. (2003) *Teaching in Further Education: An Outline of Principles and Practice.* 6th edn. London: Continuum.
> Tennant, M. (1997) *Psychology and Adult Learning.* 2nd edn. London: Routledge.

More detailed accounts of learning drawn from the psychological schools considered in this chapter can be found in the readings below.

A clear behaviourist account of learning is offered by Skinner:

> Skinner, B. F. (1954) 'The science of learning and the art of teaching', *Harvard Educational Review,* 24, 86–97. (**Reading 2.1**)

Bruner's work has extended for over 50 years now and has powerfully promoted a 'cultural psychology' focused on the creation of understanding. See, for example:

> Bruner, J. (1990) *Acts of Meaning.* Cambridge, MA: Harvard University Press.

Vygotsky's own discussion of the 'zone of proximal development':

> Fisher, R. (2013) *Teaching Thinking: Philosophical Enquiry in the Classroom.* London: Bloomsbury, 2–26. (**Reading 2.4**)

Vygotsky, L. S. (1978) *Mind in Society: The Development of Higher Psychological Processes.* Cambridge, MA: Harvard University Press, 84–90. (Reading 2.2)

Wells, G. (2008) 'Dialogue, Inquiry and the Construction of Learning Communities'. In B. Linguard, J. Nixon and S. Ranson (eds) *Transforming Learning in Schools and Communities.* London: Continuum, 236–42. (Reading 2.3)

Domains and taxonomies of learning

For a comprehensive overview of taxonomies of thinking, including a summary of the SOLO and Bloom's taxonomy, see:

Moseley, D., Baumfield, V., Elliott, J., Gregson, M., Higgins, S., Miller, J. and Newton, P. (2005) *Frameworks for Thinking.* Cambridge: Cambridge University Press.

For a helpful revision of the original work of Bloom and his associates on the development of policy in the FAVE sector, see:

Bloom, B. S. (1956) *Taxonomy of Educational Objectives: The Classification of Educational Goals. Handbook 1. The Cognitive Domain.* New York: McKay.

Learning and education

This section looked at some of the risks associated with becoming gripped by one way of thinking about education above all others. For a more detailed consideration of risks associated with talk of learning as opposed to education, see:

Biesta, G. (2005) 'Against learning. Reclaiming a language for education in an age of learning', *Nordisk Pedagogik,* 25, 54–66.

—(2006) *Beyond Learning: Democratic Education for a Human Future.* London: Paradigm.

For an account of how the idea of learning styles can limit our thinking about learning and education, see:

Nixon, L., Gregson, M., Spedding, P. (2007) 'Challenging the intuitive appeal of learning styles'. Later published as 'Pedagogy and the intuitive appeal of learning styles in post-compulsory education in England', *Journal of Vocational Education and Training,* 59 (1), 39–50 (Reading 2.5).

The associated website, **reflectiveteaching.co.uk**, offers a wealth of supplementary resources including reflective activities, research briefings, advice on further reading and downloadable diagrams, figures and checklists from the book. It also features a compendium of educational terms, links to useful websites, policy and curriculum documents, and showcases examples of excellent research and practice.

Reflection
How can we develop the quality of our teaching?

3

We teach to change the world.
(Brookfield, 1995: 1)

Introduction

When we think carefully about our teaching, we demonstrate our commitment to improving our professional practice. We want to find out about the consequences of our actions. We need, therefore, a commitment to the systematic questioning of our teaching as a basis for development (Stenhouse, 1975). We should be concerned to question and test theory in practice in the use of these qualities. What do the following TLRP principles mean to you in supporting your practice?

TLRP principles

Principle 1: Effective teaching and learning equips learners for life in its broadest sense. Learning should aim to help people develop the intellectual, personal and social resources that will enable them to participate as active citizens and flourish as individuals in a diverse and changing society. This implies adopting a broad view of learning outcomes and ensuring that equity and social justice are taken seriously.

Principle 9: Effective teaching and learning depends on teacher learning. The need for lecturers, teachers, trainers and co-workers to learn continuously in order to develop their knowledge and skill, and to adapt and develop their roles, especially through practice-based inquiry, should be recognized and supported.

Principle 10: Effective teaching and learning demands consistent policy frameworks with support for teaching and learning as the primary focus. Policies at national, institutional and local levels need to recognize the fundamental importance of teaching and learning. They should be designed to create effective learning environments in which all learners can thrive.

When we are newcomers to the study of education, we are asked to undertake teaching practice where we may be placed with experienced colleagues and given the opportunity to work with their students over short intensive periods of time. We may be asked to undertake microtraining or microteaching practice during our training. We also talk about 'good practice', which can refer to a code of conduct, an underpinning approach or standards for which we must strive. Professional standards are usually based on ideas of good practice and set out what practitioners can aim to achieve, starting with standards for new entrants to the profession, through to those who have gained experience and teaching qualifications. In addition to the standards which define what people should do, there is a set of skills and attributes which relate to how people should behave, and qualities they should possess. This second set of skills and attributes may help define a set of values, and begin to define good practice in our work.

This chapter will examine the philosophical and theoretical roots of reflective practice and discuss how reflective practice can be used in professional practice. We will argue that reflecting on our practice is something that should be done with our peers and colleagues and, through this, help to develop our practice jointly. We will also outline how reflecting on our practice can lead to action which will provide evidence to inform that practice and upon which other colleagues can in turn develop theirs.

1 Why critically reflect on practice?

Why should we reflect critically on our daily practice (Dewey, 1916, Reading 3.2)? What can it achieve? There are two main reasons for doing this. The first is that we often have practices that are convenient in the short term but in the long term do not actually help people to learn effectively. For example, many students ask for handouts when they attend a formal learning situation or for the PowerPoint presentation to be uploaded on an intranet. Handouts and downloaded files enable students to catch up on any missed session and they enable the teacher to clarify what is to be covered in a session. Now, with the increasing use of information technology, there is almost a competition to see how beautiful and entertaining these handouts and electronic resources can be. Yet many students take the handout or save the link and then ignore the content. How a handout or electronic resource is *used* is important for how well a person will *learn*. Simply having a set of handouts or links to websites will not guarantee that, as if by osmosis, the content will transfer to someone's brain! We think this encourages a 'grab and go' approach to learning. So, if we think good teaching means having lots of smart-looking handouts and interactive web pages for our students because they think they have the content of the course, then in the long run they will not learn so much and we may have to develop further teaching sessions to help them cover the material.

A second and more fundamental reason for thinking critically is that we do not teach in a vacuum. We are products of complex social and personal circumstances that affect anything we do (Calderhead, 1994, Reading 3.1). Some of the things that we think are a result of the influences of ideology and society, what Gramsci (1971) called hegemony. For example, in the Western world, there is a prevailing view that intelligence is important and that qualifications are vital for good jobs. The kind of education we have often determines the kind of qualifications we subsequently gain and the type of work we do. People in positions of power who make decisions about the education system in the UK, including those in government, the legal system and the professions, have been overwhelmingly beneficiaries of a system that values particular types of education and qualification. This system continually reproduces what is desired for those who have been on the receiving end of it. This situation is hegemonic. We do not often question the underlying idea that education and qualifications are in themselves 'good things'. In other words, the state system provides the context in which some of our values are reinforced and others are neglected.

Now, some of our assumptions are a lot easier to question than others. If we say that we think meeting students' needs is very important, most people reading this book would agree with this view. However, if we then say that meeting students' needs means always doing what the students want, people might start to challenge this. What if a learner has a very narrow definition of what is needed? What if we know that there is a whole range of alternatives that the learner simply has never heard of? It becomes easy to challenge us on this view. However, if we claim that being learner-centred is a fundamental value in our teaching, it would be hard to challenge us, and we would certainly resist such challenges. Yet when we begin to look very carefully at that statement, we can start to see many assumptions that may be quite false. Are we sure that the students' needs are paramount? It may be that the learner does not *need* something but likes to have certain desires satisfied. For example, a learner may wish to have a set of notes for every session. This is not absolutely necessary, but it is something that she has come to expect. This is where a learner's needs are actually 'wants' that are misplaced. What if we think we are meeting students' needs when really we are teaching in our preferred way and it does not take account of the students' needs? The teaching/learning situation is one where the tutor wields power, not just in explicit ways like deciding if particular work meets assessment standards, but in less obvious ways, such as deciding what will be learnt, and how.

A colleague who had worked in what was then known as adult basic education for many years believed that students should not have to work for qualifications in literacy and numeracy because it was more important to them to learn that they had dignity and that they should have confidence in themselves. She felt that having to undertake work that was assessed would only remind them of their previous failures. Yet when Wordpower and Numberpower (qualifications in basic skills) were first introduced, she found that her students developed a lot of confidence by achieving these, and it was through publicly recognized awards that they felt they could gain self-respect. Her previous assumptions had been based on challenges to the establishment and the value of qualifications. She had not thought of how the students wanted to belong to that establishment. Now, we could go further and question whether people should need qualifications to earn self-respect and this leads to the current debates about lifelong learning and the need for a workforce that is qualified.

1.1 Scenario

Case study 3.1 Using reflective practice to improve the quality of our teaching

Maria rushes into the class a few minutes late. She switches off her mobile, puts her heavy bag by her side filled with resources and assignments to assess and settles down for the evening session of her course. She teaches psychology part-time at a local college and is working towards a teaching qualification. The teaching course runs over two years and she is in the final term. She joins a group of three other students who are all working in the post-compulsory sector. Nadine teaches numeracy, Mark teaches hairdressing and Sunil works in a community centre nearby, mainly with young parents.

The four students are in a learning set which was set up when they joined the course last year. They meet weekly and are given various tasks to perform. Recently, they have been involved in action learning for their projects, the last major assignment they need to complete. Tonight, it is Maria's turn to discuss an aspect of her practice, which the other members of the group can help her think about so that she can take action.

Maria tells the group that she has noticed that the students who are taking her psychology course for a vocational qualification in care in the community really struggle with many of the requirements. They really hate anything to do with statistics, which is an essential component of the programme. She has tried to make the sessions light-hearted, but this does not seem to help.

At this point, Nadine asks Maria to describe what happens in a typical session. Are all the students avoiding statistics? How do they respond when Maria introduces the topic? Has she noticed if certain students don't come to these sessions? Mark asks what happens with the other more academic courses she teaches; is it a problem there too? Sunil asks how Maria feels about statistics; did she enjoy it when she was taught it? How confident is she when teaching it to others?

Maria begins to feel uncomfortable. She hadn't really thought about her own feelings about statistics as part of what was going on in her teaching. She had a really tough time getting to grips with it and felt really intimidated at university when her lecturer asked students in turn to demonstrate a solution to a particular data analysis question. She wanted to run and hide. She often found excuses to miss some of those sessions.

During the next hour, the discussion ranges from the emotional aspect of teaching mathematical concepts, ways to make these accessible and relevant, why some students begin avoidance behaviour including making jokes, surreptitiously checking their mobile phones or simply not attending. The group begin to identify a possible way forward by suggesting that Maria introduces a topic to show when statistics can help people make decisions or even to be able to question 'facts' that they are presented with in the media.

After a while, various ideas to tackle the situation begin to emerge. Sunil is note-taker for this session and summarizes what was suggested. Maria decides to try using examples of misleading graphs and statements from the media to draw her students into discussion. She also agrees that she will reflect on her own learning experiences of statistics and see how this is influencing her practice. She will keep a blog to capture her feelings, as well as what she was observing among her students.

The group agrees who will present next time and who will take notes. It is time to go home and mark those assignments!

What was going on in that session? The same presentation could lead to completely different ideas if it was repeated, or if it had other members present. There is no view about what should be done about the situation described, but it establishes that someone's perspective on a professional matter can be 'unpacked'. The members studied reflective practice earlier in their course. They read widely about the theory of critical reflection and about being a professional. They were thinking and acting reflectively. They were becoming reflective practitioners.

Reflective activity 3.1

Think about an aspect of your practice such as your use of learning resources. How do your students respond to these? How actively engaged are they when you use them? If possible, discuss with your colleagues how these resources are used in your setting and identify if there are any unintended consequences from their use.

You might like to discuss your assumptions about the benefits and difficulties in using certain resources such as downloadable PowerPoint and course material, or whether other resources present challenges such as handouts, models or artefacts that are not easily transported to community settings.

What assumptions are you making about the reason for using such resources? What underlying rationale is there for using the resources as you do? Are there, for example, set materials that all staff must use on a particular course or programme? Why do these have to be aligned to a set format? Is there trust in your own professional standards or does your institution adopt a quality control approach to these materials? If so, why?

So far, we have suggested that it is possible to challenge our taken-for-granted assumptions about meeting learner needs because this may not be the most appropriate course of action to take. Another result of trying to meet students' needs is that it is almost impossible to achieve this for everyone. It is important not to be too self-critical by the idea that we should be meeting all our students' needs. Brookfield (1998) reminds us that:

> A critically reflective educator knows that while meeting everyone's needs sounds compassionate and learner-centred it is pedagogically unsound and psychologically demoralising. She knows that clinging to this assumption will only cause her to carry around a permanent burden of guilt at her inability to live up to this impossible task. (p. 133)

So, when we reflect, we may not only challenge our assumptions about why we do what we do, we can also help ourselves identify where we feel lacking and why we may be setting ourselves unnecessarily unachievable standards. How can we reflect on our approaches to our practice? What can we do? What can we uncover in the process?

1.2 Thinking reflectively

There are numerous models of reflective practice and we can outline only some of them. Calderhead (1994, Reading 3.1) has identified many versions in the literature, including reflection-in-action, reflection-on-action (Schon, 1983, 1987), deliberative reflection (Grimmett et al., 1990) and critical reflection (Brookfield, 1995). All of these are processes that help foster enquiry into all aspects of our teaching, including the cognitive, behavioural and affective aspects. These are all linked in the practice of teaching, but what exactly should we be examining?

To challenge our assumptions, we have to begin by *thinking* reflectively. What is this, exactly? One of the earliest exponents of thinking reflectively was John Dewey (1916,

1933, Reading 3.2). His writing is accessible, thought-provoking and relevant, even though he was writing in the early part of last century. Dewey understood that we are always trying to work out what to do in an experimental way and we can think reflectively to help us do this. In other words, he was very much aware of the practical implications for thinking.

Dewey identified five general features of reflective thinking, including: perplexity, confusion, doubt due to the fact we are usually in situations where we don't know all the relevant factors; thinking about possible reasons for this situation; looking at all the evidence from the situation currently; devising a tentative hypothesis of what we could try and do to make a change; and finally actually taking action.

For example, if we had a group of students who were thinking of dropping out from their studies, we may wonder how to tackle this. Instead of assuming that it is their problem, we may start to doubt the view that in any programme of learning, there will be drop-out and be perplexed why that is. By thinking about possible reasons for a situation and looking at it from a variety of angles we can begin to come up with some ideas. This is what Dewey calls 'conjectural anticipation'. In our example, we may begin to wonder if our drop-out rate had anything to do with the clash between assessment deadlines and busy times for families like holy festivals and holidays. We may wonder if our drop-out rate had something to do with difficulties in public transport, or difficulties with finance. We may want to research the students' perspectives, how they see the situation, as well as obtaining facts about transport, childcare, ability to pay, and the timing of major festivals and holidays. We need to come up with a possible reason (or set of reasons) for our situation, which we can then use to begin finding ways to deal with it. Once we have our facts and figures and people's perceptions, we can begin to think of ways of dealing with our problem of drop-out. We may decide that we should alter the timing of the programme, or seek a college-wide solution to some of the transport difficulties and financial arrangements. We do not yet know if these ideas will work, but by taking action we are testing the hypothesis. What we do may not to lead to what we thought would happen, but now, when we look at the consequences of our action, we are doing so in a more focused way. We are hoping to *learn* from what we have done.

There are two points to note about Dewey's approach. The first is that the use of careful survey and elaboration makes this a *reflective* approach rather than a simple rushing into a trial-and-error approach to action. Second, Dewey suggested that hypotheses are formulated and then *tested* through taking action. By doing this, we take an *inquisitive* approach to our actions in the world. As teachers, we can use this approach to take action based on our reflections. In other words, we can learn from our experiences, be proactive in trying out new ideas and solutions to existing problems, and be aware that any action we take leads to new challenges. For Dewey, you can't think reflectively without acting in the first place. The two are inextricably linked. We can spend time working out what an issue or problem is, and we can spend time thinking about what to do about this, but these can only work if we are doing something – in this case, teaching!

Thinking reflectively can be quite a dangerous undertaking. We are actively challenging the comfortable, taken-for-granted parts of our professional selves. The words that Dewey, back in 1916 and 1933, uses to capture such demands are significant:

> … one can think reflectively only when one is willing to *endure* suspense and to *undergo* the *trouble* of searching. To many persons both *suspense of judgement* and *intellectual*

search are *disagreeable,* they want to get them ended as soon as possible. They cultivate over-positive and dogmatic habit of mind, or feel perhaps that a condition of *doubt* will be regarded as evidence of *mental inferiority.* It is at the point where *examination* and *test* enter into investigation that the difference between reflective thought and bad thinking comes in ... to be *genuinely thoughtful,* we must be willing to *sustain* and *protract* that state of doubt which is the *stimulus to thorough inquiry.* (1933: 15–16; 1916: 176, our italics)

In our example at the beginning of this chapter, Maria will learn from her experience, particularly if she is thinking reflectively. However, what can help her to learn beyond the survival stage? She could easily try out different approaches but this could simply be 'shots in the dark'. In other words, what can she do to avoid simply focusing on the context of her practice but rather to 'problematize' this practice? To progress, she needs to systematically question her understanding of the situation at hand. We suggest that Dewey's approach to thinking reflectively can lead to a more experimental approach where we take action but also observe the consequences of our actions and, very importantly, work with our colleagues so that our experiences and understanding can be used by others.

Experimentation can often lead to consequences that require further action. For example, suppose we are trying to improve the way our students learn effectively. One collaborative project, from Joint Practice Development (see Gregson et al., 2015, Reading 16.1 for a fuller explanation). *Enabling further learning through available technology* (Barton and Butcher, 2012) started with the problem that online delivery was criticized by Ofsted as being inconsistent and ineffective. They decided to see how students actually used the virtual learning environment (VLE) and then developed effective methods with their colleagues through the use of question-and-answer strategies. This idea made use of existing strategies (question and answer) but applied them in a new context (the VLE), thus experimenting with a solution and testing a previous successful method further. This particular study led the practitioners to the view that:

No one person or research has any clue or direction on how to make it [VLE to enhance deep learning] work, rather a collection of possible means in which to employ the concepts in different ways in the attempt to meet learner need. (Barton and Butcher, 2012: 6)

2 Critical reflection: Practical ways to begin reflecting

One of the great exponents of critical reflection is Mezirow. His fundamental approach is based upon the idea that we should critically reflect on our assumptions (CRA) so that we have a principled approach to our thinking; in other words, it is impartial, consistent and non-arbitrary. This is a tall order. If we do begin to adopt this approach, the results will be transformative. Mezirow called critical reflection of assumptions and self-reflection on assumptions the 'emancipatory dimensions of adult learning' (1998: 191). Yet how do we manage to critically reflect?

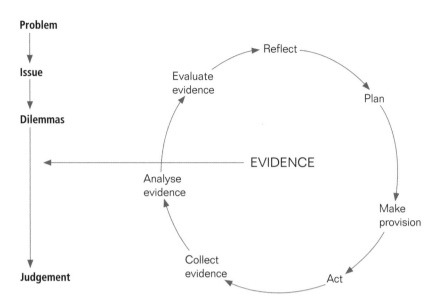

Problem

Issue

Dilemmas

Judgement

Reflect

Evaluate
evidence

Plan

EVIDENCE

Analyse
evidence

Make
provision

Collect
evidence

Act

Figure 3.1
Evidence informed
practice

This model provides an opportunity to step back from the urgency of dealing with the problem, task or incident. More importantly, by working with a group of colleagues or peers, it is possible to reframe the incident using a variety of perspectives which the individuals in that group offer. This is an important aspect of reflective practice. It is very difficult to reveal our own assumptions without the help of a 'critical friend'.

Critical incident analysis

One way to begin this process is to start with a 'critical incident'. This idea was developed by Flanagan (1954) and essentially asks us to think of an example which especially illustrates a general point. So if we want to think about what it is like to be a learner, we can think of a situation where we recently acquired a new skill.

Reflective activity 3.2

Yvonne began learning British Sign Language a few years ago while working at the City Lit, which has a Centre for Deaf People. She wanted to learn to communicate with her deaf colleagues, particularly as they had started working together on a course for sign language teachers, all of whom were deaf. She was excited by communicating through showing facial expressions but also the immense difficulty in trying to read someone else's finger-spelling. She enjoyed trying out the signs in pairs and small groups. Yet Yvonne felt completely useless when it came to watching her tutor finger-spell and to take it in turns to say what he had just said. Critical incident analysis would ask: what were the characteristics of that situation which helped her to learn? What was difficult? Is there anything about these characteristics that we think we could attend to with our own students?

So what can be learned from this particular example? If *we* remember feeling anxious about trying out our new skill in public, perhaps in front of our fellow

---

students, then why do we ask our *students* to do this? Can we justify putting them through such emotional terror? If we think it really is important for people to practise their new skill, is there a way we could enable them to do this without an 'audience'? These are the kinds of question we can ask when we have a critical incident to analyse. In this way, we identify problems, based on our own experiences, for us to examine further.

Brookfield's critical lenses

Brookfield (1995) suggests that we can look at a situation from our own viewpoint, from our colleagues' viewpoint, from our students' viewpoint and from theoretical literature. He calls these the four critical lenses. Brookfield identifies critical reflection as a fundamental approach to teaching. He suggests that not only teachers but also students should develop an approach which demands the 'hunt for assumptions'. It is like detective work, seeking out clues to our current behaviour.

Case study 3.2 Reflective practice through Joint Practice Development

Derbyshire Adult Community Education Service became involved in a project which sought to encourage tutors and managers to change their practice through participation in an action learning research project where they were encouraged to take a risk, try something new and be supported to experiment. They were trying to identify what they could do when tutors may have been graded with a Level 2 (i.e. their practice was assessed as 'good') but no subsequent action was taken to share or improve their teaching. The researchers needed to address what was being assumed about the practice of their peers when it had been graded as being good and also about whether this good practice could be further developed. By supporting tutors to try out something new, the researchers found that joint practice development did lead to changes in practice and found some evidence that this also affected the ways in which students learnt.

2.1 Drawing upon everyday experience

There is a widely held perception that theory and practice are mutually exclusive and one is of no help to the other. Indeed, many readers may be thinking that this section is going to get too theoretical and that perhaps they can skim it, or put it away for another day! In her research with basic education practitioners (Hillier, 1994), Yvonne found that many practitioners involved in the study mentioned that they did not read books on educational theory but they did have their own ideas. Their daily practice was steeped in theory but they would not have been able to articulate it. Theory, on the other hand, could and did describe and explain much of their practice. We do have ideas of theories in use and taken-for-granted ideas about what we do, ideas which can be seen as 'knowing how' and 'knowing that', and occasionally ideas about 'knowing why' (Ryle, 1945).

If you are currently taking a course in how to teach, you will have noticed that you have many similarities with your colleagues' ideas, but also many differences. In many cases, we simply do not know the 'best way' to do something, or why certain situations occur. Now, we can have our 'hunches' and these are the basis of our informal theories. These informal theories contrast with the formal theories which are given status because they have been publicly examined and because we tend to think that theory, and in particular anything scientific, must be true. Brookfield, as ever, provides a timely reminder that if we think about what he calls 'universal theory', i.e. formal public theory, it does not help us adapt to local conditions, in which, 'students' actions contradict our beautifully reasoned analysis' (Brookfield, 1995: 209).

Once again, the idea of tacit knowledge is apparent when we think of how much professionals know. Polanyi (1962) once said 'we know more than we can tell'. If you have observed an experienced colleague teach, that person will have an enormous amount of personal knowledge which is being operationalized. If you then ask your colleague to provide a running commentary on why she was behaving in the way she did, she would find it extremely difficult to do so. This is because she is using what Schön (1983) called 'knowledge in action', and needs to step out of that in order to talk about it.

Another example of public and private knowledge was demonstrated by Nonaka and Takeuchi (1995). They found that people joining a new organization are socialized into certain ways of doing things quite quickly. Some of these procedures are public knowledge; for example, in a further education college, filling in learning contracts must be done, and everyone who is involved in teaching a group of students is told about it. However, there are implicit things that are not even discussed, often involving how people relate to each other, or what they wear. Yet newcomers work out for themselves, for example, what the dress code is. If asked, people may stop and think and then discuss 'this is how we do things around here', but this knowledge is often implicit and has been acquired without an induction programme to spell it out. An interesting activity for us is to try and think about what is publicly known by our colleagues about our workplace and what we seem to know without having talked about it.

We have seen in the example of Maria how a specific problem can be examined in terms of what assumptions are being brought to bear when she identifies it as a problem. These assumptions, be they profound or workaday, constitute the theoretical basis of her actions. There is no practice without theory, even if it is unstated. In this example, the theory includes ideas about emotional aspects of learning. We can look at an individual lecturer's perceptions of the purposes of education and training and the way in which qualifications are so necessary for young people entering the workplace. We could therefore consider the motivation of both lecturer and students. In short, we have in this example a microcosm of the situation of teaching adults and young people, which can be analysed using existing theories from a number of disciplines including social science, philosophy, history and politics.

Sometimes we define one thing by what it is not, and theory and practice are sometimes seen to be opposites – that practice deals with concrete, immediate realities and theory deals with general, abstract concepts. This is quite misleading. Carr (1986) argued that the assumptions that practice is non-theoretical and theory is non-practical underestimate the 'extent to which those who engage in educational practices have to reflect upon, and hence theorize about, what, in general, they are trying to do' (p. 162).

What, in fact, is happening is 'theory-guided practice' where what we do presupposes a conceptual framework, even if we are not terribly good at articulating it or are even aware of it. In fact, Griffin (1989) goes so far as to claim that our practice and our theory are interlinked:

> There is no adult education practice that does not express theory and no adult education theory that does not arise directly from adult education practice … the knowledge base would be the practice. (p. 136)

The link between theory and practice therefore means that theory is 'grounded' in practice and the latter is not some kind of 'thoughtless behaviour which exists separately from theory' (Carr and Kemmis, 1986: 113). When we teach, our practice is formed by our experience – by the way we make sense of what we do. If we try out a new way of teaching, the results of trying this new way help us decide whether or not to use it in the future. We develop knowledge which can be called practical knowledge, and this is concerned with 'appropriate action in the world' (Usher and Bryant, 1989).

When we think about our practice, we act upon certain material things such as handouts, computers, all manner of learning resources. We are therefore using technical knowhow when producing and using these materials. However, the way in which we choose to put these resources to use in practice is an interaction between us as human beings and these materials. We have to make judgements about how best to use our materials (learning resources) with the students we have in our groups and to draw upon the learning theories we outlined in the preceding chapter. We suggest there is a particular approach which involves making judgements about what to do, when and how in ways which address deep and enduring purposes of education. In other words, we are embarking on a much broader and deeper endeavour than simply using a set of technical skills. This approach goes beyond the mere application of technical skills because our practice means more than this. Educational practice must take account of the importance of the pursuit of the 'human good' (Carr, 1986).

Let us introduce some terms which help us to define what we mean by practice. Nowadays there is a danger of assuming that we all know what educational practice is, whereby we accept our common-sense understandings of it (see Carr, 1995). Yet, like theory, it is much more complex and subject to different conceptualizations. The Greeks had a richer understanding of this. Aristotle called technical skills *techne*. Technical skills, he argued, can help us to make material objects but they cannot tell us what to do in our actions and interactions in the social world. *Techne* involves knowledge about the materials we work with and the techniques we can apply to work with those materials to produce the end object we are trying to make. However, making things does not simply involve following a recipe. *Techne* is guided by *poiesis,* the production or fabrication of *things*, which are already known prior to the action taken to produce them. This is perhaps best seen as a kind of instrumental or rule following action. It involves exercising a particular kind of judgement, *poiesis,* about the application of our technical knowledge to this particular *thing* or piece of material for the particular purpose in hand as we are engaged in the process of making it. When we make a cake, there are all manner of handy rules about what to do to create the perfect example, but in the process of making it, experienced cooks take decisions to adjust what they are doing as they can see that the mixture requires action – for example, when adding eggs the mixture may curdle. When we teach, we adjust all the time to the ways in which our students are responding and this knowledge is also derived from experience. So *poiesis* is a broader form of knowledge than *techne* and is gained from experience. Biesta (2015, Reading 1.1) provides an analysis of how important *poiesis* is in our professional practice.

With teaching, we do not actually bring about the creation of material products. When we talk about the practice of teaching, we are talking about acting in the social world. As we noted above, this has a moral dimension in educational practice. So for us the interesting term is *praxis,* which is concerned with the 'human good'. *Praxis* is not a form of 'technically correct' behaviour – it is much deeper than that. It is concerned with ethical, social and political action. When we think of *praxis,* we therefore begin to think about how we are influenced by our culture, our upbringing, and our socially situated selves. We act in this world in ways that are defined by our personalities, our religion or philosophy, and by our ideologies, much of which we are unaware. One of the major proponents of *praxis* was Freire (1971, 2002) whose work with poor people in Brazil led him to see that their need to gain literacy was not simply so that they could read and write, but so that they could take action in the world to improve their situation. *Praxis* is therefore concerned with political action. It is something that Carr and Kemmis (1986) describe thus:

> Praxis has its roots in the commitment of the practitioner to wise and prudent action in a practical, concrete, historical situation. Praxis is always risky; it requires that the practitioner makes a wise and prudent practical judgement about how to act in this situation. (pp. 190–2)

So *poiesis* is non-reflective action which leads to the creation of something. It does involve judgements about materials and things. It doesn't, though, consider pursuing the 'moral good'. *Praxis,* on the other hand, is a reflective form of action which is capable of transforming the theory that influences it and is completely bound up with the pursuit of the 'human good'. This kind of action is therefore not going to lead to a specific output in the way that making a cake or a pot will; it is not neutral and it is not simple. It is all about a process that leads to a goal which itself is often highly contested.

Knowledge about teaching is not the abstract, generalized kind but is 'situational' in that it is 'socially located, very often complex and problematic and consciously and intentionally carried out' (Usher and Bryant, 1989: 82). This can be called 'informal theory'. However, it is often taken for granted, it may be seen as simple common sense and is private and unique to the practitioner. So we need to try and make explicit the implicit nature of this theory, and once it has been made explicit we can critically examine it. Without critical analysis, informal theories held by practitioners and their practical knowledge arising from their experiences risk 'remaining at the level of anecdotal, idiosyncratic reminiscence' (Brookfield, 1993: 75).

For educational practice to take the form of *praxis* rather than mere *techne*, we need to reflect critically on our practice. The process of critical reflection can take many forms, as we showed earlier in this chapter. However, to ensure that our educational practice does benefit from our critical reflections, we need to adopt a form of reflective practice that comprises certain key characteristics we will now outline.

3 Critical reflection: Principles and values

3.1 Seven characteristics of reflective practice

So far in this chapter we have discussed the importance of reflecting on our practice in order to become effective. We have suggested that it is by practice that we can further develop and test our theories, both those we have held informally and those which are explicit and formal. We have provided examples where people can develop their practice jointly. We believe that reflective practice is a key factor in achieving good practice in our professional lives. We have set out reasons why we support reflective practice. We can now turn to examining the principal characteristics of this practice, following Pollard (2013), who has identified seven key characteristics of reflective practice:

1 **Reflective teaching implies an active concern with aims and consequences, as well as means and technical efficiency.**

If we want to find out whether what we know and do is effective, or indeed if we want to test knowledge, then we need a way to draw upon the tacit as well as explicit nature of that knowledge. Research, therefore, in FAVE should draw upon the wealth of professional knowledge that resides within the people who work in the sector. A fundamental approach to developing our practice stems from examining carefully or researching what we do. Such research does not have to be of the large-scale variety, as most of us do not have access to such opportunities. However, we agree with Stenhouse (1975, Reading 3.3), Elliot (1981), Fielding (2005) and Coffield (2008) when we say that research-informed practice is something we can achieve ourselves and which can help inform our peers.

2 **Reflective teaching is applied in a cyclical or spiral process, in which teachers monitor, evaluate and revise their own practice continually.**

One approach to examining and developing our practice can be achieved through action research (Pring, 2004, Reading 3.4). Here, we identify an issue that we wish to address and take action, collaboratively, to address it, but all the time monitoring and changing what we do. Action research is about making a difference but doing so in a way that is informed by careful research. It aims to enable people to improve their own practice, rather than have improvements done to them. It is self-critical, located in an approach aiming to develop practice via systematic enquiry and learning. It is a deliberate attempt to examine the way in which something is being undertaken, with a view to making changes to that process as the research goes along. It is inherently bound up with reflective practice, in which a group of colleagues may challenge the taken-for-granted and try to create a rationale for their practice (Hillier and Jameson, 2003).

3 **Reflective teaching requires competence in methods of evidence-informed classroom enquiry, to support the progressive development of higher standards of teaching.**

Our first starting point of identifying an issue we wish to pursue should lead us to examine what has already been researched and reported. We therefore need to make use of such evidence, through undertaking searches of printed material in books, journals, reports and through internet searches.

We then need to be able to gather our *own* evidence. There are many ways to gain experience in this, from reading about research methodology to undertaking formal programmes of research training. For example, in England, a research network set up to enable practitioners from FAVE to use and undertake their own research, the Learning and Skills Research Network (LSRN), developed a toolkit to help practitioners undertake research in an informed way (Morris and Norman, 2004). The JPD programme sponsored by the Education and Training Foundation (ETF) pioneered a systematic approach to gathering research evidence and improving teaching and learning in the FAVE sector. However, data gathering is not enough. We need to be able to analyse the data that we have. This requires a sound knowledge of data analysis techniques and, importantly, an understanding of the limits of any approach undertaken.

Finally, we need to be able to evaluate our own research and that of others. Most reported research does not fully cover the stops and starts and messiness of research, or indeed the decisions taken that inevitably provide one perspective over another (Hillier and Jameson, 2003).

4 **Reflective teaching requires attitudes of open-mindedness, responsibility and wholeheartedness.**

How do we know what is 'good'? We need to apply a critical approach to both our practice and the theory that informs it. If discussion on critical theory seems removed from our own teaching, let us return to our first example of critical reflection. When we think of Maria, we have to ask ourselves whether there is an underlying viewpoint, an ideology which is operating and directing all of us to gaze in a particular direction. If we look ahead, we do not see what is behind us. We need to direct our gaze to the areas out of our view. What happens if we do reflectively criticize our taken-for-granted thoughts? What happens to the action as a result? It requires reflection on our experiences so that 'formal study is informed by some appreciation of reality' (Brookfield, 1990: 50). Brookfield recommends that we can go beyond the 'nitty gritty' of our daily practice in the classroom or training room by 'questioning and then replacing or reframing an assumption which is accepted as representing dominant common sense by a majority' (1993: 66).

It is all very well saying that we can think reflectively and try out solutions to problems we have identified, but how do we know we have identified the real problems? Our definition of the problem arising from a given situation may not be the same as your view: who is 'right'? Furthermore, our identification of a problem and the solution may simply relate to what is called 'technical rationality' (Schön, 1983) – in other words, we are finding a means to an end. We want our students to learn in an efficient way. We may not be taking into account the notions of equity, or challenging what it is the students should learn, and why. What about practising in ways that are 'morally good'? Here, we are moving away from the idea that we simply have to find efficient ways to go about the business of teaching and learning, to the idea that there are things that we *should* do – that is, there is a *normative* aspect to our theory and practice.

We discussed earlier in this chapter that *praxis* involves an emphasis on commitment to action. However, commitment to action is still not enough if we are searching for the wisest course of action. How do we know that our practice is prudent? For this, we need another approach where our action has been informed by reflection which makes judgements about what is the 'best' way. This is the Greek term *phronesis*. It means practical knowledge that is defined as rightness of action. It aims to go beyond practice which is routine, habitual or unquestioned. It requires acting 'rightly and appropriately' (Carr and Kemmis, 1986: 32) and a 'prudent understanding of variable situations with a view to what is to be done' (McCarthy, 1984: 2). Of course, what is appropriate cannot be easily established and is open to challenge. Yet searching for ways to act rightly and appropriately is an important goal for us. It is a constant search and ensures that we do not become complacent. Carr, in articulating the importance of *phronesis* for Aristotle, described it as 'the most supreme intellectual virtue and an indispensable feature of practice' (1986: 171).

We are not suggesting that we can discover one right way morally. We know that there are cultural differences in how we define what is morally right. We can, however, be open to debate about the moral and ethical dimension of our work. It is only by acknowledging the difficulties we encounter in deciding how to act in this world rightly and appropriately that we can begin to work towards achieving this goal. So, our search for reflective teaching is based upon an ancient Greek concept of *phronesis*. Without it, the person 'who lacks *phronesis* may be technically accountable but never morally answerable' (Carr, 1986: 171). Standards help direct the way in which we undertake our professional practice and begin to help us identify and debate our code of practice as professionals who facilitate the learning of others. We do not think we should consider these values as given or unproblematic. We believe they should form the basis of a professional dialogue, continually reminding us that we are searching for practice which is never complacent.

5 **Reflective teaching is based on teacher judgement, informed by evidence and insights from other research.**

Evidence-informed classroom enquiry provides an opportunity for small-scale research by practitioners to be systematically developed into larger-scale research studies, but it can also provide important nuggets of local insights upon which practitioners can continue to experiment. In England, the success of the Learning and Skills Improvement Service (LSIS) Joint Practice Development (JPD) programme, the National Research and Development Centre for Adult Literacy, Language and Numeracy (NRDC) and the LSRN practitioner projects provide a growing body of evidence from research into FAVE which we can draw upon. This approach is used internationally, for example, in Australia with the National Centre for Vocational Education Research (NCVER) supported practitioner research projects (NCVER, 2014)

6 Reflective teaching, professional learning and personal fulfilment are enhanced through collaboration and dialogue with colleagues.

This approach relates to a concept of professional practice. Elliot (1991) wrote that all worthwhile professional learning is experiential. We should look at real practical situations which are problematic, complex and open to a variety of interpretations from differing points of view. This provides opportunities to develop capacities which are fundamental to competent professional practice. Thus our acquisition of knowledge proceeds interactively with reflecting about practical situations.

It is one thing to think reflectively about our practice and use this in a wise way. Have we established that critical reflection can actually change practice? Can we change practice and make it more effective, more underpinned by theories that are the best we have? Our informal theories have little likelihood of developing into 'good practice' if they are not critically examined and tested. Talking to colleagues about what we do 'unwraps the shroud of silence in which our practice is wrapped' (Brookfield, 1998: 136). If we reflect critically, we can begin to formulate propositions from our own personal, informal theories which then become public and testable. We can then begin to advance both our practical and theoretical knowledge, taking into account the important interplay between what is happening in practice and what sense is being made of our practice by others. Examining our practice is, as Popper noted, 'not the enemy of theoretical knowledge but the incentive to it' (1962: 222).

By reflecting critically, instead of continuing with our feelings of self-doubt, that we are imposters in our classrooms, or that we are failing as teachers and racked with guilt, we can become positive in our search for new understandings of our practice and more ways to deal with the challenges that confront us continually. We take control over our professional practice, acknowledging that we cannot transform everything, but aware that we can identify the spheres in which we can. It is a truly emancipatory process.

7 Reflective teaching enables teachers to creatively mediate externally developed frameworks for teaching and learning.

Intimately connected with reflective practice, then, is the way in which we act as professionals. One of the characteristics of professional behaviour is adhering to a set of values and views about how to practise, as seen by the TLRP principles we discuss throughout this book. The FAVE sector can draw upon a number of professional practices, as it comprises such a vast array of specialist subjects.

However, within the teaching and learning arena, the main source of an articulated code of practice is the set standards (Education and Training Foundation, 2014) which include a requirement that professional practitioners engage in continuous professional development, with the aim of improving their skills and deepening their knowledge.

As the standards focus on the role of the professional, you may find that you are required to keep a professional diary, or learning log, throughout your teacher training programmes. We will not prescribe how you should keep such a log, or even create exercises for you to undertake upon reading any chapter in this book. However, we do suggest that you write down thoughts as and when they occur to you, as you will be surprised at progress in your thinking as time goes by, and these 'scribbles' will provide you with an important source of information when you are asked to look back over your programme and identify how you have developed your thinking and understanding of this vast and complex area.

3.2 Developing joint practice

Earlier in this chapter we drew attention to the limitations of solitary or, at best, pairs of practitioners engaging in reflective practice and we showed through our case studies how collaborative reflection in groups is a powerful way to bring together different perspectives to bear upon the understanding of a problem or issue in practice. We encourage you to explore with colleagues to develop your ideas and knowledge about your professional practice and indeed, we argue that working together to critically examine practice and then take steps to change this in an exploratory way is a fundamental part of being a professional teacher. We will include examples drawn from the LSIS JPD programme throughout the book to illustrate what we mean by collaborative reflective practice and how you might go about it in a research-informed and systematic way. Below we set out more fully the main features of JPD.

JPD is a practitioner-centred approach to improving teaching, learning and assessment (TLA) which:

> ... takes account of the existing practice of teachers who are trying to learn new ways of working and acknowledges the effort of those who are trying to support them. It also underscores the necessity of mutual engagement, which lies at the heart of the complex task of opening up and sharing practices with others. (Michael Fielding et al., 2005: 72)

JPD differs from more traditional approaches to CPD, which assumes there is an expert in possession of the knowledge to be transferred to the teacher, who is seen in deficit in respect of these new ideas or practices. JPD recognizes the power of knowledge gained from educational research to improve TLA. It balances the knowledge gained from educational research with the local knowledge and individual insight of education leaders and teachers working in particular settings. At the heart of the JPD approach is the idea that when teachers, education leaders and organizations learn from one another as they *experiment* with putting research findings into practice, real change can happen.

In the introduction, we outlined four guiding principles for JPD. These are for practitioners to:

1 Make space for trust, openness and honesty.

2 Work to establish a shared understanding of the education problem and how it makes educational sense for it to be addressed.

3 Share the experience of trying out interventions/innovative practices.

4 Critically review overall progress together.

JPD begins with the recognition that finding new and better ways of working need not discount the merits of current practice. Instead it encourages education leaders and teachers to collaborate in adapting well-researched innovations and ideas and incorporating these into existing aspects of their work together in mutually supportive ways. This approach, supported by our ideas on critically reflecting on practice, provides the cornerstone for our approach to teaching in FAVE.

Reflective activity 3.3

Think about a situation in your teaching that perplexes or challenges you. Write down an example of this and begin to identify from your understanding of this chapter what the issues are, from your own perspective, from that of your students and from the wider context. Discuss this with a colleague, or preferably a small group of colleagues who are aware of the process of reflection and who can help analyse the situation from different perspectives. Remember to think about the possible action that you can take and agree to meet again to see how the next steps affect your practice. Also try and keep a log of your thoughts and actions, as well as any reading that you do. The log doesn't have to be a formal diary and you may want to look at some websites and blogs or engage with social networks in your own context (see Chapter 17).

Conclusion

By now, many of you may be wondering exactly what you can rely upon when thinking about the most appropriate course of action with your students. We have suggested that you have underlying private theories about why things work and therefore how to teach, but these are not tested by others, if they are even articulated. We then argued that this informal theory is subject to all sorts of 'deceptions', influences of culture and ideology which create assumptions that are not easily identified and therefore not easily challenged. As Crotty (1996: 280) noted: 'When we attempt to describe what we have never had to describe before, language fails us.' So what is to be done?

Perhaps a starting point is to think of professional practice as a journey. At the beginning, you have to be 'kitted up'; in other words, you have to have the necessary equipment and knowledge about how to plan your journey and what to take with you. This is like initial professional education and training. However, once you start travelling, you will meet different situations and people; you will naturally grow older and will have found particular strategies and methods to help you on your way. This is experience which you gain and from which, if you reflect critically, you can learn. There is also a lot of information that you can obtain along the way, too. This is the formal knowledge that is public, a bit like tourist information, maps and timetables. You have to make use of them to plan your particular journey, and you will come to know some of this information very well. Yet your choice of mode of travel may not be the most effective. Sometimes you will not know this until you meet up with other fellow travellers.

Even though we can never know just how much we're cooking the data of our memories and experiences to produce images and renditions that confirm our own prejudices and instincts, the critical journey has to start somewhere, and examining our autobiographies as adult students is one obvious and fruitful (though usually neglected) point of departure (Brookfield, 1998: 135).

This chapter started with a practical situation. It then discussed what a reflective process was. This raised questions about thinking reflectively and how we, as practitioners, have many informal theories about our professional work. This led to thinking about theory and what it is and how it can help us. The idea of professionalism and competence was discussed, showing that professionals continually seek more knowledge about how to improve their practice. In this way, we realize that not only do we teach but we constantly learn about our teaching. Throughout this book, you will be asked to think of yourself as a learner. What does it feel like? Can you remember when you struggled to learn something? Can you remember when you learned something easily? Can you use your experience when you work with your own students? In other words, can you reflect on your experience and learn from it, transferring your knowledge about learning into knowledge about teaching? Can you teach reflectively?

We are accountable to many people when we teach: students, colleagues, funding providers, members of communities, and we know that the demands of the various 'stake-holders' are often competing. Critical reflection does not claim to offer easy answers to these deeply serious and complex problems. It is something that Maslow (1968) described as 'the crucial, unresolved, human questions'. As Eraut (1994) carefully points out, learning from experience is quite problematic. What, precisely, do we learn from experience? We may learn to repeat past mistakes, simply because we have not even thought that there could be alternative ways of doing things.

So, perhaps we can argue that it is not the fact that we can change the world through critical reflection, or indeed can guarantee that we will change our daily practice, but that we have a more developed view about what we do than before we began to think reflectively. Our position is now 'informed by other positions' (Warnke, 1987: 169). We can draw upon different forms of learning: learning from initial education and training; learning from books and formal, public knowledge; and learning from experience.

As we have shown in this chapter, we need to take account of our potential to foster active citizenship not just for our students but for ourselves. We need to recognize how our own professional practice must continually be challenged and developed and we must finally recognize that we are part of a complex system that is influenced by policies at every level of our work in FAVE.

Key readings

Books which discuss key aspects of becoming a reflective teacher:

Brookfield, S. D. (1995) *Becoming a Critically Reflective Teacher*. San Francisco: Jossey-Bass.

Carr, W. and Kemmis, S. (1986) *Becoming Critical*. Lewes: Falmer.

A classic text on how human beings think and learn:

Dewey, J. (1916) *How We Think: A Restatement of the Relation of Reflective Teaching in the Educative Process*. Chicago: Henry Regnery.

For a useful analysis of how professionals think and learn, see:

Eraut, M. (1994) *Developing Professional Knowledge and Competence*. London: Falmer.

A helpful discussion of the processes and conditions necessary to change and improve professional practice:

Fielding, M., Bragg, S., Craig, J., Cunningham, I.., Eraut, M., Gillinson. S., Horne, M., Robinson, C. and Thorp, J. (2005) *Factors Influencing the Transfer of Good Practice*. London: Department for Education and Skills RR 615.

Seminal texts in the development of thinking about reflective practice:

Schön, D. (1983) *The Reflective Practitioner*. San Francisco: Jossey-Bass.

—(1987) *Educating the Reflective Practitioner: Toward a New Design for Teaching and Learning in the Professions*. San Francisco: Jossey-Bass.

For an insightful introduction to curriculum theory and curriculum development, see:

Stenhouse, L. (1975) *An Introduction to Curriculum Research and Development*. London: Heinemann.

The following readings can be found in the accompanying reader to this textbook:

For James Calderhead's five areas of research on teaching and learning to teach, see **Reading 3.1**, edited from:

Calderhead, J. (1994) 'Can the complexities of teaching be accounted for in terms of competences? Contrasting views of professional practice from research and policy'. Mimeo produced for an Economic and Social Research Council symposium on teacher competence, 1–2.

John Dewey considers the relationship between reflective thinking and the sort of challenges people face in **Reading 3.2**, edited from:

> Dewey, J. (1916) *Democracy and Education.* New York: Free Press, 176–7.
> —(1933) *How We Think: A Restatement of the Relation of Reflective Thinking to the Educative Process.* Chicago: Henry Regnery, 15–16.

For Lawrence Stenhouse's article about 'The teacher as researcher' see **Reading 3.3**, edited from:

> Stenhouse, L. (1975*) An Introduction to Curriculum Research and Development.* London: Heinemann, 143–57.

To see Richard Pring's theories on the development of practice, look at **Reading 3.4**, edited from:

> Pring, R. (2000) *Philosophy of Educational Research.* Continuum: London, 130–4.

The associated website, **reflectiveteaching.co.uk**, offers a wealth of supplementary resources including reflective activities, research briefings, advice on further reading and downloadable diagrams, figures and checklists from the book. It also features a compendium of educational terms, links to useful websites, policy and curriculum documents, and showcases examples of excellent research and practice.

Principles

What are the foundations of effective teaching and learning?

4

Introduction

In Chapter 1 we draw attention to how, as a teacher, you will be faced with complex and unfolding situations in your practice when it may not be clear what you should do for the best. This raises the interesting question of what *do* you do when you don't know what to do? Any situation we meet in our professional practice involves managing dilemmas and making decisions. We often talk about the need to think carefully and of the need to draw upon previous educational experiences to exercise good judgements and act upon those judgements (Biesta, 2015, Reading 1.1). At the same time, we must monitor the consequences of our actions upon the students in the light of evidence. As we explained in Chapters 1 and 3, we believe that the development of good educational practice involves engaging with educational values and guiding principles to help us to deal with the numerous issues and dilemmas we face in our practice as teachers in careful and critically reflective ways.

We have already suggested that educational practice is far more than a set of technical skills and it is important to think carefully about what we do, why, and what happens as a result. This is because our educational practice should fundamentally involve a moral dimension alongside an obligation to act in pursuit of the human good. Heilbronn (2011, Reading 4.1) points out that it is important for teachers in the development of practical judgement and the wisdom and capacity 'to do the right thing and at the right time'. She shows how Aristotle's work on practical judgement foregrounds enduring qualities required in combining experience and analysis in practical contexts. She goes on to identify three dimensions of practical judgement: ethics, flexibility and personal rootedness (the character, dispositions and qualities to act in ways informed by the teacher's personal experiences and educational values). She draws attention to the moral purposes of teaching, which always require the teacher to make careful judgements in multidimensional and often continuingly emerging situations. (Heilbronn, 2011, Reading 4.1). This is what makes teaching so interesting and such a responsibility.

This view does not always sit comfortably with notions of effective teaching, which are used, for example, in many standards and inspection regimes. In talking about good education we can carelessly speak of effective, successful, good, best, excellent and outstanding practice as though they all carry the same values and imply the same meaning. For example, in your professional role you will be expected to teach effectively, you will be judged by your students, colleagues and by quality assurance managers of external inspectors appointed to ensure that all students experience successful learning. But what does it mean to teach effectively? How will you know that you have done so? How does anyone inspecting teaching in the wide variety of contexts in FAVE identify good or outstanding educational practice? In this chapter, we will discuss how our approach to educational practice can relate to notions of effective practice through application of guiding principles developed as part of the Teaching and Learning Research Programme (TLRP) (James and Pollard, 2006).

Over the past 50 years in England, politicians and policymakers across all sectors of education have increasingly legislated the work of teachers. This increased attention could be seen as a positive development signalling a real concern for the quality of education and the importance of teacher professionalism. Governments in many countries have established a series of measures including central curriculum prescription and highly specified assessment regimes, testing, inspection, league tables and a plethora of internal mechanisms for micro-management and 'quality' control. As part of this drive to monitor and control the work of teachers, politicians and policymakers are now turning their attention to teacher education. This welcome recognition that the quality of teacher education is central to the quality of education in general could also be viewed more pessimistically as establishing more control over the education system and the practice of education.

There is another way to describe this issue. Instead of being welcome, there is growing concern that damage is being done. Ball (2003) calls this the rise of 'performativity' – a culture or system of accountability which uses public comparisons of performance as a means of control. In such regimes, he argues, the performances of individuals serve as measures of productivity and output which represent the 'worth, quality or value of an individual or organisation' (Ball, 2003: 49). For Ball, the current technologies of education reform are devices for changing the meaning of practice and of social relations that exist within practice. He claims that these tensions and contradictions serve to divert the energies and attention of teachers away from important issues in teaching and learning towards instrumental 'fabrications of compliance'.

Coffield (2006) argues that, in England, education policy overload from successive governments is doing more harm than good. He points to the dilemmas that teachers face in balancing the intensification of demands to increase their direct engagement with students with other competing imperatives. He describes the toll that pressures to conduct research and curriculum development alongside requirements to collect and record quality assurance and performance data as part of the constant preparation for short-notice inspections is having on teachers across the sector.

As many of you – new to teaching or experienced – discover, the push towards compliance can be compelling. It takes confidence and courage to resist the call of 'teaching to the test'. The continual call to 'genuflect' to the hegemony of league tables can appear plausible and offer attractive 'survival tactics' to beginning and experienced teachers alike. In this culture it is all too easy to feel that enduring educational values are being eroded, distorted and even trivialized. At times like these, therefore, it is important for us to be clear about what we mean by 'good education'. In the context of the FAVE sector, Ecclestone suggests that:

> … performativity accompanied by a subtle ideology of 'risk' and 'risk aversion' … produces a 'minimalist pedagogy', based on low expectations of learners' potential for intrinsic motivation or critical autonomy … Low expectations combined with micro-disciplinary practices associated with assessment and quality assurance regimes lead to increased safety and compliance in learning activities. (Ecclestone, 2002: 182)

More subtly still, she argues, such approaches encourage us to see good education solely in terms of economic necessities and priorities. Using examples from Finland, Sahlberg (2011) offers an alternative model of education (Sahlberg, 2011, **Reading 4.2**) where teachers have more autonomy.

Biesta (2010) points out how performative technologies attempt to change the way we think about the role of human relationships in education and diminish the importance of educational values and pedagogies which aim to develop individual character and ethics exemplified by a concern for the collective as well as the individual good. He argues that:

> Although the question of good education is a difficult and contentious question, I believe that it is also the most central and most important question we can and should ask … Education be it in the form of schooling, workplace learning or vocational training, or learning through life is by its very nature a process with direction and purpose. (Biesta, 2010: 2)

It is important to remember that, despite living in a world of increasing centralized control, prescription and surveillance, the capacity for wise judgement and the exercise of practical wisdom (*phronesis*) are vital to good educational practice. We must hold on to educational practice as a creative process, making use of educational evidence informed by educational theory while remaining open to testing out new ideas.

In our view, having the courage to take action, based on wise educational judgements, in the pursuit of educational ends and the human good, can and should become the hallmark of good education to which we all aspire.

In the first part of this book we have recognized the need for evidence-informed and principled approaches to initial teacher education and continuing professional development. We have also argued that educational practice cannot be reduced to the simple or instrumental application of concepts, theories, ideas or tips for teachers. Instrumental approaches to the professional development of teachers, often presented in the form of recipes, which on the face of it appear to offer simple solutions that are intuitively appealing and seem to be easy and cheap to implement, are seldom what they seem. Such recipes for good teaching can prove difficult and sometimes quite impossible to put into practice in the wide variety of contexts that constitute the FAVE sector. This is largely because the instrumental application of recipes or tips either overlooks or significantly underestimates the amount of professional knowledge and additional learning and support that you and your colleagues in the sector will need to develop in order to put good ideas into practice in educationally sound and sustainable ways.

Reflective activity 4.1

How many times have you or a colleague come across what you thought was a good educational idea only to find that it was really difficult to put into practice? What are the reasons for this? This might have been because it was an idea that looked great on paper but turned out to be lacking in substance; or that it was not supported by robust educational research; or that it was too theoretical; or that it was simply devoid of educational theory and research altogether! The problem might have been because you felt isolated in trying to put the idea into practice or that you felt someone else's new idea was considered to be 'the best in town' and was being forced upon you (Goldacre, 2013). Which, if any, of the reasons above do you think most often account for this difficulty?

Goldacre reminds us that *teaching* should be driving the research agenda by identifying questions that need to be answered. In Chapter 1 and this chapter we have already recognized the realities and complexities of teaching and the importance of teachers' professional judgement. We have also recognized ways that enduring educational issues are overlooked as a consequence of the rise of unprecedented centralized curriculum regimes, where the agency and professionalism of the teacher is reduced (Coffield, 2006; Ball, 2008).

We have suggested that educational practice involves making moral judgements about what to do in complex and unfolding situations for the good of the individual and for the collective good. So even if we do know that a particular action is likely to lead to a particular outcome, that outcome might not be in the interests of individuals or groups of students in those circumstances at that time. We cannot therefore assume that the identification of a set of universal laws of 'what works' will be possible or even desirable in informing our practice. The danger of such approaches to the improvement of teaching, learning and assessment in the sector is that under-researched and under-examined ideas can be (and have been) rolled out on a 'one size fits all' basis, sometimes to the detriment of good educational practice and often with educational costs to learners and financial costs to public funds (Pollard, 2014).

James and Pollard (2006) point to a growing body of research evidence from around the world that the most significant means of improving the performance of national education systems is through encouraging and supporting the on-going development of creativity, excellence, research and innovation in teachers and their teaching (Hattie, 2009, Reading 4.3) alongside the development of 'principled educational practice' (Pollard, 2014). We are the main creators of professional knowledge and improving educational practice resides in our capacity to scrutinize ideas, theories, ethical values and empirical evidence as an integral part of what we do as teachers. This involves strengthening the shared professional language (i.e. discourse) we use when we talk about teaching, learning and assessment well enough for us to make sure that we understand it ourselves and for this discourse to be able to stand up to scrutiny, argument and evidence from others. At the same time, we need to encourage and enable our colleagues to present, share and justify their professional practice in research and evidence-informed, accessible and collaborative ways (Goldacre, 2013).

As we discussed in Chapter 1 of this book, we found ourselves working in the FAVE sector in different countries and our entry to the teaching profession was via a variety of routes. As we have worked closely together in researching and writing this book, we have found that we share a lot of common ground in relation to what we think education is *for* and how we think it should be practised. As we noted in Chapter 3, the fundamental principle of reflecting on our teaching is to take forward ideas about our practice and to share our experiences so that the community of practitioners to which we belong can also test out our ideas and growing understanding of our practice and theirs.

In the following section, we discuss two frameworks for thinking and talking about principled approaches to the initial and continuing professional development of teachers. We begin with TLRP principles developed by Pollard and his associates. Then we go on to discuss Biesta's (2010, 2012) 'three dimensions of education'. It is worth restating that neither of these are offered as 'cookbook' recipes which will lead to instant success, but as focusing devices for thinking and talking about the development of educational practice. They are research, theory and evidence-informed ideas that can be used to encourage and guide future experimentation and practice. They are also offered as 'evidence-informed educational principles' (Pollard, 2013) or 'dimensions of education' (Biesta, 2012) which can be used to support the development of teachers' professional educational judgement.

1 Evidence-informed principles

Each of the TLRP ten principles described in this chapter has an extensive research base – they are 'evidence-informed'. TLRP's ten principles are an attempt to pick out prominent patterns from the complexity of teaching and learning, and to shed light on them. As we have already explained, such principles are best regarded as working statements of what we *think* we understand at this point in time, based upon evidence drawn from the TLRP programme and other sources of research. The overarching guide in the development of James and Pollard's (2006) framework is Principle 1, which is concerned with the enduring purposes of education and issues and dilemmas in educational practice. The next cluster of principles relate to curriculum, pedagogy and assessment, which the TLRP framework takes to be key aspects of teacher expertise, with a further cluster focusing on the personal and social processes which underpin learning. The final two principles endeavour to frame enabling conditions for success in practice and policy. Figure 4.1 represents the ten principles holistically.

2 TLRP's principles

2.1 Education for life

The first principle, which is an overarching statement, invites us to consider the following:

Principle 1: Effective teaching and learning equips learners for life in its broadest sense. Learning should aim to help people develop the intellectual, personal and social resources that will enable them to participate as active citizens and flourish as individuals in a diverse and changing society. This implies adopting a broad view of learning outcomes and ensuring that equity and social justice are taken seriously.

What does this mean? We believe that effective pedagogy in this context means 'good education practice'. This involves a value judgement about what we should be working towards and this is not simply limited to teaching in a learning environment without any thought of the wider issues. Indeed, the TLRP programme suggested that empirical evidence is not sufficient for decision-making in policy or practice, for it is always driven by values even if these are not explicit. James and Biesta argue that:

Effective teaching and learning

10 Effective teaching and learning demands consistent policy frameworks with support for teaching and learning as the primary focus. Policies at national, institutional and local levels need to recognize the fundamental importance of teaching and learning. They should be designed to create effective learning environments in which all learners can thrive. (Chapters 5, 8, 9, 14, 16 and 17)

1 Effective teaching and learning equips learners for life in its broadest sense. Learning should aim to help people develop the intellectual, personal and social resources that will enable them to participate as active citizens and flourish as individuals in a diverse and changing society. This implies adopting a broad view of learning outcomes and ensuring that equity and social justice are taken seriously. (Chapters 1, 9 and 15)

9 Effective teaching and learning depends on teacher learning. The need for lecturers, teachers, trainers and co-workers to learn continuously in order to develop their knowledge and skills, and to adapt and develop their roles, especially through classroom inquiry, should be recognized and supported. (Chapters 1, 3, 16 and 17)

2 Effective teaching and learning engages with valued forms of knowledge. Teaching and learning should engage with the big ideas, facts, processes, language and narratives of subjects so that learners understand what constitutes quality and standards in particular disciplines. (Chapters 9 and 10)

8 Effective teaching and learning recognizes the significance of informal learning. Informal learning, such as learning out of college and other formal educational settings, should be recognized as at least as significant as formal learning and should therefore be valued and used appropriately in formal processes. (Chapters 2, 5, 8 and 15)

3 Effective teaching and learning recognizes the importance of prior experience and learning. Teaching and learning should take account of what the learner knows already in order to plan their next steps. This includes building on personal and cultural experiences of different groups of learners. (Chapters 2 and 10)

7 Effective teaching and learning fosters both individual and social processes and outcomes. Learning is a social activity. Learners should be encouraged and helped to work with others, to share ideas and build knowledge together. Consulting learners about their learning and giving them a voice is both an expectation and a right. (Chapters 3, 6, 7, 12 and 15)

6 Effective teaching and learning promotes the active engagement of the learner. A chief goal of teaching and learning should be the promotion of learners' independence and autonomy. This involves acquiring a repertoire of learning strategies and practices, developing positive attitudes towards learning, and confidence in oneself as a good learner. (Chapters 2, 7, 11 and 13)

5 Effective teaching and learning needs assessment to be congruent with learning. Assessment should help to advance learning as well as determine whether learning has taken place. It should be designed and carried out so that it measures learning outcomes in a dependable way and also provides feedback for future learning. (Chapters 13 and 14)

4 Effective teaching and learning requires teachers to scaffold learning. Teachers should provide activities which support learners as they move forward, not just intellectually but also socially and emotionally, so that once these supports are removed, learning is secure. (Chapters 6, 11 and 12)

Figure 4.1 Ten evidence-informed educational principles for effective teaching and learning.

> It is important to supplement judgements about learning effectiveness with judgements about the value of learning and to make issues of effectiveness subordinate to issues of value. (James and Biesta, 2007: 147)

Education, in other words, can make an enormous difference to the people we become. In their study of further education experiences, *Transforming Learning Cultures*, James and Biesta (2007) recognize the way in which institutional conditions enable or constrain opportunities for independent learning. The Nuffield Review of 14–19 undertook a study of provision for young people and produced a number of research papers relating to the value of education for this age group (Pring et al., Reading 4.4). The *Learning Lives* project (Biesta et al., 2010) studied learners across the life-course using a combination of evidence from a large-scale cohort study and case study interviews reviewing people's learning careers over time. The research showed the lifelong reach of people's educational experience and demonstrated the durability of attitudes deriving from their early school experiences. In particular, the way people talk about their learning and educational experiences frames the development of their identity, self-confidence and agency in later life. Other quantitative studies reinforce this analysis to demonstrate the wider benefits of learning (Feinstein et al., 2008). Schuller and Watson (2009) draw upon a wide range of research evidence to direct attention to the importance of adults having access to learning across the course of their lives.

We, as teachers, have a unique privilege and responsibility to contribute to the lives of our students and help them develop, even if their initial experiences in the school system were unsuccessful. That is why this principle on 'education for life' is so important. As we have argued above, teaching has moral purpose, wherever we practice in the education spectrum.

2.2 Valued knowledge

Principle 2: Effective teaching and learning engages with valued forms of knowledge. Teaching and learning should engage with the big ideas, facts, processes, language and narratives of subjects so that learners understand what constitutes quality and standards in particular disciplines.

What should we teach? What subject do we specialize in? What are the subjects that are deemed to be fundamental to all learning (such as literacy, numeracy and language) and how do emerging areas become part of the curriculum? There has always been debate about what a curriculum should consist of, how it should be organized; what constitutes valued knowledge in a subject or field; how such knowledge can be represented and communicated to learners; and how learners' knowledge, understanding and skills can be identified and evaluated (see Chapter 9). Indeed, some forms of knowledge can be more valued than others. Learning in the workplace, for example, is often deemed to be of lower status than 'academic' knowledge acquired through the study of theories and ideas contained in literature. The value of practical experience and development of wise judgement often goes unrecognized as an important and valued form of knowledge.

Subject knowledge is undoubtedly of enormous significance in teachers' professional practice (see Chapter 9). In FAVE, there is the further complication that a 'national curriculum' as such does not exist. There are bodies of knowledge, lists of skills and competences that are required for a particular vocational area. There are codes of practice and conduct that must be adhered to (think, for example, of a heating engineer needing to meet health and safety standards as well as being a registered plumber). In adult and community education, there may be no specific curriculum as such but an agreed agenda for the group of students and their teacher to cover in a series of evening sessions. Yet underlying this is an expectation that the teacher possesses the subject knowledge and that the students will be able to build their own knowledge and experience as a result of being involved in the learning programme.

Such debates reflect the dominant priorities and relays of power that privilege some forms of knowledge over others in our culture, together with the capacity of particular stakeholders to promote their views. Analysts of such processes characterize the curriculum as a contested, social construction, with any particular settlement being influenced by the balance of power of the time. The early work of Young (1971) and Bernstein (1971) describe this phenomenon in the context of history of UK curriculum 'reform'. Goodson (1989) demonstrates the significance of this perspective in the USA and elsewhere.

2.3 Prior experience

Principle 3: Effective teaching and learning recognizes the importance of prior experience and learning. Teaching and learning should take account of what the learner knows already in order to plan their next steps. This includes building on personal and cultural experiences of different groups of learners.

Our students are adults and young people. They evidently have experience and prior knowledge when they engage with learning programmes. A famous quote by Ausubel put this clearly:

> If I had to reduce all of educational psychology to just one principle, I would say this:
> 'The most important single factor affecting learning is what the learner already knows.
> Ascertain this, and teach him [sic] accordingly.' (1968: vi)

How do you manage the diverse demands of your learners? You may have an open access evening class with adults who come from all walks of life and have different levels of subject knowledge. How do you run, for example, a French Conversation class with people who spend time in France and have in the past achieved a high level of French at 'A' level or university along with those who are very new to the language and are reluctant to speak and show themselves up? How do you know what people already know when they join one of your classes? People may even know 'the wrong things'. For example, one TLRP project developed and evaluated sequences for teaching science concepts and complemented this with banks of diagnostic questions to identify misconceptions (Millar et al., 2006). The researchers found that carefully designed probing questions can illuminate students' understanding of key concepts, and misconceptions and can inform judgements about next steps in teaching. Many fundamental science ideas increase only slowly, so that pitching an appropriate level of challenge is essential. Such evidence suggests that the sequencing of content knowledge within a programme of learning is important. Although this project worked with school children, adults too need time to acquire new knowledge and understanding. One Joint Practice Development project funded by the Education and Training Foundation in England developed a programme of continuing professional development which focused on formative assessment to identify learner achievement and next steps to success (see **reflectiveteaching.co.uk**).

www. C

2.4 Scaffolding understanding

Principle 4: Effective teaching and learning requires teachers to scaffold learning. Teachers should provide activities which support learners as they move forward, not just intellectually but also socially and emotionally, so that once these supports are removed, learning is secure.

In Chapter 2 we considered different theories of learning and their origins, their strengths and their weaknesses in informing educational practice. In Chapter 13 we illustrate through the work of Wiliam (2010) and Clarke (2001, 2008) how formative assessment can help to close the gap between current and potential levels of student learning and achievement. In Chapter 2 we also saw how the use of the term scaffolding in teaching can be used to help learners learn from each other and consolidate their learning in a systematic way.

Case study 4.1 Experience of an FE Curriculum Manager

An FE Curriculum Manager worked with Heads of Department and Curriculum Leaders, using the principles of JPD (Fielding et al., 2005) to devise a cross-curriculum planning project where subject specialists and literacy specialists learned about and planned the curriculum together to help develop language and literacy skills through the teaching of vocational subjects. As part of the process, practitioners became the 'advanced other' for each other at different times and stages in the project as each teacher learned more about other curricula. As a result, teachers were able to identify opportunities for synergy and consolidation across the FE curriculum (see **reflectiveteaching.co.uk**).

www. C

TLRP's fourth principle emphasizes provision of 'intellectual, social *and* emotional support'. The TLRP argues that social and emotional factors are also important, such as those associated with social expectations and feelings of personal security, for example (see Immordino and Damasio, 2007). Because our learning is intrinsically personal, intellectual progress is enabled or constrained by such factors and reflective teachers will consider how to provide for each of the intellectual, social *and* emotional dimensions of learning. Brockbank and McGill (2007) emphasize the importance of the affective domain in relation to planning and developing strategies to help people learn.

A crucial contribution to scaffolded learning derives from dialogue between teacher and learners, between learners and other learners and through the feedback loops that this makes possible. We must match our language, discourse and feedback to the current understanding or capabilities of our learners and, in turn, must be informed by feedback from them (see Chapter 12).

2.5 Assessment for learning

Principle 5: Effective teaching and learning needs assessment to be congruent with learning. Assessment should help to advance learning as well as determine whether learning has taken place. It should be designed and carried out so that it measures learning outcomes in a dependable way and also provides feedback for future learning.

How do we know that our students have actually learnt what we have set out to teach them? What else have they learnt that we didn't realize they were learning? How do we prevent people learning something superficially just to 'pass the test'? How can we apply sound teaching techniques to help our students learn in ways that also help them show what they have learnt? Chapter 13 extends this analysis, when guiding principles and practical implications are discussed at length. See the work of Gibbs (1986) for examples of practical 'learning to learn' strategies. For practical examples of vocational assessment see Ecclestone (2013) and Biggs and Tang (2011). Even though many of our students have had significant experience of learning in a variety of settings, it is also the case that we can promote their learning through setting out how we will be assessing their achievements. Given that many of our students are not studying for formal qualifications or to meet sector and workplace requirements, we need to find ways to help assess their learning in a meaningful and relevant way.

However, as we have already pointed out earlier in this chapter, changes in practice are not easy to establish and research demonstrates that, although advice on specific techniques is useful in the short term, longer-term development and sustainability depends on re-evaluating beliefs about learning, reviewing the way learning activities are structured, and recognizing the effect of roles and relationships in any learning environment.

2.6 Active engagement

Principle 6: Effective teaching and learning promotes the active engagement of the learner. A chief goal of teaching and learning should be the promotion of learners' independence and autonomy. This involves acquiring a repertoire of learning strategies and practices, developing positive attitudes towards learning, and confidence in oneself as a good learner.

What can we do to help our students learn for themselves? We mainly work with adults and young people and in other aspects of their lives they are often used to taking responsibility for their families, their colleagues, as well as for themselves. They regularly tell us what they want to get out of any learning programme they are engaged in and even what kind of learner they are. Yet not all our students will have such confidence and many of them may expect the kind of learning environment they experienced as children, which may not be appropriate for them as adults.

The most pragmatic reason for emphasizing active engagement is simply that it is essential for learning. This capacity to sustain active engagement in purposive ways is encapsulated in Claxton's conception of 'building learning power' through resilience, resourcefulness, reflection and reciprocity (Claxton, 2011).

In the FAVE sector, Ecclestone (2002) found that outcomes based approaches to vocational education tended to undermine students' autonomy and encourage teachers in the sector to 'spoon-feed' their students with the information needed to demonstrate the outcomes necessary to pass the course. In Chapters 10 and 13 we point to the poverty of such pedagogical approaches and argue that the active engagement of students in the FAVE sector does not require 'spoon-feeding' but careful and creative curriculum planning informed by theories of learning and supported by a wide range of imaginative and multi-sensory resources which capture the imaginations of learners and inspire them to achieve their full potential.

Fuller and Unwin's work (2003, 2004) on expansive and restrictive learning environments and approaches to apprenticeships show that engineering apprentices who had opportunities to participate in a broad range of activities, including off-the-job courses which covered engineering theories and concepts, were in a stronger position to progress than those who only had access to on-the-job learning experiences.

The guidance provided by teacher scaffolding and formative assessment techniques can only be accurately deployed and taken up through the active engagement of the student. By now, you will see that many of the principles we have been discussing relating to planning, theories of learning, scaffolding and assessment are deeply interconnected. It is only for the purposes of focusing in depth on any one aspect that we separate them out, but in reality, we suggest that the practice of teaching should really be seen as a coherent whole.

2.7 Social relationships

Principle 7: Effective teaching and learning fosters both individual and social processes and outcomes. Learning is a social activity. Learners should be encouraged and helped to work with others, to share ideas and build knowledge together. Consulting learners about their learning and giving them a voice is both an expectation and a right.

Almost all of your teaching is conducted in a social environment. As well as thinking about each individual student, we agree with Pollard (2013) when he suggests that learning is a social as well as an individual activity. It flourishes through interaction with other people, when the conditions are right. Good teacher–student relationships underpin such conditions. Some TLRP projects used the concept of social capital (Putnam, 1995) to analyse available opportunities, while noting the formative role that previous education, as well as peer-relations, can play in the accumulation and progression of learning. Social capital relates to the benefits that people possess by being members of a variety of social groups including their families, communities of practice, their social class and their friendship groups. NIACE has developed many resources for examining how such capital can affect not only people's learning experiences but also ways in which the participation in learning can actually enhance this capital (see, for example, the wider benefits of learning in Watson and Schuller, 2009).

TLRP's studies on group work (Baines et al., 2008), teacher learning (James et al., 2007) and inclusion (Ainscow et al., 2006), among others, show that when educational institutions function as genuine learning communities, students and teachers thrive both collectively and as individuals. Experiments carried out with older students, using concept-mapping software, showed that opportunities for students to discuss their maps with others were the significant factors in raising attainment (Bevan, 2007).

It is worth repeating that Principle 7 draws attention to how 'consulting learners is both an expectation and a right'. Many of you will be familiar with discussing at the outset of any learning programme what its aims are and checking that your students are not only aware of these but that they can suggest topics or areas that they want to pursue. The social practices approach to literacy, numeracy and language (see Tett, Hamilton and Hillier, 2006; Hughes and Schwab, 2010) argues that involving students in decisions about what they need to learn, how they will judge success and how they will use their newly acquired knowledge and understanding is a fundamental aspect of thinking about literacies as being part of people's lives rather than a series of technical skills to be acquired. If gaining confidence in writing affects a person's ability to read to their children or to write a letter to the school or even apply for a job, then this approach to learning how to write appropriately is going to be far more effective (and useful) than learning a set of spellings!

Within FAVE, adult education has a long-established tradition of working within the community, fostering and developing relationships among groups and individuals and even working with them to identify their own political and social agendas (see, for example, Lovett, 1988; Mayo and Thompson, 1995). Such work has led tenants, for example, to take action to prevent local authorities or government closing down facilities, or to fight for resources that were being denied certain groups.

Another important feature in this principle is that of understanding how to foster communities of practice for learners (Lave and Wenger, 1991). You may have experienced yourself being put into groups to discuss aspects of teaching if you are undergoing a teaching qualification. You may also have experienced setting your own groups together, perhaps working on an assignment or sending emails about how to go about dealing with a particular problem or sharing ideas for group practice. Teachers do not always have to be leading the setting-up of group work and we suggest that the principle of fostering social processes is very much linked to the next principle, which acknowledges the role of learning outside of a formal environment.

2.8 Informal learning

Principle 8: Effective teaching and learning recognizes the significance of informal learning. Informal learning, such as learning outside of college and other formal educational settings, should be recognized as at least as significant as formal learning and should therefore be valued and used appropriately in formal processes.

We showed in Chapters 1 and 2 that people in FAVE learn in a huge variety of settings. Many of these are informal – for example, in libraries, in online and social networks, and simply through watching cookery programmes on television and deciding to try out new recipes. Indeed, the previous government in England undertook a consultation about informal learning and whether they should do anything specifically to support it (DIUS, 2008). Arguably, one of the characteristics about the success of informal learning is precisely that it is outside any formal remit and therefore not subject to rules and regulations or indeed inspection. On the other hand, finding ways to ensure that the wealth of opportunities can be sustained is really important (Watson and Schuller, 2009).

As the wider benefits of learning programmes demonstrate, the well-being of adults and young people has, to a large extent, been supported by informal learning and though we do not measure it or judge it for its quality, it is in many ways central to adult life.

Although this TLRP principle can be stated simply, it has profound implications and challenges. Recognition of the social and cultural dimensions of learning in many TLRP projects produced a heightened awareness of learners, relationships and contexts (see also Chapter 2). Over several years, researchers struggled with how to study, analyse and represent the learning that took place beyond formal educational settings.

In FAVE, one obvious site for such learning is in the workplace. Just think about how often we find out how to do something on our computer simply by observing that a colleague goes about a process in a way we didn't know was possible. The recognition that workplaces are legitimate environments for informal and formal learning (Billett, 2001; Fuller and Unwin, 2003) has become widely accepted in both research and policy circles. Despite this, workplace learning is often absent from debates about lifelong learning (Unwin, 2009). For Unwin the workplace is naturally an important place for individuals to demonstrate competence that takes place through a combination of formal and informal learning.

The other major site for informal learning is in any formal learning environment. This may seem strange, but think about how often you come away from any learning activity having discovered something that was not part of the original plan, or you had a chance encounter by the photocopier or in the corridor. Clearly we are not suggesting that we should stop formal learning activities and favour the serendipity of chance meetings of people in car parks, photocopying rooms or cafes, but we do need to think about the prevalence of this form of learning and, where possible, we should consider ways to make use of it. Those of you who have experienced going to conferences will know that it is often during the coffee breaks that sharing of ideas and meeting new people leads to new activities rather than the actual input from plenary speakers or individual presentations.

Finally, it is important to acknowledge the 'hidden curriculum' within any formal learning situation. This is where people learn the unwritten rules including what to wear, what to say and who seems to be the one with the authority. People very soon learn what they have to do and what they can get away with not doing, including how to get away with keeping their mobiles on and discreetly texting, or how to avoid being asked to do something. Even mature adults find out how to get round completing their learning plans or at least how to say the 'right things' to help their tutor be observed in a positive light by her peers or an inspector!

2.9 Teacher learning

Principle 9: Effective teaching and learning depends on teacher learning. The need for lecturers, teachers, trainers and co-workers to learn continuously in order to develop their knowledge and skill, and to adapt and develop their roles, especially through practice-based inquiry, should be recognized and supported.

We cannot even begin to consider ourselves to be professional practitioners if we do not commit to an ongoing search to develop our practice and our understanding of the theory and research which can inform such practice. Indeed, this principle provides the rationale for this book as a whole. We need to be reflective, and commit to our own learning, because this enhances our effectiveness in supporting our students.

Teacher learning is concerned with both what we do *and* how we think. Effective forms of teaching depend not only on behavioural change and the acquisition of new knowledge about pedagogy, but also on the development of values and understanding. With the right leadership and support, such learning is particularly effective in the workplace and through participation in collaborative activities with other teachers (see Chapters 3 and 16, in particular). How can we make judgements that are wise if we do not continue to ask questions about our practice and learn from research and debate from our colleagues?

A summary of common themes within the TLRP suggests:

1 Learning involves the acquisition of knowledge and skills *and* participation in social processes. Thus the development of supportive professional cultures is vitally important. Within colleges, the focus is often the department or team. However, the very cohesion of these groups can create insularity and inhibit change. Rich and dynamic learning environments need to provide opportunities for boundary crossings, and to encourage learning from others in different communities of practice (see Chapters 3 and 17).

2 Teachers are most ready to accept ideas for change if these resonate with their existing or previous beliefs and experience. However, this does not necessarily make them 'right' or appropriate. Teachers need to develop knowledge and skills to evaluate evidence and the confidence to challenge taken-for-granted assumptions, including their own. This is difficult (see Chapter 3) and it is often helpful to involve outsiders, perhaps researchers from universities or visiting teachers from other institutions. Teachers need to be assured that it is acceptable and often fruitful to take risks – so a culture of trust and openness is crucial.

3 As we pointed out earlier in this chapter, evidence from research about effective practice is not always enough or sufficiently accessible for teachers to use as a basis for action. Findings often need to be transformed into practical and concrete strategies that can be tried out. This may involve the production of concise and user-friendly materials, although ideas are often mediated best by talk and personal contacts with other teachers who have had some success in using them (James, 2005: 107–8).

2.10 Policy frameworks

Principle 10: Effective teaching and learning demands consistent policy frameworks with support for teaching and learning as the primary focus. Policies at national, institutional and local levels need to recognize the fundamental importance of teaching and learning. They should be designed to create effective learning environments in which all learners can thrive.

How much do you know about the policies at national and international levels affecting what you do in your daily practice? For example, are you teaching a qualification that is undergoing change from coursework-assessed to final examination-based assessment? Where has this idea come from and why is the system being changed now? Are you involved in working with apprenticeships and why are the criteria for supporting these being debated? Do you have to work hard to retain your students in your programme and are you admonished if too many of them leave, even if they have perfectly legitimate reasons to do so? All of these situations relate to the overarching policy context in which FAVE is operated.

There is growing international awareness of the significance of the coherence, or otherwise, of national policy systems. Hodgson and Spours (2011) argue that curriculum requirements in FAVE need to articulate assessment processes and qualifications. They draw attention to how these need to be supported by programmes of initial and continuing teacher education, effective teacher recruitment, promotion and retention policies. The CAVTL report (2013) makes similar points where it emphasizes that above all forms and systems of national vocational education provision must ultimately be focused on the contribution they can make to effective learning.

Policy in FAVE

In the current economic and political climate, the presence or absence of spaces where differences can be discussed and constructive argument can take place will influence how and how well public sector professionals adapt to contemporary challenges in complex and uncertain situations. Improved efficiency, effectiveness and value for public money in the future will depend upon creating such spaces where research-informed judgements can be arrived at on the basis of evidence, considered from a plurality of perspectives. Making room for open and constructive argument and improvement is particularly important because it can help us to rehearse in public life different ways of seeing complex situations (Andrews, 2009: 22).

Reflective activity 4.2

Look at the principles in this chapter. Describe what these mean in your own context. Give examples from your own practice where you can see how you are working within the ideas contained in any given principle.

---

3 Three dimensions of education

Biesta's (2010, 2012) three dimensions of education offer another way of looking at the purposes and principles for good education. These aim to help teachers to consider the different purposes or dimensions of education which they can take into consideration when making judgements about educational practice. These dimensions of education are also open to adaptation to different contexts, as we initially discussed in Chapter 1 and expand on in Chapters 13 and 14. Biesta's dimensions of education were adapted for FAVE contexts and presented to the national Commission for Adult and Vocational Teaching and Learning (CAVTL) (Gregson, 2013) as presented below.

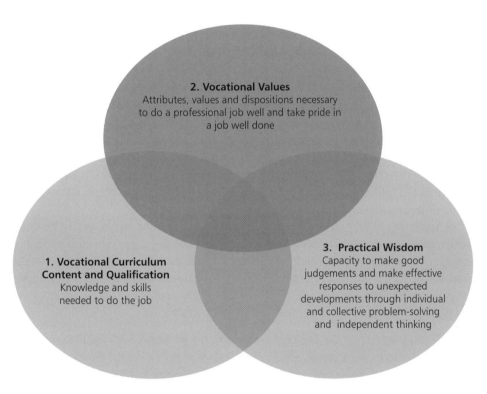

Figure 4.2
Adapted from Biesta (2010) *Good Education in an Age of Measurement*

The central point to note from the above adaptation of Biesta's (2010, 2012) work is that teachers in FAVE need opportunities for initial and continuing professional development that enable them to carefully balance the above three competing demands in making judgements about educational practice.

The findings of CAVTL recommended that opportunities for the initial and continuing professional development of teachers need to:

1 Enable and encourage teachers in the FAVE sector to acquire high levels of subject specialist knowledge – the knowledge and skills needed to do the job so that they can pass this on to their students as they pursue their qualifications (Figure 4.2, Circle 1).

2 Develop the values of FAVE which are characterized by the disposition to do a job well for its own sake and taking pride in a job well done (Figure 4.2, Circle 2).

3 Draw upon practical wisdom (see above and Chapter 3 on *phronesis*) and the well-developed capacities for systematic situated practical problem-solving, i.e. the capacity to respond effectively to unexpected developments through collective learning in order to share and solve problems individually and collectively through independent and critical thinking (Figure 4.2, Circle 3).

In addition, the Commission recommended that initial and continuing professional development of teachers in FAVE should encourage a strong commitment to becoming a professional vocational teacher, enacting vocational educational values in practice, with a clear sense of pride in supporting the achievements of students, apprentices, teachers and trainers (CAVTL, Reading 11.3).

3.1 What does this mean for someone working in FAVE?

Changing and improving professional practice is not as easy as it sounds. Voices from across the field of educational research warn that such development is hard won and that what appear to be quick fixes seldom, if ever, fix anything and never quickly. For example, Gardner et al. (2008) note that 'Quick fixes suit the political desire to regain support when public disquiet with standards undermines it' (p. 92).

As Tomlinson (2007) and Coffield (2007) point out, since the mid to late 1970s quick fixes in education are nothing new. What is relatively new, they argue is the unprecedented volume of policy initiatives which have swept through the FAVE sector over the last 30 years and at such a rate that practitioners barely have time to implement one educational policy initiative, let alone evaluate, it before the next one comes along! This situation was described as 'raining policy' by Hillier and Jameson (2006).

> Rather than waiting for the verdict of evaluations, the ministerial response to previous policy tends to be more policy; but the sheer volume of policy and the tensions created by conflicts within policy now constitute one of the main barriers to progress … The post compulsory sector is currently saturated with policies which deflect resources and energies from the central tasks of teaching and learning. Government ministers do not need to be persuaded of this argument, it is their practice that needs to change. (Coffield, 2007: 12–13)

Through the work of Clark (1997, 2000), Newman (2000, 2001, 2005) and Kooiman (2003), Coffield (2007) points to the obvious dangers of framing educational policy in terms of a stereotyped and demonized past, giving way to a visionary and idealized policy future akin to some 'road to Damascus' conversion. He also warns of the pitfalls of assuming that one dominant educational policy model of improvement for the sector is being imposed from above. The picture, he cautions, is much less deliberate and far more complicated. In order to stop educational policy from 'running ever faster down the wrong road' (see Chapter 14), Coffield argues, it will be important not only to build upon the strengths of FAVE but also to face up to where educational policy is going wrong and to be able to respond appropriately. What is urgently needed is 'a change in the culture of government at the highest level because those who demand continuous change from others are exactly those most in need of changing their own practices' (2007: 19). Such fundamental changes in political and policy practices will have to be learned by all of us and that will take time, courage and require patience. We will all need to critically examine how we have thought and talked about improving teaching and learning in the past and we will all need to learn how to think, talk and go about improving teaching and learning across the sector differently in the future. This will require the creation of physical and metaphorical spaces where we can make room for argument and where we can admit and learn from past, unfolding current mistakes. Indeed Keep (2011) suggests that if policy implementation is not scrutinized for its unintended outcomes as well as its specified goals, we are in danger of doing 'more of the same, with less, forever' (Keep, 2011: 33).

Talking about the practicalities involved in the improvement of practice openly, 'out loud and together' can help to achieve real and sustainable improvements beyond the expense and pretensions of political 'quick fixes'. Data from the Learning and Skills Improvement Service (LSIS) policy seminars and research projects in England (LSIS 2009a, 2009b, 2013) suggest that facing dilemmas and differences of opinion openly and together in sometimes difficult and often uncertain situations will require the professional development and support of leaders, practitioners and key partners who can make sense of options and build relationships across the spectrum of organizations which constitute the sector. The same data show that such people will need to be capable of creating effective and coherent strategies for the improvement of teaching, learning and research in the sector and be clearly committed to publicly defending collaborative educational values in practice at both local and national level for the collective good.

We need to be both realistic and optimistic about this goal. Although achieving *principled* educational coherence is difficult, incremental progress can be, and is being, made as governments realize its significance. It remains important that all those with an interest in effective teaching and learning – students, teachers, researchers, policymakers and the public at large – continue to strive together to establish socially just policies that truly support learning for the diverse needs of all learners in our communities.

> Participants in policy making all do so from different positions in space–time, with difference experiences, stakes, values, norms and beliefs. The possibility of creative action may become a reality only if they manage to create some common or shared understandings on why they seek cooperation and collective action at all. The essential process therefore is the joint construction of problems as a condition for joint responses. (Hoppe, 2010: 50)

> ## Reflective activity 4.3
> Think about an aspect of your practice that has been particularly challenging. What research evidence is available to support your professional development to address this issue? Discuss with your colleague or mentor an action plan that can begin to help you gather evidence and begin addressing this issue using research-informed evidence.

Conclusion

In this chapter we have introduced TLRP's ten evidence-informed principles which were developed to support the judgements of teachers and others in working towards high-quality teaching and learning. We have also introduced Biesta's (2010, 2012) dimensions of education.

The relevance and application of particular principles may change in relation to the specific circumstances or issues which we will be confronted by in the future, but we hope that your developing practice and critical reflection and research into this practice will further refine and test out these principles. For now, the TLRP ten principles can be used to structure reflection because they engage with the enduring issues which we currently face. When that is done, there is often a gap between aspiration and achievement. This gives pause for thought, and can lead to new insights and developments.

This first section of our book has outlined our own values and journeys into FAVE, preliminary examination of theories of learning and why critical reflection is such an important component of our professional practice, together with research-informed principles derived from the work of our peers and colleagues. These ideas provide the basis for our next section which examines key aspects of educational practice in greater detail.

Key readings

The TLRP principles

For an introduction to the ten TLRP principles and commentary which explains how the ten Evidence-Informed Principles for Effective Teaching and Learning were developed, see:

> James, M. and Pollard, A. (2006) *Improving Teaching and Learning in Schools: A Commentary by the Teaching and Learning Research Programme.* London: TLRP.

For an extended academic review of the ten TLRP Evidence-Informed Principles for Effective Teaching and Learning together with international commentaries, see:

> James, M. and Pollard, A. (2012) *Principles for Effective Pedagogy: International Responses to Evidence from the UK Teaching and Learning Research Programme.* London: Routledge.

Simple summaries of TLRP's findings in the form of teacher guide, poster, DVD and commentary can be found at: **tlrp.org/findings** or at **reflectiveteaching.co.uk**

Ruth Heilbronn's explanation of practical judgement, as well as its roots in Aristotle's philosophy, can be seen in **Reading 4.1**, edited from:

> Heilbronn, R. (2011) 'The Nature of Practice-based Knowledge and Understanding'. In R. Heilbronn and J. Yandell (eds) *Critical Practice in Teacher Education: A Study of Professional Learning*. London: London University, Institute of Education (IOE), 7–9.

For a discussion on an alternate model of education, see Pasi Sahlberg's article on 'What the world can learn from educational change in Finland' **Reading 4.2**, edited from:

> Sahlberg, P. (2011) *Finnish Lessons: What Can the World Learn from Educational Change in Finland*. New York: Teachers College Press, 1–6, 140–5.

John Hattie's comparison and synopsis of teaching strategies and their levels of effectiveness can be seen in **Reading 4.3,** edited from:

> Hattie, J. (2009) *Visible Learning: A Synthesis of Meta-Analyses Relating to Achievement*. Abingdon: Routledge, 1–3, 236–40, 244.

Reading 4.4: Nuffield (2009) 'The Nuffield Review of 14–19 Education and Training Summary' **nuffieldfoundation.org/14-19review**.

A summary of a major review of 14–19 education funded by the Nuffield Foundation can be found in:

> Pring, R., Hayward, G., Hodgson, A., Johnson, J., Keep, E., Oancea, A., Rees, G., Spours K. and Wilde S. (2009) *Education for All: The Future of Education and Training for 14–19 Year Olds*. London: Routledge.

For an insightful introduction to enduring issues and debates in the nature and purpose of education, see:

> Biesta, G. (2010) *Good Education in an Age of Measurement*. London: Paradigm Publishers. (**Also see Reading 1.1**)

For an overview of the FAVE system in England together with recommendations on how best to sustain adults and their learning throughout the life-course, see:

> Schuller, T. and Watson, D. (2009) *Learning Through Life: Inquiry into the Future for Lifelong Learning*. Leicester: NIACE.

For a thought-provoking analysis of the growth of managerialism in education and educational inequality, see:

> Ball, S. (2008a) *The Education Debate: Policy and Politics in the Twenty-First Century*. London: Policy Press.

Ball, S. (2008b) *The More Things Change ...: Educational Research, Social Class and 'Interlocking' Inequalities*. London: University of London, Institute of Education (IOE).

For a seminal discussion of issues in the organization of education and the development of knowledge, see:

Bernstein, B. (1971) 'On the Classification and Framing of Educational Knowledge'. In M. F. D. Young (ed.) *Knowledge and Control*. London: Collier-Macmillan.

For a discussion of the development of learning cultures in Further Education colleges in England which recognizes the way in which institutional conditions enable or constrain opportunities for independent learning, see:

James, D. and Biesta, G. (2007) *Improving Learning Cultures in Further Education*. London: Routledge.

 The associated website, **reflectiveteaching.co.uk**, offers a wealth of supplementary resources including reflective activities, research briefings, advice on further reading and downloadable diagrams, figures and checklists from the book. It also features a compendium of educational terms, links to useful websites, policy and curriculum documents, and showcases examples of excellent research and practice.

 In particular, consult the two supplementary chapters on the **reflectiveteaching.co.uk** website. These chapters consider the topics of Enquiry and Techniques of enquiry. They will help you plan, implement and reflect upon any research-informed improvement work you undertake as part of your professional development as a teacher.

part two

Creating conditions for learning

Part Two concerns the creation of classroom environments to support high-quality teaching and learning.

We begin by analysing the bigger picture in FAVE. We consider the circumstances which impinge on FAVE organizations and the communities they serve (Chapter 5). We note the ways in which people contribute to and challenge such circumstances through their actions.

We then move to the heart of educational activity in classrooms, workshops and other FAVE contexts with a focus on teacher–student relationships and classroom climate (Chapter 6). We suggest 'good relationships' are enabling and play a central part in our endeavour to achieve the good educational practice we have outlined in Part One. Chapter 7 builds further and illustrates how positive cycles of behaviour can be created through firmness, fairness and engaging students in the curriculum.

Finally, we consider a range of learning spaces (Chapter 8) in FAVE organizations and beyond, as well as affordances they offer for formal and informal learning. In addition to the basic dimensions of classroom organization, this chapter also addresses the use of technology, student organization, and team-working with colleagues including technicians and learning support assistants.

Contexts
What is, and what might be?

5

Introduction

What is it like working in the FAVE sector? Who makes decisions about what we teach, where we teach and who we teach? What factors have influenced the educational experiences of our students before we encounter them? This chapter provides a brief review of some of the contextual factors which are important in FAVE and of how teachers, students, communities and employers respond. We argue that the influence of social context is central to teaching, learning and assessment in FAVE and that teachers need to be aware of issues of social structures and contexts, because they are an important contributing element of reflective teaching. The influence of social structures and contexts is felt at many levels, from the big picture of government policies to the detail of community, education, local cultures, institutional cultures and individual circumstances. We will return to these ideas in Chapter 16 when we examine the underpinning concepts of our professional practice and how these influences from the bigger picture can shape our day-to-day practice.

A second purpose of the chapter is to explore some concepts concerning the relationships between individuals and society. The chapter is very deliberately set out in two parts. The first, social context, emphasizes the ideas, social structures and distribution of resources which *structure* action in various ways. The second part, people and agency, is concerned with the factors which, in various senses, *enable* action by individual teachers and students.

TLRP principles

The following two principles are of relevance to this chapter on the broader contexts in which teaching and learning take place:

Principle 8: Effective teaching and learning recognizes the significance of informal learning. Informal learning, such as learning out of college and no other formal educational settings, should be recognized as at least as significant as formal learning and should therefore be valued and used appropriately in formal processes.

Principle 10: Effective teaching and learning demands consistent policy frameworks with support for teaching and learning as the primary focus. Policies at national, institutional and local levels need to recognize the fundamental importance of teaching and learning. They should be designed to create effective learning environments in which all learners can thrive.

Throughout this book we argue that there is a dynamic relationship between society as a whole and the people who are centrally involved in education. There is a constant interplay of social forces and individual actions (see, for example, Giddens, 1984). We point out how the decisions and actions which people make and take in their lives are constrained by social structures and by the historical processes which bring about such structures. Yet each individual has a unique sense of self, derived from his or her personal history or biography. We argue that individuals have a degree of free will in acting and in developing understandings with others and that sets of these understandings, which endure over time, form the basis of cultures. Such understandings, we claim, can also lead to challenges to established social structures and thus to future changes. The ways in which these processes play out, we argue, is significantly influenced by the circumstances of various social groups in terms of power, wealth, status and opportunities (Ainley, 1993; Bloomer, 1986; Mills, 1959, Reading 5.1). Individuals, each with their own backgrounds and identities, will react to such factors in a variety of ways. People in powerful positions may believe that their position is inherited by right or earned by merit. Others who are less fortunate may accept the social order or even aspire to success in its terms. Some people believe that being able to question existing social arrangements is a fundamental right in democratic societies.

We begin this chapter by outlining the historic boundaries between vocational and academic education. We show how these boundaries have resulted in structural inequalities – for example, as evidenced by wide disparities in the funding of FAVE provision in comparison to that of the schools sector. From this position we consider more fully how historical and current political and policy developments in the sector have shaped educational beliefs, ideals and practices and we encourage practitioners across the sector to participate in constructive debate around how current and proposed policy and practice reforms in education encourage some practices and constrain others.

In Britain the traditional or narrow view of vocational education as '*training*' continues to perpetuate differences in wealth, power and social control (see Keep, 2011; Green and Janmaat, 2011, Reading 5.2). Teachers and students reflect subjective perceptions, values, identities, life narratives and imagined futures. We explore the presence or absence of the exercise of agency and voice and how actions are or are not simply determined by circumstances.

The particular historical era in which we happen to live is significant. Following the Second World War, the UK economy was still the third-largest in the world (after the US and Soviet Union). It is now the sixth-largest and living standards have trebled and life-expectancy has steadily risen. Education is now seen as a critical factor in ensuring economic productivity and competitiveness. Education policy is developed and implemented in response to the pressures and demands of globalization (see OECD, 2013). Some economists predict that in the future, competition from countries such as China, India and Brazil is likely to continue to force structural changes in the UK and other economies. However Elliott and Lemert (2006) caution us to be sceptical of the 'myth of the powerless state' and remind us that conceptualizing globalization solely in terms of an external force prevents us from seeing the wide variety of ways in which individuals, neighbourhoods and communities can respond to and mediate the potential effects of globalizing forces in their everyday lives. Harvey (1996) warns us to be wary of 'globaloney' and reminds us that many of the doctrines of globalization have been subject to considerable criticism.

In recent decades, global forces have resulted in increasingly interventionist education policies from governments of both left and right political persuasions. The forms of intervention have differed in scale but the current rate of political and policy intervention in education in England is both remarkable and unprecedented (Coffield, 2006: 2). Educational provision may be influenced by the circumstances of globalization but it is not determined by them. As Giddens points out, 'globalization invades local contexts, it does not destroy them' (Giddens, 2011: 367–8). He argues that new forms of identity and self-expression emerge from and are bound up in globalizing forces. National education policy is inevitably implemented at the local level and is received and interpreted differently at that level. In other words, the political, cultural and ideological forces operate in the sites of practice at the local level (Hoppe, 2010). There is an enduring ebb and flow in social change, a process of tension and struggle. It is the product of a constant interaction between agency and circumstance, voluntarism and determinism, biography and history (Mills, 1959, Reading 5.1). There have been times when people (teachers and their students) have acted to stand up for their educational values. For example, in the 1980s during times of swingeing cuts, many teachers and their students took to the streets to defend their centres against being closed down (Hamilton and Hillier, 2006).

As we pointed out in Chapter 4, in all of this a reflective practitioner engaged in the implementation of education policy at the local level has obligations and responsibilities to take action, based on wise educational judgements, in the pursuit of educational values and ends and the human good. Taking action in pursuit of the values and purposes of good education in such circumstances requires teachers in FAVE to be committed to the development of these qualities on an individual and collective basis.

We cannot predict the future and the roles which education in FAVE contexts may be called upon to fulfil, but we can predict the character and the qualities of the teachers and the nature of the wise educational judgements they will be required to make in response to unexpected and unpredictable challenges in the pursuit of good vocational education. For example, given the environmental challenges facing the world, it would not be surprising if FAVE organizations were one day required to play an increasing role in introducing more sustainable ways of life to new generations. At the moment, governments sometimes appear to merely pay lip service to this issue, but events could make it a much higher priority.

1 Social context

We now consider four aspects of the social context which are particularly significant for practice in FAVE: ideology, culture, opportunity and accountability. The influence of each can be traced at national, regional, local and organizational levels so that, although such issues sometimes seem distant, they shape educational activity in very real ways. We have already noted that some of these influences are so deeply ingrained we are not usually aware of them, but it is important to recognize their influence and also our ability to take action, where necessary. For example, if your organization is introducing a new quality assurance process, what is its purpose? Who is it aimed at and what are the unintended consequence of its introduction? Why is it being introduced and how different is it from previous procedures? Underpinning such a new procedure are a number of factors, not least an ideological viewpoint about how quality is desirable in FAVE and how it can be measured.

1.1 Ideology

People often talk about ideology but, as with numerous terms used in education, there are various meanings and uses. A dictionary definition of ideology states that it means a 'way of thinking'. However, particular sets of ideas are often used, consciously or unconsciously, to promote and legitimize the interests of specific groups of people. Indeed, if a particular way of thinking about a society is dominant at any point in time, it is likely to be an important influence on education and on our actions. It may determine the types of FAVE organizations which are created, produce a particular curriculum emphasis and even begin to frame the ways in which we think about our work and the ways in which we relate to our students. To understand and compare education policies on a national and international level, we need to be mindful of the complex relationships between ideas, the way such ideas are disseminated and the ways in which they are made sense of in different contexts.

Concepts and the language used to describe them can be slippery. They can be often exported from one 'discourse' into another in order to convey quite a different meaning. When we talk about discourse, we mean the ways in which we use language to frame our reality (see Fairclough, 2003; Gee et al., 1996). The way in which we talk about people who have difficulties in reading or writing, for example, shows what we believe about their situation. They can be 'illiterate' or people 'with difficulties'. The study of the history of mental health shows a range of views about what it means to have a learning disability, where people in the past were called 'idiots', then educationally subnormal and now, far more fairly and acceptably, people with a particular condition. The discourses of governments in England across the political spectrum appear to assume that academic performance is the most important and only goal of education policy. Such discourses are populated by terms such as 'beacon colleges', 'choice', 'traditional values' and the 'marketizing' of relations between FAVE organizations. While on the surface these may be intuitively appealing, on closer inspection they often prove to have very different and sometimes much less benign meanings in practice (Ball, 2006, 2008).

It is important to remember that all discourses put forward certain concepts at the expense of others, so it is useful to try to identify what is being excluded, displaced or even derided in the dominant educational discourses of our time. Education comprises a raft of ideological struggles and people take up entrenched positions and engage in little more than 'discourses of derision' (Ball, 2006, 2008). Such discourses often use exaggeration, preposterous images, ridicule, crass stereotypes and caricatures, which are then presented to the public as an accurate depiction of reality. Ball illustrates how this 'deployment of derision is a way of creating rhetorical spaces within which to articulate reform' (2008: 96). The danger is, as Bernstein (1996) puts it, 'Every time a discourse moves there is space for ideology to play' (p. 24).

Discourses of derision are unlikely to be genuinely educational. They would certainly not be particularly helpful in bringing about 'good education' and human flourishing through a 'life devoted to right living through the pursuit of the human good', which we discussed through the work of Carr (1995) and Biesta (2012) in Chapter 4.

It helps us to understand our own ideology if we use international comparisons to enable us to put our 'taken-for-granted' assumptions into perspective and consider alternatives. A study by the LLAKES research centre in London (Green and Janmaat, 2011, Reading 5.2) analysed the values and assumptions underpinning education policies in the Western world. They identify three main positions:

- **Neo-liberal** – with core beliefs in individual opportunities and rewards based on merit (English-speaking countries, particularly UK and USA).

- **Social Market** – with solidarity depending more on the state and less on civil society (NW continental Europe, including Belgium, France, Germany, Netherlands).

- **Social Democratic** – with egalitarian and solidaristic values and higher levels of social and political trust (Nordic countries, such as Denmark, Finland, Norway, Sweden).

Particular beliefs and values permeate perception and decision-making in these societies, and throw up a wide range of issues. A common question in some parts of the UK asks why do we widely admire the achievements of the Nordic countries but in reality do so little to emulate them?

Some historians and sociologists have argued (for example, Simon, 1992; Ball, 2006) that forms of educational organization can best be understood in terms of the reproduction of social class structures and patterns of advantage and disadvantage. Indeed, authors such as Althusser (1971) see education systems within capitalist societies as forms of an 'ideological state apparatus' designed to achieve broader social control in the interests of powerful elites. On the other hand, sociologists such as Kogan (1978) and Archer (1979) have argued that educational policies and provision are the product of competing interest groups and that control and power is more diffuse.

Case study 5.1 A short history of the secondary school system

In England, Wales and Northern Ireland after the Second World War, different types of secondary school were established: grammar schools, technical schools and secondary moderns. Pupils were selected for each of these schools on merit, based on how they performed in 'eleven plus' tests. However, it was not long before this 'tripartite' system came to be criticized for favouring well-off families whose children were over-represented in the grammar schools. This led to proposals for the introduction of a system of common secondary schools, which would be 'comprehensive' in that there was to be no selection of students. By the 1960s this view had become the new orthodoxy and, with support from all major political parties, comprehensive schools supported by local education authorities became the norm in most of England, Scotland and Wales. The commitment to the meritocratic ideal of 'opportunities for all' was distinctive, but comprehensives were criticized in the 1990s for being too complacent or, as an English minister once put it, 'bog standard'. The coalition government in England in 2010 urged that schools should become responsive to their local communities by breaking free from local authorities and establishing themselves as independent academies. Competition between such schools is expected to improve the performance of the system overall. However the establishment of academies is a matter of considerable continuing controversy and dispute. This has important implications for the FAVE sector as many of our students' first educational experiences were shaped in the school sector.

Ideologies flourish not just in the structure of schools and colleges but in the curriculum, teaching methods, assessment requirements and many other issues. You will see this in the ways in which your own students are encouraged to gain certain qualifications rather than others, or whether an examination at the end of a full programme of study is considered to have higher status than one involving coursework throughout. These differences of opinion, which are derived from deep ideological ideas, can be seen in a wider context in national and international policymaking. There is considerable struggle for control between politicians, civil servants and professionals over education policy (Ball, 1990, 2006, 2008; Keep, 2011). Tension can still be seen in animated media debates and moral panics about education issues (cries of 'dumbing down' when examination results are released annually), uneasy relationships between researchers and policymakers, and regular 'shake ups' of government education departments (in Finland, Sahlberg, 2011, Reading 4.2; in the UK, there has been a high turnover of ministers of education in recent years). Currently, politicians have taken to claiming that their policies are 'evidence-based', though the academic community is sometimes rather sceptical of this assertion. The commitment in principle to the use of evidence to inform policy and practice is an important development but, as we argue in Chapter 4, evidence can only tell us about the past, not the present or the future. Evidence can tell us that something has 'worked' in a particular situation for someone else; it cannot tell us if or how we should use that in the complex and unfolding situations which face teachers in FAVE on a daily basis. For that we need to exercise good judgement in our educational practice as well as to understand that we are constantly testing out those judgements and decisions. We can, though, draw upon a number of bodies of research from organizations such as the Economic and Social Research Council (ESRC), the British Academy and, in education, the UK Strategic Forum for Research in Education (SFRE), Campaign for Evidence-Based Education (CEBE) and British Educational Research Association (BERA).

Even at national levels, ideologies interact with culture and identity as well as with material interests. For example, in England, as we will see in the discussion of accountability later in this chapter, the big story of the last 30 years has been the growth of centralized control over the education system. But this is not quite the same in Scotland, Northern Ireland or Wales, where devolution has enabled the centralist tendencies of the English system to be significantly moderated. Further afield, in countries such as Australia, Canada and the United States, the federal nature of the political system adds a further level of complexity and influence where state and territory jurisdictions also have some bearing upon education as well as federal or commonwealth government sources. No ideology is all-powerful, and countervailing ideas emerge over time, based on their own power bases and social movements.

In summary, current ideas, perspectives or beliefs are not necessarily reflected in public debate and education policy. While basic issues are likely to remain much the same, the way in which they are addressed will change and change again over your teaching career. Societies and dominant ideologies are never static, but we hope that being aware of the influence of ideology makes it more likely that you will be able to evaluate the values or interests that may lie behind new ideas, policies, practices or other proposals as they arise.

It is important to remember that no one, including ourselves, is immune to the influences of ideologies. For instance, professional ideologies are always likely to remain strong among teachers; they represent commitments, ideals *and* interests. We as reflective teachers should be open-minded enough to constructively critique our own beliefs, as well as those of others.

Reflective activity 5.1

Reflecting on your own place of work, can you identify one aspect of practice that is shaped by an ideology? Do you think this ideology has a positive or negative impact on the education of students? If so, why?

1.2 Culture

What does culture mean to you? Is it about enjoying certain activities such as going to the opera ('highbrow') or knowing what cutlery to use in an expensive restaurant? Is it about blending in with social ways (knowing how to 'let your hair down' and have a good 'knees-up') or what to do when being introduced to someone for the first time? Cultures can be seen as sets of shared perspectives (Hofstede, 1987). They often develop from collective activity and from the creative responses of groups to situations. Furthermore, cultures endure over time and represent sets of perspectives, values and practices into which individuals are likely to be socialized.

For our students, cultures are strongly influenced by films, television, games, popular music, mobile phones, social networking and other popular culture and technologies as well as their family and social backgrounds. We will discuss these differences more in Chapter 12, but cultural differences can be seen in the way some students will not use direct eye contact, or others will be uncomfortable in joining in a discussion to criticize a piece of writing by a famous author. Almost all cultures have notions of respect and a set of rules, or norms, which apply – although these are often not only different across cultures, they can even be quite oppositional.

Cultural diversity encompasses many divisions such as ethnicity, language, religion, social class, gender, sexuality, political or personal values. These differences are particularly prevalent in many inner-city FAVE organizations and we need to explore the relationship between cultures in our students' home lives, communities, hobbies, employment and friendship groups. Research has shown problems arising when working-class cultures are regarded as being deficient (see, for example, Gorard et al., 1998). Similarly, institutionalized forms of racism are likely to result if teachers fail to take appropriate account of the perspectives of ethnic groups (Harris, 1995; Hughes and Schwab, 2010). Stereotypical perceptions of teachers may also have gender or sexuality dimensions that could impinge in a number of ways on the educational opportunities of all students (see Chapter 15).

Not only are there cultural differences among groups of people, but you will see differing cultures *within* departments in FAVE organizations. Teachers' allegiances and identities tend to be strongly influenced by subject departments (see for example, Becher and Trowler (2002), who talked about academic tribes and territories in higher education), but may also reflect other departmental divides including sixth forms versus generic FE, specialist language, literacy and numeracy subjects, student support and special educational needs (Hamilton and Hillier, 2006). While the complexity of FAVE organizations creates more opportunities for sub-groups to form among the workforce, FE college principals and other senior managers across the sector will be concerned to develop and maintain a shared understanding of 'the way we do things here'.

Cultures in educational settings have a huge impact on learning and behaviour (Wells, 2007; Bruner, 1986, 1990, Reading 5.3; see also Chapter 2). For example, some students have grown up in families that highly value the achievement of qualifications, whereas others may have experienced the culture of having employment as being an important outcome when leaving school. These concepts and artefacts frame and mediate understanding and shape development. Students' sense of identity as individuals may change as a result of their participation in FAVE and this may conflict with their previous social, economic or cultural experiences. Students from traditionally low-participation families in higher education have been found to feel that higher education is 'not for me', particularly if they were being encouraged to study in high-status universities (Reay at al., 2007; Callender and Wilkinson, 2012).

Of course, you, as a teacher, are also subject to these cultural influences. You may find yourself having to adapt to the organizational culture in which you work. This may be a challenge. If you are used to working in a very free-flowing way and then join an organization which has intense micromanagement, you may find it difficult to 'fit in' (Jameson and Hillier, 2004, Reading 5.4). Cultures can be exclusive as well as inclusive, particularly when organizations assert a narrow range of goals. There are, however, opportunities to 'belong'. FAVE organizations can helpfully be seen as 'communities of practice' (Wenger, 1999) which evolve and maintain strong norms of behaviour and thought. People joining organizations within FAVE soon learn how to conduct themselves and there may be a process of 'cognitive apprenticeship' (Rogoff, 1990) as new understanding is acquired.

Cultures can both enable and constrain learning (Bathmaker, 2014, Reading 11.6). Indeed, they are likely to afford different opportunities for particular individuals and groups. FAVE develops in response to conditions, some of which we *can* control. For example, knowing what resources are available and how you make the most of them can be an important influence on the quality of the teaching environment. Knowing who to approach in order to ensure your students have all the support and resources they need is an important aspect of your practice and this is not always easy if you are working part-time in outreach centres.

> ### Reflective activity 5.2
> Reflecting on your own place of work, can you identify two or three cultural concerns that your organization does or should address? Do you think your organization addresses these concerns fully, partially, or do you think they are ignored? Why do you think this is?

1.3 Opportunity

It has been said that education cannot compensate for society (Bernstein, 1971) even though teachers and others aspire to create opportunities for their students to contribute to the meritocratic ideal to which most contemporary societies subscribe. However, the challenge of creating such opportunities through education is not to be underestimated.

International comparison shows that health, social and educational problems are closely related to inequality within wealthy countries, as shown in OECD reports (2013). These relative positions are measured regularly by international agencies and draw from data within each country on issues such as social relations, life expectancy, mental health, obesity and, not least, educational performance.

In the case of the UK, there was a substantial rise in inequality during the 1980s and in recent years the incomes of top earners have continued to increase far more than lower-paid workers (Sibieta, 2011). Economists debate factors such as changes in employment opportunities, returns from high-level skills and education, regional differences and demographic patterns to explain the increasing polarization of rich and poor in the UK. The direct consequences of government policies on tax and benefits may moderate such structural factors, but the UK's recent experience is of a low level of intergenerational mobility (Bynner and Parsons, 2006). In other words, the circumstance of parents tends to be reproduced for their children. Longitudinal studies of cohorts of children who are now adults have shown that social mobility has stalled and there is a very strong correlation between the social group and income level of a child's family and his/her subsequent own position (Bynner and Parsons, 2006; Feinstein et al., 2008).

Bourdieu (1977) argues that overall social status is significantly affected by three forms of capital, each of which can be transferred from one generation to another. Economic capital concerns access to material assets. Social capital focuses on relationships in the family, community or wider society, which offer contacts, networks and support. Cultural capital relates to the understanding, knowledge and capabilities of individuals to act within particular social settings. The seeds of difference are sown in the ways in which young children are brought up. Reay (2000) illuminates how mothers in different circumstances deploy emotional capital to support their children, and she suggests that generational reserves are built up over time.

Families provide economic, social, cultural, linguistic and emotional resources. These affect the experiences, opportunities and expectations that are made available to the next generation. It is impossible for education to compensate for society and yet the particular needs of our students still have to be met. This is a moral imperative as well as a professional responsibility. Whatever the nature of the overall context around us, we need to search for ways to provide the best possible educational opportunities for our students. Despite the statistics, there are many examples of people whose lives have been transformed through the influence of teachers.

The bigger picture may seem divorced from our everyday practice. What does the influence of opportunity mean to our FAVE context? As we mentioned earlier, the resources which are available in FAVE organizations make a big difference in the creation of learning opportunities. We outline four types here: people, buildings, equipment and materials, and these provide concrete examples of the ways in which opportunity affects our students.

Many people are involved in the life of successful FAVE organizations. Apart from the principal, heads of department, curriculum managers and other senior managers and the teaching staff, there are many others, such as cleaners, catering staff, administration staff, student guidance and support staff and caretakers, who all have very important roles to play.

Buildings are also an important influence on what goes on in FAVE organizations (see Chapter 8). At its most obvious, buildings constrain decisions about numbers and types of classes because of the number and nature of the classrooms that are available. This often affects class sizes and forms of curriculum and teaching organization. It is impossible to teach a lab-based science course in a community hall that has multiple purposes! The quality of the environment will also be influenced by aesthetic considerations, and FAVE organizations vary considerably in terms of the degree of consideration that is given to this issue. Teachers are likely to be concerned about the quality of the learning environment within their classrooms, departments and FAVE organizations and will aim to maximize the learning potential of the spaces which they have available. Hillier and Jameson (2004, 2006) show that part-time teachers do all they can to minimize the effect of poor quality teaching spaces and their action is another example of the ways in which people interact with their environments to make a difference to the quality of the educational experience of their students.

Equipment and materials enable us to provide learning experiences of various sorts. For example, for FAVE organizations, maintaining up-to-date and relevant vocational education curricula across all subjects involves working closely with funding organizations. This includes working with employers, sponsors and local communities to secure appropriate resources to support our students' achievement and progression across vocational areas.

The most challenging form of equipment for FAVE organizations relates to capital equipment and information technology. This is fast-moving in terms of specialist machinery and equipment to support the teaching of vocational subjects such as engineering, agriculture, hairdressing, art and design, dance, media, sports science, etc., and more generic ICT hardware and software to support student achievement. Variation in these aspects of provision between FAVE organizations is often considerable.

UK FAVE organizations have locally managed budgets in which income from government is distributed annually on the basis of a formula. This allocates a certain amount for each student enrolled, plus allowances in respect of social disadvantage or special educational needs. Expenditure is the responsibility of the Principal, senior management team and governors. However, once fixed costs are taken out of the overall budget, education managers in FAVE organizations often have relatively small sums to spend at their discretion. Indeed, the salaries of teachers and other staff account for the major share of the budget, followed by costs of building maintenance and running costs. Only a relatively small percentage is left for books, equipment and materials and discretionary expenditure.

The key factor in FAVE organizations' budgets remains the number of students enrolled. Each FAVE organization's position in the quasi-market for student enrolments in its area is crucial to its resource base, hence the pressure for performance in formal assessments and in developing a positive local reputation.

Resources structure the material conditions in which teachers work and the opportunities they can provide for students. However, the actions they take are also likely to be influenced by the degree of autonomy which they feel they have. For this reason, we now focus on the issue of accountability.

1.4 Accountability

Teachers are paid to provide professional educational services. However, the degree of accountability and external control to which they have been subjected has varied historically over past decades. Each country has its national inspection system, but the form and role of these vary considerably.

Teachers are coming under increasing pressure to 'increase their accountability' and to demonstrate competent performance against centrally defined criteria. In the 1980s in England, the Conservative government reduced the influence of the 'producers' (seen as teacher unions, administrators and theorists) to enable educational provision to be shaped by the 'consumers' (seen as parents and industry, though with little direct reference to students). Under the New Labour administration from the late 1990s, the emphasis moved to modern performance management systems. Following the devolution in UK and in Ireland, differences in this performativity culture are evident (see Hodgson, Spours and Waring, 2011).

Case study 5.2 The shaping of further, adult and vocational education (FAVE)

In FAVE, attempts to shape vocational education in the UK have had a long and chequered history. This dates back to the formation of the craft guilds and apprenticeship schemes of the industrial revolution, to the establishment of the Mechanics' and Miners' Institutes in the nineteenth century, through to the introduction of the technical colleges in the 1950s–1960s, on to the incorporation of colleges of the national network of Further Education colleges in 1993.

The explicit introduction of the concept 'learning to learn' into the vocational educational curriculum through the Manpower Services Commission's (MSC) Youth Training

---

Scheme (YTS) in 1983 marked a significant milestone in the process of state-driven curriculum reform in that, for the first time, aspects of meta-cognitive thinking were seen as having legitimate links to vocational education. A series of government agencies and political imperatives have since attempted to reshape the educational goals, curriculum content and structure of post-16 education in a variety of ways. The institutional evolution of state attempts to reform vocational education has included the incorporation of the Manpower Services Commission into the Employment Department (ED), which in turn was amalgamated with the Department of Employment (DoE) which then became the Department for Employment and Education (DfEE) the Department for Employment and Skills (DfES) and eventually split between the Department for Education (DfE) and the Department for Business, Innovation and Skills (BIS) as the main regulatory bodies for the sector. It is interesting to note that throughout the various constituencies and histories of these policymaking and regulatory bodies, what has remained constant is the development and promotion of policies for educational reform, which conflate the aims of vocational training with the predominantly liberal aims of adult education in the UK and the needs of the economy.

The new vocationalism of the 1980s was heralded by an employer-dominated training regime for young people based on the notion that the working class needed to improve their skills to meet the needs of employers and the market. Another dominant idea at the time was the belief in the power of technology (as opposed to political activity) to open up new opportunities for social mobility.

Armitage et al. (2012) argue that the period from 1989 to the early part of the twenty-first century can be seen as one of 'containment', in that the number of young people in FAVE increased dramatically. Calls to increase the school leaving age in England met with little criticism. Qualifications are now required for jobs that used to be considered 'unskilled'. Vocational education is now closely and narrowly associated with employability. The education versus training debate continues as the gulf between academic and vocational education widens. At the same time learning has become framed in highly individualized terms and the world of lifelong learning has become populated by isolated individuals in a context which Biesta (2005) has described as the 'learnification' of education, where educational values are pushed to the margins.

However, England retains a powerful interventionist capacity in the form of the national inspection system through the Office for Standards in Education (Ofsted) (see Ofsted, 2012). Ofsted contracts teams of inspectors to make a structured report on every individual FAVE organizations in a regular cycle. Comparative data from FAVE organizations serving similar socioeconomic communities and baseline data from the FAVE organizations being inspected are used to evaluate levels of performance and improvement. The strongest sanction available to Ofsted is that a college be placed in 'special measures'. This means that it is deemed to have been failing to meet expected performance standards under the present management. Support or even an alternative leadership team may be provided.

The issue of accountability crystallizes many issues concerning the relationship between education and society. Should education be a relatively autonomous system or should it be under tight forms of control? Should teachers simply carry out centrally determined instructions, or should they develop and exercise professional judgement? (See Chapters 4 and 17). What, indeed, is the role of local democratic institutions in this? And who should pay for the accountability system? The history of our education system provides many fascinating instances of attempts to reconcile such dilemmas (Silver, 1980; Hyland and Merrill, 2003; Hodgson, Spours and Wareham, 2011) and there are plenty of related current issues which a reflective teacher might consider.

Reflective activity 5.3

How should you act? To whom do you feel you should be accountable? Think about your students, employers, parents, colleagues, your principal or chief executive, local or national government, the media, inspectors and yourself. Discuss this with a colleague and identify where you pay most attention. Is this different from what your manager or students expect of you? Are there tensions in meeting different expectations and how do you try to resolve these?

2 People and agency

We now turn to the individual and personal factors which influence our professional practice in FAVE. For instance, classroom life can be seen as being created by ourselves as teachers and our students as we respond to the situations in which we find ourselves. As well as understanding something of the factors affecting the social context of FAVE organizations, we also need to consider how we and our students respond. Such responses reflect subjective perceptions, beliefs, values, commitments, identities, life narratives and imagined futures. This is where agency and voice come to the fore, where our actions are not simply determined by our circumstances but as an interplay between the way things are and our power to take action. We begin by focusing on teachers.

2.1 Teachers

Teachers hold a particular position in FAVE organizations. Each of us is unique, with particular cultural and material experiences making up our biography (Sikes, Measor and Woods, 1985). And our sense of self influences our personality and perspectives (Goodson, 2007). Our development continues throughout our life, but early formative experiences remain important. Indeed, personal qualities such as having the capacity to empathize and the confidence to project and assert ourselves are so important in teaching. Much of what we will be able to achieve in our classrooms, workshops and other FAVE settings will be influenced by these characteristics. We all have strengths and weaknesses and most of us would agree that classroom life tends to reveal these fairly quickly. Reflective teaching has, therefore, a great deal to do with facing such features of ourselves in a constructive and objective manner and in a way which incorporates a continuous capacity to change and develop.

Being able to review the relationship of 'what is' and 'what ought to be' helps us examine our aims our educational values and philosophies (see Chapter 4). While there has always been a good deal of idealism in commitment to teaching, there has also always been a concern with practical realism. Indeed, a very important factor which influences our perceptions in the classroom/workshop is that we have to cope, personally as well as professionally, with the vocational education contexts in which we work (Hyland, 2011). For this reason, we would suggest that a fundamental element of coping or survival in FAVE contexts is very deeply personal, for it involves a particular image of ourselves acting in the challenging situations which classrooms and other vocational education contexts represent. We must remember that what it is possible to do in classrooms and other vocational education contexts is constrained by the basic facts of large numbers of students, limited resources, compulsory attendance, curriculum and assessment frame-works and other external expectations which exist about what should and should not take place. Our 'social work' role in supporting students as they struggle to balance employment, family and educational commitments is considerable (Webb and Vulliamy, 2002). In such circumstances, we face acute dilemmas between our personal and professional concerns and practical possibilities. We are forced to juggle with priorities as we manage the stress which is often involved with classroom situations (Lumby and Foskett, 2003).

Contemporary policy calls for a lightening of constraints on teachers so that they are able to exercise professional judgement in a wider range of circumstances. However inspection regimes, tightly prescribed assessment regimes, target-driven funding systems and league tables can operate to shape the practice of teachers in less than helpful ways (see Chapter 14).

In recent years considerable attention has been paid to providing stronger continuity in professional development, so that the situation of a student teacher, newly qualified teacher, established teacher and advanced practitioner is now reasonably well defined (Institute for Learning, 2009). This may offer a sense of continuity for a career profes-sional, and certainly enables governments to provide more systematic forms of support and direction for teachers' continuing professional development. Recent work in relation to the use of Joint Practice Development (JPD) as an integral part of teachers' CPD (see Chapter 16) is an important component of our professional practice. Yet the status of teaching as a profession has become increasingly contested in England under the present coalition government. The statutory requirement for teachers across the FAVE sector to have a professional teaching qualification was revoked in August 2013, calling into question the future of university-based teacher education in England (see Appleby and Hillier, 2012).

We also need to consider our position as employees where we have legal, contractual and economic interests to maintain, protect and develop (Lawn and Grace, 1987). We may be required to undertake activities which are additional to basic classroom teaching, such as attendance at staff planning meetings and open days/evenings. Given such activity, surveys of working hours regularly record that teachers work far in excess of their contractual obligation (Hillier and Jameson, 2006, Reading 5.4; Taubman, 2013). A balance has to be struck between educational expectations and what it is reasonable to ask of people who happen to earn their living from teaching. Indeed, principals and senior management teams have a duty to manage the FAVE workforce with regard to their well-being. We have our own personal lives outside the classroom and our independent identities, which are often challenged by work and the complexities of modern society (Maclure, 2000). Many of us have significant family responsibilities, as well as other interests.

2.2 Students

Students embody and are influenced by a huge range of circumstances and prior experiences. These include factors such as gender, social class, race, language development, learning disposition, health, and types of parental and peer support. As we saw earlier, patterns of advantage and disadvantage are very significant. However, such factors do not determine consequences.

Students have a unique 'biography', and the ways in which they feel about themselves and present themselves in FAVE organizations will be influenced by their understandings of previous cultural, social and material experience in their families and elsewhere (Bruner, 1986). Through their compulsory education, from age 5 to 16, most children develop a relatively clear sense of their identity as learners. Indeed, pre-school experience and social processes in the primary school lead them to perceive themselves as relative learning failures or successes. The foundations of their learning disposition and stance as a lifelong learner become established, and there is no doubt that this is the crucial age phase for educational investment (Karoly et al., 1998), as demonstrated by initiatives in England such as Sure Start and the development of Children's Centres. As young people progress through secondary schools, with their complex systems of setting, banding, options and pathways, their self-perceptions are further reinforced or modified (see also Lawrence, 1987). At the point of leaving schooling and entering the world of college or work, young people's learning and life trajectories are well established before they participate in FAVE. Older learners, too, have been influenced by their varied life experiences. We must remember that we are shaping long-term life-chances and identities of our students as well as working towards immediate targets for performance (Feinstein et al., 2008). The key issue is how students respond to their circumstances, and here we play a crucial role in supporting them.

Students have to survive in classrooms and other FAVE situations in which they may well feel insecure. Peer culture and the support of friends are considerable resources in this. However, this can also pose dilemmas in classroom and workshop situations when students attempt to please both their peers and their teacher. Creative strategies are called for and these may cover a range from conformity through negotiation to rejection. The agency of students is played out in the immediacy of the classroom/workshop and teachers have unique opportunities to influence factors such as motivation, approaches to learning and to subject knowledge (Ecclestone, 2013; Bathmaker, 2014 Reading 11.6).

Above all, though, we must never forget that people are placed in the role of 'students' for only part of each day. It is no wonder that families, friends, relationships, television, film, computer games, music, fashion or sport are important to them. We must aim to work with an understanding of the culture of our students. If connections can be made, then student culture can itself provide an excellent motivational hook into engagement in FAVE contexts.

Employers, families and friends can play a particularly important role in supporting a student. They are often thought of as supplementary teachers, with an advantageous 1:1 teaching ratio, and such support is certainly a major factor in pre-school development and early literacy. However, perhaps the most important role for employers, families and friends today is in providing a source of stable emotional support for each student as he or she encounters new challenges in FAVE contexts. Reay (2000) provides a fascinating analysis of this as a form of 'emotional capital'. FAVE organizations are increasingly pressured places, and there is a need for someone to really nurture the developing student from day to day, year to year. It is not necessary to be well-off financially to do this. Often the most valuable contributions are probably time, patience, understanding and care. There is also an increasing understanding that all families and communities, including those that may seem disadvantaged, have 'funds of knowledge' that should be tapped into to enhance students' learning (Moll and Greenberg, 1990). Social circumstances do, however, radically affect participation (Crozier and Reay, 2005; Vincent, 1996, 2000) and the voices of students can sometimes be inadequately recognized (Crozier, 2000).

Reflective activity 5.2

What does the meaning and significance of 'agency' have for you and for students? Share your own educational biography with a colleague with whom you feel secure. Taking it in turns, take time to provide a narrative of how you moved through your education, meeting different teachers, growing up, finding some learning difficult but succeeding in others. Identify and focus on some key episodes or turning points which enabled your to progress. Explore, if you can, the actions you took and the encouragement or support you received from others.

You might like to consider a small number of students you know. Try to identify to what extent are they able to exercise agency in relation to their circumstances and goals, and how you might be able to help?

Conclusion

This chapter examined the relationship between society as a whole and the people who are centrally involved in education. This is because FAVE practices in classroom/workshop and other settings are influenced by the social circumstances within which they occur. However, we also argued that individuals can, and will, have effects on future social changes as they exercise their personal agency, though the degree of influence ebbs and flows depending on the roles occupied and at different phases of history.

Understanding the influence of context in FAVE contributes to the principle that we can all 'make a difference' within our society. Professional commitment and good educational judgement are very important. As professional educators we should not be passive receptors of externally determined prescription. Education is enhanced when our social awareness complements our teaching and when our professional actions are taken seriously.

This fundamental belief in the commitment, quality and constructive role of teachers underpins our book. Our analysis is optimistic because we can see that education depends on the professionalism of teachers with both the courage and character to do the right thing at the right time in the pursuit of good educational ends.

Key readings

We begin with the theoretical framework which informs this book, with its juxtaposition of social context and individual agency.

Mills, C. W. (1959) *The Sociological Imagination*. New York: Oxford University Press, 111–13. (Reading 5.1)

For a comparative analysis of educational values in different countries, their effects on provision and on what seems possible, see:

Green, A., Preston, J. and Janmaat, J. G. (2006) *Education, Equality and Social Cohesion: A Comparative Analysis*. London: Palgrave. (Reading 5.2)

The work of Pierre Bourdieu has influenced ways of understanding different forms of cultural, social and emotional capital, alongside the economic, through which social differences are perpetuated.

Bourdieu, P. and Passeron, J. C. (1977) *Reproduction in Education, Society and Culture*. London: Sage Publications Ltd.

Stephen Ball has documented policies and practices in the reproduction of social class and other forms of differentiation, with particular reference to secondary education.

Ball, S. (2006) *Education Policy and Social Class*. London: Routledge.

An important international study of the consequences of inequality:

Wilkinson, R. and Pickett, K. (2010) *The Spirit Level: Why Equality is Better for Everyone*. London: Penguin.

Jerome Bruner gives a rich account of how culture and biography effects educational outputs.

Bruner, J. S. (2006) *In Search of Pedagogy Volume II: The Selected Works of Jerome S. Bruner*. New York: Routledge, 145–6. (Reading 5.3)

To review the contemporary challenges and pleasures of being a teacher, see:

Jameson, J., Hillier, Y., Betts, D. (2004) *The Ragged-Trousered Philanthropy of LSC Part-time Staff*. Presented at the British Educational Research Association Conference, UMITST, Manchester, 16–18 September. (Reading 5.4)

Shain, F. and Gleeson, D. (1999) 'Under new management: changing conceptions of teacher professionalism and policy in the further education sector', *Journal of Education Policy,* 14 (4), 445–62. (Reading 14.3)

The associated website, **reflectiveteaching.co.uk**, offers a wealth of supplementary resources including reflective activities, research briefings, advice on further reading and downloadable diagrams, figures and checklists from the book. It also features a compendium of educational terms, links to useful websites, policy and curriculum documents, and showcases examples of excellent research and practice.

Relationships

How are we getting on together?

6

Introduction

Just because we teach adults and young people, we should not assume we will have good relationships in a classroom or that our sessions will be easy to manage. Students begin programmes of study in FAVE for numerous reasons and are likely to turn up to study with a variety of issues and a history. This history may often include disappointment, perceived failure and frustration with the kind of education they have experienced before. Although the education in the FAVE sector is likely to be quite different from the school sector and may not even take place in a classroom, students may project their past experiences onto the new educational setting. This chapter will focus on the importance of maintaining positive relationships with our students and the following chapter (Chapter 7) will discuss how we manage the behaviour of our students. These two chapters are linked and we suggest you may like to read them together. For ease of use we shall use the word 'classroom' in this chapter, although learning may be taking place in classrooms, lecture theatres, seminar rooms, workshops, workplaces, studios, salons, community centres and even corridors.

TLRP principles

Two TLRP principles underpin classroom relationships as a foundation for learning:

Principle 4: Effective teaching and learning requires teachers to scaffold learning. Teachers should provide activities which support learners as they move forward, not just intellectually but also socially and emotionally, so that once these supports are removed, learning is secure.

Principle 7: Effective teaching and learning fosters both individual and social processes and outcomes. Learning is a social activity. Learners should be encouraged and helped to work with others, to share ideas and build knowledge together. Consulting learners about their learning and giving them a voice is both an expectation and a right.

If you are a student teacher, you may feel worried about how you will manage the behaviour of your students and how you should treat them. Even if you are very experienced, making sure that your relationship with and between your students is positive is challenging. This chapter will examine the ways in which teachers and their students relate to each other. It provides insights to ensure that such relationships are rewarding.

Codes and principles of interaction are significant in contributing to the social, ethical and moral education of students and their ability to become active citizens in a democracy (Coffield and Williamson, 2011). In a sense, good citizenship in the classroom can act as a model for responsible, active citizenship in life. Teachers and students can negotiate their roles and responsibilities in an equitable way.

This chapter is structured in four main parts. It begins with detailed discussions of classroom relationships and the roles of rules, routines and fairness. This understanding is then directly applied to teaching and learning processes of curriculum, teacher and student action, and developmental cycles in class relationships over time. We then move on to discuss teacher expectations and professional skills, particularly for maintaining classroom authority. Finally, we examine classroom climate, which includes specific sections on emotional security, self-esteem and inclusion.

1 Classroom relationships

1.1 The working consensus

Good classroom relationships are based on recognition of the legitimate interests of others and on a mutual exchange of dignity between the teacher and students in a class. There evolves, in other words, a reciprocal, but often tacit, recognition of the needs of the other in coping with classroom life (Pollard, 2014; Cooper and Baynham, 2005, Reading 6.1). Sometimes teachers and students have the capacity to make life very difficult for each other and a pragmatic basis for negotiation does help. However, shared understandings about working together do not just appear. We have to work hard to establish the rules, understandings, routines and rituals which will structure behaviour in our classrooms. It is down to us to develop and take account of the nature of our relationships. Adults and young people expect teachers to act competently in ways which they regard as fair and which will enable them to progress with their education (Gipps and MacGilchrist, 1999, Reading 6.2).

1.2 Rules and initial encounters

Students will normally expect us to set boundaries and expectations, and these can often be expressed as ground rules which could be a small number of formal, overt rules adjusted for the type of students and the educational setting. Often, these can (and should) be derived from whole-institution or faculty policy and practices. We might, for instance, promote three overarching rules on:

- treating others as we would want to be treated (e.g. respect, support, empathy)
- committing ourselves to learning (e.g. positive thinking, effort, resilience)
- behaviour in college and classroom (e.g. attendance, work completion, respect for teacher and students)

These ground rules should demonstrate and affirm that the classroom will be a place of respect, which establishes forms of interpersonal relationships in the classroom where learners can thrive. By providing such a secure framework, we also provide emotional and psychological safety.

The first few weeks of contact with a class, the period of 'initial encounters' (Ball, 1981), is a particularly important opportunity during which a teacher can take initiatives, introduce rules and establish positive relationships. There is often a honeymoon period when teachers attempt to establish their requirements. The students are likely to have hopes that this course, this teacher, this learning is going to help them progress and to improve their life. They will have made a decision to join this particular study programme out of a combination of optimism and necessity. If their expectations of progress are not met, they are likely to lose trust in the teacher and the course that they are on. The behavioural expectations and the teacher's capacity to enforce them are normally tested by the students before long, for students will usually want to find out how much they will need to commit to succeed and how the teacher will react when students resist. For example, you may find that students use their mobile phones and other devices even when the ground rules prohibit this and such situations require your action if you are to maintain the agreed rules. This is where a sense of fair play occurs. Adults with commitments elsewhere may need to be able to respond to calls – for example, if they have sick children – but decisions about what is acceptable and appropriate are not always easily agreed upon. Chapter 7 provides some useful suggestions for setting up ground rules with your students.

1.3 Classroom routines

Classroom routines enable us to operationalize overarching rules and apply their principles to concrete activities. We have our own favoured routines and these will certainly vary according to the setting and age of our students. In FAVE likely routines will include:

- Introducing lessons
- Setting work
- Collecting work
- Absence
- Punctuality
- Collecting homework
- Plenary sessions
- Group work
- Class discussion
- Question and answer

Routines, in other words, are multipurpose procedures which put rules and understandings into practice. The expectations which are embedded in the routines do always need to be maintained. Without routines, your hard-won understandings may be eroded and your students may not engage with the learning activity. Routines are a major focus of negotiation in arriving at a working and workable consensus.

1.4 Identifying routines and understandings

If you are a student teacher, you may find that your students have already established a set of understandings with their previous teacher. You will need to be aware of these, but also create your own routines and tacit understandings, and this is often quite difficult if you are not solely responsible for your group of students. Even experienced teachers will work with students who have experienced different routines and understandings from their previous settings or with different teachers.

It is not a good idea to assume that, having developed an understanding of key expectations, there is no further need to do anything about them. You will need to review and evaluate them as the programme proceeds. You might ask yourself which rules and routines need reinforcement or adjustment and how you might prioritize such developments. For example, if your students' previous teacher always starts the session with a PowerPoint presentation and you want to use a starter activity to stimulate discussion and check how much the students have recalled from the session before, then you are introducing a change to the standard pattern of teaching and also establishing your own signal that you are ready to teach and you want the students to focus.

1.5 Being fair

In all rules, our actions should be regarded as being fair. There is nothing more important than being seen, by students, to have acted with fairness (Bennett, 2011, Reading 6.3). This occurs because of their ultimate vulnerability to teacher power. This can be particularly pertinent in FAVE settings as there are likely to be students present who have had poor experiences in previous school or on previous courses, and may well have experienced failure. They will often experience a negative judgement from a teacher as confirmation that they are going to fail again or that the system is against them. Students need to be assured that their teachers will act reasonably. If a teacher or student teacher does act without consideration of existing rules, routines and understandings, this is likely to produce a negative response from students.

2 Relationships for learning

2.1 Curriculum and relationships

We suggest that successful teaching occurs when the learners are *learning*. When this happens, both teachers and students feel fulfilled and the quality of their relationship is enhanced. Good relationships not only contribute to the conditions which make learning possible, they are also reinforced by success. A major contribution to good classroom relationships is the provision of an interesting and appropriate curriculum (i.e. the content of our learning programmes, see Chapter 9), with suitable learning experiences and high-quality feedback. Here we focus on the way in which curriculum is particularly significant for the development of relationships. Coffield and Williamson argue that a curriculum rooted in the challenges of today encourages students to engage in democratic processes, in essence to find their voice and understand that they can improve the world (Coffield and Williamson, 2011).

One way to good relationships is to think of students as individual learners with different goals and needs. Rather than assume a 'one size fits all' programme, you may find that you are encouraged to develop personalized learning approaches which focus on each student and requires 'tailor-made' programmes of learning. This is a tall order, particularly if the programme of learning has set requirements to meet a vocational qualification or sector standards. Yet how can you establish a relationship with each student if you are not aware of their own goals, what they have already achieved and how you may best help them make progress? It is a good idea to consult your students on their experiences of teaching and learning. This information supplies a basic type of feedback on their motivation and can be set alongside other diagnostic information about learning achievements and difficulties. Indeed, many colleges now make use of diagnostic tests, particularly in relation to literacy, numeracy and language, so that they can ensure that students begin their studies on an appropriate programme. Although the primary focus of such testing is for recruitment and selection, it does enable teachers to tailor their sessions and plan for a more personalized programme of learning.

Even within a programme of learning, students have different views about the activities they enjoy or find beneficial and those which they dislike or find confusing or unhelpful. We are not suggesting that you avoid activities just because some students find them challenging. Indeed, it is often when students are struggling or finding something challenging that they are actually moving from a comfortable feeling to one which is actually helping them learn new skills or knowledge. The reflective activity below involves making comparisons between classroom activities. Such comparisons are useful because they often highlight hidden issues.

Reflective activity 6.1

One method, suitable for students for whom writing is not difficult, is simply to ask them to write a comparison of two activities which you choose. It may be worth structuring this at the beginning by suggesting notes are made under headings such as the ones below:

	Good things	Bad things
Activity 1		
Activity 2		

An alternative method would be to carry out a similar exercise verbally. Fairly open questions might be used, such as 'What things do you like doing best in class?' and 'What things don't you like doing?'. These, if followed up sensitively by further enquiries to obtain reasons (and the results recorded), should soon show up the students' criteria and patterns in their opinions about your provision. The recording is important, for, when there is no record to reflect on, it is very easy to fail to fully appreciate the messages one may be being offered.

This activity will help your future planning and provision and could be analysed to identify any patterns in your students' perspectives. If some students seem to be poorly motivated, to lack interest or to dispute the value of an activity, then you will need to consider possible alternative means to achieve the same learning outcomes, or even point students towards further support from professional sources. For example, group work may appeal to many students, but those who are particularly shy may find having to work in a more interactive way is stressful. This is a sensitive issue, as students do need to engage in a variety of activities including socializing with peers as well as with you, the teacher. However, there may be a number of factors involved in this situation which you may be unaware of, or indeed, have little power to intervene; being able to determine what you can do and what the student – and possibly other professionals or colleagues – can do is an important part of your professional decision-making.

2.2 Student perspectives of teachers

All students have views about their teachers. This is a fairly well-researched issue and enquiry into it can provide information about the way students feel about the quality of relationships and education in their classroom. Research has consistently shown that students like teachers who are kind, consistent, efficient at organizing and teaching, patient, fair and who have a sense of humour (Brockbank and McGill, 1998). They dislike teachers who are domineering, boring, unkind, unpredictable and unfair. Strict/soft are two common constructs which students use, with 'strict but fair' often being positively valued. 'Softness' is usually regarded as a sign of weakness. Predictability is also usually important and students are often expert interpreters of the 'moods' of their teachers. Indeed, more generally, student feedback to teachers has been found to be both relatively accurate and reliable. However, the recent development of students commenting on their teachers through social networking sites does show how the balance of power is shifting in educational settings. 'Rate my teacher', for example, can lead to numerous problems including libellous statements, stress for teachers and even closure of classes if students decide to leave.

2.3 Teacher and student actions

Drawing upon Pollard et al. (2014), Figure 6.1 provides a simple model for reflecting on the types of action which teachers and students make in classrooms when a working consensus exists. The most important distinction is between actions which are bounded by the understandings which have been negotiated and those which are not. Five basic 'types of action' can be identified.

Conformity. These actions, by teachers or students, are 'as expected'. They are according to the tacit conventions and agreements of the working consensus.

Routine deviance/low-level disruption. This is the type of low-level disruption or minor misdemeanour which is accepted as being part of normal student behaviour. Lateness,

Figure 6.1
A classification of
types of teacher
and student
classroom action

Teacher Acts			Student Acts	
Unilateral	Within the working consensus			Unilateral
Non-legitimate censure	Legitimate routine censure	Conformity	Legitimate routine deviance	Non-legitimate rule-framed disorder

talking at inappropriate times, 'having a laugh', 'daydreaming and texting on mobile phones' might be examples. Such activities are partly expected by teachers and are not normally intended as a challenge. They are thus within the bounds of the working consensus. It is important for support staff to also be aware of such boundaries.

Routine censure. This is the typical teacher response to routine deviance, a mild reprimand. It will be regarded by the students as legitimate, insofar as such a reprimand will not threaten the dignity of a student nor be employed inappropriately. For example, texting during class happens regularly and requires some gentle but firm reminders. Censures of this type are also within the bounds of the working consensus – they are expected. The teacher is doing his or her job.

Non-legitimate disorder. This is a type of student action which teachers dislike and find hard to understand. It often occurs when a student or a group of students seek to disrupt a classroom situation. They are particularly prone to do this if students perceive themselves to have been treated unfairly or feel that their dignity has been undermined. Action of this type usually reflects the cultural rules of peer groups and can be used to build up a type of 'solidarity' or an alternative source of positive self-esteem. Students who only want to sit with their friends and resist being split up during group work may develop a sense of being hard done by. Many adult students would respond badly to this as they would feel that they are being treated like schoolchildren.

Non-legitimate censure. This is the type of teacher action which students dislike and cannot understand. It often occurs when a teacher loses his or her temper or feels under great pressure. The effect of such actions is that the students feel attacked and unable to cope. They perceive teacher power being used without justification. Such actions lie outside the bounds of the working consensus and are likely to lead to a breakdown in relationships. Teachers who lose their temper or 'blow hot and cold' may find their relationship with their students strained.

The central argument is that 'good relationships' are based on the existence of a negotiated sense of acceptability and fairness which teachers and students share. We discuss ways to deal with these difficult situations in greater detail in Chapter 7.

2.4 Patterns in student actions

Students' actions might range from conforming to rules, engaging in routine deviance and mischief, to acting in unilateral and disorderly ways. These patterns are indeed commonly found in classrooms, as in other walks of life. They do not relate solely to working with young people. Adults in educational settings can argue and even fight! After all, students' actions simply reflect strategies of agreement, negotiation or challenge.

If the quality of both interpersonal relationships *and* curriculum provision is high, then the parameters of student behaviour and engagement are likely to improve. If interpersonal relationships are poor and curriculum provision is inappropriate, then the result is likely to be an increase in disruption, a decrease in learning and the growth of dissatisfaction with education. Overall, social differentiation and exclusion are likely to increase, as you act to deal with disengaged students who may then become 'labelled' as disruptive or problematic.

2.5 Positive and negative cycles

As you get to know your students better you will undoubtedly notice any changes, even minor, in relationships with your class. Consider the model of a positive cycle of teaching and learning in Figure 6.2, a model seen from the student perspective (Pollard, 2014).

In this model Pollard suggests, first, that teacher initiatives lead to learners enjoying a sense of their own dignity and value. Second, students are stimulated by the curriculum or learning activities provided for them by the teacher. These are judged to be interesting and appear likely to satisfy their interest in learning. Third, the situation is regarded as being fair. There are two aspects of fairness here, relating to the way students are managed and to the nature of the tasks which they are asked to undertake. Let us assume that the students and teacher are operating within established organizational and social frameworks and that thus they have both negotiated and both understand the parameters of permissible action. Everyone agrees and is clear about what is expected of them. The other aspect of fairness concerns the appropriateness of the match between the task which the students are faced with and their ability and motivation to do it. If the task is well matched and attractively presented, then students are likely to accept its challenges and attempt to grapple with them enthusiastically. The students' interests are satisfied by teacher provision and

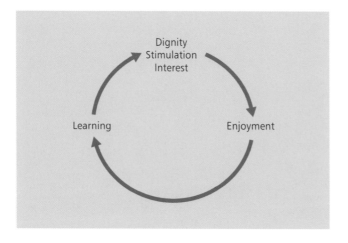

Figure 6.2
A positive cycle of teaching, learning and relationships

action from the start. The crucial result of this enjoyment and learning is that the teacher's interests are also satisfied. If you are able to achieve this quality of relationships, you will find your teaching is effective, your confidence and enjoyment increases. In turn this will help you to inject more energy and care into your teaching and this will fuel another cycle. A cyclical process of reinforcement is created which can then spiral upwards into a higher and higher quality of learning experiences. You will experience many occasions where this positive cycle occurs and it is a potent source of reinforcement of your chosen profession.

On the other hand, things can go wrong if the initiatives you take inadvertently seem to threaten your students' interests. We must also recognize the existence of negative cycles which, instead of spiralling upwards, can lead to a decline into suspicion, hostility and unpleasantness. Again this can be represented by a model seen from the student perspective (Figure 6.3).

In this model it is suggested that teacher initiatives which are not well thought through can threaten the students' interests on three counts. Students may feel affronted, they may switch off, and they may feel their teacher has acted unfairly. Students may feel powerless in such situations, but they do have a degree of collective defensive power and this 'collective solidarity' is likely to be used to neutralize the perceived damage done by their teacher, with resistance in the form of low-level disruption such as whispering to friends, making sarcastic remarks, absence, non-completion of tasks, lateness, psychological disengagement and occupying oneself with a mobile phone or other gadget. At the same time, the teacher will begin to experience lower confidence and diminishing enjoyment and this often leads to increasing stress and behaviour problems. It is exhausting trying to foster learning in this situation. Yet we all have times when things don't go as well as planned and it is important to remember that we are not 'perfect' teachers. We do, though, need to take action to stem any further downward movement.

If things seem to be deteriorating, it is tempting to perceive the causes of disruption as being exclusively to do with particular students. However, reflection on our own actions in respect of the working consensus and the quality of curriculum provision may provide another set of issues for consideration. These issues are, to a great extent, within our own control as teachers. It is at times like this when sharing our experiences are important.

Figure 6.3
A negative cycle of teaching, learning and relationships

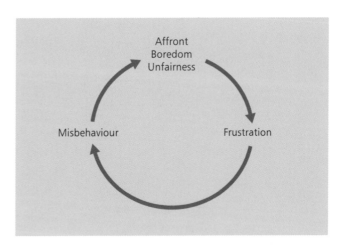

Affront
Boredom
Unfairness

Misbehaviour

Frustration

Asking a colleague to come and observe provides really helpful feedback on the way we respond to the students and they respond to us. These are situations to be shared rather than to be kept to ourselves and worried about.

3 Teacher feelings, expectations and skills

3.1 Teacher perspectives

So far in this chapter, we have suggested the importance of taking account of the perspectives, feelings and position of your students. Now it is time to change the focus onto ourselves as teachers, for our self-image is just as important to maintain as the self-image of the student. Good teaching has never been easy, for to some extent it has always meant placing our students' needs before our own. However, classroom relationships are a very special and subtle phenomenon. On the one hand, a working consensus is related to disciplinary issues and problems which are likely to confront us. On the other hand, the quality of relationships can provide a continuous sense of personal reward and self-fulfilment.

If our own feelings as teachers are also an important factor in maintaining a positive working consensus, then ways of monitoring our feelings may be useful. Reflective activity 6.2 suggests keeping a personal diary (not in the way you may have been asked for your teaching qualification – this is more focused on your own feelings). This does not have to be complicated or a burden and could take the form of jotting down a few notes/key words to remind you of a critical incident or event. This has been used by classroom researchers over many years (Moon, 1999) and is a tried-and-tested way of reflexively taking stock of life as it unfolds. Talking with colleagues and friends can also be immensely valuable and supportive. To care for others, you must also look after yourself (Hyland, 2011). This is true in any form of leadership role and teachers lead the learning of the students in their classes.

Reflective activity 6.2

Start keeping a diary. As we recommended above, this does not have to be an elaborate, time-consuming one, but simply a personal statement of how things have gone and how you felt. The major focus of the diary in this case will obviously be on relationships. It is very common for such reflections to focus in more detail on particular disciplinary issues or on interaction with specific individuals. It should be written professionally, with awareness of ethical issues and the feelings of other classroom participants.

Diary-keeping tends to heighten awareness and, at the same time, it supplies a document which can be of great value in reviewing events.

Once a diary has been kept for a fortnight or so, you might set aside some time to read it carefully and to reflect upon it with a view to drawing reasonably balanced conclusions regarding yourself and your future planning for the classroom. It would be better still to discuss the issues raised with a colleague or friend.

3.2 Expectations of others

The expectations of teachers for the learners in their charge have long been recognized as contributing to student achievements. The classic study of this, by Rosenthal and Jacobson (1968), which focused on schools, suggested that a 'self-fulfilling prophecy' could be set up, in which children who were believed to be 'bright' would do well but, where negative expectations existed, then children would underperform. Indeed, although the ways in which teacher expectations influence student behaviour and attainment is highly complex, there is a broad consensus that high expectations can have a very positive effect (see Chapter 15).

Reflective activity 6.3

Keep a diary of critical classroom events, observations and personal feelings, particularly regarding the behaviour of a range of students with different attitudes to learning. (This is a different diary from the previous one in reflective activity 6.2.)

Review your diary some weeks later. This will trigger a personal recall of events and feelings, and enable you to construct a meaningful (and evidence-informed) story of how classroom relationships developed. Did your students' behaviour remain within the bounds of the working consensus that you had previously established with them? Or were some students acting beyond these limits so that they actually challenged your authority? If so, which students and with whom? Could you feel the engagement of the class ebb and flow over the period? What helped them to become more settled? What disturbed them? Can you relate these patterns to the things that you did, or felt? How did these changes affect particular groups of students?

While we should aim to raise the expectations and look for positive points for potential development in our students, there are also dangers from the existence of negative expectations. For instance, stereotyping is the attribution of particular characteristics to members of a group, and is often used negatively. Thus sex role stereotyping might be found, say, in college science classrooms, with women being encouraged to support the practical by helping and keeping the lab tidy while men engage in leading the experiment.

Bias is a further source of unequal treatment of students. It might refer to images and ideas in books and in other resources which suggest the superiority or inferiority of certain groups of people (see Chapters 8 and 15). However, educational procedures can also be biased in themselves. For example there has been a long-standing debate about bias in intelligence tests and such questions are recurring with regard to assessment procedures. This debate has focused on class, gender and cultural bias at various times and is closely associated with the ways in which disadvantages can be 'institutionalized'. The institutionalization of disadvantage refers to situations in which social arrangements and procedures are established and taken for granted, despite the fact that they may systematically disadvantage a particular social group. Epstein (1993) has provided a particularly clear analysis of this with regard to racism.

3.3 Professional skills

As a teacher, you will develop and refine your professional practice over many years. It is helpful to remember that even though an experienced teacher can seemingly act with minimal effort, this has been achieved through much practice and reflection which is often not apparent, yet they have been deeply involved in thinking reflectively and acting upon this. It is just so ingrained that it looks unconscious. Indeed, one model of professional development suggests we move from being unconsciously incompetent to unconsciously competent (Benner, 2001) and Dreyfus and Dreyfus (1986) argue that we move from being novices to experts, the latter often appearing to act unthinkingly when the reverse is true (see Chapter 16). For an extended discussion around the qualities of a great teacher, see Bennett (2012) on how we develop justice, courage, patience and wisdom.

> ## Case study 6.1 Effects of non-verbal communication
>
> Jeannette has just walked into her workshop. She is aware that her non-verbal behaviour such as facial expression, use of eye contact, posture, gesture and movement has an effect on her students, who monitor her almost continuously for indications of her intentions. They seem to be able to pick up on changes in her mood. She has had a difficult time recently with a car that keeps breaking down, a cat that is unwell, and her brother going to live abroad in the next few weeks. Even though she tries really hard, she finds it difficult to walk in with a smile on her face every day. However, what she can do is show exactly when she wants the students to quieten down ready to begin the session. She knows that simply by standing quietly with her tools ready to demonstrate a particular process, her students understand the signal that she is ready to begin.

A skilful teacher is thus aware of, and manages, her non-verbal behaviour as a form of communication to students. It is thus possible, without saying a word, to convey confidence or anxiety, calmness or tension, satisfaction or displeasure through the ways in which we present ourselves. A skilful teacher can silence a whole lecture theatre by establishing firm eye contact with one or two individuals in the room. The others sense that there is a connection between the teacher and the audience. The lecture hall becomes quiet. A less skilful teacher might struggle even in a smaller class to achieve this, especially if they scan the room constantly, moving their eyes from side to side, front to back and – crucially – restlessly avoiding connection. The way we stand conveys information to our students. If we are standing tall and firm, we send out a signal that we are in charge. If we look apologetic, or hunch our shoulders, we convey a message that we are insecure or unsure. Body language, of course, has many cultural overtones and what we think is being assertive may be taken for being overbearing in another culture. However, being aware of how we come across to students helps us when we want to direct our students in our sessions. It is usually better to be quietly confident, although in some situations, often with younger learners, a more active and even 'off the wall' gesture can be very effective!

Verbal capabilities represent another group of skills. Most obviously, there is the capacity to project your voice within a classroom environment. This is not necessarily to do with volume, but is certainly related to clarity in both the form and content of what is said. Pitching your voice appropriately, so that it is not strained but can be heard, is extremely important and can be developed to improve effectiveness. When under pressure or anxious, people tend to speak more quickly and with a higher pitch. Our voices tend to warble if we are feeling inadequate and we often find our mouths go dry when we are feeling under stress, which results in our voice changing. Voice training should certainly be considered if this becomes a problem. Through the ways in which we speak, we are also able to convey feelings of enthusiasm, confidence or concern so that we can reinforce the substantive message we intend to communicate (see Chapter 12).

An equally important skill is the ability to listen to and interpret what is said by students. The most important dimension of this is to maintain openness to what is said, rather than 'hearing what we expect to hear'. This is by no means easy. But it is an essential skill if an effective feedback loop from students to teacher is to be maintained. Without it, we cannot learn from student perspectives and the appropriateness of our teaching will inevitably be impaired (see Chapters 12 and 15).

The ways in which we behave, speak and listen combine authority and accessibility. It is essential that students respect the role and knowledge of their teachers, but also that they feel able to engage openly with them. Experienced teachers monitor this balance and are able, drawing on their professional skills, to make on-going and contextually appropriate adjustments. In these ways we can establish classroom climates which are effective for learning.

3.4 Classroom authority

We enact our teaching role on behalf of employers, communities and others in society more broadly. In that sense, the powerful position we hold is socially ascribed. The main point of developing good relationships with the class as a whole is that this authority should be accepted by the students. Only then can the power of a teacher be converted into an authentic and practically useful authority. Authority, in other words, is based on acceptance of the role of the teacher – what is called the legitimation of teacher power. Even in more informal settings, where we are acting in a more facilitating role, there is still an exercise of power operating in the setting. Ultimately, we are responsible for the health and safety of our students and are empowered to take action in a number of ways that demonstrate our exercise of power.

4 Enhancing classroom climate

In this chapter so far, we have focused on classroom relationships from student and teacher perspectives, on the interaction between them and on the professional capabilities which are called for. It is now time to consider the classroom as an environment for learning, using the concept of classroom climate. In this section, we will also review how the classroom environment can support self-esteem and make inclusive provision for all students. We discuss this in more detail in Chapter 8.

4.1 Classroom climate and emotional security

The influence of classroom environments on teachers and students has been a research topic for many years. One obvious question which emerged was how to define the 'environment'. Contemporary advances in neurobiology draw connections between social, emotional, cognitive and biological factors. For example, authors of an article entitled 'We feel, therefore we learn' explain that:

> Modern biology reveals humans to be fundamentally emotional and social creatures ... The relationship between learning, emotion and body state runs much deeper than many educators realize. It is not that emotions rule our cognition, nor that rational thought does not exist. It is rather, that the original purpose for which our brains evolved was to manage our physiology, to optimize our survival and to allow us to flourish ... But there is another layer to the problem of surviving and flourishing, [for] as brains and the minds they support became more complex, the problem became not only dealing with one's own self but managing social interactions and relationships ... The physiology of emotion and its consequent processes of feeling have enormous repercussions for the way we learn. (Immordino-Yang and Damsio, 2007: 3–9)

Put another way, the feelings which students develop about classroom life, about their teachers and about learning itself have profound educational implications. We are unlikely to 'open up' for learning unless we feel personally secure (Brockbank and McGill, 1998).

And yet, as we have seen, life in classrooms is inherently challenging for students because of the crowds, praise and power which characterize them. Students in FAVE settings have often experienced education as a process in which they are relatively powerless, constantly evaluated and often fail. We have to attend to the social and emotional dimensions of our student experiences as a foundation for the development of a sense of belonging and to engender constructive approaches to learning.

Enduring insights on the social and emotional foundations of secure relationships are provided by the work of Rogers on counselling (1969, 1980). Three basic qualities are required if a warm, person-centred relationship is to be established: acceptance, genuineness and empathy. When we apply this to teaching, acceptance involves acknowledging and receiving students as they are; genuineness implies that such acceptance is real and heartfelt; while empathy suggests that a teacher is able to appreciate what classroom events feel like to students. Rogers introduced the challenging idea of providing unconditional positive regard for his clients and perhaps this can also provide an ideal for what teachers should offer students. Good relationships are, according to Rogers, founded on understanding and on giving.

Rogers' three qualities have much in common with the three key attitudes of the reflective teacher, discussed in Chapter 3. Being able to demonstrate acceptance and genuinely empathize requires open-mindedness and a wholehearted commitment to the students in our class. It also necessitates responsibility when considering the long-term consequences of our feelings and actions. However, this analysis is not really adequate as a guide to classroom relationships because additional factors are involved. For a number of reasons, the warmth and positive regard which teachers may wish to offer their class can rarely be completely unconditional. In the first place, we are constrained by our responsibility for ensuring that the students learn adequately and appropriately. Second, we may be responsible for relatively large numbers of students where the challenges of class management and discipline condition our actions. Third, the fact that we ourselves have feelings, concerns and interests in the classroom means that we, too, need to feel the benefit of a degree of acceptance, genuineness and empathy if we are to give of our best.

Good relationships in classrooms and FAVE settings can earn the respect of our students by demonstrating empathy and understanding *and* by establishing a framework of order and authority. It is a finely judged balance between two necessary elements. If, as reflective teachers, we are to take full account of the social and emotional climate in our classrooms, we need a form of analysis which recognizes this subtlety. It must recognize both the importance of interpersonal understandings and also the inevitable power struggle between teachers and students.

4.2 Supporting students' confidence and self-esteem

Students often feel vulnerable in classrooms, particularly because of their past experience of education and the power teachers use to control and evaluate. This affects how students experience education and their openness to new learning. Indeed, it is often suggested that people only learn effectively if their self-esteem is positive (Roberts, 2002). We need to reflect on how we use our power and on how this use affects our students.

There are two basic aspects of this. First there is the positive aspect of how we use our power constructively to encourage, to reinforce appropriate student actions and to enhance their self-esteem. Second, however, there is the potential for the destructive use of such power. This particularly concerns the manner in which teachers act when 'rules' are broken. This can be negative and damaging, but skilful and aware teachers will aim to make any necessary disciplinary points yet still preserve the dignity of each student. We suggest activities below to monitor each of these aspects, starting with being positive.

Being positive involves constant attempts to build on success by offering suitable challenges and making maximum use of our students' achievements to generate still more. This policy assumes that each student will have some successes. Sometimes a student's successes may be difficult to identify. This is where by working with individual students in mind, we can create shared targets which are achievable and easily assessed. For example, with basic English and maths programmes, what seem like small steps may provide immense satisfaction to our students, but we need to notice them and capture them (see Chapter 14).

A further type of reflection on relationships concerns the degree of involvement by students, which brings us to the notion of what we have called the inclusive classroom. We discuss this more fully in Chapter 15.

4.3 Developing an inclusive classroom

An inclusive classroom is one which is consciously designed to enable students to act as full participants in class activities and also to feel themselves to be a valued members of the class. In the context of curriculum pressures, relatively large class sizes and the requirements of many assessment procedures, it is difficult to achieve. One feature which often causes problems is that there are variations in both the quantity and quality of teacher attention that is given to different categories of student. It is very understandable if teachers tend to deal first with students whose needs press most or whose actions necessitate an immediate response. However, the problem which then arises is that some other students may be consistently passed over (Collins, 1996). We have a responsibility to ensure our effort is distributed in proportion to the needs of all our students.

Classes also vary in the degree to which differences between students and their abilities are valued. Such differences between people do exist, but a contrast can be drawn between classrooms in which the strengths and weaknesses of each student are recognized and in which the particular level of achievement of each student is accepted as a starting point, and classrooms in which specific qualities or abilities are regarded as being of more value than others in absolute terms. Stress is often on levels of attainment rather than on the effort which students may have made. Indeed, relative attainments can even become institutionalized through inflexible 'ability' grouping systems; the ethos becomes competitive rather than co-operative, and the success of some students is made possible only at the cost of the relative failure of others. The overall effect is to marginalize and exclude some students while the work of others is praised and regarded as setting a standard to which other students should aspire. This can have very negative consequences for students' perceptions of themselves as learners.

Quality of work and standards of achievement are crucially important considerations, but there are also many other factors to bear in mind. For instance, we would suggest that an inclusive classroom will produce better classroom relationships and more understanding and respect for others than one which emphasizes the particular success of a few. Such issues are particularly significant when specific assessment knowledge is gathered. In FAVE settings there is tremendous pressure to link every learning objective with a qualification, leading to employability, evidencing a skill that employers need. This means that students feel the constant pressure of evaluation and judgement. They also often experience learning as very functional and unexpansive. (It is a challenge to value and celebrate students' more subtle strengths and achievements – see Chapter 14.)

Reflective activity 6.4

Consider a group of students in one of your settings. Write a short profile of their characteristics. What do you know about their previous educational experiences? How much do they socialize with each other during your session? Do some students interact more with others? Can you see any patterns in the ways in which your students engage with you and with each other?

Conclusion

Good relationships are closely connected to classroom management, effective teaching and student well-being. They provide a foundation for learning, are enjoyable to participate in and pre-empt trouble. Positive classroom relationships are a considerable source of teacher and student fulfilment. In this chapter we have emphasized that classroom relationships need to be worked at constantly. These relationships cannot be left to chance. We hear too often from teachers about particular groups or classes that 'they were a good group, they really gelled', or the converse, 'they were a nightmare; they really didn't want to learn'. We have proposed a methodology for working on these relationships through the various reflective activities. We hope that you will be able to use these activities to improve relationships; this will result in better learning for your students. However, it is worth noting that while this will benefit you and your students, there is a pressing need for leaders and managers of the system, of organizations, and of departments (in addition to leaders of classrooms) to understand and enable professional learning. Individual reflection, leading to action and review, is only a small part of reflective practice. It is essential that reflection is also public and social; it is essential that leaders and managers make time to organize reflection, so that staff can genuinely develop their practice. Reynolds and Vince argue that being reflective is not simply a technique to be learned and sometimes applied, but rather that it should be part of what it means to be a manager (Reynolds and Vince, 2007). This is all the more important if the management task is to manage education. So, in our view, the reflective activities described in this chapter are more powerful if carried out with other teachers so that practice can be developed, tested and refined with others in genuine professional learning communities. This follows the principles of Joint Practice Development (JPD) – a theme we follow throughout this book.

Perhaps, too, an expectation of being caring towards each other may spread among the students and be of longer-term benefit for society more generally.

Finally, we should note that there are sometimes students with whom more specific efforts to develop good relationships may need to be made. Such cases might include particularly able students who may become bored; students who find studying difficult and may become frustrated; students who have special educational needs; students who find their new educational setting intimidating; and students who have been upset by events in their lives over which they have little control, such as a bereavement, a break-up of a marriage, unemployment, underachievement or even sexual or physical abuse. Such students need very sensitive and empathic attention and they may need special help to express their feelings, to put them in perspective, to realize that their teacher and others care about them and to feel that they have tangible and appropriate targets to strive for in their lives. Such care may enable a student to take control of the situation, with the support of their teacher, to the extent that this is possible. However, teachers should guard against being amateur therapists. Psychologists and social workers are available and they should be approached to give advice if circumstances require their help.

This chapter has focused on the social nature of teaching and learning. We have argued that we must consider how we interact with our students both explicitly but also through the signals that our non-verbal behaviour portrays. We have also suggested that our students do not learn in isolation and that teaching and learning are both parts of a complex social practice.

Key readings

To help you focus your reflection on classroom relationships and relationships for learning, the discussions below provide useful concepts and ideas:

Cooper, B. – Emotions and Learning Piece. (Reading 6.1)

Cooper, B. and Baynham, M. (2005) 'Rites of passage embedding meaningful language, literacy and numeracy skills in skilled trades courses through significant and transforming relationships.' Natural Research and Development Centre for Adult Literacy and Numeracy. London: NRDC.

Rogers, C. (1969) *Freedom to Learn*. New York: Merrill.

Withall, J. (1949) 'The development of a technique for the measurement of social-emotional climate in classrooms', *Journal of Experimental Education,* 17, 347–61.

The role 'student consultation' and 'voice' can play in establishing relationships for learning is considered in:

Rudduck, J. and McIntyre, D. (2007) *Improving Learning Through Consulting Students*. TLRP's Improving Learning series. London: Routledge.

Teacher thinking and professional skills to enhance the classroom climate

The teacher's role in leading the development of learning relationships is explored in:

Bennett, T. (2012) *Teacher: Mastering the Art and Craft of Teaching*. London: Continuum, 71–121. (Reading 6.3)

Coffield, F. and Williamson, B. (2011) *From Exam Factories to Communities of Discovery: The Democratic Route*. London: University of London, Institute of Education (IOE).

Cowie, H. and Wallace, P. (2000) *Peer Support in Action: From Bystanding to Standing By*. London: Sage Publications Ltd.

Gipps, C. and MacGilchrist, B. (1999) 'Primary School Learners'. In P. Mortimore (ed.) *Understanding Pedagogy and Its Impact on Learning*. London: Paul Chapman, 52–5. (Reading 6.2)

Humphreys, T. (1995) *A Different Kind of Teacher*. London: Cassell.

Mental Health Foundation (2005) *A Bright Future for All*. London: Mental Health Foundation.

Watkins, C. (2005) *Classrooms as Learning Communities*. London: Routledge.

For a detailed consideration of establishing positive relationships between teachers and support staff, from both perspectives, see:

Fox, G. (1998) *A Handbook for Learning Support Assistants*. London: David Fulton.
Watkinson, A. (2003) *Managing Teaching Assistants*. London: Routledge.

The associated website, **reflectiveteaching.co.uk**, offers a wealth of supplementary resources including reflective activities, research briefings, advice on further reading and downloadable diagrams, figures and checklists from the book. It also features a compendium of educational terms, links to useful websites, policy and curriculum documents, and showcases examples of excellent research and practice.

Engagement
How are we managing behaviour?

7

Introduction

How do you manage behaviour in your class? If you work with adults in community settings it's likely to be easier than with 16–18-year-olds in FE settings. Student teachers are often worried in the early stages of teaching that they won't be able to cope with, manage and include all of their students in meaningful educational activities. Central to this chapter is the idea that good behaviour is most easily obtained and maintained by ensuring that all students are fully engaged in their education. If your focus is on achieving a positive climate for teaching, learning and assessment (TLA) which draws upon creative and inclusive approaches, you are much more likely to prevent problems arising. This is not always easy, since classrooms are complex places where unexpected events can unfold very quickly (Doyle, 1977, Reading 7.1). Throughout this chapter we discuss working with young people but many of the challenges and issues do apply to adults, although in different ways.

TLRP principles

Principle 6: Effective teaching and learning promotes the active engagement of the learner. A chief goal of teaching and learning should be the promotion of learners' independence and autonomy. This involves acquiring a repertoire of learning strategies and practices, developing positive attitudes towards learning, and confidence in oneself as a good learner.

Principle 7: Effective teaching and learning fosters both individual and social processes and outcomes. Learning is a social activity. Learners should be encouraged and helped to work with others, to share ideas and build knowledge together. Consulting learners about their learning and giving them a voice is both an expectation and a right.

---

1 Understanding classroom behaviour

We believe the key to achieving a positive climate for education is the development of good relationships between teachers and students. Coffield (2008) talks about:

> … a climate of mutual trust and respect which allows for rich, warm and personal exchanges; a language which both parties can use to deepen their understanding of T & L; feedback which publicly affirms the positive regard in which every learner is held and which also challenges every student to move his or her learning forward; dialogue which 'scaffolds' the understanding of learners, enabling them to go beyond their tutors and the information given; dialogue among tutors about T & L which leads to T & L communities; and the incorporation by tutors and learners of a broad range of perspectives on how people learn. (Coffield, 2008: 39)

An emphasis on high expectations and motivation is important and keeping students engaged in appropriately challenging and interesting activities helps to make sure behaviour problems are minimized. Coffield (2009) uses the metaphor of a tandem to illustrate how tutors and students working in partnership will get the best out of education and explores the idea of upward and downward spirals to represent ways in which tutors may motivate or demotivate their students. Although these ideas are based on teaching 14–18-year-olds, the same principles are relevant in other contexts of FAVE. The ways in which learning environments are managed in adult and community education may well have different emphases. Disturbances to learning may be less about misbehaviour and more about ensuring that diversity is celebrated and prejudiced behaviours are tackled. In the context of adult learning, students are more likely to stop coming to sessions if they feel unsafe or uneasy because of the behaviours of others.

It is important to put classroom behaviour and management in the context of the whole organization. You should always find out about and understand the ethos and values of the organization you teach in. At the very least, get copies of the organization's behaviour policies and talk with senior managers and other staff about how those policies are put into practice. Following behavioural guidelines laid down in the organization's policy is an important step towards ensuring that all the staff adopt a coherent and consistent approach to behaviour. The report by Mitchell et al. (FEDA, 1998), *Ain't Misbehavin*, offers sound advice for teachers and managers developing whole organizational approaches to classroom management. In this chapter, we examine the management of behaviour by looking at what goes on in the classroom, what teachers can do themselves to create appropriate environments to influence good behaviour, and we conclude with practical examples of strategies to use when things begin to get tricky.

As we discussed in Chapter 6, good classroom management matters both in terms of fulfilling your professional role and enjoying your professional work. Surviving as a teacher is not possible if discipline and progress in learning cannot be achieved.

The most constructive way of achieving classroom management is to teach the class well so that positive cycles of learning and behaviour are created (see Chapter 6). For most of us, most of the time, regardless of where or who we teach, classrooms are safe, caring environments where lots of productive, lively educational experiences are played out. That said, reports from teachers that the behaviour of some young people has become more challenging cannot be ignored. Equally important is not to stigmatize people who may be disturbed or troubled by events or circumstances beyond the influence of the educational organization. Chapters 6, 7 and 15 offer suggestions for building good relationships, behaviour and inclusion for all, and these should remain key objectives for democratic education.

You may find that students who cause exceptional trouble are often those with various personal and social difficulties (Duckworth, 2013, Reading 7.4). These may be symptomatic of deeper problems and it is important to maintain a sense of perspective and try to think beyond what is happening at the time. It can be difficult for people whose life-chances slip further away through failure in education or who need extra support at a particular point in time. Competing demands on your time, confidence in dealing with certain issues, your qualifications and expertise or even your right to intervene can certainly be a worry. It's important to be realistic about what is possible. Sometimes it may be simply impossible to meet your students' needs within normal forms of provision and supplementary assistance may be required. You shouldn't be reluctant to seek help from colleagues, senior staff or specialist experts when appropriate. We argue that working together with colleagues, for example in joint practice development, can also provide enormous support as you endeavour to find ways to deal with challenges you are facing.

Classroom behaviour for some of us becomes high stakes because it is a public issue as well as, potentially, a private challenge to any teacher. We hear a lot in newspapers and other media about 'declining discipline' and about how young people today are 'up to no good'. In fact, the concern has a long history and has been articulated in almost every era in which public education has existed. We need, therefore, to keep it in perspective. Most educational environments are, for the most part, well-ordered places where good relationships, courteous behaviour and positive attitudes to learning are developed. Nevertheless, the moral panic about behaviour is likely to endure.

You shouldn't feel isolated if experiencing difficulty in achieving and maintaining a good classroom climate where everyone works to develop and maintain productive relationships. If you have concerns, colleagues in your team or department should be a first source of support and more senior staff can also be called upon as appropriate. In some organizations, particular roles exist to lead on behaviour policy and practice. Students' increased access to technology beyond and within the classroom can sometimes act to exacerbate problematic behaviour with inappropriate messaging on social media or, in extreme cases, cyber-bullying.

The professional associations in England which represent teachers and unions such as the University and College Union (UCU) and the Association of Teachers and Lecturers (ATL) are helpful in offering support on classroom management, for they know just how important it is. For example, the ATL offers professional development programmes on behaviour in its *Learning Zone* and has published an excellent guide to constructive professional practice (Watkins, 2011).

If the fundamentals which underpin good classroom planning and management are understood, routines established and creative and challenging TLA activities in place, then such problems are unlikely to arise.

From the teacher perspective, to understand classroom behaviour we should first do what we can to appreciate the circumstances of our students and then think about the educational provision we develop in the diverse educational establishments that FAVE operates in. The latter constitutes the environment, the context, to which our students' behaviour is a response.

1.1 Understanding young people

This section may be of most interest to those working in schools and colleges or with young people 'not in education, employment or training' (NEET). We need here to take stock of the issues raised in Chapters 1, 2 and 4 and to recognize that students in the same classroom may have very different home circumstances. Contemporary societies are seeing extreme differences in wealth and in the associated forms of cultural capital. Some families maintain a stable parent structure, while others are more complex and sustain more fragmented interrelationships. Some students have a great eagerness to learn, while others will feel deeply uneasy or may even be frightened. As they get older, some students will receive significant support and interest while others will find that their efforts may be treated as being of little interest. It is very easy to succumb to stereotypes in trying to make sense of the complexity of people's lives, but this really should be resisted. Being poor does not denote a lack of commitment to children, just as being well off doesn't in itself produce valuable support. Each form of social difference – class, gender, ethnicity, disability, wealth, sexual orientation – is simply a circumstance which needs to be recognized. As teachers, we have to do what we can to understand the prior experiences of the students we teach.

1.2 Providing an engaging environment

As a teacher in FAVE, where you work and the age of your students will impact upon the ways in which you manage and create the learning environment. For some, our students are willing and eager participants for whom educational experiences are welcomed and valued, for others learning is something to be endured and survived with coping strategies developed to get through the day.

Taking into account the context of where you teach and reviewing the following dimensions of the learning environment will help you to develop practice around maximizing student engagement:

Curriculum – it is crucial that students find the curriculum relevant and interesting. This will have a positive impact on their commitment and behaviour and if they don't, then they will seek diversions or opt out of learning all together. This is particularly tricky when knowledge and skills need to be mastered over time and finding creative and innovate ways of teaching to ensure students remain motivated is essential. Chapters 8 and 9 focus on curriculum.

Pedagogy – young students in particular tend to be aware of how they are being controlled, of the rules, routines and rituals of the classroom, the fairness which should underpin them and the security which they offer and on occasions the desire to 'flaunt' them. Beyond this, they will hope for pedagogies which are participatory, make the subject matter interesting, support success in learning and enable enjoyment. Chapters 11 and 12 address such issues. If the learning environment doesn't support this, older learners who are not 'required' to be there may simply stop attending rather than misbehave. In the context of FAVE, patterns of non-attendance which disrupt or stop education signal a concern equal to that of the disruptive behaviour of younger students.

Assessment – anxiety about being judged by others is commonplace. For adult returners, hard-to-reach learners, the experience of being classified may not be a happy one and needs to be managed with care and sensitivity. On the other hand, assessment practices and feedback which enable empowerment and progress in learning are likely to be greatly welcomed. Taking an authentic interest in your students' progress is key to creating a successful learning environment.

Relationships with others – this dimension is essentially about relationships between peers, which can be fraught and challenging for some students. Feeling accepted by a peer group is very important for surviving a programme of study and is manifested in 'having friends'. However people can also be unkind and some students may become isolated or may even be bullied. Even in less formal educational environments, cliques can prevail, and confident characters can be oppressive, especially to those who find it difficult to fit in. Developing ground rules with everyone in the group will help you to create a climate in which everyone is valued and respected, but you need to continue to be watchful to ensure that the experienced environment lives up to these expectations.

2 Establishing authority

Establishing authority over a class is partly about self-belief – that is, acting with confidence as a teacher, and partly about capability in the sense of being professionally competent in the core skills of teaching. This means being able to interpret and analyse classroom events as they develop so that adjustments are possible (Cowley, 2010, **Reading 7.2**). Underlying all these qualities, as we saw in Chapter 6, are the relationships which we develop with students and being seen to act fairly. This will differ depending upon the circumstances and context of your teaching. This can commonly include age and gender in many FAVE settings, with more complex social customs and traditions coming into play across different adult and community education settings.

Of course, the difficulty is that competence and understanding take time to develop and while books of this sort can support such processes, there is no substitute for direct experience. Student teachers and beginning teachers face the difficult challenge of working on their competence and understanding while at the same time needing to teach their groups and classes.

In this section, we focus on four issues which support the establishment of classroom authority: expectations, self-presentation, use of language and strategic repertoire.

2.1 Expectations

Students, just like most of us, are extremely good at sensing the beliefs, motivations and dispositions of others. Teachers who presume that students are up to no good and cannot be trusted are likely to engender similarly guarded responses. On the other hand, if a teacher conveys a set of expectations which presumes capability and projects realistic goals towards success, then it is likely that students will respond.

We need to take control of our own expectations, and to review these carefully, particularly in relation to our personal theories about our students' behaviour. Beliefs of any sort evolve in the light of experience, but can also be culturally and personally embedded. Contrasting ideas of people as inherently good or bad have long histories within contemporary cultures and may even be found within some educational settings. To establish authority, teachers need to be cautious about unquestioned beliefs, in whatever form they may emerge. In the long term, neither being too soft nor being too strict will work. The most realistic and effective strategy is to consistently presume the best from students while carefully taking notice of what's actually happening.

Expectations for behaviour in respect of classroom rules should be made explicit, modelled and reinforced (Chaplain, 2003, Reading 7.3). Whenever things begin to slide, or if established understandings are challenged, then such rules need to be reasserted. The setting of ground rules together with your students can be helpful here. As discussed in Chapter 2 on learning, it helps to credit students with what they do, rather than focus on deficits and failures. In the context of our teaching, something as seemingly straightforward as punctuality needs to be carefully nuanced in respect of individual circumstances. Late arrival doesn't necessarily mean students don't care about their education or are demotivated; they might have caring responsibilities, travel long distances, work shift patterns or any number of reasons. Likewise, rules about mobile phones need to be flexible and accommodating to different needs, contexts and activities.

Setting high expectations about behaviour, as for learning, is an important foundation for establishing teacher authority.

2.2 Self-presentation

Teachers who are able to project themselves so that students take for granted that they are in charge, have a valuable skill. There is an important element of self-confidence in this and student teachers, in particular, may sometimes find it difficult to enact the change from the student role to the teacher role. Perhaps this is not surprising, for a huge change in rights and responsibilities is involved. An important starting point is to believe in yourself as a teacher.

Judgement is needed about self-presentation because the process of establishing authority, as we saw in Chapter 6, is essentially one of negotiation between the teacher and the class. Authenticity is an important contribution to any negotiation and it is likely that, in the challenges of the classroom, attempts by novice teachers to bluff and pretend that they are hugely experienced will be found out. It is usually wise to progress carefully and 'with' the students wherever possible. This doesn't mean you should not act the part and fulfil the teacher role, as students will expect this.

Professional skills, as reviewed in Chapter 6, come into their own here – for they are all related to demonstration of classroom competence. Non-verbal skills relate to such things as gesture, posture, movement, position in the room, facial expression, etc. and will be actively interpreted by students. The intended impression might be one of confidence and competence, but you will need to consider how this is achieved. How do you feel? How do you move within the classroom? Voice control is particularly crucial, for changing the pitch, volume, projection and intensity can convey meaning. If your voice is to be used in this way then it may require some training and time to develop. Teachers, like singers and actors, can learn to use their diaphragm to project a chest voice, to breathe more deeply and speak more slowly so that their voice and their message is carried more effectively (see

Chapter 6). Crucially the skill of really listening to students and understanding what they have to say is critical to the establishment of authority, which is the basis of its legitimacy.

A final and more general area of presentational skill is that of acting as though on stage. In this sense it is the ability to convey what we mean by being a teacher so that expectations are clear and relationships can be negotiated. Don't underestimate the power of turning your class into an audience when appropriate. As an audience they will feed your self-presentation and, if you actively observe and listen to your audience, you will know exactly where your efforts are misfiring.

The skills reviewed above are necessary but are not sufficient. A self-confident performer who lacks purpose and gets practical matters wrong (for example, mixes up students' names, plans sessions badly, loses student work or acts unfairly) will not be able to manage a class. A teacher has to be purposive as well as skilled and must understand the ends of education as well as the means.

2.3 Language

We may need to be assertive, but we also need to bear in mind our broader educational purposes. Every time we speak to students, for whatever purpose, we have educational opportunities. In relation to behaviour, the aim is to keep them on track as effectively as possible as a means to educational ends.

Rogers (2011: 83) identifies seven ways in which language could be used to support good discipline:

1 Keep corrective interaction as least-intrusive as possible.

2 Avoid unnecessary confrontation.

3 Keep a respectful, positive tone of voice wherever possible.

4 Keep corrective language positive where possible.

5 Restore working relationships with a reprimanded student as quickly as possible.

6 Follow up with students on matters beyond the classroom context.

7 If we need to communicate frustration, or even anger, do so assertively rather than aggressively.

Misbehaviours (day-dreaming, calling out, gossiping, lateness, making too much noise) are aspects of what we call low-level disruption. Such behaviours should be met with non-confrontational censure designed constructively to assert classroom rules while protecting the dignity of the student. Possible responses include:

- Communicating calmness and a measured response.

- Using humour to defuse the situation.

- Inviting correction, for example with 'when … and then'.

- Minimizing denials, for example from overuse of 'can't', 'won't'.

- Avoiding humiliation, for example from sarcasm.

- Avoiding aggression, for example through pointing fingers, shouting.
- Being firm and fair, but brief, in asserting the correct behaviour.

To establish our authority as teachers, even with the pressure of the busy classroom, we must carefully think about what we say and how we say it. To build productive learning behaviour we need to:

- *Connect personally* with relevant student/s.
- *Identify the behaviour* which needs to change.
- *Encourage re-engagement* with curricular intentions.
- *Minimize disruption* to others.
- *Follow through* to ensure conformity.

Measured and constructive assertiveness combined with an interesting and engaging curriculum can sustain and reinforce good order, which helps the establishment of authority. Intemperate use of language can provoke poor discipline and is likely to undermine authority. Rogers warns teachers not to get out of control, something students may describe where the teacher has 'lost it'. Such uncontrolled use of power is a long way from establishing authority. Crucially, the latter rests on non-legitimacy.

Cowley (2010), makes similar points in her book, *Getting the Buggers to Behave*, particularly suitable for those working with younger students (see also Reading 7.2). Vizard (2007) focuses on managing behaviour in FE and, in addition to offering a range of practical strategies, also offers a good starting point in relation to creating positive learning environments and making a strong first impression.

2.4 Strategic repertoire

Teacher strategies become more intrusive as they feel the need to draw on their authority and assert their power. Experienced teachers are aware of a repertoire of strategies on which they can draw to establish and maintain appropriate student behaviour. Strategies identified by Rogers (2011) can be considered in three groups. These reflect minimal, routine and assertive levels of teacher action.

Minimal intrusion strategies

The usefulness of these strategies rests on the existence of well-understood rules and good classroom relationships. In some FAVE contexts learning contracts are drawn up with students at the beginning of a programme and/or ground rules are established. If these relationships are in place, good behaviour can be achieved with simple reminders. Three of Rogers' minimal strategies are:

- **Tactical ignoring** – you are aware of, but temporarily ignore, minor misdemeanours while focusing on and affirming positive behaviours. Students should then come into line.

- **Incidental language** – where you remind students of classroom rules without attributing blame to anyone. Because rules are established and accepted, students self-adjust to conform.

- **Take-up time** – after a rule reminder or request, you move away to give students time to cooperate. By doing this you communicate trust (although you are likely to keep an eye on progress!).

Routine strategies

This group of strategies reflects the ebb and flow of teacher–student interaction and the fact that relationships are always dynamic. A little jostling and testing of boundaries is to be expected. The strategies below are typical of those which teachers use to frame and control classroom situations, particularly when students may have non-curricular activities in mind!

- **Behavioural direction** – expected behaviours are directly, positively and briefly communicated: 'Can we all come back into the main group now', 'All paying attention to me now please'.

- **Rule reminder** – rather than 'picking on' a particular transgressor, the teacher reminds everyone of a rule; this is better still if it comes from the ground rules generated by everyone. For example, the teacher might say: 'Remember we all agreed that we would start our session promptly after the break …'

- **Prefacing** – with awareness of potential misbehaviour, this strategy can be used to anticipate and frame activities without being too heavy-handed. On setting up or at suitable moments, the teacher interacts with relevant students to show awareness, to nip unwanted aspects in the bud, and to redirect attention back to activity in question.

- **Distraction** – this strategy involves deliberately drawing attention to something that is going well and thus bypassing something which might be problematic. With the class refocused, the difficulty fades away or can be quietly dealt with.

- **Direct questions** – such questions challenge students to justify themselves and to take responsibility: 'What should you be doing now?' 'How are you meant to …?' 'Where should you put the …?' Such questions may be the starting point for discussion and clarification of rules.

- **Directed 'choices'** – these are student options which are circumscribed by established rules and routines. Indeed, the choice is a condition of satisfying such understandings: 'Yes we'll have our break once this activity is completed.'

Assertive strategies

The strategies in this group depend on teachers asserting their authority and 'standing up' to students in various ways. While they are less negotiative, they still make reference to established understandings and rules. However, they leave students in no doubt that the teacher is in charge.

- **Blocking** – this is an important strategy to maintain focus on important behavioural issues in the face of all sorts of distraction tactics which may be deployed by students: 'Hold on. Now let's get to the point about what really happened', 'I'll hear you one at a time. John … Sam …'

- **Assertion** – this strategy calmly deploys verbal and non-verbal skills and draws on reserves of self-confidence to defend and promote a principle about behaviour which has been threatened: 'We don't accept language of that sort here.' The stance should be non-aggressive. There may need to be a sequence of blocking and assertion moves as the complexity of student feelings, explanations and actions is worked through. This strategy can be particularly important when teachers have to deal with incidents of prejudice, when it can really help to use a strategy which stops the action and signals to everyone that the incident and issues surrounding it are serious and will be returned to. This is known as a 'holding response', such as: 'Talking that way will not be tolerated and I want you to stop. There is no place for that type of behaviour here. We'll return to this in our next session.' This will give you time to develop a more measured response rather than reacting to the situation in the 'heat of the moment'. Even more significantly, it gives you time to plan a 'pedagogical response' and lets everyone know that you have taken the incident seriously and the incident has not been dropped. Examples of pedagogical responses include planning sessions or topic areas which directly address the particular prejudice, reviewing the materials and activities which recognize dimensions of difference including class, gender, ethnicity, disability, wealth, sexual orientation and gender realignment. Material and resources available to support you include 'Show Racism the Red Card Pack for Initial Teacher Trainers' and the Stonewall site for challenging homophobic bullying. In some adult education settings, there may be groups of students who have come from areas of conflict in their previous environments who are now sitting next to a previous enemy. These situations require great skill and understanding and the resources cited above may provide helpful advice in dealing with such tensions within the classroom.

- **Command** – the distinguishing characteristic of a command is that it is simply that: a direct instruction. To be effective, a command needs to be delivered in a clear and direct way, and to be followed up immediately: 'Louise, please put the mobile phone down, you know the rules.' Eye contact, proximity and firm tone of voice will all convey the seriousness of your intentions. This strategy is one of direct intervention and should not be common in classroom use. If it is, it may be a sign that relationships are breaking down. Ineffectually demanding things from an alienated class should be avoided at all costs. To be effective, commands draw on mutual respect and trust. If you work in educational settings where young people are learning and growing up, unquestioning obedience is rarely obtainable!

Our power is always circumscribed but, as the ones with responsibility, we have the task of analysing and interpreting what is going on and taking action if necessary.

3 Skills for engagement

This section draws upon curriculum planning and preparing teaching sessions which is discussed in Chapter 10. We outline seven skills relating to the maintenance and development of teaching sessions: gaining attention, framing, withitness, overlapping, pacing, orchestration and consistency. Many of the issues in this and the following section on managing classroom episodes are also addressed in Chapter 11. There will be significant differences in the way in which you use or don't use these skills depending upon the context of your work. Managing the learning environment and building relationships with energetic 16-year-old apprentices may call upon very different skills than those you would apply to build the confidence and skills of asylum-seekers in an ESOL class.

3.1 Gaining attention

For those working with adult learners this is rarely an issue. However, it's often one of the first problems to confront a student teacher working in formal FE settings with 16–18-year-olds. When students are in the classroom, talking or texting, how do you get them to stop what they are doing and turn their attention to you? Established teachers are likely to have at least one routine for this. Closing the door, switching the lights off and on or a single, sharp clap of the hands may cut though the noise and produce a short pause which creates an opportunity to take the initiative. On a sports field where speech might not carry well, a whistle is the conventional tool. Sadly, things are rarely so simple and gaining attention often has to be worked for.

To understand why this is, it is worth considering what is at stake. When young people are milling about and talking among themselves they are free of adult constraints and able to indulge in all the excitements and diversions of peer culture. The switch signal given by the teacher is an interruption in this freedom. It is an assertion, based on the teacher's authority, that the time has now come for them to assume the role of 'students' again. They are to set aside what they were previously doing, and must now accept the rules, routines and expectations of the classroom.

As with so many aspects of teaching, it is helpful to think of building up a repertoire of ways of gaining attention so that various strategies are available. While a clear, firm command may be part of the repertoire, it is important to avoid uncontrolled shouting, or to take any other action which could be interpreted as desperation or weakness. Remember to pay attention to your pitch of voice and speed of talking. For student teachers, it is very good practice to study the strategies used by established teachers and to discuss their routines with them. One very simple course of action is to ensure that you arrive in the classroom before your students, putting you in control, as well as enabling you to welcome the group.

3.2 Framing

Framing indicates the extent to which situations or events are structured by expectations. It may apply in particular settings, or from moment to moment within a lesson. For instance, you might compare the strong framing which often exists in a hushed library with the weak framing which exists in classrooms during a break. For some purposes, such as during the introduction to a teaching session, you might want the frame to be strong to ensure tight control and attention. On other occasions, such as for group problem-solving discussions, a weaker overall frame may be perfectly acceptable and will enable students to take initiatives to fulfil learning objectives. Situations of difficulty often arise where strong framing is expected by a teacher but students act as if the framing is weak. If this happens, you need to act quickly to redefine the rules in play.

The ability to manage the strength of behavioural framing over time has a great deal to do with classroom discipline. It sustains expectations and avoids a lurch from routine to routine. In particular, skilful management provides a means of pre-empting serious difficulties through giving clear expectations about acceptable behaviour. By its very nature, though, the development of such understandings cannot be rushed and frequently needs to be reviewed explicitly by teachers and students. Once again, ground rules and the consequences of breaking them can be helpful here.

If you teach in very informal settings it is likely that you will deliberately want to create an environment which is more relaxed. If students are opting in to education, it is possible to have a much weaker frame as students self-regulate behaviour and need a flexible environment which responds to the wide range of needs they may bring to the group.

3.3 Withitness

Withitness (Kounin, 1970) describes the capacity of teachers to be aware of the wide variety of things which are simultaneously going on in a classroom. This is a constant challenge for any teacher and can be a particular strain for a new teacher until the skill is acquired. Teachers who are 'with-it' are said to 'have eyes in the back of their head'. They are able to anticipate and to see where help is needed. They are able to nip trouble in the bud. They are skilful at scanning the class while helping individuals and they position themselves accordingly. They are alert and can act fast. They can sense the way a class is responding, re-establish the framework of expectations if necessary and act to maintain a positive atmosphere.

3.4 Overlapping

Kounin describes the skill of being able to do more than one thing at the same time as overlapping, similar to the popular term multitasking. Most teachers have to think about and do more than one thing at a time. Decisions have to be made very rapidly. Frequently scanning the class, even while helping one individual, should enable the teacher to identify and reinforce appropriate behaviour or to anticipate and intervene at the first signs of trouble.

3.5 Pacing

Pacing a lesson is another important skill. Pacing involves making appropriate judgements about the timing and phasing of the organization, manner and content of lessons. Decisions have to be made about when to begin and end an activity and how much time to leave for tidying up or a plenary discussion. It is easy to get involved in activities, forget about the clock and suddenly find that it is break time. More complex educational judgements are necessary in relation to learning activities and the various phases of a typical session – for example, the motivation generated at the start of an activity has to be sustained throughout. There may also be a need for incubation and developmental phases in which students think about the activities, explore ideas and then tackle tasks. From time to time there may be a need for a restructuring phase where objectives and procedures may need to be clarified further. Finally, there may be a review phase for reinforcing good effort or for reflecting on overall progress.

Flexibility and exercising judgement about pacing are vitally important as they depend crucially on being sensitive to how students are responding to activities. If they are immersed and productively engaged, then you might decide to extend or run the activity into the next session. If students seem to be becoming bored, frustrated or listless, then it is usually wise to restructure or review the activity or to move on to something new. If students are becoming too high, excited and distracted, then it may be useful to review and maybe redirect them into an activity which calms them down by re-channelling their energies.

3.6 Orchestration

Here we are using the term 'orchestration' to refer to the way in which a teacher works with the whole class rather like a conductor controls an orchestra or a stand-up comedian plays an audience. Whether you are adopting whole-class, individual or group teaching strategies, part of your job is to maximize the time that all the individuals in the class are on task and paying attention. Involving all students in the learning activities of a classroom involves developing the sensitivity to be able to read how individual students are responding and to be able to anticipate the most effective way of maintaining interest or re-engaging attention. This will differ from individual to individual and in different contexts. Bored behaviour might arise because a task is too easy or too difficult (see Chapter 10 on differentiation). On the other hand, some students may be highly motivated by an activity which others find tedious and dull. In all cases you have to be aware of everything that is happening in your classroom and be prepared to act accordingly. This may involve a differentiated response in which some students are allowed to continue with what they are doing while a new focus is found for others. There is a range of ways of motivating all the individuals in the class (Scruton and Ferguson, 2014). As discussed in the next section, working with a class of individuals may involve being able to respond to many, if not all, of their responses at the same time.

3.7 Consistency

Consistency is necessary in the promotion of classroom rules, routines and expectations. After all, in the domain of the classroom, the teacher often acts as government, police, judge and jury all rolled into one. Students are one of the crowd and remain subject to the teacher's right to evaluate and power to punish. If we are inconsistent, we will reduce the integrity of our working consensus and the sense of fairness on which it is based. This, in turn, can lead to a variety of subsequent control difficulties and to risk-avoidance strategies.

Students will feel vulnerable unless they can rely on teacher consistency and fairness. With such security, students are more likely to open themselves up to the challenges and risks of new learning. Being consistent is central to providing an underlying structure for high quality student learning.

Reflective activity 7.1

Investigating classroom management skills

Ask a colleague to observe you in a teaching session and to make notes on the way in which you manage students. They could watch out for examples of gaining attention, framing, withitness, overlapping, pacing, orchestration and maintaining consistency. Discuss the session together afterwards.

Alternatively, set up a video camera to record a session which you take. Analyse the playback in terms of the issues above.

---

4 Managing classroom episodes

Flow is an important summary criterion which can be used to describe classroom management. By flow we mean the degree of continuity and coherence which is achieved in a learning session. It implies steady, continuous movement in a particular direction. We should work with students to develop a coherent sense of purpose within our classes; organize our classrooms in ways which are consistent with those purposes; and manage students, phases and events so that learning objectives are cumulatively reinforced.

In this section we discuss five issues which pose particular management challenges to the flow of sessions. We discuss beginnings of sessions; their development; transitions between phases of sessions or between sessions themselves; and the endings of sessions. We also consider strategies for dealing with the unexpected.

4.1 Beginnings

The beginning of a session is often seen as important because of the way in which it sets a tone. The next important goal is usually to introduce and interest students in the planned activities; to provide them with a clear indication of the learning objectives of the session, a clear understanding of what they are expected to do; and to structure the activity in practical, organizational terms.

Context is significant here; if you are working in a 'drop-in' centre or studio/workshop, a very different approach may be adopted, as students 'come and go' and interact with you and their peers in very different ways. Although you have to plan carefully for the individual requirements of your students, the nature and structure of this type of education rarely results in behaviour disturbances.

4.2 Development

However carefully the session begins, how does it develop? Students will expect to find progression which will maintain their interest and engagement with curricular tasks. This is a clear example of how good behaviour can be seen as a product of good teaching – in this case, of appropriate curriculum planning (see Chapter 10).

4.3 Transitions

Transitions are a regular cause of control difficulties, particularly for trainee teachers. This often arises when expectations about behaviour concerning one activity have to be left behind and those of the new one have yet to be established. In these circumstances, an experienced teacher is likely to plan carefully, involve available support staff if required, take an initiative early and structure the transition carefully.

For example, it can be a challenge when students are on courses with practical and theory sessions, such as sport, dance, catering, and where the practical session is more valued by students than the theory. When a range of practical activities are in full flow and suddenly students have to get changed for a theory session in another room, then it is important to break down a transition such as this into three discrete stages. First, in antici-pating problems before they arise; second, in pre-structuring the next phase; and finally, in interesting students in the next phase so that they are drawn through and into it. These principles (anticipate, pre-structure and engage) can apply to any transition.

4.4 Endings

Ending a session is a further management issue; any equipment used should be put away and the classroom tidied up ready for future sessions. The second aspect relates to disci-pline and control. People can sometimes get a little 'high' at the end of a session when they look forward to whatever follows. This, combined with the chores of tidying up, can require a degree of awareness and firmness from the teacher. This is much less likely to be an issue when working with adults, although here it may be getting them to leave that is often the challenge!

Overall, a carefully thought-out and well-executed ending to a session will contribute to the flow of activities by providing an ordered exit, by reinforcing learning and by building up the sense of 'belonging' within the class as a whole.

4.5 The unexpected

Unpredictability is a challenging feature for student and experienced teachers alike. It is difficult to predict student reactions to questions, how they will respond to specific activities or how long it will take for a class to complete an activity. These are skills which are acquired over time and with experience. However, in any classroom there is the continuous possibility of internal and external interruptions – for example, there may be changes in the normal schedule or a potential breakdown in equipment. Experienced teachers learn to plan ahead, to anticipate potential difficulties and to have a range of strategies for dealing with the unexpected. In this section we consider how teachers might deal with the unexpected in terms of both learning outcomes and 'crises'.

A classroom crisis is a clear example of the unexpected. Crises can come in many forms, from someone being ill, interruptions from outside, student disagreements, to students challenging the teacher's authority and judgement. Despite the wide-ranging issues which are raised, there are three fairly simple principles which can be applied from the classroom-management point of view.

The first priority is to minimize the disturbance. A student who is ill, hurt or upset cannot be given the attention they require by a teacher who has continuing classroom responsibilities. Help from support staff or another colleague should be called in either to deal with the problem or to relieve the class teacher to deal with it. In this way disturbance to the classroom flow can be minimized and those in need of undivided attention can receive it. The organization should have an identified procedure for how to handle crises. Usually a student teacher has a full-time teacher to call upon. Of course, in less formal environments other colleagues may not be on hand; usually students in the class will be able to deal and regulate the situation with you.

The second step for handling a crisis is to maximize reassurance. Other students can be upset when something unexpected happens. The third strategy involves pausing for sufficient thought before making a judgement about how to act. Obviously, this depends on what has happened and some events require immediate action. However, if it is possible to gain time to think about the issues outside the heat of the moment, then it may produce more authoritative and constructive decisions. Blocking and holding responses may be helpful here.

As teachers in FAVE, the sheer diversity of the context and settings in which we teach can present unexpected events and issues, and things that apply in one context rarely, if ever, are experienced in another. For example, if you are working with students in offender learning, peer relationships can be volatile, as can the effects of being away from family and friends, being moved to another prison, or having privileges revoked. Community education can bring challenges around attendance and relationship-building when people are in difficult and transient situations coping with homelessness, addiction, or low self-esteem, which can erupt into fighting and disagreement. Alongside this may be issues around personal hygiene, acceptable behaviour and boundaries.

5 Cycles of behaviour

In dealing with behavioural problems the most effective strategy is, without doubt, to try to prevent them from happening in the first place. The incidence of inappropriate behaviour is likely to be significantly reduced by following some basic rules of thumb to improve student engagement. We talked about building positive cycles in Chapter 6. Here we make suggestions to help sustain this approach.

Figure 7.1
Checklist for pre-empting disturbances and improving engagement.

1   Be clear about general class rules and what constitutes acceptable behaviour.
2   Be sure to 'give credit' for appropriate behaviour.
3   Select tasks and activities that offer appropriate challenges and interests, but which also enable students to achieve success.
4   Have clear learning objectives and make sure students understand these.
5   Explain the activity or task clearly and be sure that everyone knows what to do and how to do it.
6   Be supportive of any problems encountered and provide feedback.
7   Show approval of appropriate work and reward effort.
8   Be consistent and be positive.

Unfortunately, while the strategies identified above should significantly reduce the incidence of misbehaviour, they may not prevent it in all circumstances. Consequently it's important to develop in your repertoire a range of strategies for dealing with inappropriate behaviour before it develops into anything worse.

5.1 Managing challenging behaviour – avoiding a negative cycle

Although crises will be rare, there may be behavioural problems which gradually erode good relationships and threaten the way in which the classroom operates. In this section we present them in terms of recurring challenges which even the most experienced teacher may have to deal with. The aim, of course, would be to anticipate undesirable behaviour and to 'nip it in the bud' so that it does not lead to a negative cycle. Below we offer strategies in five progressive stages. The emphasis, naturally, is on prevention and personal safety.

1 If inappropriate behaviour occurs only once and seems relatively minor:
- indicate that you have noticed and disapprove of the behaviour – eye contact and a shake of the head.

2 If repeated:
- Make sustained eye contact, use more emphatic non-verbal gestures.
- Move towards the student.
- Invite the student to participate – ask a question or encourage a comment, direct the focus onto work to be done.

3 If persistent, in addition to the responses above:
- Name the student firmly and positively.
- Move to the student.
- Stop the action.
- Find out the facts if the situation is ambiguous; avoid jumping to conclusions.
- Briefly identify the inappropriate behaviour, comment on the *behaviour* (not the student), keep voice low and controlled, avoid nagging/lecturing.
- Clearly state the desired behaviour, and expect a compliant response.
- Distance the student from the situation – avoid a contagious spread, a public clash and an 'audience' which can provoke 'showing-off'.
- Focus on the principle individual involved; don't be drawn into discussion with a group – followers will conform if you control the leader.
- Deal with the situation as quickly and neatly as possible; don't be drawn into long arguments; don't let the situation distract your attention from the rest of the class and the goals of your lesson.

4 If 'punishment' is judged to be necessary:
- Ensure that the punishments you consider are consistent with organization policies and established classroom norms.
- Be sure that the punishment you decide upon is appropriate and will be seen to be 'fair'.
- Avoid indiscriminate punishment of class or group which would be deemed 'unfair'.
- Be confident that you can implement the punishment as announced.

5. Closure/after the event:
- Take those involved to one side, perhaps individually, and present them with 'the problem'– preserve their dignity, avoid 'supporters' chipping in.
- Encourage the student to identify what had been wrong, thus sharing responsibility.

- If you have acted inappropriately in any way, then apologize, so you are seen to be fair.
- Invite the student to draw up a 'contract' for the future.
- If privileges are to be withdrawn, show how they can be earned back.
- Provide new opportunities to earn praise.
- Conclude with 'peace-terms' which are clear to all parties.

The point of all this is to be 'firm but fair'. You, as the teacher, are responsible and must take control. But you have to act appropriately and negotiate a new foundation for future conformity and a sustainable, positive relationship.

It is important to record and analyse the behaviour and try to identify the possible causes before major action is taken. Keeping a diary or notes of events you can record the conditions, characteristics and consequences of the behaviour and produce evidence for future action.

Reflective activity 7.2

Recording incidents of ongoing 'problem' behaviour

Keep a record of when you experience difficult or challenging behaviour. Use the checklist below to help you identify the characteristics of the situation

Conditions: When exactly does the disruption occur?
- Is it random or regular?
- Is there a pattern with a particular student?
- Is there a pattern regarding a particular task?
- Is there a pattern with a particular teacher?

Characteristics: What exactly happens?
- Is it a verbal reaction?
- Is it a physical reaction?

Consequences: What are the effects?
- On the student, the teacher?
- On the class, the organization?
- Do others join in, ignore, retaliate?

Such major, persistent problems are best discussed with other colleagues and a common strategy worked out in line with the organization's behaviour policy. This might also involve parents, carers, employers, community members and the whole class, if necessary, so that a consistent approach can be adopted.

Whether a problem is associated with an individual student or most of the class, a consistent, balanced, firm and constructive approach is essential which will, hopefully, provide security for the students as well as yourself. Remember that people respond to situations and experiences differently. We, as teachers, structure such experiences. If students respond problematically, we must reflect on the experiences that we provide rather than simply trying to apportion blame elsewhere.

5.2 Principles for classroom management

The following may help you to think about and act upon managing the complex behaviours that take place in your classroom and help minimize the occurrence of types of behaviours which interrupt the learning of others. Take care to have clearly stated boundaries of acceptable behaviour and respond promptly and firmly to those who test boundaries. Ensure the motivation of students to learn is valued, with high expectations set and maintained. Provide a stimulating and appropriately differentiated curriculum where groups and individuals are skilfully managed. Create a positive atmosphere and climate for learning based on a sense of community and shared values. Consider how you might achieve the highest possible degree of consensus about standards of behaviour among staff, students and others involved in the education process and how you promote values of mutual respect, self-discipline and social responsibility.

At a wider level, holistic whole organizational approaches are recommended. Organizational and classroom misbehaviour should, above all, be pre-empted where purposeful communities of people exist, with teachers acting sensitively, skilfully and authoritatively to maintain the values, rules, expectations and activities which provide an infrastructure for high-quality education.

The Elton Report includes a statement of eleven 'principles of classroom management' (DES, 1989: 71) which reflect much good sense and experience. We include them below in the form of questions for use in planning, undertaking and reflecting on classroom practice, and we have added a question on modelling non-prejudiced behaviour.

Can we say how and if we:

1   Know our students as individuals: names, personalities, interests, friendship groups, responsibilities and concerns in their lives which may impact upon their education?

2   Plan and organize the space in which we teach and plan our lessons to keep students interested and minimize the opportunities for disruption: furniture layout, student groupings, matching of work, pacing lessons, enthusiasm, humour?

3   Involve students in establishing ground rules for classroom behaviour and routinely reinforce why they are necessary?

4   Act flexibly to take advantage of unexpected events rather than being thrown by them?

5   Continually observe or 'scan' the way in which students act, participate, include others in the class?

6   Remain aware of, and control our own behaviour including stance and tone of voice?

7   Model appropriate non-prejudiced behaviour through the language we use and the pedagogical responses we take to tackle prejudice head-on?

8   Model the standards of courtesy that we expect from our students?

9   Emphasize the positive, including praise for good behaviour as well as good work?

10   Make sparing and consistent use of reprimands – being firm not aggressive, targeting the right student, using private not public reprimands, being fair and consistent, avoiding sarcasm and idle threats?

11   Make sparing and consistent use of punishments – avoiding whole-group punishment and student humiliation which breed resentment?

12   Analyse our own classroom management performance and learn from it?

Conclusion

This chapter has examined aspects of behaviour management which help to establish and sustain conditions for successful learning. Such issues are of great concern to us as teachers because they underpin our effectiveness. Most of us gradually grow in confidence and competence with such challenges and 'good discipline' is, above all, the product of professional expertise. If you are a student teacher you should allow yourself time to learn, experiment, and learn some more. Direct experience is irreplaceable in developing competence, but there is also much to be said for sharing ideas, problems and successes through discussion with tutors, peers and mentors. Classroom management is an absolutely necessary means to an end, but it is not the end itself.

We have shown in this chapter numerous strategies to help manage student behaviour in effective and non-judgemental ways. We suggest that respecting our students' behaviour is a key component of managing it, particularly when we consider our own role in being able to defuse tense situations, or even how we, inadvertently, can contribute to these. We have outlined the range of practices with a view to developing confidence in dealing with demanding situations.

Key readings

For advice on developing whole organizational approaches to classroom management, see:

Mitchell, C., Pride, D., Howard, L. and Pride, B. (1998) *Ain't Misbehavin':
    Managing Disruptive Behaviour*. London: Further Education Development
    Agency.

For an analysis of the difficulties of classroom teaching, with some useful pointers to making it easier:

Reading 7.1 – edited from Doyle, W. (1977) 'Learning the classroom environment: an
    ecological analysis', *Journal of Teacher Education,* 8, XXVIII (6), 51–4.

There are many books which provide practical and effective advice on classroom strategies to achieve good behaviour. For example:

> **Reading 7.2** – edited from Cowley, S. (2010) *Getting the Buggers to Behave*. London: Continuum, 39–53.

For an analysis of language and discipline, look at Bill Rogers' book on classroom behaviour:

> Rogers, B. (2011) *Classroom Behaviour: A Practical Guide to Effective Teaching, Behaviour Management and Colleague Support*. London: Sage Publications Ltd.

A thought-provoking reading for maintaining discipline and managing behaviour can be seen in:

> Scruton, J. and Ferguson, B. (2014) *Teaching and Supporting Adult Learners*. Northwich: Critical Publishing.

Vicky Duckworth provides a helpful discussion of how students who cause exceptional classroom disruption are often those with multiple disadvantage and profound personal and social difficulties:

> Duckworth, V. (2013) *Learning Trajectories, Violence and Empowerment Amongst Adult Basic Skills Learners*. London: Routledge. **(Reading 7.4)**

A useful and practical book for handling behaviour and discipline specifically in the FE sector:

> Vizard, D. (2007) *How to Manage Behaviour in Further Education*. London: Sage Publications Ltd.

For an exploration of how the careful use of rules, routines and rituals can contribute enormously to creating a positive environment for learning, see:

> **Reading 7.3** – edited from Chaplain, R. (2003) *Teaching Without Disruption in the Primary School*. New York: Routledge, 140–55; also in *Teaching Without Disruption in the Secondary School*. New York: Routledge

For additional information on Jacob Kounin and his philosophy on 'withitness', see:

> Kounin, J. (1970) *Discipline and Group Management in Classrooms*. New York: Holt, Rinehart and Winston.

The use of force to control or restrain students is discussed in updated guidance from the ATL. A short overview defines the 'use of force', puts it in the context of a whole organization policy and offers advice for teachers on how to deal with malicious allegations.

> Watkins, C. (2011) *Managing Classroom Behaviour*. London: ATL.

Tackling racist behaviour and bullying

When you are developing a pedagogical response to racist behaviour and bullying, good practical ideas for sessions can be found on the following websites and publications. Both adopt a practical and theoretically sound approach to these issues. They both include support notes and discussions for teachers.

Show Racism the Red Card Pack for Initial Teacher Trainers
Good practical ideas for sessions to support work with learners. Also includes support notes for teachers. See: **reflectiveteaching.co.uk**

Insted – A really useful place to find resources and materials to stimulate discussion about equality and diversity topics. It also contains helpful articles on national identity, Islamophobia, religion and education. Also check out the links page which identifies some wonderful resources to support learners for whom English is a second language.
See: **reflectiveteaching.co.uk**

STONEWALL the Lesbian, Gay and Bisexual Charity
See: **reflectiveteaching.co.uk**

Resources to counter homophobic bullying available on Teachernet.gov.uk
See: **reflectiveteaching.co.uk**

The associated website, **reflectiveteaching.co.uk**, offers a wealth of supplementary resources including reflective activities, research briefings, advice on further reading and downloadable diagrams, figures and checklists from the book. It also features a compendium of educational terms, links to useful websites, policy and curriculum documents, and showcases examples of excellent research and practice.

Spaces

How are we creating environments for learning?

8

Introduction

The educational spaces in FAVE are as numerous and diverse as the students. Learning environments encompass physical space, the resources and strategies you select and the way in which you use them (Bransford et al., 1999, **Reading 8.1**). Equally important are ways in which relationships are shaped, the behaviours you encourage, the values you embody in the way you act and the atmosphere/culture that is created. Your subject and pedagogical knowledge, your creativity, the way you work with other teachers, beliefs about your students' capabilities and how much you care about their education all contribute to educational environments. This chapter considers how spaces can become effective educational environments, where teachers' agency can maximize democratic, creative and inclusive spaces and environments where education can thrive.

TLRP principles

Two of the TLRP principles outlined below are of relevance to this chapter:

Principle 8: Effective teaching and learning recognizes the significance of informal learning. Informal learning, such as learning outside of college and other formal educational settings, should be recognized as at least as significant as formal learning and should therefore be valued and used appropriately in formal processes.

Principle 10: Effective teaching and learning demands consistent policy frameworks with support for teaching and learning as the primary focus. Policies at national, institutional and local levels need to recognize the fundamental importance of teaching and learning. They should be designed to create effective learning environments in which all learners can thrive.

The core space for many teachers in FAVE is the classroom/training room or the workshop/studio and a key concern is how that space is organized to the best advantage for teaching, learning and assessment (TLA) to flourish. The physical and human resources of the classroom need to support and reinforce the teacher's values, aims, curriculum and syllabus demands. A FAVE teacher works in traditional classrooms, sports fields, workshops, music studios, operating theatres, factory floors, private homes and community buildings. We will refer to these formal education spaces as the 'classroom'.

These are not the only spaces where our students learn. Students spend most of their time in environments other than formal education or training and most have the potential to contribute to their learning. In addition to classic learning spaces such as home, work or pub, institutions such as museums, libraries, music and sports venues offer more formalized 'out of the classroom' learning experiences. Television, new media, mobile technologies and specific virtual learning environments (VLEs) now play an increasingly significant role in supporting learning both informally and formally (Laurillard, 2008; Pachler, 2013; Peechey, 2012). Although the FAVE teacher works mainly with young people and adults, the home remains a significant influence on learning regardless of whether our students are parents, carers or children.

In this chapter we will see that not only is there a range of possible spaces for learning but that each has affordances or constraints for particular purposes. The term affordances, with its origins in Gestalt psychology, was first coined by Gibson (1977) in developing an ecological approach to perception. It has been widely adopted in education, particularly in relation to educational technologies, to express the inherent potential for learning which an environment or tool offers. Constraints may restrict learning in an environment, space or tool. Fuller and Unwin introduce the concept of expansive and restrictive environments in workplace learning (2004, 2009, 2015). At one end of the continuum are expansive environments where employers value and provide education for all of their workers: spaces are provided for education; mentoring and coaching models prevail; hierarchies are flattened in order to encourage ideas from the bottom up. In contrast, restrictive environments fail to provide education at work or the support and integration for education to happen off-site: employees' ideas are not taken seriously, with only the views and ideas of senior staff seen to have value.

Exploiting the affordances and minimizing the constraints for learning can be achieved in part by good planning. Teachers work proactively to develop environments and spaces that are accessible, welcoming, relevant and engaging to all students. An inclusive classroom is one which creates a sense of learning community where productive TLA takes place and students feel valued and motivated (Dzubinski et al., 2012). A focus on enabling students to develop their English, language and maths skills is also important, as low attainment in these areas can be a major barrier to future success. Planning should incorporate reference to cultural dimensions of diversity (Spenceley, 2014).

1 Environments for learning

1.1 What is a learning environment?

If we think about a learning environment with the student at the heart, we need to consider the complex layers which exist within and around any learning space which can, in turn, affect a person's development. The ecological systems theory of Bronfenbrenner (1979; 1993) gives us one way to think about these layers and how they interact, starting with students and their relationships at home, with peers and in formal education. Beyond this lies the larger social system and beyond this again the wider cultural values, customs and laws within which the student operates. Thinking about a student's environment in this way makes it clear that no learning space can be considered in isolation. There are connections between the various settings and communities involved in a student's life. Of course, these interconnections change over time and the ways in which people, resources and space typically interact in FAVE have some similarities, but are also distinct.

1.2 Formal and informal learning environments

The classroom provides a structured and formal learning environment, which can be subject to a number of constraints. Less formal environments such as museums, theatres, music venues or outdoor learning spaces can provide opportunities to work outside such constraints. These can provide:

- an immediate and novel context for learning;
- an alternative source of curriculum delivery, allowing repackaging of the curriculum through a museum's object collections for art and humanities programmes, 'A' level law students visiting the local court, ESOL students practising spoken English in a café;
- a chance to ensure that the curriculum does not restrict students' learning;
- objects and environments that can form the basis for inquiry and knowledge-building, allowing students a chance to follow and explore their interests, and encouraging a mastery approach to learning;
- students with the chance to develop more engagement and autonomy in knowledge-building, through handling and questioning objects.

Many teachers, especially those in voluntary and community education, have worked very successfully and creatively within less formal environments. For those working in predominately formal environments, engaging in less formal contexts can present challenges when faced by curriculum demands (coverage versus content) and policies and procedures which make working 'off-site' seem deliberately difficult. Using different learning spaces requires you to think about both practical organizational concerns and the pedagogical perspective on what enables effective learning. Informal spaces can also provide distractions from learning and if the pedagogy underpinning such choices is not sufficiently robust, learning can be reduced to 'edu-tainment'.

Often teachers in FAVE are dealing with students' negative experiences of formal schooling. For many, FAVE represents a second chance at education which, in turn, places even greater responsibility on teachers to provide caring, inclusive and, above all, productive educational spaces and environments for learning.

The interaction between home and where we teach can also be an important influence on learning. Students spend hours on their smartphones and computers or watching television and lifestyles are influenced by advertising, television, the 'cult of celebrity' and the internet. People may identify and participate in virtual communities. How much they learn will depend on whether people are passive or active in their stance and how new cultural experiences are interpreted and used (Ivanic et al., 2004).

2 Organizing the classroom for learning

2.1 The classroom as a learning environment

For teachers in FAVE, the classroom presents many more challenges than the classroom familiar to colleagues in schools. It is rare even in the relatively stable and formal environment of an FE college for teachers to exclusively have their own teaching space. Almost without exception this will be shared with other teachers who may or may not be from the same subject or vocational area. This presents challenges for the ways in which the space is used. It may be possible to create an environment which reflects the subject we teach in terms of what is on the walls, displays of student work, or it may be that we work in neutral spaces made available to multiple areas of study and where 'customizing' the space is not possible.

For others, it may be that the classroom changes from session to session, timetabling clashes, programmes of study put on at the last minute or double bookings. Those of us who teach out in the community may regularly have different venues as and when courses are recruited and may use rooms in community centres and public spaces. It is not easy to teach in rooms that are cramped, unsuitable for the subject being studied, that are too hot/cold, inaccessible or badly lit, yet we still have to manage. However, many specialist colleges have state-of-the-art facilities in particular subject areas: studios, salons, simulation stations and in the training facilities of private companies.

The physical aspects of the classroom environment interact with the teacher's intentions for learning, and that careful consideration of the interaction of these elements is necessary in creating an 'inclusive classroom'.

Reflective activity 8.1

Together with another teacher, either from a different subject or a different context, analyse the classroom(s) in which you both teach most often. Each of you should have one or more particular learning activities in mind, and you should work together to analyse each other's classrooms in this context. Share the problems and issues that are pertinent to your circumstances. You may find the questions in Checklist 8.1 helpful, which focus on the use of affordances to support learning.

Environmental factors such as classroom temperature, acoustics and lighting may affect students' ability to engage in learning. There is a limit to what individual teachers can do to control such factors, but maintaining good ventilation, preventing over-lighting of students' workstations, and ensuring students sit where they cannot see a 'glare spot' on the interactive whiteboard are all important.

This is where the experienced teacher makes a difference – providing, where appropriate, tea/coffee, time spent before class starts, time built into session where portable displays are used, student work displayed, mobile technologies utilized, music, involving the group in lobbying for more resources.

Figure 8.1
Checklist of
affordances to
support learning.

1 *Design*. What are the main design features of the room, and how do they affect its aesthetic feel?
2 *Potential affordances*. What are the possibilities and constraints for active learning in the classroom? Can you move the tables to enable discussion? What are the possibilities and issues for display on walls, on windows, on flat surfaces, off the ceiling?
3 *Purposes*. Do displays stimulate and inform? Do they provide opportunities for students to interact with them – for example, by posing questions? Do displays only show finished products or do they also reveal processes and value hard work – for example, displaying drafts and then finished products. Do they provide a stimulus for discussion (such as thinking walls, or word mats), sharing problems, or giving mutual support and advice? Do they provide a stimulus for structuring inquiry, from devising questions to testing ideas?
4 *Quality*. Do classroom displays show that the students' work is valued? Do they provide a model which students may apply to their own work? Is there a 'working wall' which enables on-going contributions by students?
5 *Practicality*. Is the classroom environment as practical as it can be to maintain?

Making changes to your classroom is not always possible and is particularly difficult for student and agency teachers who may not know how to access the system – for example, to ask about changing lighting, layout or using displays. Given the increasingly large numbers of teachers on casual contracts, this is a situation which may well worsen.

2.2 Use of resources

Active, inclusive, student-centred learning requires a range of relevant resources to support learning in innovative and constructive ways. Resources can:

- motivate, inspire and focus students' attention;
- provide a basis for discussion, or be designed to enable students to learn independently;
- stimulate, explain, instruct, or demonstrate procedures and ideas;
- enable students to access information;
- enable students to learn in manageable steps;
- help students to recall, consolidate and extend their learning;
- support assessment of students' understanding.

The more traditional the setting for your teaching, the more likely processes and procedures for ordering, storing and distributing resources will be. Even with centrally managed resources, laptops have lost their charge, the printer is out of ink or the library is shut. It's common for shared resources not to be put back where they are usually stored or for photocopying not to arrive on time. Despite collective responsibility for providing resources, most teachers work independently to manage and plan for the resources they need to bring learning to life.

When selecting resources four possible criteria might be considered:

- *Appropriateness*. What resources are needed to support the learning processes which are expected to take place?

- *Availability*. What resources are available? What is in the classroom, the organization, the community, businesses, libraries, museums? Are there cost, time or transport factors to be considered?

- *Storage*. How are classroom resources stored? Which should be under teacher control? Which should be openly available to the students? Which are stored by the technician? Are they clearly labelled and safely stored?

- *Maintenance*. What maintenance is required? Is there a system for seeing that this is done? In the case of ICT and specialist equipment, where is the expertise and technical support located and how can this be accessed?

2.3 Use of space

Space in classrooms can be limited, yet has to allow for changes in organizational strategies – for instance, between whole-class, group or pair work and the associated implications for seating and working. Interactive whiteboards, laptop computers and mobile technologies used in some FAVE classrooms can also create particular demands on space and determine the use of whole-class or individual learning.

As discussed earlier, teachers in FAVE are much less likely than their school counter-parts to have a classroom where space is 'owned', thereby enabling flexibility in the look and layout of the room and appropriateness for the learning activity. Despite this, you still need to carefully examine the requirements of particular TLA activities and how to adapt the space accordingly.

If you do use the same classroom on a regular basis it may be worthwhile to consider developing a classroom plan using classroom design software (e.g. **teacher.scholastic.com/ tools/class_setup/**). Layout plans can help when exploring the affordances and constraints of space when planning for teaching, learning and assessment.

Figure 8.2 highlights some of the ways in which resources can be used to enhance learning and offers alternatives to address limitations. These are in addition to sports facilities, specialized workshops and equipment.

Even in formal FAVE contexts it's very likely that you are entering a classroom where another group and teacher are spilling out with little or no time to move furniture before your students arrive. However, you still need to plan how to use the space – at the very least, if you know in advance which classroom you are using, go and visit when it is empty. Ask yourself questions about the position of screens or boards, do they work, are they static or movable, how many chairs and tables are there, can they be moved easily, do the windows and or blinds open/shut, do the radiators have controls, what is the usual layout of the furniture, is the room messy or tidy, what are the noise levels like?

`WWW.`

Figure 8.2 Resources to support learning

Resource	Description	Uses	Advantages	Limitations	Alternatives
Mobile Technologies which includes access to internet and a range of other functions	Smartphones iPads, Tablets Laptops with functions like: • internet • social networking • camera/video • email • calculators • word process • note-taking • texting • speakerphone	• in classroom and on trips • when computers are unavailable • researching topics • capturing images – alternative to writing • exchanging ideas and info • educational sites	• increasing number own smartphones • quick/easy source • educational Facebook or email groups • connects to students lives • easy to use • space saving	• still not everyone owns them • distraction • connectivity • not enough reading on topics	• desktop computer • articles • books • camera
Education Visits Local Regional National International	Trip to a place or event with curricular significance	• develop topic and concepts • real world experience • team building • modelling	• can bring learning to life • value added • hands-on	• unfocused tasks • not relevant to study • health and safety	• on-line tours • bringing visitors into the classroom • research texts • research online
Handouts	Paper resource used to support teaching and learning, supplements information not easily available to students	• definitions, key terms, information • posing questions • case studies • instructions • background data, statistics, diagrams • revision/homework tasks	• cheap • can be copied, reused, stored • cuts down on note taking	• can lead to superficial learning • poorly produced/copied	• electronic versions • Power Point slides • flipchart • whiteboard • lecture and note taking

	film, music, interviews, documentaries, popular culture	• inserted into teaching activity • discussion stimulus • illustrates skills, techniques etc. • revision and practice at 'own pace': pause, rewind etc	• downloadable • free • brings field 'experts' and places into the classroom • connects with students' lives • available on mobiles	• anyone can upload material • may contain misleading info • can be overused • copyright • need internet connection	• CDs • guest speakers • hands-on demonstration
Whiteboard or Flipchart	Various sized fixed or portable wipe-clean board or paper	• supports development of session • Q & A • concept maps • plenaries • presentations • group work • posters • focusing device	• no technical issues • cheap • re-useable • individual mini whiteboards • used spontaneously	• needs legible writing and good grammar • non-permanent • one record only	• interactive whiteboard • iPads • paper
People	Any person who makes a contribution to learning – other teachers, external speakers, support staff, librarians, student group	• guest speakers • developing specific expertise • concept and subject development • support and guidance • role model • scaffolding learning • targeting specific support • cross curricular planning	• connects life experience • relevant • develops social skills • motivational • interactive • doesn't depend on technology • team teaching	• depends on people 'buying in' • teacher needs to be able to create condition for peer support and learning • availability of outside speakers • bias	• technology e.g. YouTube • study books • handbooks
World Wide Web	Global computer network providing information, networks and communication facilities	• research • data • Subject-relevant sites • educational sites	• instantly accessible data and information • downloadable • can be stored in different formats	• technical issues • overwhelming • unreliable sources • explicit material • membership fees for some sites	• libraries • paper-based resources • experts

Resource	Description	Uses	Advantages	Limitations	Alternatives
Out of class ● Outside spaces, parks, countryside, coast, etc. ● Computer room ● Library sites	Educational activities which take place outside of regular 'classroom'	● develop topic and concepts ● develop expression using natural resources e.g. painting, poetry, ● holistic subject development ● to enable whole class access to facility e.g. computer suite, library	● novel ● inspiring ● creative ● real world ● inclusive	● needs to be planned ahead ● health and safety ● weather ● availability ● distractions	● outside speakers ● sound, visual, smell, tactile – objects and materials brought into class
Models	3-dimensional representation of person, object or structure often on a smaller scale than original	● studying anatomy e.g. skeleton, heart, eyes, dummies ● world and science e.g atoms, landscapes, engines, buildings, equations ● art e.g. life model, fruit, plants, ● architecture/design ● making models ● theory building	● ethical ● accessible ● allows for repetition of procedures e.g. resuscitation	● off-scale ● whole class viewing of small-scale model ● insufficient ● can be expensive ● hygiene ● availability	● photos, graphics, illustrations ● electronic modelling ● real thing
PowerPoint	Presentation software	● To structure whole class presentations and lectures ● Sound and vision ● Slide show ● To produce posters ● lesson plan template	● present information in variety of ways and layouts ● can insert film clips, photos, charts, tables, ● links to multi media ● can download slides and share ● permanent record ● interactive	● 'death by PowerPoint' ● requires computer access	● Prezi – requires internet connection

	Description	Teaching uses	Benefits	Considerations	Examples
Everyday items	Readily available items e.g. student work, games, newspapers, magazines, household objects, food	• starter activities • to bring learning to life • making abstract ideas concrete • stimulus and props • to support, reinforce learning • develops cognitive, affective and psychomotor skills	• readily available • cheap • connects to students' lives • can involve students in developing the resources • bespoke	• ensuring relevance • gimmick • currency	• computer-based games • downloads of news items, articles, • TV, DVDs, CDs
Popular Culture	Film, TV, radio, art, music, literature				
Smart Board	Computer-based web enabled display board	• supports development of session • audio-visual aid – plays CDs, DVDs, presentation software, hyperlinks • Q & A • focusing device • research in real time possible • concept and topic development	• interactive when used actively with students • dynamic tool which stores any changes as lesson unfolds • provides a record to share with learners • cuts down on paper-based activities	• cost • availability • technical difficulties • can become teacher-centred • doesn't ensure learning in itself • can become screen only • requires training to optimize use	• conventional whiteboard • PowerPoint • mobile technologies
DVDs	Storage device for film, images, information, files	• play film for educational stimulus • connect learning to popular culture • create digital portfolios, learning diaries, CVs			• USB • YouTube • dropbox • iCloud • CDs • paper-based materials

You may be in an even more difficult situation and only get to know which room you are in shortly before the class starts or, worse still, have to find a space because you're double-booked or not even booked at all. You will need a range of workable solutions and strategies to help mitigate some of these shortcomings.

When planning a classroom layout, it is important to create opportunities for meaningful dialogue between and with students which enables peer and teacher support at whole-class, group or pair level (Mercer and Littleton, 2007). Interactive whiteboards can be effective tools to promote dialogic teaching at whole-class level (Warwick, Hennessy and Mercer, 2011). This requires you to consider if the screen is accessible to all students and whether the classroom is organized to promote high-quality discussion at whole-class level with the interactive whiteboard as a stimulus. Likewise, sitting in rows is not conducive to small-group discussion. It can be tempting to merely focus on the logistics of an activity, but if the classroom is not organized in such a way as to promote student talk, then a teacher may miss opportunities to support students' learning.

Whatever approach is taken to resource management or classroom layout, it's important to consider health and safety implications.

2.4 Use of time

However well organized your classroom and resources are, when students start to use that space, it can lead to a significant amount of 'evaporated time', and may require analysis of the way in which space, resources and students' use of these are designed and managed.

Time available for curriculum activity is the remaining time in each teaching/learning session, once it has properly started, excluding interruptions and time to pack up at the end of the lesson. Students who have paid fees to attend a learning programme are particularly aware of the need for good time management (Harper, 2013). Encouraging students to take on more responsibility for organizing themselves, their classroom and their resources is important, as it can enhance their learning time and reduce their reliance on you, giving you more time to focus on students' learning. Alternatively, you may adopt different strategies to try and maximize time available for learning.

Time spent in active learning is the second key issue. To maximize learning in which students are actively engaged, it is important to ensure there is a *variety* of *stimulating* tasks over time. You should avoid 'satiation' – in other words, letting students get bored by monotonous or repetitive activities. Variety relates to the pedagogical decisions you make and you need to plan and organize this to ensure that all students remain engaged and motivated throughout.

'Flip' teaching is a form of blended learning which encompasses any use of technology to leverage the learning in a classroom, enabling the teacher to spend more time inter-acting with learners. This is commonly done by the teacher creating or selecting a video on a topic which is viewed by students prior to the class then discussed/analysed together in class. Alternatively, extension activities of lessons in the form of video or texts are shared on social media sites, enabling students to further develop their learning and interests.

3 Using technology for learning

The classroom environment consists of its physical environment and social systems informed by the prevailing values and culture of the organization. The ways in which resources are organized and used will reflect these interlinked elements. This too is true of information and communications technology (ICT) resources, which are now integral to teaching and learning and our students' lives (Edwards, 2012, Reading 8.2).

3.1 ICT in formal education settings

ICT in computer suites

ICT suites enable all students to use a specific piece of software at the same time, sharing experiences and benefiting from common input from the teacher; they can be used very specifically for the teaching of computing skills, and the numbers of computers available should ensure equitable access to ICT resources. However, their use has been criticized because such use can be rather artificial and skill-focused. In organizations where computer suites are the main location of computers, careful thought has to be given to their effective and equitable use by classes. Timetabling is a necessary constraint but, while recognizing such limitations, teachers need to judge how to get the most from the affordances that suites offer.

In FAVE contexts, mobile technologies are much more likely to be the norm than computer suites and, given the above finding from Ofsted, such use of ICT is likely to be more relevant and effective in contributing to student learning. As more and more staff and students own smartphones/tablets alongside improved connectivity and lower tariffs, it is likely that these will become an increasingly used resource to support learning. As Coffield remarks in his research with young FE students:

> Technology's biggest impact on their lives, however, is not so much in terms of the number of gadgets they own. It has affected where and how they study. (Coffield, 2009: 51)

ICT in the classroom

The general availability of ICT resources in the classroom can be one strong determinant of whether they are likely to be used readily by students to support their learning. However, simply having ICT in the classroom does not determine its effective use for students' learning.

Laurillard (2008) presents a compelling argument for digital technologies and their role in achieving our ambitions for education. She summarizes her discussion by recommending that we:

> Give pedagogy back to the teachers. Embrace technology as part of the solution. Begin with the ambition and use the technology to achieve it … build the tools and resources that enable teachers to be the creative, adaptive, learning professionals that they want to be. (Laurillard, 2008: 34)

Teachers are absolutely crucial to exploiting the potential of classroom technologies (Sutherland, John and Robertson, 2006). A good example is that of the interactive whiteboard (IWB), a digital hub through which other technologies can be channelled, as orchestrated by the teacher and the students. Tools such as this have no agency; they don't insist that a teacher or student adopts a particular approach to their use. They offer a range of affordances and constraints for learning and these are determined by two things: the functionality of the device(s); and how both teachers and students see that functionality as providing opportunities for, or barriers to, learning. Teachers who adopt an interactive, dialogic pedagogy will perceive the affordances and constraints of particular hardware and software very differently from those who favour a more didactic pedagogy.

The constraints on the uses of ICT in classrooms derive not only from the pedagogic intentions of teachers or the availability of ICT hardware and software, but from other features of the learners or the setting. The fundamental question for the teacher has to be: 'Will this use of ICT in the lesson enhance the students' learning?' If the answer is 'yes' then there are several pedagogical and practical considerations to consider.

Figure 8.3
Checklist of the pedagogical and practical implications of the classroom use of ICT.

- Has e-safety been considered? In particular, do all devices you plan to use have appropriate internet site blocking?
- Is some direct teaching in relation to e-safety a necessary feature of the lesson? (see **ofsted.gov.uk/resources/safe-use-of-new-technologies**)
- Have you considered how the use of ICT resources may impact on the time management of your lesson (e.g. set-up time, time on task)?
- Have you planned for the procedural aspects of ICT use in the lesson (e.g. numbers of students to a computer, physical placement of computer resources, possible circulation of groups to a single resource such as the IWB)?
- Are any password systems, used to access devices, clear for the students?
- Are the devices fully charged? (This is a particularly important consideration where laptop or mobile device charging units may not be in your classroom.)
- Is the software that you plan to use actually on each of the devices the students will be using?
- Have you considered whether the students are able to store their own work in progress, and know how to do so?

Reflective activity 8.2

Use the previous checklist to analyse how you use ICT resources in your setting. Share with a colleague your experiences and together identify how your use affects the ways in which your students learn and also your own teaching practices.

3.2 ICT beyond formal education settings

An increasing amount of time is spent on educational activity which takes place in the virtual world, with many students using learning platforms to store their work, respond to learning tasks, research, complete homework and communicate with their teacher and their peers (Sutherland, John and Robertson, 2006; Pachler, 2013; Peechey, 2012). Many students are very comfortable with technology, especially YouTube, Facebook, Twitter, Google, wiggio, blogs and podcasts, and regularly access smartphones, iPods, iPads, gaming consoles, televisions and computers (Selwyn et al., 2005)

Students' use of technologies, both in formal and informal settings, *can* be complementary in terms of students' learning (Kent and Facer, 2004), and this is true even where use focuses on areas not normally associated with academic activity, such as social networking and gaming. Handheld technologies can form a locus of such activity and the use of devices that provide both 'educational' activities and wider opportunities to engage with non-educational software can create a situation in which learning seems to fit with other activities carried out on the device. With the rise of devices such as the iPad, iPod and android variants as both classroom and home tools, this engagement between the teacher's pedagogical intentions and the students' everyday activity on the device is now becoming more common. The ubiquity of such devices – providing easy access to the internet, video and audio material, games for learning, applications with specific foci, social communication and e-books and the digital literacies that underpin their use – contributes to the idea that their use for learning is natural, both in educational settings and at home (Kress, 2010, Reading 8.3). There is a shift in emphasis here from teaching to learning, and from the product to the process of learning, as students need to focus on how and where to acquire, store and utilize knowledge rather than to remember it all (Salmon, 2013; Laurillard, 2008), and to do this both in and out of formal education contexts.

We must remember that not everyone possesses these devices and we must also remember that recent trends, for example in cyber-bullying, can pervade environments primarily set up for educational activities.

4 Managing people

People in the FAVE classroom need to be managed in ways which are most appropriate for supporting the teaching, learning and assessment activities which have been planned. This does not only involve students and the teacher but also classroom assistants, other support staff and sometimes volunteers.

4.1 Organizing students

When you make choices about organizing students for teaching purposes you have to consider both pedagogical and practical considerations alongside the overriding principle of fitness for purpose. Pedagogical considerations will include your general aims and how these inform classroom ethos and procedures, as well as the learning objectives for the task and students. Practical factors include the number of students, the size of the room and the availability of resources. A joinery workshop in an FE college, for example, is a very different working space from an ESOL classroom in a community centre and provides different affordances and constraints on the ways in which students might be organized for activities.

Here we set out the three main organizational choices available to us: class work, group work and individual work, identifying the main characteristics of each. (For further discussion of the pedagogic strategies associated with each of these three forms of organization, see Chapter 11.)

Class work

This is the strong form of organization for starting and ending a lesson; for giving out administrative instructions; for introducing learning objectives, tasks and activities; for the direct teaching of specific concepts and knowledge; for demonstrating and for extending and reviewing work. Whole-class elements to lessons should be seen as part of a flexible repertoire that a teacher has with respect to student organization.

Whole-class activity is generally assumed to be teacher-centred and what most whole-class activities have in common is that the teacher generally remains the focus of control. But there is a continuum of teacher dominance even when the whole class is involved in the same activity, and these sessions can be highly interactive (Hillier, 2012; Armitage et al., 2012). At one end of the continuum is the situation where the teacher talks and the students listen, take notes or copy from the board. At the other, the teacher plans to give control of the activity to the students who may teach by, for example, reporting what they have learned, demonstrating the result of an activity, offering solutions for problem-solving, discussing alternative or conflicting ideas, and asking questions. These activities can create a sense of class identity and shared endeavour. Again, it is the teacher's pedagogic framework that will determine how whole-class elements of lessons proceed; some will encourage students' active participation in *all* elements of a lesson, while others may be reticent to do so.

Using whole-class organizational procedures may give you a chance to teach the class more directly and economically than when working with groups. For instance, you may be able to stimulate students' thinking by sharing lesson objectives, exploring ideas, asking more 'probing' questions, modelling quality answers and supporting review, assessment and reflection on their learning. However, class work can challenge both the teacher and the listener. It is difficult to match the instruction appropriately to students' differing needs. There is a tendency for teaching to be pitched at the 'middle', potentially failing those capable of more and those needing support. Some students may be reluctant to face the risks involved in contributing to the whole class, while the ability of listeners to remain focused on one speaker is limited and affected both by the listeners' motivation and the speaker's skill. There is evidence of teachers addressing questions only to students in a V-shaped wedge in the centre of the room, or to particular groups or individuals (Wragg, 2000). An awareness of these potential difficulties should help teachers to tailor the length and nature of whole-class elements of lessons to the learning needs of their students.

Many teachers in FAVE are working exclusively with adults and the conditions for classroom organization encompass different power relations, class size, motivation and behaviour. It is still important to think about how everyone will interact, how you will include quiet students, 'odd' students, avoid cliques and manage the ones who know it all (see Chapter 7).

Group work

Group work is often recommended for developing students' social and language skills and to support, challenge and extend their learning together or in subject or vocational areas where practical work is required. Group work can provide opportunities to observe students' learning more closely and, through questioning or providing information, to support them as they move forward. This approach draws particularly on social constructivist psychology (see Chapter 2). Groups are likely to exist in some form in most classrooms.

Types of group work purposes include:

- *Task groups*. The teacher decides on a group of students to work together on a particular task or learning objective. Students in the group may or may not normally sit or work together and are likely to be given specific group roles, such as recorder or researcher.

- *Teaching groups*. Groups can also be used for group teaching purposes, where the teacher instructs students who are at the same stage, doing the same task, at the same time. This may be followed by the students working individually. Such a system can be an economical use of teacher instruction time and resources. The teaching may be directive or be based on a problem-solving activity.

- *Seating groups*. This is a very common form of grouping, where a number of students sit together around a table, usually in a four or six. Such an arrangement is flexible, allowing students to work individually and to socialize when appropriate. The central question for the teacher here is: 'If the students are not actually working together, is this arrangement beneficial to their learning?'

- *Collaborative groups*. This is used where there is a shared group aim, work is done together and the outcome is a combined product – perhaps in the form of a model, completed experiment, story or problem solved. Importantly, it involves students working and talking together, sharing their ideas and explaining their reasoning (Jacques, 2000; Hillier, 2012; Armitage, 2012). The collaboration can also lead to a number of different outcomes from individuals or pairs. Although less teacher-centred than teaching groups, teachers may observe students and, as a result, plan to intervene to support learning.

- *Reciprocal teaching*. This form of collaboration occurs when students work in pairs, one taking the role of teacher partner, offering evaluation, and feedback. This approach is particularly evident in subjects like PE, drama and languages which involve 'performance'. The teacher supports by intervening to develop the quality of the evaluation and feedback.

Group work most frequently fails where students do not have a clear sense of purpose or appropriate skills to work together effectively.

Individual work

Whether or not students are *seated* in groups, they spend a great deal of classroom time working individually. They may be learning via tasks which require them to work alone or demonstrating the results of their learning in individual outcomes.

Working individually may be the dominant mode in many lessons and particularly prevalent in literacy, numeracy and ESOL sessions. The teacher's role in supporting activity and scaffolding learning is probably even more intense than it is when students are working in groups, but it does have the potential advantage that such support and scaffolding is targeted on the specific learning needs of an individual. As a result, it is likely to be highly productive for learning (see Chapter 12).

However, there are potential problems. If you rely heavily on setting individual work, you may find that similar teaching points have to be explained on many separate occasions. Working with each individual separately inevitably means that only a limited amount of time can be spent with any one student, and often this time can be spent monitoring students' work, rather than in developing their understanding. It is particularly important to think of individual work, as with whole-class work, as part of the repertoire of organizational alternatives open to you at particular points in a lesson. You must ask yourself: 'What am I hoping to achieve by getting the students to work individually at this point in the lesson? Is this the best form of organization for the task, or for my intended outcomes?'

Professional judgement is essential in ensuring that, whatever organizational strategy you consider – whole-class, group or individual – it is consistent with learning goals and evidence of effectiveness. Each approach within a teacher's repertoire has a different purpose and specific potential.

Reflective activity 8.3

Discuss the following scenarios with another teacher and consider how you might develop practical strategies for making the most of the classroom environment and maximizing opportunities for students to get the most out of their education:

- An ESOL class of 10 students with 15 weekly two-hour sessions 6–8 p.m. in a computer room in the local FE college.
- A group of 15 engineering apprentices who use 'the training room' one day per week in a large engineering company's premises.
- A drop-in adult literacy class which takes place over a number of rooms in a rural community centre.
- Thirty 16–18-year-olds in a BTEC Sports Studies class who have theory sessions in a 25-seater classroom which is used by other sports-related classes.
- Offenders using the Education Room – a dedicated classroom within a maximum security prison.
- Twenty mature students on a two-year part-time degree in education and training with a three-hour session once per week in a demountable classroom 6–9 p.m. in the car park of an FE college.
- Thinking about the space in which you teach, how do you create the best conditions possible for a productive learning environment?

We now go on to consider how teachers can liaise and work with other adults and support staff, in and beyond the classroom.

4.2 Working with adults

There is little research about the role of classroom support workers in FAVE (Bailey and Robson, 2004). In her discussion of a number of 'outstanding' lessons in the lifelong learning sector, Harper describes learning support workers as a key resource for success:

> The success of very good teamwork [is] between the different professionals. Not just an 'extra pair of hands', the learning support assistants' contribution was integral to the success of the lesson. Planning had very evidently involved the identification of the learning support assistants' role and specialist knowledge and skills. Students were clearly familiar with the pattern of working and benefitted from the close working relationships between these professionals. (Harper, 2013: 16)

If you are working with support staff or with technicians, remember that your relationship needs to be one that is both respectful but clear – for example, who makes decisions about what to do and when in the learning session. It is your responsibility as the teacher, but support staff particularly appreciate being consulted as they, too, have experience and knowledge derived from working in educational settings. You are working together for the benefit of your learners.

Conclusion

In this chapter, two major points about learning spaces have been made. First, all contexts and settings (whether directly experienced or virtual) provide conditions which influence learning (James and Biesta, 2007, Reading 8.4). Some will enable learning to flourish, while others may inhibit such development. So, when you organize your own classroom environment you should consider the likely overall effect on your primary objective of supporting learning.

Second, classrooms are far from being isolated entities. Rather, they are contextualized by many other influences on students' lives. Among the most obvious are the educational organization as a whole, the family, the workplace and communities. These factors are encompassed by wider cultural, economic, technological, social and political conditions.

Effective classroom organization requires consideration of the physical environment, resources, technologies, structures, routines, processes and people that are intended to progress student learning. Such factors, as well as the organization of students themselves, must be considered in relation to their capacity to enable or constrain learning.

Awareness of the range of influences on student learning and appropriate organization of classroom provision will help inform your professional practice and enable you to provide an effective learning environment. We have discussed how environments have a profound effect on our teaching effectiveness and the ways in which our students can be provided with high-quality learning experiences. We have drawn attention to the ways that such environments are both formally constructed in educational settings, but also in the ways in which other affordances interact with these – for example, in the ways in which our students bring their own use of mobile phones, iPads, social networking sites into the educational arena. The informal environment, then, has as much to do with our reflection on creating educational spaces as that within which we practise in our more formal educational settings. These settings can be supported through the funding regimes, inspection regimes and through policies created by national and local governments to support particularly the use of technology in learning.

Key readings

Environments for learning and organizing the classroom

Understanding of the conditions which enable learning, development and performance have been enhanced by ecological analyses which trace contextual influences. Classic here is:

Bronfenbrenner, U. (1979) *The Ecology of Human Development: Experiments by Nature and Design.* Cambridge, MA: Harvard University Press.

For further detail around the relationships between environments and actions, the 'theory of affordances' with its origins in Gestalt psychology was coined by Gibson in developing an ecological approach to perception:

> Gibson, E. J. (1977) 'The Theory of Affordances'. In R. Shaw and J. Bransford (eds) *Perceiving, Acting and Knowing*. Hillsdale, NJ: Lawrence Erlbaum.

Understanding this in the context of workplace learning, Fuller and Unwin introduced the concept of 'expansive and restrictive' environments and its effect upon learning. For an up-to-date discussion, see:

> Fuller, A. and Unwin, L. (2015) *Creating and Managing Expansive Learning Environments: Improving Vocational and Professional Education*. London: Routledge.

For an analysis of the impact that effective learning environments have upon practice, see:

> **Reading 8.1** – edited from Bransford, J. D., Brown, A. L. and Cocking, R. R. (1999) *How People Learn: Brain, Mind, Experience and School*. Washington, DC: National Academy Press, xvi–xix.

For a summary of learning environments and teaching practices in the context of FAVE, see:

> Hillier, Y. (2012) *Reflective Teaching in Further and Adult Education*. 3rd edn. London: Continuum.

For insights into the relationship between formal and informal learning and a discussion of the effects of the passive and active learning of adults and how new cultural experiences are interpreted and used, see:

> Ivanic, R., Appleby, Y., Hodge, R., Tusting, K. and Barton, D. (2004) *Listening to Learners: Practitioner Research on the Adult Learners' Project*. London: NRDC.

As all practitioners know, circumstances vary in different classrooms and judgement has to be applied to select appropriate forms of classroom organization and layout for the purposes which the teacher has in mind. For insights into these challenges and opportunities, see:

> Coffield, F. (2009) *All you ever Wanted to know about Learning and Teaching but were too Cool to ask*. London: Learning and Skills Network (LSN).
>
> Mercer, N. and Littleton, K. (2007) *Dialogue and the Development of Children's Thinking: A Socio-cultural Approach*. London: Routledge.

Using technology for learning both in formal and informal settings is a key concern and teachers are absolutely crucial to exploiting the potential of classroom technologies. An invitation for teachers to consider the environment of their classrooms and available resources and to reflect creatively on possibilities and constraints for teaching and learning activities is in:

> **Reading 8.2** – edited from Edwards, A. (2012) *New Technology and Education.* London: Continuum, 86–8.

Arguments for the use of digital technologies and discussions on how new textual learning spaces and modes of communication are being created can be found in:

> **Reading 8.3** – edited from Kress, G. (2010) 'The Profound Shift of Digital Literacies'. In J. Gillen and D. Barton (eds) *Digital Literacies. TLRP – Technology Enhanced Learning.* London: University of London, Institute of Education (IOE), 2–3.

> Kent, N. A. and Facer, K. L. (2004) 'Different worlds? children's home and school computer use', *Journal of Computer Assisted Learning,* 20 (6), 440–55.

> Laurillard, D. (2008) 'Digital technologies and their role in achieving our ambitions for education' (Inaugural Professorial Lecture). London: University of London, Institute of Education (IOE).

> Sutherland, R., John, P. and Robertson, S. (2006) 'Using computers to enhance learning: integrating ICT into everyday classroom practices', *Teaching and Learning Research Briefing*, 19.

Managing people both in terms of organizing students and working with adults is an important aspect of creating good environments for learning. See Chapter 11 for an extended discussion of pedagogy, student development, whole-group discussion, questioning and small group working. For a practical introduction to effective whole-class, group and individual work, see:

> Armitage, A., Evershed, J., Hayes, D., Hudson, A., Kent, J., Lawes, S., Poma, S. and Renwick, M. (2012) *Teaching and Training in Lifelong Learning.* Berks: Open University Press.

> Hillier, Y. (2012) *Reflective Teaching in Further and Adult Education.* 3rd edn. London: Continuum.

Consideration of the productive implementation of learning support workers in FAVE and professional teamwork can be seen in:

> Bailey, B and Robson, J. (2004) 'Learning support workers in further education in England: a hidden revolution?', *Journal of Further and Higher Education,* 28 (4).

> Harper, H. (2013) *Outstanding Teaching in Lifelong Learning.* London: Oxford University Press/McGraw-Hill Education.

For discussion on the ways in which learning cultures might be transformed and on how, through such transformations, learning might be improved:

Reading 8.4 – edited from James, D. and Biesta, G. (2007) *Improving Learning Cultures in Further Education*. London: Routledge.

The associated website, **reflectiveteaching.co.uk**, offers a wealth of supplementary resources including reflective activities, research briefings, advice on further reading and downloadable diagrams, figures and checklists from the book. It also features a compendium of educational terms, links to useful websites, policy and curriculum documents, and showcases examples of excellent research and practice.

part three

Teaching for learning

Part Three supports the development of practice across the three classic dimensions of teaching: curriculum, pedagogy and assessment.

We begin in Chapter 9 by reviewing aspects of curriculum design and development and the role of subject knowledge. Chapter 10 puts these ideas into action and supports the development and evaluation of programmes of study, schemes of work and lesson plans. Chapter 11 offers ways of understanding the art, craft and science of pedagogy and the development of a pedagogic repertoire. Chapter 12 extends this with an introduction to the vital role of talking, listening, and the development of literacies across the curriculum.

We argue that communication plays a central role in the development of thinking and learning for teachers and their students. Finally, this part concludes by demonstrating how assessment can underpin teaching and learning processes in very constructive ways (Chapter 13).

Curriculum
What is to be taught and learned?

9

Introduction

The curriculum that teachers develop and deliver and students experience in the FAVE sector is shaped by a number of factors including Awarding Body (AB) criteria, professional body requirements as well as the syllabi for national qualification such as 'A' levels, GCSEs and BTECs. Non-qualification programmes, primarily those aimed at adults for general education, have no prescribed curriculum as such and the provision can be determined by the students who participate in a leisure class, although it can be determined by an agency or society (Hamilton and Hillier, 2006, Reading 9.1). For example, people can learn to sail and gain internationally recognized qualifications through the Royal Yachting Association (RYA). Each level of qualification does have a set curriculum which must meet not just national but international standards and protocols.

In the compulsory education sector national curricula play a central role of ensuring students acquire a range of knowledge. As we will discuss in Chapters 13 and 14, the curriculum can result in teachers 'teaching to the test' and feeling constrained in the level of autonomy they have in being innovative and creative in their choice of topics within the national curriculum. In the FAVE sector, even though the need to satisfy a national curriculum is not as acute, a similar balance has to be struck in relation to meeting a broader set of interests and concerns beyond professional body requirements and the qualification structure (Young, 2013, Reading 9.2).

In this chapter, we introduce enduring concepts and principles of curriculum design, teaching, learning and assessment (TLA), mediation and innovation on which curriculum development can be based. This will help equip you, as a reflective teacher, in your career-long engagement with curricular issues.

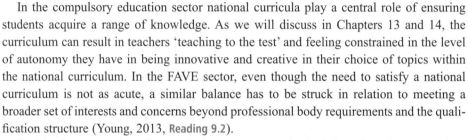

TLRP principles

Two TLRP principles underpin this focus on curricular requirements:

Principle 2: Effective teaching and learning engages with valued forms of knowledge. Teaching and learning should engage with the big ideas, facts, processes, language and narratives of subjects so that learners understand what constitutes quality and standards in particular disciplines.

Principle 10: Effective teaching and learning demands consistent policy frameworks with support for teaching and learning as the primary focus. Policies at national, institutional and local levels need to recognize the fundamental importance of teaching and learning. They should be designed to create effective learning environments in which all learners can thrive.

1 What do we mean by curriculum?

There are three ways to think about this term.

The official curriculum. This is the explicitly stated programme of learning, and will probably incorporate a national curriculum which has been endorsed by government or professional body requirements. The course of study is likely to have three elements: a specified curriculum content; an expected sequence or progression to cover this content; and a system of testing to make explicit the students' achievement. The FAVE sector is influenced by the school sector, where for many years national curricula within the UK have been structured by key stage programmes of study for core and foundation subjects in combination with attainment targets for particular levels, national assessment and examination requirements. The official school curriculum thus reflects a historically specific combination of national requirements and more local commitments and decisions. The students who go on to study within the FAVE sector have therefore been exposed to certain forms of learning, certain requirements and – in the last two decades in England – endless testing and comparison with national targets.

The hidden curriculum. People learn many things that have not been explicitly planned for, known as tacit learning. For example, people will have learnt as children about the role of the teacher and they will have developed attitudes towards learning and schooling. Children may also acquire ideas about the ways boys or girls should behave, or about differences because of being black or white, middle-class or working-class. Such ideas reflect the way in which values are conveyed through interaction and language associated with teaching and learning processes. The hidden curriculum is implicit within education procedures and curriculum materials, and can exert a powerful influence on people through its influence on self-image and expectations. Think how in government publications, care is taken to choose a range of people to be inclusive in the images portrayed and how different such images were in past decades. Although hidden, the influences are not subtle and one of the important considerations we must make when creating resources is what messages, intended or unintended, we are giving (see Chapter 15).

The experienced curriculum. Despite our planning, what sense do our students actually make of our provision? Arguably, it is the way that our students *experience* the curriculum that has the most educational impact. Thinking about curricular provision from the perspectives of a deliberately wide range of learners is a helpful check when we review our planning, whether it is for a single lesson, series of lessons, or even for a whole programme. For example, if we are teaching food technology, using a variety of foods that do not contravene strict religious beliefs would ensure that all students can successfully cover the requirements of the programme. It is important to choose age-appropriate topics if you are working with a group of adults aged between 18 and 80. Using images of slim, young women when designing clothes is not helpful, particularly if your students are all middle-aged and possibly no longer slim!

The curriculum is therefore far more than a series of lessons – it is the whole provision and experience offered to our students. To understand more fully the role of curriculum in the FAVE sector, we now discuss the factors influencing curriculum development and its delivery. It is highly unusual for a teacher in FAVE to have much say in the curriculum required for students on qualification programmes, but there is much scope for those working particularly in adult education.

1.1 Factors enabling and constraining curriculum development and delivery in the FAVE sector

Figure 9.1
Depicting many
of the factors
which contribute
to curriculum
development.

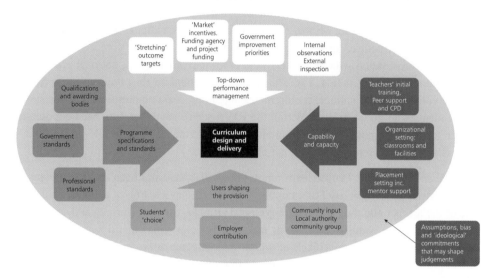

Figure 9.1 depicts many of the factors which contribute to curriculum development. On the left-hand side we can see the influence of the qualifications framework. Standards are regularly reviewed by the appropriate body and it is important to keep abreast of any changes. However, the influence of specifications and standards on the curriculum is strong and one which holds little opportunity for teachers to challenge. Usually the standards and specifications have resulted from consultation and development by sector body leaders and managers and you may find opportunities to respond to such consultations when revised standards are being developed.

The influence of top-down performance management is another strong set of factors influencing curriculum design and delivery. A prime example of this is how the government targets for adults and young people to hold certain levels of qualifications drives provision through the funding mechanism. In other words, those qualifications which contribute to targets may be funded, whereas those that do not will require students themselves to pay fees to cover the full costs of the programme. If certain classroom subjects are 'cheaper' to offer, have more recognition for employers and contribute to government targets, they are more likely to appear on college prospectuses than those that do not recruit many students, require additional funding to cover the costs of the subject being taught and do not lead to success in relation to meeting government targets or indeed national benchmarks. Conversely, some subject areas that were underfunded in the past have thrived if they have become part of a national strategy. The way in which adult literacy, numeracy and language has become mainstreamed within FAVE is a clear example of the influence of government in the past two decades (see below). The inspection regime (see Chapter 14) also influences what is taught and what is left out.

Teachers need to be specialists in their subject area and qualified to teach. Students need appropriate facilities, particularly in vocational areas, as well as access to relevant work experience. This capacity-building and making use of existing capability within the workforce and within the infrastructure is a key element in curriculum design. Think how the rise of technology has required colleges and institutions to acquire new computers and software and train staff to use them effectively, and how programmes have both incorporated and adapted to the fast-changing technological landscape.

Reflective activity 9.1

Try to find old prospectuses from your college or organization to see how the curriculum on offer has changed to reflect the changes in the way we use computers and how students are given opportunities to acquire the necessary skills and knowledge to keep pace with these changes. It is also interesting to see how certain subjects have changed in the way they are named and framed, as well as the content of their programmes. In the 1970s, people wanting to learn how to decorate cakes attended 'Cake Decoration' classes. Today they attend 'Sugarcraft' sessions. What other examples can you identify from these prospectuses?

The final source of influence on curriculum design and delivery actually reflects what students and other stakeholders want. For example, a community college may offer a series of programmes on self-help for young families, or sustainability in horticulture to reflect the interests of its local community. Another may provide courses on learning to use computers for retired people, or language classes for people newly arrived in the country. FAVE colleges are usually closely linked to the industries and services within their catchment areas and employers may fund their employees to attend certain bespoke programmes as well as more traditional provision relating to vocational qualifications. Most colleges and training providers have staff whose specific role is to engage with employers.

Reflective activity 9.2

Review the factors that influence curriculum design and delivery above. Identify the five or six factors that you see influencing the curriculum you deliver. Evaluate the impact these factors have on shaping your delivery of the curriculum. What enables your delivery and what constrains your delivery?

1.2 Factors shaping adult literacies

We noted above that the curriculum can change due to a variety of influences. Adult literacy, language and numeracy provides an interesting example of how the curriculum evolved in FAVE provision from the 1960s to the present day (Hamilton and Hillier, 2006, Reading 9.1). The table below shows key moments during this period and what effect these had on the curriculum. It is important to note that there was no formal curriculum, provision or indeed professional development for teachers at the beginning and it was through the effort of local managers and part-time tutors that the initial curriculum was developed, although those involved at the time would not have used this term.

Figure 9.2 How factors influencing curriculum design and delivery have shaped the teaching and learning in adult literacy and numeracy in England from the 1970s until 2010.

Phase	Key events and factors influencing Literacies curricula	Implications for curriculum design, delivery and development	Three main forces shaping curriculum planning and delivery (see Fig. 9.1 above)
One: 1970s	1973: Russell Report – help the disadvantaged. 1975: BBC TV series *On The Move* – supporting building skills in literacy. By 1976, 15,000 adults receiving literacy tuition across England and Wales.	Education offered by volunteers – classes in make-do settings: primary schools, warehouses, college corridors and canteens. No formal curriculum, resourses often taken from other sectors (primary and secondary) or created. Informal support networks begin to form. High teacher autonomy. Limited support for teachers. Little formal funding available.	**High student demand stimulated by *On The Move*, a BBC TV series** **No formal training available** **No formal funding available**
Two: 1980s	**1980**: Adult literacy expanded to include numeracy and become known as Adult Basic Education (ABE). **1984**: ESOL added to the remit of the national agency, now know as the Adult Literacy and Basic Skills Unit (ALBSU). ALBSU became the 'official voice' for sector **1985**: ALBSU estimated that 110,000 adults received tuition. **1985**: Research and Practice in Adult Literacy (RaPAL) was founded. RaPAL campaigns for the rights of all adults to have access to the full range of literacies in their lives. Funding from the Manpower Services Commissions (MSC) and the European Social Fund (ESF). Estimates of 85,000 adults in ABE tuition. Funding continually under review by central government. Agency existence remains precarious.	Education offered by volunteers – classes in 'make do' settings: primary schools, warehouses, college corridors and canteens. No formal curriculum, resources often taken from primary and secondary sectors or created. Informal support networks begin to form. High teacher autonomy. Research begins to become available from RaPAL. Some funding available.	**Funding from MSC and ESF** **Focus on link between literacy and work** **No formal training available** **No formal curricula**

Phase	Key events and factors influencing Literacies curricula	Implications for curriculum design, delivery and development	Three main forces shaping curriculum planning and delivery (see Fig. 9.1 above)
Three: 1989–99	1992: FE colleges removed from local government control. Adult Literacies became a designated area of vocational study within FE guaranteed free to all students. LEA retains responsibility for non-vocational adult leisure courses. Community education begins to reduce as funding cuts. 1993: ALBSU reports importance of Basic Skills to employers in the last five years. 1995: ALBSU becomes Basic Skills Agency (BSA). 'Basic Skills' courses become eligible for funding in relation to vocational courses. Funding related to the colleges brings funding regime, vocational outcomes and qualification and formal audit. By 1996, 319,402 people were currently receiving tuition in England, two-thirds of whom were in further education.	Education offered by volunteers and trained teachers. Classes begin to become part of the formal college offer. Still many 'make-do' contexts. Some guidance of curricula. Beginnings of formal audit and quality control measures. Funding becoming more stable.	**Funding more stable** **Training increase** Qualifications more widely available **Quality and audit systems**
Four: 1997–2006	International Literacy Survey (IALS) suggested 7 million adults were in need of Adult Literacies. Moser Report, 'A Fresh Start' – recommended a new Basic Skills strategy The Adult Basic Skills Strategy Unit (ABSSU) was set up directly within the Department for Education and Skills (DfES) and 'Skills for Life' strategy agreed. National Research and Development Centre (NRDC) established prioritizing evidence-informed practice.	Education offered by more trained teachers and volunteers. Classes become integrated part of other programmes. Still some 'make-do' contexts. National curricula have massive impact on shaping how adult literacies conceived, taught and audited. Formal audit and quality control measures come to shape practice. Funding becomes fairly stable.	**National curricula** Shape sessions presenting literacies as sets of discreet skills. **Training course** Well established and widely used. **'Stretching' targets and audit procedures.** Curricula, qualifications make cross-organizational comparison possible.

Phase	Key events and factors influencing Literacies curricula	Implications for curriculum design, delivery and development	Three main forces shaping curriculum planning and delivery (see Fig. 9.1 above)
	Core Curricula for Literacy, Numeracy and ESOL published. National qualifications at L1 and L2 introduced. Stable and generous funding made available by Treasury for the 'Skills for Life'. Promotional campaign *Gremlins*. Consolidation of 'target culture'. Consolidation of 'quality' systems, internal and external. 'Pelting torrent' of government initiatives		
Five: 2010–	Rise of functional skills Return of GCSE English Language. Entrenchment of 'target culture'. Consolidation of 'quality' systems – graded lesson observations and inspection. Rhetoric of devolved control.		

Alongside these particular feature are the cultural attitudes, bias and 'ideological' commitments shaping judgements.

Adapted from Hamilton, M. and Hillier, Y. (2006) *The Changing Faces of Adult Literacy, Language and Numeracy*. Stoke-on-Trent: Trentham Books.

The influences on the curriculum can be seen from the four directions outlined in Figure 9.1 at different times throughout this period. In the chart, you will see that early on, there was no infrastructure for provision of Adult Literacy Language and Numeracy (ALLN) and it was not until the 1990s that there was a formal curriculum and qualification structure. The factors having most influence were those from the individual teachers, managers, community agencies and the students themselves. Only in the mid-1990s, when international tests and rank ordering of nation states took place, did government priorities explicitly cover ALLN. This led to a huge capacity-building exercise from 2000 onwards, with prescribed qualifications for teachers and students. The early influence of users (both students and teachers) was overtaken by the increasing specification and top-down management. Yet one lasting influence of this story has been how ALLN curriculum and particularly the student-centred approach to teaching have influenced good practice in FAVE generally. Many of the early practitioners of ALLN moved into teacher training and management and they took with them their experience of creating a pedagogy and curriculum to influence a much wider range of teaching in the sector.

1.3 Student voice and the curriculum

It is possible for students and teachers to influence the curriculum. Our second case study arises from a similar starting point to the adult literacies example shown above. Here we examine a specific area, art and design, and how it was the site of a major disruption in the relationship between students, teachers and government authorities. In 1968, there was great student unrest across many countries and many university and college staff joined in. They were angry with the way that the curriculum was controlled by privileged members of society and they also argued that the curriculum did not equip them to live fulfilled, economically successful lives. One area that epitomizes the struggle was in art education. The following account is drawn from a newspaper article 'What the art students want' written by Peter Wilby, a journalist with a particular interest in education, for the *Observer*, 6 October 1968. The Hornsey College of Art students began their protest on 28 May 1968. This can be seen in the context of the May 1968 student riots in Paris which were larger in scale and also included various workers and farmers protesting against De Gaulle's government.

> What began as just another student sit-in over local rights and grievances, ranging from the state of the lavatories to demands for sabbatical leave, became a highly articulate and enlightened debate about the whole purpose and meaning of art education.
> (Wilby, 1968)

The debate led to the use of guard dogs at both Guildford and Hornsey Schools of Art to keep rebel students and staff out. Hornsey had to stay closed until 23rd October due to the damage the sit-in caused. At Guilford, 39 members of staff were suspended for sympathizing with the rebel students. The students appeared on television and radio in what one student called a 'public relations job for art education'. The rebel students claimed they were protesting against 'education for obsolescence'. The protesters were in sympathy with Dr Leach's Reith lecture where he had argued that every skill, technique, piece of specialized knowledge may be rendered valueless in our lifetimes. However, who could decide what skills would be useful? As one art teacher pointed out: 'Industry itself cannot predict what kind of art graduate it will need in three years' time; techniques change too quickly.'

The National Advisory Council on Art Education had aimed to change the art and design curriculum, making it a 'more respectable structure for art education'. The Coldstream Report was published in 1960 and proposed a more broad liberal education rather than one based on a nineteenth-century craft tradition. Students had been examined by an external body and included narrow categories: Book Production; Dress; Embroidery (Hand); Embroidery (Hand and Design); Interior Decoration; Jewellery; Mosaic; Painting; Pottery; Pottery (Hand); Sculpture and Pottery; Shoe Design. There was a tension between a curriculum based on particular specialist skills which could quickly go out of date and a liberal curriculum which seemed disconnected to the practice of art and design both in college and industry.

Coldstream introduced the Diploma in Art and Design (Dip AD) where students specialized in one area from fine arts (painting and sculpture), three-dimensional design, graphic design or textile design. But some time was also spent on liberal studies such a psychology, English or sociology. Attempts to make the curriculum more respectable resulted in college curricula that more closely resembled those used in universities. Instead of doing a predetermined course a student would be given a tutor who would set them a problem which the student could solve using their initiative; it might require any combination of paint, textiles, metals, plastics. Students would discover specialist skills through the project. The revolutionaries called this a 'network system'.

> For example a student might decide to design a table and chair. At the drawing stage, at which he would try to present his ideas and inspiration to the tutor, would involve problems of graphic design. Later, in considering whether wood, plastics or metal was the most suitable medium for transmitting his ideas, he would investigate the properties of widely different materials. Upholstering the chair would involve problems of textile design. Finally, in considering marketing and production problems, the student would think about function of a table and chair in its social context. (Wilby, 1968)

It is hard to imagine students arguing against their curriculum today. However, the curriculum they experience is very much linked to the developments achieved from 1968. In many subject areas, problem-based learning or project-based approaches to covering the curriculum have evolved.

Any decision about what to teach, why and how is fraught with tension and differences of opinion between students, teachers, families, employers, professional bodies and governments. In FAVE, the need to include the employers' demands is particularly acute. In recent years, governments have attempted to place employers at the heart of decisions about what should be taught. The creation of Foundation Degrees in 2000, for example, was predicated on the involvement of employers to help fashion qualifications for technical and professional employees. Keep (2011) has outlined some of the many problems associated with fashioning programmes of vocational learning by stakeholders such as employers and governments. Among these are the notion that employers are seen to have rights but no actual responsibility for the curriculum, and a belief that vocational qualifications are simply a mechanism to ensure economic success for the country.

Given that the curriculum – explicit or hidden – is so contested, how can we best develop it so that our students benefit and meet their personal goals while at the same time meeting the requirements of the sector or system in which we all work? We now provide some underlying principles for curriculum provision.

2 Principles for curriculum provision

2.1 Knowledge, development and curriculum

The educational role of curricular provision relates to three basic, enduring considerations (Pollard, 2014). They are fundamental to all curricular deliberation:

- the nature of knowledge;
- the needs of learners; and crucially,
- the interactions between them.

These elements were highlighted in the first chapter of an Expert Panel report on England's national curriculum (DfE, 2011). An edited version is reproduced below:

> Subject knowledge can be seen as representing the accumulated experience of the past and a representation of this for the future. The concepts, facts, processes, language, narratives and conventions of each subject constitute socially refined forms of knowledge – knowledge that is regarded as 'powerful' in our society (Young, 2013, **Reading 9.2**). Established knowledge is highly codified, with disciplines, associations, professions and specialist institutions. Many contemporary bodies of knowledge are more mobile, with innovation and change being characteristic features.
>
> However, education is also about the development of individual learners [in colleges and training organizations as students and trainees]. There are many dimensions to such development including the personal, social and emotional as well as the physical, neurological and cognitive … The significance of the development of individuals over time has increasingly been recognized in recent years. Longitudinal research has demonstrated the lasting consequences of high quality early learning experiences (Sylva et al., 2010) and a Foresight Report (Feinstein et al., 2008) affirms the trajectories of 'learning through life' and the economic and wider benefits of such learning.

Education can be seen, at its simplest, as the product of interaction between socially valued knowledge and individual development. It occurs through learner experience of both of these key elements. Education, through the school curriculum mediates and structures these processes. The core expertise of teachers is to reach between and facilitate a productive interaction of knowledge and development. As James and Pollard (2012) put it, effective teaching 'engages with valued forms of knowledge' and also 'equips learners for life in its broadest sense' (see Chapter 4). This argument is represented in Figure 9.3 below.

Pollard (2014) argued that some people emphasize subject knowledge and discount the significance of more developmental aspects of education. And there are also many who foreground the development of skills, competencies and dispositions while asserting that contemporary knowledge changes so fast that 'learning how to learn' is all that is necessary. But these are unhelpful polarizations, for it is impossible to conceptualize 'learning to learn' except in relation to some substantive purpose. Both elements, knowledge and development, are essential considerations in relation to curricular provision.

The two elements are not, however, equally significant at every age. In particular, developmental aspects and basic skills are more crucial for young children, while appropriate understanding of more differentiated subject knowledge, concepts and skills becomes more important for older students. The curriculum is quite different and more dispersed in FAVE compared with that in early years, primary and secondary education, although the underlying issues apply to all ages and phases.

Figure 9.3
Education: the
interaction of
knowledge,
development and
curriculum.

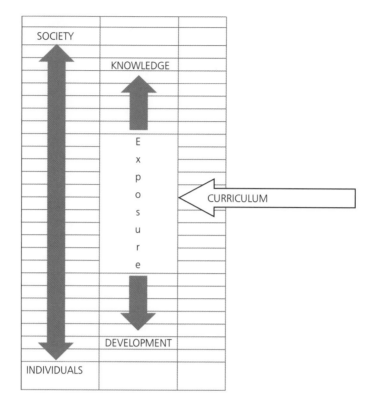

2.2 Aims and values

What is the purpose of a curriculum? What role does it serve? Legislation may define overall educational goals and high-level statements set expectations for the curricular frameworks in England, Scotland, Wales and Northern Ireland and in many countries internationally. They are essentially ethical, moral and political statements, which make transparent the values and ambitions to which a nation aspires. Of course, in FAVE there is still no 'national curriculum', but each country does define economic and social goals which steer the curriculum funded and supported within the sector. Most research and academic analysis of the curriculum has centred on the school sector, but the Nuffield 14–19 Review (Pring et al., 2009, Reading 4.4) provides an important example of the way in which the curriculum has been influenced by the school sector developments.

Historical study and international comparison (Meyer et al., 1992; National Foundation for Educational Research, 2011) reveal some common themes in relation to what can broadly be termed social, economic, personal, cultural and environmental goals. This can also be illustrated by comparison of the educational aims proposed within four sectoral reviews from England in Figure 9.4 below.

Figure 9.4 A comparison of educational aims across sectors.

	Expert Panel Report for the National Curriculum Review (DfE, 2011)	Early Years Review (Tickell, 2011)	Cambridge Primary Review (Alexander, 2010)	Nuffield 14–19 Review (Pring et al., 2009)
Social and economic	Provide opportunities for participation in a broad range of educational experiences and the acquisition of knowledge and appreciation in the arts, sciences and humanities, and of high quality academic and vocational qualifications at the end of compulsory schooling Satisfy future economic needs for individuals and for the workforce as a whole, including the development of secure knowledge and skills in communication, literacy and mathematics and confidence in acquiring new knowledge and skills	*Communication and language* Expressive arts and design Mathematics Understanding the world	Exploring, knowing, understanding and making sense Fostering skill	Knowledge and understanding Practical capabilities
Personal	Support personal development and empowerment so that each pupil is able to develop as a healthy, balanced and self-confident individual and fulfil their educational potential	*Personal, social and emotional development* *Physical development*	Well-being Engagement Empowerment Autonomy	Personal fulfilment Moral seriousness
Cultural	Appreciate national cultures, traditions and values, while recognizing diversity and encouraging responsible citizenship		Empowering local, national and global citizenship Celebrating culture and community	Community relatedness
Environmental	Promote understanding of sustainability in the stewardship of resources locally, nationally and globally		Promoting interdependence and sustainability	

The representation in Figure 9.4 shows the enduring importance of knowledge and skills in satisfying social and economic goals in all sectors, prominent concerns for policymakers, industry and the media. There is also a very strong emphasis on personal development in all sectors, which is often a particular commitment for parents and educationalists. The table also shows the awareness which exists about citizenship during schooling and suggests that environmental concern is emerging. Secondary education's need to focus on knowledge and skill in preparation for formal examinations and the social and economic demands of the workplace link very closely to the FAVE sector priorities.

Educational aims are sought through college policies and can be traced in specific programmes of study, lessons and everyday provision (see Chapter 10). If we have clear and transparent educational goals, our students are more likely to understand these, and there is mounting international evidence that this is reflected in enhanced outcomes. Indeed, clarity informs evaluative review of provision and increases accountability (Pollard, 2014).

3 Curriculum analysis and development

Given that the curriculum has primarily been examined from the perspective of compulsory schooling, it is no surprise that the key tenets of curriculum development have evolved from definitive studies in that sector. We now discuss these ideas in relation to their influence on the FAVE sector.

There are four building blocks of a curriculum for learning: knowledge, concepts, skills and attitudes. This framework originally derived from a report by the then inspectorate of schools in England and Wales (HMI 1985), *The Curriculum for 5 to 16*, which introduced the four elements in the following terms:

Knowledge: Selections of that which is worth knowing and of interest. 'That which is taught should be worth knowing, comprehensible, capable of sustaining [students'] interest and useful to them at their particular stage of development and in the future' (p. 37).

Concepts: The 'big ideas' which inform a subject, or generalizations which enable students to classify, organize and predict – to understand patterns, relationships and meanings, e.g. flow, change, consequence, temperature, refraction, power, energy.

Skills: The capacity or competence to perform a task, e.g. personal/social (listening, collaborating, reflecting), physical/practical (running, writing, cutting), intellectual (observing, reasoning, imagining), communication (oracy, literacy, numeracy).

Attitudes: The overt expression of values and personal qualities, e.g. reliability, initiative, self-discipline, tolerance, resilience, resourcefulness.

3.1 Knowledge

Underpinning curricula is the need to understanding the nature of knowledge. There are three basic positions with roots back to the philosophy, psychology and sociology of education.

First, there are those who argue that particular 'forms of knowledge' exist. These are thought to be distinguishable, philosophically, by the different ways of thinking and kinds of evidence which are employed in investigating them (Hirst, 1965; Peters, 1966). These forms are thought to be based on *a priori* differences, i.e. logical and inherent differences. Such a view has been referred to as 'rationalist' (Blenkin and Kelly, 1981) and is often used to legitimate traditional curriculum subjects (Wilson, 2000). For example, science has a set of principles for testing hypotheses about the world, whereas literature may draw upon theories of language and how it both shapes and portrays our experiences in the world.

Second, there are those who emphasize the ways in which knowledge is socially constructed by individuals and groups in interaction together and with their environment, and by successively restructuring their understanding through these experiences (Berger and Luckman, 1967; Light and Littleton, 1999). This view has resonance with the psychology of Piaget, Vygotsky and Bruner (see Chapter 2).

Finally, knowledge can be seen in sociological terms as being defined by powerful groups who define certain types of understanding as being important or of high status. They may attempt to control access to some forms of knowledge, particularly those associated with power (Young, 1971; Bernstein, 1971), but they may also try to insist on the exposure of students to particular forms of knowledge which are deemed appropriate.

Of course, these views of knowledge are not discrete and any one person's perspective may draw on several of them, or even on them all. Young (2013, Reading 9.2) makes an important distinction between 'knowledge of the powerful', which draws attention to the third usage above that is associated with status, and 'powerful knowledge', which has echoes of the first usage above and is associated with specialist understanding that is capable of application in a wide variety of contexts. He argues that providing access to such powerful knowledge is the main purpose of schooling. For example, some subjects studied at 'A' level and beyond have higher status (physics) compared with a similar level (media studies). People who have studied philosophy, politics and economics (PPE) at university often move into careers in the Civil Service and government, where their knowledge is not only powerful but is also of the powerful. On the other hand, a few years ago plumbing was seen to be an important vocational area to study as politicians in the UK government debated the need for such skills and knowledge to drive the economic success of the UK forward. Its status relative to PPE, however, is far lower, reflecting not only the vocational/academic divide in this country but also social values and the influence on who becomes powerful. The important point is that the different emphasis which is placed on particular views of knowledge tends to reflect social values, and these *can* and often *do* influence the structure and content of the curriculum.

Notwithstanding debates on how subject knowledge is actually used, a high degree of consistency has been established on the ways in which subjects provide the organizational frameworks for national curriculum requirements in countries around the world. In reviewing the comparative work of Meyer and Kamens (1992), Ross (2001) suggests that 'local variations have been ironed out as a pattern of international conformity has prevailed' (p. 129). Ross indicates that national curricula generally feature the following subjects: one or more national languages; mathematics; science; some form of social science; and aesthetic education in some form, though this is less firmly established than the other four areas. A contemporary archive on international curriculum and assessment frameworks is hosted by NFER and confirms the breadth and subject-based organization of knowledge in countries around the world (see inca.org.uk). This consistency is less visible in the FAVE sector, although initial vocational education often incorporates wider subject areas than a narrow focus on the particular industry for which the students are preparing.

3.2 Concepts

Concepts enable the most important ideas and deep structure of knowledge and understanding in each subject to be presented in concise ways. This avoids long lists of curriculum content which sometimes bedevil attempts to represent a subject domain, and which can seem overwhelming both to teachers and their students.

Elliott (1976) made the case in terms of:

The information explosion – which generates new facts at such a rate that it is futile to try to keep up. An alternative is thus to select facts to support conceptual development.

Concepts for learning – for new situations are rarely entirely novel and we are able to use our store of conceptual understanding to interpret and make sense of new experiences.

Concepts as organizers – because they provide a map of knowledge which breaks down the randomness of experience and enables us to understand it.

Concepts as anchorage points – in providing stability for exploration of the subject and enabling cumulative understanding by learners.

The arts are, arguably, even better prepared for a conceptually based curriculum through the legacy of analysis and connoisseurship which distinguishes quality (Pollard, 2014). Music and art have conceptual languages accumulated over hundreds of years. In some cases, such powers of discrimination have been codified, as in the case of dance and movement where Rudolf Laban (1879–1958) developed an exceptional analysis based on the concepts of body, effort, shape and space.

Through the provision of a robust and valid framework of key concepts, it is possible to maintain the integrity of subjects and their parent disciplines in very concise ways. The subject associations, which are often subdivided in relation to particular sectors, play an invaluable role here.

Beyond the significance of concepts as a useful focusing device in curriculum planning and provision, concepts really earn their place because of their capacity to illuminate and render accessible the deep structure of subject knowledge. Recent research in higher education, such as that by Entwistle (2009), has documented 'ways of thinking and practising in the subject' (WTPS) and the development of 'deep understanding' through making transparent the conceptual frameworks of each discipline. 'Threshold concepts', which unlock disciplinary understanding, have been identified, as have the barriers posed by forms of 'troublesome knowledge' (Meyer, Land and Davies, 2008).

Concepts, then – to return to HMI's (1985) definition – enable learners to classify, organize and predict and to understand patterns, relationships and meanings within subjects. They are epistemological tools in support of high-quality, authentic learning.

If we want our students to be able to use computational skills, for example, we need them not only to follow the rules of addition, subtraction, multiplication and division – they also need to know about some underlying principles, such as the order in which you place the numbers to undertake the computation. This in turn relates to concepts of conservation. These deeper concepts are actually useful in a variety of other contexts and provide the framework for being able to undertake any number of computations and to arrive at solutions via a variety of means.

3.3 Skills

A skill is 'the capacity or competence to perform a task' (HMI, 1985: 38) but in the context of curriculum planning, use of the term has become more complex and applied in different ways:

Physical skills normally refers to bodily coordination such as running, catching, etc. and to fine motor skills such as writing, sewing, drawing or typing.

Basic skills usually refers to communication, literacy and numeracy, and sometimes includes the use of technology.

Personal skills typically includes capabilities such as self-awareness, reflection, thinking and problem-solving, as well as interpersonal awareness, cooperation and leadership with others.

Study skills tends to be a specific set of capabilities focused on managing one's own learning, such as observing, interpreting, classifying, memorizing, prioritizing.

Subject skills highlights particular capabilities required for learning in subject domains, such as mapping in geography, experimenting in science and empathizing in drama.

Vocational skills identifies requirements for particular avenues of potential employment and career, such as nursing, business, computer programming or farming.

Although skills identified in these classifications often overlap, they are sets of capabilities which complement and extend a curriculum which is expressed in terms of subject knowledge. An innovative contemporary project on this is *Opening Minds* promoted by the Royal Society of Arts. This competence framework focuses on citizenship, learning, relating to people, managing situations and managing information and emphasizes the ability to understand and to do, rather than just the transmission of knowledge.

One way of thinking about this is in terms of a classic distinction between declarative knowledge and procedural knowledge. If the former sets out that which is known, the latter describes how it is developed and used. This distinction between 'knowing that' and 'knowing how' was drawn by Gilbert Ryle (1945). His argument asserts the significance of skills, procedures and learning activities in the development of knowledge. He also shows how, in terms of moving beyond the dry recitation of facts towards application and relevance to life, the capacity to apply knowledge is vital. There is no doubt, then, that skills provide a distinct and valuable element of curriculum provision.

Figure 9.5
The four capacities of Scotland's *Curriculum for Excellence.*

Successful learners

with
· enthusiasm and motivation for learning
· determination to reach high standards of achievement
· openness to new thinking and ideas

and able to
· use literacy, communication and numeracy skills
· use technology for learning
· think creatively and independently
· learn independently and as part of a group
· make reasoned evaluations
· link and apply different kinds of learning in new situations

Confident individuals

with
· self-respect
· a sense of physical, mental and emotional well-being
· secure values and beliefs

and able to
· relate to others and manage themselves
· pursue a healthy and active lifestyle
· be self aware
· develop and communicate their own beliefs and view of the world
· live as independently as they can
· assess risk and take informed decisions
· achieve success in different areas of activity

To enable all young people to become

Responsible citizens

with
· respect for others
· commitment to participate responsibility in political, social and cultural life

and able to
· develop knowledge and understanding of the world and Scotland's place in it
· understand different beliefs and cultures
· make informed choices and decisions
· evaluate environmental, scientific and technological issues
· develop informed, ethical views of complex issues

Effective contributors

with
· an enterprising attitude
· reliance
· self-reliance

and able to
· communicate in different ways and in different settings
· work in partnership and in teams
· take the initiative and lead
· apply critical thinking in new contexts
· create and develop
· solve problems

However, as we have seen, bodies of knowledge and associated conceptual tools represent the accumulated understanding of our societies and therefore demand attention. Thus, skills alone are unlikely to justify presentation as a complete curriculum. But skills add enormous value to engagement with subjects. Indeed, they support the development of subject knowledge, are realized through it, and contribute to its transfer and application into practice.

Systematic and embedded provision for skill development is thus a vital element of learning within any curriculum. It is often thought about in cross-curricular terms and such provision can be made at classroom, college or national levels.

Figure 9.5 shows the way that Scotland has conceptualized the curriculum. You can see that it implies a clear purpose in ensuring young people are independent, socially aware and responsible citizens. This curriculum extends into the FAVE sector. The Scottish Literacies Wheel (Learning Connections, 2005) also takes the individual as a member of society at its heart and the curriculum outlined in the wheel aims to help people who need to develop their literacies to be part of Scottish society, not just in economic terms, but in relation to contributing to their families and community.

3.4 Attitudes

Attitudes are 'the overt expression, in a variety of situations, of values and personal qualities' (HMI, 1985: 41). These include honesty, reliability, initiative, self-discipline and tolerance which 'may be encouraged in the formal curriculum and the informal'. Clearly, this relates to the significance of the 'hidden curriculum' to which we drew attention at the beginning of this chapter. In recent years, there has been particular awareness of citizenship. Attitudes to health, exercise and diet have been prominent too, and it is predictable that pressure will grow for colleges to introduce their students to sustainability issues. Values and priorities reflect particular social, cultural and economic priorities. Over the years of your career these will ebb and flow as governments change and social norms evolve. They may also vary depending on the particular circumstances and ambitions of the communities which a college serves.

This brings us back to the issues raised in Chapter 2, where we noted how culture and language frame the interpretation of our experience and how attitudes are influenced by family, community, peers, school, college and the media. The overall effect is that people form, or are socialized into adopting, attitudes which reflect the influence of significant others in their lives.

There is, after all, probably nothing more important for lifelong learning than the confidence of learners in tackling new learning challenges. In Chapter 2 again, we saw how important it is for learners to believe in their potential to learn and to improve. Claxton has cogently argued that it is possible to 'build learning power' in schools by nurturing attributes such as resilience, resourcefulness, reflection and reciprocity (Claxton, 2002, 2011). As he puts it:

- *Resilience* covers aspects of the learner's emotional and experiential engagement with the subject matter of learning.
- *Resourcefulness* embraces the main cognitive skills and dispositions of learning.

- *Reciprocity* covers the social and interpersonal side of learning.
- *Reflectiveness* covers the strategic and self-managing sides of learning. (Claxton et al., 2011: 40)

Through such careful attention to learning itself, a 'supple learning mind' can be created (see Figure 9.6 below).

Figure 9.6
The supple learning mind (from Claxton et al., 2011).

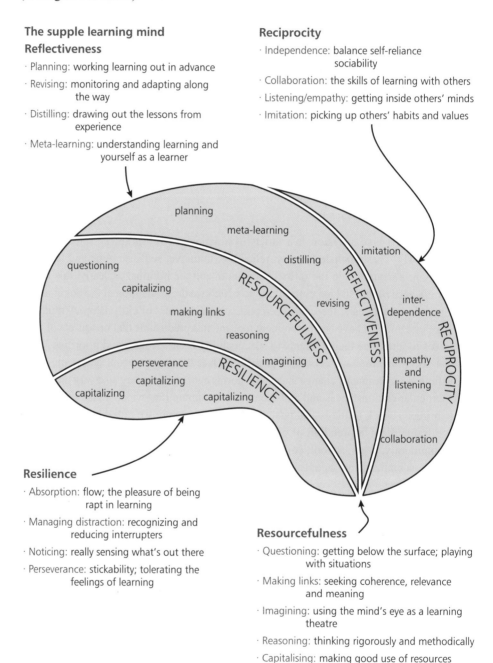

The supple learning mind
Reflectiveness

· Planning: working learning out in advance

· Revising: monitoring and adapting along the way

· Distilling: drawing out the lessons from experience

· Meta-learning: understanding learning and yourself as a learner

Reciprocity

· Independence: balance self-reliance sociability

· Collaboration: the skills of learning with others

· Listening/empathy: getting inside others' minds

· Imitation: picking up others' habits and values

Resilience

· Absorption: flow; the pleasure of being rapt in learning

· Managing distraction: recognizing and reducing interrupters

· Noticing: really sensing what's out there

· Perseverance: stickability; tolerating the feelings of learning

Resourcefulness

· Questioning: getting below the surface; playing with situations

· Making links: seeking coherence, relevance and meaning

· Imagining: using the mind's eye as a learning theatre

· Reasoning: thinking rigorously and methodically

· Capitalising: making good use of resources

These attributes are closely associated with 'learning how to learn' (James et al., 2007) and are viewed by many as being essential for learning in the twenty-first century.

3.5 A balanced curriculum

A rounded curriculum will provide balance between knowledge, concepts, skills and attitudes in curriculum design, ensuring that each has its place. This is important for those who frame national curricular frameworks in terms of classroom provision. Reflective activity 9.3 suggests a way of mapping the elements of learning within an area of curriculum provision.

Reflective activity 9.3

Consider knowledge, concepts, skills and attitudes in planned schemes of work. Select topics within a programme of study in a subject area. Working on your own or preferably with a colleague, identify and list the knowledge, concepts, skills and attitudes which are targeted for development.

TOPICS	Knowledge	Concepts	Skills	Attitudes

How easy was it to identify elements in the four categories? Which were explicit, and which implicit? Has the activity led you to refine or extend your plans? How could the framework be used to take stock of your students' learning in your classroom?

---

4 Subject knowledge

We have discussed what a curriculum is and how it is always contestable due to the varied interests of numerous stakeholders. We now analyse the content of the curriculum – in other words, what do we need to know about our subject and how to teach it in order for the curriculum to be delivered?

Teachers with good subject knowledge are able to make more secure judgements about the *appropriate* teaching of knowledge, concepts, skills and attitudes. Indeed, international research studies such as the meta-analysis of Hattie (2009, Reading 4.3) suggest that the subject knowledge of teachers is an extremely important influence on student attainment. Perhaps this is not surprising, but simply having a lot of specialist knowledge is *not* sufficient for effective teaching.

Shulman (1986) identified three forms of subject knowledge:

- *Content knowledge* – knowledge of the subject held by the teacher.
- *Pedagogic content knowledge* – knowledge of how to use content knowledge for teaching purposes.
- *Curricular knowledge* – knowledge of curriculum structures and materials.

4.1 Content knowledge

Content knowledge refers to the kind of knowledge that we gain from our own schooling, university and college courses or from personal research and interest. It can be subdivided into two aspects, the substantive and syntactic, as defined by Schwab (1978).

- The *substantive* aspect of subject matter knowledge relates to a foundational understanding of facts, concepts and principles of a subject and the way in which they are organized.
- The *syntactic* aspect relates to knowledge about why such knowledge is deemed important and is justified.

Knowledge about the chemical structure of benzene and how its resultant properties are used in the pharmaceutical industry would be an example of substantive knowledge in history. Knowing how this knowledge has been arrived at through the use of experimental testing and an understanding of the ways in which pharmaceutical companies report their experiments and the resulting relative validity of such evidence would be an example of syntactic knowledge of history.

Such knowledge is not always accessible from memory, and we often must refresh and develop our substantive knowledge of topics before planning and teaching. For example, when planning to teach a topic on childhood illnesses, we might research both older and modern cures drawing on historical resources. Such sources might include schemes of work, textbooks, a library or the internet. Topics such as this may only be taught annually or even biannually and we develop our knowledge each time they occur, helping to invigorate our own interest which then enthuses our learners.

4.2 Pedagogical content knowledge

Pedagogical content knowledge is Shulman's (1986) second form of subject knowledge, which he described as 'subject matter knowledge for teaching'. It does not simply reflect understanding of a subject, or even of how to teach. Rather, it is knowledge of how to combine both in relation to a particular domain. It is thus a specific category of teacher knowledge.

We draw on our pedagogical content knowledge when deciding how we will introduce a new idea or develop our students' knowledge or skills in relation to a specific aspect of a subject. We often make use of everyday objects to represent the topic we are introducing

– for example, we could use a grapefruit, apple and orange to show how the earth and moon rotate around the sun to help our students acquire knowledge in an accessible way.

Teaching another person what you know involves finding ways of *representing* subject matter to assist their learning, as well as being aware of the new representations that are subsequently developed. New conceptual developments can be seen as 'transformations' (Shulman, 1986). These transformations take many forms and are:

> ... the most powerful analogies, illustrations, examples, explanations and demonstrations – in a word, the ways of representing and formulating the subject that make it comprehensible to others. (Shulman, 1986: 9)

With experience, we develop a representational 'repertoire' for the subject we teach which may itself enrich and extend our own subject understanding. It is often claimed that a good way to understand something is to try to teach it. This repertoire is part of the result of 'thinking like a teacher' about a subject and is, of course, significantly helped by our own conceptual understanding. In any one lesson we may use a number of different strategies of this kind. The successes and failures of our transformations in making learning meaningful for our students, individually and as a group, add to our knowledge of the subject and of how it may be learned, in particular of subject-specific difficulties which our students may experience.

4.3 Curricular knowledge

Curricular knowledge is Shulman's third form of teacher knowledge and perhaps the simplest.

It relates to programmes of study, syllabuses, schemes of work, resources, technologies and instructional materials through which curricular objectives may be realized. The selection of such material is often structured by college policies, but rests on teacher judgement in respect of more specific activities and lessons.

For most teachers, curricular knowledge is much easier to acquire than content knowledge or pedagogic content knowledge. Indeed, some would argue that, while curricular knowledge can be obtained from textbooks, the internet or from school and national curriculum documentation, the acquisition of content knowledge calls for sustained study and pedagogical content knowledge requires extensive experience. You will find it easy to download examples of session plans, schemes of work and indeed, your college or organization may well have set resources, plans and instructional materials that you are required to use. These will provide you with a framework within which to work, but do remember that you are applying your own knowledge about what to teach and how best to do so as well.

4.4 Applying subject knowledge

As we have seen, having decided what it is that students should learn, we draw upon our subject matter knowledge and pedagogical content knowledge in relation to a particular group of students when we decide what they need to do in a particular lesson.

For example, we may be introducing the use of apostrophes to our literacy students. We know how these are used, how they are misused and how confusing this can be. We also know through our experience that trying to cover all the uses of an apostrophe in one teaching session is counterproductive. We could use a set of worksheets which cover each use of an apostrophe in successive sessions. We could take photographs of misuses of apostrophes and ask our students to spot where these occur (greengrocer shops are particularly relevant here!). We certainly will want our students to write some sentences themselves where they have to use apostrophes.

More generally, experienced teachers with thorough subject knowledge have been found to be more likely to adapt and modify textbooks and other published materials where they find the organization of content and the representations of concepts unsatisfactory (Hashweh, 1987). Teachers with deep subject knowledge were also more likely to identify where learners might misunderstand, to recognize dawning insights and to see where connections might be made within the subject and with other subject areas.

Rowland, Turner, Thwaites and Huckstep (2009) formalized this understanding through the development of what they call a 'knowledge quartet'. Their framework has its empirical origins in observations of trainee and beginning teachers teaching mathematics (Turner, 2009). The quartet highlights four aspects of subject knowledge:

Foundation – content knowledge in substantive and syntactic forms, which enables and circumscribes the available teaching repertoire.

Transformation – the capacity to re-present content knowledge in ways that are pedagogically powerful, as described above.

Connection – the expert teacher's awareness of the structures and sequencing of knowledge, so that particular elements can be related to a more holistic understanding.

Contingency – the teacher's capacity to respond to classroom events and pupil actions in ways which, though unexpected, still build towards understanding.

This work on mathematical content knowledge found that trainee and beginning teachers did not always use the most appropriate representations in their teaching and did not always make connections that would support the mathematical understanding of their students. However, when helped to reflect on the mathematical content of their teaching using the knowledge quartet framework as a tool, teachers often identified such limitations in their practice and suggested how they might make improvements (Turner, 2009).

Conclusion

Any curriculum reflects values, views of knowledge and of learning. The specification of a national curriculum in schools and a plethora of vocational curricula in colleges and workplaces raises the immediate question, 'Whose curriculum is it?' (Unwin, 2009, Reading 9.3). Dominant opinions and influence can change over time and they are not always clear-cut or coherent. Ambiguities and dissonances within and between the different agencies that govern education are also commonplace. You, as teachers, have views on such matters, perhaps based on study, experience, evidence and reflection. Your professional contribution to the educational debates is valuable alongside subject and other professional associations.

The official curriculum of any country is a very different thing from the curriculum found in colleges or in subject areas, which includes the hidden curriculum and the curriculum-as-experienced by students. There is enormous scope for creativity, adaption and extension in the formal curriculum.

We must use our professional expertise to manage a constructive interaction between what the knowledge society deems to be important and the specific needs of our students. In the next chapter we focus on the practical implementation of the curriculum through policies, programmes of study, schemes of work, lesson planning and evaluation.

This chapter has discussed the importance of knowledge and how it is generated for learning through the curriculum. Even though FAVE is not normally subject to national curricula in the ways that the school sector is, there are numerous requirements to meet industry standards, qualification requirements and professional body standards.

Key readings

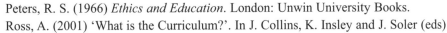
Examinations of different types of knowledge and how these shape curricula:

Hamilton M. and Hillier Y. (2006) 'Curriculum and Method'. In *Changing Faces of Adult Literacy, Numeracy and Language*. Stoke-on-Trent: Trentham Books. (Reading 9.1)

Peters, R. S. (1966) *Ethics and Education*. London: Unwin University Books.

Ross, A. (2001) 'What is the Curriculum?'. In J. Collins, K. Insley and J. Soler (eds) *Developing Pedagogy*. London: Paul Chapman.

Wilson, J. (2000) *Key Issues in Education and Teaching*. London: Cassell.

Guy Claxton's discussion of 'building learning power' explores how the curriculum can be developed to support active and independent learning:

Claxton, G., Chambers, M., Powell, G. and Lucas, B. (2011) *The Learning Powered School: Pioneering 21st Century Education*. Bristol: TLO.

An important contribution to higher levels of learning in the curriculum can be found in:

> Land, R., Meyer, J. and Smith, J. (eds) (2008) *Threshold Concepts within the Disciplines*. Rotterdam: Sense Publishers.

Support for specialist subject teaching can be found in

The Higher Education Academy (HEA) **head.ac.uk**

The Education and Training Foundation (ETF) **etf.org.uk**

For a further discussion on the problems teachers, students, employers and governments have encountered in attempting to fashion an agreed curriculum for vocational learning, see:

> Feinstein, L., Vorhaus, J. and Sabates, R. (2008) *Learning Through Life: Future Challenges*. Foresight Mental Capital and Wellbeing Project. London: The Government Office for Science.
>
> Fuller, A. and Unwin, L. (2003) 'Learning as apprentices in the contemporary UK workplace: creating and managing expansive and restrictive participation', *Journal of Education and Work*, 16 (4), 407–26.
>
> Keep, E. (2011) 'The English Policy Narrative'. In A. Hodgson, K. Spours and M. Waring (eds) *Post-Compulsory Education and Lifelong Learning Across the United Kingdom: Policy, Organisation and Governance*. London: University of London, Institute of Education (IOE).
>
> Unwin, L. (2009) *Sensuality, Sustainability and Social Justice: Vocational Education in Changing Times*. Professorial Inaugural Lecture. London: University of London, Institute of Education (IOE). 4 February. (Reading 9.3)

For Michael Young's debate on the role of subject knowledge and his distinction between the 'knowledge of the powerful' and 'powerful knowledge', see:

> Reading 9.2 – edited from Young, M. (2013) *Powerful Knowledge in Education*. London: London: University of London, Institute of Education (IOE).

Reference to official websites for UK countries that provide information about national curricula and links to subject can be found at **reflectiveteaching.co.uk**.

The associated website, **reflectiveteaching.co.uk**, offers a wealth of supplementary resources including reflective activities, research briefings, advice on further reading and downloadable diagrams, figures and checklists from the book. It also features a compendium of educational terms, links to useful websites, policy and curriculum documents, and showcases examples of excellent research and practice.

Planning
How are we implementing the curriculum?

10

Introduction

This chapter is a discussion of educational practice. It focuses upon the strategies that teachers use to plan and organize the ways in which teaching, learning and assessment (TLA) will take place, whatever their 'classroom' might look like. It also considers programme planning cycles and the role of student voice within this cycle. We begin to explore how teachers can use observations and formative and summative evaluation to inform curriculum planning, curriculum development and the improvement of practice during and at the end of the planning cycle. We extend this discussion in Chapter 15. Practical strategies for planning and examples will be used to explore key issues. For instance, we draw attention to the need to be flexible in our planning to allow for changes in response to learners' needs and evidence from practice, which emerges during a lesson. We emphasize the need to ensure that curriculum and lesson planning is pedagogically sound and never rigid, overly bureaucratic or instrumental. We point to the importance of well-developed curriculum and lesson plans which allow room for creative teaching, interpretation and the exercise of educational judgement (Harper, 2013, Reading 10.1).

> ## TLRP principles
>
> Two TLRP principles underpin our approach to providing high-quality curricular experiences:
>
> **Principle 2: Effective teaching and learning engages with valued forms of knowledge.** Teaching and learning should engage with the big ideas, facts, processes, language and narratives of subjects so that learners understand what constitutes quality and standards in particular disciplines.
>
> **Principle 3: Effective teaching and learning recognizes the importance of prior experience and learning.** Teaching and learning should take account of what the learner knows already in order to plan their next steps. This includes building on personal and cultural experiences of different groups of learners.

Putting a curriculum into practice is never a straightforward or linear process. Good curriculum design is a necessary first step, but even a well-designed curriculum can fail to be translated into effective practice if it is not sufficiently well understood or 'owned' by teachers. A rigid curriculum does not allow or encourage teachers to exercise their professional educational judgement in the everyday complexities and realities of their classroom practice.

Creativity and imagination contribute to successful educational experiences for students. Passion and enthusiasm for teaching, excellent subject knowledge and a positive classroom environment further enhance this experience. It is you, the teacher, who brings the curriculum to life. It is easier to be imaginative and responsive if you are also secure in your subject specialist knowledge and in your grasp of good pedagogical practice (see Chapter 11). This is one of the reasons why good planning is both necessary and enabling for teachers and their students.

1 The FAVE curriculum

Planning is at the heart of good teaching, learning and assessment (TLA) and is strongly connected to purpose. When planning, teachers should ask themselves: When does it make sense to do something this way? Harper identifies excellent planning as a feature of all 'outstanding' lessons. She also points out that 'teachers' planning is informed by their assumptions, values and beliefs' (2013: 9).

Despite the wide range of subject and vocational areas, there are many similarities in the curricula offered across schools, sixth forms, colleges, training organizations, adult and community learning and other providers in England. There are, however, also important differences of emphasis. In FAVE, curricula can be determined by a myriad of awarding bodies (ABs) responsible for vocational and academic qualifications and funding streams as well as by national and local initiatives and needs.

Irrespective of national requirements (see Chapter 9), curriculum planning should be influenced by the overall philosophy and aims of FAVE. Many organizations emphasize personal development and state their aim to ensure that each student achieves their potential and that each develops into a well-rounded, successful, caring and knowledgeable person. Organizational goals (as seen in mission statements and annual reports) reflect the overall philosophy and aims in FAVE institutions and can provide more detailed guidance for practical implementation. However, it is important to remember that despite the stated aims and intentions of national and individual organizational policies, they can have unintended consequences in practice (see Chapter 11).

The configuration of the timetable is an important planning decision which can enable or prohibit aspects of planning. The first step, then, is to define the basic framework. What should be the pattern of the teaching week? How long is a teaching session? Where do the breaks come? How long are the breaks? Making decisions about start and finish times may involve considerations of travelling time, the operation of transport, childcare, availability of specialist workrooms, etc. Other decisions about organization include where are there opportunities for cross-curricular planning and team teaching? How will subject and vocational teams work with specialists to develop the English, language, maths and ICT needs of students? All of these decisions will be reflected in the timetable and may enable or constrain possibilities for creative and pedagogically sound planning. The same decisions (particularly those related to funding) can have significant consequences for the contact time that is available for face-to-face teaching and student learning (Berliner, 1990, Reading 10.2).

More recent discussions involve consideration of the proportion of time that should be available for face-to-face contact with students, independent study, group work, open learning and online or distance learning to provide the best outcomes for students.

In most educational organizations, curriculum planning is managed in three time frames:

- long-term (whole courses, stages or phases);
- medium-term (yearly, termly or half-termly); and
- short-term (fortnightly, weekly or for specific lessons or sequences of teaching).

Many teachers, especially those connected to programmes with accredited qualifications, may have little choice about what they teach in terms of the curriculum content. This is usually determined externally in the form of a prescribed syllabus for the course, while others – often in adult and community education – have much greater freedom in terms of what they teach. However all teachers have choices about the ways in which they can bring the curriculum to life through creative planning in the teaching of topics and concepts within and across lessons. This is planning in the short term and the main focus of discussion for this chapter.

Curriculum planning is not a once-and-for-all affair. The curriculum needs to be reviewed and revised to make sure it is relevant, up-to-date and enabling so that all students can achieve their potential. It is a recognized good practice to link this review process closely in with the process of whole organization improvement planning and evaluation (see Chapter 14).

2 Long-term planning

2.1 Programmes of study – making it real

Long-term planning of programmes of study must develop with awareness of national and organizational requirements. Many teachers in FAVE have a strong frame for their work in the shape of specifications or a prescribed syllabus with tightly specified curriculum content. These are set by the various ABs and examination boards. Organizations offering FAVE courses and qualifications are now widely regarded as being in a market for students. This means that every provider is expected to make their provision attractive and viable to students, who are often referred to as customers. Subject teams have to select appropriate accredited courses. Once these have been chosen, course specifications are used to create and design ways of putting these specifications into practice through carefully planned programmes of study. According to Coffield and Williamson (2011), there are '144 awarding bodies, which offer qualifications at GCSE, 'A' level and in all vocational areas. In all, there are over 9,700 different accredited qualifications' (p. 47).

Some ABs and examination boards offer large quantities of support materials. However, teachers and departments need to decide how to respond to such provision, which has at times been criticized for narrowing the curriculum and diminishing rather than enhancing pedagogy (see Chapter 11). While provision in FAVE is not constrained by the national curriculum, responding to national systems for qualifications and accountability remains high. Specifications set by awarding bodies and exam boards remain extremely influential in the planning process. The raising of the school leaving age in September 2013 in England may have further implications for curriculum planning in FAVE in the UK. Ofsted also has a stake here. In inspecting provision Ofsted has the task of ensuring providers have enrolled students onto the appropriate programme of study.

As teachers we need to feel confident and able to plan in relation to the specifications set out by ABs and others and we need to have the space and power to do this. Teachers need to be encouraged and able to engage in the art and craft of curriculum planning if they are to bring these specifications to life in ways which inspire and engage students and which ignite in them a passion for the study of the subject. The potential risks of instrumentalism and the inhibiting constraints of prescribed curriculum from ABs needs to be recognized and addressed in programmes of initial and continuing teacher education and by curriculum leaders and curriculum planners across the FAVE sector.

Many students in our sector have never experienced educational success and we should plan for this to happen. This is often best achieved through incremental experiences of success and achievement. Planning decisions have to be made for sound educational reasons rather than for purely financial, bureaucratic or instrumental ones. There can be a tension between the two and we should be confident in the stance we take.

Reflective activity 10.1

What evidence of long-term planning exists in your setting? Find examples of national programmes of study and, if possible, see if you can obtain earlier versions which show evidence of the changes to long-term planning that have taken place. Discuss with a colleague what this means for your own practice.

---

3 Medium-term planning

3.1 Schemes of work

As a member of a curriculum team, you will need to think about what content needs to be covered in your subject or vocational area term by term. You may find the following questions useful. What sequence of topics will be offered? What level will lessons be pitched at? What teaching, learning and assessment strategies will be selected? What can be covered face to face? Where are the opportunities for independent learning? In FAVE an increasing significance is placed upon planning for learning through the ways in which we foreground and develop English, language, maths and ICT in your vocational or subject specialist curriculum (see Chapter 12). You may find it helpful to engage in some joint planning with some of your colleagues at this stage to plan for learning across curriculum areas.

Schemes of work provide a practical curriculum plan for each subject or vocational area of learning. As such, they enable strategic planning and review of the curriculum. They are likely to incorporate, but may also adapt and supplement, the programmes of study in awarding body and examining board specifications. Schemes of work draw upon other published resources and are frequently modified in the light of both experience and curriculum initiatives. A key intention is that schemes of work should give a clear indication of how *progression* in learning is provided in relation to each subject or area of learning. Teachers will also be concerned to ensure that the curriculum is presented in ways that are *relevant* to students.

We recommend that each scheme of work should address four basic issues:

- *What do we teach?* Here you should try to outline knowledge, concepts, skills and attitudes to be developed, links between subjects and cross-curricular elements including the development of English, language, maths and ICT.

- *How do we teach?* Here you should try to cover how the curriculum and learning processes are to be organized, units of work, learning activities and processes, forms of grouping to provide differentiation, resources needed, time allocations and opportunities for assessment.

- *When do we teach?* Here you should try to address the issues of curriculum continuity and progression throughout appropriate stages.

- *How do we know that people are learning?* Here you should try to set out the methods and plans for monitoring progress and attainment, and for setting future learning targets.

This level of planning is usually undertaken by teachers working in subject departments and/or by class teachers individually, in pairs or in small teams. Wherever possible some cross-curricular planning with subject specialists should take place. This is especially important for the development of functional English, maths and ICT skills. There is evidence to suggest that broader cross-curricular planning can be very beneficial. Schemes of work are likely to be updated, as with all planning, on the basis of teachers' and students' views on the quality of activities, performance data, organizational change and changes in the make-up of the group and in the light of requirements from ABs and examination boards.

Schemes of work are an essential medium-term planning tool, but they need to be developed in the light of the policies and priorities of the organization as a whole. Without them we have little basis on which to define the purposes of teaching sessions or to assess learner progress.

There are many ways of setting out a scheme of work, but they tend to begin by recording the following:

Class/subject details. Brief details of the group, level, timings and the subject/curriculum/ vocational areas encompassed in the plan. Such details allow colleagues to quickly understand the context of the document.

Learning objectives. Objectives express what we intend students to learn in terms of knowledge, concepts, skills and attitudes. Learning outcomes may also be used to state what learners will be able to do as a result of the teaching and learning programme. Such statements may be used to formulate sequences or ladders of success criteria on a gradient of complexity or difficulty. These can be used to review progress and to help in understanding the level of challenge in a task. A further refinement is to specify 'must', 'should' and 'could' criteria for assessment. This is a key intersection between curriculum planning and assessment for learning (AfL, see Chapter 13).

Wk	Topic/s	Link to objectives	Activities	Resources	Assessment
1					
2					
3					
Etc ...					

Figure 10.1
Sample scheme of work.

Activities. This section indicates what students will be doing in order to satisfy the stated objectives. Only a very brief description of activities is required at this stage of planning, and this may well be set out in a tabular form with each row being assigned for a lesson-by-lesson or week-by-week description of topics to be taught and learned. Other columns may record links back to objectives, anticipated activities, necessary resources and key assessment points.

This layout provides a holistic overview of the teaching programme and makes possible 'at a glance' to review whether activities are appropriately varied and therefore likely to maintain student interest. It is also possible to begin to plan where activities will need to be differentiated and any resources which need preparation or pre-ordering can be organized so that last-minute panics are avoided.

Reflective activity 10.2

Work with a colleague to compare the activities presented in a selection of schemes of work, either for your own class or for a specific group. What are the strengths and weaknesses of the layouts used? Are the anticipated activities incremental in terms of student learning? What is the balance of types of activity? Are activities likely to enthuse and motivate learners? Are outcomes clearly articulated? Is success in key learning points described?

Which activities would you replace, what with, and why?

When planning schemes of work, it is important to remember, as we saw in Chapters 2 and 9, that learning does not necessarily occur in a smooth, upward fashion. Unpredictable developments of insight and understanding may be experienced, just as occasional periods of consolidation of previous learning will occur and be needed. You will therefore need to monitor learning and assessment activities closely to try to ensure the best balance. For example, a scheme of work will provide you with a bird's eye view of activities and tasks that might cause boredom because they are too easy, tasks where the same assessment methods are overused or used in a formulaic or repetitive way, frustration from tasks that are too hard, reassurance from consolidation tasks and excitement from tasks that are challenging but not too daunting. The scheme of work is an excellent tool when taking stock of such issues.

3.2 Progression

Progression is a powerful concept for analysing planning decisions (Haynes, 2010, Reading 10.3). Any consideration of progression needs to recognize variation, diversity and uncertainty in learning and teachers need to be able to personalize the curriculum in relation to learners' existing knowledge, concepts, skills and attitudes.

Progression focuses at more detailed level on the cognitive, psychomotor and affective challenge of each curricular element. Bloom's taxonomy of educational objectives can be used to help you plan learning tasks and activities in the cognitive domain. Contributions to Bloom's taxonomy from Bloom's associates Dave and Krathwohl in the psychomotor and affective domains of learning are also useful (see Chapter 2).

3.3 Relevance

Relevance is very important in the selection of content. People learn most effectively when they understand the purposes and context of the tasks and challenges with which they are faced. When someone complains that an activity is 'pointless', 'boring', or that they 'don't see what it's for', then the curriculum is failing to satisfy the criterion of relevance. If this is the case, motivation may fall and concentration, commitment and quality may be lost. Progress and standards of work are likely to slip unless you are able to justify the activity and bolster motivation. Even when an activity could have great relevance, it may be that it has not been adequately explained to, or appreciated by, students. One key criticism of teaching by students and inspecting staff is that very often, students have not known why they are doing an activity. We must ensure that we make our rationale explicit or visible.

It is well worth considering the value of incorporating practical activities and first-hand experience into the teaching programme through the scheme of work.

4 Short-term planning

Schemes of work are the means of strategic, medium-term curriculum planning and provide the starting place for more specific short-term lesson plans.

4.1 Lesson plans

Lesson planning is the most familiar and critical part of our everyday work as teachers. The lesson plan is the tool with which we make our planning visible to ourselves and to others. This can be as an aide memoire for the session, as a record to help us evaluate and develop future sessions and the means for us to share ideas with others. The lesson plan has more recently taken a bureaucratic function as a key inspection tool used for judgements about the 'quality' of our teaching. Student and beginning teachers may justifiably be concerned when more experienced teachers take what seems to be an off-hand or production line approach to the production of lesson plans framed in terms of rigid institutionally devised formats. Despite this, the process of lesson planning, and what we want our students to achieve as a result of the decisions we make for the lesson, lies at the very heart of being a well-prepared teacher.

The main starting place in this process is to recognize the existing understanding and motivation of your students, sometimes described in terms of their entry level to the subject, topic or the lesson. This is essential to enable you to refine specific objectives for your lessons and to ensure provision is differentiated to the needs of your students. Effective planning provides structure and security which, in turn, helps to develop your confidence and enables you to be responsive to students during the session. Good planning underpins *flexibility*.

Increasingly, education providers have standard lesson plan formats which can be helpful for staff to understand each other's work and to highlight the important elements to be included in a plan. However, as we point out in Chapter 11, such templates need to be used with considerable care if they are not to become instrumental straitjackets for lesson planning which stifle teacher creativity and overlook the need for high levels of flexibility and responsiveness.

Elements of a lesson plan are likely to include:

a) *Context and/or rationale*

b) *Learning intentions or objectives*

c) *Phases of the lesson*

d) *Learning activities and tasks*

e) *Success criteria*

f) *Resources, ICT and safety*

g) *Support staff*

a) *Context and/or rationale*

It is helpful for an initial section to first summarize basic organizational information such as:

- the class and any groups within it
- the date and duration of the session/s
- the topic/s and focus of the session/s

Second, it is essential to consider the existing levels of understanding achieved by your students. This should be recorded in an appropriate way. What are the present capabilities and knowledge of your students? It may helpful to have a profile of each of your students detailing their particular needs and aspirations.

b) *Learning intentions or objectives*
It sounds obvious, but it is important to be clear about what students are expected to learn! With the move from teacher-centred approaches to student-centred learning a distinction

has been drawn between objectives and outcomes. Objectives state what the teacher plans to cover and learning outcomes tell us what the student will be able to do by the end of the lesson. Within the broader context of overall schemes of work, objectives for a lesson sequence or single lesson should be relatively focused. Clear learning intentions enable appropriate practical decisions to be made – for instance, in selecting teaching, learning and assessment activities and tasks. In essence, learning intentions are essential because everything else about the lesson depends upon them. It is vital to share them with everyone in the class (although in some circumstances it may be appropriate not to share learning intentions with students at the outset of a lesson if the point of the lesson is maintain an element of surprise). Students and classroom support workers normally need to know learning intentions if they are to understand where their learning is going, when it has been achieved and the benefits to them in terms of focus, self-esteem, confidence and motivation.

You need to think about how learning outcomes are expressed. One familiar formulation uses the opening phrase: 'By the end of the session learners will be able to …' which encourages clarity. What students will be able to do should, wherever possible, be observable, so it helps to select active verbs such as list, describe, compare, identify, explain, solve, apply, discuss or evaluate. Alternatively, outcomes can be expressed more developmentally. Students might be expected, for example, to: be aware of, have had practice in, been introduced to, have considered, developed the ability to, gained increased insight into, improved performance in, have considered or begun to analyse. As well as general outcomes for the class, you may want or need to define outcomes for particular groups or individuals.

An important skill for the teacher is to be able to write effective objectives both at programme and session level. Below is a simple formula for writing an aim/objective for a lesson. The stem (a kind of runway into the learning objective) remains the same: *The purpose of this* [lesson or session, workshop, course or event] *is…* The aim is to help you to think carefully about your intentions as the teacher. In other words, what kind of overall learning you want to take place in the session. Remember to use Bloom's taxonomy in all three domains (if appropriate) to help you to clarify your own thinking and planning as you begin to write learning aims and objectives.

Figure 10.2
Writing an aim.

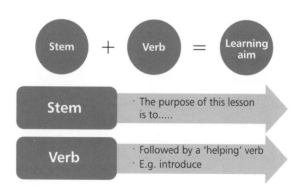

To:	To:
Introduce	Conclude
Explore – further explore	Revisit
Consolidate	Illustrate
Review	Encourage
Explain	Motivate
Outline	Build on
Develop	Revise
Examine	Demonstrate

Figure 10.3
Examples of verbs for writing learning aims.

The *verb* that follows the stem will change depending upon the subject matter, level, timing and student group. The point here is that this stem and verb combination will give you a solid foundation to develop your skill at writing appropriate aims/objectives.

It is helpful to work with someone else to begin to construct your own list of useful verbs for writing learning aims. Remember, the verbs you use should describe the teacher's intention or behaviour, for example, introduce, develop …

Learning intentions or outcomes state what you expect students will know, understand or be able to do by the end of the lesson. These need to be specific, measurable and describe the learning outcomes not the activities. The use of 'SMART' verbs is helpful:

- **S**pecific
- **M**easurable
- **A**chievable
- **R**ealistic
- **T**ime-bound

This measurability is one of the main differences between setting learning aims and learning intentions/objectives/outcomes. Remember to refer to Bloom's taxonomy again here to help you to focus your thinking. It is important that you plan activities which will enable you to know that 'understanding' has been achieved – in other words, you need to include outcomes that enable you to check that everyone understands the concept/topic being taught. Reflective activity 10.3 gives a simple formula for writing learning objectives/outcomes.

Reflective activity 10.3

- Begin to construct your own list of SMART verbs for writing learning objectives.
- Remember these verbs should describe what the learner should be able to do by the end of the session or activity.
- Keep this list with you as you plan sessions, use it and develop it further as your confidence increases.
- This list can be very helpful when planning for different levels of achievement in a session or series of sessions.
- Construct your list using the different levels in Bloom, Dave and Krathwohl.

As we have seen in Chapter 1, it is good practice to consult with learners and to share learning intentions (Rudduck and McIntyre, 2007), and also to discuss appropriate criteria for judging 'steps to success'. Clarke coined the acronym 'WILF' (what I'm looking for) and has emphasized 'active learning through formative assessment' (2008), while Hattie (2009) has gathered confirming international evidence on the significance of visible teaching and learning. Clear success criteria shared with learners also help them to get a good fix on the object of their learning and what it will look and feel like when they have accomplished it. This can empower learners to monitor, regulate and feedback on their own and each other's progress. Ask yourself: are the key learning outcomes clear and how could I share them with students?

Harper (2013) draws attention to how:

This rational and linear approach, heavily influenced by Tyler (1949) and Bloom (1956), has remained the dominant lesson plan model for a long time, despite tweaks and changing emphases over the years. Its popularity may, as suggested by John (2006: 485), be as much to do with its 'elegant simplicity' as with the prevailing political climate with its focus on accountability. The questions raised by Tyler are still being asked today, for example, 'how can we know if teachers have achieved their aims if they were not specified clearly in the first place?'. (Harper: 11)

c) *Phases of the lesson*

Thinking through the structure of a lesson or lesson sequence is one of the most important aspects of planning. Besides thinking about individual students and the lesson objectives and outcomes, it requires the application of pedagogical content knowledge (see the discussion in Chapter 9). Timing for different phases of the lesson is important for ensuring appropriate pace.

There is a well-tried three-part structure you can use for most of your lesson planning:

1. Start with a whole-class introduction. You should capture the interest and imagination of your students with an engaging starter activity, challenge or surprise designed to gain and maintain their attention. In FAVE contexts this can be a messy time with learners arriving at different times, catching up on chat, etc., and the starter should allow for this. The starter may relate to previous learning and test out whether that learning has been achieved or lead to the introduction of a new topic. Learning intentions need to

be shared and this should be done in clear, student-friendly language. Occasionally you may decide to share these later in the lesson. It is important to avoid very formulaic ways of sharing learning intentions/objectives. Harper (2013) refers to evidence from her study of outstanding lessons where none of the teachers read out a list of outcomes at the start. Although she argues that it is sensible to set the lesson in the context of previous and future lessons and to inform students of what they will be learning, she also refers to how teachers applied their professional judgement by using a different type of terminology and delaying, changing direction or building in an element of surprise. She argued that 'reading out outcomes at the start of the session is rarely associated with inspirational practice' (Harper, 2013: 107).

2. Next you should develop a range of activities that enable students to meet the learning objectives. If teaching is confined to the lower levels of Bloom's taxonomy this will lead to superficial learning; activities need to be included which will develop higher-order thinking and challenge students' capacities. Differentiation needs careful planning. Variation of activities is important with a strong emphasis on active learning strategies (Biggs, 2011; Crawley, 2011).

Action-packed but content-light lessons can be intellectually weak, while traditional, didactic or teacher-led lectures can be stimulating and successful. Once you have identified the sequence of topics, you need to plan opportunities to introduce, develop and consolidate key vocabulary, language and conceptual development in a coherent and integrated way throughout the curriculum. This is to enable ideas and language introduced in one topic to be integrated and consolidated in the next. Activities might involve the whole class, small groups, pairs or individuals. Changes of activity require the class at intervals to review their progress and refocus 'next steps'; these teacher interventions should ensure successful learning. You may plan to be working with different members of the class at different times and ways in which any support workers and peer learning may be involved and deployed to best advantage. You should visit groups to monitor, question and challenge as they work. Using your learners' experiences and interests can be valuable in creating contextualized and coherent tasks. Students in FAVE will have clear expectations, not least of all the 'cost of their education' and value for money. There is an increasing concern for teachers to be accountable for their teaching in the language and culture of what is widely described as the 'education market'.

3. The ending of the lesson is crucial. You need to allow for plenary time to summarize and review with students what has been achieved and to celebrate their achievements. Asking students to reflect on their learning can become superficial with only a cursory nod to the learning outcomes. As with the sharing of lesson outcomes, following a formulaic pattern may lead students to devise superficial responses. Encourage your students to think more deeply about what they have achieved with questions such as:

- What do you know/can do now that you didn't/couldn't at the start of the lesson?
- What have you done in the lesson to achieve the outcomes?
- How do you feel about today's lesson?

- Write down/tell the most important thing you have learned in today's lesson.
- What are you still unsure about?

This type of reflection can reveal achievement as a continuum and should increase ownership and control over students' education. In FAVE contexts, increased emphasis is given to the importance of providing opportunities for students to engage in self-assessment and to share and record their progress and achievement and their educational experiences. Traditional methods are paper-based Individual Learning Plans (ILPs) but these can be adapted electronically and also include social media and blogs.

The plenary gives you an opportunity to double-check achievement of outcomes, look ahead to future lessons and inspire students. A good finish is as important as a good start. Students should leave the lesson eager for the next and keen to continue their understanding beyond the classroom. Planning for independent learning beyond the session requires just as much as the activities in the lesson itself.

Reflective activity 10.4

For a topic you plan to teach, think about how the knowledge might be presented and how teaching might be sequenced. Using your pedagogic subject knowledge and understanding of your learners, what steps or 'chunks' might you plan for?

Identify possible tasks and activities. Experiment with the scheduling of activities to arrive at your first draft plan.

Examine the structure you are considering and identify where there will be teacher input and learner activity. What does the balance look like? Where are the opportunities for interaction?

Think about the ways in which your selection provides for progression, differentiation and inclusion.

Think about time. How many sessions will you need? Have you got enough? How does the programme divide into lessons? Will you need to keep learners together or is it possible to plan for fast and slow tracks?

Identify the elements of your proposed curriculum that are likely to be seen as highlights by the learners. Do they come at appropriate places?

Are there opportunities for you to take stock with the learners to share what has been achieved, what is working well and what barriers they are encountering?

Revise your programme as necessary.

Follow up: Keep structure under review as you plan. Make it a focus of your evaluation and adjust your planning accordingly.

---

d) *Learning activities and tasks*

Powerful and accomplished teachers are those who focus on students' cognitive engagement with the content of what it is that is being taught … (Hattie, 2012: 19)

We have come to the conclusion, that the design of instructional and assessment tasks is the fundamental determinant of the quality of teaching and learning in the classroom. (Hogan, 2012: 103)

When we plan, we must ensure that what is to be learned is set in manageable tasks and activities that match and extend learners' existing capabilities. Judgements about progression and depth of cognitive challenge in tasks are particularly significant. We have already discussed how the proposition that there are different kinds of thinking is central to the idea of cognitive challenge (see Chapter 2). Bloom (1956) identified six different kinds of thought processes in the cognitive domain. These are: recall, comprehension, application, analysis, synthesis and evaluation. The taxonomy implies a hierarchy and much of the work derived from Bloom is concerned with developing higher-order thinking in learners through activity or teacher questioning. Alternatively Bloom's classifications (or variations on them) have been used to analyse the range and variety of activity provided in classrooms. Another taxonomy developed by Biggs (1999, 2011) argued for constructive alignment of the aims of learning, the anticipated outcomes and a means of assessing the learning associated with this. His taxonomy, the SOLO taxonomy, builds on the concept of a system of structured learning outcomes and has been particularly successful in its application with higher education programmes of learning.

There is a tendency for teachers and learners to remain in comfort zones rather than take risks and stretch their capabilities. For example, it is easy to have routinized teaching activities where students can put their 'brains in neutral' and everyone gets through the session with minimal effort. Such coping strategies are exactly the reason why inspectors, government ministers and others persist in challenging the profession to have high expectations.

e) *Success criteria*

Assessment forms a vital element of every stage of planning. Without assessment and the consequent re-evaluation of planning, effective teaching cannot be developed and maintained. When planning, it is good practice to think through and record appropriate success criteria for the lesson. Objectives and outcomes are then much more likely to be borne in mind when explaining tasks, interacting with students and providing feedback.

Success criteria should specify evidence of progress/success with respect to the learning outcome. Such clarity of thinking at the planning stage allows you to share with students not only the broad lesson objectives but also to clarify specific expectations, targets and outcomes. Teacher feedback to learners can be much more precise. If learner involvement in assessing their own work is desirable, then using success criteria is a powerful tool in helping teachers to develop self-assessment as part of the learning process (Clarke, 2001).

f) *Resources, ICT and safety*

The use of checklists is recommended for making absolutely sure that all the practical necessities for a successful session are in place. Safety considerations should be made and there should be no short cuts in recording the issues anticipated and the provision made. If something does go wrong, such records assume considerable significance.

If the use of ICT is important for the lesson, a specific part of the lesson plan may be devoted to it. Clearly it would be impossible to outline how an interactive whiteboard was to be used in each phase of a lesson, though there may be phases of the lesson where its use by learners, or its combined use with other resources for demonstration purposes by the teacher, merits a reference in the lesson plan. In Chapter 8 we consider ways in which technology and mobile technologies in particular can be incorporated into your teaching.

g) *Support staff*

Effective planning is essential to get the full benefits from support staff such as learning support assistants (LSA), technicians, volunteers or anyone else who may contribute to teaching, learning and assessment. It is important that you share the nature of lesson activities with any supporting adult, and make it clear which students should be the focus of their attention. Above all, it is vital to share the learning intentions for an activity if the supporting adult is to play a full part in promoting learning (see Bailey and Robson [2004] for fuller accounts of the effective use of adult learning support). Some teachers do this verbally, but many keep a record, to which supporting adults can refer, that defines the lesson learning intentions, the activity and their role.

The topics above are likely to feature in effective lesson plans, whatever variations there may be in their presentation. Degrees of detail will vary between the novice and more experienced teachers, between exploratory and established lessons and in relation to teacher confidence generally.

Many providers have their own lesson plan template which teachers are required to use. In addition, numerous lesson plan templates and actual plans are available on the internet and as published materials. While many materials are of good quality, there are a lot of weaker publications. Any resource should therefore be carefully evaluated before use in practice. Of interest is the increasing opportunity to be involved in evaluating lesson plans through blogs and online forums. This is a useful space for teachers and student teachers to extend their professional conversations. As a rule of thumb, the more complex and bureaucratic the template, the less it is likely to be of any real use to you as a teacher.

We now move on to consider two issues which underlie all elements of lesson planning. These concern *differentiation* and *inclusion* (see Chapter 15) – in other words, how do we to design lessons which maximize meaningful connections between the knowledge to be taught and the people who are to learn?

4.2 Differentiation

The concept of differentiation highlights the cognitive demands which a curriculum or an activity makes of the learner (Haynes, 2010, **Reading 10.3**).

> If I had to reduce the whole of educational psychology to just one principle, I would say this: 'The most important single factor influencing learning is what the learner already knows. Ascertain this and teach him [sic] accordingly.' (Ausubel, 1968: vi)

Differentiation relates to the appropriateness, or otherwise, of particular tasks and activities to the learners' existing understanding and needs. How well 'matched' are learner and task? There are four key stages in planning to achieve differentiation:

- Establishing the intentions of both teacher and the student.

- Identifying the student's existing knowledge, concepts, skills and attitudes.

- Observing and interpreting the process by which the task is tackled.

- Analysing and evaluating the outcomes from the task, so that appropriate plans can be made for future learning opportunities.

A mismatch could occur at any (or all) of the stages. For example, at the first stage, a teacher could set a task for a particular purpose, but if this was not explained appropriately then the student might misunderstand. Any task might be done wrongly, or it may be done 'blindly' – i.e. without seeing the point of it. There could also be a mismatch at the second stage. The task might be too hard for a student because it requires certain knowledge or skill which they do not have. A mismatch at the third stage can be illustrated by a task which may be set with an instruction to use certain apparatus, or to present the outcome in a certain way. However, the apparatus may not be necessary and may actually confuse the student, or the style of presentation may assume some skill which the student has not yet acquired. Additional problems could also arise from a mismatch at the fourth stage. For instance, teachers often mark the end product of a person's learning; however, a high percentage of errors cannot necessarily be assumed to relate to bad work or poor learning. Indeed, errors can provide important clues about where misunderstandings may have occurred and identify areas of teaching which may be weak and in need of revision (see Chapter 13).

Various differentiation strategies can be used in lesson planning. Many books are available designed to develop your understanding and to offer practical strategies (see for example Cash, 2011; Cowley, 2013). Despite the range of methods identified, the classic distinction is between differentiation by task and differentiation by outcome.

Differentiation by task requires lesson plans in which, for all or part of the lesson, particular groups of learners will be engaged in different activities. This may be because the learners are grouped according to their attainment in a subject, or because it has been judged appropriate for particular students to focus on different topics. In such cases, the lesson plan should specify the particular groups, activities and objectives.

Differentiation by outcome calls for lesson plans in which the same basic task can be tackled in many ways, making it possible for students to respond in ways which are appropriate to their present level of knowledge, skill or understanding. A lesson plan might specify overall learning objectives but define differentiated outcomes in terms of what all, most or some learners will be expected to accomplish.

Experience will show, of course, that the neat distinction between differentiation by task and outcome is, in reality, often blurred.

It is worth bearing in mind that there are dangers in relying on differentiation by outcome too much, because it can become a euphemism for 'just seeing how well they do'. It allows teachers to avoid going through the vital process of envisaging what success or steps to success will look like for particular groups of learners within the class. However, if it is achieved, the cognitive challenge of tasks in your lessons should be matched to the cognitive needs of the learners in your class.

Equally important is to exercise caution so that we do not make self-fulfilling prophesies (see Chapters 13 and 15). Coffield reminds us:

If teachers expect to find three levels of ability, the danger is that three levels of ability are exactly what they will find. Hart et al. have usefully added the next stage in the argument: 'we **create** different types of learners by believing that there **are** different types and by teaching them accordingly (2004: 30 original emphasis). If we construct our pedagogy around the flawed and inaccurate notion of fixed ability, then the strategies adopted by our schools and classroom practices as teachers (with the aim of maximizing test results) 'are themselves implicated in creating and maintaining persistent patterns of differential achievement'. (Hart et al., 2004: 21) (Coffield, 2010: 15)

4.3 Personalization (Inclusion)

Personalization is a relatively new educational concept which reflects both cumulative international understanding about learning and contemporary commitment to reducing inequalities in outcomes. While echoing the cognitive issues associated with differentiation, it extends and broadens these to also embrace the social, emotional and motivational dimensions of learning.

The emphasis on engagement and on meeting needs of individual learners can seem daunting until you realize that the needs of many students are shared in common. In the context of lesson planning, the concept of personalization can be used to review what has been planned and to pose questions regarding the likely efficacy of the provision. In addition to tasks being appropriately differentiated, will they really engage learners, connect with their culture and expectations, and support their learning?

However, if it is achieved, inclusion should enable learners to identify with classroom activities in meaningful ways (see Chapter 15). Coffield encourages us to:

> ... embrace the expansive notion that **everyone's** capacity for learning can be enhanced: you and I can become more intelligent, we can **learn** to be more intelligent. (Coffield, 2010: 15, original emphasis)

Drawing on the work of Sennett (2008), he argues that sharing talent and working in teams is critical and this in turn helps us to become good citizens.

Coffield urges teachers to 'ensure that all students receive the rights to enhancement, inclusion and participation' (2008: 29). Through the work of Bernstein, he argues that in an effective democracy all learners have three interrelated pedagogic rights: right to enhancement; right to be included socially, intellectually, culturally and personally; and right to participate in activities leading to social change. A very simple question – but one which demands much thought – is:

> Do Level 1 and Level 2 students receive the same kind of demanding programmes, the same teaching hours and resources, as Level 3 students? If not, why not? There is nothing so practical as a good theoretical question to expose unjustifiable inequalities or poor performance by institutions. (Coffield, 2008: 29)

5 Evaluating curricular provision

This section considers three generic questions which can be used to investigate practice, with a particular focus on the application of subject knowledge in the curriculum. Addressing them will illuminate some issues on which personal improvement can be focused. As we noted in Part One, Joint Practice Development (JPD) offers a systematic approach to curricular improvement which is undertaken in collaboration with colleagues. This is attracting a lot of attention as a process of improving TLA and supporting teachers' professional development (Fielding et al., 2005; Gregson et al., 2015, **Reading 16.1**; Sebba et al., 2012).

These approaches illustrate, in different ways, TLRP's principle that 'student learning depends on teacher learning' (see Chapter 4).

5.1 Key evaluation questions

All plans, at whatever level, should be open to modification and change depending on their success in aiding the development of learning in the classroom. A reflective teacher clearly understands the intimate links between the processes of planning, teaching, assessment and evaluation (see Chapters 9, 13 and 14).

Three key evaluation questions may be posed:

- Did students learn what was expected, and why?
- How did teacher knowledge support learning?
- How did classroom activities facilitate learning?

Question 1: Did students learn what was expected, and why?
Assessment and evaluation are often confused because they are intricately entwined (see Chapters 13 and 14). For example, the question 'Did students learn what was expected?' focuses on both the learner and the teaching intentions. In order to answer the question, the reflective teacher needs assessment information on student performance. This information comes from formative assessment. *Assessment*, then, involves collecting evidence about *how* students related to particular teaching/learning experiences and *what* (if any) knowledge, understanding or skills were developed. *Evaluation*, on the other hand, considers *why* the particular teaching and learning experience supported or did not support intended or unintended learning.

Assessment and evaluation go hand in hand since it is not possible to consider the *why* without the *how* and the *what*. Evaluation of *why* student performance took the form it did should lead to deeper analysis of teacher action – and the next two questions.

Question 2: How did teacher knowledge support learning?
Evaluation of knowledge for teaching includes consideration of both subject/vocational knowledge and pedagogical knowledge (see Chapter 9) and whether these were sufficient to support learning. You will have given some thought to these issues when planning.

However, it is only possible to fully answer this evaluation question after the lesson/s has taken place. The reflective teacher will consider how well their knowledge of the subject or vocational area and their knowledge of how to make this accessible to students supported learning. Specific questions to ask include:

- Did I use appropriate and accurate language?

- Did I need to rely on textbooks or other sources of content matter?

- Did students give responses to questions or make suggestions about which I was uncertain?

- Had I predicted what students would find easy or difficult and any misconceptions they might have?

- Did my explanations and/or demonstrations aid students' understanding of the content?

- Did I use the most appropriate examples and representations?

- Did I introduce ideas in an order which enabled understanding to be built?

- Did I make connections between ideas presented in the lesson and with students' learning more generally?

This is not intended to be a definitive list, but gives an idea of the sorts of questions reflective teachers might ask which relate to their own teaching.

The precise nature of evaluative questions to ask about knowledge for teaching will vary depending on the subject matter of the teaching/learning experience being evaluated. For example, in an engineering lesson a reflective teacher might ask: 'Did the resources and examples I used portray accurate information about drilling in the North Sea?' Of essence here is that the reflective teacher considers whether their pedagogical content knowledge facilitated learning. That is, did they know enough about not only the subject but also about how to teach the subject so that students were able to learn?

The purpose of evaluating knowledge for teaching is not to identify limitations in teacher knowledge; rather, it is to understand better how to meet the educational needs of students. Having evaluated our use of language, ability to respond to learners, sequencing of content, the reflective teacher uses this analysis to inform learning and future teaching. Focusing on the way in which subject/vocational specialist knowledge and pedagogical content knowledge supports learning facilitates the development of knowledge for teaching. In this way future teaching and learning are enhanced.

Question 3: How did classroom activities facilitate learning?
The evaluation of classroom activities requires careful analysis of *how* students respond to activities, *what* they learn from them and *why* that learning takes place. Certain student and/or teacher activities may facilitate learning of some types of subject content better than others, and understanding this is important if the teacher is to develop their repertoire of teaching strategies for particular subjects.

It is also necessary to focus on individual students. For example, analysis of an activity might suggest that some people learned from physically manipulating objects while explaining what they were doing, while others learned from watching and listening. Yet others may have failed to learn through listening, but then physically manipulated the objects and learned for themselves. There are many possibilities.

Analysis of *why* activities are successful for different types of content and with different learners may lead to more generic pedagogical learning. Like the other two key evaluative questions, the answer to this question is only useful if it leads to developments in planning for teaching and learning. Provided that careful analysis is carried out, it is possible to learn about how to develop planning for teaching and learning both from activities that worked well and those that did not.

Reflective activity 10.5

Arrange for a colleague to observe a session. If you are a trainee teacher, this will be part of your programme. Ask your observer to focus specifically on one aspect of planning that is being implemented. For example, you may want your observer to focus on the way that you are starting or finishing a session. You may want to focus on your use of differentiated activities. Use the checklists included in this chapter to discuss your observed session with your colleague or mentor.

Conclusion

Underpinning every really good lesson is sound planning at a number of levels. We need to take account of curriculum requirements at national level and of whole-organization policies. These must be complemented by our understanding of the prior knowledge of our students, of our subject knowledge and pedagogic knowledge. The more experienced and confident we become in our planning, the more confident we will feel to experiment and plan for challenging lessons which match the levels at which our students are operating.

There is a strong link between planning, actually teaching in the classroom and finding out what our students have learnt (Hattie, 2012, **Reading 10.4**). The next chapters focus on examining the practicalities of how we communicate our plans with our students and assess their impact.

In this chapter, we have shown how knowledge which is to be fostered and used by our students can be developed through the curriculum and that planning what is to be taught and how we can know that learning is taking place are important elements of our practice.

Key readings

Further information regarding the taxonomies of Bloom and Biggs can be found in:

Biggs, J. (2011) *Teaching for Quality Learning in Higher Education*. Buckingham: SRHE/Open University Press.

Bloom, B. S. (1956) *Taxonomy of Educational Objectives: The Classification of Educational Goals. Handbook 1. The Cognitive Domain*. New York: McKay.

For discussions around the benefits of effective lesson planning, the following provide accessible and practical guidance:

Crawley, J. (2011) *In at the Deep End: A Survival Guide for Teachers in Post-compulsory Education.* 2nd edn. Abingdon: Routledge.

 Harper, H. (2013) *Outstanding Teaching in Lifelong Learning.* London: Oxford University Press/McGraw-Hill Education. **Reading 10.1** – Harriet Harper, 'Outstanding Teaching in the Classroom' – provides an abridged account of the key factors from this study.

Haynes, A. (2010) *The Complete Guide to Lesson Planning and Preparation.* London: Continuum.

David Berliner offers a useful insight into time management, a fundamental consideration for the classroom environment and for planning in

 Reading 10.2 – edited from Berliner, D. (1990) 'What's all the Fuss about Instructional Time?'. In M. Ben-Peretz and R. Bromme (eds) *The Nature of Time in Schools.* New York: Teacher College Press, 3–35.

Hattie draws implications from his exceptional synthesis of international evidence on effective lesson design and teaching practices. For John Hattie's essay on maximizing learning through 'mind frames', see

Reading 10.4 – edited from Hattie, J. (2012) *Visible Learning for Teachers: Maximising Impact on Learning.* Abingdon: Routledge, 1–20.

Various differentiation strategies can be used in lesson planning. Many books are available designed to develop your understanding and to offer practical strategies, see for example:

Cash, R. (2011) *Advancing Differentiation: Thinking and Learning for the 21st Century.* Minneapolis, MN: Free Spirit Publishing.

Cowley, S. (2013) *The Seven T's of Practical Differentiation.* Bristol: Sue Cowley Books Ltd.

Anthony Haynes' work on the significance of progression and differentiation for curriculum planning and classroom planning can be seen in

 Reading 10.3 – edited from Haynes, A. (2010) *The Complete Guide to Lesson Planning and Preparation.* London: Continuum, 135–47.

The link between curriculum planning and assessment is further elaborated in Chapter 13. The following offer insights around types of formative assessment and their effect on the quality of teaching:

Hogan, D. (2012) 'Yes Brian, at Long Last, there is Pedagogy in England – and in Singapore too'. In M. James and A. Pollard (eds) *Principles for Effective Pedagogy. International Responses to the UK TLRP.* London: Routledge.

Clarke, S. (2001) *Unlocking Formative Assessment: Practical Strategies for Enhancing Pupils' Learning in the Primary Classroom*. London: Hodder and Stoughton.

—(2008) *Active Learning through Formative Assessment*. London: Hodder and Stoughton.

Systematic and open evaluation of lessons is key to improvement, as Hattie's work has shown. As we noted in Part One, Joint Practice Development (JPD) offers a systematic approach to curricular improvement which is undertaken in collaboration with colleagues. The following suggest practical ways of framing this:

Fielding, M., Bragg, S., Craig, J., Cunningham, I., Eraut, M., Gillinson. S., Horne, M., Robinson, C. and Thorp, J. (2005) *Factors Influencing the Transfer of Good Practice*. London: Department for Education and Skills RR 615.

Gregson, M., Nixon, L., Spedding, P. and Kearney, S. (2015) *Helping Good Ideas Become Good Practice*. London: Bloomsbury. (Reading 16.1)

Sebba, J., Kent, P. and Tregenza, J. (2012) *Joint Practice Development (JPD.) What Does the Evidence Suggest are Effective Approaches?* Nottingham: National College for School Leadership.

The associated website, **reflectiveteaching.co.uk**, offers a wealth of supplementary resources including reflective activities, research briefings, advice on further reading and downloadable diagrams, figures and checklists from the book. It also features a compendium of educational terms, links to useful websites, policy and curriculum documents, and showcases examples of excellent research and practice.

Pedagogy
How can we develop effective strategies?

11

Introduction

The focus of this chapter is upon pedagogy. Pedagogy is a term used in education to consider what is really being taught and what is actually being learned. Pedagogy can have intended and unintended consequences. A teacher who uses predominantly teacher-centred methods may be encouraging learners to be passive recipients of other people's knowledge.

TLRP principles

Three TLRP principles underpin our focus in this chapter on teacher strategies and pedagogic repertoire:

Principle 1: Effective teaching and learning equips learners for life in its broadest sense. Learning should aim to help people develop the intellectual, personal and social resources that will enable them to participate as active citizens and flourish as individuals in a diverse and changing society. This implies adopting a broad view of learning outcomes and ensuring that equity and social justice are taken seriously.

Principle 4: Effective teaching and learning requires teachers to scaffold learning. Teachers should provide activities which support learners as they move forward, not just intellectually but also socially and emotionally, so that once these supports are removed, learning is secure.

Principle 6: Effective teaching and learning promotes the active engagement of the learner. A chief goal of teaching and learning should be the promotion of learners' independence and autonomy. This involves acquiring a repertoire of learning strategies and practices, developing positive attitudes towards learning, and confidence in oneself as a good learner.

Pedagogy refers to the interplay between a teacher's professional craft of teaching and their artful judgements about what to do for the educational good of students in the unfolding and complex situations which they encounter every day in their practice. Pedagogy also refers to the ways in which teachers use theory and research to support planning, delivery and reflection. Pedagogy asks us, as teachers, to take much into consideration when planning, delivering and reflecting on our practice. This chapter illustrates how reflecting on the art, craft and science of our pedagogy can support the development of rich educational opportunities and is divided into three main sections. Section 1 looks at vocational and subject-specialist pedagogy. Section 2 looks at pedagogy and promoting student development. We consider how pedagogy can bring the students into meaningful dialogue with the subject using teaching strategies that bring who is to be taught to engage with what is to be taught. Section 3 looks at pedagogy and whole-group and small-group working.

As teachers we constantly move back and forth between these different areas and our knowledge of the subject. We make judgements all the time about how best to support the education of our students. We give a lot of thought to which teaching strategies will support students' learning, what topics, concepts and ideas to teach, and what we and our students should aim to achieve. When we use the term pedagogy we are thinking about the complex work the teacher does in the classroom and in other FAVE contexts.

In this chapter, we explore the themes of equipping learners for life, scaffolding learning and the active engagement of learners in learning further in relation to FAVE contexts in some detail. We relate this discussion to pedagogical work mainly in relation to whole-group and small-group working with students. Alexander argues that 'teachers need a repertoire of approaches from which they select on the basis of fitness for purpose in relation to the learner, the subject-matter and the opportunities and constraints of context' (Alexander, 2008: 109). While acknowledging that the idea of repertoire is infinitely expandable, he concentrates on three broad aspects: how classrooms can be organized to afford different interactive opportunities such as whole-class work or group work; how teachers use talk to encourage different kinds of learning; how learners use talk to develop their understanding (Alexander, 2008). In this chapter we focus upon whole-group discussion, question-and-answer and small-group discussion. This allows us to explore the idea of pedagogy in terms of supporting students to think and speak for themselves. We examine how teachers can enable students to develop their own understanding, deepen the ways in which they think for themselves and increase their confidence in themselves as thinkers. We draw upon an overarching definition of pedagogy offered by the TLRP in which the authors suggest that pedagogy is the *craft, science* and *art* of teaching. We have also found the work of Carr (1987) useful in distinguishing between 'making' and 'doing' the action of teaching.

As Figure 11.1 shows, the three aspects of teaching interlock and contribute jointly to the overall concept of pedagogy (Bruner, 1996, Reading 11.1; Simon, 1982, Reading 11.2). Craft is seen as the repertoire of teachers' skills, strategies, methods, approaches and practices from which they select and to which they continue to add through a lifetime of

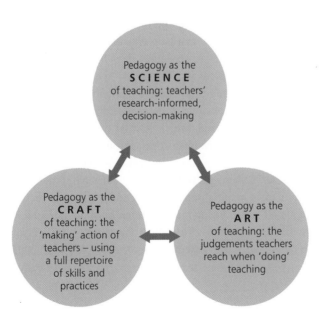

Figure 11.1
The craft, science and art of teaching.

professional work. When we see teaching as a craft, we can see the way teachers reflect on their teaching in terms of strategies and how these can help us to achieve clear aims. Science is seen as teachers' knowledge, understanding of and engagement in evaluation, reflection and research, in search of evidence to inform the professional choices and decisions they make. Art is seen in the 'doing action' of teachers, the judgements reached about what is the right thing to do in a particular context of working with particular students and is reflected in the ways these encounters are supported, as the situation demands.

Thinking about the art of teaching in terms of doing action focuses attention on the TLRP principle of 'equipping learners for life in its broadest sense'. As Coffield notes, this is concerned with the development of all students as active citizens, which means, for instance, 'expanding our conception of worthwhile learning outcomes beyond the attainment of academic qualifications' (2008: 11). Thinking of the art of teaching, 'doing action' helps us to see the important role pedagogy plays in helping students to reach an understanding that is their own.

In Chapter 4 we examined how reflecting on our teaching in terms of the three educational values of achieving qualification, socializing students and helping students to become independent thinkers could contribute to building the art of teaching. Reflecting fully on our pedagogical practice will require us to reflect on all three of these features of pedagogy: its craft, its science and its art.

1 Vocational and subject-specialist pedagogy

Pedagogy is the act of teaching a subject specialism. It is important to remember that subjects and vocational areas have developed over time and are still developing, and the boundaries between them are still evolving.

Subject and vocational specialisms can be focused upon traditional academic subjects such as history or chemistry, or they can be work-related as in a vocational subject such as hairdressing or carpentry. There are obviously links between the teaching of traditional and vocational subjects. In both areas we focus upon 'what it is to be taught' – the *subject knowledge*, the concepts, knowledge and understanding that relate to the subject. The term 'vocational' alerts us to the dimensions of education that are particularly important to a calling to do something in the world, which is what the original Latin root of the word vocation means. We prefer to use the term vocational education because we take the view that becoming able to do anything well in the world involves more than just training. The craft of tuning an engine, plastering a wall or cutting curly hair builds a number of learned skills that play a big part in helping people to do good work when they meet both routine ordinary and exceptional cases. Vocational education must do more than equip students to produce essays on the first principles of a subject specialism; it must also focus on helping students to put this knowledge into practice (see for example Eraut, 2005).

1.1 Vocational pedagogy

What is vocational education? Sennett uses the term *craftsmanship* to describe the craftwork done by any human being in the following terms:

> Craftsmanship names an enduring, basic impulse to do a good job well for its own sake. Craftsmanship cuts a far wider swath than skilled manual labour; it serves the computer programmer, the doctor, and the artist ... Every good craftsman conducts a dialogue between concrete practices and thinking; this dialogue evolves into sustained habits, and these habits establish a rhythm between problem solving and problem finding. (Sennett, 2008: 9)

Education plays a significant role in helping students to establish the sustained habits and ways of thinking that equip them to both solve and find problems in subject-specialist vocational areas. The key point to which Sennett draws attention is that a vocational education can also build insight into being a good person. If this statement appears lofty and sets unrealistic ambitions for vocational education, Hyde offers a neat summary of just what the educated craftsman knows about what is of value.

> They know how to negotiate between autonomy and authority (as one must in any workshop); how to work not against resistant forces but with them (as did the engineers who first drilled tunnels beneath the Thames); how to complete their tasks using 'minimum force' (as do all chefs who must chop vegetables); how to meet people and things with sympathetic imagination (as does the glassblower whose 'corporeal anticipation' lets her stay one step ahead of the molten glass); and above all they know how to play, for it is in play that we find the origin of the dialogue the craftsman conducts with materials like clay and glass. (Hyde, 2008)

Vocational education therefore has the potential to equip students for the work of life in the broadest sense. Pring's (1999) observation that the current forms of vocational education in England are too instrumental, uninspiring and narrowly focused indicates that that this potential has, as yet, not been realized.

Corson's distinction between 'education for work' and 'training for work' helps us to reflect critically on how we plan and support a vocational pedagogy that nurtures vocational professionals. According to Corson, if we focus on training for work we lose sight of much of what education requires and it seems reasonable that employers alone can give students what they need to become craftsmen. Corson argues that vocational education must include 'training for work' but it must be much more than just training:

> Being educated demands more than being highly trained; it involves the possession of a body of knowledge along with a conceptual scheme to raise that body of knowledge above the level of a collection of disjointed facts. (Corson, 1985: 291)

Sennett foregrounds the 'joined-up-ness' of the practice and thinking of vocational professionals. When we combine this with Alexander's emphasis on dialogue, we begin to see the fundamental importance of working together to identify, address and create new working practices. In pedagogical terms, it reminds us of the importance of whole-group, small-group discussion and question-and-answer in helping students build vocation-specific problem-solving and problem-finding skills together.

Huddleston and Unwin (2007) identify five areas to teaching, learning and assessment. When planning for and delivering competence-based programmes it is helpful to pay particular attention to the following questions in **reflective activity 11.1** below.

Reflective activity 11.1

Evaluating current vocational learning practice

Work with a colleague to consider the following questions:

- How will you develop learning support materials that individual students can access according to their needs?
- How will you establish support structures that allow students to identify the work-based 'learning opportunities' to help them build portfolios containing the right kind of evidence?
- How will you balance the desire to meet employers and students' preferences with the need to ensure the students are engaged in a coherent and rich programme of study?
- How will you give students opportunities to participate in whole-group and small-group discussion to discuss problems?
- How will you give students opportunities to work collaboratively, using joint practice development, on problem-solving and problem-finding?

(Developed from Huddleston and Unwin, 2007)

1.2 Teaching core concepts in vocational and subject-specialist areas

How do we help our students to 'develop the intellectual, personal and social resources that will enable them to participate as active citizens and flourish as individuals in a diverse and changing society?' (TLRP Principle 1).

To do this, we need to avoid what Bernstein called 'socially empty pedagogies' (1996) – in other words, where we teach such transferable skills as being socially motivated without fully understanding or critically evaluating them. We need to avoid teaching a narrow range of skill or knowledge that does not enable our students to practice their chosen vocational area as fully engaged members of society. The CAVTL report (2013, Reading 11.3) particularly emphasized the need to have a direct 'line of sight' to vocational practice in the workplace and also to encourage a collaborative approach to dealing with unexpected situations and problems that arise in the workplace. The challenge for us is, as far as possible, to use our pedagogic knowledge to bring all these aspects of practice together.

Young has called for us to 'bring knowledge back into vocational education' (2008: 174). He argues that the vocational education should serve two purposes. These dual purposes of are the acquisition of:

- occupationally related knowledge and skills.

- knowledge as a basis for progression to higher education or new occupations (not necessarily available in the workplace).

(Young, 2008: 174–6)

We often have to work with 'bloated' programme specifications that can be traced back to education policy priorities (Oates, 2010). The longer the list of targets to be achieved, the bigger the risk that students of both vocational and traditional academic subjects become disorientated and lose focus on what really matters. We therefore need to distinguish between what could be taught and what core concepts and ideas must be taught. We need to step back and spend some time thinking about what are the key concepts, the 'tricky bits', the ideas and practices that students need in order to get to grips with the subject in a meaningful way. This will involve carefully analysing current pedagogic practice to identify the main elements of the programme that students really need to deeply understand. **Reflective activity 11.2** should help you to identify the key elements of what is to be taught in our subject-specialist and vocational pedagogy.

Reflective activity 11.2

Identifying and teaching core concepts and practices

Use the following prompt questions to help you identify and plan to teach the concepts and practices at the heart of your subject:

- **What are key knowledge concepts, principles, operations in your subject?**
  Concepts and principles might include conservation of mass, elasticity and metaphor. Concepts comprise the key operations that need to be understood – for example, in mathematics working with vectors.

- **What elements are essential to progression to deep understanding of your subject?**
  For example, threshold concepts such as conservation in arithmetic computation, subject and object in sentence construction, tolerances in engineering.

- **Is sequence of your teaching of concepts, ideas of skills arranged in logical sequence?**
  Are there topics that you know you will need to return to in order to consolidate or deepen the students' understanding? For example, introducing the use of the subjunctive in French and building on previous verb tenses.

- **Do the pedagogical elements, what is to be taught and how it will be taught, reinforce one another?**
  Are there opportunities to consolidate previous learning? For example, use of light in art and photography, rise in democracy in European history and current areas of conflict.

- **What do your students need to know and be able to do to be good/ outstanding at different levels of study?**
  Meeting qualification levels for example between GCSE, AS and 'A' levels, distinguishing between merit and distinction in BTEC.

> ● **What are the 'tricky' concepts, ideas and skills to teach?**
> How much time do you realistically need to teach these topics? For example, use of apostrophes in English, genres in literature, fractions, percentages and decimals in mathematics.
>
> Will you need to repeat the exploration of the topic using a number of different teaching strategies?
> (Developed from Coffield, 2011)

Having identified these key elements, you will need to go on to consider how best to teach, reinforce and consolidate learning. It involves considering how much time it will realistically take to teach the topic effectively (see Chapter 10). You will need to make careful decisions on how best to mediate or moderate external demands and avoid teaching in narrow or instrumental ways. Below is a list of strategies that you may find helpful.

Figure 11.2
Learning and teaching strategies used within vocational education.

Learning and teaching strategies used within vocational education

- Learning by watching
- Learning by imitating
- Learning by practising ('trial and error')
- Learning through feedback
- Learning through conversation
- Learning by teaching and helping
- Learning by real-world problem-solving
- Learning through enquiry
- Learning by thinking critically and producing knowledge
- Learning by listening, transcribing and remembering
- Learning by drafting and sketching
- Learning by reflecting
- Learning on the fly
- Learning by being coached
- Learning by competing
- Learning through virtual environments
- Learning through simulation and role play
- Learning through games.

Lucas, Spencer and Claxton (2012: 58–85)

2 Pedagogy and student development

Dewey (1916) criticizes any form of instruction which aims to merely instil facts in learners' minds but does not encourage genuine thinking. Teachers in FAVE are particularly well placed to understand students' learning holistically. Teachers in our sector are acutely aware of the interconnections between experience and subjects studied. The extent to which life experience may be enriched or 'fertilized', to use Dewey's metaphor, by FAVE learning is explored in the following case study. It exemplifies TLRP Principle 3 which links teaching to prior or life experience and learning and 'includes building on personal and cultural experiences of different groups of learners' (TLRP Principle 3). In the case study, we see a STEM teacher, Robert, carrying out practitioner research that aimed to develop his pedagogic practice.

Case study 11.1 Robert's case study

Robert: The problem I sought to investigate and address was the under-achievement of one cohort of IT students. I conducted the study over a four-month period while I taught full-time at an inner city FE college. The students in the cohort where I carried out my research were studying for a BTEC Level 3 extended Diploma in IT. The students entered the programme with a mixture of qualifications, some GCSEs and some Level 2 qualifications in IT. Only two or three students in the group had already achieved Level 2 in English or Maths.

During my research I gathered evidence about the problem and impact of my changes to how I taught my learners from:

1 pre-enrolment interviews at the start of the course;
2 keeping a teacher diary, including reflections on tutorial work with individual
   students and small groups of students, and the use made of formative feedback;
3 survey and interview with students;
4 careful analysis of student assignments and final grades.

From my interviews and observations I found that all the students were keenly aware of the power of IT and technology to shape the modern world. They all recognized the role of smartphones, tablets, PCs and games consoles in keeping them informed and entertained. They talked enthusiastically about fixing computers and helping their families and friends to 'get online' and use IT. It was common for the students to express the ambition to work in the IT industry and most aspired to study IT at university.

From my interviews, classroom observations and analysis of their assignments I singled out two ways in which the students studied or thought about studying that were barriers to progress. First, students tended to always look to me for the 'correct' answer, even for simple or free-thinking tasks. They wanted spoon-feeding. My conversations with colleagues indicated that this phenomenon of teacher dependence was experienced across the department. Second, the draft assignments submitted were commonly generated through a combination of 'Wikipedia cut and paste' and 'thesaurus/translator abuse'. I thought that this attitude to learning demonstrated many of the characteristics of 'surface learning' – that is, finding out the shape of the assignment and then putting together a thin facsimile that matched the assignment criteria.

I began to experiment with pedagogical ways to bring together the students' life experience and the IT curriculum. One of my key aims was to change the students' attitude to learning. I began to experiment with a range of collaborative group tasks that established an environment where students could question one another's thinking about a topic and explore associations between key concepts, and produce a shared understanding of the topic. I also used peer checking, support and challenge to build their confidence in the key concepts and my own pre-prepared questions to explore the depth of understanding achieved. The students were then able to apply this theoretical learning to suggest solutions to 'real-world' IT problems.

When I reflected on the impact of my changes to pedagogic practice, I found that the collaborative ways of learning the students already used in their home lives to help family and friends with IT problems could be applied to classroom tasks through group working. I found that students benefitted from working with peers to build their understanding and apply this knowledge to real-world situations. Organizing the session in this way encouraged individual students to think more deeply about concepts and ideas. These group tasks combined with real-world problems also had a positive impact on their self-esteem and attitude to studying. The contrast with the surface approach was notable in the quality of assignments that were produced later.

2.1 Analysis of case study

Looking at Robert's experience in terms of the broad definition of pedagogy, two themes stand out. First, by bringing life experience into classroom through collaborative small-group activities, real-life IT problems help to make the learning real for students. Robert's case study also demonstrated that life experience is not always empowering. In this case, students had learned ways of studying prior to attending college that acted as a barrier to their own success.

The case study illustrates that this way of teaching took much more time for Robert to prepare and deliver than the traditional lecture model. In his overall reflections on the project Robert raised concerns that it might not always be possible to work in this way with tight deadlines and a crowded curriculum. These remarks illustrate the importance of the broad definition of pedagogy as art, craft and science. Organizational and/or policy constraints might limit our ability to do what we see to be appropriate for the needs of our students.

3 Discussion in groups and question-and-answer

There is a growing body of research, both internationally and recently in the UK, which supports the view that by working in groups, where students use talk for learning (Alexander, 2008, Reading 11.4), can improve students' academic performance and attitudes to learning. Galton summarizes the key benefits to students working in groups as follows:

- The process promotes independent thinking, such that students gain a sense of control over their learning.
- It can develop speaking and listening skills, allowing students to share feelings and ideas.

- It can encourage positive self-esteem, allowing students to build confidence in their own abilities.

- It can improve classroom relationships, enhancing students' sense of social responsibility. (Galton, 2007: 110)

In this section we concentrate on group working and talk for learning. We focus on two of the most effective teaching strategies we can use to bring student experience and the topic together through talk for learning: whole-group discussion and small-group discussion. These strategies organize the interaction between students while giving them a chance to think for themselves and relate their experience to the educational topic and make sense of it together with their peers. The power of these teaching strategies is only matched by the challenges they present to us in planning and delivering them effectively.

3.1 Whole-group discussion

How can we use group work to develop our students thinking and learning? Lipman and colleagues (2003) have developed the *Community of Enquiry* teaching technique that aims to encourage people to become better thinkers in collaboration with others. This technique has been used successfully in a number of FAVE settings. Lipman argues that this technique gives students the chance to practice three kinds of 'thinking'.

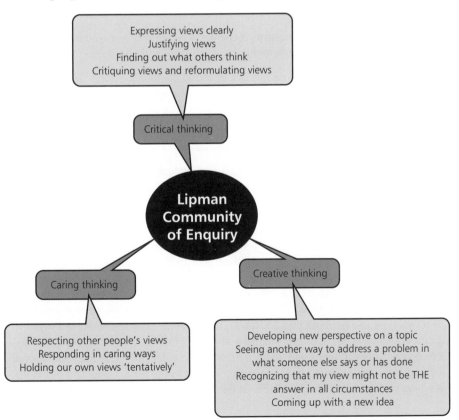

Figure 11.3 Opportunities for learning associated with Community of Enquiry (adapted from Lipman, 2003).

The idea of a community of enquiry has been developed into a set of steps very much like a recipe to develop group discussion. The advantage of this format is that it gives us a clear sequence of steps to follow – particularly useful when we want to try a new strategy out. Like all good cooks, we might choose to use only some of the steps, given the circumstances and what we judge to be achievable within the students' expectations and the time available.

Figure 11.4
Steps in planning
and facilitating
a community of
enquiry.

Steps in planning and facilitating a community of enquiry

Preliminaries – begin with all participants sitting in a circle. The facilitator attempts to create the right environment.

Stimulus – introduce the stimulus: a video clip, painting, poem, selected because in some way it explores the topic.

Thinking time and question-forming – use 'think, pair, share' to support students to develop a number of questions in response to the stimulus.

Airing and comparing questions – the teacher scribes the questions, asks for clarification of the thinking behind the questions.

Question choosing – students vote to pick the best question to focus their discussion.

Beginning enquiry – question reintroduced. They begin to tease out the issues behind the question.

Developing/reviewing the enquiry – a chance to widen and deepen thinking, to consider counter-examples, other different but related issues and questions.

End summarizing enquiry – each member of the community offers 'last words' on the topic. This is typically a sentence that sums up something that has stood out from the discussion for them.

(Adapted from Fisher, 2003)

The following case study offers some insights into the use of community of enquiry.

Case study 11.2 Louise's case study

Louise: I work with disengaged young people and I decided to try out a community of enquiry to encourage students to share their prior experience and their hopes for the future.

I wanted the group to discuss their experiences of education, to air and share their concerns. This was one session from a year-long informal programme that sought to help young people get back into education. I had already taught and worked with this group once a week for about six months and we had built up a good rapport. This was a diverse group of students with many different reasons for previously poor educational experiences. I was surprised by the students' interest in the subject area and found this teaching method had powerful effects on both the young people and myself.

When I came into the lesson and asked them to push all the tables back and form a circle, the group became very quiet. I told them I was going to show them a quick video and then we were going to have a discussion. They settled down, still very quiet.

I showed them a clip of Vicky Pollard from *Little Britain* (a British television programme) returning to her old school on stage in assembly. David Walliams played the teacher, interviewing her about her life. Vicky went through what had happened to her since leaving school – several children by different fathers, drug and alcohol issues and how much she hated school.

By the end of the clip the students were all laughing and joking. I asked them for a list of barriers to learning Vicky faced and they came up with almost all of them, 11 or 12 in total. They were really enjoying the process, although were still unsure of where it was leading them.

Once they had all the barriers to learning, I told them about the focus of the session. I sent them away for 4 minutes (2 minutes each) in pairs to discuss their experiences of school. This could have gone on for much longer. They really enjoyed having a safe space to discuss their own educational experiences and barriers to learning. Once this had finished, I asked each pair to come up with a question that we could discuss to enable me to find out how they felt about school and college. They came up with:

- Why do people feel out of place in school?
- Did you ever feel intimidated moving from school to college?
- How do you overcome prejudice/racism in school and college?

They voted for the second question and spent half an hour discussing it. Some of the discussion was so moving I was almost reduced to tears. They needed very little facilitation. They discussed bullying, lack of respect from teachers and how great it felt to be given a second chance. They discussed what they liked and didn't like about both school and college. Their responses were mature and measured and they were respectful of each other's feelings.

From start to finish this whole experience lasted one hour. It felt like we were in a bubble together, it felt like we had shared something real. I could see the lift that the entire experience had given the group as a whole and the individual students.

In this case study we see that opportunities are opened up for caring, critical and creative thinking. Thinking more carefully about their own experience and building trust in each other as a group of students made it possible for the students to speak out loud about their real experiences of education. It helped the students to identify some of the barriers to education the school system had put in their way, how personal circumstances had got in the way of studying, but also how they themselves had played an active part in disengaging from school. Finally, this activity opened up opportunities for the students to explore the idea of returning to studying full-time and what this might involve for them.

> ### Reflective activity 11.3
> **Planning to use a community of enquiry**
> With a colleague, read through Louise's case study and the steps in planning and facilitating a community of enquiry. Working together, identify a topic in your curriculum that demands higher-order thinking. Plan a community of enquiry around a key topic or concept. Also spend some time identifying what factors you need to look out for to help you evaluate the impact of the activity. If possible deliver your first communities of enquiry with a colleague. Then reflect together on the impact this strategy had and how it you could further develop your confidence in delivering a community of enquiry.

3.2 Question-and-answer in whole groups

As teachers we ask a great many questions and students enjoy, worry about or avoid answering them. Spending time reflecting on how to plan, deliver and manage a question-and-answer session will therefore have a big impact on your confidence and effectiveness as a teacher (Perrot, 1982, Reading 11.5; Alexander, 2008, Reading 11.4). It could also really help you to engage and include all of your students and give them the opportunity to build their understanding.

In order to reflect carefully about your current practice it is useful to look at the question-and-answer session in relation to three themes. These themes bring different aspects of question-and-answer sessions into sharp focus. They will help you to design your questions, plan how to organize a question-and-answer session and give a solid justification for what you are doing. When you then reflect back on what you have tried out, you will be in a better position to judge whether you achieved what you set out to achieve and explore why things went well or didn't go as expected and/or how they could be developed further.

The three ways to reflect upon question-and-answer sessions considered in this section are:

- The purpose behind asking questions.
- Crafting your questions.
- Making the most of your question-and-answer sessions.

The purpose behind asking the questions

Questions can be grouped in terms of many different purposes or functions. Biesta's three purposes of qualification, socialization and individualization give a clear set of domains that help us to think about questions (Biesta, 2011, Readings 1.1 and 8.4).

Questions that help students to achieve their qualifications

These questions relate to exploring and building confidence in the skills, attitudes, concepts and knowledge that are at the heart of achieving the formal qualification being studied.

- Questions to stimulate interest in a topic.
- Questions to find out what students already know about a topic.
- Questions to explore a particular curriculum topic or issue.
- Questions to structure the exploration of topic to build understanding.
- Questions that probe understanding and explore how understanding of the topic could have got sidetracked.
- Questions that give students the opportunity to reflect on information.

Questions that help students understand and explore their place in their vocation and social role as a student and member of a democratic community

- Questions to encourage students to think about values involved in their chosen specialism.
- Questions to encourage peer learning.
- Questions which centre on relationships between students or between a teacher and the students (e.g. 'How do you feel about doing this assignment?').
- Questions to find out what students know about how the vocational subject is practised or to help them explore their place in the group or as part of the college or professional community:
  - to encourage shy members to integrate by participating (e.g. 'Jan, you've got a new grandchild too, haven't you?')
  - to show interest in and value for group members (e.g. 'You had a good idea, Norita. Will you tell us?')
  - to develop respect for each others' views (e.g. 'What do you think you would have done?')

Questions that encourage students to think for themselves, develop their own voice as individuals

- Questions to explore the implications of an academic topic for how they think about their own lives.
- Questions that inspire wonder and ask students to imagine how things could be.

- Questions that encourage learners to build their individual skills as a scholar.
- Questions that allow students to express their individual ideas, views and interests.
- Questions that encourage students to reflect upon and develop or reconsider their own views.
- Questions to find out what students know.
- Questions to inspire students to be creative.

In the classroom, the use of question-and-answer will mostly concentrate on supporting students to build their understanding of the topics in order to achieve their qualifications. Reminding ourselves of the role question-and-answer can also play in helping to build understanding of social roles and to develop an individual voice helps us to reflect on how our classrooms can be rich places of education, not simply rote-learning.

3.3 Crafting questions

Key to crafting your questions so that they make sense to your students is being clear about the level of difficulty associated with them. When you have an idea of what answering the question involves, you will be better able to target your questions to students in ways that encourage participation, allowing everyone to achieve but also helping you to challenge and extend thinking. Being clear about the level of challenge associated with your questions can therefore help you to create an inclusive classroom where all are able to participate.

Adapting Bloom's taxonomy of educational objectives (cognitive domain) to the topic of questioning gives us a way to talk about the level of difficulty associated with the questions and is in the spirit of Bloom's original aim of improving 'communication and practice among educators' (Mosley et al., 2005). If you want to facilitate a relatively low-level educational experience, ask a simple question. Difficult questions demand more complicated responses and are likely to develop deeper educational experiences. There are times when you will want to ask simple, uncomplicated questions and others where you want to be more searching and promote deeper levels of responses from your students (see Chapter 10).

The following questions will help you craft your questions:

Questions for recall

At the recall level, use these stems to help you craft your questions:

- What happened after…?
- How many…?
- What is…?
- Who was it that…?

- Can you name...?
- Find the meaning of...
- Describe what happened after...
- Who spoke to...?
- Which is true or false...?

Questions for comprehension

At the comprehension level, use these stems to help you craft your questions:

- Can you write in your own words...?
- How would you explain...?
- Can you write a brief outline...?
- What do you think could have happened next...?
- Who do you think...?
- What was the main idea...?
- Can you clarify...?
- Can you illustrate...?
- Does everyone act in the way that...?

Questions for application

At the application level, use these stems to help you craft your questions:

- Do you know of another instance where...?
- Can you group by characteristics such as...?
- Which factors would you change if...?
- What questions would you ask of...?
- From the information given, can you develop a set of instructions about...?

Questions for analysis

At the analysis level, use these stems to help you craft your questions:

- Which of the three scenarios described is least likely to happen in the future?
- If ... happened, what might the ending have been?
- How is ... similar to...?
- What do you see as other possible outcomes?
- Why did ... changes occur?
- Can you explain what must have happened when...?

- What are some or the problems of…?
- Can you distinguish between…?
- What were some of the motives behind…?
- What was the turning point?
- What was the problem with…?

Questions for synthesis

At the synthesis comprehension level, use these stems to help you craft your questions:

- Can you design a … to…?
- Can you see a possible solution to…?
- If you had access to all resources, how would you deal with…?
- Why don't you devise your own way to…?
- What would happen if…?
- How many ways can you…?
- Can you create new and unusual uses for…?
- Can you develop a proposal which would…?

Questions for evaluation

At the evaluation level, use these stems to help you craft your questions:

- Is there a better solution to…?
- Judge the value of…
- What do you think about…?
- Can you defend your position about…?
- Do you think … is a good or bad thing?
- How would you have handled…?
- What changes to … would you recommend?
- Do you believe …?
- How would you feel if…?
- What are the pros and cons of…?
- Why is … of value?
- What are the alternatives?
- Who will gain and who will lose?

(Adapted from Pohl [2001] *Learning to Think, Thinking to Learn*)

> **Reflective activity 11.4**
>
> **Devising your own questions**
>
> With a colleague, where possible, use the prompts above develop a set of questions to help you teach a key topic. Try out the questions in your separate classrooms and then come back together to evaluate how well the questions worked to confirm learning, identify instances of misunderstanding that could then be corrected. How could you improve this group of questions further?

3.4 Making the most of question-and-answer sessions

It is all very well asking questions, but how do we ensure that everyone joins in? Below are seven practical techniques to help you include all students in question-and-answer sessions.

1) 'Quick-fire' question-and-answer sessions

These sessions can be fun, entertaining and unpredictable. The teacher fires off questions to students and works on the response to build the whole-class consideration of the topic. These sessions are also relatively unstructured and rely upon the teacher to respond quickly and sensibly. Thinking on your feet is invigorating. You should use 'no hands up' (see below) wherever possible. Even in these fairly freely structured sessions there are some important points to keep in mind and planning will help. Try to avoid Initiation/Response/Evaluation (IRE) pattern in a question-and-answer session (Teacher: 'Name one cause of WWII.' Student: 'Economic instability.' Teacher: 'Correct.') Instead use an Initiation/Response/Follow-Up (IRF) pattern to organize the discussion of questions and answers.

The Initiation/Response/Follow-Up pattern can be supported in the following ways:

- Question basketball – i.e. passing the question on: 'Joe, pick out one good element in Sarah's answer. What would you add?'

- Get more out of the initial response to the question: 'Can you say that in another way?', 'Can you say a bit more about that?', 'Could you give us an example?', 'Can you say why you think that?', 'Is that always the case?', 'I'm not sure I understand. Can you make it clearer?', 'Does this remind you of anything we found when we were studying…?'

- Invite students to collaborate in their individual answers to build whole-group understanding of an aspect of a topic. Start with an answer to a basic question and build on this: *'Say a little bit more about…'*, 'Can anyone else help?', 'Can we accept that answer?', 'How does that fit with your idea, Susan?', 'You've nearly got it. Can anyone else explain the last step?', 'Does that help us with…', 'Can we think of a better way to put that?'

- Echo – *'So you think that…'* You can use this to confirm learning. Or you can misunderstand on purpose to give students the chance to demonstrate further understanding by correcting your mistake.

- Non-verbal invitations: eye contact, tilt of the head, nod.
- Make a personal contribution from your own experience: *'I remember…'*
- Clarifying ideas makes the key point easier to grasp and encourages students to consider viewpoints: *'I can tell that is the case because…'*
- Make a suggestion: *'You could try…'*
- Reflect on topics: *' Yes, I sometimes think that…'*
- Offer information or make an observation on a topic: *'It might be useful to know that…'*
- Speculating on a given subject encourages students to explore ideas and understand that uncertainty is a normal stage in the thinking process.

The problem with quick-fire question-and-answer sessions is that the questions can often be met with silence, 'don't know', half-answers or incorrect answer. If you use 'hands up' to pick out a student to answer your question there is a real danger that you will end up ignoring half of the class and reinforcing student perceptions about who is clever and who is stupid.

2) Think, pair, group, share

Gibbs (1981) offers us a very useful formula to help teachers to encourage students to produce thoughtful answers to questions. He offers a series of stages in generating answers that teachers can follow to either generate answers from pairs or threes or small groups. Gibbs also puts forward a number of carefully crafted statements that teachers can use to help them to encourage careful thinking by students. The example below is adapted from a study skills programme and focuses on note-taking. You should think about how to adapt this approach to the teaching of your own subject specialism. The strength of Gibbs' approach is that it starts with student experience.

Figure 11.5
Think, pair, group, share activity.

Working alone (5 minutes)	Using the prompt sheet of statements. Mark the statements strongly agree, agree, disagree. Now adapt the statements so that they fit even more closely with what you think.
Working in pairs (10 minutes)	Working with your neighbour, compare your responses. Where do you agree/disagree? If you have responded differently, what are the reasons?
Working in fours (30 minutes)	Now form a group of four. Briefly see where you agree/disagree. Does this matter? Are there ways in which members of your group cope that you are not aware of? Jot down any interesting or important points for the plenary.
Plenary (15 minutes)	Each group to pick one statement you thought particularly important and tell the group what emerged from your discussion.

3) Random student selector system: No hands up!
Black and Wiliam (1998b, 2002) stress the importance of including all students in question-and-answer sessions. They suggest a simple, cost-effective way to randomly select students to answer questions, by writing their names on lollipop sticks. Picking out a stick from the pot provides the name of the student who will be asked to answer the question.

Five ways of using random name selection:

● Pick one name at a time.

● Pick two names at a time.

● Get the students to pick a name.

● Pick a name after you have asked the question (truly random).

● Pick names before you ask the question (then aim 'right level' question at the learners picked).

There is an app called 'stick pick' which undertakes this activity.

4) All-student response systems: Mini white boards. Red cards/Yellow cards/Green cards.
Black and Wiliam also promote the use of whole-group response systems. Mini white boards allow all students to answer a question at the same time. All can see the variety of answers. Teachers can assess the level of learning, students can learn from each other.

Four ways to use mini white boards:

● Students work individually to write an answer on the mini white board.

● Students work in pairs to come up with an answer presented on one white board.

● Use mini white boards as multiple choice answer recorders: A, B, C, D.

● Students draw a cartoon to represent a key idea.

5) Concept cartoons
Students are given a choice between different possible answers and are asked to vote for the option they prefer and justify their choice. The concept cartoon works to focus the small-group discussion. They help students to explore views without personally being associated with them. (See Figure 11.6)

6) Students come up with questions to ask each other or the teacher
As we have discussed in Chapter 2, a social constructivist view of learning would advocate learners taking a more active role by initiating discussion, asking questions and making the learning their own. Strategies for organizing talk in ways that provide students with more space in which to initiate, extend and elaborate personal meanings are important. It is often difficult to engage, motivate and include large groups of students in a single discussion.

Encouraging students to formulate and ask questions for themselves and each other can help to include all learners. But students need guidance and practice in asking questions. You could use a simplified version of Bloom's taxonomy to help students ask their own questions. You could use the questions suggested above to help students.

Figure 11.6
Example: concept
cartoon.

7) Round-up statements

This is a useful questioning activity for use at the end of a session. It allows you to capture the most significant thing each student has learned in the session. The fact that members of the group might repeat what others have said prior to their turn can be seen as an advantage as it serves to remind everyone of what that main point is. Follow the steps set out below.

1 Tell the group that they will be asked to give an individual summary in no more than of couple of sentences that sum up the most significant thing they have learned in the session.

2 Tell the group that you will go round the group one person at a time and they will have the opportunity to share what they have found to be most important with the group.

3 Give the group a couple of minutes' silent thinking time by themselves about what they are going to say.

4 Ask each individual to share their summary with the group.

5 Give yourself a minute or two at the end of this summary activity to confirm the main point and possibly make links to the next session.

You might find a student does not want to contribute. You may choose to let this pass or you may wish to come back to the student at the end of the statements and ask them to say which has been the most frequently stated point.

Reflective activity 11.5

Practical techniques using question-and-answer to include all students

Reflecting on the learners you teach and the upcoming topics you have to teach, review the techniques outlined above to help you use question-and-answer to include all learners. Identify one strategy that seems to fit well with the group of learners and the session you will be teaching. Try the questioning strategy out and reflect on its impact.

---

4 Working with small groups

Small-group discussion typically occurs in groups of four and six learners. These small groups are then given a task to complete. The small-group discussions commonly lead on to a whole-group plenary discussion where the small groups feedback the outcomes of their discussions. This plenary is normally led by the teacher. This plenary discussion gives the teacher a chance to draw out the main themes and issues relating to topic of session while checking and confirming student understanding (Hamilton and Hillier, 2006, Reading 9.1).

Your main task in planning, delivering and assessing these small-group activities is creating an environment where high-quality discussion has room to develop. When students work in small groups they have the opportunity to discuss what a topic means, express views about it and learn from each other (peer learning). They can also address each other's misconceptions and challenge 'easy' answers. This small-group environment can be a safe place to collaboratively build understanding. Small-group discussion can be a powerful way to help students work toward achieving their qualifications, building their confidence in the social 'skills' of co-operation and developing an identity in the social role of being a scholar. It can also contribute to the student's development of their own voice – a voice that is heard and respected by others.

In this section we investigate small-group discussion in order to help you make the most of the possibilities for education that this way of teaching can open up. First we set out the structure and process of small-group discussion. This will help you to plan your small-group discussion activity. Second, we look briefly at the kinds of justification you can give for using small-group discussion in your lesson plan rationale. Finally we look at focused evaluation of your small-group discussion work. This will help you to look carefully at areas where discussion can go wrong and help you to begin to think how these difficulties can be addressed.

4.1 Structure and process

You can look at small-group discussion as being structured by four explicit and sequential stages: exposition and topic introduction, organization and task introduction, small-group action and plenary reflection. Figure 11.7 may help you to learn each stage in terms of your resource preparation, your input and the work of your students.

Figure 11.7
Structure of a
small-group
discussion.
(Developed from
Avon Collaborative
Learning Project
[Avon County
Council, 1993]).

Exposition and topic introduction
In the up-front exposition the teacher introduces the key concepts or ideas to be explored in the small-group discussions.

May use video, demonstration or examples of some kind.

Organization and task introduction
The teacher:

- introduces the small-group discussion task to the whole class.
- introduces the particular task that each small group will discuss.
- splits the whole group into small groups (mixed ability, friendship or random).
- introduces support, stimulus materials.
- gives a clear idea of the expected output from the small-group discussion to feedback to the whole group.

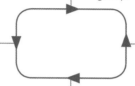

Plenary reflection
The plenary review gives students the chance to share the outputs from their discussion of the topic with the whole class.

This collaborative space gives the teacher and students a chance to review the outputs. The teacher can stress the important aspects of what is said and build on this, where relevant relating this to assessment tasks.

Small-group action
In this phase the students work on the task set. The task should stimulate focused discussion among the small group.

The teacher can circulate around the groups supporting and monitoring the discussion.

4.2 Benefits of small-group discussion

Why use small-group discussion? Benefits could include:

- Developing understanding of a concept.
- Making links between the concept and everyday experience.
- Giving students the space to express themselves.
- Practising respect for others, encouraging others, nurturing not criticizing ideas.
- Learning to tolerate opposition to individual opinions.
- Learning to collaborate: actively listen, turn-taking.

- Reaching a shared answer that can be justified.
- Communicating clearly and concisely.

Even if we are clear about the benefits of small-group discussion, there are a number of factors which may prevent this being successful. For example, we may have created a pleasant diversion from learning where people get together and have a lovely chat but not about the topic in question! The aim of the activity or indeed the instructions and resources to undertake the activity may not be clear to your students. Your students may not be confident in working in this way, or there may be some students who do not participate and others who dominate. One way to evaluate your use of small-group working is to consider the following:

Reflective activity 11.6

In order to help you reflect on the way students work together in small-group activities you can ask them to consider their own contributions. Use a self-assessment exercise to focus the reflection of your students. The resulting discussion can help you reflect on how you could develop and support small group working. To support this process the following questions could be useful:

- How well did I try to include others?
- How well did I listen to other people's ideas?
- How well did I express my feelings?
- How well did I share my feelings?
- How well did I show respect for other people's ideas and feelings?
- Did I ask questions?
- Did I use an appropriate level of voice?
- Did I disagree with others without putting them down?

In my opinion today's discussion was…
I think I was…
Next time I would like to…

Conclusion

In this chapter we have looked at what we mean by the use of the term pedagogy. One of the lessons to draw from our consideration of pedagogy is how when one aspect of pedagogy comes to dominate all others, practice becomes thin and limiting. Overemphasizing knowledge can result in rote learning; overemphasizing student needs can reduce education to a kind of self-preoccupied, feel-good therapy; an overemphasis on situated learning can lead to narrow limited and isolated learning. For student teachers or teachers who find themselves thrown into a FAVE context at the deep end, in situations where such distortions are already at work, reflecting on pedagogy offers a way to look critically at what is happening and see how pedagogy might be developed to open up richer educational opportunities.

The fact that pedagogy is something we do means that our practice is already tangled up in constraints and opportunities. Robert's case study showed how ordinary experience can be enriched when pedagogy brings together students' everyday skills to address real-world tasks. Our case studies illustrate the importance of reflecting carefully on our pedagogical practice and shows what is important. It asks us to consider how we will match up the experience of students with topics and the way they are taught. Finally, the discussion in this chapter has demonstrated the importance of carefully considering the challenges our pedagogy will need to negotiate or confront. These might include student attitudes to education acquired in the past or the unrealistic expectations of policy. The possibility of pedagogy opening up educational opportunities will be enhanced by our careful reflection. It is these reflections that help us to plan what we do, justify our decisions, help us reflect on what has happened and what we should choose to do next.

Throughout this chapter we have drawn attention to the role that a careful consideration of what is to be taught and what is to be learnt must play in our professional practice. We have shown how consideration of what is to be learnt affects people's lives in many important ways including learning in preparation for work, for family life and for health and well-being. We have also argued that we must consider not only the pedagogic content of our teaching sessions but also the emotional aspect of working with our learners. Finally, we have drawn attention to the importance of enabling our students to be independent and autonomous, i.e. actively taking responsibility for their own learning.

Key readings

Vocational and subject-specialist pedagogy

TLRP's overall findings, including 'ten principles for effective teaching and learning'. These are discussed in Chapter 4 of this book. For a simple explanation of the idea of pedagogy seen as science, craft and art, and an exposition of 'conceptual tools' for tackling enduring educational issues, see:

> Pollard, A. (ed.) (2010) *Professionalism and Pedagogy: A Contemporary Opportunity.* London: TLRP.

Alexander offers a detailed consideration of pedagogy that builds on Simon's initial discussion of the lack of pedagogy in the UK:

> Alexander, R. J. (2008) *Essays on Pedagogy.* Abingdon: Routledge, 109–13. (Reading 11.4)

> Simon, B. (1981) 'Why no Pedagogy in England?'. In B. Simon and W. Taylor (eds) *Education in the Eighties: The Central Issues.* London: Batsford, 128–40. (Reading 11.2)

Bruner offers an account of how the culture of educational institutions is shaped by and helps to shape the boarder culture:

> Bruner, J. S. (1996) *The Culture of Education*. Cambridge, MA: Harvard University Press, 45–50. **(Reading 11.1)**

Vocational education has multiple purposes and potentials. Further reading for this topic can be found in the following texts:

> Bathmaker, A. M. (2014) '"Applied", "technical" and "vocational": Constructions of knowledge in vocational education'. BERA PCLL event (BERA.ac.uk) **(Reading 11.6)**
> CAVTL (2012) Extract from *Report on Vocational Education.* **(Reading 11.3)**
> Pring, R. (1999) *Closing the Gap: Liberal Education and Vocational Preparation.* London: Hodder and Stoughton.
> Sennett, R. (2008) *The Craftsman.* London: Allen Lane.

Lipman offers a detailed account of the theoretical commitments behind community of enquiry. Fisher offers a more direct consideration of the practical steps to take to make community of enquiry work in the classroom:

> Fisher, R. (2013) *Teaching Thinking: Philosophical Enquiry in the Classroom.* London: Bloomsbury, 2–26. **(Reading 2.4)**
> Lipman, M. (2003) *Thinking in Education*. Cambridge: Cambridge University Press.

The readings below offer a more detailed consideration of the use of question-and-answer:

> Black, P. and Wiliam, D. (2002) *Working Inside the Black Box: Assessment for Learning in the Classroom.* London: King's College.
> Gibbs, G. (1981) *Teaching Students to Learn: A Student-Centred Approach*. Milton Keynes: Open University Press.
> Perrot, E. (1982) *Effective Teaching: A Practical Guide to Improving Your Teaching.* London: Longman, 56–91. **(Reading 11.5)**

In one way or another, most of Reflective Teaching's chapters are concerned with pedagogy. For readings on more specific issues – such as relationships, engagement, behaviour, assessment, etc. – please consult the relevant chapter.

The associated website, **reflectiveteaching.co.uk**, offers a wealth of supplementary resources including reflective activities, research briefings, advice on further reading and downloadable diagrams, figures and checklists from the book. It also features a compendium of educational terms, links to useful websites, policy and curriculum documents, and showcases examples of excellent research and practice.

Communication
How does language support learning?

12

Introduction

> Whatever else people do when they come together – whether they play, fight, make love or make automobiles – they talk. We live in a world of language … Hardly a moment of our waking lives is free from words, even in our dreams we talk and are talked to … The possession of language, perhaps more than any other attribute, distinguishes humans from other animals. According to the philosophy expressed in the myths and religions of many peoples, language is the source of human life and power. (Fromkin et al., 2013: 1)

Through the means of spoken, written and symbolic language, in songs, symbols, stories, dance and drama, our ancestors have passed on to us what they believed in, what they feared, what they hoped for, what they could do and what they knew. Language has therefore helped us to acquire the knowledge and skills we needed in the past. It will no doubt play an important part in the acquisition of the knowledge and skills we need now and will need in the future (Duncan, 2012, **Reading 12.1**).

TLRP principles

Three TLRP principles are relevant to this chapter:

Principle 3: Effective teaching and learning recognizes the importance of prior experience and learning. Teaching and learning should take account of what the learner knows already in order to plan their next steps. This includes building on personal and cultural experiences of different groups of learners.

Principle 4: Effective teaching and learning requires teachers to scaffold learning. Teachers should provide activities which support learners as they move forward, not just intellectually but also socially and emotionally, so that once these supports are removed, learning is secure.

Principle 8: Effective teaching and learning recognizes the significance of informal learning. Informal learning, such as learning outside of college and other formal educational settings, should be recognized as at least as significant as formal learning and should therefore be valued and used appropriately in formal processes.

The Russian psychologist Vygotsky (1986) draws attention to the important connections which exist between our language and our thinking. The Austrian philosopher Wittgenstein (1922) argues that the limits of our language mean the limits of our world. However as Geertz (1985) reminds us, to accept as a starting point that the limits of our language mean the limits of our world is not to suggest that the reach of our minds, of what we can say, think, appreciate and judge, is trapped within the borders of our society, our country, our class or our time. On the contrary, it is to see that the reach of our minds, the range of signs we 'manage to interpret is what defines the intellectual, emotional, and moral space within which we live' (Geertz, 1985: 263).

Language also has important links to inclusion (see Chapter 15). The more we can imagine and understand 'other worlds' and what it might be like to be other people, the clearer we become to ourselves, both in terms of what we see in others that seems remote to us, as well as that which we see in others that seems familiar (Geertz, 1985).

This chapter is about communication and what it means for each of us as teachers and learners. It will try to capture the language that is part of how we teach and learn: the interactions, the conversations, the reading and the writing. We will argue that language is both *how* we teach and *what* we teach. This is crucial: language is part of whatever we teach – whether plastering or Persian poetry – whether we are explicitly aware of it or not. This chapter explores how we use language in learning and teaching and what we, as teachers, need to *know* about language. We argue that *all* teachers need to know something about language, not because we need to become expert language teachers, but because language is part of learning.

We will examine 'speaking and listening', literacy development, language variety and multilingualism. This chapter will also introduce the term *foregrounding* to describe the act of highlighting and developing language in the teaching of any subject.

1 Language

Every page of this book offers, in one form or another, definitions, explanations or demonstrations of learning in a wide variety of FAVE contexts. The act of defining or understanding learning is endless. Language is no simpler to pin down. Languages are systems of communication, where signs represent meaning. Language is collaborative, follows structures and systems of organization and is infinitely generative; signs, symbols, gestures or words can be put into an infinite number of combinations, making language mind-blowingly creative. Language pre-exists each one of us and plays an integral part in socialization, and yet language is also influenced, reformed, recreated by individual use. We are thus both created *by* and creators *of* language. Many linguists (and non-linguists) see our humanity as located in our language use.

Whenever we talk about learning, therefore, we are talking about learning in our world of language. Language is how we develop, express, exchange, debate and record ideas. It is how we develop thoughts alone or in groups. It is how we communicate with others sitting together or separated by miles, years or millennia. Language is how we form, understand, represent and negotiate our identities. A teacher conceptualizes and plans using language and then puts that plan into action using language: making statements, modelling and demonstrating, asking questions, giving instructions, using written materials, generating discussions, asking for feedback, assessing learning, making announcements, organizing activities, reading and writing on student work. Students may listen, read, speak and write, processing meanings, understanding implications, drawing conclusions and recording ideas in words and sentences. Students make, annotate, and share notes and have conversations. All this (and so much more) means that there are things we can and should be doing in our teaching to ensure that the way we use language to communicate the subjects we teach lights up our 'classrooms' and engages, inspires and instils a passion for learning the subject, as well as providing an initiation into particular ways of thinking about and 'doing' the subject. However, how we develop language in the wide variety of FAVE contexts in which we teach can become (often inadvertently) constrained by the policy, funding and prescribed practice (Gregson and Nixon, 2011, **Reading 12.2**).

Reflective activity 12.1

Speaking and listening

Think back to the last time you taught or, if you are new to teaching, the last time you were in a teaching session as a student. Imagine you are there now, watching the session. Who is speaking and to whom are they speaking? Who else is speaking? When does the teacher speak and why? When do students speak and why? Try to trace the patterns of speaking and listening. Imagine a ball of wool being unravelled, starting from the first person you heard speak and linking them to the person or people they were addressing, and then from that person to the next. Perhaps there are many different balls of wool being unravelled, of different colours, as several different conversations or patterns of speaking and listening play out at once. Perhaps you don't hear anything at all, but are looking at people communicating using British Sign Language or other types of sign language. Perhaps you are D/deaf or hearing-impaired yourself and are used to reading 'speaking and listening' and understanding it to mean patterns of communication whether 'voiced' or not.

How can we understand 'speaking and listening' in learning environments? We have already started this discussion of group work in Chapter 11, and the analysis of questions and questioning in Chapters 10 and 13. Here, we will look at four aspects of 'speaking and listening' in learning: deaf awareness, learning through conversation, giving instructions and teacher listening.

1.1 Deaf awareness

We have put 'speaking and listening' in inverted commas to remind ourselves that not everyone can talk or hear. Many D/deaf or hearing-impaired people hold conversations through British Sign Language or other regionally based forms of sign language (such as American Sign Language or Australian Sign Language). These are different languages but share features: they are all languages that use space and the movement of face, head, hands and body. They are not versions of, or based on, English, but are distinct languages with, for example, completely different grammars. Some deaf or hearing-impaired people lip-read – that is, watching the movements of a speaker's mouth to understand conversations in English – and some deaf or hearing-impaired people use speech.

One way, then, that we can understand 'speaking and listening' in learning environments is to remember that there are many different ways to communicate, and a teacher needs to be prepared for them all. Overall, most D/deaf teachers recommend that when working with D/deaf learners, start by asking them what they need. This may include working with a sign language interpreter, who may need to position themselves carefully in the room between you and the learners, or at times may need to be closer to the learners, or this may include reminding everyone to face a lip-reading learner, and not cover their mouth, when speaking to them. It may mean reminding everyone to address the D/deaf learners and not their signer. We will return to this in Chapter 15. For now, we need to remember that speaking and listening or conversation happens differently for different people.

1.2 Learning through conversation: A reading circle model

Much of the discussion on group work (see Chapters 10 and 11) presents an idea of learning through conversation in pairs, small groups or larger groups, discussing, collaborating, and negotiating our way to new understandings. Research on reading circles in adult literacy education (Duncan, 2012) argues that when people get together to talk about a book, they are not simply telling each other about conclusions they have already drawn, but rather they are drawing conclusions as they talk together. Crucially, they are developing understandings and forming interpretations as they are talking to each other, through their conversation ('*What did you think she meant by that*?' '*Was she trying to put him down*'?). This means that people engaged in reading circles are not only talking *about* their reading together, but they are doing some of the interpretative work of reading together. They are reading *collaboratively*; they are learning through talking.

Harvey and Daniels (2009) argue for a reading or 'inquiry' circle model across the curriculum. They observe that working in small, peer-led, dialogue-based groups encourages greater learner autonomy, increased engagement and deeper understanding. Specialists in compulsory schooling (like Harvey and Daniels) argue that an inquiry/ reading circle approach develops the social skills of the participants. We could also argue that this kind of autonomous, small-group, discussion-based approach is a particularly adult way of learning because it involves self-management, draws on existing experience/ expertise, and encourages peer teaching and learning.

1.3 Giving instructions

Think back to the last time you gave instructions in a teaching session. How did you do it? Did they achieve what you wanted them to achieve? We asked five experienced teachers to share their strategies with us and this is what they said:

- **Be clear yourself what you want students to do**. Think through the details. If you are giving instructions for a small-group activity, how many people in each group? What do you want them to do? How long will you give them? How do you want to organize feedback? Do you want them all to write something or just one person? Think about all these details ahead of time, before you start giving instructions.

- **Plan in advance what you are going to say and the order in which you will say it**. For example, do you want people to read a task and then find a partner? Or find a partner and read the task with the partner? Be careful of asking students to do something while you are still giving instructions – they will be moving around and may not hear the rest of what you have to say. You might want to give instructions in small stages. For example: 'Find a partner.' Then wait for them to find partners before continuing: 'Now compare your notes.'

- **Say as little as possible**. Imagine a teacher standing up and giving these instructions: *'Now I think I'd like you to find a partner. Yes, look around and find someone. It could be anyone. I really want you to find a partner. Come on, it could be anyone. We've done this recently. And when you have managed to find someone, yes that's right, that's what I'm saying, you need to get your sheets of notes out of your bags ... get them out, and compare them, compare your notes with each other. I want you to look at what you have and compare them ...'* These instructions could be confusing, particularly for less-confident English speakers or those using a BSL interpreter. The key messages are hidden in waffle. Instructions like this are also likely to encourage students to switch off; too much is being said of too little importance. Using simple sentences and the imperative tense – for example: 'Find a partner', 'Discuss the key issue', Compare your notes' – is much more likely to be effective.

- **Provide written or other visual back-up for spoken/signed instructions**. Some students will find it hard to follow even pared-down instructions. Written instructions displayed on a PowerPoint presentation, a whiteboard, on handouts or cards can help. This can also support literacy and language development by helping to identify core vocabulary and specialist language and spelling.

- **No matter how clear you think your instructions are, some students may be unsure.** Make sure you observe and monitor student activity carefully to check and clarify any areas of apparent confusion or uncertainty.

- **Some teachers like to check that their oral instructions have been understood by asking a member of the group to recap the instructions to the group.** This can allow you to assess understanding of the instructions and provide further reinforcement (repetition) of the instructions.

In many teaching situations it is not only teachers who give instructions. Students will also sometimes need to give instructions and we can help them develop this vital communication skill by modelling good practice ourselves and/or critically examining a set of guidelines such as those above.

1.4 Teacher listening

There is a lot written about teacher talk, but less about teacher listening. Yet listening (or watching, in the case of lip-readers or users of sign language) is one of the most important teaching skills. A teacher needs to hear (or notice) as much as possible about what is going on in the room. This is an aspect of 'withitness' (Chapter 7), of being in control of the environment. It sounds easy. Listen carefully, focus, be alert, but what happens if …

a) One student makes a homophobic comment to another. You don't hear but both students think you did.

b) You ask a question. One student offers the correct answer several times. You don't hear, but then you do hear another student and praise this student for having the correct answer.

Both have the potential for serious repercussions. In the first situation, both students may think you condone this behaviour, encouraging the perpetrator and further diminishing the victim. In the second, the student who first offered the correct answer may feel victimized and discouraged, may be less likely to respond in the future, and may even lose interest in the course.

Yet, how do we avoid these? Simply by practice or experience? Perhaps. However it is also about how we move around a teaching space, how we concentrate, how we get to know our students. Teacher listening also relates to ground rules and discipline (see Chapters 6 and 7): the more everyone is used to conventions of ordered turn-taking, the better chance a teacher has of hearing and allowing students to know when and how they can be heard.

Sheeba Faisal, a student teacher on a post-compulsory teacher education course, wrote about this issue in a piece of reflective writing:

Case study 12.1 Responding to students' answers

This stems from the feedback I received from my tutor after my first observation. Her feedback on my use of questioning techniques really stood out for me. This is because before that I never really thought about it, what I was doing wrong when learners were responding to my questions. Her comments were as follows:

> Be careful of when you reformulate or repeat learners' answers for the benefit of the others – this can be effective but you must be clear that they gave the right answer in the first place. Several times, after you reformulated a response, the learner muttered 'that's what I said', and seemed offended, as if they thought that you were implying they gave the wrong answer and you were giving the correct one. Clarify by saying something like: 'Exactly, excellent answer, did you all hear what X said?' This can make a huge difference to how cooperative groups are. (Observation 1 Feedback)

As I read her comments I realized what I was doing wrong – I was not praising or acknowledging the learners' correct answers and so they did not know whether they were right or not.

Sheeba wrote later about how she tried to reformulate or repeat students' responses less and instead acknowledged them as correct or useful responses and, if she felt the others hadn't heard, asked the students to repeat their responses themselves.

Reflective activity 12.2

In section 1, on the ways we use language, we have explored a number of topics: deaf awareness, learning through conversation, giving instructions, teacher listening. Thinking about your own working context, identify the theme that is most relevant to developing your practice. Reread the section and identify one suggestion that you could use to further develop your use of language. In relation to one of your teaching sessions, plan to try out the recommendation in practice. Remember to make time to review the impact of this change after this session.

---

2 Literacy: Reading and writing

Literacy (reading and writing) is an aspect of language. In English, as in many languages, just as we can say or hear words, we can write or read them and pass them on to someone far away from us, in time or place. The majority of the world's population now lives in literate societies, which means that reading and writing texts of all kinds is an integral part of how we operate socially, culturally, politically and, many would argue, cognitively. To say we live in a literate society means written texts are everywhere and highly valued. It does not, however, mean that everyone can read or write, or that everyone reads and writes to the same degree, in the same way, or in the same contexts.

Over the past hundred years literacy expectations have risen dramatically in much of the world. In many parts of the world (including Britain) the cultural expectation is that all children are taught to read and write and so the assumption is that all adults are able to read and write. However, many adults cannot read and write, and many more cannot read and write to the 'levels' expected at the end of compulsory schooling. The expectation of universal literacy means that those who read and write less than most are considered to have literacy problems or difficulties (Brandt, 2001). Literacy difficulties are sometimes attributed to cognitive disorders or learning disabilities and sometimes to the 'failure' of schools or society. These can certainly be factors: learning difficulties or disabilities can affect literacy use and learning, and schools, families and societies can indeed 'fail' children by not providing them with adequate support, opportunity or methods to learn to read and write.

Yet this view still hides what is most important: that our minds simply seem to work quite differently when it comes to processing and producing written language. Some people would learn to read and write with no instruction at all, some need more support, and for some people learning to read and write is a lifelong struggle (Duncan, 2012, Reading 12.1). We are different, just as we are different when it comes to hand–eye coordination or perception of musical pitch. For hundreds of years people have learnt to read at different ages, in different contexts, and using different methods. For literacy teachers this means we have to keep thinking of ways to help both children and adults learn to read and write. For the organization of adult education, this means that we will always need provision in adult literacy, no matter how effective schools are at teaching children to read and write, because some people will miss bits of schooling and others will need a bit longer to learn. And for any teacher in the FAVE sector, this means that the students in our classes will have dramatically different literacy confidences, experiences, strengths and development needs. We cannot assume that reading and writing is easy or straightforward for anyone or everyone.

So, how can we understand literacy development needs? The English adult literacy national core curriculum (Adult Literacy Core Curriculum, 2001) divides literacy into three aspects: word, sentence and text. Word-level includes spelling, decoding individual words and handwriting or use of keyboards. Sentence-level includes punctuation and syntax, and text-level includes overall communicative coherence of the text, paragraphing, grasp of genre and critical reading. Though the word, sentence and text levels certainly overlap, many adult literacy teachers find this way of conceptualizing literacy valuable for reminding us of just how much literacy involves. For example, rather than looking at a piece of writing and noticing spelling errors, as many of us tend to do, we are reminded to think about what the writer is doing at the level of the sentence and text as well as how well the writer is using linking words, or addressing a particular audience (Hughes and Schwab, 2010). This could be called a skills-based approach, as the word/sentence/text-level division can be seen as breaking literacy down into a set of skills to be mastered. As an approach it has been criticized for the way in which it can reduce the acquisition of language down to tick lists of instrumental skills developed, demonstrated and relentlessly assessed through the overuse of worksheets (death by worksheet!).

Another way of understanding literacy is to see it as a social or cultural practice – that is, something which is part of social life, something done differently by different people and in different contexts. Rather than seeing literacy as a set of skills located within the individual, this view positions literacy as a highly contextualized and variable social practice (Barton, 2007; Barton, Hamilton and Ivanic, 2000). We read and write for different purposes, in different ways and in widely different contexts.

Let's look at reading and writing more closely, to think about what they involve and how they feature in our teaching.

2.1 Reading

Reading is making sense of written language. It is decoding a written code, turning marks on the page (or the screen, or a wall, or a scroll) into sounds, words, meanings, emotion, knowledge, communication. Reading can be giving voice to written words, sentences, texts, and it can be understanding, thinking about or acting on those words, sentences and texts. Remembering the word/sentence/text-level division, we read words by looking at individual letters, groups of letters or whole words and turning these into sounds and/or meaning. Sentence and text-level reading is about putting these words together to create larger meanings. Sentence and text-level reading involves acts of interpretation

– interpreting, for example, that 'she' means the young woman described two paragraphs earlier, or that a sign left on a door saying 'I have gone to find you. I will be right back' means 'Stay here!'.

Reading can make us smile or cry. It can be how we communicate with those far from us in time and place, how we learn (and teach), how we escape and dream, how we can be alone or in communion with others. Reading is a way we can *be* other people, if for just a few hours or even minutes, and how we can understand others better. It is something we do with our brains, our minds, our hearts, our families, our communities. It is something we can do alone or in groups, silently or aloud. It has been argued that reading is therefore a cognitive act, a communicative act, an educational act, an affective act and an imaginative act (Duncan, 2012). Our reading practices vary greatly. Think of all the reading you have done today. This may include bills, instructions on a bottle of medicine, a train schedule, a text, an email or a chapter from a novel.

2.2 Writing

Writing could be seen as the other side of the reading coin: producing those marks on the page, forming those letters, chunks of letters, words, sentences and texts. Word-level writing includes spelling and handwriting or keyboard/texting skills, sentence-level includes word order and use of punctuation, and text-level includes the coherence and cohesion of the entire text as a piece of communication. Text-level writing also includes engagement with a particular audience, register, appropriate vocabulary and genre or text-type: are we writing a report or a poem? A formal letter or a short story? Writing is recording and writing is composing. 'Writing a book' is different from 'writing down my address' largely because of the level of cognitive demand and the extent to which the writing is complex, original or creative.

Reflective activity 12.3

Reading and writing in your teaching

Think of the very last session you have taught or attended as a student, and identify ALL the reading involved. Include what you read from a board, from the walls, handouts, other instructions, reading silently and aloud. Just think of what happens in the session. Make a list. Now add anything that was assigned as homework. Now add anything else to do with the logistics or administration of the course. Is it more or less than you thought?

Now do the same for writing.

Does this mean we teach reading and writing?

Adult literacy teachers spend a lot of time developing their skills in teaching reading and writing, in working with adults with varying degrees of confidence and experience in reading and writing. Most have undertaken specialist teacher training (see Hughes and

Schwab, 2010). But what about other teachers – those of us who teach Chinese or history, hairdressing or construction, those of us with classrooms filled with reading and writing: are we teachers of reading and writing? One answer is 'no', of course we are not literacy teachers; we are teachers of Chinese or history, hairdressing or construction. Another answer is, well 'yes', we are teachers of the reading and writing which is part of teaching Chinese or history, hairdressing or construction.

If we think about it, we may find that these are the same answers. We teach our subjects and this means teaching the reading and writing (and speaking and listening) which is already part of our subjects, our teaching and our assessment. This kind of language work is sometimes called embedding, to emphasize the idea that one set of skills (for example word-level reading) is part of the practice of a vocational subject (for example hairdressing). We have chosen not to use the term embedding here because of how this approach to language development was reduced to highly instrumental mapping of skills onto lesson plans for the purposes of inspection/internal auditing. In this book we are not interested in the act of adding or inserting one set of skills into another, but rather bringing to the fore what is already there, but often ignored or unseen. We are calling this foregrounding.

2.3 Foregrounding literacy

Foregrounding means *noticing* all the reading and writing involved in our teaching (including assessment); *not assuming* that everyone finds reading or writing easy or straightforward; *being explicit* about what is required, highlighting important steps to success, particularly around literacy conventions (how does a report have to be structured?); and developing reading and writing skills and practices as appropriate. In this way, we can develop the reading and writing skills and practices which are already within the subjects we are teaching and the ways we are assessing. Let's look at some case studies of how teachers have done this.

Case study 12.2 Improving spelling – suggested strategies

Miriam teaches sociology on an Access to Education course at a large FE college. When marking the students' first assignments, she noticed that the majority of the group made quite a few spelling errors, some with new, specialized vocabulary and some with more day-to-day works (like 'necessary' or 'privilege'). After speaking to several colleagues, both Access tutors and literacy specialists, Miriam decided to start each session with a five-minute 'spelling strategies' starter/activity. At the beginning Miriam led the sessions herself, initially distributing a list of words which students had misspelt in assignments (no names, just words) and asking them to learn to spell the top ten for the next week. She started the week with a spelling quiz and then asked the group how they had learnt the words. This generated three different spelling strategies: 1) writing the words ten times each; 2) asking a friend or partner to quiz them orally; and 3) writing the words on post-its displayed above the sink in the kitchen and next to the medicine cabinet in

---

the bathroom. Miriam encouraged each learner to choose one of these strategies and try it as a way to learn the next five words on their group list. Gradually, as the weeks went by, they gathered and explored over 12 different strategies and found that some learners prefer using the same strategy all the time, while others use a different strategy depending on the nature of the word (preferring, for example, to divide up long Latinate words – like communication – into syllables, com- mu- ni- ca- tion [* there are different ways to divide this word; some would divide it as 'comm- u- ni- ca- tion]). As the weeks went by, there was also a shift from Miriam managing their spelling work each week to different students volunteering to take the lead. The students continued to compile the lists of words they wanted to learn to spell.

This is an example of a teacher foregrounding word-level writing skills (spelling). The teacher noticed that she was requiring them to spell words and that most learners had difficulties. She was explicit about the importance of spelling as part of any academic or professional activity ('there are always more specialist words to learn') and she worked with the students to develop this skill – and develop the study skills required for them to continue developing this skill independently.

Case study 12.3 Identifying difficulties with literacy requirements 1

Teacher educators Izabella and Nicolai work on an in-service post-compulsory teacher training course. They have noticed that the literacy requirements of the course's assessment (the written assignments) are more demanding – or different – from the literacy requirements for the rest of the course participation (reading texts, writing lesson plans, creating resources, etc.). They are also aware that many trainee teachers on the course have not studied at an HE level before or have studied in a context with greatly different conventions for written assignments (for example, a science degree in England or a literature degree in Latin America). They identified two key areas of difficulty: synthesis of theory and classroom experience, and referencing. They decided to foreground synthesis by providing models of assignments with effective synthesis and asked trainees to identify and debate characteristics of effective synthesis. They then asked trainees to compare this literacy skill with their existing experience and identify areas to develop individually, in pairs or in further sessions. This was an hour-long session, part of their normal teaching time, just after they introduced the new assignment. Izabella and Nicolai decided to organize a separate workshop on referencing. They asked a colleague to deliver this, and sat in so that they had a good sense of the approach taken and could run this session themselves next time if necessary.

They foregrounded text-level writing skills, by noticing what they were requiring students to do, realizing that many had difficulties with this, being explicit about what they meant and developing these skills in focused sessions.

Here are two briefer examples.

Case study 12.4 Identifying difficulties with literacy requirements 2

Gertrude, who teaches business studies, found that nearly all her students had trouble using full stops, i.e. knowing where one sentence ends and another begins. She feels confident in this area herself and over the years has developed a range of activities, from doing focused input on sentence structure (subjects and predicates), to having students write sentences on rolls of receipt paper (taken from supermarket tills) and debate about where to make the cut between one sentence and another, and why. She feels this is an area she needs to keep coming back to and plans to introduce some peer-led activities.

Many teachers are not so confident in this aspect of writing. Often, if you are a confident writer, you may think it's obvious where one sentence ends and another begins. It may feel 'logical'. Yet, for people who have not grown up reading and writing with confidence, or who find this area confusing for various reasons, it is far from logical. A sentence is a unit of writing, not of speech, and so those confident in speaking but not writing will not have internalized its logic. It is rarely helpful to say that a sentence is 'one thought' or that a full stop marks a 'breath.' Speak to an adult literacy teaching colleague to get some more ideas.

Case study 12.5 Identifying difficulties with literacy requirements 3

Marco teaches a beginners' course in DIY. Within this, there are key terms, key items of specialist vocabulary which students need to be able to read and write (with accurate spelling). This is part of the subject: getting these terms clear. Marco has noticed that for some, reading and spelling are challenging, so at the end of each session, he asks the group to identify any new key words, make posters of them to display on the walls and record them in individual vocabulary books. As students arrive in the classroom each week, he talks with them individually and asks them if they want to have a go at reading out words from the posters to develop their recognition or decoding of these words.

This is an example of foregrounding word-level reading and spelling, as well as wider vocabulary development. Marco is also using a mixture of whole-group activities, one-to-one teaching and independent study.

Talking to teachers

We talked to experienced teachers to see what they had learnt so far about foregrounding literacy. This is what they said.

- We see different things when we look at print. Some people will see the words jump around and move, which could be to do with eyesight or learning disabilities like dyslexia. I've found it always pays to ask people to describe what they see when they look at a piece of text.

- I have learnt about the avoidance tactics of those not confident in their literacy. If someone always goes to the toilet, or has forgotten their glasses whenever there is some reading to be done, then it usually means you need to have a talk.

- The conventions for written assignments vary *hugely* from context to another. Someone might just be used to writing in a certain way, from their past educational or professional experience, and have no idea what you mean by 'an essay' or 'a paragraph'. Always be really clear about the requirements of pieces of writing. Don't assume anything. Examples help.

- Those diagnosed with dyslexia are still all different. Some might prefer reading on lightly coloured paper, or using coloured overlays, but some might not. You need to ask. Also people react very differently to the idea of being labelled as dyslexic. Some find it a huge relief, others a bind. And never assume that those who are not labelled as dyslexic have no problems with reading and writing. Many do.

- Someone may struggle with reading but not writing, or with writing but not reading, or with some aspects of reading or writing but not others. Keep noticing and talking.

- It may be an obvious point, but having difficulties reading and writing has nothing to do with 'intelligence'. A student may be very talented in your subject area but have difficulties reading or writing, and so you need to be careful that your assessment manages to assess their learning in your subject, not their literacy.

- We read at dramatically different paces, and a slower reader is not necessarily a 'worse' or 'less skilled' reader. A quicker reader doesn't necessarily understand more of what they are reading.

These teachers stressed these ideas come from observing, thinking, noticing, and asking questions of both learners and other teachers.

We are arguing that to teach any subject well, we need to make sure we are foregrounding the reading and writing which is part of its learning and teaching. To do this, we need to know that literacy is not a given, not easy for everyone, not one universal set of skills, but determined by different practices and their varied conventions. We need to know that we can think of language on word, sentence and text levels.

3 Language and diversity

We have discussed the importance of foregrounding reading and writing, but there is another important dimension to communication and this relates to the diverse languages and ways of speaking that we and our students employ. We should recognize that there is not just one 'English' but a variety of 'Englishes' (Bragg, 2003) and that it is likely many of our students will be users of either other varieties of English or other languages altogether. We need to remember the potential diversity of language use within any group.

3.1 Language variety

The two case studies below can help us to pick out important aspect of the technical phrase 'language variety' – that is, they can help us to see what this phrase means. Read through the case studies and think what they say to you about the range of ways people speak English to say what they mean.

Case study 12.6 Language variety

Geraldine is a 17-year-old woman who lives with her family on an official Travellers' site in an inner London borough. At home she speaks mainly Irish English, the variety spoken by her parents and extended family. Her linguistic heritage also includes knowledge of Gammon, the traditional language of the Irish Traveller community. In social contexts outside the Traveller community, the greatest influence on her speech is London English, a rich vernacular which itself reflects the diverse influence of generations of native and settled communities. As a writer of formal texts, Geraldine uses Standard English, which she aspires to use more confidently in the hope of getting a qualification and a job.

Dulcie, having been brought up in rural Jamaica, is a speaker of Jamaican Creole, a language used by the whole community for everyday communication but not for official or formal purposes, when Standard Jamaican English would be employed. This was the variety which was used in the media and taught in school. Dulcie switches between these two varieties depending on whom she is speaking to, and her written English draws on both varieties, together with the London English she has heard all around her for the last 40 years. (Hughes and Schwab, 2010: 99–100).

These two case studies provide a sense of the meaning of language variety. Irish English, Jamaican Creole and Standard Jamaican English are all varieties (also known as dialects) of English. So are Scottish Standard English, Newcastle English and Kenyan English. Languages have always existed in multiple varieties, because languages by their very nature change over time, and they change differently in different areas or within different communities. How they change and how quickly they change depends on population density, contact with other languages and a range of cultural, social and political factors. Some varieties have developed in specific sociopolitical situations. The Jamaican Creole mentioned above could be seen as the product of the slave trade, producing a variety which combines a largely (but not exclusively) English-based vocabulary with features of West African grammatical structures.

When we talk about *a language* – German, Hindi, Spanish – there are really dozens, if not hundreds of different varieties of that language. 'Standard' varieties (Standard English, for example) are the varieties with more prestige, power and the stamp of being 'the correct version' within a certain context. Standard English (or Standard English English, if we want to differentiate it from Standard American English or Standard Scottish English) is the variety which developed from the English used in the triangle between Oxford, Cambridge and London, as printing, the universities and the sense of London as the capital of a nation state grew.

It is important to remember that a variety of a language is not the same as an accent. Accent is about how we pronounce words. Three people speaking Standard English may all have different accents. Imagine a woman from Newcastle, a woman from Wales and a man from Liverpool at a university exam board. They will probably all be speaking Standard English, because this is the variety of English usually used in academic contexts. But their accents, how they pronounce words and the intonation they use in phrases will all be quite different.

Varieties of a language differ (to a greater or lesser extent) in their vocabularies and grammar. After the meeting, the woman from Newcastle may go and meet some friends for a meal. She and her friends may speak Newcastle English, using some of the characteristic vocabulary and grammar of this particular variety of English.

Do all teachers really need to know this? Isn't this more something for a linguistics degree? Let's think of it a different way. Is it important for teachers to know that there are different varieties of any language, including English, and that these varieties can have different grammatical conventions or that varieties are afforded vastly different social status or prestige, and that one's use of a particular language variety is closely bound with identity? We will have many students whose mother tongue is English, and this really means that their mother tongues are of a range of different varieties of English, some more similar to Standard English (hereafter SE) than others. Many people will be aware of the differences between their varieties and SE and will be skilled at switching between the two, in speaking and writing, in different contexts. Others may be less able to do this.

In the majority of educational contexts, it is expected that teachers and students use SE (or the comparative standard language when outside of England). With very few exceptions, written assessments are expected to be in SE. Non-standard grammar (i.e. using grammatical conventions from other varieties of English) will usually be identified as 'grammatical mistakes'. Take these sentences from three different pieces of student writing on a Pre-Access course at an FE college:

Yesterday she walk to hospital.
My sister, she love to travel.
We done it carefully.

Each sentence correctly follows the grammatical conventions of a different variety of English. They would all be seen as containing errors, though, if the writer were intending to write in SE. As a teacher marking this work, what would you do?

If you simply cross out or correct the 'errors', the writers in each case could feel confused or that their home variety of English was being insulted or devalued (or that they and their families are being insulted or devalued). If you leave these sentences as they are, and say nothing, would that help the students, assuming they were each intending to write in SE? If they are on a Pre-Access course, they are likely to be interested in going further in formal education, perhaps to university. So, once again, what would you do?

The answer probably lies in discussion and explanation. The teacher and the student both need to know that this is an issue of language variety, of power and of standardization. The teacher needs to know that the errors are not random, nor are they about 'sloppiness'. The student may not be aware of the grammatical differences between different varieties of English. Or they may be trying to learn SE grammar but still be unsure. The key here is having discussions, in a group or individually; explaining, asking and opening up learning (rather than just crossing out and therefore closing down). The impact of using a non-standard variety of English in a poem is likely to be different from the impact it would have in a job application letter to a large multinational company. Explanation of language variety (and the history of the English language) can free us from feeling that our choices are between failing or conforming to the one way of 'being correct', and see instead that it can be a question of equipping and empowering.

Case study 12.7 Foregrounding features of language variety

Ria teaches drama. Her students produce two types of written work: a play and an essay on twentieth-century drama. When Ria first looked at Mary's essay, she thought it was just full of mistakes, missing 's's and 'ed's. Then, when she saw the range of vocabulary used in Mary's play, she began to realize that Mary may be writing in a Caribbean variety of English. She sat down with Mary in tutorial time and asked her about the vocabulary, which led to a discussion about Mary's variety of English. Mary described how she had deliberately used her own language variety to give a Caribbean voice to the play but was trying to use SE for her essay. While she was using SE vocabulary, the grammar she was using was a mixture of SE and the grammar conventions of her own variety. Ria met with Mary three more times that term and together they identified differences between the grammar conventions of SE and Mary's variety (for example, how the past tense is indicated). Mary used this new grammatical awareness to develop both the play and the essay and Ria used it to provide more focused and useful feedback on Mary's work. Mary completed her play and the following term the drama group performed it, with Mary coaching the group on their use of her language variety.

Viv teaches 'A' level religious studies. He has noticed non-standard grammar in several of his students' assignments. His grandmother speaks a Yorkshire variety of English and he has a long-standing interest in language change, so he is aware of issues to do with SE, language variety and power. He felt it was too important to try to skirt around. He decided to spend two hours of their whole-group class time to really tackle this issue, starting from a history of the English language to show that English has always been made up of different varieties, and there have always been tensions between the standard and non-standard varieties in terms of identity and political power. He then asked the students to do some research on their own varieties (even if they felt, as one or two did, that their own variety was SE) and present it to the group, including at least one grammar difference and one vocabulary difference. He referred back to this work in his individual and whole-group feedback.

Talking to teachers

Once again, we talked to experienced teachers to see what they have learnt about language variety and foregrounding.

- Students may have a sense that their own varieties of English are inferior or 'broken' and so introducing the issue can be very sensitive. They also may not realize that the written work they produce contains a mixture of standard and non-standard features.

- Language variety is a literacy issue because the smaller differences between other varieties of English and SE are rarely noticed in speaking, but suddenly stand out as mistakes in writing.

- I often use short stories written in other varieties of English as a way into discussions about how we all choose the form of language we use, depending on the context and the impact we want to make.

- Once you get into talking about different varieties of English, you realize how much the multilingual and 'monolingual' students have in common: how everyone 'code-switches' at times and how every language is really made up of different varieties which are valued unequally.

3.2 Multilingualism

The students that we teach speak/use different varieties of English. The students that we teach may also speak/use different languages. Just as some of our students speak varieties of English as their first and only language, some will have spoken English along with other language since childhood, growing up in bilingual or multilingual households or learning English as a small child. Others will have grown up using another language or languages and learnt English as older children or adults, and others still will have only recently started to learn English. Some may have been living in English-speaking regions for a long time but your class may be their first experience of an English language (micro) community. The possible combinations are infinite.

In a study of multilingualism and 'heritage languages' in the United States, Valdes (2005) refers to 'a continuum of language users'. He is describing a continuum of language competence (how effectively someone can communicate in a language, spoken and written) and use, running from no knowledge or use to complete fluency and regular use. Valdes argues that for members of immigrant communities, both their English and 'heritage' language (for example, Spanish) use runs along this continuum. A newly arrived immigrant may, for example, use Spanish fluently and English not at all. A third-generation member of the Latino community may use English fluently and Spanish not at all. Between these two are all possible combinations of English and Spanish use, bound up with issues of identity, education, family and work roles and membership of other communities. Many learners in the FAVE sector will be using two, three or more languages, each for different reasons, in different contexts, with different levels of confidence and, importantly, which relate to different elements of their identities.

Key issue 1: English language development

We are assuming teaching in an English language context and that, apart from language classes, the main language of instruction is English.

The first thing to remember is that many people who speak English as an additional language are completely confident and competent in their English language use. This may be because it is one of their multiple mother tongues, because they have learnt English as a child and/or because they are skilled language learners and users. This is a simple but integral point. Being multilingual does not mean that someone needs support with their English.

At the same time, of course, there are people who do see themselves as working on their English, from those newly learning English to those who feel they are on the everlasting journey of getting to grips with the subtleties of grammar or vocabulary. Every teacher therefore needs to be able to observe and discuss potential English language support needs and be able to use foregrounding to support learners who feel they need English language support.

Case study 12.8 Addressing individuals' language needs

Najlaa is teaching cake decorating in a small community setting. One of her learners, George, is newer to learning English and does not use English much outside of class. When monitoring individual and small-group work, Najlaa has noticed that George is not always able to follow the instructions she gives orally to the class, and has trouble following what other students are saying in pair work if they speak quickly. She has also noticed that he is more confident processing information in written form. As a result, she has started providing written back-up of her instructions, in simplified form, and/or repeating the instructions she gives orally to the whole group by speaking one-to-one with George – making sure she says as little as possible, keeping the instructions simple and carefully staged. She has also talked to George one-to-one, asking him to let her know if he doesn't understand her, and asking if he is interested in taking ESOL classes. She found that he has just enrolled in an ESOL class in the same college and, with George's permission, will try to make contact with his ESOL teacher. She also recommended that George keep a vocabulary book to record and practise the key words connected with cake decorating.

Sandro teaches philosophy in an adult education institution. He asks his students to write a short weekly essay on themes from the readings and class discussion. One of his students, Diana, is an ex-journalist from Columbia. Her academic literacy and overall English language accuracy are strong but she makes mistakes with double negatives (e.g. 'They do not do nothing'). Sandro noticed this in both her writing and contributions to class discussions. When providing feedback on her written work, he highlights instances of her use of the double negative using a pink highlighter. In tutorials, they look through her work and Sandro asks Diana why he has used the pink highlighter. She knows at once what he is referring to as she knows the rule about double negatives in English (different from Spanish) and makes it a personal goal to proofread her work with this in mind. On Diana's request, Sandra has also agreed to correct her use of double negatives in class discussions. They are going to see how it goes.

Key issue 2: The other languages

Multilingual students may well have English language development needs, but this isn't the only thing we need to know about them. Multilingual learners also use their other languages with varied degrees of competence and confidence, in different contexts and with different personal meanings. What do we need to know about how our students use and feel about their other languages?

Many linguists believe that the use and development of one language will benefit the use and development of another language (see for example Cook, 2003; Cummings, 2005; Mehmedbegovic, 2003). This is both about overall cognitive development (the idea that learning and using languages develops our brains in certain ways) and about developing particular linguistic and metalinguistic competencies (memory, ear, understanding of language functions and grammatical structures, development of language learning study skills). This means that for most multilingual people, developing their other languages will also benefit their English language development.

Secondly, research in school settings (for example, with bilingual book projects) suggests that besides the above-mentioned cognitive/linguistic benefits, encouraging the use and development of learners' other languages (which may be called their home, heritage or community languages) can benefit learners' engagement in the classroom, whatever they are learning. Within a formal educational setting, acknowledgement of, and respect for, home languages and cultures can affirm the identity of the learner, allowing her to feel that she is someone who belongs and can achieve – or 'shine' (Mehmedbegovic, 2007, 2012). This could mean performing a scene from a play in their home language; creating a bilingual book; or teaching other students about their languages, whether greetings or something more (Dakin, 2012; Mehmedbegovic, 2007, 2012; Kenner et al., 2007, 2008a, 2008b). We can also encourage conversations about the use and development of students' other languages to encourage all learners to feel they can excel in the subjects we teach and in the wider learning environment.

Finally, multilingual learners may carry with them skills and understandings honed through their use of several languages which could be of use to other learners, both monolingual and multilingual. This is both a form of peer learning and a way of valuing learners' expertise and experience. Someone who has worked hard to learn their fourth language at the age of 40 may have useful tips or ideas to help someone else learn new subject-specific items of vocabulary. Someone who switches between languages as he moves between different communities may be able to help another learner grasp the idea that every piece of writing is written according to particular genre conventions.

Case study 12.9 Connecting learning in the class with learning in life

Maho teaches an introduction to poetry class as part of an adult 'return to study programme'. Her students also take literacy, study skills, ICT and maths classes and all hope to build towards university entrance. Maho is working on the learner-chosen topic of 'war poetry' and has collected five different poems and songs to examine with the group. She also asked each student to find or write a war poem, either in English or another language. An Iranian woman brought in a poem in Farsi about the recent war in Iran. She read it aloud to the group in Farsi and then read out her own in-progress translation, asking for help from the group as she searched for some words. She then re-read the poem in Farsi as the group sat, silent and transfixed. This led to a discussion about the effect of the sounds of words, independent from their meaning (an important poetry learning point, Maho felt) and also to a discussion about how the wars which members of the group had experienced, and the languages used to make sense of them, are part of our identities and are underneath everything else that we will ever do (this was a theme of the poem, the Iranian woman explained). Later, Maho observed that the Iranian woman was more involved in the poetry sessions and in a tutorial she spoke about how important it was for her to 'connect the learning in the class with the learning of my life'.

Maho had not seen her open invitation for learners to recite poetry in their other languages as foregrounding; she had seen it as part of understanding the relationships between poetry, culture and identity. Yet the way this activity used and valued other languages helped some students engage more meaningfully with the poetry class and helped one student to understand how her development in both English and Farsi was central to her development as an adult learner.

Talking to teachers

We asked a sample of experienced teachers: 'What have you learnt about multilingualism?'

- Doing several things at once is harder in a foreign language. This means it can be harder for some students to listen, look at a PowerPoint slide and take notes at the same time.

- It is really difficult to make sense of grammatical mistakes without an overall explanation. It took me years to realize that just correcting missing articles or mistakes with tenses was really not very useful. Now I either just mark them with a 'vt' for verb tense or 'sm' for 'something missing' and ask the student to think about what they think I'm getting at and then work from there, or I notice patterns and build to a mini-grammar lesson with the help of a colleague. Patterns help people make sense of things.

- I've built up a tiny bit of knowledge about the grammatical/syntactic systems of different languages, i.e. which ones don't have articles, or which ones have a more fluid sentence structure. This helps me to better understand and react to students' mistakes.

- Some students may not feel they can talk about their home languages, or may even see being multilingual as an asset. I usually try to raise this as a point, so they get to see who speaks which languages and so they feel more confident about putting it down on their CV and realize that in speaking more than one language, they can do something amazing – something I wish I could do!

Conclusion

We have tried to start where other chapters have left off in an exploration of speaking and listening in the classroom and we have examined reading and writing. In doing so, our aim has been to point to some of the challenges for teachers and for learners in engaging in vocational and adult education in an austere economic climate (Thompson and Tuckett, 2011, **Reading 12.3**). Reading and writing led us to think about foregrounding: how we are all teachers of the reading and writing which is part of our subjects, teaching or assessment. We then realized that we needed to think more about language, and discussed language variety and multilingualism, both presenting more opportunities for foregrounding and for thinking about speaking and listening, reading and writing in a different way.

There are other things we can foreground: numeracy and ICT, for example. Just as we have tried to notice all the reading and writing in our teaching, we could identify our use of numeracy or ICT and foreground, using the examples here as a guide (see Griffiths and Stone [2013] for an introduction to issues in foregrounding maths/numeracy). There is also much more to be said about diversity and communication: about the use of British Sign Language, about how blind people read, about dyslexia and cognitive impairment. We will pick this up, and recommend further reading, in Chapter 15.

None of this is easy, and a great deal of it may be outside of the usual delineations of our professional expertise. *'I'm a photography teacher. Do I really need to get my head around all this?'* Yes, we think so, but remember that we also see teacher education as a lifelong process, never-ending, provisional and endlessly problematic. We can find CPD courses on language and literacy, on numeracy or ICT. We can read books (see below) and we can work with colleagues with other specialisms (like adult literacy, ESOL and numeracy teachers).

Key readings

This edited book contains chapters from a range of adult numeracy experts on the best ways to support adults with their maths/numeracy. Intended as a guide for specialist numeracy teachers, it also works very well as an overview on numeracy/mathematics issues for teachers of all subjects:

Griffiths, G. and Stone, R. (eds) (2013) *Teaching Adult Numeracy: Principles and Practice.* Maidenhead: Open University Press.

This edited book contains chapters from a range of adult literacy experts on the best ways to support adult language development. Intended as a guide for specialist English/literacy teachers, it also works very well as an overview on language issues for teachers of all subjects:

Hughes, N. and Schwab, I. (eds) (2010) *Teaching Adult Literacy: Principles and Practice.* Maidenhead: McGraw Hill/Open University Press.

This edited book contains chapters from a range of adult ESOL experts on the best ways to support adult language development. Intended as a guide for specialist ESOL teachers, it also works very well as an overview on language issues for teachers of all subjects:

Paton, A. and Wilkins, M. (eds) (2009) *Teaching Adult ESOL: Principles and Practice*. Maidenhead: Open University Press.

This book examines reading in adult life, how adults develop their reading and provides an overview of adult literacy issues and provision. It will help place adult literacy needs and desires in a broader historical context:

Duncan, S. (2012) 'Reading Circles as Ideal Pedagogy'. In *Reading Circles, Novels and Adult Reading Development*. London: Continuum/Bloomsbury. **(Reading 12.1)**

This edited book contains chapters from a range of perspectives (child and adult) on best practice in supporting those from migrant and refugee backgrounds in educational contexts:

Mallows, D. (ed.) (2012) *Innovations in English Language Teaching for Migrants and Refugees*. London: The British Council.

The following readings explore the way policy does and could shape the way literacies are taught:

Gregson, M. and Nixon, L. (2011) 'Unlocking the potential of Skills for Life (SfL) tutors and learners: a critical evaluation of the implementation of SfL Policy in England', *Teaching in Lifelong Learning*. CETTS Journal. Huddersfield: University of Huddersfield Press. **(Reading 12.2)**

Thomson, A. and Tuckett, A. (2010) *Lifelong Learning in Challenging Times: An Agenda for a New Government*. London: NIACE. **(Reading 12.3)**

The associated website, **reflectiveteaching.co.uk**, offers a wealth of supplementary resources including reflective activities, research briefings, advice on further reading and downloadable diagrams, figures and checklists from the book. It also features a compendium of educational terms, links to useful websites, policy and curriculum documents, and showcases examples of excellent research and practice.

Assessment
How can assessment enhance learning?

13

Introduction

In Chapter 2, we discussed the need to understand the relationship between teaching and learning and how in educational settings we are always faced with the question of what students should learn and why they should learn it. We pointed out that it is only when we are clear about what it is that teachers and students want to achieve that we can make meaningful decisions about curriculum content. This also has implications for what kinds of relationships we need to establish between teachers and students, and between students themselves and the kinds of activities we should engage in to help us to reach our goals. As teachers, we also need to take into account the ways in which we will assess progress along the way, so that we will be able to judge whether we and our students have achieved what we aimed them to achieve. We also need to be aware of the ways in which summative assessment and accreditation can influence learners and their learning (Hamilton and Hillier, 2006, **Reading 13.1**).

> ## TLRP principles
>
> Two TLRP principles are particularly represent this chapter:
>
> **Principle 5: Effective teaching and learning needs assessment to be congruent with learning.** Assessment should help to advance learning as well as determine whether learning has taken place. It should be designed and carried out so that it measures learning outcomes in a dependable way and also provides feedback for future learning.
>
> **Principle 6: Effective teaching and learning promotes the active engagement of the learner.** A chief goal of teaching and learning should be the promotion of learners' independence and autonomy. This involves acquiring a repertoire of learning strategies and practices, developing positive attitudes towards learning, and confidence in oneself as a good learner.

In the opening chapters of this book we drew attention to the importance of educational values in FAVE and the need to balance competing purposes of education in terms of the necessity for students to develop the knowledge, skills and dispositions they need to be able to practice in a particular field – the *'qualification'* demands of practice (Biesta, 2012). This is, of course, important, but it is not the only aspect of education that matters. We also need to think carefully about how engaging in education helps us to become part of existing social, cultural and political practices and the traditions, which have shaped our society in the past and through which it will grow in the future. Biesta describes this as the *'socialization'* dimension of education.

Biesta argues that it is both necessary and desirable to introduce 'newcomers' (for example, children, apprentices of all kinds, student teachers, trainee doctors, architects, hairdressers, electricians, nursery nurses, poets, dancers, musicians, actors, chefs or adult immigrants) into existing social and professional orders and cultures. How we identify with such orders influences the development of our own individual and collective identity and in turn shapes the cultures and societies we live in.

In Chapters 1, 4 and 16 we point to the importance of a third dimension of education: the way in which education impacts on the person. This includes learning that we can and must be able to exist 'outside' of existing social and political orders, so that we can exercise the human freedom of being able to criticize and change them and address injustices and inequalities inherent within them. In this way education contributes to democracy by helping us to improve existing social, political and economic structures of power through engagement with issues of injustice and the pursuit of moral practice (Hyland, 2009, 2011; Biesta, 2012).

In this chapter and the next, we look at assessment in education from a variety of perspectives. In particular, we explore practical strategies to support formative assessment in FAVE contexts. Our main focus in this chapter is to look at how we can use assessment in ways which help our students learn and enable them to achieve their goals and reach their full potential. To do this, students need to receive feedback from others. In order to be useful, we need to offer them feedback in accessible, constructive and timely ways which not only encourage them to think critically, carefully and for themselves but also help them recognize their current progress, where they need to get to next, as well as the steps they need to take to get there (Harlen and Gipps, 1992, Reading 13.2).

Assessment that supports the process of active learning through careful and systematic planning (see Chapter 10) and thoughtful and inclusive communication (see Chapter 12), encourages students to monitor their own progress and enables them to identify, in dialogue with their teachers, their next steps to success, is widely referred to as Assessment for Learning (AfL) (Swaffield, 2011, Reading 13.3). This term is often used interchangeably with the term *formative assessment*. This chapter deliberately refers to AfL, not as a series of techniques or recipes that can be instrumentally or mechanically inserted into practice by teachers, but as a kind of social practice which *integrates* teaching, learning and assessment. While AfL does include practical techniques such as open questioning, sharing learning objectives, identifying success criteria (sometimes referred to as 'steps to success'), focused marking, wait time and 'no hands up', these techniques must always be put into assessment practice by teachers in principled and educationally sound ways which promote active learning.

This chapter is primarily concerned with how we can use assessment *for* learning, rather than assessment *of* learning (after it has supposedly taken place) though the use of summative examinations and tests, (discussed more fully in Chapter 14; see for example Assessment Reform Group, 1999, Reading 13.4). There are two main sections to this chapter. First we consider the issues of assessment, learning and teaching. We then go on to explore classroom strategies affirming assessment for learning. In the first section key issues, definitions and principles that concern the dynamics of assessment, learning and teaching are introduced and discussed. Different ways of putting formative assessment into practice are then considered in five groups. We recommend that you read both of these sections together to ensure that you develop a sound grasp of both the principles and the practices of formative assessment.

Activities associated with AfL not only provide information to be used for formative assessment purposes, but also (and probably even more importantly) these activities are learning processes in themselves. AfL is underpinned by a set of principles and key strategies, which, when put into practice, can establish an active learning culture in the classroom that helps students to see the steps they need to take to achieve success in their learning. They also help to develop students' confidence in themselves and each other as learners and encourage the development of an increasing sense of autonomy and responsibility for their learning, now and in the future (Hillier, 2012, **Reading 13.1**).

1 Assessment, learning and teaching

Rowntree (1977) advises that if you want to know the purpose of a system of education, a course of study or a single lesson – in other words, what it is *for* – then it is wise to look carefully at its assessment practices and procedures. Approaches to assessment adopted by political administrations, educational organizations or individual teachers can reveal (often despite rhetoric to the contrary) what is really valued and what is actually rewarded in practice. Assessment practices and procedures signal to students and teachers what they need to do (or not do) in order to achieve success. It is important therefore that, as teachers, we are aware of the messages that different approaches to assessment transmit to our students.

If we think back to our own experiences of being assessed at school, it is quite easy to see the impact of how we are assessed upon us as human beings and upon what is really taught and what is actually learned. For example, you may have had experience of preparing for a test, where you only learnt material that you thought would come up in the exam and which you forgot immediately afterwards. How we are assessed can also have a significant influence (positive or negative) upon who we think we are and what we think we are capable of learning and achieving, now and in the future. If you were required to take an examination such as the 'eleven plus' or some kind of entry examination to decide which kind of school or which profession, apprenticeship or vocation you were allowed entry to, you may have learnt very early on that you were 'clever' or 'a failure'. This might have led you to think of yourself as bright or smart, not very bright or smart, or even stupid. Wiliam challenges the view that being 'smart' or 'bright' is predetermined at birth, arguing: 'Smart is not something that you are, smart is something you get' (2010).

Coffield (2009: 2) also encourages us to remember that neither we nor our students are stuck with the intelligence we were born with and that we can learn to become more intelligent by engaging in learning in purposeful and thoughtful ways. Earlier in this book we discussed how education in FAVE contexts usually involves learning to do something in the world, as well as encouraging and nurturing the disposition to do it well. We have also drawn attention to how it is also about being able to stand back from the world and look critically at what is taken for granted, so that we can begin to see what we could do better and how things in the world might be different. Here we want to make the point that formative and summative assessment are important contributing factors to good education. This means that, as teachers, we need to put assessment procedures into practice in ways which reflect a strong commitment to educational values and active learning in FAVE contexts. This includes developing vocational knowledge and understanding, encouraging autonomy, and fostering values that will enable those being educated to construct and participate in the vocational communities of practice which they wish to join. It also involves fostering in our students a passionate commitment to engage in the world in the pursuit of their chosen vocations, take pride in a job well done, and nurture the character and courage to be prepared to 'challenge injustice, poverty and inequality and all the other factors which stand in the way of human flourishing and well-being' (Hyland, 2009: 13).

According to the national Commission for Adult and Vocational Training in England (CAVTL, 2013 – see Chapter 4 and Reading 11.3), approaches to assessment in FAVE should enable and encourage students to acquire well-developed capacities for careful thinking and systematic individual and collective, situated practical problem-solving. CAVTL call for the development of assessment practices and procedures across the sector that enhance student learning in ways which encourage students in FAVE to develop the capacity to respond effectively to unexpected developments in life and in the workplace through individual and collective learning, so that they can share and solve problems together in a wide range of immediate situations and in the future.

In developing our approaches to assessment, we must therefore constantly remind ourselves of the purposes of education and the nature and purposes of assessment (Rowntree, 1987; Pollard, 2010; Biesta, 2012).

1.1 Guiding principles of Assessment for Learning

Assessment of students' learning as they progress in any particular programme of study is widely known in scholarly literature and in practice as formative assessment. However, an approach which has increasingly recognized the importance of active learning was developed by Black and Wiliam (1998). Their approach came to be known as Assessment for Learning (AfL), which is based upon the principle that through assessment our students could learn how to learn (Harlen and Gipps, 1992, Reading 13.2).

Clarke (2008) identifies three kinds of assessment which are linked to different relationships between assessment and learning:

Assessment *of* Learning includes any summative test of assessment, which can result in **test scores or grades**. These might be classroom-based, college/institution-based or on a national scale. For example, in England this might take the form of a GSCE or 'A' level. Or it might take the form of a question asked in class to check student learning – for example, a question of recall/comprehension/analysis etc., such as *'Which are the odd numbers in this sequence?'* or *'When was the Battle of Hastings?'*.

Assessment *for* Learning includes any assessment practice which provides information to students about **what** to improve – for example, *'This piece of writing could be improved by better use of adjectives and using sentences of different lengths'.*

Assessment *as* Learning includes any assessment practice which extends what to improve into **how** to improve – for example, *'Use your senses to imagine how this character in the play is feeling', 'Build up a bank of descriptive adjectives and powerful verbs and use them to improve the persuasiveness of your writing', 'Look at this assignment from one of last* *year's students and pay particular attention to how they have structured their assignment and how they have used Harvard referencing to support their argument'.*

As the primary goal of assessment *for* learning is that assessment *as* learning should result (Clarke, 2008: 9), for the rest of this chapter we will use the term *formative assessment* to cover both of these aspects of assessment practice. It is worth pointing out that many of the advocates for formative assessment now have concerns about how it is being enacted in practice.

> As with anything of worth in education, formative assessment has been argued over, misinterpreted and misused. One of the problems … is that formative assessment needs to consist of quite specific techniques while at the same time allowing for experimentation and development. A too-straitjacketed approach to techniques doesn't work because the underlying aims of active learning are not guiding the practice. A flexible 'follow the principles and do your own thing' approach leads to disillusionment when things don't work very well because the specifics of the techniques have not been studied. Both aspects make or break the success of formative assessment implementation. (Clarke, 2008: 2–3)

Active learning in formative assessment requires us to collaborate with our students in planning, in deciding contexts for learning and success criteria. It also involves us in discussions with students about quality in terms of how we would recognize a good piece of work. Formative assessment includes engaging in continual paired or whole-classroom talk, in critically analysing learning as it is happening and in a constant process of careful and considered reviews of success and improvement.

The following three key principles of AfL are generated through the TLRP Learning How to Learn project (James et al., 2007). These embrace key strategies involved in formative assessment first developed by Wiliam (2006) and subsequently extended by Clarke (2008).

1 Making learning explicit

We have already discussed earlier in this chapter and in Chapter 2 the need to understand the integrated nature of teaching, learning and assessment and the importance of being clear about what teachers and students want to achieve. This is because it is only then that we can make meaningful decisions about curriculum content, pedagogical practice and assessment strategies. The AfL principle of making learning explicit involves the use of key strategies such as clarifying learning intentions and establishing student-generated and therefore student-owned criteria for success. Working together with our students in identifying clear 'steps to success' (student actions that will support achievement) and helping the students to 'see' what success might look, feel, sound or taste like, as well as helping them to identify how success will be known and how achievement will be recognized, are central aspects of formative assessment.

This means that teachers need to create a classroom culture in which all involved see ability as incremental rather than fixed. This means that we need to involve students in planning both appropriately pitched content and meaningful contexts in our lessons. We also need to enable and plan for effective classroom dialogic talk, where the teacher uses worthwhile questioning to encourage to students to think 'out loud and together' (Mercer, 1998). Involving our students in analysis and discussion about not just meeting the success criteria but how best to meet them and different ways to meet them is at the core of the process of formative assessment (Clarke, 2005, 2008).

2 Autonomous learning

Autonomous learning refers to students taking responsibility for their learning and exercising some measure of independence. This does not mean that they work on their own (although there might be occasions when they decide that this is the most appropriate thing to do). If we are to promote learning autonomy in our students, then we must grant some level of choice about what they learn and support them in identifying options and developing the skills and confidence they will need to make decisions about the options available. A key feature of autonomous learning is that students are self and peer evaluators and can decide on next steps in their learning without having to be reliant on a teacher or someone else to tell them. Realistic self-assessment is informed by knowledge of learning objectives/intentions. Being clear about criteria for success and quality are crucial to teachers and students alike. It is also important to remember that learning to self-regulate your learning is not age- or stage-dependent – it is a learnt process. Students become more autonomous learners with guidance and through regular engagement in the principles and practices of formative assessment.

3 Focusing on learning

In Chapter 2 we cautioned against oversimplistic notions of learning and the assumption that all learning is good. That is why we argue that, as teachers, we need to pay attention to the nature of the learning that is promoted and valued. In relation to the principles of formative assessment, active learning is crucial. Learning for its intrinsic worth and long-lasting value is paramount. The cornerstones of formative assessment stand in stark contrast to mechanistic and utilitarian approaches, which are solely concerned with getting marks in a test or examination, after which what was learnt is soon forgotten. The formative assessment principle of focusing on learning is closely linked to Dweck's (2006) notion of a 'growth' mindset rather than a 'performance' mindset. Focusing on active learning includes focusing on the process of learning, as well as what is to be learnt. This means establishing continual opportunities for timely review and feedback from teachers and students, focusing on recognition of success and the identification of improvement needs. As Clarke (2008) cautions, there is no point providing feedback if our students have no opportunity to put our feedback and recommendations into practice. In planning for formative assessment and feedback we need to ensure that we plan for and provide our students with time to act on feedback in classrooms, workshops, studios, workplaces and other sites of learning, wherever possible.

1.2 Key ideas

As we have seen, formative assessment is not something that happens at the end of a sequence of teaching and learning events. It is there right from the beginning of the planning stage, is dynamic and goes on throughout a lesson. As we plan for the kinds and levels of learning we intend to be achieved by our students, we decide the questions and assessment activities that will be used along the way to check that our students are successfully engaging with, and learning from, the content of the session. We also need to develop strategies and measures that help us to ensure that they are progressing towards learning intentions. In the process, we need to adjust our teaching accordingly as we identify how well our learners are progressing during the lesson. Formative and summative assessment activities can also be used at the end of the lesson and beyond to check, consolidate and build upon learning achieved.

Clarke (2001: 51–3) powerfully demonstrates how teachers' language during a lesson influences what learners see as being important and what they subsequently paid attention to in and out of class. The main point to note here is that the way assessment is *practised* shapes how our students view themselves. This has far-reaching consequences, because assessment practices have a strong influence upon whether students develop as successful learners (or not). It also determines the culture, relays of power, relationships and interactions of the classroom.

If a teacher's feedback and comments are predominantly about presentation and quantity, rather than learning intentions and quality, then 'our learning intentions and success criteria will be seen to be a lie' (Clarke, 2008: 51) because these aspects will be seen by students as being the most important. If the highest attainment in the class is valued more than the greatest achievement by an individual, and if correct answers appear to be more important than having a go, then most of the class will feel they can never succeed and will probably disengage, and the rich learning that comes through effort and risk-taking will be rare.

The development of a sound grasp of the guiding principles of formative assessment and key strategies to support the practices of formative assessment are vital to inclusive and engaging teaching. When these are coupled with maintenance of an up-to-date, relevant and well-connected body of subject specialist knowledge (see Chapter 8) and a wide repertoire of teaching methods and techniques, formative assessment and creative teaching become open and accessible to people of all ages and from all walks of life.

2 Classroom strategies

In the next section, formative assessment strategies are considered in more detail under five categories. Remember that these are interrelated. Since formative assessment is a coherent way of working, any grouping of the following practices is to some extent artificial and slightly arbitrary.

2.1 Sharing goals and identifying quality

As we have already shown, the first active element of formative assessment begins with sharing learning objectives/intentions with students. Muddled learning objectives can lead to mismatched activities and inhibit student achievement. They can also distort the focus of a lesson and make it difficult to identify success criteria and what constitutes good learning.

Learning objectives or intentions can be made explicit and shared by introducing students to a simple phrase and mnemonic to help them to identify, discuss and focus upon learning intentions/outcomes. In the schools sector, the phrase *'We are learning to…'* (WALT) is often used. While we appreciate that we must be careful to use age-appropriate language for our students, this phrase helps to identify not only what is going to be learnt but implies that it is a process. Accompanying this sharing of learning goals are 'steps to success'. These are the *process success criteria* (Clarke, 2005, 2008), which focus upon the learning processes and strategies that our students will need to be able to use as they work towards reaching their goals. Process success criteria can act as either a reminder of steps (such as working out quantities of chemicals used in making hair dye) or the elements which could help the student achieve the learning objective (e.g. writing a promotional leaflet using adjectives). Of course, not all the criteria have to be used for success to be evident. Once our students have access to the success criteria, they can think and talk about them in a formative dialogue with teachers, peers and even in intra-personal dialogue with themselves. Dialogue about process success criteria enables our students to ensure and maintain appropriate focus. They can also help to clarify understanding, identify success and determine difficulties. Discussing strategies for improvement can help students to reflect on their interim and overall progress. In other words, success criteria help students and teachers talk about learning and 'see' what success might look like. This is particularly important when we are working with students who may have had a long experience of failure in their previous educational settings (see Schwab and Hughes, 2010).

Students can be invited to generate success criteria by asking them 'How will we know we have achieved this?' Another simple phrase and mnemonic applied successfully in schools is *'What I'm looking for'* (WILF). The use of this phrase encourages students to engage in regular self-assessment and can also help you to make the learning objective or intention clear and explicit to your students. Learning intentions and process success criteria can be framed at any level and in any of the cognitive, affective and psychomotor domains of Bloom's (1956) taxonomy of educational objectives (see Chapter 10). The use of these mnemonics by Clarke and others in the schools sector may work equally well in the FAVE sector. On the other hand, or you may decide to adapt these phrases for use in the context of your practice, or you might decide to develop a new mnemonic. Either way, it is important to remember the value of finding clear and simple ways to share learning goals and process success criteria or 'steps to success' with your students.

Closed learning objectives

According to Clarke (2008), there are two main types of learning objectives: closed and open. Both have their uses depending on what we want our students to achieve and how best we can assess their progress. Learning objectives, which are complex and focused on knowledge, are often expressed in a 'closed' manner – that is, they need to be broken down incrementally in terms of their constituent parts and linked to a 'skill', a way of thinking or doing so that the process success criteria focus mainly on the skill rather than solely upon knowledge or concepts (Schwab and Hughes, 2010: 82). Examples of closed learning objectives include being able to use question marks; use an index; subtract using decomposition; use a map; define photosynthesis; recite the names of colours in French; use Pythagoras' theorem. Bloom's (1956) taxonomy of educational objectives, helpfully revised by Anderson and Krathwohl (2001), can be very helpful here in analysing and identifying the kinds and levels of learning you and your students are aiming for.

Implications for success criteria and feedback

Closed skills are assessed as being either right or wrong. For example, the quantity of sand and lime used in making cement is not a matter of judgement, but a fixed ratio. Identifying process success criteria for closed learning objectives or skills are relatively easy to plan in terms of either the steps involved or what you need to remember to do in order to achieve the learning objective. For example, to make a béchamel sauce you need to add the flour to the melted butter, then add the milk slowly until the sauce thickens. To prepare a slide to examine the cells from a swab of the lining of the mouth requires a specific process to stain the cells.

Open learning objectives

Open learning objectives refer to an aspect of learning which is neither right nor wrong. In the case of 'open' learning objectives, students' attempts are on a continuum of achievement across the programme. Open learning objectives include being able to write a persuasive argument; conduct a fair test; compare data, reports, pieces of art work or different religions; empathize in writing/role-play; discuss an effective sequence in using balance and travel in gymnastics; use effective adjectives, adverbs complex sentences; write a characterization; draw an effective conclusion. These require judgement about how well the activity has been performed or demonstrated. Once again, Anderson and Krathwohl's (2001) revision to Bloom's (1956) taxonomy can also be of use here, particularly at the higher levels of the cognitive, affective and psychomotor levels of learning.

Implications for success criteria and feedback

Open learning objectives require discussion with students using a variety of real examples as a model to avoid a minimalistic approach. Here we need to engage with our students in dialogues by asking questions such as: '*How does Monet evoke the changing light in his paintings of Rouen Cathedral?', 'How does Jane Austen convey the situation of young women in marriage?'* It helps to show students examples of work on the continuum of the extent to which each example has met the learning objectives. For instance, we may want to show two essays that discuss the contributing factors to the outbreak of the First World War – one which barely answers the question and one which not only states the main factors but discusses these critically. Students can be asked to discuss and analyse the differences and try to identify and quantify the quality of each example in terms of the learning objectives, process criteria and success criteria. Then individually or in pairs, students can look for where they best achieved each criterion for success in their own work and identify where they could improve.

Clarke (2005, 2008) reminds us that we need to be careful when we ask students to think about the learning objectives. Students tend to focus on the most concrete element in the objective and their thinking and talk is more likely to be about what they are *doing* rather than what they are *learning.* In this way, students can assume that the learning processes they have applied in one subject or activity are not relevant in another. Learning objectives uncoupled from context can help to promote vocabulary and talk focused on learning rather than just the context. This encourages students to transfer their learning to any context. For example, in the table below, if we ask our students to think about how well they discussed pollution in their town, they might not reflect on their ability to write a newspaper report but rather on what they know about pollution. The following examples are adapted from Clarke (2005, 2008).

Learning objective	Context
To write a newspaper report	about pollution in our town (research-based plus ICT skills).
To analyse data	in comparing the climate between Birmingham and Cairo, using atlas graphs.
To multiply by using repeated addition	using calculators and a variety of resources
To paint in the style of Monet	the scene in our park, first analysing his work then practising his techniques
To present a written reasoned argument including 'for' and 'against' positions	vegetarianism
To understand the needs of a human baby	by interviewing a parent about her baby
To investigate the distribution of an economic activity	by interviewing a family about where they shop and how their shopping patterns have changed
To order written numerals	numbers to at least 50 using number cards
To use watercolours to create wash effects	in a painting of the sea

Figure 13.1
Learning objectives.

(Adapted from Clarke, 2005: 31; 2008: 86)

We also need to think about the 'nesting' effect of long- and short-term learning objectives – for example, where short-term examples, such as writing a newspaper report on pollution, are actually concerned with much longer-term objectives, such as writing persuasively, using different voices for different audiences and undertaking research into topics and writing summaries of the main implications.

Figure 13.2
Long-term
learning,
short-term learning
and learning
objectives.

Long-term learning objective (often several years)	Short-term learning objective (individual lessons)	Learning objective separated from context (highlighting 'key skill' for which process success criteria are generated by students)
To be able to punctuate correctly	To be able to use question marks and full stops	Recognize symbols and their meaning
To be able to design a science experiment	To be able to record observations	Observe and notice important information
To know significant events in Tudor times	To recognize the impact of Henry VIII on people's lives	Select and organize historical information
To be able to paint in the style of Monet	To analyse and practise the artistic techniques used by Monet	Use watercolours to create wash effects

Outlined below is a framed example of a learning objective from a training department in a large engineering company in England.

Figure 13.3
Learning objectives
in context.

Learning objective:	To manufacture paper gaskets
Context:	For a gearbox
Success criteria:	Making the gasket without tearing the material
	Monitor the construction of the gasket.
	Supply two gaskets for a gearbox.
Activity (abbreviated):	Introduction, research, planning on paper, discussion, make paper gaskets by tapping lightly on the edge of the gearbox to provide a perfect outline of the gearbox.
Assessment:	Self-assessment, peer assessment and training officer assessment, producing final version of gasket.

(Todd, 2013)

Once the learning goal has been made explicit, and notions of what constitutes quality established, success criteria help students to attain the learning objectives. As we have seen, success criteria help direct students' attention and may be closed instructions ('*Write down your calculation*') or open-ended prompts ('*Use at least three ways of describing the heroine's character, such as likes and dislikes, interests, personality, attitude to others*'). Although initially we will need to model appropriate success criteria, they are most effective when students help to generate them. Ways of doing this include asking about key points to remember, comparing examples of products, presenting something that is incomplete, or the teacher 'doing it wrongly' and eliciting ways to improve a piece of work. Helping students to get into the habit of using process and success criteria enables them to clarify their aims and to continually improve.

Sharing learning goals, process and success criteria, notions of quality, and information on how their work will be evaluated, all help students to understand what they are trying to achieve. These are all elements of short-term planning (see Chapter 10). Clarke (2001, 2005, 2008) shows that students' learning improved when they were involved in discussions about what they were learning, how their work would be assessed and what would count as good work. Moreover, the lower-attaining students made greater gains than the previously higher-attaining students, indicating that some students' previous lack of success may have been as a result of not understanding what was required because they could not see what success looked like.

While it helps learners to know what they are aiming for, sometimes stating it too baldly right at the beginning of a lesson can militate against a sense of excitement, surprise or wonder. A teacher might want to capture students' interest in any number of creative ways, leading to a statement of the learning objective part-way into the lesson. In other cases, when students will be investigating or creating something, it is inappropriate to give them the 'answer' before they begin. Here an understanding of different kinds of objectives is helpful. Eisner (2002) distinguishes what he calls curriculum objectives from problem-solving and creative objectives. He argues that these categories suggest that it is not always necessary or appropriate to frame learning intentions in the form of objectives or outcomes – for example, in some cases it may be appropriate to frame learning objectives in the form of a question or a challenge. For example, a photography teacher might start the session by saying: '*Today I would like us to think about how we can best capture a dynamic image from the pictures you took last week in the college library.*' A music technology tutor might ask: '*How can we create a sound reminiscent of the 1970s?*' It is worth reiterating that at the end of the day it is teachers' creativity and judgement, not 'recipes' or formulaic approaches that are central to good education and engaging teaching, learning and assessment.

As we have indicated earlier in this chapter, students can be helped to understand what they are aiming for by seeing examples of work generated previously. Single pieces can be discussed to reveal expectations, characteristics and indications of quality, but care must be taken to avoid giving the impression that there is only one way, or that the model should be copied. Examples do not, of course, have to be limited to written work. Different kinds of products, including models, artefacts, sound recordings and videos of action, can all be used to stimulate student learning. Sharing examples of high-quality work and analysing what makes them so can be very powerful, but multiple examples are needed so that students realize there are many possible and unique manifestations of excellence.

Shared learning intentions, developing a sense of quality, and jointly creating success criteria all enable students to take responsibility for the quality of their work. This can help them to become more autonomous learners and assist them in developing self-regulation. However, it is important to note that these aspects of assessment for learning only come about when students are actively engaged in the processes of formative assessment. They do not result from the mechanistic writing-up of learning objectives, which is sometimes the outcome of dogmatic adherence to simplistically stated policy or highly prescriptive, bureaucratic centrally prescribed pro-forma for lesson plans. It is therefore crucial that the focus is kept on the learning intention, and that we do not unwittingly give the impression that other things (such as behaviour or presentation) are more important than the lesson's learning focus.

2.2 Questioning and dialogue

Formative dialogue and questioning are vital to formative assessment. It is through dialogue that students develop a sense of what they are aiming for, how to get there, and what constitutes a quality piece of work. Questioning and dialogue are integral to feedback and peer assessment and are key ways in which teachers can assess what students have learned, giving insights into their comprehension and misunderstandings. There are many resonances here with the research and educational issues discussed in Chapters 10 and 12.

Talk in the classroom not only helps to assess current understanding, but also plays an integral part in assessment that supports learning and is itself a thinking and learning process. Students and teachers alike must learn how to engage in effective dialogue. For this to be successful, certain conditions are necessary, as we show below.

Teachers ask questions to find out exactly what students know and understand already, what misconceptions they hold (Rutledge, 2010), which aspects and parts of their work provide evidence of high-quality learning, those that need strengthening and the steps to success that could further improve their work. However many questions are unnecessary, not well thought through, closed and unproductive. Closed questions imply that there is only one right answer and that the teacher knows what it is! Normally closed questions are concerned with the recall of facts or basic comprehension at the lower levels of Bloom's taxonomy, where the answer has previously been provided and normally begin with the words 'do/did/can/is/was' and so on, where the answer can be a straightforward 'yes' or 'no'. Closed questions are very limited in helping teachers to understand what individual students know or understand and can often mislead teachers into thinking that students understand more than they do. (For example, 'Is that clear? Does that make sense? Does everyone understand that?' When questions of this nature are asked in class the answer is often 'yes', but the reality of students' responses to such questions may very far from the truth.)

Questioning is central, but the quality of ensuing dialogue is highly dependent on the nature of the questions. Closed questions used to check students' recall or speed of calculation have their uses, but they do not stimulate dialogue. Instead, open-ended questions, perhaps framed to aim at generating higher-level thinking in Bloom's taxonomy, are usually more fruitful. It is worth noting that 'why', 'how' and 'what' questions are more likely to lead to discussion than 'when' or 'where' questions, but much depends on the exact phrasing. The format of questions can also be varied to good effect – for example, you might stimulate discussion and dialogue by providing a question together with a range of answers, including answers that are definitely right, definitely wrong, or ambiguous. Other approaches include asking whether and why students agree or disagree with a given statement. You might state an answer and ask the students what they think the question could have been. You might also ask students to identify which statement/shape/object is the odd one out and why.

It is also very important to plan for and allow 'wait time' (Black and Wiliam, 1998) after asking students a question. This gives students time to think and then respond. Students very quickly get into the habit of leaving the answering of questions put to the whole class to those who appear to be able to respond quickly and so they become less and less confident in themselves as learners and more and more afraid of making mistakes in public by getting the answer wrong. Wiliam (2010) powerfully demonstrates how as a result of this destructive, downward spiral of low participation and achievement, some students come to think of themselves as 'dull' or 'stupid' and that they will never able to become 'smart'. Through the experiences and practices of formative assessment Wiliam (2010) shows that students can learn to become better learners.

Other techniques for increasing involvement in dialogue involve the use of small groups. Key points here include the use of 'talk partners', where students can discuss something in pairs before sharing their thoughts and ideas with the whole group. Keeping discussions very focused and not letting them run on for too long (from 5 or 10 seconds up to 2 or 3 minutes, depending on the task) can be another way of keeping lessons on task and interesting. You might also think about frequently changing or randomly selecting 'talk partners' to ensure inclusion and prevent the formation of factions or cliques in the group.

It is also useful to establish and use ground-rules, routines and protocols to monitor and manage classroom behaviour (Schwab and Hughes, 2010; Pollard, 2013). Being able to engage in effective small group dialogue is a very valuable skill in itself, and needs to be continually practised and supported. You might think about how you could model the language you would like students to acquire and develop in your own use of written and spoken language in the classroom, workshop or studio or other educational setting.

> ## Reflective activity 13.1
>
> Really good questions and prompts for dialogue often require thinking about in advance. You might find it helpful to keep a record of useful questions, and share them with colleagues. There are a number of ways to do this, including:
>
> - invite students to elaborate: 'Say a little bit more about...'
> - echo their ideas to help students clarify their own thinking: 'So you think that...'
> - use non-verbal invitations: eye contact, tilt of the head, nod, smile, raised eyebrow(s)
> - make a personal contribution from your own experience: 'I remember...'; clarify ideas: 'I can tell this is the case because...'
> - make a suggestion – this encourages students to offer their suggestions or build on yours: 'You could try...'
> - encourage students to reflect on topics rather than simply look for the most straightforward or obvious answer: 'I sometimes think that/wonder if...'
> - offer information or make an observation on a topic: 'It might be useful to know that...', 'It might be helpful to remind you of...'
> - speculate on a given topic: ' I'm puzzled by that too...', 'What I'm not sure about here is...', 'I wonder what that means...', 'I'm not sure about the implications of that for...'
>
> Another strategy is to let the mistake or wrong answer go on to the whiteboard and wait to see what happens. Students almost invariably spot the error!
>
> Remember that questioning can be used therefore to check students' understanding before, during and after activities and questions, which are used as prompts or starting points for thinking.

2.3 Feedback and marking

Feedback to students can be given in written or verbal form. Both written and verbal feedback can focus on the outcome of an assessment task or activity (product or summative feedback) or on the process in which the student engaged to produce the product (process or formative feedback). We have already seen that feedback is most useful when it focuses on the learning objective/intention and that adopting a 'closing the gap' (Clarke, 2001) approach in classroom discussion through questioning and dialogue can help teachers to stand in the zone of proximal development (ZPD) (Vygotsky, 1934) with their students to identify the next step they need to take to move forward in their learning. Providing feedback to students in written form is no different, and many of the same principles and practices discussed above in relation to 'closing the gap' between current and potential levels of student achievement are also relevant here.

There are, however, many problems and pitfalls in providing students with written feedback. These include marking to show off assessment practice to an Ofsted inspector or external examiner, or providing too much feedback of a critical nature regarding what needs to be improved to the extent that students feel overwhelmed and simply give up. Providing feedback that is too vague or bland for students to do anything constructive with can be another pitfall, as is students not reading or acting upon feedback given. Feedback being given too late is not useful to students, nor is feedback that students do not under-stand. Remember not to treat every written assignment like an English Language test or every mathematics assignment or classroom calculation like a maths test. It is also useful to try not to introduce more than one skill or area for improvement at a time. Students also need to be given enough time to practice applying the new skills, knowledge and advice offered through feedback, so it is best to plan and build time for students to read and act on your feedback into your lessons.

Feedback can be given on first drafts of student work to help them improve their final mark or on submitted work to help students improve future assignments. Feedback should concentrate first on how well the student has addressed the learning objectives/intentions with reference to the success criteria. When marking students' work using formative assessment, a teacher cannot make learning explicit by the occasional tick or an overall mark or grade. Instead, it is important to maintain dialogue with the student beyond the classroom. On paper this can be achieved using the 'I-You' language of conversation to identify particular strengths in the student's work. For example, a teacher could write on a student's script/work:

'I like the way that you have identified the strengths and weaknesses of each of these methods.'

'You really bring the scene to life in this paragraph through your use of powerful verbs and adjectives.'

'You justify your argument well here by giving clear reasons for your position on this subject.'

'You go on to support key points in your argument with reference to relevant literature.'

You can also point to specific points for improvement by careful and constructive use of questions and sensitive use of the imperative tense to help to focus the students' thinking – for example:

'Think about how you could extend your argument here with reference to…'

'How might the work of … be relevant here?'

'What might be a counter-argument to the one you make here?'

Clarke (2001) illustrates a number of prompts to help teachers frame their 'closing the gap' comments. These include:

- reminder prompts – which simply remind the students of what could be improved: *'Say more about how you feel about this character'*.

- scaffolded prompts – for students who need more structure than a simple reminder: *'Can you describe how this person is a good friend?'* (a question); or *'Describe something that happened that showed you they were a good friend'* (a directive); or *'He showed me he was a good friend when…'* (an unfinished sentence).

- example prompts – for students who need more help: '*Choose one of these or your own: He is a good friend because he never says unkind things about me … My friend is a friend because he is always nice to me*'.

Although Clarke conducts her research in school contexts, it is not difficult to see how these prompts could be amended to FAVE contexts.

Case study 13.1 Using video to provide feedback

The following research poster provides an example of how a teacher involved in a JPD project related to teaching English to speakers of other languages (ESOL), funded by the Education and Training Foundation in England, adapted the work of Clarke (2001) in an FAVE context in relation to 'closing the gap' feedback. The teacher used video feedback software to give formative assessment to her learners by scanning each student's writing and saving it as a PDF. She then used software to annotate the scanned document. This process and supporting commentary was recorded in real time and narrated throughout the marking process. This allowed a conversation with the learner to occur during and after the marking process. The video file and annotated PDF were then uploaded by the teacher to Moodle. Each student was able to access their feedback through Moodle as often as they wished. Students reported that they were able to understand the video feedback more clearly, watched the feedback videos multiple times, enjoyed listening to the teacher's pronunciation and preferred video feedback to written feedback.

Figure 13.4
Example of a SUNCETT-ETF practitioner research poster.

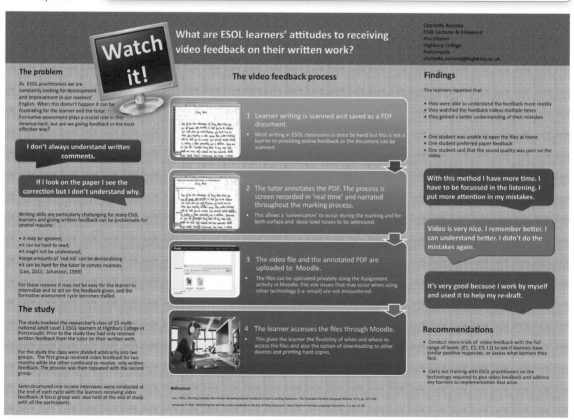

The above study demonstrates how rigorous, robust and principled approaches to formative assessment which originated in the schools sector can be adapted relatively easily by teachers working in FAVE contexts.

Some teachers have also adopted the use of short notes of tutorial discussions to indicate that oral feedback has taken place, and the use of action plans to act as a record and to demonstrate that the teacher has considered a first draft of the work. Others have adapted the weighting of assessment tasks so that a mark can be awarded for a first draft and a further mark awarded for a revised draft to reflect the extent to which the student has listened and responded to formative feedback comments and suggestions

It is important to make feedback and marking practice explicit and manageable. To balance quality with manageability, teachers have to be selective about which pieces and aspects of work they mark in detail. For example, they may spend more time at the beginning of a course to provide detailed formative comments. This not only helps to establish relationships of trust, support and the importance and legitimacy of constructive challenge, it also helps to establish a meaningful dialogue with the student. Students need to know what to expect in terms of feedback and the symbols and protocols of marking, and policy and practice need to be explained to students, mentors, employers and other stakeholders.

2.4 Self and peer assessment

People need to become their own best self-assessors. (Earl and Katz, 2008: 90)

Everyone needs to be continually learning and adapting, becoming more autonomous, self-regulating, self-monitoring learners. The classroom strategies discussed in the sections above help students to become more self-regulating learners. In particular, understanding the objective, and having a clear sense of success criteria and quality, enables students to evaluate their own work. The feedback and marking comments they have seen modelled by teachers help students to give feedback to themselves, essentially 'sitting beside' themselves reviewing their efforts (Muschamp, 1991). Self-assessment, as with so many other aspects of formative assessment, needs support and practice, so to begin with the teacher initiates formative assessment activity. However, the aim is for students to take control so that they initiate repeated moments of self-assessment, integrating the practice into the continual process of working on a task. This is where the real power of self-assessment lies – not in 'marking' completed pieces of work, but in learning to learn and to develop the ability to evaluate and improve your own work.

Similarly, peer assessment is coming to be seen as 'co-operative improvement' (Falkichov, 2001; Clarke, 2011), rather than the swapping of books to be marked in the more traditional sense. If peers look at and discuss work together, with improvements being made immediately, there is little need for over-preoccupation with grades. There is, however, the danger that, especially for less competent writers, peer assessment might become yet another literacy chore, limited by what can be expressed in writing, with consequent impoverishment of feedback. That is why it is important to think about ways in which self and peer assessment might be used in ways which do not always involve the written word.

Putting the focus on improvement also reduces the emphasis on judgement and thus lessens some of the more sensitive risks of peer assessment, including possible threats to self-esteem and opportunities for bullying. Cooperating with a peer in order to make each other's work even better helps students appreciate each other's strengths, can enhance group identity and cohesion and helps students appreciate the value of another point of view. This can help to enhance learning autonomy by encouraging students to realize that it can be very useful to seek, analyse and use another person's perspective in the development of your own thinking. It is also important that self and peer assessment should be focused, by the owner of the work indicating which particular aspect he or she is seeking help to improve.

Reflective activity 13.2

We suggest that you work with a group of students from your class and discuss with them examples of some assessments which you have made. Perhaps you could use some written work that has been produced and look at any comments and corrections you made. How do the students feel about your responses?

You could also self-consciously monitor your verbal feedback during a teaching session. Listen to your comments, observe the students' faces. How do they seem to respond? Are they delighted, wary, confused, anxious, angry, resigned?

What ways of protecting students' dignity can you develop, while still providing appropriate assessment feedback to them? Could you negotiate with the students to establish criteria by which their work will be evaluated? (See Chapter 13)

2.5 Adjusting teaching and learning

The most important factor influencing learning, according to Ausubel (1968), is what the learner already knows; therefore the teacher should take care at the start of a module/unit/lesson to establish each student's entry level – what they know or think about the topic already (see Chapter 10). This seemingly simple yet powerful observation is a key element of formative assessment with its notion of using assessment to match the next steps in learning to the learner's current achievement.

There are a number of ways in which teachers can check students' understanding before starting on a new topic. Asking students to talk about what they already know can be a useful way of identifying 'the tricky bits' in a subject (Rutledge, 2010). Rutledge uses the term *tricky bits* as a way of describing the common misunderstandings and misconceptions in a subject which students often struggle with. Being aware of and paying attention to the *tricky bits* in a subject can help the teacher to develop creative and systematic ways to address and challenge these misunderstandings and misconceptions through careful curriculum planning.

Pre- and post-lesson concept maps can provide rich information and software packages have been developed to help students to organize their ideas, make links, see connections between theories and concepts. Concept maps can be used before and after a lesson to help students to make before-and-after comparisons of how their thinking has developed during the lesson. Other ways to check students' understanding include quick quizzes (on paper or using ICT), individual or group presentations, projects, poster presentations, debates or role-play.

Another approach for gauging current understanding when students already have some knowledge is to ask them to set the questions for a class test at the end. The test itself is not actually taken, but the questions reveal the breadth and depth of current knowledge as well as misconceptions. Some teachers give students a list of the items that constitute the forthcoming topic and ask them to indicate their current understanding of each one, typically using 'traffic lights' (colouring items red, orange, green) to reflect how much they know about or how much they are interested in learning about each particular topic. This technique can be very helpful in effectively directing what is always limited teaching time, but there are two necessary conditions. First, the items must be phrased in such a way that students' responses provide valid information. For example, we don't necessarily know what we don't know about something; I may think that I understand 'photosynthesis' but I may have many misconceptions of which I am unaware. Second, students must respond honestly, and are more likely to do so if they appreciate the purpose of the task and know the consequences of their responses. If a learning culture is well established in the classroom this is unlikely to be problematic, but may be more so if the emphasis has previously been on getting everything right and being seen to be clever.

Whichever techniques are used to establish students' current knowledge and under-standing, they must be used in sufficient time for the teacher to act on what he or she finds out. There is no point using them in the first lesson of a series allocated for a particular topic if the subsequent lessons have already been planned and there is no time to make amendments.

Although it is always sensible to have some learning intentions in mind, learning is not linear and predictable, so you will need to be open-minded about unplanned worthwhile learning that may only become apparent during the learning process.

As we have already pointed out, we should be checking our students' learning and adjusting teaching minute-by-minute, lesson-by-lesson in order to maintain our 'withitness' (Pollard, 2014). There are many ways in which we can glean information about students' learning, for example:

- carefully phrased questioning that elicits important misunderstandings as well as understandings.

- listening attentively to what students say in response to questions and in dialogue and discussion.

- observing students at work.

- checking written work and other tangible evidence.

- looking at students' responses to questions on individual white boards.

- using 'ABCD' cards for every student to give a response to a multiple choice question.
- setting specifically designed tasks for each student.

There are many different adjustments a teacher can make in response to what he or she has found out about students' learning. In general terms this might involve speeding up or slowing down the learning journey, adding more steps or taking some out, refining the support which might be from materials or people, setting different tasks, or changing working groups. The practical possibilities are endless, and range from rephrasing a question or providing a different illustration to a complete rethink about the learning goal and ways to achieve it. Many adjustments are made almost instantaneously, while others may be put into operation the next lesson or the next week. Continual monitoring and adjusting means that we can keep our students' learning on track. If you only check position and progress occasionally then you might find much greater deviations in students' achievements, which may requiring a complete change of tack to get back on course.

Students, too, have an important role to place in monitoring progress and adjusting learning. We have responsibility for the whole class, but no one knows better than the individual student whether he or she needs some additional help or has grasped something and needs to move on. Students can draw upon numerous strategies such as asking a talk partner, drawing a diagram, using equipment, consulting reference material or expressing their understanding in a different way. Continual review and improvement is the essence of self-regulation, an important aspect of learning considered in relation to self-assessment. When a learning culture is well established in a classroom, workshop or studio, students clearly feel comfortable telling their teacher when a lesson is not going well so that they then work together in deciding how to improve matters.

Teachers sometimes worry about deviating from set schemes of work. The important thing to remember here is that schemes of work and plans are there to help, not hinder, learning. The aim is that students will have engaged in meaningful learning and achieved the learning intention, not that a predetermined plan has been relentlessly and unquestioningly followed. Reviewing a sequence of lessons at the end, thinking about what went well and what was less successful, will suggest changes that should be made to the plan for the next time the teacher teaches the same topic.

In summary, learning and teaching will be much more effective if the accuracy of assumed starting points is checked, the appropriateness of the proposed finishing point questioned, and position and progress monitored throughout. You can then use formative assessment and feedback to make appropriate adjustments along the way, rather than – as is so often the case – only checking learning when it is assumed everyone has arrived at the right place, for example through an end-of-topic test, by which time it is too late to address any problems.

Conclusion

In focusing on assessment to support learning, we have drawn attention to the complexity of the relationship between teaching, assessment and learning. We have pointed to the profound influence of assessment practices not only on the content of what is being learned, but, even more importantly, on the process of learning and on the student's sense of self. While it is a complex area, the three research-generated guiding principles discussed above provide sound direction and useful checks for reflective practitioners. The ways in which we assess learning at the end of phases and stages within any programme and the use we make of this information about our students' progress is the next aspect of learning which we go on to discuss in Chapter 14.

Key readings

This short book provides a useful introduction to first principles and practices of Assessment for Learning:

Black, P. and Wiliam, D. (1998) *Inside the Black Box: Raising Standards through Classroom Assessment*. London: King's College.

For a more detailed analysis of Assessment for Learning, see:

Black, P., Harrison, C., Lee, C., Marshall, B. and Wiliam, D. (2003) *Assessment for Learning: Putting It Into Practice*. Buckingham: Open University Press.

These three books and supplementary DVD provide in-depth discussion and practical examples of formative assessment in practice in the schools sector and make it quite easy to see how these examples might be adapted for use in the FAVE sector:

Clarke, S. (2005a) *Formative Assessment in Action: Weaving the Elements Together*. London: Hodder and Stoughton.

—(2005b) *Formative Assessment in the Secondary Classroom*. London: Hodder and Stoughton.

—(2008) *Active Learning through Formative Assessment*. London: Hodder Education.

—(2011) *The Power of Formative Assessment: Self-belief and Active Involvement in the Process of Learning* (DVD). Shirley Clarke Media Ltd.

Assessing for learning in higher levels of FAVE can be found in:

Biggs, J. (2011) *Teaching for Quality Learning in Higher Education*. Buckingham: SRHE/Open University Press.

Assessing adult literacy, language and numeracy can be found in:

Hughes, N. and Schwab, I. (2010) *Teaching Adult Literacy: Principles and Practice*. Maidenhead: McGraw Hill/Open University Press.

Assessing for general FAVE can be found in:

Armitage, A., Evershed, J., Hayes, D., Hudson, A., Kent, J., Lawes, S., Poma, S. and Renwick, M. (2012) *Teaching and Training in Lifelong Learning*. 4th edn. Maidenhead: Open University Press.

Crawley, J. (2011) *In at the Deep End: A Survival Guide for Teachers in Post-compulsory Education*. 2nd edn. Abingdon: Routledge.

Hamilton, M. and Hillier, Y. (2006a) 'Mapping and Tracking: Assessment and Accreditation'. In *The Changing Faces of Adult Literacy, Numeracy and Language*. Stoke-on-Trent: Trentham Books. (Reading 13.1)

Harlen, W., Gipps, C., Broadfoot, P. and Nuttall, D. (1992) 'Assessment and the improvement of education', *Curriculum Journal*, 3 (3), 217–25. (Reading 13.2)

Swaffield, S. (2011) 'Getting to the heart of authentic assessment for learning', *Assessment in Education: Principles, Policy and Practice*, 18 (4), 441–3. (Reading 13.3)

Assessment Reform Group (1999) *Assessment for Learning: Beyond the Black Box*. Cambridge: University of Cambridge School of Education, 5–8. (Reading 13.4)

The associated website, **reflectiveteaching.co.uk**, offers a wealth of supplementary resources including reflective activities, research briefings, advice on further reading and downloadable diagrams, figures and checklists from the book. It also features a compendium of educational terms, links to useful websites, policy and curriculum documents, and showcases examples of excellent research and practice.

part four

Reflecting on consequences

Part Four draws attention to what is achieved in FAVE contexts and by whom, and the consequences of what we do. It examines the consequences of our approaches to summative assessment and educational evaluation. We also look at our legal and moral obligation to take account of the differences between our students. We offer ways in which our professional practice looks at consequences not only of what we do, but to whom.

Chapter 14 reviews assessment and evaluation, paying particular attention to measuring achievement and managing accountability. Chapter 15 considers various dimensions of difference and the ways in which routine processes differentiate between people. It offers approaches to build more inclusive communities in FAVE.

Outcomes
How do we monitor student learning achievements?

14

Introduction

In this chapter we focus on how accountability in FAVE is managed and how we measure student achievement. Accountability in education derives from the process of evaluation, which essentially is concerned with identifying the *value* in an educational activity or process. We discuss the advantages and disadvantages of different approaches to educational evaluation. This includes aspects such as external inspection regimes, management information, targets and league tables. Other means of measuring educational performance and progress are explored. We also consider widely used approaches to the summative assessment of student achievement, including examinations and competence-based assessment. We then present key issues in the use of summative approaches to educational evaluation.

TLRP principles

Two TLRP principles relate to the achievement of outcomes:

Principle 5: Effective teaching and learning needs assessment to be congruent with learning. Assessment should help to advance learning as well as determine whether learning has taken place. It should be designed and carried out so that it measures learning outcomes in a dependable way and also provides feedback for future learning.

Principle 10: Effective teaching and learning demands consistent policy frameworks with support for teaching and learning as the primary focus. Policies at national, institutional and local levels need to recognize the fundamental importance of teaching and learning. They should be designed to create effective learning environments in which all learners can thrive.

In principle, the summative assessment of student learning aims to assess learning in ways that do justice to the full achievements of students and teachers. Summative assessment should be fair and manageable. It can (where appropriate) be recorded and certified using a variety of measures of impact. It is important to ensure, however, that summative assessment and evaluation measures do not have undesirable educational consequences. In this chapter we discuss methods of summative assessment and the recording and reporting of student achievement. We explore ideas, issues and principles in summative assessment and educational evaluation which we hope will be of interest and use to beginning and experienced teachers working in a variety of FAVE contexts.

We argue throughout this chapter that different ways of seeing the impact of education can bring to light different kinds of evidence of educational achievement.

1 Key issues

1.1 Accountability and improvement

A good system of education should enable people from all walks of life to fulfil their potential and encourage everyone to make a positive contribution to society. This is one of the reasons why education is often linked to considerations of democracy and ideas of social justice. However, in order to establish how 'good' a system of education is, we need to find authentic ways of evaluating its impact upon teachers and learners. Governments all over the world and across the political spectrum routinely introduce ways of 'measuring' or evaluating the impact of educational outcomes in order to demonstrate to taxpayers and voters that public money has been spent wisely and that inspection and education policy reforms are having a positive impact on teaching, learning and assessment. For example, the annual *Education at a Glance* (OECD, 2013) report provides a wealth of comparative data on this issue.

However, evaluating the impact of a system of education is often more complex and more problematic than you might imagine. Different approaches to summative assessment and educational evaluation in a system of education reflect what is considered to be important in education as well as what is not (Stenhouse, 1975; Sarason, 1990; Gregson and Nixon, 2008; Coffield, 2014, Reading 14.1). For example, some approaches to summative assessment and educational evaluation are concerned chiefly with the measurement of educational objectives (the ends or outcomes of a system of education), while others are more interested in educational processes (the means through which educational outcomes are achieved).

Accounting for the wise use of public money understandably leads politicians and policymakers to give priority to the identification and measurement of summative approaches to student achievement and to educational evaluation in terms of hard measures of impact (Gardner et al., 2008). In England, many politicians and public figures argue that such measures – including centrally devised curriculum content, nationally prescribed standards, league tables, targets, examinations and inspections – have worked in driving up standards of educational achievement. Others argue that such ways of seeing the impact of education can have perverse consequences that serve to divert our attention away from enduring educational issues and concerns, towards 'teaching to the test' or the pursuit of instrumental 'fabrications' of achievement (Ball, 2003). Such distortions of practice, Ball argues, can often manifest themselves in shallow demonstrations of compliance with centrally devised standards, public performance to external inspection regimes, narrowly prescribed curricula and the production of educationally 'thin' learning outcomes. These are often supported by highly instrumental evidence that superficial targets for achievement have been met (Elliott, 2001; Fielding et al., 2003; Pollard, 2008; Biesta, 2012; Coffield, 2008, 2014, Reading 14.2).

Wiliam (2009) notes that raising educational achievement is inextricably linked to individual quality of life and economic growth:

> The first step in the argument is to consider why we need to raise achievement. It is not because of Ofsted league tables or what is sometimes called 'the standards agenda'. It is because raising achievement matters both for individuals and for society. For the individual, higher achievement means an increased lifetime salary, improved health and longer life. For society it results in increased tax revenue, lower healthcare costs and reduced criminal justice costs. (Wiliam, 2009: 1)

Longitudinal studies have also demonstrated that people with higher levels of education and qualification have also enjoyed better health as well as higher levels of income (see Bynner et al., 2006; Feinstein et al., 2008).

Ideally, educational evaluation should be an integral part of the organization of learning. It can be carried out for the purposes of ensuring the maintenance of overall standards of performance or for identifying aspects of teaching, learning and assessment that need to be improved. This can include the criteria through which successes and failures, 'the size of the gap between educational aspiration and attainment', can be judged (Adelman and Alexander, 1981). Educational evaluation can be summative, formative, or a combination of both. Whatever form it takes, educational evaluation normally involves the systematic collection and analysis of evidence and making judgements about standards of teaching, learning and assessment based on that evidence. At its best, educational evaluation incorporates a number of viewpoints, including those of education leaders, teachers and learners. There are, however, issues, advantages and difficulties in including multiple viewpoints. Contentious issues involve deciding what the focus of the evaluation should be, whose criteria and what evidence should be used in arriving at judgements and by whom. Brynner et al. (1982: 10) argue that 'only by giving participants the opportunity to contribute to the formulation of evaluation policy can their commitment to it be assured'. Their main contention was that, as teachers will inevitably be responsible for acting upon the findings of educational evaluations and be accountable for putting their recommendations into practice, they should be given a say in deciding what form the evaluation should take. Such inclusive approaches to educational evaluation have been variously referred to as 'formative' (Scriven, 1967), 'democratic' (MacDonald and Parlett, 1973) and 'illuminative' (Parlett and Hamilton, 1972; Parlett and Dearden, 1977).

Others contend that educational evaluation must be rigorous and objective, conducted by trained inspectors who are external to the organization being evaluated. From this point of view, the main focus is upon ensuring that educational organizations are operating in ways which provide evidence of compliance with national policies and regulations. For example, in England, educational evaluation of FAVE takes the form of formal government-funded external inspections. The process begins with each FAVE organization producing a self-assessment document based upon criteria set by the Office for Standards in Education (Ofsted). These reports are made available to Ofsted in the first term of each academic year. Organizations chosen for inspection in that year are notified very shortly before the inspection visit is due to take place. Following the inspection visit, the organization is awarded a grade on the basis of evidence collected by inspectors. These grades identify areas of strength, together with those in need of improvement. The outcomes of inspections are then made public in inspection reports. In this way teachers and education leaders across FAVE in England are held to account for the standards of their practice. Organizations which fail to receive a 'good' or 'outstanding' grade and are required to improve are automatically inspected again the following year. Shain and Gleeson (1999) examine the changing nature of professional practice in the Further Education sector in England. They show how the rise of cultures of audit and inspection are leading to a strengthening of managerialist cultures and generating forms of strategic compliance among lecturers in contexts where the elusive concept of lifelong learning and accounts of a rebirth of professionalism for staff at college level are more rhetorical in nature than real.

Governments and employers place particular emphasis on student retention rates on courses, student achievement, standards of students' literacy and numeracy and the quality, currency and relevance of academic or vocational subject-specialist knowledge acquired. Results from key examinations and assessments and inspection reports are used to make judgements about the quality of teaching and learning. This puts pressure on educational organizations to perform well in public (Shain and Gleeson, 1999, Reading 14.3). Results, league tables and inspection reports are important factors informing students' judgements about where they choose to study. FAVE organizations in England that repeatedly score highly in government-funded inspections against externally set measures of performance earn autonomy in the sense that they are inspected less often and with a 'lighter touch', while those deemed to be less adequate or even failing are put under intense pressure to improve with little, if any, external support.

In contrast, in Finland, educational organizations which underperform are *supported* to improve because of the public acknowledgement of the entitlement of all communities to high-quality education in their locality (Sahlberg, 2011, Reading 4.2). The ways in which this dilemma is resolved in different countries reflects dominant educational and social values and reveals core assumptions about what is considered to be the purpose of education in each country (Biesta, 2015, Reading 1.1; Heilbronn, 2011, Reading 4.1). Governments are understandably concerned with global economic competition and the effectiveness of the national workforce over the long term. State schools are funded by taxpayers who expect good use of their public investments. The economic success of a country, including the pensions and welfare of its older citizens, is seen to depend on the education of its young people and the qualification and skills of its worforce. International comparisons of FAVE systems are conducted regularly, often on an annual basis. The interpretation of such evidence can be controversial, so it is important to remember that such comparisons can be deliberately used for political purposes. We need to be guarded and treat such comparisons with caution before arriving at any conclusions. Most attention is given to schools and higher education in these international comparisons. For example, a comparative international study of performance in the schools sector (OECD, 2011) ranked Finland as the top performing system, followed by South Korea, Hong Kong, Japan, Singapore and then the UK. Although the authors of the report advised against drawing simplistic conclusions from the study, they urged policy professionals to note that there are no magic bullets, that it is important to respect teachers, and that organizational cultures can be changed. They also pointed to the importance of education for the future, not just the present, and the recognition that no one individual stakeholder in education (i.e. parents, teachers, employers) should be regarded as being the impediments or saviours of education.

1.2 Comparing achievements

The interpretation of any assessment involves some form of comparison about performance in relation to something. For example, educational performance can be judged in relation to:

- performances of others (norm referencing).
- specified, agreed standards (criterion referencing).
- an individual's previous performance (ipsative referencing).

While the terms norm, criterion and ipsative may not be commonly used, the practices to which they refer are embedded in the assessment routines of almost all educational institutions.

Norm referencing: With norm referencing, individual students are compared with others. Performance is expressed by ranking, and giving a position in the class is common ('she came third in the class in maths'). Performance can also be expressed in relation to the rest of the group with statements such as 'he's about average' and 'she's in the bottom third'.

Knowing how a student is doing in relation to others is understandable for students and teachers alike. It is necessary when competition and selection are required. However, norm referenced assessment results give no information about the specifics of what any student knows, understands and is able to do, nor do they identify particular difficulties or point to the appropriate next steps in learning.

Criterion referencing: Criterion-referenced assessment makes judgements about a student's attainment in relation to pre-specified criteria, irrespective of the performance of other students. When criteria are made explicit, this form of assessment provides specific information about a student's learning. Criteria not yet met indicate both what students now do know and what they will need to cover to help them move to the next level or stage. The competence-based assessment system endorsed by the National Vocational Qualifications (NVQ) framework in England was based upon a form of criterion referencing described as 'success/performance criteria'. However it is worth noting that NVQ success criteria were based on a rather narrow, reductionist view of learning which has little, if anything, to do with the principles and practices of formative assessment discussed in the previous chapter.

Criterion- and norm-referenced approaches are interrelated in that the criteria take into account what it is reasonable to expect for students at a particular stage of their education, so notions of norm referencing underlie criterion referencing. Norm and criterion referencing are easily associated with notions of success and failure, whether this is judged in relation to others' performance, or the setting of particular standards, benchmarks or cut-off points in a criterion-referenced system.

Ipsative referencing: The word 'ipsative' comes from Latin 'ipse' meaning self. Although this is not a common term, teachers use ipsative-referenced assessment all the time as judgements are made about a student's performance in relation to their previous achievements. This works best for detailed assessment when the teacher knows the student well, can identify specific improvements, and guide next steps at an appropriate degree of challenge.

Ipsative assessment is very supportive of learning, and seeks to motivate *all* students, however they are judged through norm- or criterion-referenced assessment. This is the most inclusive and enabling form of assessment, since it values and challenges those at both extremes of the attainment range and everyone in between (see Chapter 15). It provides direct feedback for a personal learning orientation seeking 'mastery'. (See Schwab and Hughes [2010] for the ways in which ipsative assessment is used in adult literacy, language and numeracy.)

In reflecting on the three bases for comparison, it may be helpful to think about the Olympic Games, where ipsative, criterion and norm referencing are all in evidence. Ipsative referencing underpins preparation for the Olympic Games, as athletes strive to improve on their 'personal best'. Criterion referencing is then often used in relation to qualifying for an event, when athletes do, or do not, satisfy the standard. In the finals, the awarding of medals is norm-referenced for those who come first, second and third. Recognition is also sometimes given to athletes who produce their best-ever performance, but it is the norm-referenced gold medals that are paramount rather than ipsative-referenced personal bests, no matter how remarkable these may be.

> ## Reflective activity 14.1
> Think of a student in your class or a student you know well. Consider when it would be useful and appropriate to use norm-, criterion- and ipsative-referenced assessment. Now list all the different assessments that the student has experienced, and identify the basis of comparison for each. How closely does what happens match what you thought would be useful and appropriate?

1.3 Validity, reliability and dependability

How do you know that you can trust an assessment outcome? How do you know that an assessment instrument actually measures what it is supposed to measure? Here we review three important factors that underpin these questions (see also Mansell and James, 2009; Hillier, 2012).

Validity: This concept is of central importance. The key question to ask in relation to the validity of an assessment is: Does the instrument or method of assessment actually measure what it claims to measure? This is known as construct validity. So, for example: 'Is a written multiple choice test a valid way of assessing students' ability to write effectively?' The answer is 'probably not', because many other forms of knowledge, skills and understanding are involved in writing beyond those needed to complete a multiple choice test. And even though such an assessment method might be considered to have higher construct validity as a measure of, say, knowledge of grammar or spelling, it is also important to acknowledge that some students do not perform consistently in stressful and somewhat artificial situations but may do better when applying their knowledge in a more authentic writing activity.

While we are interested in test results themselves, it is actually the inferences that we draw from outcomes of assessment that make them so crucial. Results of assessment are used to make decisions about, for example: what to teach next; the adequacy of the progress that a student is making; appropriate next stages in terms of educational experience; levels of attainment reached; and the quality of teaching in FAVE organizations, including the quality and relevance of curricula on offer. It is important to remember that the quality of summative assessment decisions inevitably depends on the nature of the assessments on which they are based.

Reliability: If a form of assessment is considered to be valid for a particular purpose, the next question becomes whether it can be used reliably and consistently. If something is reliable, it means that we can expect it to do what it claims to do on every occasion we use it. It is important to ensure that irrelevant factors do not interfere in other ways too. A common problem arises when the capabilities being assessed are interrelated. For example, the level of reading or writing demands of a particular test might constrain some students' ability to demonstrate their understanding of the subject in maths, science or history. In maths, a common problem is when the mathematical question contains a large amount of prose; a student's performance in solving the question will depend on an ability to read the question and this may interfere with being able to do the maths. This is a particularly common situation in adult classes where students may not be using English as their first language (see Chapter 12). It is not always possible to avoid assessment processes which conflate different kinds of knowledge, skills or attributes and we need to be careful in drawing conclusions from such assessment measures.

Reliability can be increased by using questions to which there is only one correct answer (as in multiple choice questions), since such questions are likely to be marked accurately and consistently. However, multiple choice questions can only assess certain kinds of knowledge and learning outcomes, so cannot be used to assess everything that is considered important. Extended writing, speaking and listening, for example, require very different assessment arrangements and are more difficult to assess reliably than factual knowledge.

Obtaining adequate reliability is particularly important when achievements are to be certificated or comparisons made, with implications for equity. Indeed, it is clearly of enormous significance for major national examination systems such as 'A' levels where student performance is measured across institutions and when standards are expected to be maintained from year to year.

Dependability: Assessment regimes are dependable when stakeholders have confidence in their ability to reliably and validly assess learning. It reflects outcomes of the struggle to achieve validity and reliability, and the perceived legitimacy of those outcomes. Mansell and James (2009) defined the dependability of assessments as follows:

> Together, maximum validity and optimal reliability contribute to the *dependability* of assessments – the confidence that can be placed in them. (Mansell and James, 2009: 12)

The central dilemma is that validity and reliability are interrelated, so strengthening one aspect often weakens another.

The search for construct validity tends to lead in the direction of assessment procedures, which are designed for routine classroom circumstances, covering a wide curriculum and using a range of assessment techniques such as question-and-answer, individual and group tasks, course work, assignments, projects, presentations and continuous assessment. Teachers' development and use of a wide range of approaches to assessment resonate with the principles of Assessment for Learning (AfL) and formative assessment, discussed in Chapter 13.

However, the drive for reliability can lead to the simplification in both assessment procedures and the range of curriculum to be assessed, so that there is more chance of comparability being attained. The result of this is an emphasis on methods, which can be tightly controlled, such as timed pen-and-paper or ICT-based tests and examinations. However these can in turn weaken their validity. When the emphasis is on certification of student attainment and organizational accountability, politicians and the media tend to stress this traditional view of reliability and focus on tests and examinations.

The validity and reliability of instruments, tasks, tests and processes are therefore crucial to overall judgements of the dependability of assessment outcomes. Where construct validity is low, assessments are likely to be regarded as partial, limited and crude because of the elements of learning which they ignore or cannot measure. Where reliability is low, assessments will be regarded as inconsistent, unfair and unreliable because of the variation in the procedures by which the assessment results were produced.

In Chapter 13 we focused on the use of formative assessment, assessment to *support learning*. This in itself, a very different goal than the *measurement of attainment* with which this chapter is concerned. A robust and dependable assessment system will be one in which there is clarity about purposes.

1.4 Effects and consequences

Because assessment outcomes are so significant in our societies, people often adjust their behaviour in attempts to secure 'good results' or to influence the interpretation of outcomes. As we pointed out earlier this chapter, this may adversely influence the practice of teachers, including factors such as what is taught, teaching and learning processes, classroom relationships and student experience (Hamilton and Hillier, 2006, Reading 13.1). These are discussed more fully below.

We have already drawn attention to the dangers of situations where summative assessment results are used as measures of performance. This brings about high-stakes situations for students, teachers, school leaders and politicians alike. We have also pointed out that there is a well-documented tendency in such circumstances for teachers and students to 'work to the test' (Stobart, 2008). In addition, we have argued that the result is likely to be a narrowing of the curriculum and, while standards in the tested areas of the curriculum may rise, overall standards across the broader curriculum may fall. For example, in the schools system, the evaluators of the national literacy and numeracy strategies in England expressed deep concerns about the narrowing of the curriculum, which they attributed to targets and high-stakes testing (Earl et al., 2003). Today, particular 'A' level subjects are seen to provide better chances of entering selective higher education institutions and this situation is partly driving both student option choices and the curriculum on offer in schools, sixth forms and FE colleges. Whatever is given prominence in high-profile assessment dominates teaching, while areas of the curriculum that do not feature in widely reported or significant tests can be sidelined. In this way, whole subjects (notably, but not only, the arts) can be devalued. Even within the high-status subjects of mathematics and English, key aspects such as investigations and oral capabilities, self-confidence, tenacity and the development of learning-to-learn strategies can receive very little attention.

High-stakes assessment can have a distorting effect not only on what is taught, but also how it is taught. Teaching 'to the test' in whatever context typically not only focuses on a narrow part of the curriculum but also involves much test preparation concentrating on examination technique, question-spotting, mark-gaining and practice questions. Many students begin their learning in FAVE contexts following less than positive experiences of summative assessment in the school system. They come to study in the sector seeking a second chance to become successful in their learning. Often they regard themselves as 'failures' and have been reduced to thinking of themselves as incompetent learners. To a large extent this may be due to national testing and evaluation regimes in the school system in England, which encourage teaching and learning 'to the test' and a system of assessment that consigns 50 per cent of students to failure if they do not demonstrate potential to achieve five good GCSE grades by time they are 16. As a result, teachers in FAVE are often faced with disaffected and disengaged learners 'whose self-confidence and self-respect have been damaged by their earlier experiences of school' (Coffield, 2008: 27). This places even greater demands on teachers in FAVE who are often expected to address 11 years of negative experiences of compulsory schooling in the space or one or two years.

Coffield argues that England 'still does not have a high quality vocational path which could offer a prestigious alternative to the academic route' (2013: 15). He points out that this seriously disadvantages the lives and life-chances of at least 50 per cent of each generation of students whose futures are not considered to be as important or politically sensitive as their 'A' level counterparts. In a small-scale study of students in the FAVE sector in England Coffield shows that:

> … students have become worried, nervous and mark-hungry. A few of them appear to be obsessed with testing and its significance for their future … The only model of learning which these students mentioned in their writing was the official one of acquisition, where learning is seen as gaining possession of knowledge, skills and qualifications, just as people acquire watches, cars and iPods. (Coffield, 2009: 56–7).

Through the work of Freire, he notes how this instrumental approach reduces education to a banking model, an act of depositing, in which the teacher makes deposits which the students 'patiently receive, memorise and repeat … where the scope of action allowed to the students extends only as far as receiving, filing and storing the deposits' (Freire,

1972: 45–6). Coffield argues that casualties in all of this are students themselves who become diminished rather than enhanced by their experiences of summative assessment in education. They are, he observes, 'filed and stored away ... passive recipients of knowledge, robbed of creativity' (Coffield, 2009: 57).

The ways in which assessment results influence the expectations teachers have of students, students have of each other, and students have of themselves are still not yet fully researched. Repeated testing, including practice tests, seems to reinforce the low self-image of lower-attaining students, which subsequently widens the gap between higher- and lower-attaining students.

There is little doubt that formal assessment procedures have long-term effects on students. In part, these may be seen as positive, in that the quality of teaching and learning may be enhanced. Reflective teachers would be well advised to watch carefully for effects which could damage both the self-image and self-confidence of students and have other divisive consequences.

2 Summative and formative educational evaluation

We have outlined above how summative assessment can have far-reaching implications not only for systems of education but also for the societies which shape them and are, in turn, shaped by them. However well-intentioned, accountability mechanisms based on summative assessment results can have unintended and negative consequences, detracting from the aim of educational improvement. This phenomenon can be seen at all levels, from the single classroom to the nation state (Shain and Gleeson, 1999, Reading 14.3). This is particularly likely when the 'stakes' are high. While tensions created by assessment attempting to serve multiple purposes will always exist, difficulties can be identified and may be ameliorated by awareness and understanding of key issues discussed below.

The assessment of learning for summative and overall evaluative purposes can be carried out in a number of ways, and in this section we consider four main approaches.

2.1 Statutory tests and examinations

In the UK, in FAVE contexts, formal assessment and testing often takes place at the end of modules or units of study and normally at the end of a course. Such outcomes are also used to track the performance of FAVE organizations and the effectiveness of the FAVE education system as a whole. In England, the publication of the Wolf Report (2013) is leading to a sharp increase in the numbers of students in FAVE settings pursuing formally examined GSCE qualifications in English and mathematics.

Examination and other summatively assessed outcome results are part of contemporary inspection and accountability structures as well as representing the personal achievement of individual students. As we have already noted, summative assessment is extremely 'high-stakes', and the policies and practices of most FAVE organizations are highly geared to maximize the results of such measures.

Developing high-quality tests and examinations is a complex and specialized activity. Test development involves not only the writing and carrying out of pilot studies of test items but also all the production of mark schemes and moderation arrangements, the training and monitoring of markers, the procedures for students requiring special arrangements, and much more. Examination boards, awarding bodies and test development agencies typically have great expertise, many years of experience, and are supported by active research divisions, as well as being regulated themselves.

However, testing is not an exact science. Black and Wiliam draw attention to the 'very limited reliability of external tests, which command a degree of confidence which they do not deserve' (1998a: 158). Undoubtedly some students are misclassified, although which individuals and how many in total will always be open to question. Wiliam (2001) estimates that at least 30 per cent of students could be given the wrong grade.

Another problem arising from external testing is the risk of grade inflation. Questions often raised by the press include: Are these students really much better than those of previous years? Is it really that standards are going up, or in another sense are standards actually dropping because exams are getting easier? To counter such fears, exam boards set grade boundaries using examiners' judgements of the quality of work from year to year. They also work to achieve comparable outcomes across subjects and they use statistical modelling to try to account for other contextual factors.

Despite such efforts, the trend of exam performance is a frequent focus for political debate. In England, in the days following the publication of national test results, teachers are often cast by the media in a 'lose–lose' situation where, if student achievement rises, the headlines proclaim that examinations and assessment procedures are too easy; on the other hand, if student performance decreases, the headlines criticise teachers for the fall of standards in teaching and student achievement.

2.2 National and organizational surveys of system performance and student voice

The outcomes of individual students' performance are often aggregated and used as measures of evaluating and comparing the performance of individual FAVE organizations or of national FAVE systems as a whole. This is common in 'neo-liberal' educational systems (Green and Janmaat, 2011 Reading 5.2) where system-wide improvement is expected to come from competition between FAVE organizations. However, as we have seen, this conflates assessment aims so that judgements about the learning of individuals become entangled in measures of whole FAVE organizations or the FAVE system itself. As Harlen et al. (1992) argue, such conflation of aims can have significant unintended consequences.

National surveys of students in the UK engaged in programmes of higher education are conducted annually and results are used to construct and publish league tables of universities. While league tables can be helpful in providing potential students with feedback from previous students regarding their experiences of learning at a particular institution, we have also pointed out that they can contribute to the notion of education as a market. 'In essence education is not a market and it suffers if it is treated as such' (Coffield, 2008: 1). High-stakes testing regimes and league tables 'pit college against college and colleague against colleague' and this in turn 'prevents the widespread emergence of communities of learning' (Coffield, 2013: 20).

Internal organizational surveys of student performance often take the form of questionnaires to students. While these can provide quantitative data regarding aspects of student satisfaction, discussion groups and learning logs can offer a much more powerful way of accessing the voice of learners and help teachers and education leaders to identify aspects of practice in need of improvement. Yet as Coffield points out, 'students are seasoned observers of teachers and are adept in spotting differences between them as well as the strengths and weaknesses of individuals' (Coffield, 2009: 55). Fielding makes a similar point where he argues that we need to work with our students to enable them to collaborate with their tutors in the quest for continuous improvement (Fielding, 2008).

2.3 Non-statutory tests and tasks

There are many tests and tasks that teachers can and do use on an optional basis. Some of these were developed to assist with the monitoring of progress between points of statutory assessment, and are marked by the teachers of the students being tested. This activity itself gives teachers an insight into the statutory assessment process, helps them become more familiar with standards, and provides them with detailed information about each student's performance. These activities are often formative in nature, as we noted in Chapter 13.

2.4 Teacher assessment

Another approach to summative assessment is periodic teacher assessment. Teachers can make judgements about an individual student's level of attainment against national frameworks. This is often used when deciding whether a student should attempt a particular level of qualification, such as with GCSEs in England. However, such a classification provides very little information about what the student actually understands and is able to do.

Although tests and tasks can be used to inform teacher assessment, the true value of teacher assessment is that a wide range of evidence is taken into account, thus increasing validity, so test results should not be given overdue prominence. If we know the individual circumstances of our students, then we can make judgements about their progress which cannot necessarily be ascertained from the more formal assessment regimes.

If, as teachers, our assessment is to be used for summative and comparative purposes, then the development of our understanding of standards is crucial for its reliability. Once we have made provisional judgements, moderation is required to ensure fairness to students and that the data produced is useful. Systems of moderation often help ensure the comparability of assessment across a wider area. In FAVE, moderation processes often involve examining a percentage sample of student work from across each cohort covering the full range of achievement from fail/borderline fail to 'outstanding' (i.e. 'outstanding' is usually taken to be attainment of over 70 per cent of the marks available). Students' scripts are normally first-marked by the teacher who taught the student and then second-marked by another teacher who may or may not know the student in question. Both teachers then arrive at an agreed grade. Samples of student grades from across cohorts are then moderated by teachers from other FAVE organizations who teach the same or similar modules. Differences in grades awarded are noted and discussed in detail to identify how the consistency of grading might be strengthened. The sample of work is then presented for external examination. External examiners are often invited, respected and experienced teachers from other educational organizations offering courses and programmes of a similar nature, or external verifiers appointed by an awarding body (AB). The main purpose of external examination/external verification is to ensure that students' work meets the standards expected in different educational organizations offering similar courses in different parts of the country.

Reflective activity 14.2

How are the programmes you teach assessed and moderated? What process of moderation is used in your organization or for your qualification system? If you have experience of moderation, what challenges have you experienced undertaking this role?

---

3 Using summative and formative educational evaluation

An enormous amount of time, energy and money is expended on assessment, yet students' learning is only improved if assessment information is actually used, rather than simply collected (see Chapter 13). A key point to note here is that assessment information is used in a wide variety of ways, by different people, and for different purposes.

3.1 Supporting student progress

As we have repeatedly seen in this book, it is crucial to build on students' current knowledge and understanding. It is important that at the start of any module or unit of work we need to use assessment information to establish each student's entry level to the subject. When teaching any lesson, we can use assessment information formatively to adapt our teaching depending on the students' responses. At the end of each lesson we can note – probably on the plans themselves or in a reflective diary – things that need to be taken account of in the next lesson. These may apply to all or just some of the students and could be about the need to reinforce a particular concept, or omit a planned activity since the learning objective it was designed to support is already well grasped.

Towards the end of a unit or module we may devise a particular assessment activity focusing on the key learning objectives for that unit or module, and we may use the last period of time near the end of a unit or course to extend the work or review unit or course objectives, as the students' remaining learning needs and any areas of misunderstanding or misconceptions emerge. After a unit, module of work or course has been completed, notes will again be made to inform both the future teaching of that unit to other groups, and the future teaching of related units to the same group of students.

Teachers in FAVE in England often use a Personal Learning Plan (PLP) to work in collaboration with their students to monitor student effort, progress and achievement against agreed standards. Review of the PLP usually begins with student self-assessment of their progress towards national/module standards. This self-assessment process and supporting evidence to support judgements arrived at by the student are brought to an individual tutorial and act as a focus for professional, vocational or personal dialogue and target-setting with the tutor to enable the identification of next actions or next steps in the student's future development.

Numerical assessment data, perhaps in the form of levels or grades awarded, can be used as part of the PLP process for tracking progress over time. PLP data can be used periodically to monitor the attainment of both individuals and groups and these can be compared with both their previous and target attainment, and judgements made about whether they are on an appropriate learning trajectory, falling behind or exceeding expecta-tions. Different scenarios could lead to different actions to support learning – for example, reviewing and revising initial expectations, providing additional support or extending the challenge. Similarly when expectations for a unit, module or course of work have been set in terms of what 'all', 'most' and 'some' of the students should attain, recording names against each category enables student tracking but without recourse to levels or grades. It is important to remember that, despite their apparent attractiveness, numbers are a very blunt instrument when trying to represent student learning.

3.2 Transfer and transition

Assessment information can support effective transition when students move from one level to another. It provides important information when students want to move from one FAVE organization to another or when they progress into higher education or employment. It is vital that key information is passed on in a manageable way and at times when the information can be used effectively. This can take the form of transcripts of students' achievement and/or personal references.

People who complete FAVE courses may move into work or undertake further study, apprenticeships provided by employers and industry training centres, a tradi-tional vocational education route into skilled employment, or into college or university education. For many FAVE students, contemporary economic circumstances are much more challenging than they have been for some time. Other aspects of student progress and achievement which are not usually measured in formal assessment regimes include resil-ience, determination, self-confidence, self-respect, creativity, flexibility and a continuing commitment to learning to learn. However, these are vital aspects of character in relation to finding work or moving to higher levels of study.

3.3 Whole-organization improvement and accountability

We have already drawn attention to how a prominent use of assessment evidence in recent years, particularly in the English education system, has been in relation to targets. National targets have been set and then cascaded down FAVE organizations, with funding closely tied to the achievement of such targets. Performance target and outcome data are hugely influential on organizational policies and practices, as well as being central to account-ability mechanisms. This is a worldwide trend, though 'England arguably has more data and more sophisticated data than any other jurisdiction in the world' (Earl and Fullan, 2003: 385).

National examinations, tests and related assessments of every student on many occasions during their school career have generated huge amounts of data, at the same time as developments in information technology have enabled large-scale data storage, sophisticated analysis and detailed reporting. Alongside this, the high profile now given to accountability in education has spawned huge industries using management information systems for the assessment of data for organizational improvement and accountability. College principals, education leaders and inspectors regularly use this assessment data as a driver for organizational improvement. This can provide opportunities to mediate and explain information to students, employers and others.

Preoccupations with targets, data collection and outcomes-driven funding can, however, have serious unintended consequences. Data can be extremely helpful in making informed decisions (Ofsted, 2008), but can also misleading and open to misinterpretation. Nevertheless, a basic understanding of evaluation and assessment data and their strengths, weaknesses and related issues is essential for all teachers and educational leaders in helping them to identify aspects of their practice in need of improvement. A balance must be struck, therefore, between putting teaching and learning at the heart of what we do and ensuring that data collection does not become too onerous. Data should not be used as a stick to beat teachers with, but as a focus for productive, open, honest and constructive professional dialogue, where all concerned are mutually accountable and responsible for securing improvements in teaching and learning.

Data derived from assessment is sometimes referred to as 'performance data', a term that encompasses:

Raw and aggregated attainment data
Value-added data
Contextual value-added data.

Attainment data can be generated by teacher assessment, tasks, tests and examinations, and peer observation, and typically attention is given to certain key indicators – for example, the attaining of a particular level, or higher grades in a combination of subjects, or the point score from a number of subjects, or the achievement of a higher grade through peer observation. When raw data from individual students are aggregated, other indicators are possible – for example, the percentage of students attaining five or more good grades.

Value-added data takes account of the fact that students have differing starting points, and so two students with the same raw score at the end of a stage could have made very different progress or even none at all. Value-added data is applicable for both individuals and large groups of students and is particularly relevant when comparing organizations whose students on intake were already attaining very differently. Contextual value-added data takes the notion further, by not only considering students' prior attainment but also taking account of other factors such as gender, ethnicity, special educational needs, and a proxy for social deprivation such as the postcodes or districts where students live. Many people regard contextual value-added data as being a much better measure of organizational performance than raw scores (Schagen and Hutchinson, 2003) although it is worth bearing in mind that value-added data also requires understanding and careful interpretation. Performance data may be aggregated, analysed and used to produce league tables. These often attract considerable media attention and are promoted as enabling students and employers to make judgements about different providers and so inform choice. This, in turn, puts market pressure on organizations to improve. However, as we have argued, the reliability of such analyses cannot be taken for granted.

Reflective activity 14.3

Try to identify where data is held in your organization, in your region and, where possible, in your country. Where could you find information about comparative achievement of your own students? Does your organization require you to use benchmarks and if so, how and what do you do?

---

4 Records and reporting

4.1 Keeping records

All teachers need to take decisions about *what* aspects of students' activity and learning achievements should be recorded, and *how* they should be recorded.

What should be recorded?

There are multiple purposes of assessment and recording. As a minimum, records must meet legal requirements, which normally require organizations to keep 'curricular' records on every student. These formally record academic achievements, modules/units/assignments outcomes, skills, abilities and progress, and are a subset of the fuller educational records that must be maintained for each individual. This requirement could probably be met by simply keeping a copy of all tutorial records, moderation records and reports and cohort assessment profiles. However, this is unlikely to be sufficient to support our students' learning, Nor is it likely to satisfy the requirements of inspectors and others, who will expect to see close analysis of retention, achievement and other data regarding individual student starting points, evidence of differentiated support to enable each student to achieve their full potential, and measures of individual and group progress.

Beyond the legal minimum, within any organization teachers might keep a variety of different records, each with particular purposes and uses. These might include:

- evidence of teacher planning the next steps in teaching and learning.
- evidence of what a student knows, understands and can do, and the progress that he or she has made.
- evidence that students are aware of the progress they are making.
- evidence of target-setting.
- evidence to inform discussions with mentors or employers.
- accurate information about a student's attainment, progress and learning needs that can be passed on to the next teacher.
- evidence to assist with end-of-year or statutory teacher assessments.
- evidence to inform revisions to medium-term plans and schemes of work in the light of student feedback.
- evidence of evaluations on the effectiveness of teaching.
- evidence of the identification and issues and actions taken in progressing the organization's improvement plans.

(Adapted from Swaffield, 2000)

Case study 14.1 How should records be kept?

How should records be kept?
This question concerns manageability and the use of records. It is useful to think of the range of forms that records can take, as in Figure 14.1.

Along with whatever recording systems the organization decides upon, teachers will keep records to assist in their day-to-day teaching and to contribute to the whole-organization system monitoring. In most countries there are moves towards increasing access to records. For instance, in England, teachers can keep personal records solely for their own use, but any record which may be seen by or transferred to other teachers or other professionals must be made available on request. This can help teachers develop the habit of recording achievement in a positive format. The issue reflects general ethical concerns about the central accumulation and recording of information about individuals, whether medical, financial, criminal or anything else. Indeed, most of us would probably want to know what was being kept on us and many people take the view that this is a legitimate right. Continuous awareness of the possible audiences for teacher-created records is necessary, and FAVE organizations in Europe should consider the implications of the requirements of the Data Protection Act, 1998, and the Freedom of Information Act, 2000.

Figure 14.1 Screenshot of examples of PLPs, cohort analysis, improvement plans.

Surname	Forename	Interview and Induction Stage	Tutorial 1		Tutorial 2		Final Attainment stage
		Potential Attainment Grade	Current Achievement Grade	Next Stage Achievement Target	Current Achievement Grade	Next Stage Achievement Target	Final Attainment Grade
Dimmick	Charlie	1	2	1	2	1	2
Freeman	Lewis	1	3	2	2	1	1
Goff	Sam	2	3	2	3	2	3
Hatty	Tony	2	2	2	3	2	2
Hazlett	Sandra	2	3	2	3	2	3
King	John	1	3	2	3	2	2
Mann	Claire	1	3	2	2	1	2
Peterson	Robert	2	3	2	3	2	2
Stevens	Zoe	2	2	2	2	1	2

4.2 Reporting to employers, mentors and other stakeholders

Families and employers are hugely significant in students' lives – as, of course, is informal learning in other settings. For these reasons, if teachers are able to inform, learn from and work with such significant others, the improvement in learning outcomes for students is likely to be considerable (Desforges, 2003; Goodall and Vorhaus, 2010).

However, the ways in which we report the progress of our students are influenced by two seemingly contradictory sets of expectations. The first makes the assumption that in FAVE, employers and mentors are often *partners* with teachers in supporting the learning of each student. Employers and mentors may be routinely invited into the organization at recruitment and selection stages of a course and at other key progression points, including programme boards and assessment boards. Tutorial discussions are likely to include consideration of assessment processes in relation to the progress of students and with reference to the standards of their work and their achievements to date.

One of the most explicit ways of manifesting the partnership model is through the processes which a FAVE organization adopts in reporting students' achievements. Steering groups, focus groups, open days/evenings, employability events, interim reports, phone calls, emails, individual face-to-face discussions and so on can all strengthen the relationship between students and teachers, while also addressing employer expectations about access and information. Some of the best practice involves the students as active participants – for example, through employers/previous students attending recruitment fairs and first appointment events and contributing to written reports and evaluations.

The second expectation is based on an image of employers as *consumers* of vocational education, having contracted with the college or training organization for the provision of educational services to their current or potential apprentice, employee or potential employee. As such, employers and other stakeholders require a report of outcomes, through which the FAVE organization can be held accountable for student progress. Most FAVE organizations make provision that reflects elements of both these approaches. While the partnership model of FAVE is professionally acknowledged as contributing very constructively to student learning in FAVE contexts, the consumer model is increasingly underwritten through litigation and the establishment of sector-led employer organizations.

Additional information is required for students who have undergone grading against national standards assessments, and comparative information about same age/subjects at the organization and nationally must be available on request. Such requirements feed the consumer model of education. The partnership aspect is most clearly demonstrated by the inclusion within reports of targets for the future, and the provision of advice about specific ways in which employers can help.

However, it is by no means clear how this tension between partnership and consumerist models will develop over time, particularly in view of severe cutbacks in funding and the significant raising of fee levels for FAVE and university courses.

Conclusion

We have argued in this chapter that the summative assessment of student achievement and approaches to educational evaluation are crucial, complex and increasingly controversial. It is of vital importance to the students themselves, as their lives and life-chances can be significantly affected by the outcomes of summative assessment. Summative student assessment can also shape self-image, self-respect, confidence and motivation. The process of summatively assessing students' learning is therefore complex and requires careful professional judgement.

Summative assessment and outcomes-based approaches to educational evaluation also often have implications for FAVE organizations, teachers and heads of department, as their work is increasingly judged on the basis of students' results in formal summative assessments. In England, FAVE providers can be closed if their performance is deemed to be unsatisfactory by Ofsted inspectors, with consequences that spread beyond the organization to the surrounding community.

We need a secure understanding of issues in summative assessment and educational evaluation so that we can make the best decisions for our students' learning, and engage in informed dialogue with colleagues, students, employers, mentors, inspectors, policy-makers and the public.

Key readings

Books that provide overview of assessment are listed for Chapter 13 but are also relevant for this chapter. Readings given below are more focused on the summative purposes of assessment, but may also relate to issues discussed in the previous chapter.

Biesta provides a an insightful analysis of the ways in which assessment and evaluation practices are directing attention away for enduring educational issues:

Biesta, G. (2010) *Good Education in an Age of Measurement*. London: Paradigm Publishers.

Mansell, W. and James, M. (2009) 'Assessment in Schools: Fit for Purpose?'. A Commentary by the Teaching and Learning Research Programme. London: Economic and School Science Research Council Teaching and Learning Research Programme.

For a detailed consideration of aspects of evalaution policy, including strategies, orgamization, reporting and action, see:

Brynner, J., McCormick, R. and Nuttal, D. (1982) *Organisation and Use of Evaluation*. Milton Keynes: Open University Press.

For a careful and accessible discussion of why teaching and learning should regain its rightful place as the main priority in the FAVE sector, see:

Coffield, F. (2008) *Just Suppose Teaching and Learning Became the First Priority*. London: Learning and Skills Network.

In this edited book Parlett and Dearden provide practical examples of alternative approaches to educational evaluation:

Parlett, M. and Dearden, G. (eds) (1977) *Introduction to Illuminative Evaluation: Studies in Higher Education*. Cardiff-by-the-Sea, CA: Pacific Soundings Press.

For a thought-provoking illustration of how long-standing educational structures, coupled with the need of various stakeholders in education to defend their power, stifles education reform efforts, see:

Sarason, S. B. (1990) *The Predictable Failure of Educational Reform: Can We Change Course Before It's Too Late?* San Francisco: Jossey-Bass.

Much of the literature for further reading suggested for Chapters 13 and 14 will also be relevant here.

For a consideration of the impact of widely used summative approaches to educational evaluation upon teaching and learning, see:

Gregson, M. and Nixon, L. (2009) 'Assessing effectiveness: ways of seeing impact', *International Journal of Interdisciplinary Social Sciences,* 21 (3). **(Reading 14.1)**

A powerful critique of current government policies alongside a considered response:

Reading 14.2 – edited from Coffield, F. (2014) *Beyond Bulimic Learning.* London: University of London, Institute of Education (IOE), 162–6.

For a thought-provoking consideration of the rise of managerialsim in the FAVE sector, see:

Shain F. and Gleeson, D. (1999) 'Under new management: changing conceptions of teacher professionalism and policy in the further education sector', *Journal of Education Policy,* 14 (4), 445–62. **(Reading 14.3)**

The associated website, **reflectiveteaching.co.uk**, offers a wealth of supplementary resources including reflective activities, research briefings, advice on further reading and downloadable diagrams, figures and checklists from the book. It also features a compendium of educational terms, links to useful websites, policy and curriculum documents, and showcases examples of excellent research and practice.

Inclusion
How do we manage equality and diversity?

15

Introduction

> Inclusive education requires the transformation of what has been common practice in schools and colleges, to ensure all learners can be successful in achieving their social and academic potential. Historical inequalities exist and have existed throughout human history. A human rights perspective, which has gained support in the years since the UN Declaration of Human Rights (1948), demands that the world move forward to embrace a collaborative future where people and our environments are placed before profits. All are born into humankind, so all have a right to grow up and receive their education together. Breaking down the barriers that prevent this is an important part of human progress and the development of a sustainable future. (Rieser, 2011: 156)

This is a chapter about what inclusion means in the context of teaching and learning. It is a chapter about how people are included and excluded in educational contexts. It is a chapter about how we are different and how we are the same. It is about understanding people better as we come to understand teaching and learning better. It explores how education can exclude, discriminate and marginalize people as well as how it can enhance, enrich and expand all of our lives. Our starting points are that diversity is a reality and a very welcome one, and that inclusive practice, the desire and commitment to make sure every person is given the best opportunities to learn and achieve, is at the core of 'good' teaching (Richardson, 2009, Reading 15.1). This chapter offers an opportunity to consolidate everything you have read in this book so far. It also invites you to think carefully about the diversity of your students; about prejudice, discrimination, bullying and exclusion; about meeting needs and understanding disability; about multiculturalism and racism; and about our particular take on the concept of 'inclusive pedagogy'.

TLRP principles

Three TLRP principles are relevant to this chapter:

Principle 3: Effective teaching and learning recognizes the importance of prior experience and learning. Teaching and learning should take account of what the learner knows already in order to plan their next steps. This includes building on personal and cultural experiences of different groups of learners.

Principle 4: Effective teaching and learning requires teachers to scaffold learning. Teachers should provide activities which support learners as they move forward, not just intellectually but also socially and emotionally, so that once these supports are removed, learning is secure.

Principle 7: Effective teaching and learning fosters both individual and social processes and outcomes. Learning is a social activity. Learners should be encouraged and helped to work with others, to share ideas and build knowledge together. Consulting learners about their learning and giving them a voice is both an expectation and a right.

---

1 Diversity: How we are different

Diversity is how we are different. We are all different and we are different in so many ways. Imagine a class you have taught or are teaching now. Imagine a class at a prison or a community centre near you. Imagine a class you have been a member of, or a class you have dreamt of joining but never managed to. Think about all the ways in which the people gathered are different. We may be of different ages and have different educational backgrounds. We may have different purposes for joining the group, different motivations, interests and passions. We may be of different ethnic backgrounds, genders and faiths. We may have different sexualities, different family and financial circumstances. We may use different languages and have varying confidences with reading and writing.

We may be physically different; some of us may be fitter, stronger or able to run faster or jump higher. We certainly smell different, because our body chemistry and diets are different and we have different washing routines and products. We may have different needs in terms of mobility; some of us may walk and others may use wheelchairs. Some of us may be D/deaf or blind to varying degrees. Our health is likely to be different; some of us may have long-term conditions which require medication, make us tired or cause us pain. Some of us will be marathon runners and others will struggle to run a few metres to a bus. We get different amounts of sleep. We are of different ages. Our mental health will be different; some of us will be dealing with anxiety, depression or schizophrenia. Some of us may be suffering from addiction, be living, or have lived, with addicts. Some of us may have specific learning difficulties, like dyslexia, and others may have learning disabilities and need support with the tasks of daily life. We will be different in terms of our legal statuses in this country; some of us may be refugees, some may be undergoing asylum proceedings, others will have been granted leave to remain, some will have been citizens from birth and others will have been recently granted citizenship. Some of us may be under threat of deportation.

We will also be different in how and where we live. Some of us live alone and some with others. Some of us are in prison or on parole, some in safe housing and some living in shop doorways. Some have substantial caring duties, for children, vulnerable adults or the elderly. Some of us are lonely. Some are pregnant, breastfeeding or with small children who keep us awake most nights. Some of us go to sleep surrounded by people we love; others are far away from those they love. Some have been told their love is wrong.

Some of us feel confident in educational settings, feeling that we know what is expected and that we belong. Others of us feel unsure, insecure, or that we are not sure that we are the sort of people who are meant to be here. Some of us have talents in other areas – music, art, cooking, sport – and find this a source of strength. Some of us may be searching for our talents and some may have been told (many times) that we are stupid or useless. Some of us may have come to the class to make friends, to give our lives some structure or to learn a particular skill. Some of us are there as a first step in a bigger life plan.

We are different in what we find easy, in what we find difficult, in what we find stimulating, or challenging, or boring, or important, or not important. We are different in where we have been, who we have spoken to, what we have read, seen or heard. We are different in the weather we like, in the experiences we hold and remember, in what we feel is normal or in where we feel accepted. We are different in how we smile and in how we dance and in how we kiss. We are different in how we make rice or what we eat for breakfast. We are different in our experiences, tastes, preferences, in our priorities, life plans and desires. We are different in our moods and in what makes us happy or unhappy. We are different in what and how we see.

These are only some ways in which we are different; these are all ways that learners in your groups may be different. Crucially they are all ways in which we can be the same. These are all things we can have in common, ways that we can feel united with others, despite more obvious or assumed differences. The chief task of this chapter – and one of the most important tasks of any teacher, in any teaching situation – is to think about what these differences, and similarities, mean for teaching and learning (Richardson, 2009, Reading 15.1).

Reflective activity 15.1

Think about the differences mentioned above, and others you may think of. What do these mean for you as a learner? As a teacher? How do things look different when viewed from these two different perspectives?

Some of these differences mean that we may focus on different examples, different activities or elements to our curricula. If a language teacher knows that several members of a group are homeless, then they would probably decide not to do topics around 'describe your home' and instead ask people to describe a room in the teaching centre, a library or a nearby café. If a biology teacher knows that several quieter members of the group are passionate about music, they may try to focus on music examples when describing how the ear works and even try to encourage some of the students to play or perform their music as part of an example. People will learn in different ways or at different paces. A floristry teacher may be aware that some members of the group have well-developed study skills for learning the names of plants while others are not sure where to start, so she may pair up students as 'study skills buddies' to share ideas or give more individual support to those who need it.

Every single way we are different, mentioned above, could have an impact on why and how someone learns. They could have an impact on attendance or on whether someone can do homework. One key message is that teachers need to be sensitive to potential differences and keep reflecting on what these differences could mean for how each learner learns and the implications of this for their role as teachers. Another message is that our diversity is itself diverse; our differences mean different things for teaching and learning. Some differences can mean that some of us are made more vulnerable, and others more powerful. Some differences can mean that some opportunities are open to some of us and not others and so diversity is related to fairness, justice and equity. This is what is usually understood by discrimination. Difference is also how some are excluded. We will examine discrimination and exclusion next.

2 Discrimination, prejudice, bullying and exclusion

2.1 Discrimination and the law

Discrimination is usually understood as the prejudicial, or less favourable, treatment of individuals because of their membership of, perceived membership of, or association with a specific group or category. If someone refuses to let me enrol on a college course because I am of a particular religion, this would usually be considered to be *direct discrimination*. If I am allowed to enrol on the course, but it is only offered on a particular day that would usually preclude people of a certain religion being able to attend, then this could be considered *indirect discrimination*.

Legislation exists in many countries to define discrimination and outlaw it in relation to specific aspects of diversity. In the United Kingdom, the Equality Act of 2010 was a very important piece of legislation. It drew together, clarified and, in some cases, extended existing separate items of legislation around equality, diversity and discrimination, and it attempted to do so in more easily understandable language. Interestingly, it starts by setting out the 'public sector duty regarding socio-economic inequalities' (all quotations are from the official Equality Act website; see Bibliography), aiming to ensure that the goal of reducing socio-economic inequality is central to all public decision-making. In this way, the Act is framed by an awareness of the large socio-economic inequalities which form the background against which acts of discrimination occur.

The Equality Act 2010 identifies nine 'protected characteristics' or aspects of diversity, and sets out legislation around how workplaces, education providers and other organizations cannot discriminate against someone (or harass or victimize; see discussion later) on the basis of these characteristics. The 'protected characteristics' are: age; disability; gender reassignment; marriage and civil partnership; pregnancy and maternity; race; religion or belief; sex; and sexual orientation. We will explore each of these characteristics briefly here, both in terms of what the Equality Act says about them and what we can add from the perspective of adult educators.

Age

Age is not a protected characteristic in compulsory schooling. This means that pupils at a school can indeed be treated differently on the basis of their age (so 5-year-olds are treated differently from 12-year-olds and so on). Age *is* a protected characteristic in further and higher education. What does this mean for retired learners and courses geared towards employability? Or older learners when funding is focused increasingly on younger learners? Do we, as teachers, treat our learners differently because of their ages? Do we have different expectations? Schuller and Watson (2009, Reading 15.2) point to the importance of being able to access educational opportunities throughout our lives.

Disability

The Act offers a legal definition of disability: as a 'physical or mental impairment' which 'has a substantial and long-term adverse effect on [someone's] ability to carry out day-to-day activities'. Long-term means 12 months or more. The act stipulates that further and higher education institutions have a 'duty to make reasonable adjustments' to support those with disabilities in their studies. According to this definition, a long-term illness, like cancer, could be considered a disability, while breaking a leg normally would not be. This definition of disability, and the legal requirement for 'reasonable adjustments', shapes policy and practice in the FAVE sector. We will return to disability later in this chapter, but what is crucial here is that the Act makes it clear that the onus is on the educational organization to meet the needs of a disabled person. If I am blind and want to access a course, a college cannot tell me that their courses are not for blind people; it has to try to make the 'reasonable adjustments' required to allow me to access the course. The legislation around disability is therefore at once complex (What is a reasonable adjustment? Reasonable to whom? What affects someone's ability to carry out day-to-day activities?) and yet provides a clear statement of policy: if you are disabled and want to join a course, the provider of that course has a duty to accommodate you.

Gender reassignment

Someone fits the protected characteristic of gender reassignment if they are 'proposing to undergo, is undergoing or has undergone a process (or part of a process) for the purpose of reassigning the person's sex by changing physiological or other attributes of sex'. This means that someone who was born a man and who has become, or is going to become, a woman, or vice versa, is protected from discrimination, harassment or victimization, such as other students refusing to call her by her female name. Also if someone is going into hospital for gender reassignment, a workplace or educational institution is required to treat them as they would any other person who going into hospital for an operation. If a teacher has someone in their group who is planning to undergo gender reassignment, then the teacher needs to talk to that person about what, if anything, they want to tell the other students.

Marriage and civil partnership

In workplaces, this can mean that someone who is in a civil partnership cannot be treated less favourably than someone in a marriage (for example, being granted a leave request when a spouse or civil partner is in hospital having a serious operation). The issue of marriage, civil partnership and non-married life is also an important one in FAVE in terms of inclusive practice. If a language teacher (or a history teacher or any other teacher) focuses all their examples on heterosexual married life, this is likely to alienate those who are not married, not heterosexual or simply not interested in family life.

Pregnancy and maternity

This means that a woman cannot be treated less favourably because she is pregnant, has given birth (within 26 weeks) and/or is breastfeeding. In workplaces, this provides crucial protection around maternity leave. In FAVE, it means that teachers need to work with their pregnant and breastfeeding students to work out how they can meet deadlines and fulfil course requirements.

Race

The Equality Act 2010 states that 'race includes a) colour b) nationality and c) ethnic or national origins'. This definition reflects contemporary usage of the term 'race' in Britain today and highlights its complexity. The Act makes it clear that discrimination on the basis of race is illegal. Race and racism will be discussed later in this chapter.

Religion or belief

The Act's definition of religion or philosophical belief stresses that religion includes a lack of religion and belief a lack of belief. The Act makes it clear that colleges and other FAVE institutions are therefore required to ensure that they are not discriminating against students on the basis of their faith, or lack of faith. Some Muslim students need to pray five times a day and this has led to many further education colleges creating prayer rooms so that students don't miss parts of their lessons because they have to travel to mosques. These prayer rooms are usually called 'multifaith prayer or meditation rooms' because to mark them only for Muslim students could be seen as discriminating against those of other faiths or none. The line between what is accommodating some faiths or beliefs and what is compromising others may seem blurred at times, but it could be helpful to remember that discrimination is about disadvantage, not about someone feeling more or less comfortable with a topic of conversation. For example, discussing a homosexual author in a literature class may (or may not) make a particular learner from a certain Christian group feel uncomfortable, but this is not discrimination. Determining what constitutes religious discrimination can also be complex, because one faith – Christianity, Islam and Judaism make good examples – is usually made up of many different forms and interpretations.

Sex

Sex is a physiological category, being a man or being a woman. Women cannot be treated less favourably than men and vice versa. In FAVE, this raises the issue of women-only and men-only classes, for example (taking two examples from a further education college in Greater London) 'Fresh Start for Women' – a return-to-study programme for women who have been out of education for some time, or 'Men's Talk' – a discussion group for men with learning disabilities. The former is only for women and the latter only for men, and yet these are not usually seen as examples of sexual discrimination, but rather examples of an educational offer designed to support learners with particular needs (women who may feel unconfident about returning to study and may want the support of an all-female group, or men who may want to talk about issues to do with masculinity, sexuality or dating in the company of other men with learning disabilities). Nevertheless, these classes *could* be seen as discriminatory, particularly if they left a gap in the provision.

Sexual orientation

This is about sexual orientation: heterosexual, homosexual or bisexual. Discrimination on the basis of sexual orientation is illegal. In terms of teaching and broader inclusion issues, this raises important questions. Are ESOL classes using materials exclusively based on heterosexual married couples and traditional families treating those who are not hetero-sexual less favourably? Some teachers and sociologists talk about the invisible heterosexual norm. This means that classrooms which many teachers and students may think are 'sexual orientation neutral' are actually full of talk of husbands and wives (heterosexual family norms) while there is no equivalent presence of homosexual or bisexual lives.

The specificity around these nine protected characteristics does not mean that they are the only way we can see diversity or discrimination. These are certainly not the only ways that people suffer discrimination. The act itself acknowledges the underlying socio-economic basis of much discrimination, but it is perhaps within the nature of a capitalist society that we cannot really deal with it; we cannot take anyone to court for discrimi-nation when someone gets paid £6.50 per hour to do their job while another person gets paid £2,000 per hour to do their job.

Reflective activity 15.2

Review the nine 'protected characteristics' identified by the Equality Act 2010. Reflecting on the practice of your organization, identify one way of working in your organization that works well in tackling discrimination and making sure that those associated with the protected characteristic feel safe, are included and are able to get the best out of their education opportunity. What lesson can you draw from this successful example for the wider practice organization?

2.2 Prejudice

We should perhaps stop and think about the relationship between prejudice and discrimi-nation. Prejudice is *pre-judging* groups or individuals of people, usually based on stereotyping. It is an extension of what our minds do all the time, of what we do to make sense of the mass of information we are faced with every day. Our minds group things into categories based on our observations and experiences. Children very soon learn that, for example, older people usually have wrinkles. Having a prejudice does not neces-sarily mean that we act in a discriminatory way. Someone could have the prejudice that women are 'over-emotional', but as long as this person does not act on this prejudice – for example, refusing to hire women – this is not discrimination.

Some say that the legal framework offered by the Equality Act 2010 is so important because we will always have prejudices, so the important thing is to be clear on what constitutes discrimination in order to avoid it. We cannot avoid prejudice, perhaps, but we can and should avoid discrimination. Is that right? But, a note of caution: it is not always, or often, easy to tell when we have prejudices and when we may be putting those prejudices into discriminatory action.

Let's look at an example. A teacher may have a prejudice but may not see it as a prejudice, rather that her experience has led her to believe that most young Indian women are highly reflective and hard-working, while most young football-playing men are restless and find it hard to concentrate. If this teacher sees one of the students, a young woman of Indian heritage, looking out the window of her philosophy class, she may be likely to think this young woman is in the process of thinking deeply – exactly what she should be doing in a philosophy class. If the same teacher sees another student, a young football-playing man, doing exactly the same thing (looking out of the window), she may be more likely to interpret it as daydreaming, not concentrating, being 'off-task'.

These small acts of interpretation can influence teacher assumptions and expectations. They can influence how the teacher treats each student (in the above case, perhaps the teachers would be more likely to ask the woman more challenging questions and the man less challenging questions) and how the students, in turn, respond and react to the teacher and the class. This can produce what is often called 'self-fulfilling prophecy' – the teacher thinks one student will achieve more highly and so they do (because the teacher has treated that student differently). Given that so much of our work as teachers is about judgement, interpretation and different acts of assessment, we need to be very careful about what prejudices we may carry and how they may play out in our actions (Gregson, Nixon and Spedding, 2011, Reading 15.3). This needs serious vigilance, particularly when we think about how and why we differentiate (see Chapter 10).

2.3 Bullying

Discrimination, direct and indirect, is not the only form of 'prohibited conduct' referred to in the Equality Act 2010; the act (and similar legislation of this kind internationally) also refers to 'harassment' and 'victimization', defined as 'unwanted contact', 'violations of dignity' and/or 'creating an intimidating, hostile, degrading, or offensive environment' for someone. Within education, particularly compulsory schooling, there is discourse around bullying, defined in similar terms. Kidscape (Kidscape, 2013) defines bullying in this way: 'Bullying is the use of aggression with the intention of hurting another person. Bullying results in pain and distress to the victim' (Kidscape, 2013). Bullying happens for reasons related to the protected characteristics and, for others, around perceived difference and vulnerability, and affects around 40 per cent of children (Kidscape, 2012). Young people identified as lesbian, gay, bisexual or transgender are even more likely to be bullied (Smith, 2011; Stonewall, 2006, 2009). Anti-bullying training and policies is therefore a large part of understanding inclusion in compulsory schooling (Duncan, 2011).

Bullying is far less talked about in FAVE, but this doesn't mean it isn't present. Bullying occurs *within* both younger and older FAVE groups in similar ways as in compulsory schooling, as well as in students' lives outside of the educational context in the abuse students may suffer outside of education, such as domestic violence (see, for example, Duckworth, 2012). Additionally, and significantly, many learners within FAVE carry with them the experiences of being bullied at school or forms of abuse in their past lives. The consequences of this past abuse are often still felt very much in the present in the form of low self-worth and this can have a significant impact on learning. Some people have spent many years being told over and over that they are stupid or worthless. Some may never have been praised for doing something in their lives. This is worth remembering when thinking about the power of praise and encouragement and simply how transformative it can be to convince a student that they are indeed someone who can succeed in learning.

2.4 Exclusion

Discrimination excludes, bullying excludes, and small acts of teacher interpretation based on prejudice exclude. Thinking about inclusion, therefore, involves thinking broadly about exclusion: about who is excluded and why. If I run a class in a room on the fourth floor of an old building with no lifts, I may be excluding people who cannot climb stairs. If my modern Chinese history class involves a lot of reading, I may be excluding someone not confident in their literacy. If I address all my questions to the front-row students in a class, I may be excluding the rest. We will examine exclusion by logistics, communication, assessment, advice and guidance and expectations.

Logistics exclude through: times and days of sessions, buildings, location, cost of classes, materials and transport, qualifications requirements (and which qualifications are given value and which are not). *Someone living far away from an adult education centre, with little public transport, is excluded, as is someone who works on rotating shifts and cannot commit to a weekly timeslot.* Teachers and institutions need to be aware of these factors by talking to existing students, looking at why students leave courses, analysing retention and completion data in a meaningful way and doing outreach work.

Communication excludes through: language, literacy, terminology, communication requirements for those with sensory disabilities, ICT literacy, communication conventions. *Someone with no ICT literacy may be excluded from a programme which communicates with its students via email or requires online application.* Teachers constantly need to be aware of varied language and communication demands in their courses and student needs in relation to these (see Chapter 12).

Assessment excludes through: language and literacy requirements and conventions, understanding of, or desire for, types of formal assessment. *Someone who doesn't want to take an exam may be excluded from provision where you can only go to the next level if you take an exam. Someone may be excluded by failing an assessment exercise for* *which the conventions were not properly explained.* We need to think carefully about what and how we are assessing and be explicit about assessment requirements (see Chapter 13).

Advice/guidance/'social capital' excludes through: lack of information. How you find out which course to take help you enter a chosen career? How do you know which subjects you need to take to study a certain subject at university? What courses or subjects will carry greater weight than others? What if you don't know anyone working in a certain career or anyone who has studied at university? Some people have a great deal of 'social capital' in this respect because they have existing knowledge and they have contact with people who have the relevant expertise and experience. Other people do not have this knowledge and may not know who to turn to for advice. This means that advice and guidance offered by FAVE institutions and by individual teachers (in collaboration with other professionals) is of crucial importance to inclusion.

Expectations exclude through: teachers' expectations and students' expectations of themselves and each other, the expectations of significant others in students' past and present lives.

Case study 15.1 A teacher's expectations of a student

Carla teaches A-level Chemistry in an FE college. She has seen that Lorraine is interested in nails, boys, fashion, etc. She doesn't expect Lorraine to excel in Chemistry. She's keeping an eye on her in case she is disruptive. She doesn't expect Lorraine to do very well and so avoids giving her the more difficult problems.

Put in this way, it's easy to see what's wrong here, but not so easy, always, to tell when we are doing something similar ourselves. Keep asking yourself questions, and remember that it is possible to have high expectations of everyone without losing sight of possible support needs.

Reflective activity 15.3

Using the case study above, discuss with a colleague what you would do in this situation.

2.5 Five aspects of inclusive practice

- Be aware of the Equality Act 2010 (or equivalent national legislation).
- Be aware of, and shape as appropriate, institutional policies and practice.
- Make students aware of institutional and individual class expectations and rules.
- Actively work against discrimination and exclusion in planning, delivery, management and assessment of teaching.

- Actively work against all forms of exclusion in outreach work and in the planning and design of courses.

- Reflect continuously on your own prejudices, assumptions and expectations and what these could mean for your teaching.

3 Disability and 'special' or 'additional' educational needs

Earlier in this chapter we explored the human differences which mean that we all have particular or distinct needs when it comes to teaching and learning. But do some of us have more significant or pressing needs than others? Another way inclusive educational practice is understood is how educational environments, and teachers, are able to support those identified as having additional or special learning needs, and those who are considered disabled. This chapter will explore what is understood by disability, special or additional learning needs, and what these could mean for us as teachers.

It might be helpful to start by thinking of a spectrum of needs, from someone with caring responsibilities who needs a course that starts after 9.30 a.m. to someone with profound and multiple learning difficulties that mean they are severely limited in their ability to communicate with others. Within this spectrum there are hundreds, if not thousands, of needs which affect learning: needs around communication; needs around mobility; pain management, medication and physical health; mental health needs; needs around cognitive impairment or learning disabilities; and needs around behaviour and life circumstances (including caring responsibilities, homelessness and addiction).

These needs are classified within educational institutions in different ways, most commonly under the labels of special educational needs (SEN), additional educational needs, learning support needs or disability. There is some overlap between these labels – for example, visual impairment is likely to be included under all four. They do, however, also aim to cover some different territory: an English language need would be classified in some institutions as an Additional Educational Need or Learning Support Need, but it is certainly not a disability. Within FAVE it is probably most common to hear reference to disability and disability support, so we will start by thinking about disability.

3.1 Disability

We have already looked, briefly, at the definition of disability in the Equality Act 2010: an impairment that has a 'substantial and long-term adverse effect on [someone's] ability to carry out normal day-to-day activities'. This can therefore include mental health issues such as depression, physical health issues such as epilepsy, physical disabilities such as loss or lack of limbs, sensory disabilities such as visual or auditory impairments, and learning difficulties and disabilities. This is the legal framework for understanding disability in terms of how support needs are understood and met. Many FAVE institutions have a disability coordinator or disability support officer who would work with students and teachers to provide the necessary support. We will look at some examples later in this section.

Disability studies is also an expanding area of sociological study and political activism (see, for example, Goodley, Hughes and Davis, 2012). Disability studies theorists analyse shifts in culturally dominant models of disability, from a religious model where disability could be seen as a punishment or gift from God, to a medical model where the disability is located within the individual, as someone with 'something wrong' with them which needs to be 'fixed', to the social model which locates the disability within the social context, its expectations of what is 'normal,' and society's inability to adapt to people who are considered to be different. From the perspective of the social model of disability, it is society's (and its institutions') rigidity which are the 'disabling' problem, not any one individual.

The social model has also been criticized for both neglecting the potential pain of the individual and lacking a model for an affirmative individual identity as a disabled person. As a result, the affirmative model has gained ground over the past ten years, with a much stronger political focus on disabled people as oppressed peoples where their disability is neither a personal tragedy, nor located externally and somehow separate from individual identity. Its focus is on one's identity as a disabled person (Swain and French, 2000; Cameron, 2010; Hodkinson and Vickerman, 2009). The term 'disabled person' is now preferred by most disabled people (rather than a person with disabilities) to reflect the stance that a disabled person has been disabled by society and this act of disabling is core, not incidental, to individual identity.

As indicated above, disability is broad and includes much of what is also classified as SEN, additional or learning support needs. We will look at a few examples of the kind of needs we might find. We cannot, of course, cover everything, but will instead provide one or two examples and some overall guidelines.

Physical needs may include mobility, dexterity, fatigue and pain – for example, a student with a medical condition which means they are unable to sit down for long periods of time. This student may need to stand up and walk around during sessions and may sometimes need to leave sessions to lie down in a prearranged space. Her teacher is in constant dialogue with her and their institution's disability coordinator about how best to meet her needs.

Sensory needs include visual impairment and D/deaf culture which affect how someone can move, see or hear – for example, someone who is profoundly Deaf and uses British Sign Language is likely to come to college with a BSL interpreter and a note-taker. The BSL interpreter may want to see the teacher's materials in advance to familiarize herself with specialist vocabulary. Every session the teacher, BSL interpreter and student carefully consider where each should be located in relation to the others, so that the Deaf student can see her and the interpreter at the same time. The teacher and other students are mindful of the Deaf student's needs in terms of careful turn-taking in discussions (not talking over each other, for example). The teacher may well have worked with D/deaf students before and has attended D/deaf awareness training, but as the needs of D/deaf students vary greatly, the teacher had a long discussion with the Deaf student about their needs at the beginning of the course. (See British Deaf Association website, 2013; Action on Hearing Loss website, 2013; and Marschark and Spencer, 2011; RNIB, 2013, for information for supporting blind or visually impaired students.)

Mental health needs include depression, anxiety, and conditions such as schizophrenia. Mental health needs can mean someone misses sessions or may find some activities (such as presentations) extremely difficult. Discrete provision for adults with mental health issues is quite common, both within specialist hospitals and in the community. Teachers working in these institutions are likely to have specialist training in working with adults with mental health issues, and this training is offered more and more in 'mainstream' FAVE institutions. As with all the needs we are discussing, individual needs vary greatly – for example, two people dealing with the same disability may have very different needs. Additionally, mental health needs may not be immediately apparent; people may not have had formal diagnoses, or may not wish to disclose their information (for fear of discrimination). Every and any class in FAVE is likely to contain students with mental health issues (see Mind, 2012).

Autism. This is how the National Autistic Society website (The National Autistic Society, 2013) defines and explains autism:

> **Autism is a lifelong developmental disability that affects how a person communicates with, and relates to, other people. It also affects how they make sense of the world around them.** It is a spectrum condition, which means that, while all people with autism share certain difficulties, their condition will affect them in different ways. Some people with autism are able to live relatively independent lives but others may have accompanying learning disabilities and need a lifetime of specialist support. People with autism may also experience over or under sensitivity to sounds, touch, tastes, smells, light or colours. Asperger's syndrome is a form of autism. People with Asperger's syndrome are often of average or above average intelligence. They have fewer problems with speech but may still have difficulties with understanding and processing language.

We are using this definition because it is so clear and the condition of autism is so complex. Because it is a spectrum condition, it is likely that no matter what subject you teach, at what levels or where, you will have students with autism or Asperger's syndrome in your classes. While those with autism may share certain characteristic needs, such as difficulties relating to others, their individual needs will be very different. Once again, to work out how best to meet the needs of students with autism we recommend talking to the student, his carers or support workers (if appropriate) and a disability coordinator. The National Autistic Society website (National Autistic Society, 2013) is also useful.

3.2 Specific learning difficulties

Include dyslexia, dyscalculia and dyspraxia – for example, dyslexia includes particular difficulties with processing written language. Those diagnosed with dyslexia have different needs (some may not like to read from white paper, others may be happy reading on white paper) and also feel differently about their diagnosis. For some, diagnosis was 'liberating! … I was called stupid for years at school because I couldn't read and spell and now I understand I'm not stupid; I'm just dyslexic'. Others feel differently: 'I don't want to be told I'm this or I'm that. I can't do this or that.' Dyslexia theorists and experts also disagree – dramatically (see Rice and Brooks, 2004; Herrington, 2010) and some theorists deny that there is such a thing as dyslexia at all.

This is another complex area, but extremely important for us as FAVE teachers to engage with, because there are a great many learners on FAVE courses who have already been diagnosed as dyslexic, feel they are dyslexic, or feel they have specific difficulties reading and writing. As teachers in FAVE, we need to know how to organize dyslexia assessments (usually through our organizations) and the benefits for students of formal diagnosis, which potentially include extra time for exams, one-to-one support workers and financial assistance with learning materials. We should also be aware that not all difficulties with reading and writing come under the umbrella of dyslexia, and reading and writing are challenging for many people, for many different reasons (Appleby, 2010, Reading 15.4).

3.3 Learning disabilities

Learning disabilities, sometimes called 'global learning difficulties or disabilities' (to distinguish them from *specific* learning difficulties), or cognitive impairments are often classified as mild, moderate, severe, or profound and multiple. These categories were once distinguished by notions of IQ, but are now more often understood in terms of a person's ability to live independently. Learning disabilities are distinct from mental health issues or medical conditions such as epilepsy, but many people with learning disabilities also have epilepsy or other health problems and/or mental health issues. Within FAVE, there is discrete provision for those with learning disabilities (such as life and work skills courses, gardening, catering) and there are learners with learning disabilities in 'mainstream' classes. A student with moderate or severe learning difficulties in an adult literacy class, for example, may need more support with understanding tasks and may need more repetition and reinforcement than 'most' students (Duncan, 2010; Wilson and Hunter, 2007).

3.4 Understanding and meeting specific or additional learning needs

The above are only a few examples of the many thousands of particular, additional or special needs which our students could present. For each, there is a great deal that a teacher needs to learn, which is a good example of why teacher education just has to be ongoing (and challenging). Here is a reminder of our key messages.

The terms and categories used above (disability, visual impairment, dyslexia) are part of an attempt to better understand and build expertise around particular needs, but, as with most labels, what is labelled is still very diverse. We still need to remember that everyone is different. What one visually impaired learner may need will be different from that of another learner. This means we need to start from each individual: asking, learning, assessing. Beware of assumptions and low expectations. Just because we are supporting doesn't mean we should not also be challenging.

Case study 15.2 Understanding individual needs

As a new teacher working with groups of moderate and severe learning disabilities, Sam was first surprised not to be given a sheet of paper with information, or a 'diagnosis' of the impairment of each person, to guide her in meeting their needs. Yet, she soon came to feel that even if such a document existed, it would be of little use since everyone is so different, including those who may have the same official 'condition', and a label could distract from assessing individual needs by working directly with that individual. Both positions – wanting information about a particular disability, and seeing such information as potentially perilous – are common, and the debate continues. One way of looking at it would be to say that any information we get about the nature of someone's disability can certainly be useful, as long as it does not: a) replace information coming directly from that person (talking to them) and your ongoing assessment of needs; and b) limit our expectations of that student or encourage them to limit their expectations of themselves.

To support any of our students, we need to work in collaboration with other professionals: disability support workers, support workers, health professionals, advice and guidance professionals, financial advisors and others, within and outside of our institutions. This includes people working alongside us in the classroom. We may have teaching assistants or other teachers in our classes to offer general support for any or all of our learners. This means we need to figure out how best to work with the other practitioner, to make the most of this resource. Alternatively, we may have a learning support assistant assigned to a particular student (with, for example, challenging behavioural needs), and again, we need to figure out how best to make use of them and ensure that their presence does not get in the way of that student's interaction with other students. A student may also come along with a key worker or carer (someone who supports their travel, for example), and again this requires careful thought about what works best. Some students may interact better when their key worker is outside the room; for others, it may be better for the key worker to be next to them at all times. Once again, the message is to talk, try and assess.

4 Multiculturalism and fighting racism

There are different degrees of multiculturalism and while it is common for a class of adults in an inner city location to contain over a dozen different languages and ethnicities and a handful of different faiths, this is not quite the case for all adult education groups around the country. Nevertheless, all our classes *are* multicultural. Every single group contains people who could be seen belonging to different cultures, including cultures associated with region, urban/rural, age, language use and origin, religion, ethnic origin and class. We need to foreground the multiculturalism that is around us, incorporate it into our curricula and pedagogies. We also need to recognize, unfortunately, that while 'race' or ethnicity is a slippery and contested term, racism is another reality which needs constant thought and attention from teachers.

We would like to draw upon three perspectives on multiculturalism and anti-racism. The first are the ideas of Guo and Jamal (2006), whose writing about Canadian universities seems relevant to FAVE. They argue that 'integrating cultural diversity into adult learning' (p. 126) can follow three models of action. The first they call 'a framework for individual diversity development' (p. 228), a type of teachers' continuing professional development (CPD) and reflective practice in order to develop our awareness of other cultures as broadly *and* deeply as possible. This is about individual teacher development involving questioning and 'risk-taking'.

The second is the multicultural educational model whereby the teachers 'respond to the cultural diversity' by 'content integration' (p. 129) (adding content and perspectives to the curriculum from represented groups); by making explicit the values and power structures in knowledge production (so learners are aware of the cultural nature of knowledge production and value); by 'prejudice reduction' through teaching greater awareness of different groups; through 'equity pedagogy', where 'teachers can provide opportunities for students to learn in different ways' and 'from content that is relevant and meaningful to them'; and 'by encouraging them to think critically about the perspectives that underpin curriculum content and materials' (pp. 129–30). Crucially, this 'multicultural education model' involves creating 'an empowering learning culture and social structure' in *the whole organization*, with all parts of the organization working together to provide a positive, supportive, inclusive environment. Finally, Guo and Jamal's third model – the 'anti-racist educational model' (p. 131) – complements the teacher development and whole-organization action drives of the first two models by introducing a focus on the existing barriers and encouraging teachers and students to understand and interrogate their own 'values and assumptions'.

Mirza and Meetoo (2012) examine the needs of trainee teachers in the English teacher education system. Their focus is those training to teach in primary or secondary education, though, once again, their points seem equally relevant to those teaching or training to teach adults. They discuss the *multiplicity* of racism, using a quotation from Fredman (2001: 2) on 'racisms': 'There is no single racism, but multiple racisms; colour racism must be examined together with cultural racism, which includes ethnicity, religion and language.' Mirza and Meetoo also highlight the simultaneous reality and unreality of race:

> It is now generally accepted that there is no scientific or biological foundation for racial difference. Thus 'race' is deemed a social construct (hence the quotation marks). When people use the term 'black' to self-identify, it is understood not to constitute a real or fixed (essential) 'race' category. Instead, it is a politically contested umbrella term that has come to mean post-colonial peoples who are visibly and politically positioned as racialised 'others' [...] 'Race' is therefore not about objective measurable physical and social characteristics, but about relationships of domination and subordination. (Mirza and Meetoo, 2012: 4)

They stress that racism is not just the 'hatred and violence' but rather:

> ... it is the micro everyday behaviours and attitudes that maintain the macro social structures of racism. The unwitting process whereby thoughtless, everyday discriminatory practices become an ingrained part of the ethos or culture of an organisation has been referred to as 'institutional racism'. (Mirza and Meetoo, 2012: 4–5)

Mirza and Meetoo go on make recommendations that inclusive practice therefore means 'embedded multicultural and anti-racist teacher training', 'developing inclusive classroom pedagogy with cultural relevant curricula' and 'enhancing race equality and diversity through challenging professional practice and leadership' (2012: 60).

Finally, we'd like to turn to one of the most influential British theorists of racism and education, David Gillborn. Gillborn uses a Critical Race Theory approach to analyse racial inequality in the British education system. Drawing on the work of Dalgado and Stefancic (2000), he explains 'the starting point for CRT is a focus on racism; in particular its central importance in society and its routine (often unrecognised) character' (Gillborn, 2008a: 27). Gillborn analyses data on achievement across different age groups and between different racial groups to argue that assessment systems, teacher expectations, school-level decisions about discipline and other forms of institutional racism amount to a racist 'conspiracy'. This is an analysis of compulsory schooling rather than FAVE, but the messages for our sector are clear: a) we are dealing with young people and adults who have been the victim of institutional racism in schools; and b) institutional racism is likely to be operating within FAVE in a similar way.

Case study 15.3 Multiculturalism and tackling prejudice – what teachers can do

So, what can or should we, as teachers, trainee teachers and teacher educators, be doing? This is the question posed to David Gillborn and this was his reply:

> I suppose my advice (from a CRT perspective) would be always question the deficit analysis/explanation and to be self-critical about how your own actions/assumptions might (inadvertently) feed the process. So, for example, if a school finds that it's excluding kids from group X more than other groups – don't automatically assume it's the kids or their parents. Could there be problems in the school? In its treatment of kids in that group? In the assumptions that teachers bring to that group? Are group X 'expected' to be trouble? Are there supports that could be put in place to check whether kids in group X are getting into trouble lower down the conflict ladder? Do group X exclusion offences look different to other groups? If group Y aren't doing well in maths, have you spoken to kids/parents in group Y to find out what they think of maths or how they explain the problem?
>
> Basically, because most policy-makers and practitioners are white and not aware of race issues and stereotyping, when we make policies, design curricula, make assessments, or discipline kids, our actions will often end up disadvantaging some minority groups, not because we're rabid racists or bad people, but because our actions embody beliefs or assumptions that we just don't recognise or understand. So when there's a problem, we need to look for ways it could reflect things we do. It's good pedagogy, because the things WE do are the things we CAN change most easily – if we're interested. (Gillborn, 2013)

To better understand just how important this message is, let's remind ourselves how finely 'culture' can be sliced and, when we think of racism, remember that we could be talking about discrimination in terms of religion, class, accent, immigration status, which part of the city someone lives in, whether their parents are addicts or not, long-term unemployed or not, mental health issues, sexuality, and so on (see, for example, the work of Derrington [2011] on Gypsy, Roma and Traveller pupils, and Candappa [2011] with asylum-seekers). The warning is the same. We need to be constantly alert to the possibility that we ourselves are discriminating against those we are meant to be helping.

Conclusion

What is inclusive pedagogy?

Making sure we are not discriminatory, though, is only part of what it means recognize the multicultural or diverse nature of our worlds and classes. We also need to use that diversity in how and what we teach. This is what we mean by 'inclusive pedagogy'. We are going to look briefly at two aspects of inclusive pedagogy. The first is promoting understanding. The second aspect is the idea that good practice in inclusive education *is* good practice in any kind of education – this is: to teach, we need to teach inclusively. We cannot imagine that we could be doing any kind of good teaching job without inclusive practice.

In Chapter 12 through the work of Geertz (1985) we made the very simple point that we need diversity to learn. We learn by coming across, and coming to understand, difference. And in a more complex way, we can see that other ways of doing things, other ways of seeing things, other experiences and approaches are what we need to challenge and develop our thinking, within and across subject areas, and to help us grow and develop as human beings.

So while we have talked in this chapter of the importance of fighting racism, we also remember what we have learnt and can learn from other 'races', ethnicities, faiths or cultures. While we have discussed the policies which are in place to make sure that D/deaf or visual impaired students can study, we also need to remember what we could learn from how others communicate. We can enrich our curricula and learning methods by using the diversity in our groups and more broadly in the worlds around us. This means making sure we are representing the communities around us (whether making sure we celebrate female physicists as well as male, or Caribbean poets as well as Irish), as well as making sure our whole curriculum reflects our learners (What do we study in history? How can we understand the history and developments of mathematics, engineering, construction, hairdressing, nursing, beauty therapy?). Diversity is about looking carefully at the local as well as the global. We can challenge each other. We can learn from each other and the different points of view we hold. What can we learn from a debate about abortion if everyone feels the same?

Inclusive teaching is better teaching

We all learn and teach better through inclusive practice. Inclusive teaching is simply better teaching. Key messages for inclusive education include: careful assessment, creative teaching, checking learning, carefully chosen or designed resources, careful watch on differentiation or personalization, working from individual needs, being careful of assumptions and prejudice – these are the ways we can teach better with any group of people, whatever their needs or perceived lack of needs. Good practice in teaching *is* inclusive practice (Appleby, 2001, Reading 15.4). This does not mean 'one size fits all', but rather recognizes that every single classroom is full of all sorts of difference (think back to the beginning of this chapter) and so we always need to be assessing need, we always need to be learning more about our students, and we always need to be working reflectively with colleagues.

Key readings

This website offers clarifications, analysis and advice around the Equality Act 2010:

> Equality and Human Rights Commission (website offering guidance on the Equality Act 2010), **equalityhumanrights.com/legal-and-policy/equality-act/**

For an overview of the intersecting areas of SEN, inclusion and diversity and how teaching can acknowledge and include differences, see:

> Appleby, A. (2010) 'Who are the Learners?'. In N. Hughes and I. Schwab (eds) *Teaching Adult Literacy: Principles and Practice.* London: University of London, Institute of Education (IOE), 29–47. (Reading 15.4)
>
> Frederickson, N. and Cline, T. (2009) *Special Educational Needs, Inclusion and Diversity.* 2nd edn. Maidenhead: McGraw Hill/Open University Press.
>
> Richardson, R. (2009) *Holding Together.* Stoke-on-Trent: Trentham Books, 24, 26–8. (Reading 15.1)

Tackling prejudice and thinking carefully about what it means to teach in 'anti-racist' ways and establish inclusive learning environments:

> Spedding P., Gregson, M. and Nixon, L. (2011) *Tackling Prejudice Together.* Presentation at University of Sunderland, Faculty of Education and Society Conference, 5 September. (Reading 15.3)
>
> Gillborn, D. (2008a) 'Developing Antiracist School Policy'. In M. Pollock (ed.) *Everyday Antiracism: Getting Real About Racism in School.* New York: The New Press, 246–51.
>
> Candappa, M. (2011) 'Invisibility and Otherness: Asylum-seeking and Refugee Students in the Classroom'. In G. Richards and F. Armstrong (eds) *Teaching and Learning in Diverse and Inclusive Classrooms.* London: Routledge, 156–69.

Understand disability, society, how these issue shape classroom practice and how more inclusive practice can be established:

Duckworth, V. (2013) *Learning Trajectories, Violence and Empowerment Amongst Adult Basic Skills Learners.* London: Routledge.

Goodley, D., Hughes, B. and Davis, L. (eds) (2012) *Disability and Social Theory: New Developments and Directions.* London: Palgrave Macmillan.

Marschark, M. and Spencer, P. E. (2011) *The Oxford Handbook of Deaf Studies, Language, and Education.* 2nd edn. Oxford: Oxford University Press.

The idea and ideals of diversity and inclusion from different and challenging perspectives are described and evaluated in the following:

Derrington, C. (2011) 'Supporting Gypsy, Roma and Traveller Pupils'. In G. Richards and F. Armstrong (eds) *Teaching and Learning in Diverse and Inclusive Classrooms.* London: Routledge, 156–69.

Richards, G. and Armstrong, F. (eds) (2011) *Teaching and Learning in Diverse and Inclusive Classrooms.* London: Routledge.

Schuller and Watson's reading reminds us of just how important the policy context and funding arrangement are to providing learning opportunities for all learners throughout their lives:

Schuller, S. and Watson, D. (2009) *Learning Through Life: Inquiry into the Future for Lifelong Learning.* Leicester: NIACE. **(Reading 15.2)**

The associated website, **reflectiveteaching.co.uk**, offers a wealth of supplementary resources including reflective activities, research briefings, advice on further reading and downloadable diagrams, figures and checklists from the book. It also features a compendium of educational terms, links to useful websites, policy and curriculum documents, and showcases examples of excellent research and practice.

part five

Deepening understanding

Part Five integrates major themes through discussion of teacher expertise and professionalism.

Chapter 16 integrates key themes from previous chapters into a holistic conceptual framework of enduring issues in teaching and learning. It examines these through three case studies relating to the dimensions of teaching: curriculum, pedagogy and assessment. The chapter also presents dimensions of expert thinking. In Chapter 17, we show how professionalism is a contested concept, but we offer a variety of ways in which readers can foster their own professional practice.

Expertise
Conceptual tools for career-long fascination?

16

Introduction: A conceptual framework for deepening expertise

You may now have reached a point where you are starting to feel more confident about your teaching. At this stage you may also be more familiar with the ideas and the theories in this book and are now looking for ways in which to develop your practice further. This chapter begins with an overview of what it means to develop our 'expertise' in the FAVE sector. We consider some of the career paths you might follow and offer a few practical insights through illustrative case studies of some of the choices and judgements you might be asked to make along the way.

Every sector in education today is complex, challenging, subject to almost continuous change. Arguably the FAVE sector suffers from change more than the others because of its links to employers, the economy, and changes in technology and in the workplace (see Coffield, 2014, 2015, Reading 1.2). As we saw in Chapter 4 (Sahlberg, 2012, Reading 4.2; Hattie, 2009, Reading 4.3), it is now internationally recognized more than ever before that 'teachers matter'. Wiliam (2009) focuses on the development of teacher expertise and on teachers' professional development activity. He suggests that the content of teachers' professional development strategies should concentrate on teaching strategies of proven effectiveness and processes of classroom application.

Analyses on the statistical effect sizes and different teaching and learning strategies have been referred to throughout this book. Such findings offer important insights into good teaching. However, specific findings such as these need to become integrated more holistically into teachers' routine practices and ways of thinking. This brings us to a discussion of the progressive development and deepening of teacher expertise.

TLRP principles

The following TLRP principles are of particular relevance to this chapter on expertise in teaching and learning in the FAVE sector:

Principle 2: Effective teaching and learning engages with valued forms of knowledge. Teaching and learning should engage with the big ideas, facts, processes, language and narratives of subjects so that learners understand what constitutes quality and standards in particular disciplines.

Principle 9: Effective teaching and learning depends on teacher learning. The need for lecturers, teachers, trainers and co-workers to learn continuously in order to develop their knowledge and skill, and to adapt and develop their roles, especially through practice-based inquiry, should be recognized and supported.

Principle 10: Effective teaching and learning demands consistent policy frameworks with support for teaching and learning as the primary focus. Policies at national, institutional and local levels need to recognize the fundamental importance of teaching and learning. They should be designed to create effective learning environments in which all learners can thrive.

In Part One of this book and in Section 1 of this chapter, we explore what we mean by the notion of expertise and what it means to become educationally wise (Biesta, 2015, Reading 1.1), and the importance of teachers' development of practical wisdom (Heilbron, 2011, Reading 4.1). In Section 2, we offer some ideas about how you might begin to manage your career as a teacher in proactive and forward-thinking ways. In Section 3 we discuss how teachers can learn to get better at what they do through collaborative and individual research and engagement in the scholarship of teaching and learning. We go on to explore how this might be done using the principles of Joint Practice Development (JPD) (Gregson et al., 2015, Reading 16.1) as well as through other approaches to educational research. This involves a discussion of different notions of scholarship in education, what counts as good research, and how different forms of scholarship might be systematically applied in programmes of practitioner research.

We aim to bring a number of fundamental threads of this book together in this chapter in order to answer the question of how, over time, teachers can systematically develop their educational expertise in a community of scholars and in a genuine spirit of discovery. This is not something that is only important in the initial education teachers receive. It is a career-long process through which teachers, individually and together with others, deepen their understanding of what it means to be a teacher, enhance their ability to reflect, and through this develop their ability to make wise judgements about their practice. (We will return to the idea of wisdom – and, more specifically, the idea of educational wisdom – later in this chapter.)

To see the development of our expertise as a career-long process is not to suggest that this is an enormous or onerous task for which we need a whole career. It is rather intended to highlight that teachers do not and should not stop learning once they enter the profession. In order to remain motivated (which can from time to time be really difficult) and to ensure that your standards of teaching remain at the highest level possible, you will need to continue to develop your professional knowledge and practice. It is also important that you keep renewing and developing your engagement with the research so that you can keep up to date with developments in the discipline of education and with questions of what it means to practise good education. A career-long fascination for teaching, learning and research is at the heart of this process.

In addition to the TLRP principles in Chapter 4, we considered three dimensions of educational practice: 'qualification, subjectification and socialisation' (Biesta, 2009). As your career progresses you might find that each of these principles and dimensions of practice pulls you in a different direction at different times. Depending on the context and culture in which you work, you may have more or less control over these dimensions. For example, a funding and inspection regime may oblige senior managers in an organization to be primarily concerned with ensuring that student recruitment, retention and achievement targets are met, but this is not necessarily sufficient to bring about a good educational experience for our students. Through the work of Newman (1889), Finlay (2008) argues that the aim of professional education in higher education (we would also argue in all sectors of education) should be that it is not only useful but that it should also enable people to develop intellectual capacities and dispositions to take what they have learned in familiar settings into different and unfamiliar situations to develop new ways of thinking and working.

For Newman a good education is always useful, but a useful education is not always good. (Finlay, 2008: 18).

Coffield (2008) illustrates this powerfully through the following case study:

> I was sitting in the back row of a class of electrical apprentices in a German vocational school … About twenty 18/19-year-olds were studying part of the core curriculum – German literature – and on this particular Friday morning they were taking turns to read out loud from Goethe's *Faust* … When the class finished I asked … (one of the students) … what was the relevance to his future working life as an electrician of Goethe's *Faust*? He thought for a moment and then whispered back: 'Electricians have souls too, you know'. (Coffield, 2008: 43)

From this example we can see that in providing a good education for our students we need to attend not only to the knowledge and skills they need to do a job well for its own sake, but also to the knowledge, skills and virtues they will need to help them to lead a fulfilled life in the future. Good vocational education should therefore not only enable students to do a job well in the present, but also develop the intellectual capacities, dispositions and 'virtues' they will need in order to think well and act well individually and with others when faced with unexpected developments, dilemmas or unfamiliar situations in the future (Coffield, 2014, Reading 1.2; CAVTL, 2013, Reading 11.3).

Becoming a professional teacher therefore involves much more than just introducing you to the knowledge and techniques of teaching and learning you need in order to teach well in the early stages of your career. It also requires you to engage with the discipline of education throughout your career. This involves upholding the values of educational practice and always being able and prepared to challenge 'taken-for-granted' assumptions about what should be done in the field of education and in the other subjects and disciplines that you teach. You will also need to be able and prepared to justify the positions you take and the judgements you make as a professional teacher (Hillier and Jameson, 2003, Reading 16.2).

In Chapter 14 we discussed how achievement in education is often taken to be the result of a combination of good teaching, student 'ability' and effort. The underlying assumption here is that, through education, individual ability is identified and developed so that everyone can reach their potential and lead a fulfilled life. However, as we saw in Chapter 15, there is considerable evidence that educational under-achievement is not equally distributed across all social groups, indicating that social mobility and social justice are more available through education to some of us than to others. Such dilemmas and contradictions are among the many enduring issues we have to face in education. As teachers, we need to develop the wisdom and expertise to deal with such issues in our professional practice in the most educationally sound ways possible.

Becoming a reflective teacher in the FAVE sector involves us in engaging in a particular way of life and a set of educational practices, particular ways of working, thinking and going about what we do. The work we do plays an important part in carrying forward the ideas and crafts of those who have gone before us. It also critically examines old ways of thinking and working to create new thinking and new practices. In this way our work both sustains and transforms communities, societies and the regional and national economies in which we live. No matter what they teach, good teachers come to care about the practice of education. When we ignite the first spark of interest in our students; when we fire their imagination; when we watch them develop a sense of belonging; when we see them realize the possibilities offered by the subject or craft they have chosen to pursue; when we observe how they have developed a passion for and pride in their work; when we watch them grow in confidence; when we see them recognize the virtue of doing something well for its own sake and when we know how we have contributed to all of this ... we become good teachers.

As teachers, we participate in educational practices together with our students by engaging in partnerships based upon cooperation and in traditions and vocational practices which not only transcend us as individuals but are also deeply alive in the present, stretch back to the past and, through our combined efforts, can be extended into the future (Dunne, 2005). In doing so, we discover the rewards that come from mutual engagement and the embodiment of the practices that each of us come to pursue, including the practice of leading a fulfilled life.

> In looking at education into a practice ... I would of course want to see it as being *in itself* in a very strong sense a *moral education* in so far as properly conducted it involves ... the learning not only of skills but of virtues. (Dunne, 2005: 155, author italics)

Throughout this book we argue that in pursuing the internal 'goods' of educational practice, including those outlined above, we need to develop virtues and qualities to guide the sometimes difficult and often wonderful decisions we need to make in our practice as teachers. In the course of your career you will almost certainly find yourself faced with many complex dilemmas and issues, including the notion that education can and should be a commercial practice rather than a moral one.

As a beginning teacher you are naturally most likely to be concerned about the immediacies of your educational practice, including how to plan and teach a good lesson, how to learn from a lesson that did not go so well, how to deal with unexpected developments in the classroom/workshop, as well as dealing with many policy and structural changes which regularly impact upon the work of teachers and education mangers across the sector (Hargreaves, 2007, Reading 16.3). As your career as a teacher develops, you are likely to be asked take on new roles and responsibilities, often involving wider aspects of educational leadership including developing departmental/organizational policies and strategic decision-making. Each new role will undoubtedly present you with different possibilities, problems and difficult decisions.

The quality of the judgements you make in these situations will play a significant part in your professional life and in the lives of your students. A key aspect of developing your expertise as a teacher is to learn how to balance your competing teaching, learning, assessment, preparing for external evaluation/inspection administration and research responsibilities.

In previous chapters we have pointed to the need for professionals involved in any area of practice to have the knowledge and skills to be able to carry out that practice in the world in ways that demonstrate their commitment to the shared values and norms necessary to do it well. In the case of the practice of education, this means going about our work in ways that are in the interests of and for the good of all our students. As teachers, therefore, we have an obligation to teach well and to continue to develop and improve our practice beyond our experiences of initial teacher education. But the question then becomes: how do you know what you need to do to improve in your practice and how should you go about improving it?

To say that teachers should reflect, and that reflection will help to make their work better, assumes that teachers have the time to reflect and that they have opportunities to act upon the outcomes of their reflections. This, however, has become quite a contentious assumption, since nowadays the work of teachers, not only in the FAVE sector but in many other sectors of education, and not only in the UK but in many countries around the world, is increasingly being regulated and controlled from the outside (Biesta, 2015, Reading 1.1; Coffield, 2014, Reading 1.2)

1 Standards and the development of expertise

One of the main devices in the development of professional practice is the introduction of standards and the enforcement of such standards through a regime of testing, measurement and inspection. The idea of standards is, of course, helpful. Standards of practice across the professions aim to provide clarity about what people who are practising in a particular profession might be expected to do and how and how well and at what stage they might be expected to do it.

In England, there are different sets of professional standards for practitioners who teach non-higher education courses (The Professional Standards for Further Education Teachers and Trainers in England, Education and Training Foundation, 2014) and for those who teach programmes of higher education in the FAVE sector (The UK Professional Standards Framework, Higher Education Academy, 2011). Both identify the importance of the evaluation of practice, a commitment to continuing professional development, as well as the importance of drawing upon research to improve practice in education.

Taken literally, standards define what constitutes good practice. However, in the field of education in England, until recently such standards have tended to be developed and defined in a bureaucratic 'top-down' basis. These have functioned more often than not as means to restrain the scope teachers have for professional judgement and creativity in their teaching, rather than enhance it (Hargreaves, 2007, Reading 16.3). At best, professional standards in education can and should act as an instrument to enhance reflection, encourage good educational judgement and value, and promote the agency of teachers to make good educational decisions in the context of their practice (see for example Jeffrey and Troman, 2012). 'Agency' here refers to the extent to which teachers are able to give direction to their own practice and the extent to which, together with others, they can give direction to the development of their work together.

It is important to note that professional standards and other policy initiatives which aim for improvements in education inevitably depend upon the willingness and expertise of teachers to reflect upon how best to enact them in practice. Clearly the conditions under which teachers have the scope for reflection and contextualization are crucial to the development of their practice. In other words, the ways in which teachers interpret, implement, adapt and evaluate policy initiatives in education (including standards of practice for teachers) are vital to the success and impact of education policy in general (O'Leary, 2013, Reading 16.4; Coffield, 2014, Reading 1.2).

We usually refer to someone being an expert if they have developed an extensive range of knowledge and an extended repertoire of skills in their subject or chosen field of practice. A novice is usually considered to be someone just entering the field who has fairly basic levels of knowledge, understanding and skills and usually very little experience.

Much has been written about how we develop expertise and a variety of models have been developed to represent how people progress from being novices to experts. The model developed by Dreyfus and Dreyfus (1986) is one of the better-known. It was originally focused upon the development of clinical skills, but it is regarded as having relevance to the development of professional practice in other disciplines and fields of study. This model represents five stages in the development of professional practice:

1 Novice

2 Advanced beginner

3 Competent

4 Proficient

5 Expert

Novices and beginners depend on rules and principles set out by their professional code in order to practise (and indeed are usually judged as being able to practise on this basis). When they become more competent, they are more familiar with the rules and principles and act upon these in a more holistic way. They also have their own previous experiences to draw upon to inform the ways in which they enact their professional codes. Experts invariably have a store of professional knowledge, experience and understanding which helps them deal with the complex, difficult situations that are less subject to routinized standards and practices. They are usually more autonomous in their approach and they also have a wealth of knowledge that they can share with others. This is particularly important when helping new generations of novices and advanced beginners enter the profession.

Case study 16.1 The advanced beginner

James is a guitarist who studied at a local FE college for his vocational qualification; since gaining his degree and working in a variety of contexts, he has become a trainee teacher at the same college. He has a deep knowledge of music but is now finding out how to encourage young people to develop their musical talents of voice and instrument for the same vocational qualification that he originally gained at the college.

James has a group of students who are preparing for a concert. They are a vocals group and need to be able to sing in harmony, to sing in a particular key and be able to find the most appropriate key for their individual performance. They are keen to work on their performances.

James starts with exercises to warm up their voices. He decides to ask them to sing intervals, which some of the students find difficult. He sings along with them until they become more familiar with what is required and he asks each student to then sing the intervals he suggests. James then makes it even more demanding by asking them to sing a semitone higher or lower than the original key. The students do everything he asks them to do, albeit with some gentle persuasion as the tasks increase in difficulty.

James knows all about the health and safety requirements of warming up before singing. He also knows about the importance of being able to sing in different keys, and to be able to identify intervals, as these help students to sing any song regardless of how demanding these may be. While watching and listening carefully to his students' attempts to sing intervals and semitones, he decided to change his original plan and spend more time on the warm-up exercises, practising intervals and semitones. This was the appropriate thing to do at this point as he knew it would provide a better platform upon which to build his students' vocal performances.

He has many ideas to try out in future sessions and a deep level of professionalism gained from his experiences working outside of FAVE. He is not only a newly qualified teacher but also a professional musician. His professional journey as a teacher in FAVE is beginning and is supported by a range of understanding and knowledge from his previous work and his own learning.

As his students were so cooperative, he has yet to learn what to do with a group that is not so attentive.

Question: How could James plan and manage a session on vocal performance with a less motivated group?

Hattie (2003) applies this notion of expertise to teaching and identifies five attributes of expert teachers:

- They identify essential representations of their subject.
- They guide learning through classroom interactions.
- They monitor learning and provide feedback.
- They attend to emotional attributes.
- They influence student outcomes.

Reflective activity 16.1

Thinking about the attributes of expert teachers

Think about Hattie's five attributes of expert teachers. Identify at least one experienced expert teacher in your institution and ask if you can spend some time observing one or more of their classes/workshops. As you observe, ask yourself the following questions:

- Can you see one or more of these attributes in their teaching?
- Ask your expert colleagues whether they would add or remove anything from Hattie's list and why?

- Use this discussion as the basis for considering your own journey from novice to expert teacher. Where would you place yourself on the novice–expert spectrum and why?
- Identify up to three aspects of your practice you would like to develop further.

Hattie argues that the level of a teacher's expertise has an impact on the quality of student learning. He claims that students who are taught by experts develop more coherent and integrated understandings of concepts and therefore higher levels of abstraction in their thinking.

We suggest that reflective practice can develop our transition from being novices in the field to being competent practitioners and, where possible, experts. Not everyone reading this book will spend their whole careers in FAVE but we anticipate that much of the knowledge, skill and understanding that is gained from time spent in this field of education will be able to be transferred to other careers and activities.

We have discussed throughout our book how we can think about what we do when we teach. As a teacher, you will already have well-developed knowledge and skills in your subject(s) or in the vocational area(s) you teach. You may even have studied your subject at masters degree or a PhD level. On the other hand, you may have entered the field of education as a learning support assistant or vocational assessor without qualifications in English, mathematics or in any other subjects where the sources of your expertise are grounded in your vocational practice and acquired experience. An important aspect of developing our expertise involves examining and deepening our knowledge of our subject specialism. Berliner (1986) points to the importance of teachers developing both the knowledge of their subject as well as the knowledge of how to teach it. He goes on to argue that expert teachers use different mental schema (ways of thinking) about problems and dilemmas and that they notice cues that a novice may tend to overlook.

Case study 16.2 The experienced teacher

Donna is a curriculum leader of a mathematics department in a large FE college. A recent national government policy initiative has released funding for CPD training and supporting materials for teachers of functional mathematics in the college to enable them to teach mathematics at the higher level of General Certificate of Education (GCSE). Donna has already started to work with her team to begin to plan the GCSE curriculum for next year. She attends some CPD training events and as part of one of the workshops discovers that the new GCSE curriculum for mathematics is unlike the old modular GCSE curriculum, which allowed different aspects of mathematics to be taught and assessed separately on a modular basis. Instead, the new GCSE mathematics curriculum has been designed on a linear model. Here, examination of the course replaces modular assessment and this has implications for the way in which the subject will be taught. An integrated approach will be required rather than simply teaching topics which are immediately assessed.

Question: What should Donna do? What might be the likely consequences of this decision and how should she attend to these?

For those of you teaching higher education in FAVE, you will be aware of the differences between demands on your counterparts who teach in higher education institutions (HEIs) and your own institution. Generally there are usually more opportunities for colleagues in HEIs to undertake research and scholarly activity than in the FAVE sector. In FAVE, the expectation is less concerned with you being research-active and more concerned with your ability to draw upon research to improve practice. We strongly argue that this is a serious omission, as practitioner-research can generate unique insights into practice, which an outsider may not be able to access. Supported practitioner research in FAVE, as we have seen for example through JPD, can make real and sustainable improvements in practice. At the same time it is important to be aware that practitioner-research in education has been the subject of considerable criticism. Such criticisms include accusations that it is often unsystematic with poor research design, lack of objectivity, lack of scholarship and rigour, and, in some cases, the absence of robust indicators of impact (Tooley et al., 1998).

There is a long-standing culture in the UK and elsewhere that teaching and educational research are different forms of practice requiring different knowledge, skills and virtues. Through the work of Bass (1998), McCarthy challenges the traditional consignment of teaching and research to different domains of practice. Echoing the above authors, she challenges the traditional 'teaching versus research' debate in order to extend the meaning of scholarship in education to include the full scope of academic work in that field of practice.

We take the view that the purpose of engaging in the scholarship of teaching and learning (SoTL) (Murray, 2008) is that we can get better at educational practice and that this involves getting better at teaching, learning, assessment and research in education together. For us, scholarship and pedagogical research and development in education and the scholarship of subject specialist or disciplinary knowledge are central components of the development of expertise in FAVE. These issues are discussed more fully in Section 3.

It is all very well suggesting that expertise can be developed through time spent in the field of education and through keeping up to date with our subject specialist area, but how do we know what approach will ensure that we develop sound ideas and knowledge? We want to avoid becoming 'set in our ways' or disillusioned by the 'same old, same old' situations we meet in our professional lives. In other words, we want to develop a kind of expertise that is open-minded and able to support our teaching and that of our colleagues. Below we set out our argument for developing *wisdom* together in the practice of education.

1.1 Becoming educationally wise

Sennett (2008) points out that most of us, whatever our vocation, don't just want to 'get by' in our work, we want to get better and better at what we do. If we put it in more formal language, we can say that reflective teaching is a central element in the improvement of education.

Hickson (2011) acknowledges that largely individual models of reflection can result in people being 'seduced by their own stories and beliefs' (2001: 832). Thompson and Pascal

(2011) argue that the idea of reflective teaching and models of reflective practice have become oversimplified and under-theorized in ways which separate thought and action and miss crucial 'sociological' elements of reflective practice. Echoing Gingell and Winch (2004), they are critical of 'technical-rational' approaches to reflective practice, which 'attempt to apply engineering-type, problem-solving approaches to human relations' (2004: 313). Following Carr (1995), they criticize literature on reflective practice, for the way in which it has overemphasized individual reflective practice and overlooks the importance of more collective forms of reflection and, in doing so, misses opportunities for collective deliberation and decision-making in the light of evidence.

> Human existence is fundamentally social. Social issues should not therefore be seen as merely a backdrop or a set of minor contextual features. The social context is a primary feature of human reality. There is therefore a need to see personal reflection as not only an interpersonal matter, but also part of a broader context of cultural formations and structural relations. (Thompson and Pascal, 2011: 318).

They conclude that 'traditional' understandings of reflective practice need to move beyond the work of Schön (1987) and others to establish more sociologically informed, collective and critically reflective approaches based upon dialogue, including considerations and deliberations about practice arrived at together, in context and in the light of evidence.

That is why it is not only important that student teachers work actively at learning to reflect upon and in their practice on their own. It also means that experienced teachers should continue to think carefully about their work, alone and with their colleagues – for example, in the form of what, earlier in this book, we have described as Joint Practice Development (JPD).

In one respect, the message we have put forward in the preceding chapters has been a very simple one: It might help if you not just *do*, but if, from time to time, you also reflect upon what you do (Biesta, 2015, Reading 1.1). This applies not only in your teaching, but also to the work you do together with colleagues, such as when you teach together or when you are jointly involved in researching your practice, engaged in curriculum development, planning for teaching, learning and assessment, organizing or providing student support. In all cases, thinking about what you do and thinking together and working collaboratively with others can help us to do things better.

The basic message is that things may go better when you think carefully about them, when you share your thinking with others and when you genuinely try to help each other to improve your practice in a spirit of critical professional friendship. We have, in the preceding chapters, also revealed some of the complexities of introducing reflection in your teaching. We have partly done this through showing the different aspects of education that are worthy of reflection, such as curriculum, pedagogy and assessment, or contexts, spaces and relationships. And we have done this by identifying dimensions that could and should be taken in consideration when we reflect on the purpose of education and the nature of our teaching, such as, for example, the need for inclusive, responsive, responsible and democratic ways of working.

The three key terms we use in this chapter are reflection, judgement and wisdom. Reflection has to do with the ways in which we think carefully about what we do – alone and together with others. Judgement focuses in on one particular aspect of reflection, namely our engagement with the question how to do things and with the question what is to be done – the question of purpose. Judgements are not about the application of rules or about following prescriptions, but are about applying knowledge, standards, principles and theories to the always concrete and often complex and unfolding situations in which teachers work. In a sense, these are the unique situations in which we find ourselves with our students day to day, minute by minute. Wisdom refers to the way in which, over time, a teacher begins to embody their capacity for good educational judgement so that it becomes part of their whole professional self.

For example, if two nautical engineering apprentices were using their mobile phones constantly during a workshop, it would be tempting to simply ask them to turn them off and pay attention. However, if the teacher decided to ask them why they were needing to use their phones so much, it might transpire that one had an elderly relative undergoing surgery and the other was chatting to his mates. The two circumstances require strategies which are deemed to be fair to all those involved. Jumping to conclusions in the heat of the moment without reflecting on the underlying issue is likely to lead to further difficulty. Why do people use their phones during a teaching session? What protocols and exceptions need to be established? What expectations of behaviour do we and our students have in this context? Expertise provides an understanding of when to dispense with hard-and-fast rules and when to stick to them (Heilbronn, 2011, Reading 4.1).

We suggest that it is in relation to developing practical judgement that JPD has a potential key role to play in moving our thinking beyond individual reflective practice, beyond the notion of a solitary, contemplative individual activity towards a more active, collaborative, practice-focused, research- and evidence-based approach. This is because people are different and hold different views and can negotiate these differences as they practice together. Again, Biesta's (2009, 2010a) three dimensions of education and the ten TLRP principles can play a role in helping to focus the conversations of teachers collaborating in improving practice.

We introduced the idea of JPD in Chapter 3. We noted how important it is to reflect and develop practice through interaction with peers. JPD provides a different and, we argue, more meaningful and practical ways to improve our practice and to demonstrate that we meet professional requirements. In your colleges and institutions there are funds to support continuing professional development (CPD) and again, this is an important facet of being a professional (of which more in Chapter 17).

The following case study is offered as an illustration of the complex problems experienced teachers and education leaders regularly encounter. This highlights the difficult decisions they have to make in the face of limited budgets, competing priorities and external pressures and imperatives.

Case study 16.3 The expert education leader

Richard has just moved into his new job as an HE curriculum manager in a Further Education college in England. He has managed to secure some CPD funding to enable staff teaching on HE programmes at his own college and in two other colleges nearby to engage in CPD activities which will enable them to gain recognition under the UK Standards framework (2011), which will confer a level of Fellowship from the Higher Education Academy (HEA) upon staff who participate in the CPD project. He has organized a CPD event for staff from all three colleges so that they can meet to plan how they will be able to use this funding. Although staff are keen to gain the recognition, they are hard pressed to find the time to complete the paperwork required. Richard has arranged two guest speakers to contribute to the event.

The first guest speaker suggests that all three colleges might use the JPD approach to CPD to address areas of practice where teaching and learning could be improved and to work together across the colleges to research and improve these, while, at the same time, generating evidence of research activity for the HEA A5 area of professional practice:

Engage in continuing professional development in subjects/disciplines and their pedagogy, incorporating scholarship and the evaluation of professional practice.

The second guest speaker describes how, in their college, the Human Resources department designed and delivered a series of two-hour sessions on a variety of topics including safeguarding, which all HE staff in the college were required to attend in order to generate evidence of engagement in CPD in their subjects/disciplines, demonstrate their scholarship and their ability to reflect upon and evaluate professional practice and so meet the HEA A5 area of professional practice.

Some people have already started to complete the HEA paperwork on their own with the intention of just getting it out of the way so that they can gain the HEA status they need to satisfy the requirements of the next round of inspection/reviews.

Question: What should Richard do? What might be the likely consequences of this decision and how should he attend to these?

Aspects of the above example lend support to Sarason's (1990) claim that long-standing structures and unchallenged traditional practices in education, coupled with the need of various groups to defend their power, can stifle and distort even the most well-intentioned initiatives intended to improve educational practice.

2 Managing your career and your professional development

Programmes for the initial and continuing professional development for teachers in the FAVE sector are a relatively new phenomenon. For example, it is only in the past 40 years

Figure 16.1 Approaches to CPD: strengths and limitations

Model of CPD	Characteristics of this approach to CPD	Main aim of this approach to CPD	Main strengths of this approach to CPD	Main limitations of this approach to CPD
In-house CPD events and development days	Workshop or collection of workshops organized by education leaders where an internal/external 'expert' tells everyone what to do. 'Expert' tells staff what 'best practice ' is.	To showcase 'best practice' in teaching and learning. Often used to inform staff of changes in their administrative managerial procedures and responsibilities – e.g. timetabling, registers, Ofsted requirements.	Quick way of raising awareness of 'best practice' across the organization. Networking among staff.	Little or no support for participants after the event to put the idea into practice. Focus is on attendance not impact on practice. Links to robust research weak. Vulnerable to 'fad and gimmick' and hard sell from experts/'gurus'. Risk of events focusing primarily on updating procedures and responsibilities rather than teaching and learning. Limited interactivity. Students rarely involved. Flow of influence from the top down.
Conferences	Organizational-led themed event. Research-led themed event, at a regional, national or international level.	Information-giving. Opportunity to focus upon theme or issue. Large-scale event, which brings delegates from the same or a number of organizations together. Opportunity to share and scrutinize ideas and findings. Can be sector-specific.	Up-to-date information shared. Prominent researchers often indicate future direction for the development of educational practice. Opportunities for an international perspective on common problems available. Opportunities to promote research and the sector. Networking for delegates.	Highly dependent on conference organization and the calibre of the speakers. Can be expensive and elitist. Time-consuming: travel time/time away from work. The 'academic' nature of some research might make the links to practical application hard to recognize. Potential future impact on frontline practice promoted but not supported. Focus in some instances on research 'on education' not 'for education'. Limited interactivity. Little or no support for participants after the event to put the ideas into practice. Students rarely involved.

Mentoring	Experienced member of staff provides mentor support. Outside agency provides mentor training/support.	To enable new staff to develop their practice through one-to-one mentoring support. Experienced member of staff able to model and share 'good practice' with new members of staff through feedback on practice.	Uses in-house, existing knowledge and expertise as the basis of CPD. Can be relatively inexpensive. Potential to provide individualized and flexible support. Novice receives direct instruction on how to develop practice from mentor. Focus on the development of day-to-day practice in context. Interactive in nature.	Highly dependent on the quality of the mentor's knowledge and skills. Relationships usually hierarchical. One-way flow of influence and expertise from mentor. Taken-for-granted practices can be perpetuated. Can inhibit the development of reflective critical attitude. Links to research tenuous. Often under-trained and under-resourced. Students rarely involved.
Joint practice development	Shared experience where the focus is on the development of local practice. Two or more people interacting and influencing each other. Mutual development of practice not a simple 'transfer' of practice. Research experienced support for the development of ideas and interventions. Time and space to talk about teaching and learning.	The main focus is on the development of practice. Joint identification of an aspect of practice for improvement. Looks to educational research for ideas/support/interventions. Shared experience of changing practice. Shared experience of evaluating impact. Collaborative discussion of issues, possible solutions and reflection on impact. Based on an 'opt-in' rather than 'imposed' model.	Impact focused on local practice. Collaboration allows participants to learn from each other and to develop social capital, reciprocity and trust. Research-informed input and evidence challenges thinking. Focused on the development of local practice. Opportunity to select projects that respond to local, regional or national priorities. Reach beyond immediate participants. The flow of influence is two-way. It is interactive, iterative and incremental. Relatively inexpensive. Builds upon existing in-house knowledge and expertise. Potential sustainability – staff and students can use the approach on different projects. Strong horizontal impact between staff at the same level within the organization. Students can be directly involved in design and implementation of project and evaluation of impact.	Realistic allocation of time resource required. Requires research experienced guidance and support to help staff engage with research literature. Not a 'quick fix' but a 'slow burn'. Risk of outcomes of JPD research being disseminated in ways which do not reflect the guiding principles and core practices of JPD.

that governments and universities in the UK, Australasia and the USA have formalized programmes for the professional development of teachers. Before that time, knowledge of the vocational or subject-specialist qualification was considered both a necessary and sufficient condition in order to be able to teach. Indeed, such credentials were considered to be more important than engagement with the discipline and scholarship of education and knowledge about how to teach. However, interest in the development of professional standards for teachers in the FAVE sector and the regulation of their practice has increased in line with the recognition of the importance of their role in contributing to the economic and social life of the neighbourhoods, towns, cities, regions and countries in which teachers work. Equally, the influence of teachers across the FAVE sector in offering 'second chances' to people who have had less-than-positive experiences in the schools sector is now widely accepted.

The career paths of teachers across the FAVE sector vary according to the nature of their full-time or part-time contracts, their subject specialisms or disciplines, the different work-loading arrangements and the different staff development policies which operate in different institutions of education. To sum up, a key to the successful management of your career in the FAVE sector is the ability to think carefully about your practice, be committed to the improvement of teaching and learning, and be aware of the many opportunities for teachers' CPD available to you.

It is customary for leaders of education to use CPD budgets to update the subject and pedagogical knowledge of their staff. Usually this involves attending time-consuming, often expensive, courses, conferences or other events where someone who is considered (or considers themselves) to be 'an expert' tells everyone else in attendance what to do.

While CPD events and networks are helpful in raising awareness of new developments, exchanging ideas and sharing resources – arguably a necessary first step in improving practice – they are not enough to guarantee it. This is because a lot more 'new learning' (Eraut, 2004) has to take place before knowledge is transferred well enough to bring about real changes in practice. Eraut uses the metaphor of an iceberg to explain how practice really changes. He argues that abstract, theoretical knowledge and information about a 'good practice' constitutes only one-eighth of the knowledge needed to put a 'good idea' into practice and that the remaining seven-eighths represents the amount of *new* learning needed to realize real change.

We have already pointed out how the recognition that changing and improving practice involves more than the simple transfer of information or somebody else telling you what to do. This idea is central to the principles of JPD. The JPD approach to CPD acknowledges that change takes time. It respects the existing knowledge of teachers and recognizes the reality that putting ideas into practice places greater demands upon the relationships of those involved in the processes of change and those responsible for the practices of improvement than is involved in just telling somebody else what to do (Gregson et al., 2015, Reading 16.1).

In view of the above, we argue education leaders may need to think carefully about the extent to which existing, taken-for-granted approaches to CPD can be justified in terms of value for money.

Figure 16.1 identifies the main strengths and limitations associated with a range of approaches to CPD in the FAVE sector: their strengths and limitations.

Your institution may have a Human Resources (HR) or CPD department which offers an induction into teaching in the organization, often comprising a short course over one or two days. Often attendance at such induction and safeguarding modules are compulsory and function as a useful introduction to the organization for beginning teachers. It is a good idea to make contact with your HR or CPD department as early as you can, because they invariably have a range of professional development programmes on offer to support teaching, learning and course administration. These may range from providing you with copies of the institution's promotion and staff appraisal polices, stand-alone workshops, whole-organization staff development days and conferences, through to fully accredited professional teaching qualifications

Throughout your career you will normally be expected to provide evidence of how you are continuing to develop your professional practice as well as demonstrating your contribution to, and impact upon, student learning. You may also be expected to show how your research and scholarly work in the form of research conference papers/posters and publications is contributing to your practice and to the achievements of learners. As we mentioned earlier in this chapter, a useful place to start is to look to any national professional standards which are used to regulate your practice.

2.1 Professional values and attributes

The following descriptors from the Professional Standards for Further Education Teachers and Trainers in England (2014) indicate the knowledge, understanding, professional skills, values and attributes to which a professional teacher or trainer in the FAVE sector is expected to be committed.

Establishing and working towards milestones in your career is important to the development of your expertise as a teacher. You will need to be able to provide evidence of significant developments in your practice and the impact of your research and practice upon students' learning.

Reflective activity 16.2

Identifying your own level of expertise
The following questions offer a useful first focus.

Questions
1 Which aspects of the standards are you most confident about in your practice?
2 What sources of evidence are you able to provide to demonstrate this?
3 Which aspects of the standards do you need to prioritize as part of your professional development?
4 Who could help you with this development?
5 In what ways do the standards align with your institutions policy on staff promotion?
6 How might the standards assist you in preparing for promotion?

Professional standards for further education teachers and trainers in England

Develop your own judgement of what works and does not work in your teaching and training.

1   Reflect on what works best in your teaching and learning to meet the diverse needs of learners.
2   Evaluate and challenge your practice, values and beliefs.
3   Inspire, motivate and raise aspirations of learners through your enthusiasm and knowledge.
4   Be creative and innovative in selecting and adapting strategies to help learners to learn.
5   Value and promote social and cultural diversity equality of opportunity and inclusion.
6   Build positive and collaborative relationships with colleagues and learners.

Professional knowledge and understanding

Develop deep and critically informed knowledge and understanding in theory and practice.

7   Maintain and update knowledge of your subject and/or vocational area.
8   Maintain and update your knowledge of educational research to develop evidenced-based practice.
9   Apply theoretical understanding of teaching, learning and assessment drawing on research and other evidence.
10 Evaluate your practice with others and assess its impact on learning.
11 Manage and promote positive learner behaviour.
12 Understand the teaching and professional role and your responsibilities.

Professional skills

Develop your expertise and skills to ensure the best outcomes for learners.

13 Motivate and inspire learners to promote achievement and develop their skills to enable progression.
14 Plan and deliver effective learning programmes for diverse groups or individuals in a safe and inclusive environment.
15 Promote the benefits of technology and support learners in its use.
16 Address mathematics and English of learners and work creatively to overcome individual barriers to learning.
17 Enable learners to share responsibility for their own learning and assessment, setting goals that stretch and challenge.
18 Apply appropriate and fair methods of assessment and provide constructive and timely feedback to support progression and achievement.
19 Maintain and update your teaching and training expertise and vocational skills through collaboration with employers.
20 Contribute to organizational development and quality improvement through collaboration with others.

As you progress through your career, identify and take opportunities to develop your skills and expertise by making the most of mentoring and opportunities for critical professional friendship where more experienced colleagues can offer you advice and support in developing your skills in teaching and your research. Hillier (2012) outlines some of the many ways to develop your expertise, including acting as an external examiners or verifiers for other institutions or awarding bodies, participating in institution-wide committees, working parties, steering groups, assessment boards, or embarking on higher degrees in your subject specialism or in the discipline of education. In addition, you might decide to develop a specific aspect of your practice – for example, in the use of ICT. On the other hand, you may decide to develop your academic leadership by leading the development of a new aspect of the curriculum or a new programme or successfully leading the team through a major accreditation, validation or inspection process.

As you take advantage of opportunities such as those described above, remember to document them carefully. It is a good idea to keep a portfolio of your achievements that includes a record of all of the professional development you attend and, where possible, the impact these have had upon your developing career (see Reflective activity 16.3), and that you update your curriculum vitae (CV) on a regular basis to reflect your on-going professional development. Remember to link CPD activities to developments in the depth and breadth of your expertise as you move from beginning teacher to advanced practitioner/expert. It's also a good idea to write a personal statement about your practice as a whole, so that you can not only specify particular examples of development but can also demonstrate how these activities are underpinned by the principles and values of being a professional in FAVE.

Reflective activity 16.3

Developing a portfolio of your teaching achievements

Read through the following strategies for presenting a summary of your teaching adapted from Hillier (2012). Think about how you might use or adapt these ideas to summarize your achievements in applying for consideration for a promotion or for inclusion in your teaching portfolio.

Write a short statement about what educational values matter to you and why. This might develop over time as you teach in different contexts and gain more experience and expertise. For example:

'It is important that students get a sense of the history of the subject/vocational area they are studying, the current thinking and practice in the subject/vocational area, as well as a sense of possibilities in the future direction of the subject/vocational area.'

'In my teaching I try to bring the subject/vocational area alive and generate an interest in and a passion for its study. Student participation and creative interactivity are the key to igniting this passion and interest.'

'My current professional development priority is to capture the educational potential of new technologies.'

Maintain up-to-date records of your teaching, course reviews, student feedback from evaluations and how you have responded, projects, initiatives or innovations you have led/managed. Include numbers of students taught, teaching methods, and resources you have adapted or developed and used, comment on how you ensure that your subject specialist knowledge, knowledge of teaching and how you check that the content of the curriculum is up to date and how you keep abreast of developments in your subject/vocational area by engaging in research, subscribing to professional journals, and so on.

You might also include how you adopt a student-centred approach in your teaching, how you develop positive professional relationships with your students, examples of how you have helped a student in difficulty through to successful achievement, examples of your students' accomplishments on completing their studies, how you help students from diverse cultural backgrounds to feel valued and included your classes/workshops, and how you use formative and summative feedback to students to enable them to reach their full potential.

In addition, you might demonstrate your commitment to research and scholarship in your subject-specialist discipline/vocational area or in the field of education by listing examples of how your teaching has been influenced by your own research or the research of others, including examples of formal feedback and recognition you have received from your peers, together with the impact of your engagement with research upon your students' learning. You might mention conferences or courses you have attended, books or articles you have read. Describe how you use technology in your teaching and the impact of this upon the learning of your students and their subsequent achievements. Keep a record of any indicators of national, regional or local indicators of esteem in the form of any invitations you have received to speak about teaching, learning and research at conferences, workshops and seminars.

Describe any innovations you have made in your teaching, funding grants you have received and any awards you or your students have won. Document any influence you have had on institutional, departmental or team decisions and policies.

Present your documentary evidence as a narrative/supporting statement on your CV and/or application form, which tells the story of your teaching and its development and provides convincing, coherent and compelling evidence to support the points you make.

2.2 Scholarship and research in FAVE

There are a number of views about how and why we should conduct research and engage in scholarship in FAVE. Scholarship in education in general can be taken to be the process through which teachers conduct and publish research on the teaching and learning of their specialist subject/discipline/vocational area or indeed carry out research on the practice of education in its own right. It can also be regarded as being primarily about raising the profile and status of the profession of teachers and teaching, as well as that of researchers and research.

From another point of view, it can be understood as the scholarly ways in which teachers make use of research and literature in the field of teaching and learning to inform their practice, or the ways in which teachers come to teach in more research-informed ways or more knowledgeably. It can also be a means through which the quality of teaching can be assessed. Some authors see scholarship and research in education as a critical and intellectual activity. Others claim that research in teaching is essentially about the pursuit of 'excellent' practice.

Hodkinson and James (2003) challenge the notion of the existence of some kind of universalized models of 'excellence' and 'good practice' in teaching. They argue that what constitutes effective teaching and learning cannot be straightforwardly associated with the idea that 'what works' in one educational setting will automatically 'work' in another. Coffield (2014) describes as 'ill-conceived' and 'ineffectual' the notion that teaching can and will be improved simply by identifying and disseminating what is considered to be 'best practice' in teaching and learning. No matter how broadly or narrowly we construe the remit of research and scholarship in education, what goes on in classrooms and in other sites of teaching and learning in the FAVE sector, we argue, cannot be fully understood without the clear recognition of the complex and inter-related nature of teaching, learning and research. The important role that teachers' professional judgements play in all of this and in the development of educationally sound practice should not be underestimated

Scholarship and research in the field of education often starts with the identification of a problem in educational practice that needs to be investigated. Subsequently questions are generated about the potential nature of the problem and so the process of research begins. However, problems in educational practice are often considered to be the sole province of bad teachers or something good teachers just do not have to face. Another popular notion is that if you have a problem in teaching, you probably need and want to fix it – and quickly. In the field of higher education, McCarthy (2008) argues that shifting the status of problems in teaching away from deficit pathologies of practice (which it is often assumed can be addressed by simple technical remedies or 'recipes for teaching') toward systematic and on-going investigation can and should be a key aspect of scholarship and research in teaching and learning.

However, as we have already discussed, there are those in the academy who would argue that teaching and research are two very different practices. Some would even go as far as to say that teaching is of much lower status in the field of education than research. A consequence of this is that teaching can become relegated to some kind of lowly technical transmission of disciplinary knowledge and research can become elevated to an elite status practised only by a privileged few. In this way the language of teaching and learning is used to replace the language of the discipline and practices of education (Biesta, 2004).

Brew (2006: 18) draws attention to the fact that what is often described as the 'traditional' relationship between teaching and research is far from traditional, and how the idea that teaching and research should be seen as separate is a relative newcomer in the study of education. He shows how the 'traditional' view of the relationship between teaching and research sets teaching and research in false opposition to each other and assumes that they can and should inhabit separate domains and forms of practice, competing with each other in terms of 'time, resources and space' (Brew, 2007: 1).

Brew goes on to illustrate how research has popularly been seen as taking place in a disciplinary research culture in which academics, researchers and postgraduate research students in HEIs and universities carry out the job of generating knowledge. From this perspective, teaching is seen as taking place in classrooms, lecture theatres and other educational settings where the job of teachers is seen to be to transmit knowledge generated by others.

Brown (2002) shows how this viewpoint has come to dominate education in the UK and elsewhere. He explains how this has led to unprecedentedly centralized curriculum regimes, where the pedagogical role is construed as lowly in a management hierarchy. In this climate, he contends, teachers have come to be seen as minor technicians where the overall goals of education are set in advance and framed instrumentally in terms of the needs of the national economy. In such circumstances, he shows how curriculum materials become remotely pre-packaged by alleged disciplinary specialists and equally distant experts formulate pedagogical methods. The teacher's job, therefore, becomes reduced to the technical supervision of the 'methodical insertion of ordered facts into the minds of students' (Brown, 2002: 46).

The problem with this position is that educational research becomes removed from and inaccessible to the world of educational practice. The conditions for a 'perfect storm' are therefore created, where educational research sits on the actual and virtual shelves of academic researchers while educational practice goes on in ways which are uninformed by educational research (Sarason, 1990; Gregson and Nixon, 2009).

As you develop greater expertise in teaching and learning, think about the ways in which your career reflects your commitment to research and scholarship teaching and learning and what evidence you could use to demonstrate this commitment.

Reflective activity 16.4

Thinking about professional standards

The following excerpts from the Professional Standards for Further Education Teachers and Trainers in England (2014) provide a useful guide to for thinking about how you might articulate and evidence your developing teaching and pedagogical expertise over time.

Evidencing Area 8 of the Professional Standards for Further Education Teachers and Trainers in England: Maintain and update your knowledge of educational research to develop evidenced-based practice.

This area is concerned with the enhancement of teaching and learning through the maintenance and updating of subject specialist knowledge through engaging in continuing professional development in subjects/disciplines/vocational areas and in their pedagogy. It also involves using research and scholarship to evaluate and improve your own practice.

Question: How might you draw on these elements of the standards to demonstrate that you have become a better teacher through continuing professional development, research and the critical evaluation of your teaching and learning practices?

Evidencing Area 1 of the Professional Standards for Further Education Teachers and Trainers in England: Reflect on what works best in your teaching and learning to meet the diverse needs of learners.

This area is concerned with your ability to think carefully about the impact of your teaching upon learners and their learning in the light of evidence from your practice and engagement with ideas from your own research and that of others to arrive at principled, informed and carefully considered judgements about what to do, when and why. This area foregrounds the importance of direct professional involvement in inquiry into teaching and learning practices to support the individual's own professional development and to enhance teaching and learning.

Question: What evidence can you provide to demonstrate that your teaching is informed and characterized by the values in Area 1?

For example, you might consider and apply the findings from studies, reading, personal research possibly in collaboration with a colleague and/or with your own students to identify how you might enhance your practice and improve student learning.

On the other hand, you might decide to use research in your own subject/discipline/vocational area to enhance the curriculum. This might include reading research, theory and practice in the field of curriculum design in order to provide a rationale for the design and development of the curriculum and its delivery.

2.3 The connection between teaching, learning and research

Bearing in mind the contested nature of scholarship of teaching and learning, it is worth noting how the teaching, learning and research can be connected. Scholarship in teaching and learning can connect research in the field of subject-specialist, disciplinary or vocational knowledge with teaching and pedagogical development. The scholarship of teaching and learning connects pedagogic development with pedagogical research. In other words, by finding out more from systematic and robust research in education and scholarship about how learning takes place, we can identify pedagogical interventions, ideas and approaches which are more likely to be successful, and avoid those which are not.

3 The scholarship of teaching, learning and academic promotion

Some teachers in the FAVE sector are more active in the research and scholarship of teaching and learning than others. There are a number of reasons why teachers in the FAVE sector do not engage in research. Prominent among these are the sheer pressures of high teaching workloads and the fact that little, if any, time or funding is made available to support and enable teachers in the FAVE sector to engage in research. However, research activity and publication can contribute to opportunities for promotion, so it is a good idea to familiarize yourself with your institution's policy and guidelines on the promotion of academic staff. Such documents provide you with insights into the levels of skill and achievements required to progress from one academic level to the next.

There is a relative consensus among academics (HEA, 2009) that promotion should be the main way that excellence in teaching should be rewarded. However, this is not always the case in practice, and many teachers in the FAVE sector find themselves having to move out of teaching roles and into education management and leadership posts in order to gain promotion. Coffield (2008) points to difficulties and dangers of this situation. He argues that as education managers and leaders become more removed from teaching and learning, their priorities and the decisions they make as a result can become less concerned with educational values and more with commercial ones reflecting the values, imperatives, language and practices of the market.

Throughout this book we have explored theories and concepts of curriculum, assessment and teaching. In this section we look at strategies for pulling all of these together in order to support you in developing a coherent narrative around your continuing professional development.

In Chapter 4 and in each of the subsequent chapters we have linked our discussions to principles of teaching and learning from the Teaching and Learning Research Programme (TRLP) funded by UK Economic Social Research Council (ESRC), the UK's largest and most expansive initiative in education research.

Reflective activity 16.5

Thinking about your current level of practice

Taking into account all that we have considered in this chapter about approaches for developing, extending and evidencing your expertise in the FAVE sector, think about where you would locate your current practice in relation to the following areas and what evidence you could present in support of your location on each of these aspects of practice.

- Impact on students
- Individual teaching and learning development
- Curriculum development
- Research and scholarship of teaching and learning
- Research activity in your subject specialism/discipline/vocational area
- Leadership

Conclusion

In this chapter we have explored the nature and dynamics of the development of expertise in the FAVE sector and the role that CPD plays in deepening our understandings of teaching, learning and research. We have considered some of the milestones you encounter as you develop in your career as a teacher and the value of planning well ahead in relation to your career trajectory and in harnessing potential opportunities for promotion in your teaching.

One of the most important messages we would like you take from engaging with the ideas in this chapter and in this book is that the importance of ensuring that the evidence you generate and use to demonstrate your developing expertise in your teaching is supported by robust educational research and clear indicators of the impact of your work.

We have considered in particular the Professional Standards for Further Education Teachers and Trainers in England (Education and Training Foundation, 2014). We have noted the value and importance these and other standards for teachers attach to the careful and considered evaluation of practice and a commitment to continuing professional development as a core to professional teaching practice in FAVE. The ten principles emerging from the UK's Teaching and Learning Research Programme (TLRP) introduced earlier in this book (see Chapter 4) provide another useful framework for informing your own research and scholarship of teaching and learning in the context of your practice and those of your colleagues, your department and your institution. You may even consider using the principles of JPD as guide to CPD activity with a colleague, in your team/department or across your organization.

It is our firm belief that education leaders and teachers can and should use the knowledge, expertise and talents of existing staff, alongside robust educational research and the resources they already have available, to build and support the development of collaborative and mutually responsible relationships and arrangements which are capable of supporting sustainable improvements educational practice. We have drawn attention to the potential of more collaborative ways of improving practice through JPD (Gregson et al., 2015). We suggest that JPD can help to make real and sustainable improvements in teaching, learning and assessment as an integral part of an organization's CPD strategy. Improving your practice is about making and taking judgements in the complex and unfolding situations we encounter in our everyday teaching. We have highlighted shortcomings in framing the concept of reflection solely in terms of individual teachers thinking about their own practice (see for example Thompson and Pascal, 2012) and pointed to the need for more pragmatic and cooperative ways of making sense of our work and improving what we do together with our students (Sennett, 2012). In the following chapter, we will discuss how our actions and our understanding inform our professional practice and what being a professional entails.

Key readings

Many of the key readings for Chapter 3 on reflective practice are very relevant to this chapter, including Calderhead **(Reading 3.1)** and Dewey **(Reading 3.2).**

Key readings for Chapter 4 on the principles for effective teaching and learning are also highly pertinent to enduring issues in education which have been identified – see for example Hattie **(Reading 4.3).**

We offer supplementary suggestions on the specific issue of expertise. For a philosophical overview of the nature of expertise, see:

> Winch, C. (2012) *Dimensions of Expertise: A Conceptual Exploration of Vocational Knowledge.* London: Continuum.

For a developmental account of how expertise evolves through the interaction of practice and analysis and an examination of the dynamics and processes involved in the transfer of knowledge from education to workplace settings, see:

> Eraut, M. (2004) 'Transfer of Knowledge Education and Workplace Settings'. In H. Rainbird (ed.) *Workplace Learning in Context.* London: Routledge.

Written in a clear and engaging style, this edited book presents a powerful critique of current government policies and presents a useful discussion on the notion of the development of teacher judgement, expertise and 'best practice':

> Coffield, F. (ed.) (2014) *Beyond Bulimic Learning.* London: London University, Institute of Education (IOE).

See also:

> Jeffrey, B. and Troman, G. (eds) (2012) *Performativity in UK Education: Ethnographic Cases of Its Effects, Agency and Reconstructions.* Painswick: E&E Publishing.

For a discussion on an alternative model of educational change and the importance of teachers, see Pasi Sahlberg's article on 'What the world can learn from educational change in Finland **(Reading 4.2)** – edited from:

> Sahlberg, P. (2011) *Finnish Lessons: What Can the World Learn from Educational Change in Finland?.* New York: Teachers College Press, 1–6, 140–5.

Hattie provides a synopsis of meta-analyses of quantitative educational research achievements and identifies key factors in raising student achievement encouragingly, consonant in general with the results of qualitative research which draws attention to the crucial role of teacher development in improving student achievement:

> Hattie, J. (2009) *Visible Learning: A Synthesis of Over 800 Meta-Analyses Relating to Achievement.* London: Routledge.

In this inaugural professorial lecture, Wiliam (2007) focuses on the development of teacher expertise and on teachers' professional development activity. He suggests that the content of teachers' professional development strategies should concentrate on teaching strategies of proven effectiveness and processes of classroom application.

> Wiliam, D. (2009) *Assessment for Learning: Why, what and how?* Inaugural lecture. University of London, Institute of Education (IOE), 24 April.

This journal article discusses how the language of education is being replaced by the language of learning and the potential consequences of this shift:

> Biesta, G. (2004) 'Against learning. reclaiming a language for education in an age of learning', *Nordic Studies in Education*, 23, 70, 82.

Hodkinson, P. M. and James, D. (2003*)* 'Transforming learning cultures in further
    education', *Journal of Vocational Education and Training*, 55 (4), 389–406.

For a discussion on scholarship of teaching and learning and the purposes of education,
see:

Finlay, I. (2008) 'What's Learning for? Interrogating the Scholarship of Teaching and
    Learning'. In R. Murray (ed.) *The Scholarship of Teaching and Learning in Higher
    Education.* Maidenhead: Open University Press.

This chapter in an edited book provides a careful consideration of the internal 'goods'
and 'desired outcomes' of education:

Dunne, J. (2005) 'What's the Good of Education'. In W. Carr (ed.). *The
    RoutledgeFalmer Reader in Philosophy of Education.* London: Routledge.

Also in Gregson, M., Nixon, L., Spedding, P. and Kearney, S. (forthcoming, 2015)
    Helping Research Findings Become Good Practice. London: Bloomsbury Press.
    (Reading 16.1)

Hargreaves, A. (2007) *The Persistence of Presentism and the Struggle for Lasting
    Improvement.* Professorial Lecture. London: University of London, Institute of
    Education (IOE). 24 January. **(Reading 16.3)**

Hillier, Y. and Jameson, J. (2003) *Empowering Researchers in Further Education.*
    Stoke-on-Trent: Trentham Books. **(Reading 16.2)**

O'Leary, M. (2013) *Classroom Observation: A Guide to the Effective Observation of
    Teaching and Learning.* London: Routledge. **(Reading 16.4)**

The Deepening Expertise section of **reflectiveteaching.co.uk** is being developed to provide
links to websites which extend understanding and application of particular concepts.

The associated website, **reflectiveteaching.co.uk**, offers a wealth of supplementary
resources including reflective activities, research briefings, advice on further reading
and downloadable diagrams, figures and checklists from the book. It also features a
compendium of educational terms, links to useful websites, policy and curriculum
documents, and showcases examples of excellent research and practice.

Professionalism

How does reflective teaching contribute to society, and to ourselves?

17

Introduction

Historically there is a long-standing tradition of civic responsibility among teachers in all parts of the UK and elsewhere, and the contribution to public life that socially aware professional educators have made is considerable. We have already pointed out that teaching reflects moral purpose and has significant social consequences for the societies we live in. For these reasons, commitments to educational enquiry, equity and social justice are promoted by the professional bodies that represent and, in some cases, regulate the work of teachers in the FAVE sector.

Becoming a reflective teacher in the FAVE sector involves us in engaging in a particular way of life and a set of educational practices, particular ways of working, thinking and going about what we do. In doing so, we begin to develop practical wisdom, the ability and virtue to be able to do the right thing at the right time in both familiar and unexpected situations (Biesta, 2011, Reading 1.1; Heilbronn, 2011, Reading 4.1; Wiliam, 2007, Reading 17.1). The quality of the judgements you make in these situations will play a significant part in your professional life and in the lives of your students. You will need to keep up to date with research and developments in the vocational or academic practices that you teach. You will need to ensure that you also keep up to date with research and developments in the discipline and practices of education. In the previous chapter, we developed our argument that the professionality of teachers is not just technical but also normative. We showed the relationship between reflection, judgement and wisdom based on the distinction between the technical and the normative expertise teachers need to have. In this chapter we highlight the career-long dimension of becoming educationally wise through professional development. We also return to our original values and principles where we argue that this complex, messy professional practice in which we undertake our daily work is situated in a social world full of tension and competing demands, making it frankly highly contested and associated with a lower status than other well-established professions.

TLRP principles

Two principles in particular have particularly influenced our approach to this chapter.

Principle 9: Effective teaching and learning depends on teacher learning. The need for lecturers, teachers, trainers and co-workers to learn continuously in order to develop their knowledge and skill, and to adapt and develop their roles, especially through practice-based inquiry, should be recognized and supported.

Principle 10: Effective teaching and learning demands consistent policy frameworks with support for teaching and learning as the primary focus. Policies at national, institutional and local levels need to recognize the fundamental importance of teaching and learning. They should be designed to create effective learning environments in which all learners can thrive.

We begin with a few examples to open up discussion of some of the dilemmas you may encounter as you begin to find your feet as a teacher.

Case study 17.1 CPD

It is the end of the year. You have managed to teach your programmes successfully. Your learners have achieved their qualifications, your learners have obtained vocational qualifications, and some of them have been successful in gaining employment. Others have gone on to apply for further education and training. Your evening class learners have been very satisfied with their progress and wish to enrol for other programmes next year. You look back over the year and from the evaluations of your learners, peers and your own records, you realize that there are some areas of your professional practice that you wish to develop. You are unsure how best to use technology effectively in your teaching. You are really not quite sure about the changes to qualifications being introduced and how you should be assessing your learners' work. You know there are new developments in your curriculum area and you wish to know more about them. How will you go about developing and improving your practice?

Case study 17.2 Inspection

Here is another scenario: The inspectors are visiting your institution. There is a great deal of preparation by the institution to provide evidence that the programmes of learning are of the appropriate quality. Part of this preparation involves an observation of your teaching by your line manager in readiness for the inspection. You are given a pro-forma which outlines the areas she will be concentrating on. You discuss the appropriate time for her to visit your group. After the session she arranges to provide you with feedback. When you sit down together she asks you how you thought the session went. You describe what you are happy with and the parts of the session where you know things could have gone better. She agrees, and then begins to identify aspects of your teaching that could be developed. She has noticed that you answer the questions you have just asked your learners if they hesitate even for a second. They do not get the chance to answer before you step in. Your writing on the whiteboard is difficult to read from the back of the room. There were a few typographical errors in your PowerPoint and handouts. The younger learners have not engaged with the topic and have been disruptive in your session.

As a result of your observation, your line manager suggests that you may wish to join in the staff development programme offered in the institution. It will provide you with an opportunity to meet other tutors and to share aspects of your practice, both those that are successful and those which continue to challenge. In particular, there is a new series of seminars on dealing with 14–19-year-olds that may be particularly helpful for some of your programmes next year.

She also suggests that you might like to join a professional network in your subject area that you are already aware of. She gives you a number of websites that you may find useful and makes an arrangement to meet with you during the next term so that you can update her on your progress and discuss some of the ideas that you have got from your search and networking.

How will you use this feedback to improve your practice? What will you give priority to and why?

These are two examples where individuals can look for ways to improve their professional practice. The first originates from a personal decision that there are aspects of the practice which can be developed. The second results from a line manager's recommendation. There are many reasons why you may be asked to take part in formal professional development, not simply because someone thinks that you are not teaching appropriately. Professional development can help your practice in your personal search to achieve high standards in teaching, which will maximize the learning that will take place in your classes.

We have talked about professional practice throughout this book – but what exactly do we mean by being professional?

1 Being professional

Developing professional practice suggests that we know what it is to be a professional. When you ask a neighbour whether the local plumber did a good job, you may be told that it was 'very professional'. When you visit the dentist, you may conclude that her skill in filling your tooth and the way in which she talked to you was 'very professional'. What exactly does it mean to be a professional?

In many occupations, being professional involves meeting strict criteria, including having entry qualifications before being able to practise. The medical and legal professions are prime examples where, following a number of years of initial training, further training is undertaken while practising, until people become fully qualified and certified to practise. In other occupations, being professional includes taking examinations to become members of a professional body, and again this membership licenses people to practise. Once qualified and practising, people maintain their professional practice through further training and development, called continuing education (CE) or CPD. Professional practice is therefore seen to be practice that has met threshold standards, is continually developed, and takes account of new research and development in the field.

Most of you reading this book will be specialists who also teach. You may be an electrician, linguist, beautician, accountant or counsellor. You will therefore also need to manage the adherence to your subject-specialist professional requirements as well as meeting those of the sector in which you work. This situation is often described as 'dual professionalism'. You may find, then, that your CPD centres on developing your subject knowledge or keeping updated with current changes in that area. Yet you also need to consider your teaching and how this can be developed. One argument for developing practice is that you are not a specialist who then has to think about teaching, but that your practice is a coherent whole (i.e. you teach plumbing or creative writing because you are a teaching plumber or creative writer or hairdresser, etc). This approach helps you think reflectively and creatively in a different way from one which focuses on a separate identity as teacher and subject or vocational specialist.

Many professions have specific codes of practice that members must adhere to. The medical profession, in particular, is governed by a council, Acts of Parliament and ethical committees. Before 1999 there was no equivalent body for those who work in post-compulsory education. There was no requirement for staff to be qualified to teach. Indeed, if people did gain a teaching qualification, it was not seen to be equivalent to that required by teachers in the schools sector and thus the status of the workforce was compromised (see for example Appleby and Hillier, 2012; Bathmaker and Avis, 2005; James and Biesta, 2007). You might like to find the appropriate institutional support for professional practice of staff and possibly any membership organization which represents or advocates for professionals in the FAVE sector where you are.

Professionalism is a very slippery term. It means so many different things and when applied to teaching in post-compulsory education, it becomes even more contested. In the field of professionalism in further and higher education staff, some authors provides a careful summary of characteristics of professionalism, including having autonomy, agency and practising according to codes of conduct. A University and College Union (UCU) paper towards a policy on professionalism (Taubman, 2013) identifies common elements, including people dealing with 'complex and unpredictable situations', having specialist knowledge and expertise, given trust by stakeholders, and an expectation that they will demonstrate a high level of personal integrity (UCU, 2013: 2). The Lingfield Review of Professionalism (Lingfield, 2012) identified ten criteria which underpin professionalism:

1   Master of a complex discipline.

2   Continuous enhancement of expertise.

3   Acceptance that the field of expertise is a vocation to be pursued selflessly for the benefit of others.

4   Public accountability for high standards of capability and conduct.

5   Membership of a group earning and deserving the respect of the community.

6   Membership of a defined group with similar skills, transcending local loyalties to achieve national and international recognition.

7   Acceptance of responsibility for the competence and good conduct of other members of the professional group.

8   Membership of a group which accepts responsibility for planning succession by future generations.

9   Membership of a group which seeks continuously to extend and improve its field of knowledge.

10 Membership of a group deserving an above-average standard of living.

One of the sources of tension for any group of professionals is how to manage their own autonomy against a set of expectations by their stakeholders and peers (Sahlberg et al., 2012, Reading 17.2). It is not good belonging to a 'club' of like-minded people if their practice is not in the interests of the wider community. In the past, some well-established professions like the medical profession have been accused of 'closing ranks' to preserve their conditions of service, instead of scrutinizing and improving their practice. Another problem is how professions are controlled by government policy and how much leeway they can hold in making decisions on their own behalf without interference by others who have no experience or knowledge of their profession. This tension is particularly apparent within teaching and the health professions. Given that people are drawn from a huge range of backgrounds, operate in different settings and have a variety of roles, their commitment, knowledge and expertise is a strength. Yet as Ball (2012) argues, education today is viewed as a commodity which can be bought and sold, and an increasing managerialism accompanies development. People internalize the processes of quality assurance which feature meeting targets and monitoring inputs and outputs, and UCU goes as far as to suggest that professionals have become 'reinvented as units … whose performance and productivity are constantly being audited so these can be enhanced' (UCU, 2013: 5).

The idea that professionals should be closely monitored and adhere to a set of measurable standards is very different from one that acknowledges the autonomy that professionals require in order to develop their practice. Eric Hoyle (1974) first drew the powerful distinction between 'restricted' and 'extended' professionalism.

- *Restricted professionalism* describes the competence underpinning core effectiveness. Skills and perspectives are derived from immediate classroom experience; and workplace learning occurs gradually, but largely passively. Consideration of teaching methods tends to be private and personal autonomy may be protected. Involvement in professional development is infrequent and each teacher prefers to develop in his or her own way.

- *Extended professionalism* envisages that skills and understanding are developed from the interaction of practical experience and analysis, including theory; there is awareness of social, economic and political contexts which impinge on education; and workplace events are considered in relation to policies and overall educational purposes. Teaching methods are shared with colleagues and reviewed in terms of research-informed principles. High value is placed on professional collaboration and on networking in sectoral or subject associations. Pedagogic repertoire and subject knowledge are kept up to date in active, committed and open-minded ways.

These contrastive models of teacher professionalism still resonate. For example, a review by Menter et al. (2010, Reading 17.3) for the Scottish Government used the restricted–extended spectrum in summarizing distinctions between four conceptions of professionalism. This is summarized in Figure 17.1 below:

Crowther (2011) examines a number of models of professionalism including the Professional Capital Model (Hargreaves and Fullan, 2012), an integrated competency

Restricted professionalism	Extended professionalism		
The effective teacher	The reflective teacher	The enquiring teacher	The transformative teacher

Figure 17.1
Models of teacher professionalism and practice.

model (Australia VET system), the expansive learning environment model (Fuller and Unwin, 2009) and the Teaching Standards model. Each of these has its attractions and deficits in both capturing what goes on in professional development but also what should occur. Crowther concludes that we need a model but, perhaps more importantly, a practice that represents the 'values, dispositions, traditions and contexts in which we work in an integrated way' (Crowther, 2011: 16)

Lingfield (2012) in his *Review of Professionalism in Further Education* recognized the breadth and maturity of the FE sector. Aware of the morale in the sector, he acknowledges that the role that teachers across the sectors play is pivotal in providing a better service to learners (2012: 23). He also notes that staff need to be 'treated with greater care and respect' (2012: 19), particularly given the confidence and structural deficit within the sector, which his report hoped to address by offering enhanced status through its recommendations. This report led to a number of radical changes to the support for teachers in the sector. Colleges have become responsible for making decisions about CPD and qualification requirements rather than a national requirement and registration through other statutory bodies.

In other countries, there are similar bodies that have been sent up to support and monitor the quality of provision. For example, in Australia, each state has its own system but there is also an overarching national body. As in England, these bodies change as governments change and it is important to keep abreast of these changes as their policies and directives impinge directly on your own professional practice, particularly in relation to regimes of inspection of quality and requirements for professional qualifications.

1.1 Professionals and society

We do not practise in isolation and, as we argued in Chapters 3 and 4, we have an important role as teachers in acknowledging the power that we possess to change people's lives while also recognizing the constraints under which we practice. Many of the debates about what professionals should do and to whom they should be accountable relate to this issue. Given that we can and do make educational judgements about our students that can affect their subsequent course of action (for example, going on to higher education or work), we do clearly need to be accountable for our actions. We have already outlined ways in which this occurs, including our system of inspection, our system of examination and qualification and through the quality assurance processes in the institutions in which we work. We are accountable to our fellow citizens for the ways in which we have been employed and how we have spent the funding raised through taxation or fees.

Yet we are also working within an educational system that has underlying values and functions. For example, Pollard (2014) suggests that an education system could create wealth, reproduce culture, work towards social justice, individual rights and environmental sustainability. As Keep (2011) argues, in the FAVE sector, the focus on wealth creation and economic success has driven the system to such an extent that numerous myths have developed (for example, that globalization is a threat that we must counter through using qualifications in the FAVE sector). How does this imperative sit with the aim of achieving social justice, or enhancing individual rights? What is our role in working towards these often conflicting aims?

This is where our own imperative to act in educationally wise ways comes to the fore. This is not to suggest that we will be able to solve all the problems of the world if we reflect on our practice or, indeed, if we work together to examine our practice through JPD. Neither is it helpful to sit back and blame our managers or government policymakers for all the wrongs in the world and take no action. We have discussed the value of using our own agency in Chapter 3. The next section outlines in practical ways how we can take action in very concrete ways in our journey of being a FAVE professional.

1.2 What can you expect from your institution?

We do not always know what we need to do to develop our professional practice. Sometimes there are specific requirements made by our institution – for example, we may be required to attend a Health and Safety workshop or a staff seminar on Safeguarding. We may be offered a programme of staff development that is voluntary. How do we make judgements about what to attend? Why should we attend? If you have a full-time or fractional appointment in your institution, you will be asked to take part in an appraisal of your professional practice. Appraisals are meant to identify how you have met the targets set from the last appraisal, to review your performance, to check that your job description is accurate, and to identify any changes that have taken place. You will be asked to consider the strengths and weaknesses of your performance and will set new targets for the coming period. If you have undertaken any development activities during the last period, you will be asked to consider how much effect these have had on your performance.

If you are an hourly paid tutor, you may not be given an appraisal but you may be asked to meet with your programme leader, course coordinator, or curriculum manager to discuss your teaching. You may be observed at regular intervals (O'Leary, 2013, Reading 16.4), almost certainly the first time you work for an institution and then possibly once every two to three years afterwards. Institutions have different quality assurance procedures and demands in this regard. With any form of appraisal, the important thing is to think of how it can work for you. What development do you think would help you do your job better? If you are asked to take on a completely new group of learners without any support regarding their teaching and learning requirements, then you are going to find it a difficult and challenging job. You must also take responsibility for finding out about your learners and part of your professional practice concerns keeping up to date with pedagogical issues, including how to work with varying groups of learners.

If you have not been given any information about new curriculum developments, make sure that you go and talk to your curriculum coordinator or line manager. Sometimes, these colleagues are so overwhelmed with their own work that they have not managed to ensure that all staff, particularly those who only work a small number of hours per week, are kept informed. Is there a college intranet (internal network) where you can log in and obtain news and information? You have responsibility for keeping yourself informed as well as relying upon others to pass that information to you.

In all colleges and adult education institutions there is a governing body with staff representation. Make sure that you know who your staff governor is. Keep up to date with developments at an organization-wide level by reading minutes of formal meetings in the college as well as your own programme area team meetings. In this way you can make sure that your views are represented. Staff in institutions who are fractional and hourly paid provide a large amount of the teaching, but by the nature of their contracts and other responsibilities elsewhere, they have less opportunity to be involved in decision-making. This in no way reflects their lack of commitment. Recent research has identified that part-time hourly paid staff continue to feel isolated and estranged from their institutions, even though they also value support from their line managers and have immense commitment to their learners (Hillier and Jameson, 2004a, 2006). Full-time staff, too, must ensure that their views are heard, as it is often too easy to become bogged down with all the day-to-day activities. Otherwise decisions will be made by others that may subsequently be difficult to implement.

Being responsible for keeping up to date and playing an active part in decision-making processes in an organization are part of the role of a professional teacher or tutor.

2 Analysing our practice: Professional standards

In many countries, standards for teaching in FAVE have been created. In England, for example, the ETF has published a set of standards (ETF, 2014) which have moved away from competence-based performance criteria to a more overarching and generic values-based approach. Depending on the structure of FAVE, different countries develop different requirements for their teaching workforce (Misra, 2011). Sometimes it is hard to work out exactly what standards require. This is where attending staff development programmes – particularly those which lead to qualifications – are so useful. You meet other tutors and trainers from a wide range of backgrounds and contexts and by sharing your own practice, can learn from your colleagues. In many programmes, you will be asked to identify your strengths and weaknesses as a practitioner, possibly at the beginning of the programme and certainly at the end, where you think about what you have learned and how you intend to apply your skills, knowledge and understanding. There is an expectation in all of the accredited programmes for developing teaching and learning that you will continue to develop professionally. No one expects that you will sit back comfortably having completed a qualification in teaching and learning and expect to repeat your practice annually until you retire.

Not everyone agrees about what good practice in teaching and learning is. You may find that colleagues in your own subject specialism disagree about how certain concepts and topics should be covered. Using technology to support learning may be an area where there are 'champions' who use it all the time and others who say that they are fighting a rearguard action against computers at the expense of the face-to-face learning in which they believe strongly. This kind of debate is healthy because it forces us all, as professionals, to examine our practice and to identify where new ideas can be implemented and evaluated. It is the very lack of discussion and argument that can stultify our practice.

In addition to standards for professional practice, we must also abide by government legislation governing safe practice. In England, for example, this includes the Every Child Matters legislation (ECM), which has five tenets that children and young people will:

- Be healthy
- Stay safe
- Enjoy and achieve
- Make a positive contribution
- Achieve economic well-being

As we showed in Chapter 15, we are also required to work within health and safety standards primarily through the Health and Safety at Work Act (1974) and the Management of Health and Safety at Work Act (1999). We are bound by equality legislation including the original Sex Discrimination Act (1975), the Race Relations Act (1976) and the Human Rights Act (1998), most of which have now been superseded by the Equality Act (2010).

Reflective activity 17.1

Find your own institution's policies concerning national legislation for regulations relating to health and safety, discrimination and inclusive and positive practice.
How do you keep up to date with any changes that take place? What does your institution offer by way of induction and professional updating? How easy is it to stay informed?

Once we have a set of professional standards, we can begin to measure how well we match up to them. One way of developing our professional practice is to review what we do at certain intervals. We evaluate our teaching and training constantly, wondering how individual sessions went, how to enable certain learners to make progress, deciding whether to change a particular workshop or develop new materials which can be used on the web. This reflection in action (Schön, 1983) has been described in Chapter 3. We need to move beyond such reflection to ensure that we stand back from the everyday experiences and place our experience in a bigger context. Have we found there are changes we should be making at a deeper level? For example, if we have noticed that our learners have learned particularly well from some of our activities and not from others, should we change our overall approach to certain topics? Have we decided that technology can be used to support some of the learning that can be done autonomously by our learners? It is not easy to analyse our practice by ourselves, but at least standards provide a framework against which we can begin to think about what we currently do and whether we could change some of our practice. We are not suggesting that we should assume that we must constantly change everything. The role of reflection in teaching and training is to affirm what works well in addition to helping us see what could be changed.

Standards are not the only means by which we can judge our professional practice. If you talk to your colleagues, you will probably find that you have quite different opinions about good practice. You would almost certainly find it challenging to work out what the standards mean and how you could demonstrate you are meeting them. Sharing practice is one of the most fundamentally rewarding, challenging and useful things that teachers and trainers can do. It is not necessary to sit down with a checklist and ask whether items can be ticked off. What is more important is to observe how other people practise, watch how other learners go about their work, read about ideas and debates in learning and teaching. If you are fortunate enough to attend conferences, you will notice that you learn more from the informal discussion during the breaks than you will necessarily do from the speakers. If your institution provides a staff conference, then do try to attend, as you are likely to benefit enormously from talking informally with your peers, either from your own programme area or from a completely different part of the provision.

2.1 Staying informed

How can you become involved in the debates about teaching and learning? How can you find out about the current issues? You may belong to a professional body in your own subject. There are, in addition, bodies that are specifically involved in the education and training of adults. For, example the National Institute of Adult and Continuing Education (NIACE), in particular, is an extremely useful source of information in England and acts as a lobby to government and policymakers. Their journal, *Adults Learning,* is written by practitioners in the field of adult education and training. There are sections on activities and conferences taking place, book reviews, website reviews and then a series of articles, sometimes about a particular feature, written by practitioners. Reading professional journals will keep you informed about the major developments and debates in the field. For those working in company training contexts, the Chartered Institute of Personnel and Development (CIDP) is a more formal body as it is a chartered institute and professionals working in these contexts must undertake a variety of accredited programmes to become members. The professional journal of CIPD is *People Management.*

In England, the Learning and Skills Research Network (LSRN) has regional groups of members interested in research in the sector who meet locally. There is an annual conference held by each active region and a number of practitioners have contributed to a publication of their research, having won an award for their papers in a series of annual conferences held nationally from 1997 to 2003 (Hillier and Thompson, 2004; Hillier and Morris, 2010).

All of these professional bodies, and a variety of others, provide information through their websites. You can usually find lists of their publications there. Reading about teaching and learning can be done through searching library catalogues, websites, visiting your local library and obtaining recommended lists from your staff development managers and curriculum managers. There are a variety of sources you can consult. There are policy documents about widening participation in learning, lifelong learning, paying fees for programmes of education. Many of these can be obtained from the Department for Education (DfE) and the Department for Business, Innovation and Skills (BIS) websites.

There are books, like this one, on general issues in teaching and learning. A Google search for a subject or author will provide another source of information about aspects of teaching and learning. Those of you who want to know more about assessment, for example, can follow this up through searching using key words such as 'assessment for learning', 'educational assessment', 'assessment' and 'adult education'.

Then there are subject-specific books and articles. Certain subjects have bodies that have their own journals. With adult basic skills, for example, the Research and Practice in Adult Literacy (RaPAL) group has a publication which, again, is written by practitioners. The *Basic Skills Bulletin,* with its counterparts *Numeracy Briefing* and *14–19 Bulletin,* offer important overviews of developments in the basic skills field. The National Research and Development Centre for Adult Literacy, Numeracy and ESOL (NRDC) regularly publishes research reports.

One of the teaching unions for further and higher education, UCU has its own journal, the *Journal for Further and Higher Education.* This is a refereed journal, which means that articles that are submitted are read by members of the editorial board before being accepted for publication. This process helps assure the quality of the papers. Another journal worth consulting is *Studies in Adult Education,* again published by NIACE, where the articles cover issues in more depth.

Research in the sector provides an important source of information and ideas and journals are often a good source of research findings, as does the companion reader to this text book (Gregson et al., 2015). There are journals which cover themes in education across the compulsory and non-compulsory divide, like the *British Journal of Educational Research* which is produced by the British Educational Research Association (BERA). Some journals have a specific focus, like technology in learning, such as in the *British Journal of Educational Technology,* or deal solely with certain aspects, such as *Studies in Educational Evaluation.* The Education Evidence Portal (EEP) is a useful website that enables you to search for recent research across the education sector. It is useful to look at how research in secondary and primary schools, for example, could inform work in colleges and vice versa. As we discussed at the start of this book, the Economic and Social Science Research Council (ESRC) Teaching and Learning Research Programme (TLRP) covered the range of education sectors and settings and published a wealth of research papers which provide useful insights as well as leading to the principles we have drawn upon in each chapter. In England, the new Education and Training Foundation (ETF) covers four main areas of professional practice: professional standards and workforce development; vocation education and training; leadership, management and governance; and research and innovation. ETF has a growing practitioner-research community and offers grants and other forms of support for researchers in the FAVE sector.

Further afield, there are international publications and agencies including the European Centre for the Development of Vocational Training (CEDEFOP) and the Australian National Council for Vocational Education and Training (NCVER), both of which have websites containing research reports. It is particularly helpful to read how different nations approach FAVE and to identify similarities but also differences that may provide opportunities for testing out ideas in your own context.

You can also read shorter articles about current issues in national broadsheet newspapers and in *The Times Education Supplement* and *The Times Higher Education.* If you belong to a union such as UCU, you will receive a newsletter which covers issues in teaching and learning and contains book reviews. The Association of Colleges (AoC) has its own publication. The Association of Teachers and Lecturers (ATL) offers support and guidance and has a learning zone for members to access.

Finally, you may find that your own institution has a newsletter that will provide information about local and regional developments. You may have curriculum meetings that you attend where information about new qualifications, new practices and procedures will be discussed. Awarding Bodies (ABs) attempt to disseminate information through newsletters, formal communications with centres and through their websites. For example, City and Guilds produces its *Broadsheet* which carries information about new awards, new appointments and celebrates success of its candidates. EdExcel has a *Policy Watch* and this is obtainable from the Pearson Research Institute. One of the more helpful guides produced twice-yearly is entitled *Who Does What? A Guide to the Main Education Agencies and Bodies and what they do,* prepared by Steve Besley. This summary contains a chart showing the 'New Post 14 Order'. You might find it useful to track this down to display on your office wall to help demystify the structure of the FAVE Sector! *Policy Watch* publications support the dissemination of policy analysis through breakfast briefings, webcasts and, naturally, social media, including Twitter.

Acting as verifiers for your own institution or for an Awarding Body (AB) can provide a good source of personal development. If you are fortunate enough to be asked to work as an external verifier or assessor for an accredited programme, you will meet colleagues from other centres. By undertaking the role of external verifier, you will have to assure yourself that their procedures for recruiting, teaching and assessing their learners are appropriate. You will therefore observe the practice of your peers. You will discuss issues about the learning situation, how to implement new curriculum developments, aspects of assessment, issues of equal opportunities and access, and generally how the field is developing. These discussions are an extremely potent source of personal development for you. We have learnt so much from acting as external verifiers and external examiners to the range of teaching and training awards. These experiences have informed our own practice and enabled us to share and disseminate practice we observed among staff in the centres we visited. If you have gained experience in your field, and can take on the role, we would certainly recommend your applying to act as external verifier for an AB. ABs must provide professional development for their staff and you therefore have access to further opportunities outside your own institution's provision.

You do not have to go outside your own organization to find opportunities to develop your own professional practice. If you have been invited to participate in college-wide committees, for example a teaching and learning committee, quality committee or equal opportunities committee, you will discuss how aspects of the college's policies are implemented and monitored. This can inform both your own practice and help you disseminate ideas widely among your peers.

Membership of steering committees and course boards can also enable you to learn from your peers. Most committees require membership from across discipline areas, or external membership, and this requirement specifically aims to foster cross-fertilization of ideas. Disseminating these ideas is particularly important if professional practice is to benefit.

2.2 Acquiring new skills and knowledge

Keeping informed by reading about new developments and keeping abreast of current debate will help you be up to date in your knowledge *about* teaching and learning for adults. However, another aspect of continually developing your professional practice is the *improvement* of your current level of skill and knowledge. An obvious example of this is where you are asked to undertake a new course which you have not taught before. Not only will you need to familiarize yourself with the requirements of the programme, but you may also need to learn about the subject matter more deeply. You may be asked to use new techniques. In many institutions, there is a move to making use of the learning resources centre. You may be asked to supply content for programmes that are being turned into web-based learning programmes and provide instruction through distance and web-based learning – something that you have not done before. Professional development involves learning new techniques and knowledge so that you can enable your learners to acquire skills and knowledge in different ways. If you do find yourself in a situation where you are unsure about what is required, what do you do? First, make sure you know who your programme coordinator and line manager are. Make sure that you take time to find out what is on offer centrally in the institution regarding professional development in teaching and learning. Do not restrict yourself to looking at accredited programmes. Your institution may have a policy of supporting its staff to learn by subsidizing learning on its mainstream programmes. This is where you could decide to investigate how to develop your own web-based learning, or to learn a new language. Remember, just as we think it important that our learners are exposed to a variety of ways to learn, so you, too, can do this and find out what it is like to be a *learner.* Not only can you honestly tell your learners that you know what it is like to juggle home, work and family commitments when studying, you can also see for yourself how other tutors and trainers work. Many good ideas for your own teaching and learning come from being in classes that have nothing to do with your own subject area. Providing you acknowledge where you have obtained your ideas, then there is no reason why you should not try out someone else's good idea in your own situation. You may find that your own portfolio is a great source of ideas to your tutors on your teaching qualification programme. You can usually tell who the teacher educators are in any group of learners, as they are always making notes about the activities they have just experienced!

> ### Case study 17.3 Facing a challenge
>
> Yvonne took up playing the piano again and embarked on a series of lessons culminating very recently in taking an exam. She experienced the profound nervousness of having to demonstrate her practical skill of playing in front of an examiner, something she hadn't done since she was a teenager. It was an extremely humbling experience and reminded her only too clearly about what it is like to face a challenge, with a deadline and a one 'performance on the day' experience. It also provided her with an opportunity to reflect on her piano teacher's approach to teaching. She appreciated the way in which her teacher instilled confidence in her ability to move to a much higher standard than she had ever thought was possible. This experience has already influenced how she works with her own students and, of course, has given her a chance to say (with feeling!) that she really does know what it is like to undertake a course of study that is demanding and not guaranteed to end in success.

2.3 Serendipity

Much of your thinking and reflection may take place completely outside your everyday practice. Some people have their ideas in the middle of the night, on the bus, running around a park or in the bath. Allowing time for the creative aspect of your thought processes to come to the fore is very important for reflective teaching. Just a chance word with a friend could give you an insight into your practice, or an idea to take away and try out with your learners.

Professional practice carries a variety of meanings. Implicit in the term is a notion of good practice (Biesta, 2010, Reading 1.1). You may have read and heard about this in your own institution, or from material described above. It is difficult to know what good practice really is and whether you are, in fact, achieving it in your own work. Throughout this book there have been suggestions about what to reflect upon in the many aspects of the complex activity of teaching and learning. What can you do to ensure that you continue to develop your practice? You do not need to take a qualification in teaching and learning to continually develop your professional practice. However, if you think this is what you want to do, what is available? Many of you reading this book will already be undertaking a teaching or training qualification. If you are very new to teaching adults, you may be taking a preliminary award. In this case, there are a number of further awards that may be available. As you gain experience, you will have the opportunity to draw upon this if you decide to work towards a higher-level qualification in teaching and training. Each Awarding Body (AB) offers qualifications which are available in a wide range of centres, with Postgraduate Certificates in Education (PGCEs) offered by higher education institutions.

All these awards work with the idea that there are general concepts of teaching and training that can be covered regardless of your subject specialism. Meeting other teachers and trainers on such programmes is a rewarding experience, where you can gain much from sharing experiences and ideas and from observing different practices. However, there are also programmes and qualifications which are subject-specific. There are times when it is particularly helpful to discuss teaching and learning issues about your own subject.

2.4 Higher degrees

You may also consider working towards higher-level qualifications that provide you with a deeper theoretical basis for your professional practice. Most universities offer opportunities to study part-time for postgraduate diplomas, masters degrees, at PhD or professional doctorate level. Many of these specialize in education or lifelong learning. Some are particularly geared towards those working in post-compulsory education. There are programmes that suit trainers rather than teachers. Some of the programmes can be studied by distance learning. The variety of postgraduate programmes is quite bewildering. If you do want to pursue a qualification at this level, you will need to obtain information from a variety of universities. Most have this information on their websites as well as through prospectuses.

Masters-level work usually requires a significant and sustained study, either in the form of a research project or a thesis. If you are not sure that you can devote the time to this, then you can often study to diploma or certificate level. The content may be similar: you just don't have to commit yourself to either undertaking an independent piece of work or to take so many modules of the full award. Certificates, Diplomas and short courses are very helpful for keeping you up to date with ideas and the theoretical underpinning. Most of these programmes carry credit which can be used towards a full award at a later stage. Many people decide to take one short course to see if they can manage the commitment of time and effort and then carry on to gain a full qualification. Others derive great benefit from the short course and do not feel any further study is possible or necessary. The important point is to decide why you want to study for an award or short course and to find out what is required in terms of level of study, time commitment and the appropriateness of the content and methods. You may find that your staff development manager can advise you about suitable courses, and even provide information about whether there is any possibility of funding for these.

With any of the courses described above, do remember to talk to a head of department or other education manager, staff development manager or curriculum manager in your organization. They may know of other colleagues who have studied these programmes and can help you decide if they are suitable for you. It may be that your organization is particularly keen to sponsor you to undertake certain awards. Even if there is no funding from your organization, you may find out about how to obtain funding or career development loans. Remember that there are many experienced colleagues in any institution who have undertaken a variety of programmes of professional development. Their experiences can help you consider more options than perhaps you would find for yourself.

Reflective activity 17.2

With a colleague, discuss your plans for professional development. You may have a process used by your organization or sector for recording this, often known as a professional development plan (PDP). What resources are available to help you pursue your plan?

3 Conclusion

Your professional practice is just one part of your life. It is influenced by who you are, your lifestyle, your circumstances, where you work and with whom. Just as we cannot talk about any one aspect of the teaching and learning situation without relating it to the larger picture, so we cannot talk about developing our own professional practice without thinking about how that fits in with the rest of our lives.

In the UK today there is a trend towards working long hours. We read about and experience high levels of stress at work. Our learners come to our sessions weary from their own busy lives. We are asked to meet more and more deadlines which become increasingly urgent. We have demands placed on us to reach a host of quality indicators. We have to become 'perfect' tutors, counsellors, guidance workers, and somehow find time to deal with all the other demands of contemporary life.

Reflection on our teaching, therefore, must also provide an opportunity to question whether what we do is adding something positive to our lives. For many, the satisfaction of watching our learners progress is enough to counteract their busy, stressful working conditions. We must take care, though, that what we believe in is enabled to flourish. If we place our learners at the centre of our professional activity, then we will find that we must challenge, from time to time, some of the policies that are implemented. We must speak out for the values that we believe in: treating people with respect, encouraging people, building confidence, celebrating success. And we must acknowledge the value in what we do and celebrate it publicly. We hope that your professional journey allows you time to reflect on the fundamental joys of adult learning and your role in it. We suggest that by pursuing your journey, you will be practising in ways that have been underpinned by all the TLRP principles as well as Biesta's three dimensions as outlined in Chapter Four.

Key readings

Many of the books suggested as further reading for Chapters 1, 3 and 5 will also be relevant here.

Indeed much of the philosophy regarding the relationship between education and democracy was set our some time ago by Dewey in:

Dewey, J. (1916) *Democracy and Education: An Introduction to the Philosophy of Education*. New York: Macmillan.

Keep's chapter in an edited book provides a powerful commentary on key issues and debates in educational policy for the FAVE sector:

Keep, E. (2011) 'The English Policy Narrative'. In A. Hodgson, K. Spours and M. Waring (eds) *Post-Compulsory Education and Lifelong Learning across the United Kingdom: Policy, Organisation and Governance.* London: University of London, Institute of Education (IOE).

This book discusses the nature and role of part-time lecturers in the FAVE sector and the contexts and conditions in which many of them work:

Hillier, Y. and Jameson, J. (2004a) *The Ragged Trousered Philanthropists.* London: LSDA.

This article offers an insightful account of research and practice networks across the FAVE sector:

Appleby, Y. and Hillier, Y. (2012) 'Exploring practice-research networks for critical professional learning', *Studies in Continuing Education,* 34 (1), 31–43.

This book raises important issues in the treatment of education as a commercial practice rather than a moral one:

Ball. S. (2012) *Global Education Inc: New Policy Networks and the Neo-liberal Imaginary.* London: Routledge.

Drawing on effective practice in Scotland and elsewhere, this literature review contributes to debates about the role of teacher education and its impact upon the experiences of learners:

Biesta, G. (2010). *Good Education in an Age of Measurement.* London: Paradigm Publishers. (Reading 1.1)

Menter, I., Hulme, M., Elliot, D. and Lewin, J. (2010) *Teacher Education in the 21st Century.* Edinburgh: Scottish Government, 21–5. (Reading 17.3)

Sahlberg, P., Furlong, J. and Munn, P. (2012) *Report of the International Review Panel on the Structure of Initial Teacher Education Provision in Ireland: Review conducted on behalf of the Department of Education and Skills.* Dublin: Higher Education Authority of Ireland, 5, 14–15. (Reading 17.2)

Wiliam, D. (2007) *Assessment for Learning: Why, what and how?* Inaugural lecture. London: University of London, Institute of Education (IOE). 24 April. (Reading 17.1)

The associated website, **reflectiveteaching.co.uk**, offers a wealth of supplementary resources including reflective activities, research briefings, advice on further reading and downloadable diagrams, figures and checklists from the book. It also features a compendium of educational terms, links to useful websites, policy and curriculum documents, and showcases examples of excellent research and practice.

Epilogue

Thirty-five years ago an observer of the English education system might have thought there were three distinct sectors for adults: further education, which provided technical and professional programmes; higher education, which taught degrees; and adult education, which provided a range of 'leisure' programmes. When I began my career in the sector we didn't have a national curriculum in schools and there was no thought that there should be anything so formal in adult education. My students in adult literacy and numeracy classes followed a range of activities but we didn't have to meet any standards, we were hardly ever visited to be observed by our managers, and the only real scrutiny came when HMI inspectors visited the institute. I remember attending numerous development sessions on Saturday mornings, all voluntarily. We didn't expect to be paid and were grateful for the tea and biscuits. Yet my career also began at a time of political change when there were huge cuts to adult education and other public services. By the time I became an organizer of adult basic education ten years later, my professional life was bound up with ducking and diving to find funds, protect classes and support my part-time colleagues and students.

The FAVE sector has grown and changed since the late 1970s. Technology has revolutionized some of the practices in the classroom and workplace and community settings. We can draw upon images and make connections with people across the world and bring these into our learning environments in ways that teachers in the late 1970s could only dream of. Yet FAVE has also become scrutinized, controlled and subject to surveillance to an overwhelming degree.

When the first edition of *Reflective Teaching in Further and Adult Education* (2002), appeared, the main learning resources in settings involved paper handouts and whiteboards, with overhead projectors that were often moved from room to room (and sometimes back again within teaching sessions!). Not everyone had access to a computer and even photocopiers were a scarce resource, particularly in adult education. Further education had already undergone structural changes in England by this time and part-time tutors were finding it increasingly harder to gain secure employment. Colleges competed with each other for students and teachers were moved onto difference contracts and conditions of service.

Yet numbers of people learning in the FAVE sector expanded during this time; they gained qualifications, moved into employment or learnt new skills to equip them for whatever phase of their life they were entering. Teachers were increasingly given access to training and development, funding and activities, and we discovered new ways to facilitate this, particularly through the development of the internet.

It is now well into the new millennium. This fourth edition in many ways can be seen as a first edition of a new and exciting series. There is an accompanying reader and website to support the book. As a group of authors writing this edition, we have enjoyed many moments of serious discussion to find our way to write a book which I hope will foster a deep commitment to our sector while recognizing that we all have much to discover and share.

This is my last book. It is time for me to hang up my metaphorical boots at the end of this particular journey. I have been humbled, delighted and amazed by the number of practitioners who have met me and told me that they have enjoyed reading the previous editions of the book. I do hope that those of you reading this new version will continue to engage with the deep and difficult questions we face in our sector. I am now going to be a student and will be spending my retirement continuing to play the piano, improving my French, walking on the South Downs – and, who knows, I may be in your class one day!

Yvonne Hillier
February 2015

Reflective activities

Chapter 6: Relationships. How are we getting on together?
6.1   Comparing activities
6.2   Keeping a diary – starting off
6.3   Keeping a diary – reflection
6.3   Profiles of experience

Chapter 7: Engagement. How are we managing behaviour?
7.1   Investigating classroom management skills
7.2   Recording incidents of ongoing 'problem' behaviour

Chapter 8: Spaces. How are we creating environments for learning?
8.1   Analysing your classroom
8.2   Using ICT in your setting
8.3   Making the most of the classroom environment

PART THREE: TEACHING FOR LEARNING
Chapter 9: Curriculum. What is to be taught and learned?
9.1   How the way we use computers has changed
9.2   Reviewing the factors that influence curriculum design and delivery
9.3   Identifying the knowledge, concepts, skills and attitudes which are targeted for development

Chapter 10: Planning. How are we implementing the curriculum?
10.1 Evidence of long-term planning in your setting
10.2 Comparing the activities presented in a selection of schemes of work
10.3 Constructing your own list of SMART verbs for writing learning objectives
10.4 Structuring and planning your teaching
10.5 Observing your lesson

Chapter 11: Pedagogy. How can we develop effective strategies?
11.1 Evaluating current vocational learning practice
11.2 Identifying and teaching core concepts and practices
11.3 Planning to use a community of enquiry
11.4 Devising your own questions
11.5 Practical techniques using question-and-answer to include all students
11.6 Reflecting on small-group working

Chapter 12: Communication. How does language support learning?
12.1 Speaking and listening
12.2 Developing your use of language
12.3 Reading and writing in your teaching

Chapter 13: Assessment. How can assessment enhance learning?
13.1 Asking really good questions
13.2 Thinking about your assessments

PART FOUR: REFLECTING ON CONSEQUENCES

Chapter 14: Outcomes. How do we monitor student learning achievements?

14.1   Using ipsative assessment

14.2   How are the programmes you teach assessed and moderated?

14.3   Identifying where data can help

Chapter 15: Inclusion. How do we manage equality and diversity?

15.1   Thinking about diversity

15.2   Reviewing the nine 'protected characteristics'

15.3   Discussing case study 15.1

PART FIVE: DEEPENING UNDERSTANDING

Chapter 16: Expertise. Conceptual tools for career-long fascination?

16.1   Thinking about the attributes of expert teachers

16.2   Identifying your own level of expertise

16.3   Developing a portfolio of your teaching achievements

16.4   Thinking about professional standards

16.5   Thinking about your current level of practice

Chapter 17: Professionalism. How does reflective teaching contribute to society, and to ourselves?

17.1   Keeping up to date with policy changes

17.2   Your plans for professional development

List of case studies and figures

Acknowledgements

We would like to thank Andrew Pollard for inviting us to contribute to the Reflective Teaching Series which will now span every facet of the education system, from teachers working with very young children through to those working with very senior adults. We have very much appreciated the generous support and encouragement offered to us by Andrew, particularly at times when he had so many pressing and competing demands on his time. Additionally we would like to extend our thanks to David Russell for kindly agreeing to write the foreword to this book and for recognizing its importance to the development of teaching, learning and assessment across the sector. We would also like to thank the many colleagues at the Education and Training Foundation who have had the foresight to see the potential of the JPD approach to practitioner research, particularly Sheila Kearney the Foundation's Head of Research, for her sustained and irreplaceable support. It has also been a privilege to work with Professor Frank Coffield who has championed the JPD approach and been both a critical friend and an inspiration throughout the work leading up to the production of this book. Thanks, too, to all at Bloomsbury who have encouraged us through various stages in the development of this book, including Alison Baker, Amy Pollard, Kasia Figiel, Phil Prestianni, Kim Storry and Giles Herman. We are also indebted to Andrew Buglass and Frances Moffatt at the University of Sunderland for helping us to prepare the manuscripts for this book and its companion book of readings in preparation for publication. We owe grateful thanks to John Pratt whose eagle eye and patience were invaluable. We have appreciated the opportunities provided to us by Bloomsbury to meet with our fellow authors and discuss our contributions to the series. Becoming part of a larger community of authors and co-authors dedicated to improving teaching and learning in a reflective and critical way has meant a great deal to us. All of us contributing to this book have families, friends, colleagues and students who have supported, encouraged and contributed in ways that have influenced our writing and provided experiences which we have drawn upon to illustrate the many issues we have raised in the book. We owe them a huge debt of thanks and although we cannot name them all, we would like to acknowledge their contribution here.

In the course of bringing this book to publication we spent a number of intense writing days together in Greenwich, finding ways to express our own deeply held beliefs and to represent those of our contributors. We did this amidst a certain amount of banality, laughter and sometimes tears. In has been a privilege to work together with such a great team on such an important project. Final thanks go to all of those who have shared this journey with us and to all of you who have made it possible.

Yvonne Hillier and Maggie Gregson
February 2015

Glossary

'A' Level	Advanced Level
AB	Awarding Body
ABE	Adult Basic Education
ACL	Adult Community Learning
AfL	Assessment for Learning
ALBSU	Adult Literacy and Basic Skills Unit
ALLN	Adult Literacy, Language and Numeracy
AoC	The Association of Colleges
ATL	Association of Teachers and Lecturers
BERA	British Educational Research Association
BIS	Department for Business and Skills
BSA	Basic Skills Agency
BSL	British Sign Language
BTEC	Business and Technology Education Council
CAVTL	Commission for Adult and Vocational Teaching and Learning
CE	Continuing Education
CEBE	Campaign for Evidence-Based Education
CEDEFOP	European Centre for the Development of Vocational Training
CELTA	Certificate in English Language Teaching
CIDP	The Chartered Institute of Personnel and Development
CPD	Continuing Professional Development
CRA	Critically reflect on our assumptions
CRT	Casual Relief Teacher
CV	Curriculum Vitae
DFE	Department for Education
DoE	The Department of Employment
DfEE	The Department for Employment and Education
DfES	The Department for Employment and Skills
Dip AD	The Diploma in Art and Design
DIUS	Department for Innovation, Universities and Skills
ECM	Every Child Matters legislation
ED	Employment Department
EEP	The education evidence portal
EPPI	The Evidence for Policy and Practice Information and Co-ordinating Centre
ESF	European Social Fund
ESOL	English for Speakers of Other Languages
ESRC	The Economic and Social Research Council
ETF	Education and Training Foundation
EU	European Union

FAVE	Further, adult and vocational education
FE	Further Education
FEDA	Further Education Development Agency
GCSE	General Certificate of Secondary Education
HE	Higher Education
HEA	Higher Education Academy
HEI	Higher Education Institution
HMI	Her Majesty's Inspectors of Schools
HR	Human Resources
IALS	International Adult Literacy Survey
ICT	Information and Communications Technology
IFL	Institute for Learning
IFLL	The Inquiry into the Future for Lifelong Learning
ILP	Individual Learning Plan
IRE	Initiation/Response/Evaluation
IWB	Interactive Whiteboard
JPD	Joint Practice Development
LA	Local Authority
LEA	Local Education Authorities
LLAKES	Centre for Learning and Life Chances in Knowledge Economies and Societies
LLL	Lifelong Learning
LSA	Learning Support Assistants
LSIS	Learning and Skills Improvement Service
LSRN	Learning and Skills Research Network
MA	Master of Arts
MSC	Manpower Services Commission
NCVER	National Centre for Vocational Education Research
NEC	National Extension College
NEET	Not in Education, Employment or Training
NIACE	The National Institute of Adult Continuing Education
NRDC	National Research and Development Centre for Adult Literacy, Language and Numeracy
OECD	Organisation for Economic Co-operation and Development
OED	The Oxford English Dictionary
OFSTED	The Office for Standards in Education
ONS	Office for National Statistics
P4C	Philosophy for Children
PCET	Post-compulsory Education and Training
PGCE	Postgraduate Certificate in Education
PIAAC	Programme for the International Assessment of Adult Competencies
PISA	Programme for International Student Assessment
PLP	Personal Learning Plan
PPE	Philosophy, Politics and Economics
RaPAL	Research and Practice in Adult Literacy
RARPA	Recognising and recording progress and achievement for adult learners in non-accredited learning
RNIB	Royal National Institute of Blind People
RYA	Royal Yachting Association
SE	Standard English
SEN	Special educational needs
SFRE	The UK Strategic Forum for Research in Education

SKOPE	The Centre for Skills, Knowledge and Organisational Performance
SMART	Specific, Measurable, Achievable, Realistic, Time Bound
SOLO	Structure of Observed Learning Outcomes
SoTL	Scholarship of Teaching and Learning
SRHE	Society for Research into Higher Education
STEM	Science, Technology, Engineering and Maths
TLA	Teaching, learning and assessment
TLRP	Teaching and Learning Research Programme
U3A	University of the Third Age
UCU	University and College Union
UKCES	UK Commission for Employment and Skills
VET	Vocational Education and Training
VLE	Virtual Learning environment
WALT	'We are learning to…'
WEA	Workers' Educational Association
WILF	'What I am looking for…'
YTS	Youth Training Scheme
ZPD	Zone of Proximal Development

Bilbiography

Action on Hearing Loss. Available from http://www.actiononhearingloss.org.uk/ (accessed December 2013).

Adelman, C. and Alexander, R. (1981) 'Who Wants to Know That? Aspects of Institutional Self-evaluation'. In R. Oxtonby (ed.) *Higher Education at the Crossroad.* Guildford: Society for Research in Higher Education, 150–8.

Andrews, R. (2009) *The Importance of Argument in Education.* Inaugural professorial lecture. London University, Institute of Education (IOE).

Appleby, Y. (2010) 'Who are the Learners?'. In N. Hughes and I. Schwab (eds) *Teaching Adult Literacy: Principles and Practice.* Maidenhead: Open University Press, 29–47

Appleby, Y. and Hillier, Y. (2012) *Exploring Practice-research Networks for Critical Professional Learning Studies in Continuing Education,* 34 (1), 31–43.

Ainley, P. (1993) *Class and Skill.* London: Cassell.

Ainscow, M., Booth, T. and Dyson, A. (2006) *Improving Schools, Developing Inclusion.* London: Routledge.

Alexander, R. J. (2008) *Essays on Pedagogy.* London: Routledge.

—(ed.) (2010) *Children, their World, their Education*: *Final Report of the Cambridge Primary Review.* London: Routledge.

Althusser, L. (1971) *Lenin and Philosophy and Other Essays.* New York: Monthly Review Press.

Anderson, L. W. and Krathwohl, D. R. (eds) (2001) *A Taxonomy for Learning, Teaching and Assessing: A Revision of Bloom's Taxonomy of Educational Objectives.* New York: Longman.

Archer, M. (1979) *The Social Origins of Educational Systems.* London: Sage Publications Ltd.

Armitage, A., Evershed, J., Hayes, D., Hudson, A., Kent, J., Lawes, S., Poma, S. and Renwick, M. (2012) *Teaching and Training in Lifelong Learning.* 4th edn. Berks: Open University Press.

Assessment Reform Group (1999) *Assessment for Learning: Beyond the Black Box.* Cambridge: University of Cambridge School of Education, 5–8

Ausubel, D. P. (1968) *Educational Psychology: A Cognitive View.* New York: Holt, Rinehart and Winston.

Ausubel, D. P., Novak, J. D. and Hanesian H. (1978) *Educational Psychology: A Cognitive View.* 2nd edn. New York: Holt, Rinehart and Winston.

Avis, J. (2010) 'Education, governance and the 'new' professionalism: radical possibilities?', *Power and Education,* 2 (2), 197–208.

Avon County Council (2003) *Collaborative Learning in Primary Schools.* Bristol: Avon County Council.

Bailey, B and Robson, J. (2004) 'Learning support workers in further education in England: a hidden revolution?', *Journal of Further and Higher Education,* 28 (4).

Baines, E., Blatchford, P., Kutnick, P., Chowne, A., Ota, C. and Berdondini, L. (2008) *Promoting Effective Group Work in the Primary Classroom: A Handbook for Teachers and Practitioners.* London: Routledge.

Ball, S. (1981) 'Initial Encounters in the Classroom and the Process of Establishment'. In P. F. Woods (ed.) *Pupil Strategies*. London: Croom Helm.

—(2003) 'The teacher's soul and the terrors of performativity', *Journal of Education Policy,* 18 (2), 215–28.

—(2006) *Education Policy and Social Class*. London: Routledge.

—(2008a) *The Education Debate: Policy and Politics in the Twenty-First Century*. London: Policy Press.

—(2008b) *The More Things Change ...: Educational Research, Social Class and 'Interlocking' Inequalities*. London: University of London, Institute of Education (IOE).

—(2012) *Global Education Inc. New Policy Networks and the Neo-liberal Imaginary*. London: Routledge.

Barker, B. (1987) 'Visions are off the agenda', *Times Educational Supplement*. 3 December, p. 4.

Barton, D. (2007) *Literacy: An Introduction to the Ecology of Written Language*. Oxford: Blackwell.

Barton, D, Hamilton, M and Ivanic, R. (eds) (2000) *Situated Literacies: Reading and Writing in Context*. London: Routledge.

Barton, I. and Butcher, C. (2012) *Enabling Further Learning Through Available Technologies*. Coventry: Learning and Skills Improvement Service.

Bass, R. (1998–9) 'The scholarship of teaching: what's the problem?', *Inventio,* 1998–9 [online journal]. Available from http://wiki.biologyscholars.org/@api/deki/files/820/=11RR Assignment2Readings.pdf (accessed 24 October 2014).

Bathmaker, A.-M. and Avis, J. (2005) 'Becoming a lecturer in further education in England: the construction of professional identity and the role of communities of practice', *Journal of Education for Teaching*, 31 (1), 47–62.

Becher T. and Trowler, P. (2002) *Academic Tribes and Territories: Intellectual Enquiry and the Cultures of Discipline*. Buckingham: SRHE: Open University Press.

Benner, P. (2001) *From Novice to Expert: Excellence and Power in Clinical Nursing Practice*. Commemorative edn. New Jersey: Prentice-Hall.

Bennett, T. (2012) *Teacher: Mastering the Art and Craft of Teaching*. London: Continuum.

Berger, P. L. and Luckman, T. (1967) *The Social Construction of Reality*. New York: Doubleday.

Berliner, D. (1986) 'In pursuit of the expert pedagogue', *Educational Researcher*, 1 (7), 5–13.

—(1990) 'What's all the Fuss about Instructional Time?'. In M. Ben-Peretz and R. Bromme (eds) *The Nature of Time in Schools*. New York: Teacher College Press, 3–35.

Bernstein, B. (1971) 'On the Classification and Framing of Educational Knowledge'. In M. F. D. Young (ed.) *Knowledge and Control*. London: Collier-Macmillan.

—(1996) *Pedagogy, Symbolic Control and Identity*. London: Taylor and Francis.

Bevan, R. (2007) 'From Black Boxes to Glass Boxes: On-screen Lin Schools with Concept Maps', *Research Briefing,* 21. London: TLRP.

Biesta, G. (2004) 'Against learning. reclaiming a language for education in an age of learning', *Nordic Studies in Education*, 23, 70–82.

—(2005) 'Against learning. reclaiming a language for education in an age of learning', *Nordisk Pedagogik*, 25, 54–66. Oslo.

—(2009) 'Good education in an age of measurement: on the need to reconnect with the question of purpose in education', *Educational Assessment, Evaluation and Accountability,* 21 (1), 33–46.

—(2010) *Good Education in an Age of Measurement*. London: Paradigm Publishers.

—(2012) 'Giving teaching back to education: responding to the disappearance of the teacher', *Phenomenology and Practice*, 6 (2), 35–49.

—(forthcoming, 2015) 'Expertise – Becoming Educationally Wise'. In M. Gregson, L. Nixon, A. Pollard and P. Spedding (eds) *Readings for Reflective Teaching in Further, Adult and Vocational Education*. London: Bloomsbury Press.

Biesta, G, Field, J., Hodkinson, P., Macleod, F. J. and Goodson, I. F. (2011) *Improving Learning through the Lifecourse: Learning Lives.* London: Routledge.

Biggs, J. (1999) *Teaching for Quality Learning in Higher Education.* Buckingham: SRHE/Open University Press.

—(2011) *Teaching for Quality Learning in Higher Education.* Buckingham: SRHE/Open University Press.

Biggs J, and Collis K. (1982) *Evaluating the Quality of Learning: The SOLO Taxonomy.* New York: Academic Press.

Biggs, J. and Tang, C. (2011) *Quality for Learning in Higher Education Society for Research in Higher Education.* Maidenhead: McGraw Hill.

Billett, S. (2001) 'Learning through work: workplace affordances and individual engagement', *Journal of Workplace Learning*, 13 (5), 209–14.

Black, P., Gardner, J. and Wiliam, D. (2008) *Joint Memorandum on Reliability of Assessments.* Submitted to the House of Commons, Children, Schools and Families Committee: Testing and Assessment. Third Report of Session 2007–2008. Vol. II. HC169–II. Norwich: The Stationery Office.

Black, P., Harrison, C., Lee, C., Marshall, B. and Wiliam, D. (2003) *Assessment for Learning: Putting it into Practice.* Buckingham: Open University Press.

Black, P. and Wiliam, D. (1998a) 'Assessment and classroom learning', *Assessment in Education*, 5 (1), 7–74.

—(1998b) *Inside the Black Box: Raising Standards through Classroom Assessment.* London: King's College.

—(2002) *Working Inside the Black Box: Assessment for Learning in the Classroom.* London: Kings College.

Blanchard, J. (2009) *Teaching, Learning and Assessment.* Maidenhead: Open University Press.

Blenkin, G. M. and Kelly, A. V. (1981) *The Primary Curriculum.* London: Harper and Row.

Bloom, B. S. (1956) *Taxonomy of Educational Objectives: The Classification of Educational Goals: Handbook 1. The Cognative Domain.* New York: McKay.

Bloomer, M. (1986) *Curriculum Making in Post-16 Education: The Social Conditions of Studentship.* London: Routledge.

Bourdieu, P. and Passeron, J. C. (1977) *Reproduction in Education, Society and Culture.* London: Sage Publications Ltd.

Brandt, D. (2001) *Literacy in American Lives.* Cambridge: Cambridge University Press.

Bransford, J. D., Brown, A. L. and Cocking, R. R. (1999) *How People Learn: Brain, Mind, Experience and School.* Washington, DC: National Academy Press, xvi–xix.

Brew, A. (2006) *Research and Teaching Beyond the Divide.* London: Palgrave MacMillan.

Brighouse, T. (1987) 'Goodbye to the Head and the History Man', *The Guardian,* 21 July, p. 11.

Brigg, S. and Fielding, M. (2005) 'It's an Equal Thing … It's about Achieving Together: Student Voices and the Possibility of a Radical Collegiality'. In H. Street and J. Temperley (eds) *Improving Schools Through Collaborative Enquiry.* London: Continuum.

British Deaf Association. Available from http://www.bda.org.uk (accessed December 2013).

British Education Research Association (2013) *Why Educational Research Matters: A Briefing to Inform Future Funding Decisions.* BERA, August 2013.

Brockbank, A. and McGill, I. (1998) *Facilitating Reflective Learning in Higher Education.* Buckingham: Open University Press.

—(2007) *Facilitating Reflective Learning in Higher Education.* 2nd edn. Buckingham: SRHE/Open University Press.

Bronfenbrenner, U. (1979) *The Ecology of Human Development: Experiments by Nature and Design.* Cambridge, MA: Harvard University Press.

—(1993) 'Ecological models of human development', *International Encyclopaedia of Education,* 3. Oxford: Elsevier.

Brookfield, S. D. (1988) *Training Educators of Adults: The Theory and Practice of Graduate Adult.* San Francisco: Jossey-Bass.

—(1990) *The Skilful Teacher.* San Francisco: Jossey-Bass.

—(1993) 'Breaking the code: engaging practitioners in critical analysis of adult education literature', *Studies in the Education of Adults*, 25, 1, 64–91.

—(1995) *Becoming a Critically Reflective Teacher.* San Francisco: Jossey-Bass.

—(1998) 'Against naive romanticism: from celebration to the critical analysis of experience', *Studies in Continuing Education*, 20 (2), 127–42.

Brown, K. (2002) *The Right to Learn: Alternatives for a Learning Society.* Routledge Falmer.

Brown, S. and McIntyre, D. (1993) *Making Sense of Teaching.* Buckingham: Open University Press.

Bruner, J. (1966) *The Process of Education.* Cambridge, MA: Harvard University Press.

—(1986) *Actual Minds, Possible Worlds.* Cambridge, MA: Harvard University Press.

—(1990) *Acts of Meaning.* Cambridge, MA: Harvard University Press.

—(1996) *The Culture of Education.* Cambridge, MA: Harvard University Press, 45–50.

—(2006) *In Search of Pedagogy Volume II: The Selected Works of Jerome S. Bruner.* New York: Routledge, 145–6.

Buckingham, D. (2000) *After the Death of Childhood: Growing up in the Age of Electronic Media.* Cambridge: Polity.

Brynner, J., McCormick, R. and Nuttal, D. (1982) *Organisation and Use of Evaluation.* Milton Keynes: Open University Press.

Bynner, J. and Parsons, S. (2006) *New Light on Literacy and Numeracy.* London: NRDC.

Calderhead, J. (1994) *Can the Complexities of Teaching be Accounted for in terms of Competences? Contrasting Views of Professional Practice from Research and Policy.* Mimeo produced for an Economic and Social Research Council symposium on teacher competence, 1–2.

Calderhead, J. and Gates, P. (eds) (1994) *Conceptualising Reflection in Teacher Development.* London: Falmer Press.

Callender, C. and Wilkingson, D. (2012) *Future Track: Part Time Higher Education Students – the Benefits of Part Time Higher Education after Three Years of Study.* London: Birkbeck.

Cameron, C. (2010) 'Nothing to do with me: Everything to do with me: Disability, self and identity'. Available from http://www.disabilityartsonline.org.uk/domains/disabilityarts.org/local/media/audio/Nothing_to_do_with_me_FINAL.pdf (accessed 24 October 2014).

Candappa, M. (2011) 'Invisibility and Otherness: Asylum-seeking and Refugee Students in the Classroom'. In G. Richards and F. Armstrong (eds) *Teaching and Learning in Diverse and Inclusive Classrooms.* London: Routledge, 156–69.

Carr, W. (1986) 'Theories of theory and practice', *Journal of Philosophy of Education*, 20 (2), 177–86.

—(1987) 'What is an educational practice?', *Journal of Philosophy of Education*, 21 (2), 163–75.

—(1986) *Becoming Critical.* Lewes: Falmer.

—(1995) 'Education and democracy: confronting the post modern challenge', *Journal of the Philosophy of Education,* 29, 75–91.

—(ed.) (2005) *Philosophy of Education.* Abingdon: Routledge-Falmer.

Cash, R. (2011) *Advancing Differentiation: Thinking & Learning for the 21st Century.* MN: Free Spirit Publishing.

Commission on Adult Vocational Teaching and Learning (CAVTL) (2013) *It's about Work … Excellent Adult Vocational Teaching and Learning: The Summary Report of the Commission on Adult Vocational Teaching and Learning.* Coventry. Learning and Skills Improvement Services (LSIS).

Chaplain, R. (2003) *Teaching Without Disruption in the Primary School.* New York: Routledge, 140–55.

Chomsky, N. (2002) *Chomsky on Democracy and Education,* C. P. Otero (ed.). London: Routledge.

—(2004) *Chomsky on MisEducation*, D. Macedo (ed.). Lanham, MD: Rowman & Littlefield Publishers.

Clarke, S. (2001) *Unlocking Formative Assessment: Practical Strategies for Enhancing Pupils' Learning in the Primary Classroom*. London: Hodder and Stoughton.

—(2005a) *Formative Assessment in Action: Weaving the Elements Together*. London: Hodder and Stoughton.

—(2005b) *Formative Assessment in the Secondary Classroom*. London: Hodder and Stoughton.

—(2008) *Active Learning through Formative Assessment*. London: Hodder and Stoughton.

—(2011) *The Power of Formative Assessment: Self-belief and Active Involvement in the Process of Learning* (DVD). Shirley Clarke Media Ltd.

Claxton, G. (2002) *Building Learning Power: Helping Young People Become Better Learners*. Bristol: TLO.

Claxton, G., Chambers, M., Powell, G. and Lucas, B. (2011) *The Learning Powered School: Pioneering 21st Century Education*. Bristol: TLO.

Coffield, F. (2007) *Running Ever Faster Down the Wrong Road: An Alternative Future for Education and Skills*. Inaugural Lecture Institute of Education, London: University of London, Institute of Education (IOE), 5 December.

—(2008) *Just Suppose Teaching and Learning Became the First Priority*. London: Learning and Skills Network (LSN).

—(2009) *All you ever Wanted to know about Learning and Teaching but were too Cool to ask*. London: Learning and Skills Network (LSN).

—(2010) *Yes, but what has Semmelweis to do with my Professional Development as a Tutor?* London: Learning and Skills Network.

—(2011) *Pedagogy, Power and Change in Vocational Education*. LSIS National Teaching and Learning Fair 11 July 2011. London: University of London, Institute of Education (IOE).

—(2013) *Can we Transform Classrooms and Colleges without Transforming the State?* Keynote address to The Future of Further Education Conference: Guildford, 22 March.

—(ed.) (2014) *Beyond Bulimic Learning*. London: University of London Institute of Education (IOE).

Coffield, F., Edward, S., Finlay, L., Hodgson, A., Spours, K. and Steer, R. (2008) *Improving Learning and Inclusion: The Impact of Policy and Policy-making on Post-Compulsory Education*. London: Routledge.

Coffield, F. and Williamson, B. (2011) *From Exam Factories to Communities of Discovery: The Democratic Route*. London: University of London, Institute of Education (IOE).

Colley, H., James, D., Tedder, M. and Diment, K. (2007) 'Learning as becoming in vocational education and training: class, gender and the role of vocational habitus', *Journal of Vocational Education and Training*, 55 (4), 471–97.

Collins, J. (1996) *The Quiet Child*. London. Cassell.

Collins, M. (1991) *Adult Education as Vocation: A Critical Role for the Adult Educator*. New York: Routledge.

The Commission on Adult Vocational Teaching and Learning (CAVTL) (2013) *It's about Work ... Excellent Adult Vocational Teaching and Learning: The Summary Report of the Commission on Adult Vocational Teaching and Learning*. London: LSIS/BIS

Cook, V. (ed.) (2003) *Effects of the Second Language on the First*. Clevedon: Multilingual Matters.

Corson, D. (1985) 'Education for work: reflections towards a theory of vocational education', *International Review of Education*, 31 (3), 283–302.

Cowan, J. (1999) *On Becoming an Innovative University Teacher*. Buckingham: Open University Press.

Cowie, H. and Wallace, P. (2000) *Peer Support in Action: From Bystanding to Standing By*. London: Sage Publications Ltd

Cowley, S. (2010) *Getting the Buggers to Behave.* 4th edn. London: Continuum.

—(2013) *The Seven T's of Practical Differentiation.* Bristol: Sue Cowley Books Ltd.

Crawley, J. (2011) *In at the Deep End: A Survival Guide for Teachers in Post Compulsory Education.* 2nd edn. Abingdon: Routledge.

Crotty, M. (1996) *Phenomenology and Nursing Research.* Melbourne: Churchill Livingstone.

Crowther, J. and Shaw, M. (2011) 'Education for Resilience and Resistance in the "Big Society"'. In D. Cole (ed.) *Surviving Economic Crises through Education.* Frankfurt Am Main: Peter Lang.

Crozier, G. (2000) *Parents and Schools: Partners or Protagonists?* Stoke-on-Trent: Trentham Books.

Crozier, G. and D. (2005) *Activating Participation: Parents and Teachers Working Towards Partnership.* Stoke-on-Trent: Trentham Books.

Cummings, J. (2005) 'A proposal for action: strategies for recognizing heritage language competence as a learning resources within the mainstream classroom', *The Modern Languages Journal,* 89, 585–92.

Curzon, L. B. (2003) *Teaching in Further Education: An Outline of Principles and Practice.* 6th edn. London: Continuum.

Dakin, J. (2012) 'Writing Bilingual Stories: Developing Children's Literacy Through Home Languages.' In D. Mallows (ed.) *Innovations in English Language Teaching for Migrants and Refugees.* London: The British Council, 11–21.

Day, C. and Gu, Q. (2010) *The New Lives of Teachers.* London: Routledge.

Dave, R. H. (1975) *Developing and Writing Behavioural Objectives.* Tucson, AZ: Educational Innovators Press.

Department for Education (2011). 'Building Engagement, Building Futures'. Available from http://webarchive.nationalarchives.gov.uk/20130401151715/https://www.education.gov.uk/publications/standard/publicationDetail/Page1/HMG-00195-2012#downloadableparts (accessed October 2013).

—(2013). 'First Statistical Release Quarterly Brief Quarter 1 2013'. Available from https://www.gov.uk/government/uploads/system/uploads/attachment_data/file/201104/Quarterly_Brief_NEET_Q1_2013_pdf.pdf (accessed October 2013).

Department for Education and Science (1973). *Russell Report on Adult Education: A Plan for Development.* London: HMSO.

—(1989) *Discipline in Schools.* Report of the Committee of Enquiry, chaired by Lord Elton. London: HMSO.

Department for Education and Skills (DfES) (2001) *Adult Literacy Core Curriculum.* London: DfES

Department for Innovation, Universities and Skills (2008) 'Informal Adult Learning, Shaping the Way Ahead'. Available from http://www.bis.gov.uk/assets/biscore/innovation/docs/s/urn-ial2008d-shaping-the-way-ahead-consultation-analysis (accessed May 2014).

Derrick, J., Howard, U., Field, J., Lavender, P., Meyer, S., Nuissi von rein, E. and Schuller, T. (2011) *Remaking Adult Learning.* London: University of London, Institute of Education (IOE).

Derrida, J. (1987) *Of Spirit: Heidegger and the Question.* London: University of Chicago Press.

Derrington, C. (2011) 'Supporting Gypsy, Roma and Traveller Pupils.' In G. Richards and F. Armstrong (eds) *Teaching and Learning in Diverse and Inclusive Classrooms.* London: Routledge, 156–69.

Dewey, J. (1916) *Democracy and Education: An Introduction to the Philosophy of Education.* New York: Macmillan.

—(1933) *How We Think: a Restatement of the Relation of Reflective Thinking to the Educative Process.* Chicago: Henry Regnery.

Doyal, L. and Harris, R. (1986) *Empiricism, Explanation and Rationality: An Introduction to the Philosophy of Social Sciences.* London: Routledge.

Dreyfuss, H. and Dreyfuss, S. (1986) *Mind Over Machine: The Power of Intuition and Expertise in the Era of the Computer.* Oxford: Blackwell.

Duckworth, V. (2013) *Learning Trajectories, Violence and Empowerment amongst Adult Basic Skills Learners*. London: Routledge.

Duncan, N. (2011) 'The Role of the School in Reducing Bullying.' In G. Richard and F. Armstrong (eds) *Teaching and Learning in Diverse and Inclusive Classrooms*. London: Routledge, 31–41.

Duncan, S. (2010) 'Literacy Learning for Adults with Global Learning Difficulties.' In N. Hughes, and I. Schwab (eds) *Teaching Adult Literacy*. Maidenhead: Open University Press.

—(2012) *Reading Circles, Novels and Adult Reading Development*. London: Bloomsbury.

Dunne, J. (1988) *The Beginnings of Social Understanding*. Oxford: Blackwell.

—(2003) 'Arguing for teaching as a practice: a reply to Alasdair MacIntyre', *Journal of the Philosophy of Education* (Special Edition: *Education and Practice*).

—(2005) 'What's the Good of Education?'. In W. Carr (ed.) *Reader in Philosophy of Education*. London Routledge.

Dweck, C. S. (2006) *Mindset: The New Psychology of Success*. New York: Ballantine.

Dzubinski, L., Hentz, B., Davis, K and Nicolaides, A (2012) 'Envisioning an adult learning graduate program for the early 21st century', *Adult Learning*, 23 (3).

Earl, L., Watson, N., Levin, B., Leithwood, K., Fullan, M. and Torrance, N. with Jantzi, D., Mascall, B. and Volante, L. (2003) *Watching and Learning 3: Final Report of the External Evaluation of England's National Literacy and Numeracy Strategies*. Toronto: Ontario Institute for Studies in Education.

Ecclestone, K. (2002) *Learning Autonomy in Post 16 Education*. London: Routledge Falmer.

Education and Training Foundation (ETF) (2014) *Professional Standards for Further Education Teachers and Trainers in England*. London: ETF.

Edwards, A. (2012) *New Technology and Education*. London: Continuum, 86–8.

Edwards, R. (1997) *Changing Places: Flexibility, Lifelong Learning and the Learning Society*. London: Routledge.

Eisner, E. W. (1985) *The Art of Educational Evaluation: A Personal View*. Lewes: Falmer Press.

—(2002) *The Arts and the Creation of Mind*. New Haven and London: Yale University Press.

Elliott, A. and Lemert, C. (2006) *The New Individualism: The Emotional Costs of Globalisation*. Abingdon: Routledge.

Elliott, G. (1976) *Teaching for Concepts. Place, Time and Society 8–11*. London: Schools Council.

Elliot, J. (1991) 'A model of professionalism and its implication for teacher education', *British Educational Research Journal*, 17 (4), 310–14.

—(2001) 'Making educational evaluation more educational', *British Educational Research Journal*, 7 (25), 555–74.

Entwistle, N. J. (2009) *Teaching for Understanding at University: Deep Approaches and Distinctive Ways of Thinking*. Basingstoke: Palgrave Macmillan.

Epstein, D. (1993) *Changing Classroom Cultures: Anti-Racism, Politics and Schools*. Stoke-on-Trent: Trentham Books.

Equality Act 2010. Available from http://www.legislation.gov.uk/ukpga/2010/15/contents (accessed December 2013).

Eraut, M. (1994) *Developing Professional Knowledge and Competence*. London: Falmer.

—(2004) 'Transfer of Knowledge between Education and Workplace Settings'. In A. Fuller, A. Munro and H. Rainbird (eds) *Workplace Learning in Context*. London: Routledge, 211–20.

Eurostat (2008). 'Adult Education Survey.' Available from http://epp.eurostat.ec.europa.eu/statistics_explained/index.php/Lifelong_learning_statistics (accessed January 2014).

Facer, K., Furlong, J., Furlong, R. and Sutherland, R. (2003) *Screenplay: Children and Computing in the Home*. London: Routledge.

Fairclough, N. (2003) *Analysing Discourse: Textual Analysis for Social Research*. London: Routledge.

Fawbert, F. (2003) *Teaching in Post-compulsory Education: Learning, Skills and Standards*. Lonodon: Continuum

—(2008) *Teaching in Post Compulsory Education*. London: Continuum.

Feinstein L., Duckworth K. and Sabates R. (eds) (2008) *Education and the Family: Passing Success Across the Generations*. Oxford: Routledge.

Feinstein, L., Vorhaus, J. and Sabates, R. (2008) *Learning Through Life: Future Challenges*. Foresight Mental Capital and Wellbeing Project. London: The Government Office for Science.

Fieldhouse, R. (1996) *A History of Modern British Adult Education*. Leicester: NIACE.

Fielding, M., Bragg, S., Craig, J., Cunningham, I., Eraut, M., Gillinson. S., Horne, M., Robinson, C. and Thorp, J. (2005) *Factors Influencing the Transfer of Good Practice*. London: Department for Education and Skills RR 615.

Finlay, I. (2008) 'What's Learning For? Interrogating the Scholarship of Teaching and Learning'. In R. Murray (ed.) *The Scholarship of Teaching and Learning in Higher Education*. Maidenhead: Open University Press.

Fisher, R. (2003) *Teaching Thinking*. London. Continuum

—(2013) *Teaching Thinking: Philosophical Enquiry in the Classroom*. London: Bloomsbury, 2–26.

Flanagan, C. (1954) 'The critical incident technique', *Psychological Bulletin,* 51 (4), 327–58.

Fox, G. (1998) *A Handbook for Learning Support Assistants*. London: David Fulton.

Frederickson, N. and Cline, T. (2009) *Special Educational Needs, Inclusion and Diversity*. 2nd edn. Maidenhead: McGraw Hill/Open University Press.

Fredman, S. (2001) *Discrimination and Human Rights: The Case of Racism*. Oxford: Oxford University Press.

Freire, P. (1972) *Pedagogy of the Oppressed*. London: Penguin Books.

—(2002) *Pedagogy of Hope: Reliving Pedagogy of the Oppressed*. London: Continuum.

Fromkin, V., Rodman, R. and Hyams, N. (2013) *An Introduction to Language*. 10th edn. New York: Heinle & Heinle Publishers.

Fuller, A. and Unwin, L. (2003) 'Learning as apprentices in the contemporary UK workplace: creating and managing expansive and restrictive participation', *Journal of Education and Work,* 16 (4), 407–26.

—(2004) 'Expansive learning environments: Integrating personal and organisational development'. Available from eprints.soton.ac.uk/55801 (accessed 24 October 2014).

—(2009) *Improving Working and Learning*. London: Routledge.

—(forthcoming, 2015) *Creating and Managing Expansive Learning Environments: Improving Vocational and Professional Education*. London: Routledge.

Galton, M. (2007) *Learning and Teaching in the Primary Classroom*. London: Paul Chapman.

Gee, J., Hull, G and Lankshear, C. (1996) *The New Work Order: Behind the Language of Capitalism*. London: Allen and Unwin.

Geertz, C. (2000) *Available Light: Anthropological Reflections on Philosophical Topics*. Princeton: Princeton University Press.

Gibbs, G. (1981) *Teaching Students to Learn. A Student Centred Approach*. Milton Keynes: Open University Press.

—(1989) *Teaching Students to Learn*. Milton Keynes: Open University Press.

Gibbs, G., Habeshaw, S. and Habeshaw, T. (1986) *53 Interesting Ways to Assess your Students*. Bristol: Technical and Education Services.

Gibson, E. J. (1977) 'The Theory of Affordances'. In R. Shaw and J. Bransford (eds) *Perceiving, Acting and Knowing*. Hillsdale, NJ: Lawrence Earlbaum.

Giddens, A. (1984) *The Constitution of Society: Outline of the Theory of Structuration*. Berkeley: University of California Press.

—(2011) *Introduction to Sociology*. New York: W. W. Norton.

Gillborn, D. (2008a) 'Developing Antiracist School Policy'. In M. Pollock (ed.) *Everyday Antiracism: Getting Real about Racism in School*, New York: The New Press, 246–51.

—(2008b) *Racism and Education: Coincidence or Conspiracy?* London: Routledge.

—(2013) Personal email correspondence with Sam Duncan, 11 June.

Gingell, J. and Winch, P. (2004) *Philosophy and Education Policy.* London: Routledge.

Gipps, C. and MacGilchrist, B. (1999) 'Primary School Learners'. In P. Mortimore (ed.) *Understanding Pedagogy and its Impact on Learning.* London: Paul Chapman, 52–5.

Goldacre, B. (2013) 'Building Evidence into Education'. Available from http://www.badscience.net/2013/03/heres-my-paper-on-evidence-and-teaching-for-the-education-minister/ (accessed 24 October 2014).

Goodley, D., Hughes, B. and Davis, L. (eds) (2012) *Disability and Social Theory: New Developments and Directions.* London: Palgrave Macmillan.

Goodson, I. (1989). 'Sponsoring the teacher's voice: teachers' lives and teacher development', *Cambridge Journal of Education*, 21 (1), 35–42.

—(2003) *Professional Knowledge Professional Lives.* Maidenhead: Open University Press.

—(2007) 'All the lonely people: the struggle for private meaning and public purpose in education', *Critical Studies in Education*, 48 (1), 131–48.

Gorard, S., Rees, G., Fevre, R. and Furlong, J. (1998) 'Society is not built by education alone: alternative routes to a learning society', *Research in Post-Compulsory Education,* 3 (1), 25–37.

Gramsci, A. (1978) *Selections from Political Writings.* London: Lawrence and Wishart.

Green, A. and Janmaat, J. (2011) *Regimes of Social Cohesion: Societies and the Crisis of Globalization.* Basingstoke: Palgrave Macmillan.

Green, A., Preston, J. and Janmaat, J. G. (2006) *Education, Equality and Social Cohesion. A Comparative Analysis.* London: Palgrave.

Gregson, M. and Nixon, L. (2009) 'Assessing effectiveness: ways of seeing impact', *International Journal of Interdisciplinary Social Sciences*, 21 (3).

—(2011) 'Unlocking the Potential of Skills for Life (SfL) tutors and learners: a critical evaluation of the implementation of SfL policy in England', *Teaching in Lifelong Learning.* CETTS Journal. Huddersfield: University of Huddersfield Press.

Gregson, M, Nixon, L, Spedding, P and Kearney, S. (forthcoming, 2015) *Helping Good Ideas Become Good Practice.* London: Bloomsbury Press.

Griffin, C. (1989) 'Cultural Studies, Critical Theory and Adult Education'. In B. Bright (ed.) *Theory and Practice in the Study of Adult Education: The Epistemological Debate.* London: Routledge, 121–40

Griffiths, G. and Stone, R. (eds) (2013) *Teaching Adult Numeracy: Principles and Practice.* Maidenhead: Open University Press.

Grimmett, P., Mackinnon, A., Erickson., G. and Riechen, T. (1990) 'Reflective Practice in Teacher Education'. In T. T. Clift, W. R. Houston, and M. Pugach (eds) *Encouraging Reflective Practice: An Analysis of Issues and Programs.* New York: Teacher College Press, 20–38.

Guo, S. and Jamal, Z. (2006) *'Toward Inclusive Education: Integrating Cultural Diversity into Adult Learning'.* Paper presented at the 36th Annual SCRUTREA Conference, 4–6 July, Trinity and All Saints College, Leads.

Hamilton, M. and Hillier, Y. (2006a) 'Mapping and Tracking: Assessment and Accreditation'. In M. Hamilton and Y. Hillier *Changing Faces of Adult Literacy, Numeracy and Language.* Stoke-on-Trent: Trentham Books, 125–38.

—(2006b) *The Changing Faces of Adult Literacy, Language and Numeracy: A Critical History.* Stoke-on-Trent: Trentham Books.

Hargreaves, A. (1998) 'The emotional practice of teaching', *Teaching and Teacher Education,* 14 (8), 835–54.

—(2007) *The Persistence of Presentism and the Struggle for Lasting Improvement.* Professorial Inaugural Lecture. London: University of London, Institute of Education (IOE).

Hargreaves, A. and Fullan, M. (2012) *Professional Capital: Transforming Teaching in Every School.* London. Routledge.

Harlen, W., Gipps, C., Broadfoot, P. and Nuttall, D. (1992) 'Assessment and the improvement of education', *Curriculum Journal*, 3 (3), 217–25.

Harper, H. (2013) *Outstanding Teaching in Lifelong Learning*. Maidenhead: Open University Press/McGraw-Hill Education.

Harris, R. (1995) 'Disappearing Language: Fragments and Fractures between Speech and Writing'. In J. Mace (ed.) *Literacy, Language and Community Publishing*. Clevedon: Multilingual Matters.

Hart, S., Dixon, A., Drummond, M.-J. and McIntyre, D. (2004) *Learning Without Limits*. Maidenhead: Open University Press.

Harvey, D. (1996) *Justice, Nature and the Geography of Difference*. Oxford: Blackwell.

Harvey, S. and Daniels, H. (2009) *Comprehension and Collaboration: Inquiry Circles in Action*. Portsmouth, NH: Heinemann.

Hashweh. M. Z. (1987) 'Effects of subject matter knowledge in the teaching of biology and physics', *Teaching and Teacher Education*, 3, 109–20.

Hattie, J. (2009) *Visible Learning. A Synthesis of Meta-Analyses Relating to Achievement*. London: Routledge.

—(2012) *Visible Learning for Teachers: Maximising Impact on Learning*. London: Routledge.

Hattie, J. and G. Yates (2014) *Visible Learning and the Science of how We learn*. Adingdon, Oxon, Routledge.

Haynes, A. (2010) *The Complete Guide to Lesson Planning and Preparation*. London: Continuum.

Heilbronn, R. (2011) 'Practical Judgement and Evidence-informed Practice'. In R. Heilbronn and J. Yandell (eds) *Critical Practice in Teacher Education: A Study of Professional Learning*. London: University of London, Institute of Education (IOE).

—(2012) 'The Nature of Practice Based Knowledge and Understanding'. In R. Heilbronn and J. Yandell (eds) *Critical Practice in Teacher Education: A Study of Professional Learning*. London: University of London, Institute of Education (IOE), 7–9.

Herrington, M. (2010) 'Dyslexia'. In N. Hughes and I. Schwab (eds) *Teaching Adult Literacy: Principles and Practice*. Maidenhead: Open University Press.

Hickson, H. (2011) 'Critical reflection: reflecting on learning to be reflective', *Reflective Practice: International and Multidisciplinary Perspectives,* 12 (6), 829–39.

Higher Education Academy (2011) 'UK Professional Standards Framework for Teaching and Supporting Learning in Higher Education'. Available from http://www.hea.ac.uk (accessed 24 October 2014).

Hillier, Y. (1994) *Informal Practitioner Theory in Adult Basic Education*. Unpublished PhD thesis, University of East London.

—(2006) *Everything you need to know about FE Policy*. London: Continuum.

—(2010) 'Counting me in and Getting on'. In Jackson, S. (ed.) *Innovations in Lifelong Learning Critical Perspectives on Diversity, Participation and Vocational Learning*. London: Routledge, 142–61

—(2012) *Reflective Teaching in Further and Adult Education*. 3rd edn. London: Continuum.

Hillier, Y. and Jameson, J. (2003) *Empowering Researchers in Further Education*. Stoke-on-Trent: Trentham Books.

—(2004) *A Rich Contract or The Ragged Trousered Philanthropists? The Deployment and Development of Part-time Staff in the Learning and Skills Sector.* London: LSDA.

—(2006) *Managing the Ragged Trousered Philanthropists*. London: LSDA.

Hillier, Y. and Morris, A. (2010) 'Critical practitioners, developing researchers: the story of practitioner research in the learning and skills sector', *Journal of Vocational Education and Training Volume,* 61 (1), 85–97.

Hillier, Y. and Thompson, A. (eds) (2004) *Readings in Post-compulsory Education: Research in Learning and Skills*. London: Continuum.

Hirst, P. (1965) *Liberal Education and The Nature of Knowledge in Philosophical Analysis and Education*. London: Routledge.

HMI Inspectorate of Schools in England and Wales (1985) *The Curriculum for 5 to 16*. London: HMSO

Hodgson, A., Spours, K. and Waring, M. (eds) (2011) *Post-Compulsory Education and Lifelong Learning across the United Kingdom: Policy, Organisation and Governance*. London: University of London, Institute of Education (IOE).

Hodkinson, A. and Vickerman, P. (2009) *Key Issues in Special Educational Needs and Inclusion*. London: Sage Publications Ltd.

Hodkinson, P. M. and James, D. (2003) 'Transforming learning cultures in further education', *Journal of Vocational Education and Training*, 55 (4), 389–406.

Hofstede, M (2001) *Culture's Consequences: Comparing Values, Behaviors, Institutions and Organizations across Nations*. 2nd edn. London: Sage Publications Ltd.

Hogan, D. (2012) 'Yes Brian, at Long Last, there is Pedagogy in England – and in Singapore too'. In M. James and A. Pollard (eds) *Principles for Effective Pedagogy. International Responses to the UK TLRP*. London: Routledge.

Hoppe, R. (2010) *The Governance of Problems: Puzzling, Powering, Participation*. Bristol: The Policy Press.

Hoyle, E. (1974) 'Professionality, Professionalism and Control in Teaching', *London: Education Review*, 3 (2), 13–9.

Huddleston, P. and Unwin, L. (2007) *Teaching and Learning in Further Education: Diversity and Change*. 3rd edn. London. Routledge.

Hughes, N. and Schwab, I. (2010a) 'Language Variety'. In N. Hughes and I. Schwab (eds) *Teaching Adult Literacy: Principles and Practice*. Maidenhead: McGraw Hill/Open University Press, 99–127.

—(2010b) *Teaching Adult Literacy: Principles and Practice*. Maidenhead: McGraw Hill/Open University Press.

Humphreys, T. (1995) *A Different Kind of Teacher*. London: Cassell.

Hyde, L. (2008) 'Making It', *New York Times*, 6 April. Available from http://www.newyorker.com/magazine/2008/07/21/making-it (accessed October 2014).

Hyland, T. (2009) 'Mindfulness and the therapeutic function of education', *Journal of Philosophy of Education*, 43, 1.

—(2011a) *Mindfulness and Learning: Celebrating the Affective Dimension of Education*. London: Springer.

—(2011b) 'Moral education, mindfulness and secularisation', *Prospero*, 17, 1.

Hyland, T. and Merrill, B. (2003) *The Changing Faces of Further Education*. London: Routledge.

Immordino-Yang, M. H. and Damasio, A. (2007) 'We feel, therefore we learn: the relevance of affective and social neuroscience to education', *Mind, Brain and Education*, 1 (1), 3–10.

Institute for Employment Studies (IES) with NIACE (2000) *Adult Learning in England: A Review*. Brighton: IES.

Institute for Learning (IFL) (2009) *2008–9 IFL Review of CPD. Making a Difference for Teachers, Trainers and Learners*. London: IFL.

Isecke, H. (2010) *Backwards Planning: Building Enduring Understanding Through Instructional Design*. Huntington Beach, CA: Shell Education.

Ivanic, R., Appleby, Y., Hodge, R., Tusting, K. and Barton, D. (2004) *Listening to Learners: Practitioner Research on the adult Learners' Project*. London: NRDC.

Jackson, S. (ed.) (2011) *Lifelong Learning and Social Justice: Communities, Work and Identities in a Globalised World*. Leicester: NIACE.

Jacques, D. (2000) *Learning in Groups*. 3rd edn. London: Kogan Page.

James, D. and Biesta, G. (2007) *Improving Learning Cultures in Further Education*. London: Routledge.

James, D. and D. Gleeson. (2007) 'Professionality in FE Learning Cultures'. In D. James and G. Biesta (eds) *Improving Learning Cultures in Further Education*. London: Routledge.

James, M. (2005) 'Insights on Teacher Learning from the Teaching and Learning Research Programme (TLRP)', *Research Papers in Education*. London: TLRP.

James, M. and Pollard, A. (2006) *Improving Teaching and Learning in Schools: A Commentary by the Teaching and Learning Research Programme*. London: TLRP.

—(2012) *Principles for Effective Pedagogy: International Responses to Evidence from the UK Teaching and Learning Research Programme*. London: Routledge

Jameson, J., Hillier, Y. and Betts, D. (2004) *The Ragged-trousered Philanthropy of LSC Part-time Staff*. Presented at the British Educational Research Association Conference, UMITST, Manchester. September 16–18.

Jarvis, P. (1990) *An International Dictionary of Adult and Continuing Education*. London: Routledge.

Jeffrey, B. and Troman, G. (eds) (2012) *Performativity in UK Education: Ethnographic Cases of its Effects, Agency and Reconstructions*. Painswick: E&E Publishing.

Karoly, L. A., Greenwood, P. W and Everingham, S. S. (eds) (1998) *Investing in Our Children: What We Know and Don't Know about the Costs and Benefits of Early Childhood Intervention*. New York: RAND.

Keep, E. (2011) 'The English Policy Narrative'. In A. Hodgson, K. Spours and M. Waring *Post-Compulsory Education and Lifelong Learning across the United Kingdom: Policy, Organisation and Governance*. London: University of London, Institute of Education (IOE), 18–38

Kenner, C., Al'Azami, S., Gregory, E. and Ruby, M. (2008) 'Bilingual poetry: expanding the cognitive and cultural dimensions of children's learning', *Literacy,* 42 (2), 92–100.

Kenner, C., Gregory, E., Ruby, M. and Al-Azami, S. (2008) 'Bilingual learning for second and third generation children', *Language, Culture and Curriculum*, 21 (2), 120–37.

Kenner, C., Ruby, M., Gregory, E. and Al-Azami, S. (2007) 'How research can link policy and practice: bilingualism as a learning resource for second and third generation children', *NALDIC Quarterly*, 5 (1), 10–13.

Kent, N. A. and Facer, K. L. (2004) 'Different worlds? children's home and school computer use', *Journal of Computer Assisted Learning*, 20 (6), 440–55

Keogh, B. and Naylor, S. (2014) 'Concept Cartoons in Science Education'. Available from www.millgatehouse.co.uk (last accessed June 2014).

Kidscape. Available from http://www.kidscape.org.uk/ (accessed December 2013).

—'Antibullying Policy for Schools'. Available from http://www.kidscape.org.uk (accessed December 2013).

Knowles, M. (1978) *The Adult Learner: A Neglected Species*. Houston: Gulf Publishing.

—(1984) *Andragogy in Action*. San Francisco: Jossey-Bass.

Kogan, M. (1978) *The Politics of Educational Change*. London: Fontana.

Kounin, J. (1970) *Discipline and Group Management in Classrooms*. New York: Holt, Rinehart and Winston.

Krathwohl, D. R., Bloom, B. S. and Masia, B. B. (1964) *Taxonomy of Educational Objectives: Handbook II: Affective Domain*. New York: David McKay Co.

Kress, G. (2010) 'The Profound Shift of Digital Literacies'. In J. Gillen and D. Barton (eds) *Digital Literacies. TLRP – Technology Enhanced Learning*. London: University of London, Institute of Education (IOE), 2–3.

Kyriacou, C. (1998) *Essential Teaching Skills*. Cheltenham: Nelson Thornes.

Land, R., Meyer, J. and Smith, J. (eds) (2008) *Threshold Concepts within the Disciplines*. Rotterdam: Sense Publishers.

Laurillard, D. (2008) *Digital Technologies and their Role in Achieving our Ambitions for Education*. Inaugural Professorial Lecture. London: University of London, Institute of Education (IOE).

Lawn, M. and Grace, G. (eds) (1987) *Teachers: The Culture and Politics of Work*. London: Falmer.

Lawrence, D. (1987) *Enhancing Self-esteem in the Classroom*. London: Paul Chapman.

Lave, J. and Wenger, E. (1991). *Situated Learning: Legitimate Peripheral Participation.* Cambridge: Cambridge University Press.

Learning and Skills Improvement Service (LSIS) (2013) *A Legacy of Learning.* Coventry: LSIS.

Learning Connections. (2005) *An Adult Literacy and Numeracy Curriculum Framework for Scotland.* Glasgow: Learning Connections: Communities Scotland.

Lifelong Learning UK (LLUK) (2010) 'The Lifelong Learning Workforce in England'. Available from http://webarchive.nationalarchives.gov.uk/20110414152025/http://www.lluk.org/england/about-the-sector/ (accessed January 2014).

Light, P. and Littleton, K. (1999) *Social Processes in Children's Learning.* Cambridge: Cambridge University Press.

Lingfield. (2012) *Professionalism in Further Education: Final Report of the Independent Review Panel.* London: BIS.

Lipman, M. (2003) *Thinking in Education.* Cambridge: Cambridge University Press.

Lovett, T. (1988) *Radical Approaches to Adult Education.* London: Routledge.

Lucas, B., Spencer E. and Claxton, G. (2012) *How to Teach Vocational Education: A Theory of Vocational Pedagogy.* London. City and Guilds

Lumby, J. and Foskett, N. (2005) *Education Policy, Leadership and Learning.* London: Sage Publications Ltd.

MacDonald, B. and Parlett, M. (1973) 'Rethinking formative evaluation: notes from the Cambridge Conference', *Cambridge Journal of Education*, 3 (1973), 74–82.

Maclure, M. (2000). 'Arguing for yourself: identity as an organising principle in teachers' jobs and lives', *British Educational Research Journal*, 19 (4), 311–22.

Mallows, D (ed.) (2012) *Innovations in English Language Teaching for Migrants and Refugees.* London: The British Council.

Mansell, W. and James, M. (2009) 'Assessment in Schools: Fit for Purpose?' A Commentary by the Teaching and learning Research Programme, London: Economic and School Science Research Council Teaching and Learning Research Programme.

Marschark, M. and Spencer, P. E. (2011) *The Oxford Handbook of Deaf Studies, Language, and Education.* 2nd edn. Oxford: Oxford University Press.

Marton, F., Hounsell, D. and Entwhistle, N. J. (eds) (1997) *The Experience of Learning.* Edinburgh: Scottish Academic Press.

Marton, F. and Saljo R. (1997) 'Approaches to Learning'. In F. Marton, D. Hounsell and N. J. Entwhistle (eds) *The Experience of Learning.* Edinburgh: Scottish Academic Press.

Maslow, A. (1968) *Towards a Psychology of Being.* New York: Van Nostrand.

Mayo, M. and Thompson J. (eds) (1995) *Adult Learning, Critical Intelligence and Social Change.* Leicester: NIACE.

McCarthy, M. (2008) 'The Scholarship of Teaching and Learning in Higher Education: An Overview'. In R. Murray (ed.) *The Scholarship of Teaching and Learning in Higher Education.* Maidenhead: Society for Research Higher Education and Open University Press.

McCarthy, T. (1984) *The Critical Theory of Jurgen Habermas.* Cambridge: Polity Press.

McGivney, V. (2001) *Fixing or Changing Patterns.* Leicester: NIACE.

Mehmedbegovic, D. (2007) '"Miss, Who Needs the Languages of Immigrants?": London's Multilingual Schools. London in Education in a Global City'. In T. Brighouse and L. Fullick (eds) *Essays from London.* London: University of London, Institute of Education (IOE).

—(2012) 'In Search of High Level Learner Engagement: Autobiographical Approaches with Children and Adults'. In D. Mallows (ed.) *Innovations in English Language Teaching for Migrants and Refugees.* London: The British Council, 65–78.

Mehmedbegovic, D. (2003) 'Researching attitudes and values attached to first language maintenance', *Language Issues*, 15 (December), *The Journal of National Association for Teaching English and Community Languages to Adults.* London.

Mental Health Foundation (2005) *A Bright Future for All.* London: Mental Health Foundation.

Menter, I., Hulme, M., Elliot, D. and Lewin, J. (2010) *Teacher Education in the 21st Century.* Edinburgh: Scottish Government.

Mercer, N. (2000) *The Guided Construction of Knowledge: Talk Amongst Teachers and Learners.* Clevedon: Multilingual Matters.

Mercer, N. and Littleton, K. (2007) *Dialogue and the Development of Children's Thinking: A Socio-cultural Approach.* London: Routledge.

Meyer, J. H. F., Land, R. and Davies, P. (2008) 'Threshold Concepts and Troublesome Knowledge (4): Issues of Variation and Variability'. In R. Land, J. H. F Meyer and J. Smith *Threshold Concepts within the Disciplines.* Rotterdam and Taipei: Sense Publishers, 59–74.

Meyer, J. W. and Kamens, D. H. (1992) 'Conclusion: Accounting for a World Curriculum'. In J. W. Meyer, D. H. Kamens and A. Benavot with Y. K. Cha and S. Y. Wong (eds) *School Knowledge for the Masses: World Models of National Primary Curricular Categories in the Twentieth Century.* London: Falmer.

Mezirow, J. (1998) 'On critical reflection', *Adult Education Quarterly*, 38 (3), 185–98.

MIND: The Mental Health Charity. Available from http://www.mind.org.uk (accessed December 2013).

Millar, R., Leach, J., Osborne, J. and Ratcliffe, M. (2006) *Improving Subject Teaching: Lessons from Research in Science Education.* London: Routledge.

Mills, C. W. (1959) *The Sociological Imagination.* New York: Oxford University Press.

Mirza, H. S. and Meetoo, V. (2012). *Respecting Difference: Race, Faith and Culture for Teacher Educators.* London: University of London, Institute of Education (IOE).

Misra, P. K. (2011).'VET teachers in Europe: policies, practices and challenges', *Journal of Vocational Education and Training*, 63 (1), 27–45.

Mitchell, C., Pride, D. Howard, L. and Pride, B. (1998) *Ain't Misbehavin', Managing Disruptive Behaviour.* London: Further Education Development Agency.

Moll, L. C. and Greenberg, J. B. (1990) 'Creating Zones of Possibilities: Combining Social Contexts for Instruction'. In L. C. Moll (ed.) *Vygotsky and Education.* Cambridge: Cambridge University Press.

Moon, J. (1999) *Reflection in Learning and Professional Development: Theory and Practice.* London: Kogan Page.

Moore, A. (2004) *The Good Teacher.* Abingdon: Routledge

Morris, A. and Norman, L. (2004) *Collaborative Research in Practice.* London: Learning and Skills Research Centre.

Moseley, D., Baumfield, V., Elliott, J., Gregson, M., Higgins, S., Miller, J. and Newton, D. P. (2005) *Frameworks for Thinking.* Cambridge: Cambridge University Press.

Murray, R. (ed.) (2008) *The Scholarship of Teaching and Learning in Higher Education.* Maidenhead: Open University Press.

Muschamp. Y. (1991) *'Pupil Self-assessment', Practical Issues in Primary Education, No. 9.* Bristol: National Primary Centre (South West).

National Centre for Vocational Education Research (2014) Available from www.ncver.edu.au (accessed October 2014).

National Foundation for Educational Research (NFER) (2011) *Report on Subject Breadth in International Jurisdictions. Review of the National Curriculum in England.* London: DfE.

National Institute for Adult and Continuing Education (NIACE) (2013) *Adult Learning Survey* Leicester: NIACE.

Nixon, L., Gregson, M. and Spedding, P. (2007) 'Challenging the Intuitive Appeal of Learning Styles'. Later published at 'Pedagogy and the Intuitive Appeal of Learning Styles in Post-Compulsory Education in England', *Journal of Vocational Education and Training*, 59 (1), 39–50.

Nonaka, I. and Takeuchi H. (1995) *The Knowledge Creating Company: How Japanese Companies Create the Dynamics of Innovation.* Oxford: Oxford University Press.

Nuffield (2009) 'The Nuffield Review of 14–19 Education and Training Summary'. Available from http://www.nuffieldfoundation.org/14-19review (accessed July 2014).

Oates, T. (2010) *Could Do Better. Using International Comparisons to Refine the National Curriculum in England.* Cambridge: Cambridge Assessment.

O'Leary, M. (2013) *Classroom Observation: A Guide to the Effective Observation of Teaching and Learning.* London: Routledge.

Ofsted (2008) *Using Data, Improving Schools.* London: Ofsted.

—(2012) *Handbook for the Inspection of Further Education and Skills from September 2012.* London: Ofsted

Organisation for Economic Co-operation and Development (OECD) (2001) *Education Policy Analysis: Education and Skills.* Paris: OECD.

—(2013a) 'Programme for International Assessment of Adult Competencies'. Available from http://www.oecd.org/site/piaac/surveyofadultskills.htm (accessed July 2014).

—(2013b) *Education at a Glance.* Paris: OECD.

Pachler, N. (2013) 'The Social-cultural Ecological Approach to Mobile Learning'. Available from: http://www.slideshare.net/servusuk/norbert-pachler-on-mobile-learning-somobnet-ubc# (accessed October 2014).

Parlett, M. and Dearden, G. (eds) (1977) *Introduction to Illuminative Evaluation: Studies in Higher Education.* California: Pacific Soundings Press.

Parlett, M. and Hamilton, D. (1972). *Evaluation as Illumination: A New Approach to the Study of Innovatory Programmes.* Occasional Paper of the Centre for Research in Education Studies. Edinburgh: University of Edinburgh.

Paton, A. and Wilkins, M. (eds) (2009) *Teaching Adult ESOL: Principles and Practice.* Maidenhead: Open University Press.

Peechey, N. (2012) 'Technology is Changing how Students Learn, Teachers say'. Learning Technologies, (1 November) [online]. Available from http://www.scoop.it/t/learning-technology/p/3165751798/technology-is-changing-how-students-learn-teachers-say (accessed October 2014).

Perrot, E. (1982) *Effective Teaching: A Practical Guide to Improving Your Teaching.* London: Longman, 56–91.

Peters, R. S. (1966) *Ethics and Education.* London: Unwin University Books.

Piaget, J. (1978) *The Development of Thought: Equilibration of Cognitive Structures.* Oxford: Basil Blackwell.

Pohl, M. (2001) *Learning to Think, Thinking to Learn: Models and Strategies to Develop a Classroom Culture of Thinking.* Cheltenham, Australia: Hawker Brownlow Education Pty Ltd.

Polanyi, M. (1962) *Personal Knowledge. Towards a Post-critical Philosophy.* London: Routledge.

Pollard, A. (2010) *Professionalism and Pedagogy: A Contemporary Opportunity.* London: TLRP.

—(2014) *Reflective Teaching in Schools.* London: Bloomsbury.

Pollard, A. and Triggs, P. (2000) *What Pupils Say: Changing Policy and Practice in Primary Education.* London: Continuum.

Popper, K. (1962) *The Open Society and its Enemies: Volume 2 Hegel and Marx.* 4th edn. London: Routledge.

Pring, R. (1999) *Closing the Gap: Liberal Education and Vocational Preparation.* London. Hodder and Stoughton.

—(2000) *Action Research and the Development of Practice. Philosophy of Educational Development.* London: Continuum, 130–4.

Pring, R., Hayward G., Hodgson, A., Johnson, J., Keep E., Oancea, A., Rees, G., Spours K. and Wilde S. (2009) *Education for All: The Future of Education and Training for 14–19 Year Olds.* London: Routledge.

Putnam, R. D. (1995) 'Bowling alone: America's declining social capital', *Journal of Democracy,* 6 (1), 65–78.

Reay, D. (2000) 'A useful extension of Bourdieu's conceptual framework? emotional capital as a way of understanding mothers' involvement in their children's education?', *The Sociological Review,* 48 (4), 568–85

Reay, D., Crozier, G and Clayton, J. (2010) '"Fitting in" or "standing out" white working class students in UK higher education', *British Education Research Journal,* 1, 1–19.

RARPA (2004) 'Recognising and Recording Achievement and Progress in Non-accredited Adult Learning'. Available from http://www.learningcurve.org.uk/courses/ladder4learning/resources/rarpatoolkit (accessed July 2014).

Reynolds, M. and Vince, R. (eds) (2007) *The Handbook of Experiential Learning and Management Education.* Oxford: Oxford University Press.

Rice, M. and Brooks, G. (2004) *Developmental Dyslexia in Adults: A Research Review.* London: NRDC.

Richards, G. and Armstrong, F. (eds) (2011) *Teaching and Learning in Diverse and Inclusive Classrooms.* London: Routledge.

Richards, M. and Light, P. (eds) (1986). *Children of Social Worlds.* Oxford: Blackwell.

Richardson, R. (2009) *Holding Together.* Stoke-on-Trent: Trentham Books, 24, 26–8.

Rieser, R. (2011) 'Disability, Human Rights and Inclusive Education, and why Inclusive Education is the only Educational Philosophy and Practice that makes Sense in Today's World'. In G. Richards and F. Armstrong (eds) *Teaching and Learning in Diverse and Inclusive Classrooms.* London: Routledge, 156–69.

RNIB. Available from www.rnib.org.uk/Pages/Home.aspx (accessed December 2013).

Roberts, R. (2002) *Self-esteem and Early Learning.* London: Paul Chapman.

Rogers, B. (2011) *Classroom Behaviour: A Practical Guide to Effective Teaching, Behaviour Management and Colleague Support.* London: Sage Publications Ltd.

Rogers, C. (1969) *Freedom to Learn.* New York: Merrill.

—(1983) *Freedom to Learn for the 1980s.* Columbus: Merrill.

Rogoff, B. (1990) *Apprenticeship in Thinking: Cognitive Development in Social Context.* Oxford: Oxford University Press.

Rosenthal, R. and Jacobson, L. (1968) *Pygmalion in the Classroom: Teacher Expectation and Pupils' Intellectual Development.* New York: Holt, Rinehart and Winston.

Ross, A. (2001) 'What is the Curriculum?'. In J. Collins, K. Insley and J. Soler (eds) *Developing Pedagogy.* London: Paul Chapman.

Rowland, S. (1987) 'Child in Control: Towards an Interpretive Model of Teaching and Learning'. In A. Pollard (ed.) *Children and their Primary Schools.* London: Falmer.

Rowland, T., Turner, F., Thwaites, A. and Huckstep, P. (2009) *Developing Primary Mathematics Teaching: Reflecting on Practice with the Knowledge Quartet.* London: Sage Publications Ltd.

Rowntree, D. (1987) *Assessing Students: How Shall we Know Them?* London: Routledge.

Rudduck, J, and McIntyre, D. (2007) *Improving Learning through Consulting Pupils.* London: Routledge.

Rutledge, N. (2010) *Primary Science: Teaching the Tricky Bits in Science.* Maidenhead: Open University Press.

Ryle, G. (1945) *The Concept of Mind* London: Hutchinson

Sahlberg, P. (2011) *Finnish Lessons: What Can the World Learn from Educational Change in Finland.* New York: Teachers College Press, 1–6, 140–5.

Salmon, G. (2013) *E-tivities: The Key to Active Online Learning.* 2nd edn. London and New York: Routledge.

Sarason, S. B. (1990) *The Predictable Failure of Educational Reform. Can we Change Course before it's too Late?* San Francisco: Jossey-Bass.

Schagen, I. and Hutchison, D. (2003) 'Adding value in educational research – the marriage of value-added measures for school improvement data and analytical power', *British Educational Research Journal,* 29 (5).

Schön, D. (1983) *The Reflective Practitioner.* San Francisco: Jossey-Bass.

—(1987) *Educating the Reflective Practitioner: Towards a new Design for Teaching and Learning in the Professions.* San Francisco: Jossey-Bass.

Schuller, S. and Watson, D. (2009) *Learning through Life: Inquiry into the Future for Lifelong Learning.* Leicester. NIACE

Schuller, T., Preston, J., Hammond, C., Brassett-Grundy, A. and Bynner, J. (2004) *The Benefits of Learning: The Impact of Education on Health, Family Life and Social Capital.* Falmer: Routledge.

Schuller, T. and Watson, D. (2009) *Learning Through Life Inquiry into the Future for Lifelong Learning.* Leicester: NIACE.

Schwab, J. (1978) 'Education and the Structure of the Disciplines'. In I. Westbury and N. J. Wilkof (eds) *Science Curriculum and Liberal Education.* Chicago: University of Chicago Press, 229–72.

Scriven, M. (1967) 'The Methodology of Evaluation'. In R. E. Stake (eds) *Perspectives of Curriculum Evaluation.* American Educational Research Association. Monograph Series on Curriculum Evaluation No. 1, 38–89. Chicago: Rand McNally.

Scruton, J. and Ferguson, B. (2014) *Teaching and Supporting Adult Learners.* Northwich: Critical Publishing.

Sebba, J., Kent, P., Tregenza, J. (2012) *Joint Practice Development (JPD). What does the Evidence Suggest are Effective Approaches?* Nottingham: National College for School Leadership.

Selwyn, N., Gorard, S. and Furlong, J. (2005) *Adult Learning in the Digital Age.* London: Routledge.

Sennett, R. (2008) *The Craftsman.* London: Penguin.

—(2012) *Together.* London: Penguin.

Sfard (1998) 'On Two Metaphors for Learning and the Dangers of Choosing Just One'. In A. Pollard *From Learning Cultures to Educational Cultures: Values and Judgements in Educational Research and Educational Improvement.* London: Continuum

Shain, F. and D. Gleeson (1999) 'Under new management: changing conceptions of teacher professionalism and policy in the further education sector', *Journal of Education Policy*, 14 (4), 445–62.

Shulman, L. S. (1986) 'Those who understand: knowledge growth in teaching', *Educational Researcher*, (February), 9–10.

Sibieta, L. (2011) *Inequality in Britain: An Explanation of Recent Trends.* London: Institute for Fiscal Studies.

Simon, B. (1981) 'Why no Pedagogy in England?'. In B. Simon and W. Taylor (eds) *Education in the Eighties: The Central Issues.* London: Batsford, 128–40.

—(1985) *Does Education Matter?* London: Lawrence and Wishart

—(1992) *What Future for Education?* London: Lawrence and Wishart.

Sikes, P., Measor, L. and Woods, P. (1985) *Teacher Careers: Crises and Continuities.* London: Falmer.

Silver, H. (1980) *Education and the Social Condition.* London: Methuen.

Skills Funding Agency (2013) 'First Statistical Release Further Education and Skills; Learner Participation, Outcomes and Highest Level of Qualification Held'. Available from http://www.thedataservice.org.uk/NR/rdonlyres/0FD0BFEB-EB53-47C4-847B-6A1AE6CEF219/0/SFR_commentary_October_2013.pdf (accessed October 2013).

Skinner, B. F. (1938) *The Behaviour of Organisms: An Experimental Analysis.* New York: Appleton-Century-Crofts.

—(1954) 'The science of learning and the art of teaching', *Harvard Educational Review,* 24, 86–97.

—(1959) *Science and Human Behaviour.* New York: Macmillan

Smith, M. (2011) 'Half a Million Unseen, Half a Million Unheard: Inclusion for Gender Identity and Sexual Orientation'. In G. Richards and F. Armstrong (eds) *Teaching and Learning in Diverse and Inclusive Classrooms.* London: Routledge, 19–30.

Sockett, H. (1976) *Approaches to Curriculum Planning Unit 16 of Course E203 Curriculum Design and Development.* Milton Keynes: Open University Press.

Spedding P., Gregson, M. and Nixon, L. (2011) *Tackling Prejudice Together.* Presentation at University of Sunderland, Faculty of Education and Society Conference, 5 September.

Spenceley, L. (2014) *Inclusion in Further Education.* Northwich: Critical Publishing.

Spendlove, S. (2012) *Putting Assessment for Learning into Practice.* London: Continuum.

Stenhouse, L. (1975) *An Introduction to Curriculum Research and Development.* London: Heinemann.

Stobart, G. (2008) *Testing Times: The Uses and Abuses of Assessment.* Abingdon: Routledge.

Stonewall (2006) *The School Report: The Experiences of Young Gay People in Britain's Schools.* London: Stonewall.

—(2009) *The Teachers' Report: Homophobic Bullying in Britain's Schools.* London: Stonewall.

Sutherland, J. and Robertson, S. (2006) 'Using computers to enhance learning: integrating ICT into everyday classroom practices', *Teaching and Learning Research Briefing,* 19.

Swaffield, S. (2000) 'Record keeping', *Primary File,* 38, 61–4.

—(2008) *Unlocking Assessment: Understanding for Reflection and Application.* Abingdon: Routledge.

—(2011) 'Getting to the heart of authentic assessment for learning', *Assessment in Education: Principles, Policy and Practice,* 18 (4), 441–3

Swain, J. and French, S. (2000) 'Towards an affirmation model of disability', *Disability and Society,* 15 (4), 569–82.

Sylva, K., Melhuish, E., Sammons, P., Siraj-Blatchford, I. and Taggart, B. (2010) *Early Childhood Matters: Evidence from the Effective Pre-school and Primary Education Project.* London: Routledge.

Taubman, D. (2013) *Towards a UCU Policy on Professionalism.* London: UCU.

Tennant, M. (1997) *Psychology and Adult Learning.* 2nd edn. London: Routledge.

Tett, L., Hamilton, M. and Hillier, Y. (2006) *Adult Literacy, Numeracy and Language: Policy, Practice and Research.* Maidenhead: McGraw Hill.

Tharp, R. and Gallimore, R. (1988) *Rousing Minds to Life: Teaching, Learning and Schooling in Social Context.* New York: Cambridge University Press.

The National Autistic Society. Available from http://www.autism.org.uk/ (accessed December 2013).

Thomas, A. and Pattison, H. (2007) *How Children Learn at Home.* London: Continuum.

Thompson, N., and Pascal, J. (2012) 'Developing critically reflective practice', *Reflective Practice: International and Multidisciplinary Perspectives,* 13 (2), 311–25.

Thomson A., Tuckett A. (2010) *Lifelong Learning in Challenging Times: An Agenda for a New Government.* London. NIACE.

Thorndike, E. L. (1911) *Human Learning.* New York: Prentice Hall.

Tickell, C. (2011) *The Early Years: Foundations for Life, Health and Learning.* London: DfE.

Todd, B. (2013) SIEMENS Engineering UK. E-mail communication to Maggie Gregson, 20th June.

Tooley, J. and Derby, D. (1998) *Educational Research A Critique: A Survey of Published Education Research.* London: Ofsted.

Turner, F. (2009) 'Growth in teacher knowledge: individual reflection and community participation', *Research in Mathematics Education,* 11 (1), 81.

Unwin, L. (2009) *Sensuality, Sustainability and Social Justice: Vocational Education in Changing Times.* Professorial Inaugural Lecture. London: University of London, Institute of Education (IOE), 4 February.

Usher, R. and Bryant, I. (1989) *Adult Education as Theory, Practice and Research: The Captive Triangle.* London: Routledge.

Valdes, G. (2005) 'Bilingualism, heritage language learners, and SLA research: opportunities lost or seized?', *The Modern Languages Journal,* 89, 410–426.

Vincent, C. (1996) *Parents and Teachers: Power and Participation.* London: Falmer.

—(2000) *Including Parents? Education, Citizenship and Parental Agency*. Buckingham: Open University Press.

Vizard, D. (2007) *How to Manage Behaviour in Further Education*. London: Sage Publications Ltd.

Vorhaus, J. (2006) 'Respecting profoundly disabled learners', *Journal of Philosophy of Education*, 40 (3), 313–28.

Vorhaus, J., Feinstein, L .and Sabates, R. (2008) *The Wider Benefits of Further and Higher Education: A Review of the Literature*. London: SKOPE

Vygotsky, L. (1934) *Thought and Language*. Cambridge, MA: MIT Press.

—(1962) *Thought and Language*. Cambridge, MA: MIT Press.

—(1986 [1978]) *Mind in Society: The Development of Higher Psychological Processes*. Cambridge, MA: Harvard University Press.

Warnke, G. (1987) *Gadamer: Hermeneutics, Tradition and Reason*. Oxford: Polity Press.

Warwick, P, Hennessy, S. and Mercer, N. (2011) 'Promoting teacher and school development through co-enquiry: developing interactive whiteboard use in a "dialogic classroom"', *Teachers and Teaching: Theory and Practice*, 17 (3), 303–24.

Watkins, C. (2005) *Classrooms as Learning Communities*. London: Routledge.

—(2011) *Managing Classroom Behaviour*. London: ATL.

Watkinson, A. (2003) *Managing Teaching Assistants*. London: Routledge.

Webb, R. and Vulliamy, G. (2002) 'The social work dimension of the primary teachers' role', *Research Papers in Education*, 17 (2), 165–84.

Wells, G. (1999) *Dialogic Inquiry: Towards a Sociocultural Practice and Theory of Education*. New York: Cambridge University Press.

—(2008) 'Dialogue, Inquiry and the Construction of Learning Communities'. In B. Linguard, J. Nixon and S. Ranson (eds) *Transforming Learning in Schools and Communities*. London: Continuum, 236–42.

Wenger, E. (1999) *Communities of Practice. Learning, Meaning and Identity*. Cambridge: Cambridge University Press.

Wertsch, J. V. (1985) *Vygotsky and the Social Formation of Mind*. Cambridge, MA: Harvard University Press.

Westwood, S. and Thomas, J. E. (1991) *The Politics of Adult Education*. Leicester: NIACE.

Wheldall, K. (1991) *Discipline in Schools: Psychological Perspectives on the Elton Report*. London: Routledge.

Wilby, P. (1968) 'What the art students want', *The Observer*, 6 October, p. 11.

Wiliam, D. (2001) *Level Best? Levels of Attainment in National Curriculum Assessment*. London: Association of Teachers and Lecturers.

—(2009) *Assessment for Learning Why, What and How?* Based in an Inaugural Professorial Lecture. London: University of London, Institute of Education (IOE), 24 April 2007.

—(2010) *The Classroom Experiment*. Episode One, BBC2, 27 September.

Wilkinson, R. and Pickett, K. (2010) *The Spirit Level: Why Equality is Better for Everyone*. London: Penguin.

Wilson, A and Hunter, K. (2007) 'Effective Learning for Adults with Learning Difficulties (A Research Report for Learning Connections, Directorate of Lifelong Learning)', The Scottish Government. Available from http://www.scotland.gov.uk/Publications/2007/11/13115549/11 (accessed October 2014).

Wilson, J. (2000) *Key Issues in Education and Teaching*. London: Cassell.

Winch, C (2012) *Dimensions of Expertise: A Conceptual Exploration of Vocational Knowledge*. London: Continuum

Withall, J. (1949). 'The development of a technique for the measurement of social-emotional climate in classrooms', *Journal of Experimental Education*, 17, 347–61.

Wittenstein, L. (2007 [1922]) *Tractacus Logico-Philosophicus.* New York: Cosimo.

Wood, D. (1988) *How Children Think and Learn.* Oxford: Blackwell.

Woods, P. (1986) *Researching the Art of Teaching.* London: Routledge.

Wragg, E. C. (2000) *Class Management.* London: Routledge.

Young, M. (1971) *Knowledge and Control: New Directions for the Sociology of Education.* London: Collier Macmillan.

—(2008) *Bringing Knowledge Back In.* London: Routledge.

—(2013) *Powerful Knowledge in Education.* London: University of London, Institute of Education (IOE).

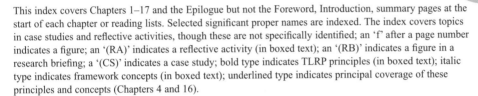

Index

This index covers Chapters 1–17 and the Epilogue but not the Foreword, Introduction, summary pages at the start of each chapter or reading lists. Selected significant proper names are indexed. The index covers topics in case studies and reflective activities, though these are not specifically identified; an 'f' after a page number indicates a figure; an '(RA)' indicates a reflective activity (in boxed text); an '(RB)' indicates a figure in a research briefing; a '(CS)' indicates a case study; bold type indicates TLRP principles (in boxed text); italic type indicates framework concepts (in boxed text); underlined type indicates principal coverage of these principles and concepts (Chapters 4 and 16).

Readings for Reflective Teaching in Further and Vocational Education: Contents list

PART ONE BECOMING A REFLECTIVE PROFESSIONAL

1. Identity. Who are we, and what do we stand for?

2. Learning. How can we understand learner development?

3. Reflection. How can we develop the quality of our teaching?

The Reflective Teaching Series

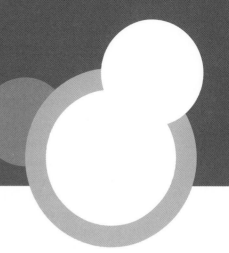

This book is one of the *Reflective Teaching Series* – applying principles of reflective practice in early, school, further, higher, adult and vocational education. Developed over three decades, the series books, companion readers and website represent the accumulated understanding of generations of teachers and educationalists. Uniquely, they offer *two* levels of support in the development of teacher expertise:

- *Comprehensive, practical guidance* on key issues – including learning, relationships, curriculum, teaching, assessment and evaluation.

- *Evidence-informed principles* to support deeper understanding.

The Reflective Teaching Series thus supports both initial steps in teaching and the development of career-long professionalism.

The series is supported by a website, **reflectiveteaching.co.uk**. For each book, this site is being developed to offer a range of resources including reflective activities, research briefings, advice on further reading and additional chapters. The site also offers generic resources such as a compendium of educational terms, links to other useful websites, and a conceptual framework for 'deepening expertise'. The latter draws on and showcases some of the UK's best educational research.

Underlying these materials, there are three key messages.

- It *is* now possible to identify teaching strategies which are more effective than others in most circumstances. Whatever the age of the learners for whom we have responsibility, we now need to be able to develop, improve, promote and defend our expertise by marshalling such evidence and by embedding enquiry, evaluation and improvement within our routine practices.

- All evidence has to be interpreted – and we do this by 'making sense'. In other words, as well as deploying effective strategies, we need to be able to pick out the underlying principles of learning and teaching to which specific policies and practices relate. As well as being practically competent, we need to be able to *understand* what is going on.

- Finally, we need to remember that education has moral purposes and social consequences. The provision we make is connected to our future as societies and to the life-chances of those in our care. The issues require very careful consideration.

The series is coordinated through meetings of the volume and series editors: Paul Ashwin, Jennifer Colwell, Maggie Gregson, Yvonne Hillier, Amy Pollard and Andrew Pollard. Each volume has an editorial team of contributors whose collective expertise and experience enable research and practice to be reviewed and applied in relation to early, school, further, higher, adult and vocational education.

The series is the first product of the Pollard Partnership, a collaboration between Andrew and Amy Pollard to maximize the beneficial use of research and evidence on public life, policymaking and professional practice.

Andrew Pollard
Bristol, February 2015